# Intellectual Heritage Reader

*Seventh Edition*

Compiled by

Robert Boughner
Ruth Crispin
Michael Dockray
Anne Marie Flanagan
Christine Flanagan
Paul Halpern
Peter Hoffer
Robert Manbeck
Barbara Bendl Reilly
Roy Robson, Editor
David Traxel

## University of the Sciences in Philadelphia

*Copley Custom Publishing Group*
Acton, Massachusetts 01720

Cover Illustration: Philadelphia Flea-Bane (*Erigeron Philadelphicum*), Figure 20 of *Engravings of Fifty Medicinal Plants Indigenous to the United States; Made after Original Drawings from Nature by W.P.C. Barton, M.D., Printed for and Published by the Publication Committee of the Philadelphia College of Pharmacy from the Original Plates in their Possession, 1832*. Courtesy of the Leopold E. Helfand Archives, University of the Sciences in Philadelphia.

Cover Design by Roy R. Robson

**Acknowledgments:**

**pp. 2–6:** From *On the Dignity of Man* by Pico Della Mirandola, translated by Charles Glenn Wallis. Copyright © by Charles Glenn Wallis. Reprinted by permission of the estate of Eleanor S. Wallis.

**pp. 19–21:** From *The Human Record: Sources of Global History*, edited by Alfred Andrea and James Overfield. Copyright © 1990 by Johns Hopkins University Press. Reprinted by permission.

**pp. 22–27:** From *Sources of the West*, Volume II, edited by Mark A. Kishlansky. Copyright © 1991 by Wall & Emerson, Inc., Toronto, Canada. Reprinted by permission of the publisher.

**p. 28–29:** From *Discoveries and Opinions of Galileo* by Galileo Galilei. Copyright © 1957 by Stillman Drake. Used by permission of Doubleday, a division of Bantam Doubleday Dell Publishing Group, Inc.

**pp. 51–58:** Reprinted by permission of the publishers and the Trustees of the Loeb Classical Library from *Cicero: Volume XVI*, Loeb Classical Library

# Contents

## Section Three: Belief and Thought

## Section Four: Nature

INTELLECTUAL HERITAGE

| | 1400–1500 | 1500–1600 | 1600–1640 | 1640–1680 | 1680–1720 |
|---|---|---|---|---|---|
| EUROPE | Renaissance Exploration | Erasmus Reformation Counter-Reformation Nation States | Shakespeare Thirty Years' War Galileo Bacon Descartes Baroque | English Revolution Rembrandt Milton | Glorious Revolution War of Spanish Succession Newton |
| AMERICA | Rise of Aztecs & Incas Columbus | Conquest of Aztecs & Incas | Jamestown & Quebec Massachusetts Bay | Navigation Acts English Acquire New York | |
| MIDDLE EAST/ WESTERN ASIA | Conquest of Constantinople by Turks | Suleiman | Peak of Safavid Culture Death of Shah Abbas | | |
| AFRICA | Decline of Mali | | Slave Trade to North America Dutch Settle West Africa | Dutch Base at Cape English Royal African Company | |
| EAST ASIA | | Hideyoshi Unites Japan | Founding of Tokugawa Shogunate Japan Expels Westerners | Fall of Ming Dynasty | Treaty of Nerchinsk |
| SOUTH ASIA | | Age of Akbar | Death of Akbar Taj Mahal | Overthrow of Shah Jahan Aurangzeb | Aurangzeb Mughal Collapse |

| | 1720–1760 | 1760–1800 | 1800–1840 |
|---|---|---|---|
| **EUROPE** | Seven Years' War Begins<br>Cabinet System of Government in England | "Spinning Jenny"<br>Enlightenment<br>French Revolution | Age of Napoleon<br>Independence of Greece<br>Romanticism<br>Revolution of 1830 in Paris |
| **AMERICA** | Great Awakening<br>French & Indian War<br>Franklin | American War of Independence<br>American Constitution<br>Jefferson | Louisiana Purchase<br>War of 18:2<br>Independence of South American Countries and Mexico<br>Age of Jackson |
| **MIDDLE EAST/ WESTERN ASIA** | Safavid Dynasty Collapses<br>Nadir Shah in Iran | Karim Khan in Iran<br>Founding of Qajar Dynasty | |
| **AFRICA** | | British Occupation of Cape Colony | British Abolish Slave Trade<br>Zulu Expansion<br>French Occupy Algiers |
| **EAST ASIA** | Ch'ien Lung in China | Ch'ien Lung in China<br>White Lotus Rebellion | Hokusai, Master Artist |
| **SOUTH ASIA** | Clive's Victories | British Siege of Ceylon | Bengal Renaissance |

| | 1840–1880 | 1880–1920 | 1920–1960 |
|---|---|---|---|
| **EUROPE** | Revolution of 1848<br>*Communist Manifesto*<br>Darwin's *Origin of the Species*<br>Unification of Germany & Italy<br>Impressionism | Dreyfus Affair<br>Origins of Cubism and Surrealism<br>World War I<br>Relativity<br>Symbolism<br>Industrialism | Weimar Republic<br>Spanish Civil War<br>Rise of Hitler<br>World War II<br>Common Market |
| **AMERICA** | American Civil War<br>Invention of Telephone | Birth of Brazilian Republic<br>Spanish American War<br>Mexican Revolution | Black Monday, 1929<br>Great Depression<br>World War II<br>Peron's Argentina |
| **MIDDLE EAST/ WESTERN ASIA** | Building of Suez Canal | World Zionist Congress<br>Balfour Declaration<br>League of Nations Mandates | Republic of Turkey<br>Kingdom of Saudi Arabia<br>Founding of Israel<br>Nasser's Revolution |
| **AFRICA** | Explorations of Livingstone<br>Conquest of Zulu | Berlin Conference on Africa<br>Boer War<br>Union of South Africa Formed<br>Italian Conquest of Tripoli | Italy Conquers Ethiopia<br>Mau Mau, Kenya |
| **EAST ASIA** | Opium War<br>Perry's Mission to Japan<br>Meiji Restoration in Japan<br>End of Japanese Feudalism | Boxer Rebellion<br>Russo-Japanese War<br>Republic of China Founded | Japanese Invasion of China<br>World War II<br>Korean War |
| **SOUTH ASIA** | Conquest of Kashmir<br>Indian Meeting<br>Victoria Named "Empress of India" | Congress Party Founded<br>Amritsar Massacre | Independence of India & Pakistan |

| | 1960–1990 | 1990–2000 |
|---|---|---|
| **EUROPE** | Fall of Khrushchev<br>Franco Dies<br>Detente<br>Gorbachev Era<br>Revolutions of 1989 | Germany Reunites<br>Channel Tunnel Opens<br>Civil War in Yugoslavia<br>Independence of Central European States<br>The Collapse of the Soviet Union |
| **AMERICA** | Cuban Missile Crisis<br>Vietnam<br>Neil Armstrong Walks on Moon<br>Watergate | The Greenspan "New Economy"<br>Globalization<br>Clinton Impeachment<br>NAFTA/WTO |
| **MIDDLE EAST/ WESTERN ASIA** | Six-Day War<br>Iranian Revolution<br>*Intifada*<br>Iran-Iraq War | Gulf War<br>Death of Jordan's King Hussein<br>Israel/Palestine (Peace Initiatives) |
| **AFRICA** | Independence of Congo and Algeria<br>War in Angola and Ethiopia<br>Famine | Genocide in Rwanda and Burundi<br>Mobutu's Fall in Congo (Zaire)<br>Famine in Sudan<br>Mandella and the end of *Apartheid* |
| **EAST ASIA** | "Cultural Revolution" in China<br>Vietnam War<br>Tiananmen Square Massacre | Hong Kong Returned to China<br>Independence of Central Asian States |
| **SOUTH ASIA** | Indira Gandhi<br>Benazir Bhutto | Fall of Suharto<br>Revolt in East Timor<br>India and Pakistan become Nuclear Powers |

*Section One*

# Birth of the Modern

ORATIO DE DIGNITATE HOMINUM

# *from* Oration on the Dignity of Man

*Giovanni Pico Della Mirandola*

EXORDIUM (INTRO)

1   Most venerable fathers, I have read in the records of the Arabians
that Abdul the Saracen, on being asked what thing on, so to
speak, the world's stage, he viewed as most greatly worthy of wonder,
answered that he viewed nothing more wonderful than man. And
Mercury's, "a great wonder, Asclepius, is man!" agrees with that opinion. On thinking over the reason for these sayings, I was not satisfied
by the many assertions made by many men concerning the outstand-
ingness of human nature: that man is the messenger between creatures, familiar with the upper and king of the lower; by the
sharpsightedness of the senses, by the hunting-power of reason, and
by the light of intelligence, the interpreter of nature; the part in
between the standstill of eternity and the flow of time; and, as the Persians say, the bond tying the world together, nay, the nuptial bond;
and, according to David, "a little lower than the angels." These reasons are great but not the chief ones, that is, they are not reasons for a
lawful claim to the highest wonder as to a prerogative. Why should
we not wonder more at the angels themselves and at the very blessed
heavenly choirs?

2   Finally, it seemed to me that I understood why man is the animal that
is most happy, and is therefore worthy of all wonder; and lastly, what
the state is that is allotted to man in the succession of things, and that
is capable of arousing envy not only in the brutes but also in the stars
and even in minds beyond the world. It is wonderful and beyond
belief. For this is the reason why man is rightly said and thought to be
a great marvel and the animal really worthy of wonder. Now hear
what it is, fathers; and with kindly ears and for the sake of your humanity, give me your close attention:

3   Now the highest Father, God the master-builder, had, by the laws of
his secret wisdom, fabricated this house, this world which we see, a
very superb temple of divinity. He had adorned the super-
celestial region with minds. He had animated the celestial globes with
eternal souls; he had filled with a diverse throng of animals the
cast-off and residual parts of the lower world. But, with the work finished, the Artisan desired that there be someone to reckon up the rea-

2

son of such a big work, to love its beauty, and to wonder at its great-ness. Accordingly, now that all things had been completed, as Moses and Timaeus testify, He lastly considered creating man. But there was nothing in the archetypes from which He could mold a new sprout, nor anything in His storehouses which He could bestow as a heritage upon a new son, nor was there an empty judiciary seat where this con-templator of the universe could sit. Everything was filled up; all things had been laid out in the highest, the lowest, and the middle orders. But it did not belong to the paternal power to have failed in the final parturition, as though exhausted by childbearing; it did not belong to wisdom, in a case of necessity, to have been tossed back and forth through want of a plan; it did not belong to the loving-kindness which was going to praise divine liberality in others to be forced to condemn itself. Finally, the best of workmen decided that that to which nothing of its very own could be given should be, in composite fashion, whatsoever had belonged individually to each and every thing. Therefore He took up man, a work of indeterminate form; and, placing him at the midpoint of the world, He spoke to him as fol-lows:

4  "We have given to thee, Adam, no fixed seat, no form of thy very own, no gift peculiarly thine, that thou mayest feel as thine own, have as thine own, possess as thine own the seat, the form, the gifts which thou thyself shalt desire. A limited nature in other creatures is con-fined within the laws written down by Us. In conformity with thy free judgment, in whose hands I have placed thee, thou art confined by no bounds; and thou wilt fix limits of nature for thyself. I have placed thee at the center of the world, that from there thou mayest more conveniently look around and see whatsoever is in the world. Neither heavenly nor earthly, neither mortal nor immortal have We made thee. Thou, like a judge appointed for being honorable, art the molder and maker of thyself; thou mayest sculpt thyself into whatever shape thou dost prefer. Thou canst grow downward into the lower natures which are brutes. Thou canst again grow upward from thy soul's reason into the higher natures which are divine."

5  O great liberality of God the Father! O great and wonderful happiness of man! It is given him to have that which he chooses and to be that which he wills. As soon as brutes are born, they bring with them, "from their dam's bag," as Lucilius says, what they are going to pos-sess. Highest spirits have been, either from the beginning or soon

after, that which they are going to be throughout everlasting eternity. At man's birth the Father placed in him every sort of seed and sprouts of every kind of life. The seeds that each man cultivates will grow and bear their fruit in him. If he cultivates vegetable seeds, he will become a plant. If the seeds of sensation, he will grow into brute. If rational, he will come out a heavenly animal. If intellectual, he will be an angel, and a son of God. And if he is not contented with the lot of any creature but takes himself up into the center of his own unity, then, made one spirit with God and settled in the solitary darkness of the Father, who is above all things, he will stand ahead of all things. Who does not wonder at this chameleon which we are? Or who at all feels more wonder at anything else whatsoever? It was not unfittingly that Asclepius the Athenian said that man was symbolized by Prometheus in the secret rites, by reason of our nature sloughing its skin and transforming itself; hence metamorphoses were popular among the Jews and the Pythagoreans.

• • •          (BOOT OMITTED)

32  I have proposed theorems about magic, too, wherein I have signified that magic is twofold. The first sort is put together by the work and authorship of demons, and is a thing, as God is true, execrable and monstrous. The other sort is, when well explored, nothing but the absolute consummation of the philosophy of nature. When the Greeks mention these, they call the first sort γοητείαν, not dignifying it in any way by the name magic. They call the second sort by its proper and peculiar name, μαγείαν, the perfect and highest wisdom, as it were. Porphyry says that in the language of the Persians, magician means the same thing as interpreter and lover of divine things means in our language. Now there is a great, or rather, fathers, there is the greatest disparity and unlikeness between these arts. Not only the Christian religion, but all laws, every well ordered state, condemn and curse the first. All wise men, all nations studious of things heavenly and divine, approve and embrace the second. The first is the most fraudulent of arts, the second is firm, faithful, and solid. Whoever cultivated the first always dissimulated it, because it would be in ignominy and disgrace of the author. From the second comes the highest splendor and glory of letters, desired in ancient times and almost always since then. No man who was a philosopher and desirous of learning good arts has ever been studious of the first. Pythagoras, Empedocles, Democritus, Plato, traveled across seas to learn the second. When they

came back, they preached it and held it chief among their esoteric doctrines. The first can be proved by no arguments nor certain founders; the second, honored as it were by most illustrious parents, has two principal founders: Xalmosis, whom Abbaris the Hyperborean imitated, and Zoroaster, not the one whom you perhaps think, but the son of Oromasus. If we question Plato as to what is the magic of each of them, he will answer in the *Alcibiades* that Zoroaster's magic is nothing but that knowledge of divine things wherein the kings of Persia educated their sons, that after the pattern of the republic of the world they might themselves be taught to rule their own republic. He will reply in the *Charmides* that the magic of Xalmosis is medicine of the soul, by which temperance is obtained for the soul, as health is obtained for the body by medicine. Afterwards Carondas, Damigeron, Apollonius, Hostanes, and Dardanus continued in their footsteps. So did Homer, whom we shall prove sometime in our *Poetic Theology* to have disguised this magic too, just as he did all other wisdoms, under the wanderings of Ulysses. Eudoxus and Hermippus continued in their footsteps. Nearly all who have examined closely the Pythagorean and Platonic mysteries have continued also. I find three among the moderns who have caught the scent of it, Alchindus the Arab, Roger Bacon, and William of Paris [of Auvergne]. Plotinus too mentions it, where he shows that the magician is the minister and not the maker of nature. That most wise man proves and asserts this second magic, so abhorring the other that, invited to the rites of evil demons, he replied that it was more fitting for them to come to him than for him to go to them, and rightly so. For as the first magic makes man subject to and delivered over to the powers of wickedness, so the second makes him their prince and lord. Finally, the first cannot claim for itself the name of either art or science. The second is full of the deepest mysteries and includes the most profound and hidden contemplation of things, and finally, the knowledge of all nature. The second, among the virtues sown by the kindness of God and planted in the world, as if calling them out from darkness into light, does not so much make wonders as carefully serve nature which makes them. Having carefully investigated the harmony of the universe, which the Greeks very expressively call συμπάθεια (sympatheia), and having looked closely into the knowledge that natures have of each other, this second magic, applying to each thing its innate charms, which are called by magicians ἴυγγες (lunges), as if it were itself the maker, discloses in public the wonders lying hidden in the recesses of the world, in the bosom of nature, in the storerooms and secrets of God. And as the farmer marries elm to vine, so the magician marries earth to heaven, that is, lower things to the qualities and virtues of higher things. Hence the first magic appears as monstrous and harmful as the second, divine and salutary. And especially because the first magic delivers man over to the enemies of God, calls him away from God, this second magic arouses that admiration at the works of God which so prepares that charity, faith, and hope most surely follow. For nothing impels more toward religion and the worship of God than assiduous contemplation of the wonders of God. When we shall have well explored these wonders by means of this natural magic we are speaking of, we shall be inspired more ardently to the worship and love of the maker, and shall be driven to sing: "The heavens are full, all the earth is full of the majesty of Thy glory."

33  And this is enough about magic, about which I have said these things because I know there are many people who, as dogs always bark at strangers, so also often condemn and hate what they do not understand.

34  I come now to those things that I have dug up from the ancient mysteries of the Hebrews and have brought forward in order to confirm the holy and Catholic faith. And lest by chance they be thought by those to whom they are unknown to be fictitious nonsense or tales about rumors, I wish everyone to understand what and of what sort they are, whence sought, by which and how famous authors they are guaranteed, and how they were stored away, how divinely inspired they are, and how necessary to us for defending religion against the rude slanders of the Hebrews. Not only do celebrated doctors of the Hebrews, but also among us Esdras, Hilary, and Origen write that Moses on the mountain received from God not only the law, which, as written down in five books, he left to posterity, but also a more secret and true interpretation of the law.

# *from* The Wisdom of the Ancients

*Francis Bacon*

## XXVI.—Prometheus, or the State of Man.

### Explained of An Overruling Profidence, and of Human Nature.

The ancients relate that man was the work of Prometheus, and formed of clay; only the artificer mixed in with the mass, particles taken from different animals. And being desirous to improve his workmanship, and endow, as well as create, the human race, he stole up to heaven with a bundle of birch-rods, and kindling them at the chariot of the Sun, thence brought down fire to the earth for the service of men.

They add that, for this meritorious act, Prometheus was repaid with ingratitude by mankind, so that, forming a conspiracy, they arraigned both him and his invention before Jupiter. But the matter was otherwise received than they imagined; for the accusation proved extremely grateful to Jupiter and the gods, insomuch that, delighted with the action, they not only indulged mankind the use of fire, but moreover conferred upon them a most acceptable and desirable present, viz: perpetual youth.

But men, foolishly overjoyed hereat, laid this present of the gods upon an ass, who, in returning back with it, being extremely thirsty, strayed to a fountain. The serpent, who was guardian thereof, would not suffer him to drink, but upon condition of receiving the burden he carried, whatever it should be. The silly ass complied, and thus the perpetual renewal of youth was, for a drop of water, transferred from men to the race of serpents.

Prometheus, not desisting from his unwarrantable practices, though now reconciled to mankind, after they were thus tricked of their present, but still continuing inveterate against Jupiter, had the boldness to attempt deceit, even in a sacrifice, and is said to have once offered up two bulls to Jupiter, but so as in the hide of one of them to wrap all the flesh and fat of both, and stuffing out the other hide only with the bones; then, in a religious and devout manner, gave Jupiter his choice of the two. Jupiter, detesting this sly fraud and hypocrisy, but having thus an opportunity of punishing the offender, purposely chose the mock bull.

7

And now giving way to revenge, but finding he could not chastise the insolence of Prometheus without afflicting the human race, (in the production whereof Prometheus had strangely and insufferably prided himself), he commanded Vulcan to form a beautiful and graceful woman, to whom every god presented a certain gift, whence she was called Pandora. They put into her hands an elegant box, containing all sorts of miseries and misfortunes; but Hope was placed at the bottom of it. With this box she first goes to Prometheus, to try if she could prevail upon him to receive and open it; but he being upon his guard, warily refused the offer. Upon this refusal, she comes to his brother Epimetheus, a man of a very different temper, who rashly and inconsiderately opens the box. When finding all kinds of miseries and misfortunes issued out of it, he grew wise too late, and with great hurry and struggle endeavored to clap the cover on again; but with all his endeavor could scarce keep in Hope, which lay at the bottom.

Lastly, Jupiter arraigned Prometheus of many heinous crimes; as that he formerly stole fire from heaven; that he contemptuously and deceitfully mocked him by a sacrifice of bones; that he despised his present, adding withal a new crime, that he attempted to ravish Pallas; for all which, he was sentenced to be bound in chains, and doomed to perpetual torments. Accordingly, by Jupiter's command, he was brought to Mount Caucasus, and there fastened to a pillar, so firmly that he could no way stir. A vulture or eagle stood by him, which in the daytime gnawed and consumed his liver; but in the night the wasted parts were supplied again; whence matter for his pain was never wanting.

They relate, however, that his punishment had an end; for Hercules sailing the ocean, in a cup, or pitcher, presented him by the Sun, came at length to Caucasus, shot the eagle with his arrows, and set Prometheus free. In certain nations, also, there were instituted particular games of the torch, to the honor of Prometheus, in which they who ran for the prize carried lighted torches; and as any one of these torches happened to go out, the bearer withdrew himself, and gave way to the next; and that person was allowed to win the prize, who first brought in his lighted torch to the goal.

EXPLANATION.—This fable contains and enforces many just and serious considerations; some whereof have been long since well observed, but some again remain perfectly untouched. Prometheus clearly and expressly signifies Providence; for of all the things in nature, the formation and endowment of man was singled out by the ancients, and esteemed the peculiar work of Providence. The reason hereof seems, 1. That the nature of man includes a mind and understanding, which is the seat of Providence. 2. That it is harsh and incredible to suppose reason and mind should be raised, and drawn out of senseless and irrational principles; whence it becomes almost inevitable, that providence is implanted in the human mind in conformity with, and by the direction and the design of the greater overruling Providence. But, 3. The principal cause is this: that man seems to be the thing in which the whole world centres, with respect to final causes; so that if he were away, all other things would stray and fluctuate, without end or intention, or become perfectly disjointed, and out of frame; for all things are made subservient to man, and he receives use and benefit from them all. Thus the revolutions, places, and periods, of the celestial bodies, serve him for distinguishing times and seasons, and for dividing the world into different regions; the meteors afford him prognostications of the weather; the winds sail our ships, drive our mills, and move our machines; and the vegetables and animals of all kinds either afford us matter for houses and habitations, clothing, food, physic; or tend to ease, or delight, to support, or refresh us; so that every thing in nature seems not made for itself, but for man.

And it is not without reason added, that the mass of matter whereof man was formed, should be mixed up with particles taken from different animals, and wrought in with the clay, because it is certain, that of all things in the universe, man is the most compounded and recompounded body; so that the ancients, not improperly, styled him a Microcosm, or little world within himself. For although the chemists have absurdly, and too literally, wrested and perverted the elegance of the term microcosm, whilst they pretend to find all kind of mineral and vegetable matters, or something corresponding to them, in man, yet it remains firm and unshaken, that the human body is, of all substances, the most mixed and organical; whence it has surprising powers and faculties; for the powers of simple bodies are but few, though certain and quick; as being little broken, or weakened, and not counterbalanced by mixture; but excellence and quantity of energy reside in mixture and composition.

Man, however, in his first origin, seems to be a defenceless, naked creature, slow in assisting himself, and standing in need of numerous things. Prometheus, therefore, hastened to the invention of fire, which supplies and administers to nearly all human uses and necessities, insomuch that, if the soul may be called the form of forms, if the hand may be called the instrument of instruments, fire may, as properly, be called the assistant of assistants, or the helper of helps; for hence proceed numberless operations, hence all the mechanic arts, and hence infinite assistances are afforded to the sciences themselves.

The manner wherein Prometheus stole this fire is properly described from the nature of the thing; he being said to have done it by applying a rod of birch to the chariot of the Sun; for birch is used in striking and beating, which clearly denotes the generation of fire to be from the violent percussions and collisions of bodies; whereby the matters struck are subtilized, rarefied, put into motion, and so prepared to receive the heat of the celestial bodies; whence they, in a clandestine and secret manner, collect and snatch fire, as it were by stealth, from the chariot of the Sun.

The next is a remarkable part of the fable, which represents that men, instead of gratitude and thanks, fell into indignation and expostulation, accusing both Prometheus and his fire to Jupiter,—and yet the accusation proved highly pleasing to Jupiter; so that he, for this reason, crowned these benefits of mankind with a new bounty. Here it may seem strange that the sin of ingratitude to a creator and benefactor, a sin so heinous as to include almost all others, should meet with approbation and reward. But the allegory has another view, and denotes, that the accusation and arraignment, both of human nature and human art among mankind, proceeds from a most noble and laudable temper of the mind, and tends to a very good purpose; whereas the contrary temper is odious to the gods, and unbeneficial in itself. For they who break into extravagant praises of human nature, and the arts in vogue, and who lay themselves out in admiring the things they already possess, and will needs have the sciences cultivated among them, to be thought absolutely perfect and complete, in the first place, show little regard to the divine nature, whilst they extol their own inventions almost as high as his perfection. In the next place, men of this temper are unserviceable and prejudicial in life, whilst they imagine themselves already got to the top of things, and there rest, without further inquiry. On the contrary, they who arraign and accuse both nature and art, and are always full of complaints against them, not only preserve a more just and modest sense of mind, but are also perpetually stirred up to fresh industry and new discoveries. Is not, then, the ignorance and fatality of mankind to be extremely pitied, whilst they remain slaves to the arrogance of a few of their own fellows, and are dotingly fond of that scrap of Grecian knowledge, the

Peripatetic philosophy; and this to such a degree, as not only to think all accusation or arraignment thereof useless, but even hold it suspect and dangerous? Certainly the procedure of Empedocles, though furious— but especially that of Democritus, (who with great modesty complained that all things were abstruse; that we know nothing; that truth lies hid in deep pits; that falsehood is strangely joined and twisted along with truth, &c.)—is to be preferred before the confident, assuming, and dogmatical school of Aristotle. Mankind are, therefore, to be admonished, that the arraignment of nature and of art is pleasing to the gods; and that a sharp and vehement accusation of Prometheus, though a creator, a founder, and a master, obtained new blessings and presents from the divine bounty, and proved more sound and serviceable than a diffusive harangue of praise and gratulation. And let men be assured that the fond opinion that they have already acquired enough, is a principal reason why they have acquired so little.

That the perpetual flower of youth should be the present which mankind received as a reward for their accusation, carries this moral: that the ancients seem not to have despaired of discovering methods, and remedies, for retarding old age, and prolonging the period of human life; but rather reckoned it among those things which, through sloth and want of diligent inquiry, perish and come to nothing, after having been once undertaken, than among such as are absolutely impossible, or placed beyond the reach of the human power. For they signify and intimate from the true use of fire, and the just and strenuous accusation and conviction of the errors of art, that the divine bounty is not wanting to men in such kind of presents, but that men indeed are wanting to themselves, and lay such an inestimable gift upon the back of a slow-paced ass; that is, upon the back of the heavy, dull, lingering thing, experience; from whose sluggish and tortoise-pace proceeds that ancient complaint of the shortness of life, and the slow advancement of arts. And certainly it may well seem, that the two faculties of reasoning and experience are not hitherto properly joined and coupled together, but to be still new gifts of the gods, separately laid, the one upon the back of a light bird, or abstract philosophy, and the other upon an ass, or slow-paced practice and trial. And yet good hopes might be conceived of this ass, if it were not for his thirst and the accidents of the way. For we judge, that if any one would constantly proceed, by a certain law and method, in the road of experience, and not by the way thirst after such experiments as make for profit or ostentation, nor exchange his burden, or quit the original design for the sake of these, he might be an useful bearer of a new and accumulated divine bounty to mankind.

That this gift of perpetual youth should pass from men to serpents, seems added by way of ornament, and illustration to the fable; perhaps intimating, at the same time, the shame it is for men, that they, with their fire, and numerous arts, cannot procure to themselves those things which nature has bestowed upon many other creatures.

The sudden reconciliation of Prometheus to mankind, after being disappointed of their hopes, contains a prudent and useful admonition. It points out the levity and temerity of men in new experiments, when, not presently succeeding, or answering to expectation, they precipitantly quit their new undertakings, hurry back to their old ones, and grow reconciled thereto.

After the fable has described the state of man, with regard to arts and intellectual matters, it passes on to religion; for after the inventing and settling of arts, follows the establishment of divine worship, which hypocrisy presently enters into and corrupts. So that by the two sacrifices we have elegantly painted the person of a man truly religious, and of an hypocrite. One of these sacrifices contained the fat, or the portion of God, used for burning and incensing; thereby denoting affection and zeal, offered up to his glory. It likewise contained the bowels, which are expressive of charity, along with the good and useful flesh. But the other contained nothing more than dry bones, which nevertheless stuffed out the hide, so as to make it resemble a fair, beautiful and magnificent sacrifice; hereby finely denoting the external and empty rites and barren ceremonies, wherewith men burden and stuff out the divine worship, —things rather intended for show and ostentation than conducing to piety. Nor are mankind simply content with this mock-worship of God, but also impose and further it upon him, as if he had chosen and ordained it. Certainly the prophet, in the person of God, has a fine expostulation, as to this matter of choice: "Is this the fasting which I have chosen, that a man should afflict his soul for a day, and bow down his head like a bulrush?"

After thus touching the state of religion, the fable next turns to manners, and the conditions of human life. And though it be a very common, yet is it a just interpretation, that Pandora denotes the pleasures and licentiousness which the cultivation and luxury of the arts of civil life introduce, as it were, by the instrumental efficacy of fire; whence the works of the voluptuary arts are properly attributed to Vulcan, the God of Fire. And hence infinite miseries and calamities have proceeded to the minds, the bodies, and the fortunes of men, together with a late repentance; and this not in each man's particular, but also in kingdoms and states; for wars, and tumults, and tyrannies, have all arisen from this same fountain, or box of Pandora.

It is worth observing, how beautifully and elegantly the fable has drawn two reigning characters in human life, and given two examples, or tablatures of them, under the persons of Prometheus and Epimetheus. The followers of Epimetheus are improvident, see not far before them, and prefer such things as are agreeable for the present; whence they are oppressed with numerous straits, difficulties, and calamities, with which they almost continually struggle; but in the mean time gratify their own temper, and, for want of a better knowledge of things, feed their minds with many vain hopes; and as with so many pleasing dreams, delight themselves, and sweeten the miseries of life.

But the followers of Prometheus are the prudent, wary men, that look into futurity, and cautiously guard against, prevent, and undermine many calamities and misfortunes. But this watchful, provident temper, is attended with a deprivation of numerous pleasures, and the loss of various delights, whilst such men debar themselves the use even of innocent things, and what is still worse, rack and torture themselves with cares, fears, and disquiets; being bound fast to the pillar of necessity, and tormented with numberless thoughts, (which for their swiftness are well compared to an eagle,) that continually wound, tear, and gnaw their liver or mind, unless, perhaps, they find some small remission by intervals or as it were at nights; but then new anxieties, dreads, and fears, soon return again, as it were in the morning. And, therefore, very few men, of either temper, have secured to themselves the advantages of providence, and kept clear of disquiets, troubles, and misfortunes.

Nor indeed can any man obtain this end without the assistance of Hercules; that is, of such fortitude and constancy of mind as stands prepared against every event, and remains indifferent to every change; looking forward without being daunted, enjoying the good without disdain, and enduring the bad without impatience. And it must be observed, that even Prometheus had not the power to free himself, but owed his deliverance to another; for no natural inbred force and fortitude could prove equal to such a task. The power of releasing him came from the utmost confines of the ocean, and from the sun; that is, from Apollo, or knowledge; and again, from a due consideration of the uncertainty, instability, and fluctuating state of human life, which is aptly represented by sailing the ocean. Accordingly, Virgil has prudently joined these two together, accounting him happy who knows the causes of things, and has conquered all his fears, apprehensions, and superstitions.

It is added, with great elegance, for supporting and confirming the human mind, that the great hero who thus delivered him sailed the ocean in a cup, or pitcher, to prevent fear, or complaint; as if, through the narrowness of our nature, or a too great fragility thereof, we were absolutely incapable of that fortitude and constancy to which Seneca finely alludes, when he says: "It is a noble thing, at once to participate in the frailty of man and the security of a god."

We have hitherto, that we might not break the connection of things, designedly omitted the last crime of Prometheus—that of attempting the chastity of Minerva—which heinous offence it doubtless was, that caused the punishment of having his liver gnawed by the vulture. The meaning seems to be this,—that when men are puffed up with arts and knowledge, they often try to subdue even the divine wisdom and bring it under the dominion of sense and reason, whence inevitably follows a perpetual and restless rending and tearing of the mind. A sober and humble distinction must, therefore, be made betwixt divine and human things, and betwixt the oracles of sense and faith, unless mankind had rather choose an heretical religion, and a fictitious and romantic philosophy.

The last particular in the fable is the Games of the Torch, instituted to Prometheus, which again relates to arts and sciences, as well as the invention of fire, for the commemoration and celebration whereof these games were held. And here we have an extremely prudent admonition, directing us to expect the perfection of the sciences from succession, and not from the swiftness and abilities of any single person; for he who is fleetest and strongest in the course may perhaps be less fit to keep his torch alight, since there is danger of its going out from too rapid as well as from too slow a motion. But this kind of contest, with the torch, seems to have been long dropped and neglected; the sciences appearing to have flourished principally in their first authors, as Aristotle, Galen, Euclid, Ptolemy, &c.; whilst their successors have done very little, or scarce made any attempts. But it were highly to be wished that these games might be renewed, to the honour of Prometheus, or human nature, and that they might excite contest, emulation, and laudable endeavours, and the design meet with such success as not to hang tottering, tremulous,and hazarded, upon the torch of any single person. Mankind, therefore, should be admonished to rouse themselves, and try and exert their own strength and chance, and not place all their dependence upon a few men, whose abilities and capacities, perhaps, are not greater than their own.

These are the particulars which appear to us shadowed out by this trite and vulgar fable, though without denying that there may be contained in it several intimations that have a surprising correspondence with the Christian mysteries. In particular, the voyage of Hercules, made in a pitcher, to release Prometheus, bears an allusion to the word of God, coming in the frail vessel of the flesh to redeem mankind. But we indulge ourselves no such liberties as these, for fear of using strange fire at the altar of the Lord.

## XXVII.—Icarus and Scylla and Charybdis, or the Middle Way.

### Explained of Mediocrity in Natural and Moral Philosophy

Mediocrity, or the holding a middle course, has been highly extolled in morality, but little in matters of science, though no less useful and proper here; whilst in politics it is held suspected, and ought to be employed with judgment. The ancients described mediocrity in manners by the course prescribed to Icarus; and in matters of the understanding by the steering betwixt Scylla and Charybdis, on account of the great difficulty and danger in passing those straits.

Icarus, being to fly across the sea, was ordered by his father neither to soar too high nor fly too low, for, as his wings were fastened together with wax, there was danger of its melting by the sun's heat in too high a flight, and of its becoming less tenacious by the moisture if he kept too near the vapor of the sea. But he, with a juvenile confidence, soared aloft, and fell down headlong.

EXPLANATION.—The fable is vulgar, and easily interpreted; for the path of virtue lies straight between excess on the one side, and defect on the other. And no wonder that excess should prove the bane of Icarus, exulting in juvenile strength and vigor; for excess is the natural vice of youth, as defect is that of old age; and if a man must perish by either, Icarus chose the better of the two; for all defects are justly esteemed more depraved than excesses. There is some magnanimity in excess, that, like a bird, claims kindred with the heavens; but defect is a reptile, that basely crawls upon the earth. It was excellently said by Heraclitus: "A dry light makes the best soul;" for if the soul contracts moisture from the earth, it perfectly degenerates and sinks. On the other hand, moderation must be observed, to prevent this fine light from burning, by its too great subtility and dryness. But these observations are common.

In matters of the understanding, it requires great skill and a particular felicity to steer clear of Scylla and Charybdis. If the ship strikes upon Scylla, it is dashed in pieces against the rocks; if upon Charybdis, it is swallowed outright. This allegory is pregnant with matter; but we shall only observe the force of it lies here, that a mean be observed in every doctrine and science, and in the rules and axioms thereof, between the rocks of distinctions and the whirlpools of universalities: for these two are the bane and shipwreck of fine geniuses and arts.

# XXVIII.—Sphinx, or Science.

**Explained of the Sciences.**

They relate that Sphinx was a monster, variously formed, having the face and voice of a virgin, the wings of a bird, and the talons of a griffin. She resided on the top of a mountain, near the city Thebes, and also beset the highways. Her manner was to lie in ambush and seize the travelers, and having them in her power, to propose to them certain dark and perplexed riddles, which it was thought she received from the Muses, and if her wretched captives could not solve and interpret these riddles, she, with great cruelty, fell upon them, in their hesitation and confusion, and tore them to pieces. This plague having reigned a long time, the Thebans at length offered their kingdom to the man who could interpret her riddles, there being no other way to subdue her. Œdipus, a penetrating and prudent man, though lame in his feet, excited by so great a reward, accepted the condition, and with a good assurance of mind, cheerfully presented himself before the monster, who directly asked him: "What creature that was, which being born four-footed, afterwards became two-footed, then three-footed, and lastly four-footed again?" Œdipus, with presence of mind, replied it was man, who, upon his first birth and infant state, crawled upon all fours in endeavoring to walk; but not long after went upright upon his two natural feet; again, in old age walked three-footed, with a stick; and at last, growing decrepit, lay four-footed confined to his bed; and having by this exact solution obtained the victory, he slew the monster, and, laying the carcass upon an ass, led her away in triumph; and upon this he was, according to the agreement, made king of Thebes.

EXPLANATION.—This is an elegant, instructive fable, and seems invented to represent science, especially as joined with practice. For science, may, without absurdity, be called a monster, being strangely gazed at and admired by the ignorant and unskilful. Her figure and form is various, by reason of the vast variety of subjects that science considers; her voice and countenance are represented female, by reason of her gay appearance and volubility of speech; wings are added, because the sciences and their inventions run and fly about in a moment, for knowledge, like light communicated from one torch to another, is presently caught and copiously diffused; sharp and hooked talons are elegantly attributed to her, because the axioms and arguments of science enter the mind, lay hold of it, fix it down, and keep it from moving or slipping away. This the sacred philosopher observed, when he said: "The words of the wise are like goads or nails driven far in." Again, all science seems placed on high, as it were on the tops of mountains that are hard to climb; for science is justly imagined a sublime and lofty thing, looking down upon ignorance from an eminence, and at the same time taking an extensive view on all sides, as is usual on the tops of mountains. Science is said to beset the highways, because through all the journey and peregrination of human life there is matter and occasion offered of contemplation.

Sphinx is said to propose various difficult questions and riddles to men, which she received from the Muses; and these questions, so long as they remain with the Muses, may very well be unaccompanied with severity, for while there is no other end of contemplation and inquiry but that of knowledge alone, the understanding is not oppressed, or driven to straits and difficulties, but expatiates and ranges at large, and even receives a degree of pleasure from doubt and variety; but after the Muses have given over their riddles to Sphinx, that is, to practice, which urges and impels to action, choice, and determination, then it is that they become torturing, severe, and trying, and, unless solved and interpreted, strangely perplex and harass the human mind, rend it every way, and perfectly tear it to pieces. All the riddles of Sphinx, therefore, have two conditions annexed, viz: dilaceration to those who do not solve them, and empire to those that do. For he who understands the thing proposed, obtains his end, and every artificer rules over his work.

Sphinx has no more than two kinds of riddles, one relating to the nature of things, the other to the nature of man; and correspondent to these, the prizes of the solution are two kinds of empire,—the empire over nature, and the empire over man. For the true and ultimate end of natural philosophy is dominion over natural things, natural bodies, remedies, machines, and numberless other particulars, though the schools, contented with what spontaneously offers, and swollen with their own discourses, neglect, and in a manner despise, both things and works.

But the riddle proposed to Œdipus, the solution whereof acquired him the Theban kingdom, regarded the nature of man; for he who has thoroughly looked into and examined human nature, may in a manner command his own fortune, and seems born to acquire dominion and rule. Accordingly, Virgil properly makes the arts of government to be the arts of the Romans. It was, therefore, extremely apposite in Augustus Cæsar to use the image of Sphinx in his signet, whether this happened by accident or by design; for he of all men was deeply versed in politics, and through the course of his life very happily solved abundance of new riddles with regard to the nature of man; and unless he had done this with great dexterity and ready address, he would frequently have been involved in imminent danger, if not destruction.

It is with the utmost elegance added in the fable, that when Sphinx was conquered, her carcass was laid upon an ass; for there is nothing so subtile and abstruse, but after being once made plain, intelligible, and common, it may be received by the slowest capacity.

We must not omit that Sphinx was conquered by a lame man, and impotent in his feet; for men usually make too much haste to the solution of Sphinx's riddles; whence it happens, that she prevailing, their minds are rather racked and torn by disputes, than invested with command by works and effects.

# On the Revolutions of the Heavenly Spheres

*Nicholas Copernicus*

POPE

I can readily imagine, Holy Father, that as soon as some people hear that in this volume, which I have written about the revolutions of the spheres of the universe, I ascribe certain motions to the terrestrial globe, they will shout that I must be immediately repudiated together with this belief. For I am not so enamored of my own opinions that I disregard what others may think of them. I am aware that a philosopher's ideas are not subject to the judgment of ordinary persons, because it is his endeavor to seek the truth in all things, to the extent permitted to human reason by God. Yet I hold that completely erroneous views should be shunned. Those who know that the consensus of many centuries has sanctioned the conception that the earth remains at rest in the middle of the heaven as its center would, I reflected, regard it as an insane pronouncement if I made the opposite assertion that the earth moves. Therefore I debated with myself for a long time whether to publish the volume which I wrote to prove the earth's motion or rather to follow the example of the Pythagoreans and certain others, who used to transmit philosophy's secrets only to kinsmen and friends, not in writing but by word of mouth. . . . When I weighed these considerations, the scorn which I had reason to fear on account of the novelty and unconventionality of my opinion almost induced me to abandon completely the work which I had undertaken.

But while I hesitated for a long time and even resisted, my friends drew me back. . . . They exhorted me no longer to refuse, on account of the fear which I felt, to make my work available for the general use of students of astronomy. The crazier my doctrine of the earth's motion now appeared to most people, the argument ran, so much the more admiration and thanks would it gain after they saw the publication of my writings dispel the fog of absurdity by most luminous proofs. Influenced therefore by these persuasive men and by this hope, in the end I allowed my friends to bring out an edition of the volume, as they had long besought me to do.

## Revolutions

. . . I have . . . no desire to conceal from Your Holiness that I was impelled to consider a different system of deducing the motions of the universe's spheres for no other reason than the realization that astronomers do not agree among themselves in their investigations of this subject. For, in the first place, they are so uncertain about the motion of the sun and moon that they cannot establish and observe a constant length even for the tropical year. Secondly, in determining the motions not only of these bodies but also of the other five planets, they do not use the same principles, assumptions, and explanations of the apparent revolutions and motions. For while some employ only homocentrics, others utilize eccentrics and epicycles, and yet they do not quite reach their goal. . . . On the contrary, their experience was just like someone taking from various places hands, feet, a head, and other pieces, very well depicted, it may be, but not for the representation of a single person; since these fragments would not belong to one another at all, a monster rather than a man would be put together from them. . . .

For a long time, then, I reflected on this confusion in the astronomical traditions concerning the derivation of the motions of the universe's spheres. I began to be annoyed that the movements of the world machine, created for our sake by the best and most systematic Artisan of all, were not understood with greater certainty by the philosophers, who otherwise examined so precisely the most insignificant trifles of this world. For this reason I undertook the task of rereading the works of all the philosophers which I could obtain to learn whether anyone had ever proposed other motions of the universe's spheres than those expounded by the teachers of astronomy in the schools. And in fact first I found in Cicero that Hicetas supposed the earth to move. Later I also discovered in Plutarch that certain others were of this opinion. I have decided to set his words down here, so that they may be available to everybody:

> Some think that the earth remains at rest. But Philolaus the Pythagorean believes that, like the sun and moon, it revolves around the fire in an oblique circle. Heraclides of Pontus and Ecphantus the Pythagorean make the earth move, not in a progressive motion, but like a wheel in a rotation from west to east about its own center.

Therefore, having obtained the opportunity from these sources, I too began to consider the mobility of the earth. And even though the idea seemed absurd, nevertheless I knew that others before me had been granted the freedom to imagine any circles whatever for the purpose of explaining the heavenly phenomena. Hence I thought that I too would be readily permitted to ascertain whether explanations sounder than those of my predecessors could be found for the revolution of the celestial spheres on the assumption of some motion of the earth.

Having thus assumed the motions which I ascribe to the earth later on in the volume, by long and intense study I finally found that if the motions of the other planets are correlated with the orbiting of the earth, and are computed for the revolution of each planet, not only do their phenomena follow therefrom but also the order and size of all the planets and spheres, and heaven itself is so linked together that in no portion of it can anything be shifted without disrupting the remaining parts and the universe as a whole. . . .

Perhaps there will be babblers who claim to be judges of astronomy although completely ignorant of the subject and, badly distorting some passage of Scripture to their purpose, will dare to find fault with my undertaking and censure it. I disregard them even to the extent of despising their criticism as unfounded. For it is not unknown that Lactantius, otherwise an illustrious writer but hardly an astronomer, speaks quite childishly about the earth's shape, when he mocks those who declared that the earth has the form of a globe. Hence scholars need not be surprised if any such persons will likewise ridicule me. Astronomy is written for astronomers.

# *from* The Two New Sciences

## Galileo Galilei

*Born in Florence and educated in Padua, Galileo Galilei (1564–1642) was one of the greatest of all of the seventeeth century scientists. His early studies of motion led him to accept the basic theories of Copernicus, the Polish astronomer who postulated that the earth was a planet that revolved around the sun. Galileo perfected the first telescope, and with it he was able to identify the moons of Jupiter and describe the lunar surface. At first Galileo was prohibited from publishing his findings, but in 1632 he received a license for the publication of* A Dialogue Between the Two Great Systems of the World, *a tract that took the form of a debate between an adherent of the old Aristotelian system and a convert to the new Copernican one. Galileo was subsequently arrested by the Inquisition, tried, condemned, and forced to recant his Copernican views.*

SAGREDO. I have always considered it to be an idle notion of the common people that in these and similar frameworks one cannot reason from the small to the large, because many mechanical devices succeed on a small scale that cannot exist in great size. Now, all reasonings about mechanics have their foundations in geometry, in which I do not see that largeness and smallness make large circles, triangles, cylinders, cones, or any other figures [or] solids subject to properties different from those of small ones: hence if the large scaffolding is built with every member proportional to its counterpart in the smaller one, and if the smaller is sound and stable under the use for which it is designed, I fail to see why the larger should not also be proof against adverse and destructive shocks that it may encounter.

SALVATI. Here you must note how conclusions that are true may seem improbable at a first glance, and yet when only some small thing is pointed out, they cast off their concealing cloaks and, thus naked and simple, gladly show off their secrets. For who does not see that a horse falling from a height of three or four braccia will break its bones, while a dog falling from the same height, or a cat from eight or ten, or even more, will suffer no harm? Thus a cricket might fall without damage from a tower, or an ant from the moon. Small children remain unhurt in falls that should break the legs, or the heads, of their elders. And just as smaller animals are proportionately stronger or more robust than larger ones, so smaller plants will sustain themselves better. I think you both know that if an oak were two hundred feet high, it could not support branches spread out similarly to those of an oak of average size. Only by a miracle could nature form a horse the size of twenty horses, or a giant ten times the height of a man—unless she greatly altered the proportions of the members, especially those of the skeleton, thickening the bones far beyond their ordinary symmetry.

Similarly, to believe that in artificial machines the large and small are equally practicable and durable is a manifest error. Thus, for example, small spires, little columns, and other solid shapes can be safely extended or heightened without risk of breaking them, whereas very large ones will go to pieces at any adverse accident, or for no more cause than that of their own weight.

> I say that that motion is equably or uniformly accelerated which, abandoning rest, adds on to itself equal momenta of swiftness in equal times.

SAGREDO. Just as it would be unreasonable for me to oppose this, or any other definition whatever assigned by any author, all [definitions] being arbitrary, so I may, without offence, doubt whether this definition, conceived and assumed in the abstract, is adapted to, suitable for, and verified in the kind of accelerated motion that heavy bodies in fact employ in falling naturally. And since it seems that the Author promises us that what he has defined is the natural motion of heavy bodies, I should like to hear you remove certain doubts that disturb my mind, so that I can then apply myself with better attention to the propositions that are expected, and their demonstrations.

SALVATI. It will be good for you and Simplicio to propound the difficulties, which I imagine will be the same ones that occurred to me when I first saw this treatise, and that our Author himself put to rest for me in our discussions, or that I removed for myself by thinking them out.

SAGREDO. I picture to myself a heavy body falling. It leaves from rest; that is, from the deprivation of any speed whatever, and enters into motion in which it goes accelerating according to the ratio of increase of time from its first instant of motion. It will have obtained, for example, eight degrees of speed in eight pulse-beats, of which at the fourth beat it will have gained four; at the second [beat], two; and at the first, one. Now, time being infinitely divisible, what follows from this? The speed being always diminished in this ratio, there will be no degree of speed, however small (or we might say, "no degree of slowness, however great"), such that the moveable will not be found to have this [at some time] after its departure from infinite slowness, that is, from rest. Thus if the degree of speed that it had at four beats of time were such that, maintaining this uniformly, it would run two miles in one hour, while with the degree of speed that it had at the second beat it would have made one mile an hour, it must be said that in instants of time closer and closer to the first [instant] of its moving from rest, it would be found to be so slow that, continuing to move with this slowness, it would not pass a mile in an hour, nor in a day, nor in a year, nor in a thousand [years], and it would not pass even one span in some still longer time. Such events I find very hard to accommodate in my imagination, when our senses show us that a heavy body in falling arrives immediately at a very great speed.

SALVATI. This is one of the difficulties that gave me pause at the outset; but not long afterward I removed it, and its removal was effected by the same experience that presently sustains it for you.

You say that it appears to you that experience shows the heavy body, having hardly left from rest, entering into a very considerable speed; and I say that this same experience makes it clear to us that the first impetuses of the falling body, however heavy it may be, are very slow indeed. Place a heavy body on some yielding material, and leave it until it has pressed as much as it can with its mere weight. It is obvious that if you now raise it one or two braccia, and then let it fall on the same material, it will make a new pressure on impact, greater than it made by its weight alone. This effect will be caused by the falling moveable in conjunction with the speed gained in fall, and will be greater and greater according as the height is greater from which the impact is made; that is, according as the speed of the striking body is greater. The amount of speed of a falling body, then, we can estimate without error from the quality and quantity of its impact.

But tell me, gentlemen: if you let a sledge fall on a pole from a height of four braccia, and it drives this, say, four inches into the ground, and will drive it much less from a height of two braccia, and still less from a height of one, and less yet from a span only; if finally it is raised but a single inch, how much more will it accomplish than it were placed on top [of the pole] without striking it at all? Certainly very little. And its effect would

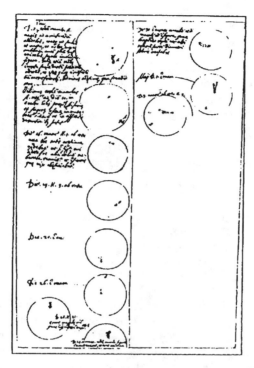

*Galileo's studies of sunspots proved that the sun rotates on its own axis just as the earth does.*

be quite imperceptible if it were lifted only the thickness of a leaf. Now, since the effect of impact is governed by the speed of a given percussent, who can doubt that its motion is very slow and minimal when its action is imperceptible? You now see how great is the force of truth, when the same experience that seemed to prove one thing at first glance assures us of the contrary when it is better considered.

But without restricting ourselves to this experience, though no doubt it is quite conclusive, it seems to me not difficult to penetrate this truth by simple reasoning. We have a heavy stone, held in the air at rest. It is freed from support and set at liberty; being heavier than air, it goes falling downward, not with uniform motion, but slowly at first and continually accelerated thereafter. Now, since speed may be increased or diminished in infinitum, what argument can persuade me that this moveable, departing from infinite slowness (which is rest), enters immediately into a speed of ten degrees rather than into one of four, or into the latter before a speed of two, or one, or one-half, or one one-hundredth? Or, in short, into all the lesser [degrees] in infinitum?

Please hear me out. I believe you would not hesitate to grant me that the acquisition of degrees of speed by the stone falling from the state of rest may occur in the same order as the diminution and loss of those same degrees when, driven by impelling force, the stone is hurled upward to the same height. But if that is so, I do not see how it can be supposed that in the diminution of speed in the ascending stone, consuming the whole speed, the stone can arrive at rest before passing through every degree of slowness.

SIMPLICIO. But if the degrees of greater and greater tardity are infinite, it will never consume them all, and this rising heavy body will never come to rest, but will move forever while always slowing down—something that is not seen to happen.

SALVATI. This would be so, Simplicio, if the moveable were to hold itself for any time in each degree; but it merely passes there, without remaining beyond an instant. And since in any finite time [temp quanto], however small, there are infinitely many instants, there are enough to correspond to the infinitely many degrees of diminished speed. It is obvious that this rising heavy body does not persist for any finite time in any one degree of speed, for if any finite time is assigned, and if the moveable had the same degree of speed at the first instant of that time and also at the last, then it could likewise be driven upward with this latter degree [of speed] through as much space [again], just as it was carried from the first [instant] to the second; and at the same rate it would pass from the second to a third, and finally, it would continue its uniform motion in infinitum.

SIMPLICIO. Truly, I should be one of those who concede that the falling heavy body vires acquirat eundo [acquires force in going], the speed increasing in the ratio of the space, while the momentum of the same percussent is doubled when it comes from double height, appear to me as propositions to be granted without repugnance or controversy.

SALVATI. And yet they are as false and impossible as [it is] that motion should be made instantaneously, and here is a very clear proof of it. When speeds have the same ratio as the spaces passed or to be passed, those spaces come to be passed in equal times, if therefore the speeds with which the falling body passed the space of four braccia were the doubles of the speeds with which it passed the first two braccia, as one space is double the other space, then the times of those passages are equal; but for the same moveable to pass the four braccia and the two in the same time cannot take place except in instantaneous motion. But we see that the falling heavy body makes its motion in time, and passes the two braccia in less [time] than the four; therefore it is false that its speed increases as the space.

The other proposition is shown to be false with the same clarity. For that which strikes being the same body, the difference and momenta of the impacts must be determined only by the difference of the speeds; if therefore the percussent coming from a double height delivers a blow of double momentum, it must strike with double speed; but double speed passes the double space in the same time, and we see the time of descent to be longer from the greater height.

SAGREDO. Too evident and too easy is this [reasoning] with which you make hidden conclusions manifest. This great facility renders the conclusions less prized than when they were under seeming contradiction. I think that people generally will little esteem ideas gained with so little trouble, in comparison with those over which long and unresolvable altercations are waged.

SALVATI. Things would not be so bad if men who show with great brevity and clarity the fallacies of propositions that have commonly been held to be true by people in general received only such bearable injury as scorn in place of thanks. What is truly unpleasant and annoying is a certain other attitude that some people habitually take. Claiming, in the same studies, at least parity with anyone that exists, these men see that the conclusions they have been putting forth as true are later exposed by someone else, and shown to be false by short and easy reasoning. I shall not call their reaction envy, which then usually transforms itself into rage and hatred against those who reveal such fallacies, but I do say that they are goaded by a desire to maintain inveterate errors rather than to permit newly discovered truths to be accepted. This desire sometimes induces them to write in contradiction to those truths of which they themselves are only too aware in their own hearts, merely to keep down the reputations of other men in the estimation of the common herd of little understanding. I have heard from our Academician not a few such false conclusions, accepted as true and [yet] easy to refute: and I have kept a record of some of these.

# *from* Letter to Christina of Tuscany: Science and Scripture

## Galileo Galilei

*The most renowned scientist at the beginning of the seventeenth century was the Italian astronomer, mathematician, and physicist Galileo Galilei (1564–1642). His discoveries about gravity, velocity, and the movement of astronomical bodies were grounded in a scientific method that ran contrary to the accepted standards for truth and authority. In the following excerpt from a letter to the Grand Duchess Christina of Tuscany (1615), Galileo defends his ideas and delineates his view of the correct line between science and scriptural authority.*

I think that in discussions of physical problems we ought to begin not from the authority of scriptural passages, but from sense-experiences and necessary demonstrations; for the holy Bible and the phenomena of nature proceed alike from the divine Word, the former as the dictate of the Holy Ghost and the latter as the observant executrix of God's commands. It is necessary for the Bible, in order to be accommodated to the understanding of every man, to speak many things which appear to differ from the absolute truth so far as the bare meaning of the words is concerned. But Nature, on the other hand, is inexorable and immutable; she never transgresses the laws imposed upon her, or cares a whit whether her abstruse reasons and methods of operation are understandable to men. For that reason it appears that nothing physical which sense-experience sets before our eyes, or which necessary demonstrations prove to us, ought to be called in question (much less condemned) upon the testimony of biblical passages which may have some different meaning beneath their words. For the Bible is not chained in every expression to conditions as strict as those which govern all physical effects; nor is God any less excellently revealed in Nature's actions than in the sacred statements of the Bible. . . .

From this I do not mean to infer that we need not have an extraordinary esteem for the passages of holy Scripture. On the contrary, having arrived at any certainties in physics, we ought to utilize these as the most appropriate aids in the true exposition of the Bible and in the investigation of those meanings which are necessarily contained therein, for these must be concordant with demonstrated truths. I should judge that the authority of the Bible was designed to persuade men of those articles and propositions which, surpassing all human reasoning, could not be made credible by science, or by any other means than through the very mouth of the Holy Spirit.

Yet even in those propositions which are not matters of faith, this authority ought to be preferred over that of all human writings which are supported only by bare assertions or probable arguments, and not set forth in a demonstrative way. This I hold to be necessary and proper to the same extent that divine wisdom surpasses all human judgment and conjecture.

But I do not feel obliged to believe that that same God who has endowed us with senses, reason, and intellect has intended to forgo their use and by some other means to give us knowledge which we can attain by them. . . .

# *from* Novum Organum

### *Francis Bacon*

The ancient authors and all others are left in undisputed possession of their honors, for we enter into no comparison of capacity or talent, but of method, and assume the part of a guide rather than of a critic.

To speak plainly, no correct judgment can be formed either of our method or its discoveries by those anticipations which are now in common use; for it is not to be required of us to submit ourselves to the judgment of the very method we ourselves arraign.

Nor is it an easy matter to deliver and explain our sentiments; for those things which are in themselves new can yet be only understood from some analogy to what is old.

Alexander Borgia said of the expedition of the French into Italy that they came with chalk in their hands to mark up their lodgings, and not with weapons to force their passage. Even so do we wish our philosophy to make its way quietly into those minds that are fit for it, and of good capacity; for we have no need of contention where we differ in first principles, and in our very notions, and even in our forms of demonstration.

We have but one simple method of delivering our sentiments, namely, we must bring men to particulars and their regular series and order, and they must for a while renounce their notions, and begin to form an acquaintance with things.

Our method and that of the sceptics agree in some respects at first setting out, but differ most widely, and are completely opposed to each other in their conclusion; for they roundly assert that nothing can be known; we, that but a small part of nature can be known, by the present method; their next step, however, is to destroy the authority of the senses and understanding, whilst we invent and supply them with assistance.

The idols and false notions which have already preoccupied the human understanding, and are deeply rooted in it, not only so beset men's minds that they become difficult of access, but even when access is obtained will again meet and trouble us in the instauration of the sciences, unless mankind when forewarned guard themselves with all possible care against them.

Four species of idols beset the human mind, to which (for distinction's sake) we have assigned names, calling the first Idols of the Tribe, the second Idols of the Den, the third Idols of the Market, the fourth Idols of the Theatre.

The formation of notions and axioms on the foundation of true induction is the only fitting remedy by which we can ward off and expel these idols. It is, however, of great service to point them out; for the doctrine of idols bears the same relation to the interpretation of nature as that of the confutation of sophisms does to common logic.

The idols of the tribe are inherent in human nature and the very tribe or race of man; for man's sense is falsely asserted to be the standard of things; on the contrary, all the perceptions both of the senses and the mind bear reference to man and not to the universe, and the human mind resembles those uneven mirrors which impart their own properties to different objects, from which rays are emitted and distort and disfigure them.

The idols of the den are those of each individual; for everybody (in addition to the errors common to the race of man) has his own individual den or cavern, which intercepts and corrupts the light of nature, either from his own peculiar and singular disposition, or from his education and intercourse with others, or from his reading, and the authority acquired by those whom he reverences and admires, or from the different impressions produced on the mind, as it happens to be preoccupied and predisposed, or equable and tranquil, and the like; so that the spirit of man (according to its several dispositions), is variable, confused, and, as it were, actuated by chance; and Heraclitus said well that men search for knowledge in lesser worlds, and not in the greater or common world.

There are also idols formed by the reciprocal intercourse and society of man with man, which we call idols of the market, from the commerce and association of men with each other; for men converse by means of language, but words are formed at the will of the generality, and there arises from a bad and unapt formation of words a wonderful obstruction to the mind. Nor can the definitions and explanations with which learned men are wont to guard and protect themselves in some instances afford a complete remedy—words still manifestly force the understanding, throw everything into confusion, and lead mankind into vain and innumerable controversies and fallacies.

Lastly, There are idols which have crept into men's minds from the various dogmas of peculiar systems of philosophy, and also from the perverted rules of demonstration and these we denominate idols of the theatre: for we regard all the systems of philosophy hitherto received or imagined, as so many plays brought out and performed, creating fictitious and theatrical worlds. Nor do we speak only of the present systems, or of the philosophy and sects of the ancients, since numerous other plays of a similar nature can be still composed and made to agree with each other, the causes of the most opposite errors being generally the same. Nor, again, do we allude merely to general systems, but also to many elements and axioms of sciences which have become inveterate by tradition implicit credence, and neglect. We must, however, discuss each species of idols more fully and distinctly in order to guard the human understanding against them.

*Section Two*

# Democracy, Power, and Oppression

# *from* The Republic

## *Plato*

*Plato (ca. 428–347 B.C.E.), an Athenian philosopher, has been a major influence on European thought. Plato's belief in the existence of transcendent truths which stood beyond the limits of time and space was made into a quasi-religious idea by Neo-Platonists during the Roman Empire and became a major influence on Augustine, one of the most important shapers of Christian theology. Ironically, Plato, who believed in rule by the few best—elitism—grew up in democratic Athens. All Athenian citizens belonged to the Assembly which governed Athens and had full political rights. Most offices were filled by lot and rotated frequently. The laws enacted by the Assembly were adjudicated by large juries also selected by lot. Plato grew up as Athenian democracy was declining and was associated with the faction in Athens which favored oligarchic government. Socrates, Plato's teacher, had been executed by the Athenian democracy for "corrupting the youth."*

## Book VI

### *The Philosophy of Government*

**SOCRATES, GLAUCON**

And what is the next question? he asked.

Surely, I said, the one which follows next in order. Inasmuch as philosophers only are able to grasp the eternal and unchangeable, and those who wander in the region of the many and variable are not philosophers, I must ask you which of the two classes should be the rulers of our State?

And how can we rightly answer that question?

Whichever of the two are best able to guard the laws and institutions of our State—let them be our guardians.

Very good.

Neither, I said, can there be any question that the guardian who is to keep anything should have eyes rather than no eyes?

There can be no question of that.

And are not those who are verily and indeed wanting in the knowledge of the true being of each thing, and who have in their souls no clear pattern, and are unable as with a painter's eye to look at the absolute truth and to that original to repair, and having perfect vision of the other world to order the laws about beauty, goodness, justice in this, if not already ordered, and to guard and preserve the order of them—are not such persons, I ask, simply blind?

Truly, he replied, they are much in that condition.

And shall they be our guardians when there are others who, besides being their equals in experience and falling short of them in no particular of virtue, also know the very truth of each thing?

There can be no reason, he said, for rejecting those who have this greatest of all great qualities; they must always have the first place unless they fail in some other respect.

Suppose, then, I said, that we determine how far they can unite this and the other excellences.

By all means.

In the first place, as we began by observing, the nature of the philosopher has to be ascertained. We must come to an understanding about him, and, when we have done so, then, if I am not mistaken, we shall also acknowledge that such a union of qualities is possible, and that those in whom they are united, and those only, should be rulers in the State.

What do you mean?

Let us suppose that philosophical minds always love knowledge of a sort which shows them the eternal nature not varying from generation and corruption.

Agreed.

And further, I said, let us agree that they are lovers of all true being; there is no part whether greater or less, or more or less honorable, which they are willing to renounce; as we said before of the lover and the man of ambition.

True.

And if they are to be what we were describing, is there not another quality which they should also possess?

What quality?

Truthfulness: they will never intentionally receive into their minds falsehood, which is their detestation, and they will love the truth.

Yes, that may be safely affirmed of them.

"May be." my friend, I replied, is not the word; say rather, "must be affirmed": for he whose nature is amorous of anything cannot help loving all that belongs or is akin to the object of his affections.

Right, he said.

And is there anything more akin to wisdom than truth?

How can there be?

Can the same nature be a lover of wisdom and a lover of falsehood?

Never.

The true lover of learning then must from his earliest youth, as far as in him lies, desire all truth?

Assuredly.

But then again, as we know by experience, he whose desires are strong in one direction will have them weaker in others; they will be like a stream which has been drawn off into another channel.

True.

He whose desires are drawn toward knowledge in every form will be absorbed in the pleasures of the soul, and will hardly feel bodily pleasure—I mean, if he be a true philosopher and not a sham one.

That is most certain.

Such a one is sure to be temperate and the reverse of covetous; for the motives which make another man desirous of having and spending, have no place in his character.

Very true.

Another criterion of the philosophical nature has also to be considered.

What is that?

There should be no secret corner of illiberality; nothing can be more antagonistic than meanness to a soul which is ever longing after the whole of things both divine and human.

Most true, he replied.

Then how can he who has magnificence of mind and is the spectator of all time and all existence, think much of human life?

He cannot.

Or can such a one account death fearful?

No, indeed.

Then the cowardly and mean nature has no part in true philosophy?

Certainly not.

Or again: can he who is harmoniously constituted, who is not covetous or mean, or a boaster, or a coward—can he, I say, ever be unjust or hard in his dealings?

Impossible.

Then you will soon observe whether a man is just and gentle, or rude and unsociable; these are the signs which distinguish even in youth the philosophical nature from the unphilosophical.

True.

There is another point which should be remarked.

What point?

Whether he has or has not a pleasure in learning; for no one will love that which gives him pain, and in which after much toil he makes little progress.

Certainly not.

And again, if he is forgetful and retains nothing of what he learns, will he not be an empty vessel?

That is certain.

Laboring in vain, he must end in hating himself and his fruitless occupation?

Yes.

Then a soul which forgets cannot be ranked among genuine philosophic natures; we must insist that the philosopher should have a good memory?

Certainly.

And once more, the inharmonious and unseemly nature can only tend to disproportion?

Undoubtedly.

And do you consider truth to be akin to proportion or to disproportion?

To proportion.

Then, besides other qualities, we must try to find a naturally well-proportioned and gracious mind, which will move spontaneously toward the true being of everything.

Certainly.

Well, and do not all these qualities, which we have been enumerating, go together, and are they not, in a manner, necessary to a soul, which is to have a full and perfect participation of being?

They are absolutely necessary, he replied.

And must not that be a blameless study which he only can pursue who has the gift of a good memory, and is quick to learn—noble, gracious, the friend of truth, justice, courage, temperance, who are his kindred?

The god of jealousy himself, he said, could find no fault with such a study.

And to men like him, I said, when perfected by years and education, and to these only you will intrust the State.

• • •

## Book VII

### *On Shadows and Realities in Education*

**SOCRATES, GLAUCON**

AND now, I said, let me show in a figure how far our nature is enlightened or unenlightened: Behold! human beings living in an underground den, which has a mouth open toward the light and reaching all along the den; here they have been from their childhood, and have their legs and necks chained so that they cannot move, and can only see before them, being prevented by the chains from turning round their heads. Above and behind them a fire is blazing at a distance, and between the fire and the prisoners there is a raised way; and you will see, if you look, a low wall built along the way, like the screen which marionette-players have in front of them, over which they show the puppets.

I see.

And do you see, I said, men passing along the wall carrying all sorts of vessels, and statues and figures of animals made of wood and stone and various materials, which appear over the wall? Some of them are talking, others silent.

You have shown me a strange image, and they are strange prisoners.

Like ourselves, I replied: and they see only their own shadows, or the shadows of one another, which the fire throws on the opposite wall of the cave?

True, he said; how could they see anything but the shadows if they were never allowed to move their heads?

And of the objects which are being carried in like manner they would only see the shadows?

Yes, he said.

And if they were able to converse with one another, would they not suppose that they were naming what was actually before them?

Very true.

And suppose further that the prison had an echo which came from the other side, would they not be sure to fancy when one of the passers-by spoke that the voice which they heard came from the passing shadow?

No question, he replied.

To them, I said, the truth would be literally nothing but the shadows of the images.

That is certain.

•   •   •

And suppose once more, that he is reluctantly dragged up a steep and rugged ascent, and held fast until he is forced into the presence of the sun himself, is he not likely to be pained and irritated? When he approaches the light his eyes will be dazzled, and he will not be able to see anything at all of what are now called realities.

Not all in a moment, he said.

He will require to grow accustomed to the sight of the upper world. And first he will see the shadows best, next the reflections of men and other objects in the water, and then the objects themselves; then he will gaze upon the light of the moon and the stars and the spangled heaven; and he will see the sky and the stars by night better than the sun or the light of the sun by day?

Certainly.

Last of all he will be able to see the sun, and not mere reflections of him in the water, but he will see him in his own proper place, and not in another; and he will contemplate him as he is.

Certainly.

He will then proceed to argue that this is he who gives the season and the years, and is the guardian of all that is in the visible world, and in a certain way the cause of all things which he and his fellows have been accustomed to behold?

Clearly, he said, he would first see the sun and then reason about him.

And when he remembered his old habitation, and the wisdom of the den and his fellow-prisoners, do you not suppose that he would felicitate himself on the change, and pity him?

Certainly, he would.

And if they were in the habit of conferring honors among themselves on those who were quickest to observe the passing shadows and to remark which of them went before, and which followed after, and which were together; and who were therefore best able to draw conclusions as to the future, do you think that he would care for such honors and glories, or envy the possessors of them? Would he not say with Homer,

> *"Better to be the poor servant of a poor master,"*

and to endure anything, rather than think as they do and live after their manner?

Yes, he said, I think that he would rather suffer anything than entertain these false notions and live in this miserable manner.

Imagine once more, I said, such a one coming suddenly out of the sun to be replaced in his old situation; would he not be certain to have his eyes full of darkness?

To be sure, he said.

And if there were a contest, and he had to compete in measuring the shadows with the prisoners who had never moved out of the den, while his sight was still weak, and before his eyes had become steady (and the time which would be needed to acquire this new habit of sight might be very considerable), would he not be ridiculous? Men would say of him that up he went and down he came without his eyes; and that it was better not even to think of ascending; and if anyone tried to loose another and lead him up to the light, let them only catch the offender, and they would put him to death.

No question, he said.

This entire allegory, I said, you may now append, dear Glaucon, to the previous argument; the prison-house is the world of sight, the light of the fire is the sun, and you will not misapprehend me if you interpret the journey upward to be the ascent of the soul into the intellectual world according to my poor belief, which, at your desire, I have expressed— whether rightly or wrongly, God knows. But, whether true or false, my opinion is that in the world of knowledge the idea of good appears last of all, and is seen only with an effort; and, when seen, is also inferred to be the universal author of all things beautiful and right, parent of light and of the lord of light in this visible world, and the immediate source of reason and truth in the intellectual; and that this is the power upon which he who would act rationally either in public or private life must have his eye fixed.

•   •   •

## Book VIII

### *Four Forms of Government*

**SOCRATES, GLAUCON**

And then democracy comes into being after the poor have conquered their opponents, slaughtering some and banishing some, while to the remainder they give an equal share of freedom and power; and this is the form of government in which the magistrates are commonly elected by lot.

Yes, he said, that is the nature of democracy, whether the revolution has been effected by arms, or whether fear has caused the opposite party to withdraw.

And now what is their manner of life, and what sort of a government have they? for as the government is, such will be the man.

Clearly, he said.

In the first place, are they not free; and is not the city full of freedom and frankness—a man may say and do what he likes?

'Tis said so, he replied.

And where freedom is, the individual is clearly able to order for himself his own life as he pleases?

Clearly.

Then in this kind of State there will be the greatest variety of human natures?

There will.

This, then, seems likely to be the fairest of States, being like an embroidered robe which is spangled with every sort of flower. And just as women and children think a variety of colors to be of all things most charming, so there are many men to whom this State, which is spangled with the manners and characters of mankind, will appear to be the fairest of States.

Yes.

Yes, my good sir, and there will be no better in which to look for a government.

Why?

Because of the liberty which reigns there—they have a complete assortment of constitutions; and he who has a mind to establish a State, as we have been doing, must go to a democracy as he would to a bazaar at which they sell them, and pick out the one that suits him; then, when he has made his choice, he may found his State.

He will be sure to have patterns enough.

And there being no necessity, I said, for you to govern in this State, even if you have the capacity, or to be governed, unless you like, or to go to war when the rest go to war, or to be at peace when others are at peace, unless you are so disposed—there being no necessity also, because some law forbids you to hold office or be a dicast, that you should not hold office or be a dicast, if you have a fancy—is not this a way of life which for the moment is supremely delightful?

For the moment, yes.

• • •

Neither does he receive or let pass into the fortress any true word of advice; if anyone says to him that some pleasures are the satisfactions of good and noble desires, and others of evil desires, and that he ought to use and honor some, and chastise and master the others—whenever this is repeated to him he shakes his head and says that they are all alike, and that one is as good as another.

Yes, he said; that is the way with him.

Yes, I said, he lives from day to day indulging the appetite of the hour; and sometimes he is lapped in drink and strains of the flute; then he becomes a water-drinker, and tries to get thin; then he takes a turn at gymnastics; sometimes idling and neglecting everything, then once more living the life of a philosopher; often he is busy with politics, and starts to his feet and says and does whatever comes into his head; and, if he is emulous of anyone who is a warrior, off he is in that direction, or of men of business, once more in that. His life has neither law nor order; and this distracted existence he terms joy and bliss and freedom; and so he goes on.

Yes, he replied, he is all liberty and equality.

• • •

And democracy has her own good, of which the insatiable desire brings her to dissolution?

What good?

Freedom, I replied; which, as they tell you in a democracy, is the glory of the State—and that therefore in a democracy alone will the freeman of nature deign to dwell.

Yes; the saying is in everybody's mouth.

I was going to observe, that the insatiable desire of this and the neglect of other things introduce the change in democracy, which occasions a demand for tyranny.

How so?

When a democracy which is thirsting for freedom has evil cup-bearers presiding over the feast, and has drunk too deeply of the strong wine of freedom, then, unless her rulers are very amenable and give a plentiful draught, she calls them to account and punishes them, and says that they are cursed oligarchs.

Yes, he replied, a very common occurrence.

Yes, I said; and loyal citizens are insultingly termed by her "slaves" who hug their chains, and men of naught; she would have subjects who are like rulers, and rulers who are like subjects: these are men after her own heart, whom she praises and honors both in private and public. Now, in such a State, can liberty have any limit?

Certainly not.

By degrees the anarchy finds a way into private houses, and ends by getting among the animals and infecting them.

How do you mean?

I mean that the father grows accustomed to descend to the level of his sons and to fear them, and the son is on a level with his father, he having no respect or reverence for either of his parents; and this is his freedom; and the metic is equal with the citizen, and the citizen with the metic, and the stranger is quite as good as either.

Yes, he said, that is the way.

And these are not the only evils, I said—there are several lesser ones: In such a state of society the master fears and flatters his scholars, and the scholars despise their masters and tutors; young and old are all alike; and the young man is on a level with the old, and is ready to compete with him in word or deed; and old men condescend to the young and are full of pleasantry and gayety; they are loth to be thought morose and authoritative, and therefore they adopt the manners of the young.

Quite true, he said.

The last extreme of popular liberty is when the slave bought with money, whether male or female, is just as free as his or her purchaser; nor must I forget to tell of the liberty and equality of the two sexes in relation to each other.

Why not, as Æschylus says, utter the word which rises to our lips?

•  •  •

And above all, I said, and as the result of all, see how sensitive the citizens become; they chafe impatiently at the least touch of authority, and at length, as you know, they cease to care even for the laws, written or unwritten; they will have no one over them.

Yes, he said, I know it too well.

Such, my friend, I said, is the fair and glorious beginning out of which springs tyranny.

# *from* Politics

## Aristotle

*Aristotle (384–322 B.C.E.), Plato's pupil, was the teacher of Alexander the Great. He wrote about many different areas of knowledge from physics and biology to ethics and politics. In spite of his considerable intellectual debt to Plato, Aristotle went his own way in methodology as well as in the conclusions he reached. He approached the question of how the ideal state should be organized by sending his students out through the various Greek city-states, collecting examples of their constitutions. He divided the constitutions into categories according to the most important differences his students found. By analyzing the results, Aristotle reached the conclusions he enunciates in the Politics. As can be seen from this selection and the one before, the ancient Greeks established the essential framework of political debate as it is still perceived in Western Civilization. In this selection Aristotle refers to "the mean" but does not explain that term. Aristotle believed that correct moral behavior involved a correct balance between opposites such as humility and pride. To be too humble or too proud would lead one to destruction. Good behavior came from limiting the excesses of either quality.*

## Book I

Every state is a community of some kind, and every community is established with a view to some good; for mankind always act in order to obtain that which they think good. But, if all communities aim at some good, the state or political community, which is the highest of all, and which embraces all the rest, aims at good in a greater degree than any other, and at the highest good.

Some people think that the qualifications of a statesman, king, householder, and master are the same, and that they differ, not in kind, but only in the number of their subjects. For example, the ruler over a few is called a master; over more, the manager of a household; over a still larger number, a statesman or king, as if there were no difference between a great household and a small state. The distinction which is made between the king and the statesman is as follows: when the government is personal, the ruler is a king; when, according to the rules of the political science, the citizens rule and are ruled in turn, then he is called a statesman.

But all this is a mistake; for governments differ in kind, as will be evident to any one who considers the matter according to the method which has hitherto guided us. As in other departments of science, so in politics, the compound should always be resolved into the simple elements or least parts of the whole. We must therefore look at the elements of which the state is composed, in order that we may see in what the different kinds of rule differ from one another, and whether any scientific result can be attained about each one of them.

• • •

## Book III

There is also a doubt as to what is to be the supreme power in the state:—Is it the multitude? Or the wealthy? Or the good? Or the one best man? Or a tyrant? Any of these alternatives seems to involve disagreeable consequences. If the poor, for example, because they are more in number, divide among themselves the property of the rich,—is not this unjust? No, by heaven (will be the reply), for the supreme authority justly willed it. But if this is not injustice, pray what is? Again, when in the first division all has been taken, and the majority divide anew the property of the minority, is it not evident, if this goes on, that they will ruin the state? Yet surely, virtue is not the ruin of those who possess her, nor is justice destructive of a state; and therefore this law of confiscation clearly cannot be just. If it were, all the acts of a tyrant must of necessity be just; for he only coerces other men by superior power, just as the multitude coerce the rich. But is it just then that the few and the wealthy should be the rulers? And what if they, in like manner, rob and plunder the people,—is this just? If so, the other case will likewise be just. But there can be no doubt that all these things are wrong and unjust.

Then ought the good to rule and have supreme power? But in that case everybody else, being excluded from power, will be dishonoured. For the offices of a state are posts of honour; and if one set of men always hold them, the rest must be deprived of them. Then will it be well that the one best man should rule? Nay, that is still more oligarchic, for the number of those who are dishonoured is thereby increased. Some one may say that it is bad in any case for a man subject as he is to all the accidents of human passion, to have the supreme power, rather than the law. But what if the law itself be democratical or oligarchical, how will that help us out of our difficulties? Not at all; the same consequences will follow.

This difficulty seems now to be sufficiently answered, but there is another akin to it. That inferior persons should have authority in greater matters than the good would appear to be a strange thing, yet the election and calling to account of the magistrates is the greatest of all. And these, as I was saying, are functions which in some states are assigned to the people, for the assembly is supreme in all such matters. Yet persons of any age, and having but a small property qualification, sit in the assembly and deliberate and judge, although for the great officers of state, such as treasurers and generals, a high qualification is required. This difficulty may be solved in the same manner as the preceding, and the present practice of democracies may be really defensible. For the power does not reside in the dicast, or senator, or ecclesiast, but in the court, and the senate, and the assembly, of which individual senators, or ecclesiasts, or dicasts, are only parts or members. And for this reason the many may claim to have a higher authority than the few; for the people, and the senate, and the courts consist of many persons, and their property collectively is greater than the property of one or of a few individuals holding great offices. But enough of this.

•  •  •

# Book IV

Now in all states there are three elements: one class is very rich, another very poor, and a third in a mean. It is admitted that moderation and the mean are best, and therefore it will clearly be best to possess the gifts of fortune in moderation; for in that condition of life men are most ready to follow rational principle. But he who neatly excels in beauty, strength, birth, or wealth, or on the other hand who is very poor, or very weak, or very much disgraced, finds it difficult to follow rational principle. Of these two the one sort grow into violent and great criminals, the others into rogues and petty rascals. And two sorts of offences correspond to them, the one committed from violence, the other from roguery. Again, the middle class is least likely to shrink from rule, or to be over-ambitious for it; both of which are injuries to the state. Again, those who have too much of the goods of fortune, strength, wealth, friends, and the like, are neither willing nor able to submit to authority. The evil begins at home; for when they are boys, by reason of the luxury in which they are brought up, they never learn even at school, the habit of obedience. On the other hand, the very poor, who are in the opposite extreme, are too degraded. So that the one class cannot obey, and can only rule despotically; the other knows not how to command and must be ruled like slaves. Thus arises a city, not of freemen, but of masters and slaves, the one despising, the other envying; and nothing can be more fatal to friendship and good fellowship in states than this: for good fellowship springs from friendship; when men are at enmity with one another, they would rather not even share the same path. But a city ought to be composed, as far as possible, of equals and similars; and these are generally the middle classes. Wherefore the city which is composed of middle-class citizens is necessarily best constituted in respect of the elements of which we say the fabric of the state naturally consists. And this is the class of citizens which is most secure in a state, for they do not, like the poor, covet their neighbours' goods: nor do others covet theirs, as the poor covet the goods of the rich; and as they neither plot against others, nor are themselves plotted against, they pass through life safely. Wisely then did Phocylides pray,— 'Many things are best in the mean; I desire to be of a middle condition in my city.'

Thus it is manifest that the best political community is formed by citizens of the middle class, and that those states are likely to be well-administered, in which the middle class is large, and stronger if possible than both the other classes, or at any rate than either singly; for the addition of the middle class turns the scale, and prevents either of the extremes from being dominant. Great then is the good fortune of a state in which the citizens have a moderate and sufficient property; for where some possess much, and the others nothing, there may arise an extreme democracy, or a pure oligarchy; or a tyranny may grow out of either extreme, either out of the most rampant democracy, or out of an oligarchy; but it is not so likely to arise out of the middle constitutions and those akin to them. I will explain the reason of this hereafter, when I speak of the revolutions of states. The mean condition of states is clearly best, for no other is free from faction; and where the middle class is large, there are least likely to be factions and dissensions. For a similar reason large states are less liable to faction than small ones, because in them the middle class is large; whereas in small states it is easy to divide all the citizens into two classes who are either rich or poor, and to leave nothing in the middle. And democracies are safer and more permanent than oligarchies, because they have a middle class which is more numerous and has a greater share in the government; for when there is no middle class, and the poor greatly exceed in number, troubles arise, and the state soon comes to an end. A proof of the superiority of the middle class is that the best legislators have been of a middle condition; for example, Solon, as his own verses testify; and Lycurgus, for he was not a king; and Charondas, and almost all legislators.

# The Laws

## *Cicero*

*Marcus Tullius Cicero (106–43 B.C.E.) was a Roman orator, statesman, and philosopher. Cicero in many ways embodied the Roman senatorial ideal and wrote as a proponent of the constitution of the Roman Republic, which was governed by a Senate made up of the Roman elite. He believed in the ideal of the gentleman scholar-citizen who lives a rich intellectual life and serves the state as needed. His loyalty to republican institutions may have provoked the enmity which caused Marc Antony to see that he was executed shortly after the assassination of Julius Caesar. Cicero articulated the doctrine of natural law, whose principles provided the foundation for Roman law. The basic view of law developed by Cicero and other Roman thinkers was the foundation for both ecclesiastical and secular law in most of Europe.*

## What Is So Trivial as Legal Advice, However Necessary?

*Atticus*: . . . Kindly begin without delay the statement of your opinions on the civil law [*jus civile*].

*Marcus*: My opinions? Well then, I believe that there have been most eminent men in our state whose customary function it was to interpret the law to the people and answer questions in regard to it, but that these men, though they have made great claims, have spent their time on unimportant details. What subject indeed is so vast as the law of the state? But what is so trivial as the task of those who give legal advice? It is, however, necessary for the people. But, while I do not consider that those who have applied themselves to this profession have lacked a conception of universal Law, yet they have carried their studies of this civil law, as it is called, only far enough to accomplish their purpose of being useful to the people. Now all this amounts to little so far as learning is concerned, though for practical purposes it is indispensable. What subject is it, then, that you are asking me to expound? To what task are you urging me? Do you want me to write a treatise on the law of eaves and house walls? Or to compose formulas for contracts and court procedure? These subjects have been carefully treated by many writers, and are of humbler character, I believe, than what is expected of me.

51

*A*: Yet if you ask what I expect of you, I consider it a logical thing that since you have already written a treatise on the constitution of the ideal State, you should also write one on its laws. For I note that this was done by your beloved Plato, whom you admire, revere above all others, and love above all others.

*M*: Is it your wish, then, that as he discussed the institutions of states and the ideal laws with Clinias and the Spartan Megillus in Crete on a summer day amid the cypress groves and forest paths of Cnossus, sometimes walking about, sometimes resting—you recall his description—we, in like manner, strolling or taking our ease among these stately poplars on the green and shady river bank, shall discuss the same subjects along somewhat broader lines than the practice of the courts calls for?

*A*: I should certainly like to hear such a conversation.

*M*: What does Quintus say?

*Quintus*: No other subject would suit me better.

*M*: And you are wise, for you must understand that in no other kind of discussion can one bring out so clearly what Nature's gifts to man are, what a wealth of most excellent possessions the human mind enjoys, what the purpose is, to strive after and accomplish which we have been born and placed in this world, what it is that unites men, and what natural fellowship there is among them. For it is only after all these things have been made clear that the origin of Law and Justice can be discovered.

*A*: Then you do not think that the science of law is to be derived from the praetor's edict, as the majority do now, or from the Twelve Tables, as people used to think, but from the deepest mysteries of philosophy?

*M*: Quite right; for in our present conversation, Pomponius, we are not trying to learn how to protect ourselves legally, or how to answer clients' questions. Such problems may be important, and in fact they are; for in former times many eminent men made a specialty of their solution, and at present one person performs this duty with the greatest authority and skill. But in our present investigation we intend to cover the whole range of universal Justice and Law in such a way that our own civil law, as it is called, will be confined to a small and narrow corner. For we must explain the nature of Justice, and this must be sought for in the nature of man; we must also consider the laws by which states ought to be governed; then we must deal with the enactments and decrees of nations which are already formulated and put in writing; and among these the civil law, as it is called, of the Roman people will not fail to find a place.

*Q*: You probe deep, and seek, as you should, the very fountainhead, to find what we are after, brother. And those who teach the civil law in any other way are teaching not so much the path of justice as of litigation.

*M*: There you are mistaken, Quintus, for it is rather ignorance of the law than knowledge of it that leads to litigation. But that will come later; now let us investigate the origins of Justice.

## Law Is the Highest Reason, Implanted in Nature

Well then, the most learned men have determined to begin with Law, and it would seem that they are right, if, according to their definition, Law is the highest reason, implanted in Nature, which commands what ought to be done and forbids the opposite. This reason, when firmly fixed and fully developed in the human mind, is Law. And so they believe that Law is intelligence, whose natural function it is to command right conduct and forbid wrongdoing. . . .

Now if this is correct, as I think it to be in general, then the origin of Justice is to be found in Law, for Law is a natural force; it is the mind and reason of the intelligent man, the standard by which Justice and Injustice are measured. But since our whole discussion has to do with the reasoning of the populace, it will sometimes be necessary to speak in the popular manner, and give the name of law to that which in written form decrees whatever it wishes, either by command or prohibition. For such is the crowd's definition of law. But in determining what Justice is, let us begin with that supreme Law which had its origin ages before any written law existed or any state had been established.

*Q*: Indeed that will be preferable and more suitable to the character of the conversation we have begun.

*M*: Well, then, shall we seek the origin of Justice itself at its fountainhead? For when that is discovered we shall undoubtedly have a standard by which the things we are seeking may be tested.

*Q*: I think that is certainly what we must do. . . .

*M*: I will not make the argument long. Your admission leads us to this: that animal which we call man, endowed with foresight and quick intelligence, complex, keen, possessing memory, full of reason and prudence, has been given a certain distinguished status by the supreme God who created him; for he is the only one among so many different kinds and varieties of living beings who has a share in reason and thought, while all the rest are deprived of it. But what is more divine, I will not say in man only, but in all heaven and earth, than reason? And reason, when it is full grown and perfected, is rightly called wisdom. Therefore, since there is nothing better than reason, and since it exists both in man and God, the first common possession of man and God is reason. But those who have reason in common must also have right reason in common. And since right reason is Law, we must believe that men have Law also in common with the gods. Further, those who share Law must also share Justice; and those who share these are to be regarded as members of the same commonwealth. If indeed they obey the same authorities and powers, this is true in a far greater degree; but as a matter of fact they do obey this celestial system, the divine mind, and the God of transcendent power. Hence we must now conceive of this whole universe as one commonwealth of which both gods and men are members. . . .

A: Ye immortal gods, how far back you go to find the origins of Justice! And you discourse so eloquently that I not only have no desire to hasten on to the consideration of the civil law, concerning which I was expecting you to speak, but I should have no objection to your spending even the entire day on your present topic: for the matters which you have taken up, no doubt merely as preparatory to another subject, are of greater import than the subject itself to which they form an introduction.

M: The points which are now being briefly touched upon are certainly important; but out of all the material of the philosophers' discussions, surely there comes nothing more valuable than the full realization that we are born for Justice, and that right is based, not upon men's opinions, but upon Nature. This fact will immediately be plain if you once get a clear conception of man's fellowship and union with his fellow men. For no single thing is so like another, so exactly its counterpart, as all of us are to one another. Nay, if bad habits and false beliefs did not twist the weaker minds and turn them in whatever direction they are inclined, no one would be so like his own self as all men would be like all others. And so, however we may define man, a single definition will apply to all. This is a sufficient proof that there is no difference in kind between man and man; for if there were, one definition could not be applicable to all men; and indeed reason, which alone raises us above the level of the beasts and enables us to draw inferences, to prove and disprove, to discuss and solve problems, and to come to conclusions, is certainly common to us all, and, though varying in what it learns, at least in the capacity to learn it is invariable. For the same things are invariably perceived by the senses, and those things which stimulate the senses, stimulate them in the same way in all men; and those rudimentary beginnings of intelligence to which I have referred, which are imprinted on our minds, are imprinted on all minds alike; and speech, the mind's interpreter, though differing in the choice of words, agrees in the sentiments expressed. In fact, there is no human being of any race who, if he finds a guide, cannot attain to virtue. . . .

The next point, then, is that we are so constituted by Nature as to share the sense of Justice with one another and to pass it on to all men. And in this whole discussion I want it understood that what I shall call Nature is that which is implanted in us by Nature; that, however, the corruption caused by bad habits is so great that the sparks of fire, so to speak, which Nature has kindled in us are extinguished by this corruption, and the vices which are their opposites spring up and are established. But if the judgments of men were in agreement with Nature, so that, as the poet [Terence] says, they considered "nothing alien to them which concern mankind," then Justice would be equally observed by all. For those creatures who have received the gift of reason from Nature have also received right reason, and therefore they have also received the gift of Law, which is right reason applied to command and prohibition. And if they have received Law, they have received Justice also. Now all men have received reason therefore all men have received Justice. . . .

Now all this is really a preface to what remains to be said in our discussion and its purpose is to make it more easily understood that Justice is inherent in nature. After I have said a few words more on this topic, I shall go on to the civil law, the subject which gives rise to all this discourse. . . .

But you see the direction this conversation is to take; our whole discourse is intended to promote the firm foundation of states, the strengthening of cities, and the curing of the ills of peoples. For that reason I want to be especially careful not to lay down first principles that have not been wisely considered and thoroughly investigated. . . .

Once more, then, before we come to the individual laws, let us look at the character and nature of Law, for fear that, though it must be the standard to which we refer everthing, we may now and then be led astray by an incorrect use of terms, and forget the rational principles on which our laws must be based.

Q: Quite so, that is the correct method of exposition.

## Law Is the Mind of God

M: Well, then, I find that it has been the opinion of the wisest men that Law is not a product of human thought, nor is it any enactment of peoples, but something eternal which rules the whole universe by its wisdom in command and prohibition. Thus they have been accustomed to say that Law is the primal and ultimate mind of God, whose reason directs all things either by compulsion or restraint. Wherefore that Law which the gods have given to the human race has been justly praised; for it is the reason and mind of a wise lawgiver applied to command and prohibition.

Q: You have touched upon this subject several times before. But before you come to the laws of peoples, please make the character of this heavenly Law clear to us, so that the waves of habit may not carry us away and sweep us into the common mode of speech on such subjects.

M: Ever since we were children, Quintus, we have learned to call, "If one summon another to court," and other rules of the same kind, laws. But we must come to the true understanding of the matter, which is as follows: this and other commands and prohibitions of nations have the power to summon to righteousness and away from wrong-doing; but this power is not merely older than the existence of nations and states, it is coeval with that God who guards and rules heaven and earth. For the divine mind cannot exist without reason, and divine reason cannot but have this power to establish right and wrong. No written law commanded that a man should take his stand on a bridge alone, against the full force of the enemy, and order the bridge broken down behind him; yet we shall not for that reason suppose that the heroic [Horatius] Cocles was not obeying the law of bravery and following its decrees in doing so noble a deed. Even if there was no written law against rape at Rome in the reign of Lucius Tarquinius, we cannot say on that account that Sextus Tarquinius did not break that eternal Law by violating Lucretia, the daughter of Lucretius! For reason did exist, derived from the nature of the universe, urging men to right conduct and diverting them from wrong-doing, and this reason did not first become law when it was written down, but when it first came into existence simultaneously with the divine mind. Wherefore the true and primal Law, applied to command and prohibition, is the right reason of supreme Jupiter.

*Q*: I agree with you, brother, that what is right and true is also eternal, and does not begin or end with written statutes.

*M*: Therefore, just as that devine mind is the supreme Law, so, when reason is perfected in man that also is Law; and this perfected reason exists in the mind of the wise man; but those rules which, in varying forms and for the need of the moment, have been formulated for the guidance of nations, bear the title of laws rather by favor than because they are really such. . . .

What of the many deadly, the many pestilential statutes which nations put in force? These no more deserve to be called laws than the rules a band of robbers might pass in their assembly. For if ignorant and unskillful men have prescribed deadly poisons instead of healing drugs, these cannot possibly be called physicians' prescriptions; neither in a nation can a statute of any sort be called a law, even though the nation, in spite of its being a ruinous regulation, has accepted it. Therefore Law is the distinction between things just and unjust, made in agreement with that primal and most ancient of all things, Nature; and in conformity to Nature's standard are framed those human laws which inflict punishment upon the wicked but defend and protect the good. . . .

So in the very beginning we must persuade our citizens that the gods are the lords and rulers of all things, and that what is done, is done by their will and authority; that they are likewise great benefactors of man, observing the character of every individual, what he does, of what wrong he is guilty, and with what intentions and with what piety he fulfills his religious duties; and that they take note of the pious and impious. For surely minds that are imbued with such ideas will not fail to form true and useful opinions. Indeed, what is more true than that no one ought to be so foolishly proud as to think that, though reason and intellect exist in himself, they do not exist in the heavens and the universe, or that those things which can hardly be understood by the highest reasoning powers of the human intellect are guided by no reason at all? In truth, the man that is not driven to gratitude by the orderly courses of the stars, the regular alternation of day and night, the gentle progress of the seasons, and the produce of the earth brought forth for our sustenance—how can such a one be accounted a man at all? And since all things that possess reason stand above those things which are without reason, and since it would be sacrilege to say that anything stands above universal Nature, we must admit that reason is inherent in Nature. Who will deny that such beliefs are useful when he remembers how often oaths are used to confirm agreements, how important to our well-being is the sanctity of treaties, how many persons are deterred from crime by the fear of divine punishment, and how sacred an association of citizens becomes when the immortal gods are made members of it, either as judges or as witnesses?

There you have the proem to the law; for that is the name given to it by Plato.

# *from* The Prince

## Niccolo Machiavelli

*Niccolo Machiavelli (1469–1527) was a citizen of Florence during the time of the Renaissance. In that era of political instability Machiavelli was an important functionary in the government in Florence, only to suffer dismissal from office, arrest, torture, and exile, during which he wrote this work, a manual for rulers on how to gain and keep power. The fact that "Machiavellian" has entered the language as a term describing a certain kind of political behavior indicates the lasting importance of Machiavelli's political thought.*

## Chapter XV

### *Of the Qualities in Respect of Which Men, and Most of All Princes, are Praised or Blamed*

It now remains for us to consider what ought to be the conduct and bearing of a Prince in relation to his subjects and friends. And since I know that many have written on this subject, I fear it may be thought presumptuous in me to write of it also; the more so, because in my treatment of it, I depart from the views that others have taken.

But since it is my object to write what shall be useful to whosoever understands it, it seems to me better to follow the real truth of things than an imaginary view of them. For many Republics and Princedoms have been imagined that were never seen or known to exist in reality. And the manner in which we live, and that in which we ought to live, are things so wide asunder, that he who quits the one to betake himself to the other is more likely to destroy than to save himself; since any one who would act up to a perfect standard of goodness in everything, must be ruined among so many who are not good. It is essential, therefore, for a Prince who desires to maintain his position, to have learned how to be other than good, and to use or not to use his goodness as necessity requires.

Laying aside, therefore, all fanciful notions concerning a Prince, and considering those only that are true, I say that all men when they are spoken of, and Princes more than others from their being set so high, are characterized by some one of those qualities which attach either praise or blame. Thus one is accounted liberal, another miserly (which word I use, rather than *avaricious*, to denote the man who is too sparing of what is his own, *avarice* being the disposition to take wrongfully what is another's); one is generous, another greedy; one cruel, another tender-hearted; one is faithless, another true to his word; one effeminate and cowardly, another high-spirited and courageous; one is courteous, another haughty; one impure, another chaste; one simple, another crafty; one firm, another facile; one grave, another frivolous; one devout, another unbelieving; and the like. Every one, I know, will admit that it would be most laudable for a Prince to be endowed with all of the above qualities that are reckoned good; but since it is impossible for him to possess or constantly practise them all, the conditions of human nature not allowing it, he must be discreet enough to know how to avoid the infamy of those vices that would deprive him of his government, and, if possible, be on his guard also against those which might not deprive him of it; though if he cannot wholly restrain himself, he may with less scruple indulge in the latter. He need never hesitate, however, to incur the reproach of those vices without which his authority can hardly be preserved; for if he well consider the whole matter, he will find that there may be a line of conduct having the appearance of virtue, to follow which would be his ruin, and that there may be another course having the appearance of vice, by following which his safety and well-being are secured.

# Chapter XVI

## *Of Liberality and Miserliness*

BEGINNING, then, with the first of the qualities above noticed, I say that it may be a good thing to be reputed liberal, but, nevertheless, that liberality without the reputation of it is hurtful; because, though it be worthily and rightly used, still if it be not known, you escape not the reproach of its opposite vice. Hence, to have credit for liberality with the world at large, you must neglect no circumstance of sumptuous display; the result being, that a Prince of a liberal disposition will consume his whole substance in things of this sort, and, after all, be obliged, if he would maintain his reputation for liberality, to burden his subjects with extraordinary taxes, and to resort to confiscations and all the other shifts whereby money is raised. But in this way he becomes hateful to his subjects, and growing impoverished is held in little esteem by any. So that in the end, having by his liberality offended many and obliged few, he is worse off than when he began, and is exposed to all his original dangers. Recognizing this, and endeavouring to retrace his steps, he at once incurs the infamy of miserliness.

A Prince, therefore, since he cannot without injury to himself practise the virtue of liberality so that it may be known, will not, if he be wise, greatly concern himself though he be called miserly. Because in time he will come to be regarded as more and more liberal, when it is seen that through his parsimony his revenues are sufficient; that he is able to defend himself against any who make war on him; that he can engage in enterprises against others without burdening his subjects; and thus exercise liberality towards all from whom he does not take, whose number is infinite, while he is miserly in respect of those only to whom he does not give, whose number is few.

In our own days we have seen no Princes accomplish great results save those who have been accounted miserly. All others have been ruined. Pope Julius II, after availing himself of his reputation for liberality to arrive at the Papacy, made no effort to preserve that reputation when making war on the King of France, but carried on all his numerous campaigns without levying from his subjects a single extraordinary tax, providing for the increased expenditure out of his long-continued savings. Had the present King of Spain been accounted liberal, he never could have engaged or succeeded in so many enterprises.

A Prince, therefore, if he is enabled thereby to forbear from plundering his subjects, to defend himself, to escape poverty and contempt, and the necessity of becoming rapacious, ought to care little though he incur the reproach of miserliness, for this is one of those vices which enable him to reign.

And should any object that Caesar by his liberality rose to power, and that many others have been advanced to the highest dignities from their having been liberal and so reputed, I reply, 'Either you are already a Prince or you seek to become one; in the former case liberality is hurtful, in the latter it is very necessary that you be thought liberal; Caesar was one of those who sought the sovereignty of Rome; but if after obtaining it he had lived on without retrenching his expenditure, he must have ruined the Empire.' And if it be further urged that many Princes reputed to have been most liberal have achieved great things with their armies, I answer that a Prince spends either what belongs to himself and his subjects, or what belongs to others; and that in the former case he ought to be sparing, but in the latter ought not to refrain from any kind of liberality. Because for a Prince who leads his armies in person and maintains them by plunder, pillage, and forced contributions, dealing as he does with the property of others this liberality is necessary, since otherwise he would not be followed by his soldiers. Of what does not belong to you or to your subjects you should, therefore, be a lavish giver, as were Cyrus, Caesar, and Alexander; for to be liberal with the property of others does not take from your reputation, but adds to it. What injures you is to give away what is your own. And there is no quality so self-destructive as liberality; for while you practise it you lose the means whereby it can be practised, and become poor and despised, or else, to avoid poverty, you become rapacious and hated. For liberality leads to one or other of these two results, against which, beyond all others, a Prince should guard.

Wherefore it is wiser to put up with the name of being miserly, which breeds ignominy, but without hate, than to be obliged, from the desire to be reckoned liberal, to incur the reproach of rapacity, which breeds hate as well as ignominy.

## Chapter XVII

### Of Cruelty and Clemency, and Whether It Is Better to Be Loved or Feared

PASSING to the other qualities above referred to, I say that every Prince should desire to be accounted merciful and not cruel. Nevertheless, he should be on his guard against the abuse of this quality of mercy. Cesare Borgia was reputed cruel, yet his cruelty restored Romagna, united it, and brought it to order and obedience; so that if we look at things in their true light, it will be seen that he was in reality far more merciful than the people of Florence, who, to avoid the imputation of cruelty, suffered Pistoja to be torn to pieces by factions.

A Prince should therefore disregard the reproach of being thought cruel where it enables him to keep his subjects united and obedient. For he who quells disorder by a very few signal examples will in the end be more merciful than he who from too great leniency permits things to take their course and so to result in rapine and bloodshed; for these hurt the whole State, whereas the severities of the Prince injure individuals only.

And for a new Prince, of all others, it is impossible to escape a name for cruelty, since new States are full of dangers. Wherefore Virgil, by the mouth of Dido, excuses the harshness of her reign on the plea that it was new, saying:—

> 'A fate unkind, and newness in my reign
> Compel me thus to guard a wide domain.'

Nevertheless, the new Prince should not be too ready of belief, nor too easily set in motion; nor should he himself be the first to raise alarms; but should so temper prudence with kindliness that too great confidence in others shall not throw him off his guard, nor groundless distrust render him insupportable.

And here comes in the question whether it is better to be loved rather than feared, or feared rather than loved. It might perhaps be answered that we should wish to be both; but since love and fear can hardly exist together, if we must choose between them, it is far safer to be feared than loved. For of men it may generally be affirmed that they are thankless, fickle, false, studious to avoid danger, greedy of gain, devoted to you while you are able to confer benefits upon them, and ready, as I said before, while danger is distant, to shed their blood, and sacrifice their property, their lives, and their children for you; but in the hour of need they turn against you. The Prince, therefore, who without otherwise securing himself builds wholly on their professions is undone. For the friendships which we buy with a price, and do not gain by greatness and nobility of character, though they be fairly earned are not made good, but fail us when we have occasion to use them.

Moreover, men are less careful how they offend him who makes himself loved than him who makes himself feared. For love is held by the tie of obligation, which, because men are a sorry breed, is broken on every whisper of private interest; but fear is bound by the apprehension of punishment which never relaxes its grasp.

Nevertheless a Prince should inspire fear in such a fashion that if he do not win love he may escape hate. For a man may very well be feared and yet not hated, and this will be the case so long as he does not meddle with the property or with the women of his citizens and subjects. And if constrained to put any to death, he should do so only when there is manifest cause or reasonable justification. But, above all, he must abstain from the property of others. For men will sooner forget the death of their father than the loss of their patrimony. Moreover, pretexts for confiscation are never to seek, and he who has once begun to live by rapine always finds reasons for taking what is not his; whereas reasons for shedding blood are fewer, and sooner exhausted.

But when a Prince is with his army, and has many soldiers under his command, he must needs disregard the reproach of cruelty, for without such a reputation in its Captain, no army can be held together or kept under any kind of control. Among other things remarkable in Hannibal this has been noted, that having a very great army, made up of men of many different nations and brought to fight in a foreign country, no dissension ever arose among the soldiers themselves, nor any mutiny against their leader, either in his good or in his evil fortunes. This we can only ascribe to the transcendent cruelty, which, joined with numberless great qualities, rendered him at once venerable and terrible in the eyes of his soldiers; for without this reputation for cruelty these other virtues would not have produced the like results.

Unreflecting writers, indeed, while they praise his achievements, have condemned the chief cause of them; but that his other merits would not by themselves have been so efficacious we may see from the case of Scipio, one of the greatest Captains, not of his own time only but of all times of which we have record, whose armies rose against him in Spain from no other cause than his too great leniency in allowing them a freedom inconsistent with military strictness. With which weakness Fabius Maximus taxed him in the Senate House, calling him the corrupter of the Roman soldiery. Again, when the Locrians were shamefully outraged by one of his lieutenants, he neither avenged them, nor punished the insolence of his officer; and this from the natural easiness of his disposition. So that it was said in the Senate by one who sought to excuse him, that there were many who knew better how to refrain from doing wrong themselves than how to correct the wrong-doing of others. This temper, however, must in time have marred the name and fame even of Scipio, had he continued in it, and retained his command. But living as he did under the control of the Senate, this hurtful quality was not merely disguised, but came to be regarded as a glory.

Returning to the question of being loved or feared, I sum up by saying, that since his being loved depends upon his subjects, while his being feared depends upon himself, a wise Prince should build on what is his own, and not on what rests with others. Only, as I have said, he must do his utmost to escape hatred.

## Chapter XVIII

### *How Princes Should Keep Faith*

EVERY one understands how praiseworthy it is in a Prince to keep faith, and to live uprightly and not craftily. Nevertheless, we see from what has taken place in our own days that Princes who have set little store by their word, but have known how to overreach men by their cunning, have accomplished great things, and in the end got the better of those who trusted to honest dealing.

Be it known, then, that there are two ways of contending, one in accordance with the laws, the other by force; the first of which is proper to men, the second to beasts. But since the first method is often ineffectual, it becomes necessary to resort to the second. A Prince should, therefore, understand how to use well both the man and the beast. And this lesson has been covertly taught by the ancient writers, who relate how Achilles and many others of these old Princes were given over to be brought up and trained by Chiron the Centaur; since the only meaning of their having for instructor one who was half man and half beast is, that it is necessary for a Prince to know how to use both natures, and that the one without the other has no stability.

But since a Prince should know how to use the beast's nature wisely, he ought of beasts to choose both the lion and the fox; for the lion cannot guard himself from the toils, nor the fox from wolves. He must therefore be a fox to discern toils, and a lion to drive off wolves.

To rely wholly on the lion is unwise; and for this reason a prudent Prince neither can nor ought to keep his word when to keep it is hurtful to him and the causes which led him to pledge it are removed. If all men were good, this would not be good advice, but since they are dishonest and do not keep faith with you, you, in return, need not keep faith with them; and no prince was ever at a loss for plausible reasons to cloak a breach of faith. Of this numberless recent instances could be given, and it might be shown how many solemn treaties and engagements have been rendered inoperative and idle through want of faith in Princes, and that he who was best known to play the fox has had the best success.

It is necessary, indeed, to put a good colour on this nature, and to be skil-ful in simulating and dissembling. But men are so simple, and governed so absolutely by their present needs, that he who wishes to deceive will never fail in finding willing dupes. One recent example I will not omit. Pope Alexander VI had no care or thought but how to deceive, and always found material to work on. No man ever had a more effective manner of asseverating, or made promises with more solemn protesta-tions, or observed them less. And yet, because he understood this side of human nature, his frauds always succeeded.

It is not essential, then, that a Prince should have all the good qualities which I have enumerated above, but it is most essential that he should seem to have them; I will even venture to affirm that if he has and invari-ably practises them all, they are hurtful, whereas the appearance of hav-ing them is useful. Thus, it is well to seem merciful, faithful, humane, religious, and upright, and also to be so; but the mind should remain so balanced that were it needful not to be so, you should be able and know how to change to the contrary.

And you are to understand that a Prince, and most of all a new Prince, cannot observe all those rules of conduct in respect whereof men are accounted good, being often forced, in order to preserve his Princedom, to act in opposition to good faith, charity, humanity, and religion. He must therefore keep his mind ready to shift as the winds and tides of For-tune turn, and, as I have already said, he ought not to quit good courses if he can help it, but should know how to follow evil courses if he must.

A Prince should therefore be very careful that nothing ever escapes his lips which is not replete with the five qualities above named, so that to see and hear him, one would think him the embodiment of mercy, good faith, integrity, humanity, and religion. And there is no virtue which it is more necessary for him to seem to possess than this last; because men in general judge rather by the eye than by the hand, for every one can see but few can touch. Every one sees what you seem, but few know what you are, and these few dare not oppose themselves to the opinion of the many who have the majesty of the State to back them up.

Moreover, in the actions of all men, and most of all of Princes, where there is no tribunal to which we can appeal, we look to results. Wherefore if a Prince succeeds in establishing and maintaining his authority, the means will always be judged honourable and be approved by every one. For the vulgar are always taken by appearances and by results, and the world is made up of the vulgar, the few only finding room when the many have no longer ground to stand on.

A certain Prince of our own days, whose name it is as well not to mention, is always preaching peace and good faith, although the mortal enemy of both; and both, had he practised them as he preaches them, would, oftener than once, have lost him his kingdom and authority.

# True Law of Free Monarchies
# *and* A Speech to Parliament

## *James I*

*James I of England reigned from 1603 to 1625, following Elizabeth I, the last of the Tudors. During the century before James came to the throne, England had become a centralized monarchy with an increasingly powerful Parliament sharing authority with the monarch. In particular, Parliament had been able to establish the precedent under the Tudors that all new taxes had to be approved by the House of Commons. James was "liberal" in the sense discussed by Machiavelli and constantly in need of new taxes which Parliament was unwilling to grant. Thus, the central theme of the reign of James was the question of whether the king was limited by legal precedents and by the will of Parliament. James thought of himself as a great philosopher and theologian and engaged in endless disputes with Parliament. This selection, written in 1598, provides the rationale James would use as king of England to assert his prerogatives and the authority by which he claimed to rule.*

## True Law

### *Prerogative and Parliament.*

According to these fundamental laws already alleged, we daily see that in the parliament (which is nothing else but the head court of the king and his vassals) the laws are but craved by his subjects, and only made by him at their [proposal] and with their advice: for albeit the king make daily statutes and ordinances, [imposing] such pains thereto as he thinks [fit], without any advice of parliament or estates, yet it lies in the power of no parliament to make any kind of law or statute, without his sceptre [that is, authority] be to it, for giving it the force of a law. . . . And as ye see it manifest that the king is over-lord of the whole land, so is he master over every person that inhabiteth the same, having power over the life and death of every one of them: for although a just prince will not take the life of any of his subjects without a clear law, yet the same laws whereby he taketh them are made by himself or his predecessors; and so the power flows always from himself. . . . Where he sees the law doubt-some or rigorous, he may interpret or mitigate the same, lest otherwise *summum jus* be *summa injuria* [the greatest right be the greatest wrong]: and therefore general laws made publicly in parliament may upon . . . [the king's] authority be mitigated and suspended upon causes only known to him.

As likewise, although I have said a good king will frame all his actions to be according to the law, yet is he not bound thereto but of his good will, and for good example-giving to his subjects. . . . So as I have already said, a good king, though he be above the law, will subject and frame his actions thereto, for example's sake to his subjects, and of his own free will, but not as subject or bound thereto.

## [A Speech before Parliament]

. . . The state of monarchy is the supremest thing upon earth: for kings are not only God's lieutenants upon earth and sit upon God's throne, but even by God himself they are called gods. There be three principal [comparisons] that illustrate the state of monarchy: one taken out of the word of God, and the two other out of the grounds of policy and philosophy. In the Scriptures kings are called gods, and so their power after a certain relation compared to the Divine power. Kings are also compared to fathers of families: for a king is truly *parens patriae* [parent of the country], the politic father of his people. And lastly, kings are compared to the head of this microcosm of the body of man. . . .

I conclude then this point touching the power of kings with this axiom of divinity, That as to dispute what God may do is blasphemy, . . . so it is sedition in subjects to dispute what a king may do in the height of his power. But just kings will ever be willing to declare what they will do, if they will not incur the curse of God. I will not be content that my power be disputed upon; but I shall ever be willing to make the reason appear of all my doings, and rule my actions according to my laws. . . .

Now the second general ground whereof I am to speak concerns the matter of grievances. . . . First then, I am not to find fault that you inform yourselves of the particular just grievances of the people; nay I must tell you, ye can neither be just nor faithful to me or to your countries that trust and employ you, if you do it not. . . . But I would wish you to be careful to avoid [these] things in the matter of grievances.

First, that you do not meddle with the main points of government: that is my craft . . . to meddle with that, were to lesson me. I am now an old king. . . .

I must not be taught my office.

Secondly, I would not have you meddle with such ancient rights of mine as I have received from my predecessors, possessing them *more majorum* [as ancestral customs]: such things I would be sorry should be accounted for grievances. All novelties are dangerous as well in a politic as in a natural body: and therefore I would be loath to be quarrelled in my ancient rights and possessions: for that were to judge me unworthy of that which my predecessors had and left me.

# *from* Leviathan

## Thomas Hobbes

*Thomas Hobbes (1588–1679) wrote* Leviathan *in 1651, two years after King Charles I of England had been beheaded by Parliamentary forces during the Civil Wars. Central to the conflict had been the question of the source of legitimate power and the limits on the prerogatives of the king. Hobbes was writing to defend monarchy, but based his arguments not on the divine right of kings, but on the nature of human society itself. Hobbes was a contemporary of Galileo and knew him. His use of human nature rather than the Bible or the teachings of the Church as the source for arguments about how political society ought to be organized can be seen to parallel Galileo's argument that truth can be ascertained by the study of nature. Hobbes's general argument could support parliamentary government or any form of sovereignty, but his argument that sovereignty is indivisible and absolute tended to favor a monarchical form of government.*

Nature hath made men so equall, in the faculties of body, and mind; as that though there bee found one man sometimes manifestly stronger in body, or of quicker mind than another; yet when all is reckoned together, the difference between man, and man, is not so considerable, as that one man can thereupon claim to himselfe any benefit, to which another may not pretend, as well as he. For as to the strength of body, the weakest has strength enough to kill the strongest, either by secret machination, or by confederacy with others, that are in the same danger with himselfe. . . .

And so as to the faculties of the mind . . . men are . . . [more] equall than unequall. . . .

From this equality of ability, ariseth equality of hope in the attaining of our Ends. And therefore if any two men desire the same thing, which neverthelesse they cannot both enjoy, they become enemies; and in the way to their End, . . . endeavour to destroy, or subdue one another. . . . If one plant, sow, build, or possesse a convenient Seat, others may probably be expected to come prepared with forces united, to dispossesse, and deprive him, not only of the fruit of his labour, but also of his life, or liberty. . . .

71

So that in the nature of man, we find three principall causes of quarrell. First, Competition; Secondly, Diffidence; Thirdly, Glory.

The first, maketh men invade for Gain; the second, for Safety; and the third, for Reputation. The first use Violence, to make themselves Masters of other men's persons, wives, children, and cattell; the second, to defend them; the third, for trifles, as a word, a smile, a different opinion, and any other signe of undervalue, either direct in their Persons, or by reflexion in their Kindred, their Friends, their Nation, their Profession, or their Name.

Hereby it is manifest, that during the time men live without a common Power to keep them all in awe, they are in that condition which is called Warre; and such a warre, as is of every man, against every man. . . .

Whatsoever therefore is consequent to a time of Warre, where every man is Enemy to every man; the same is consequent to the time, wherein men live without other security, than what their own strength, and their own invention shall furnish them withall. In such condition, there is no place for Industry; because the fruit thereof is uncertain; and consequently no Culture of the Earth; no Navigation, nor use of the commodities that may be imported by Sea; no commodious Building; no Instruments of moving, and removing such things as require much force; no Knowledge of the face of the Earth; no account of Time; no Arts; no Letters; no Society; and which is worst of all, continuall feare, and danger of violent death; And the life of man, solitary, poore, nasty, brutish, and short. . . .

The Passions that encline men to Peace, are Feare of Death; Desire of such things as are necessary to commodious living; and a Hope by their Industry to obtain them. And Reason suggesteth convenient Articles of Peace, upon which men may be drawn to agreement. . . .

And because the condition of Man, (as hath been declared in the precedent Chapter) is a condition of Warre of every one against every one; in which case every one is governed by his own Reason; and there is nothing he can make use of, that may not be a help unto him, in preserving his life against his enemyes; It followeth, that in such a condition, every man has a Right to every thing; even to one another's body. And therefore, as long as this naturall Right of every man to every thing endureth, there can be no security to any man, (how strong or wise soever he be,) of living out the time, which Nature ordinarily alloweth men to live.

. . . If there be no Power erected, or not great enough for our security; every man will and may lawfully rely on his own strength and art, for caution against all other men. . . .

The only way to erect . . . a Common Power, as may be able to defend them from the invasion of [foreigners] and the injuries of one another, and thereby to secure them in such sort, as that by their owne industrie, and by the fruites of the Earth, they may nourish themselves and live contentedly; is, to conferre all their power and strength upon one Man, or upon one Assembly of men, that may reduce all their Wills, by plurality of voices, unto one Will . . . and therein to submit their Wills, every one to his Will, and their Judgements, to his Judgement. This is more than Consent, or Concord; it is a reall Unitie of them all, in one and the same Person, made by Covenant of every man with every man, in such manner, as if every man should say to every man, *I Authorise and give up my Right of Governing my selfe, to this Man, or to this Assembly of men, on this condition, that thou give up thy Right to him, and Authorise all his Actions in like manner.* This done, the Multitude so united in one Person, is called a COMMON-WEALTH. . . . For by this Authoritie, given him by every particular man in the Common-wealth, he hath the use of so much Power and Strength . . . conferred on him, that by terror thereof, he is inabled to forme the wills of them all, to Peace at home, and mutuall [aid] against their enemies abroad. And in him consisteth the Essence of the Common-wealth; which (to define it), is *One Person, of whose Acts a great Multitude, by mutuall Covenants one with another, have made themselves every one the Author, to the end he may use the strength and means of them all, as he shall think expedient, for their Peace and Common Defence.*

And he that carryeth this Person, is called SOVERAIGNE, and said to have Soveraigne Power; and every one besides, his SUBJECT. . . .

. . . They that have already Instituted a Common-wealth, being thereby bound by Covenant . . . cannot lawfully make a new Covenant, amongst themselves, to be obedient to any other, in any thing whatsoever, without his permission. And therefore, they that are subjects to a Monarch, cannot without his leave cast off Monarchy, and return to the confusion of a disunited Multitude; nor transferre their Person from him that beareth it, to another Man, or other Assembly of men: for they . . . are bound, every man to every man, to [acknowledge] . . . that he that already is their Soveraigne, shall do, and judge fit to be done; so that [those who do not obey] break their Covenant made to that man, which is injustice: and they have also every man given the Soveraignty to him that beareth their Person; and therefore if they depose him, they take from him that which is his own, and so again it is injustice. . . . And whereas some men have pretended for their disobedience to their Soveraign, a new Covenant, made, not with men, but with God; this also is unjust: for there is no Covenant with God, but by mediation of some body that representeth God's Person; which none doth but God's Lieutenant, who hath the Soveraignty under God. But this pretence of Covenant with God, is so evident a [lie], even in the pretender's own consciences, that it is not onely an act of an unjust, but also of a vile, and unmanly disposition. . . .

. . . Consequently none of [the sovereign's] Subjects, by any pretence of forfeiture, can be freed from his Subjection.

# *from* Second Treatise on Government

## John Locke

*John Locke (1632–1704) wrote his* Second Treatise on Civil Government *in 1690, just after the Glorious Revolution of 1688 in which, without bloodshed, the English Parliament replaced James II with William III. By this act Parliament implicitly claimed the right of sovereignty for itself. Locke enunciated a theory that based state authority on the consent of the governed. His ideas were a major influence on the men who shaped the governments of the American colonies and the Constitution of the United States, as well as the* Declaration of the Rights of Man and of Citizens.

*P*olitical power is that power, which every man having in the state of nature, has given up into the hands of the society, and therein to the governors, whom the society hath set over itself, with this express or tacit trust, that it shall be employed for their good, and the preservation of their property: now this *power*, which every man has *in the state of nature*, and which he parts with to the society in all such cases where the society can secure him, is to use such means, for the preserving of his own property, as he thinks good, and nature allows him; and to punish the breach of the law of nature in others, so as (according to the best of his reason) may most conduce to the preservation of himself, and the rest of mankind. So that the *end and measure of this power*, when in every man's hands in the state of nature, being the preservation of all of his society, that is, all mankind in general, it can have no other *end or measure*, when in the hands of the magistrate, but to preserve the members of that society in their lives, liberties, and possessions; and so cannot be an absolute, arbitrary power over their lives and fortunes, which are as much as possible to be preserved; but a *power to make laws*, and annex such *penalties* to them, as may tend to the preservation of the whole, by cutting off those parts, and those only, which are so corrupt that they threaten the sound and healthy, without which no severity is lawful. And this *power has its origin only from compact*, and agreement, and the mutual consent of those who make up the community. . . .

These are the *bounds*, which the trust that is put in them by the society, and the law of God and nature, have *set to the legislative* power of every common-wealth, in all forms of government.

First, They are to govern by *promulgated established laws*, not to be varied in particular cases, but to have one rule for rich and poor, for the favourite at court, and the country man at plough.

Secondly, These *laws* also ought to be designed for no other end ultimately, but *the good of the people*.

Thirdly, They must *not raise taxes* on the *property of the people, without the consent of the people*, given by themselves, or their deputies. And this properly concerns only such governments, where the *legislative* is always in being, or at least where the people have not reserved any part of the legislative to deputies, to be from time to time chosen by themselves.

Fourthly, The *legislative* neither must *nor can transfer the power of making laws* to any body else, or place it any where, but where the people have. . . .

. . . The *legislative acts against the trust* reposed in them, when they endeavour to invade the property of the subject, and to make themselves, or any part of the community, masters, or arbitrary disposers of the lives, liberties, or fortunes of the people.

The reason why men enter into society is the preservation of their property; and the end why they chuse and authorize a legislative, is that there may be laws made, and rules set, as guards and fences to the properties of all the members of the society, to limit the power, and moderate the dominion of every part and member of the society: for since it can never be supposed to be the will of the society that the legislative should have a power to destroy that which every one designs to secure, by entering into society, and for which the people submitted themselves to legislators of their own making; whenever the *legislators endeavour to take away, and destroy the property of the people*, or to reduce them to slavery under arbitrary power, they put themselves into a state of war with the people, who are thereupon absolved from any farther obedience, and are left to the common refuge, which God hath provided for all men, against force and violence. Whensoever therefore the *legislative* shall transgress this fundamental rule of society; and either by ambition, fear, folly or corruption, *endeavour to grasp* themselves, or *put into the hands of any other, an absolute power* over the lives, liberties, and estates of the people; by this breach of trust they *forfeit the power* the people had put into their hands for quite contrary ends, and it devolves to the people, who have a right to resume their original liberty, and, by the establishment of a new legislative, (such as they shall think fit) provide for their own safety and security, which is the end for which they are in society. What I have said here, concerning the legislative in general, holds true also concerning the supreme executor, who, having a double trust put in him, both to have a part in the legislative, and the supreme execution of the law, acts against both, when he goes about to set up his own arbitrary will as the law of the society. He *acts* also *contrary to his trust*, when he either employs the force, treasure, and offices of the society, to corrupt the *representatives*, and gain them to his purposes; or openly pre-engages the *electors*, and prescribes to their choice, such, whom he has, by solicitations, threats, promises, or otherwise, won to his designs; and employs them to bring in such, who have promised beforehand what to vote, and what to enact. . . .

. . . Such *revolutions happen* not upon every little mismanagement in public affairs. *Great mistakes* in the ruling part, many wrong and inconvenient laws, and all the *slips* of human frailty, will be *borne by the people* without mutiny or murmur. But if a long train of abuses, prevarications and artifices, all tending the same way, make the design visible to the people, and they cannot but feel what they lie under, and see whither they are going; it is not to be wondered at, that they should then rouze themselves, and endeavour to put the rule into such hands which may secure to them the ends for which government was at first erected. . . .

. . . I answer, that *this doctrine* of a power in the people of providing for their safety a-new, by a new legislative, when their legislators have acted contrary to their trust, by invading their property, is the *best (de)fence against rebellion*, and the probablest means to hinder it: for *rebellion* being an opposition, not to persons, but authority, which is founded only in the constitutions and laws of the government; those, whoever they be, who by force break through, and by force justify their violation of them, are truly and properly *rebels*: for when men, by entering into society and civil government, have excluded force, and introduced laws for the preservation of property, peace, and unity amongst themselves, those who set up force again in opposition to the laws, do *rebellare*, that is, bring back again the state of war, and are properly rebels: which they who are in power, (by the pretence they have to authority, the temptation of force they have in their hands, and the flattery of those about them) being likeliest to do;

the properest way to prevent the evil, is to shew them the danger and injustice of it, who are under the greatest temptation to run into it.

The end of government is the good of mankind; and which is *best for mankind*, that the people should always be exposed to the boundless will of tyranny, or that the rulers should be sometimes liable to be opposed, when they grow exorbitant in the use of their power, and employ it for the destruction, and not the preservation of the properties of their people?

# The Declaration of Independence

*In the third session of the Second Continental Congress, Richard Henry Lee of Virginia proposed, and John Adams of Massachusetts seconded, a resolution declaring the United Colonies free and independent states; and Thomas Jefferson, John Adams, Roger Sherman, and Robert Livingstone were appointed a committee to draw up a declaration of independence. This famous document, composed almost entirely by Jefferson, was adopted unanimously on July 4, 1776.*

When in the course of human events, it becomes necessary for one people to dissolve the political bands which have connected them with another, and to assume among the Powers of the earth, the separate and equal station to which the Laws of Nature and of Nature's God entitle them, a decent respect to the opinions of mankind requires that they should declare the causes which impel them to the separation.

We hold these truths to be self-evident, that all men are created equal, that they are endowed by their Creator with certain unalienable Rights, that among these are Life, Liberty, and the pursuit of Happiness. That to secure these rights, Governments are instituted among Men, deriving their just powers from the consent of the governed, that whenever any Form of Government becomes destructive of these ends, it is the Right of the People to alter or to abolish it, and to institute new Government, laying its foundation on such principles and organizing its powers in such form, as to them shall seem most likely to effect their Safety and Happiness. Prudence, indeed, will dictate that Governments long established should not be changed for light and transient causes; and accordingly all experience hath shown, that mankind are more disposed to suffer, while evils are sufferable, than to right themselves by abolishing the forms to which they are accustomed. But when a long train of abuses and usurpations, pursuing invariably the same Object envinces a design to reduce them under absolute Despotism, it is their right, it is their duty, to throw off such Government, and to provide new Guards for their future security. Such has been the patient sufferance of these Colonies; and such is now the necessity which constrains them to alter their former Systems of Government. The history of the present King of Great Britain is a history of repeated injuries and usurpations, all having in direct object the establishment of an absolute Tyranny over these States. To prove this, let Facts be submitted to a candid world.

He has refused his Assent to Laws, the most wholesome and necessary for the public good.

He has forbidden his Governors to pass Laws of immediate and pressing importance, unless suspended in their operation till his Assent should be obtained; and when so suspended, he has utterly neglected to attend to them.

He has refused to pass other Laws for the accommodation of large districts of people, unless those people would relinquish the right of Representation in the Legislature, a right inestimable to them and formidable to tyrants only.

He has called together legislative bodies at places unusual, uncomfortable, and distant from the depository of their Public Records, for the sole purpose of fatiguing them into compliance with his measures.

He has dissolved Representative Houses repeatedly, for opposing with manly firmness his invasions on the rights of the people.

He has refused for a long time, after such dissolutions, to cause others to be elected; whereby the Legislative Powers, incapable of Annihilation, have returned to the People at large for their exercise; the State remaining in the mean time exposed to all the dangers of invasion from without, and convulsions within.

He has endeavoured to prevent the population of these States; for that purpose obstructing the Laws of Naturalization of Foreigners; refusing to pass others to encourage their migration hither, and raising the conditions of new Appropriations of Lands.

He has obstructed the Administration of Justice, by refusing his Assent to Laws for establishing Judiciary Powers.

He has made Judges dependent on his Will alone, for the tenure of their offices, and the amount and payment of their salaries.

He has erected a multitude of New Offices, and sent hither swarms of Officers to harass our People, and eat out their substance.

He has kept among us, in times of peace, Standing Armies without the Consent of our legislature.

# *from* The Social Contract

## Jean Jacques Rousseau

*More than anyone else, Jean Jacques Rousseau (1712–1778) tested the outer lim-
its of Enlightenment thought and went on to criticize its very foundations. Born
in Geneva, he spent much of his life in France (mainly in Paris), where he became
one of the philosophes who contributed to the* Encyclopedia. *Yet he also under-
mined Enlightenment thought by holding that social institutions had corrupted
people and that human beings in the state of nature were more pure, free, and
happy than in modern civilization. This line of thought provided a foundation for
the growth of Romanticism in the late eighteenth and early nineteenth centuries.
Rousseau's most important political work was* The Social Contract *(1762), in
which he argued for popular sovereignty. In the following selection from that
work, Rousseau focuses on what he considers the fundamental argument of the
book—the passage from the state of nature to the civil state by means of the social
contract.*

"The problem is to find a form of association which will defend and
protect with the whole common force the person and goods of each
associate, and in which each, while uniting himself with all, may still
obey himself alone, and remain as free as before." This is the fundamental problem of which *The Social Contract* provides the solution.

The clauses of this contract are so determined by the nature of the act that
the slightest modification would make them vain and ineffective; so that,
although they have perhaps never been formally set forth, they are everywhere the same and everywhere tacitly admitted and recognised, until,
on the violation of the social compact, each regains his original rights and
resumes his natural liberty, while losing the conventional liberty in
favour of which he renounced it.

These clauses, properly understood, may be reduced to one—the total
alienation of each associate, together with all his rights, to the whole community; for, in the first place, as each gives himself absolutely, the conditions are the same for all; and, this being so, no one has any interest in
making them burdensome to others.

Moreover, the alienation being without reserve, the union is as perfect as it can be, and no associate has anything more to demand: for, if the individuals retained certain rights, as there would be no common superior to decide between them and the public, each, being on one point his own judge, would ask to be so on all; the state of nature would thus continue, and the association would necessarily become inoperative or tyrannical.

Finally, each man, in giving himself to all, gives himself to nobody; and as there is no associate over whom he does not acquire the same right as he yields others over himself, he gains on equivalent for everything he loses, and an increase of force for the preservation of what he has.

If then we discard from the social compact what is not of its essence, we shall find that it reduces itself to the following terms—

Each of us puts his person and all his power in common under the supreme direction of the general will, and, in our corporate capacity, we receive each member as an indivisible part of the whole.

* * *

The passage from the state of nature to the civil state produces a very remarkable change in man, by substituting justice for instinct in his conduct, and giving his actions the morality they had formerly lacked. Then only, when the voice of duty takes the place of physical impulses and right of appetite, does man, who so far had considered only himself, find that he is forced to act on different principles, and to consult his reason before listening to his inclinations. Although, in this state, he deprives himself of some advantages which he got from nature, he gains in return others so great, his faculties are so stimulated and developed, his ideas so extended, his feelings so ennobled, and his whole soul so uplifted, that, did not the abuses of this new condition often degrade him below that which he left, he would be bound to bless continually the happy moment which took him from it for ever, and, instead of a stupid and unimaginative animal, made him an intelligent being and a man.

Let us draw up the whole account in terms easily commensurable. What man loses by the social contract is his natural liberty and an unlimited right to everything he tries to get and succeeds in getting; what he gains is civil liberty and the proprietorship of all he possesses. If we are to avoid mistake in weighing one against the other, we must clearly distinguish natural liberty, which is bounded only by the strength of the individual, from civil liberty, which is limited by the general will; and possession, which is merely the effect of force or the right of the first occupier, from property, which can be founded only on a positive title.

We might, over and above all this, add, to what man acquires in the civil state, moral liberty, which alone makes him truly master of himself; for the mere impulse of appetite is slavery, while obedience to a law which we prescribe to ourselves is liberty. But I have already said too much on this head, and the philosophical meaning of the word liberty does not now concern us.

# *from* The Rights of Man

## Thomas Paine

*Thomas Paine (1737–1809) was an outspoken supporter of the American and the French revolutions In this selection he attacks Edmund Burke, an opponent of the French Revolution of 1789. Burke had argued that both revolution itself, by breaking with traditional authority, and government by the many, since only the aristocracy had the ability and character to rule, are folly. After Paine published this work in England, he was forced to flee prosecution and went to France where he was a member of the Convention before he was arrested by radical Jacobins in 1793. Out of favor for his radical religious ideas, he died in obscurity in the United States.*

Among the incivilities by which nations or individuals provoke and irritate each other, Mr. Burke's pamphlet on the French Revolution is an extraordinary instance. . . . There is scarcely an epithet of abuse to be found in the English language with which Mr. Burke has not loaded the French nation and the National Assembly. Everything which rancor, prejudice, ignorance, or knowledge could suggest are poured forth in the copious fury of near four hundred pages. . . .

The two modes of government which prevail in the world are, first, government by election and representation; secondly, government by hereditary succession. The former is generally known by the name of republic; the latter by that of monarchy and aristocracy.

Those two distinct and opposite forms erect themselves on the two distinct and opposite bases of reason and ignorance. As the exercise of government requires talents and abilities, and as talents and abilities cannot have hereditary descent, it is evident that hereditary succession requires a belief from man to which his reason cannot subscribe and which can only be established upon his ignorance; and the more ignorant any country is, the better it is fitted for this species of government.

On the contrary, government in a well-constituted republic requires no belief from man beyond what his reason can give. He sees the rationale of the whole system, its origin and its operation; and as it is best supported when best understood, the human faculties act with boldness and acquire, under this form of government, a gigantic manliness.

. . . Each of those forms acts on a different base—the one moving freely by the aid of reason, the other by ignorance. . . .

All hereditary government is in its nature tyranny. A heritable crown or a heritable throne, or by what other fanciful name such things may be called, have no other significant explanation than that mankind are heritable property. To inherit a government is to inherit the people, as if they were flocks and herds. . . .

We have heard the rights of man called *a leveling* system, but the only system to which the word "leveling" is truly applicable is the hereditary monarchical system. It is a system of *mental leveling*. It indiscriminately admits every species of character to the same authority. Vice and virtue, ignorance and wisdom, in short, every quality, good or bad, is put on the same level. Kings succeed each other, not as [rational men], but as animals. It signifies not what their mental or moral characters are.

Passing over, for the present, all the evils and mischiefs which monarchy has occasioned in the world, nothing can more effectually prove its uselessness in a state of *civil government* than making it hereditary. Would we make any office hereditary that required wisdom and abilities to fill it? . . .

It requires some talents to be a common mechanic, but to be a king requires only the animal figure of a man—a sort of breathing automaton. This sort of superstition may last a few years more, but it cannot long resist the awakened reason and interest of man. . . .

As this is the order of nature, the order of government must necessarily follow it, or government will, as we see it does, degenerate into ignorance. The hereditary system, therefore, is as repugnant to human wisdom as to human rights and is as absurd as it is unjust.

As the republic of letters brings forward the best literary productions by giving to genius a fair and universal chance, so the representative system of government is calculated to produce the wisest laws by collecting wisdom where it can be found. I smile to myself when I contemplate the ridiculous insignificance into which literature and all the sciences would sink were they made hereditary, and I carry the same idea into governments. A hereditary governor is as inconsistent as a hereditary author. I know not whether Homer or Euclid had sons, but I will venture an opinion that if they had, and had left their works unfinished, those sons could not have completed them.

Do we need a stronger evidence of the absurdity of hereditary government than is seen in the descendants of those men, in any line of life, who once were famous? Is there scarcely an instance in which there is not a total reverse of character? It appears as if the tide of mental faculties flowed as far as it could in certain channels, and then forsook its course and arose in others. How irrational then is the hereditary system which establishes channels of power, in company with which wisdom refuses to flow! By continuing this absurdity, man is perpetually in contradiction with himself; he accepts for a king or a chief magistrate or a legislator a person whom he would not elect for a constable.

# Declaration of the Rights
# of Man and of Citizens

*In 1789 France was governed by an absolute monarch. Most of the high offices in the state were reserved for the aristocracy, although some offices could be purchased. Aristocrats and the clergy were exempt from taxes and subject to different laws than the vast majority of the population who made up the Third Estate. In 1789, the impending bankruptcy of the government forced the King Louis XVI to call the Estates General, which had not met for over 100 years. The French Revolution, which resulted in the execution of the king in 1793, began as a demand for a constitutional monarchy. The document below was a first step, a statement of the principles upon which the authority of the state should rest and the proper limitations of its power. At this point in the revolution the representative had defied the king and had vowed not to disband until France had a constitution.*

The Representatives of the people of FRANCE, formed into a NATIONAL ASSEMBLY, considering that ignorance, neglect, or contempt of human rights, are the sole causes of public misfortunes and corruptions of Government, have resolved to set forth in a solemn declaration, these natural, imprescriptible, and unalienable rights: that this declaration, being constantly present to the minds of the members of the body social, they may be ever kept attentive to their rights and their duties: that the acts of the legislative and executive powers of Government, being capable of being every moment compared with the end of political institutions, may be more respected: and also, that the future claims of the citizens, being directed by simple and incontestible principles, may always tend to the maintenance of the Constitution, and the general happiness.

For these reasons the NATIONAL ASSEMBLY doth recognize and declare, in the presence of the Supreme Being, and with the hope of his blessing and favor, the following sacred rights of men and of citizens:

I. *Men are born, and always continue, free, and equal in respect of their rights. Civil distinctions, therefore, can be founded only on public utility.*

II. *The end of all political associations, is, the preservation of the natural and imprescriptible rights of man; and these rights are liberty, property, security, and resistance of oppression.*

III. *The nation is essentially the source of all sovereignty; nor can any* INDIVID-UAL *or* ANY BODY OF MEN, *be entitled to any authority which is not expressly derived from it.*

IV. Political Liberty consists in the power of doing whatever does not injure another. The exercise of the natural rights of every man, has no other limits than those which are necessary to secure to every other man the free exercise of the same rights; and these limits are determinable only by the law.

V. The law ought to prohibit only actions hurtful to society. What is not prohibited by the law, should not be hindered; nor should any one be compelled to that which the law does not require.

VI. The law is an expression of the will of the community. All citizens have a right to concur, either personally, or by their representatives, in its formation. It should be the same to all, whether it protects or punishes; and *all being equal in its sight, are equally eligible to all honors, places, and employments, according to their different abilities, without any other distinction than that created by their virtues and talents.*

VII. No man should be accused, arrested, or held in confinement, except in cases determined by the law, and according to the forms which it has prescribed. All who promote, solicit, execute, or cause to be executed, arbitrary orders, ought to be punished; and every citizen called upon or apprehended by virtue of the law, ought immediately to obey, and renders himself culpable by resistance.

VIII. The law ought to impose no other penalties but such as are absolutely and evidently necessary; and no one ought to be punished, but in virtue of a law promulgated before the offence, and legally applied.

IX. Every man being presumed innocent till he has been convicted, whenever his detention becomes indispensible, all rigor [harshness] to him, more than is necessary to secure his person, ought to be provided against by the law.

X. No man ought to be molested on account of his opinions, not even on account of his *religious* opinions, provided his avowal of them does not disturb the public order established by the law.

XI. The unrestrained communication of thoughts and opinions being one of the most precious rights of man, every citizen may speak, write, and publish freely, provided he is responsible for the abuse of this liberty in cases determined by the law.

XII. A public force being necessary to give security to the rights of men and of citizens, that force is instituted for the benefit of the community, and not for the particular benefit of the persons with whom it is entrusted.

XIII. A common contribution being necessary for the support of the public force, and for defraying the other expenses of government, it ought to be divided equally among the members of the community, according to their abilities.

XIV. Every citizen has a right, either by himself or his representative, to a free voice in determining the necessity of public contributions, the appropriation of them, and their amount, mode of assessment and duration.

XV. Every community has a right to demand of all its agents, an account of their conduct.

XVI. Every community in which a separation of powers and a security of rights is not provided for, wants a constitution.

XVII. The rights to property being inviolable and sacred, no one ought to be deprived of it, except in cases of evident public necessity, legally ascertained, and on condition of a previous just indemnity.

# *from* Democracy in America

## Alexis de Tocqueville

*Alexis de Tocqueville (1805–1859) was a French aristocrat and minor govern-ment official who toured the United States in 1830. The two-volume record of his travels,* Democracy in America, *provides a perceptive analysis of American society through the eyes of a European observer. It is an invaluable record of the ways in which, only a few decades after independence, the young country had evolved a social and political system which was distinctly different than those of the European countries American immigrants had left. Of course, American society had by that time been developing for nearly two centuries and could be characterized as an amalgam of European influences which had been reshaped in the process of creating civic institutions out of frontier settlements. One funda-mental difference between the early American environment and Europe was the availability of land for settlement. This basic resource was open to anyone with the audacity and skill to fight off Native Americans and the diligence to clear away the forest and start a farm. Thus, the European landlord-peasant system was not recreated in the American colonies, which were inhabited by free farm-ers in the north, and plantation owners, slaves, and free farmers in the south.*

## Unlimited Power of the Majority in the United States, and Its Consequences

**Natural strength of the majority in democracies—Most of the Ameri-can Constitutions have increased this strength by artificial means—How this has been done—Pledged delegates—Moral power of the majority—Opinion as to its infallibility—Respect for its rights, how augmented in the United States.**

The very essence of democratic government consists in the absolute sovereignty of the majority; for there is nothing in democratic States which is capable of resisting it. Most of the American Constitutions have sought to increase this natural strength of the majority by artificial means.[1]

The legislature is, of all political institutions, the one which is most easily swayed by the wishes of the majority. The Americans determined that the members of the legislature should be elected by the people immediately, and for a very brief term, in order to subject them, not only to the general convictions, but even to the daily passions, of their constituents. The members of both houses are taken from the same class in society, and are nominated in the same manner; so that the modifications of the legislative bodies are almost as rapid and quite as irresistible as those of a single assembly. It is to a legislature thus constituted that almost all the authority of the government has been entrusted.

But whilst the law increased the strength of those authorities which of themselves were strong, it enfeebled more and more those which were naturally weak. It deprived the representatives of the executive of all stability and independence, and by subjecting them completely to the caprices of the legislature, it robbed them of the slender influence which the nature of a democratic government might have allowed them to retain. In several States the judicial power was also submitted to the elective discretion of the majority, and in all of them its existence was made to depend on the pleasure of the legislative authority, since the representatives were empowered annually to regulate the stipend of the judges.

Custom, however, has done even more than law. A proceeding which will in the end set all the guarantees of representative government at naught is becoming more and more general in the United States; it frequently happens that the electors, who choose a delegate, point out a certain line of conduct to him, and impose upon him a certain number of positive obligations which he is pledged to fulfill. With the exception of the tumult, this comes to the same thing as if the majority of the populace held its deliberations in the market-place.

Several other circumstances concur in rendering the power of the majority in America not only preponderant, but irresistible. The moral authority of the majority is partly based upon the notion that there is more intelligence and more wisdom in a great number of men collected together than in a single individual, and that the quantity of legislators is more important than their quality. The theory of equality is in fact applied to the intellect of man: and human pride is thus assailed in its last retreat by a doctrine which the minority hesitate to admit, and in which they very slowly concur. Like all other powers, and perhaps more than all other powers, the authority of the many requires the sanction of time; at first it enforces obedience by constraint, but its laws are not respected until they have long been maintained.

The right of governing society, which the majority supposes itself to derive from its superior intelligence, was introduced into the United States by the first settlers, and this idea, which would be sufficient of itself to create a free nation, has now been amalgamated with the manners of the people and the minor incidents of social intercourse.

The French, under the old monarchy, held it for a maxim (which is still a fundamental principle of the English Constitution) that the King could do no wrong; and if he did do wrong, the blame was imputed to his advisers. This notion was highly favorable to habits of obedience, and it enabled the subject to complain of the law without ceasing to love and honor the lawgiver. The Americans entertain the same opinion with respect to the majority.

The moral power of the majority is founded upon yet another principle, which is, that the interests of the many are to be preferred to those of the few. It will readily be perceived that the respect here professed for the rights of the majority must naturally increase or diminish according to the state of parties. When a nation is divided into several irreconcilable factions, the privilege of the majority is often overlooked, because it is intolerable to comply with its demands.

If there existed in America a class of citizens whom the legislating majority sought to deprive of exclusive privileges which they had possessed for ages, and to bring down from an elevated station to the level of the ranks of the multitude, it is probable that the minority would be less ready to comply with its laws. But as the United States were colonized by men holding equal rank amongst themselves, there is as yet no natural or permanent source of dissension between the interests of its different inhabitants.

There are certain communities in which the persons who constitute the minority can never hope to draw over the majority to their side, because they must then give up the very point which is at issue between them. Thus, an aristocracy can never become a majority whilst it retains its exclusive privileges, and it cannot cede its privileges without ceasing to be an aristocracy.

In the United States political questions cannot be taken up in so general and absolute a manner, and all parties are willing to recognize the rights of the majority, because they all hope to turn those rights to their own advantage at some future time. The majority therefore in that country exercises a prodigious actual authority, and a moral influence which is scarcely less preponderant; no obstacles exist which can impede or so much as retard its progress, or which can induce it to heed the complaints of those whom it crushes upon its path. This state of things is fatal in itself and dangerous for the future.

## How the Unlimited Power of the Majority Increases in America the Instability of Legislation and Administration Inherent in Democracy

**The Americans increase the mutability of the laws which is inherent in democracy by changing the legislature every year, and by investing it with unbounded authority—The same effect is produced upon the administration—In America social amelioration is conducted more energetically but less perseveringly than in Europe.**

I have already spoken of the natural defects of democratic institutions, and they all of them increase at the exact ratio of the power of the majority. To begin with the most evident of them all; the mutability of the laws is an evil inherent in democratic government, because it is natural to democracies to raise men to power in very rapid succession. But this evil is more or less sensible in proportion to the authority and the means of action which the legislature possesses.

In America the authority exercised by the legislative bodies is supreme; nothing prevents them from accomplishing their wishes with celerity, and with irresistible power, whilst they are supplied by new representatives every year. That is to say, the circumstances which contribute most powerfully to democratic instability, and which admit of the free application of caprice to every object in the State, are here in full operation. In conformity with this principle, America is, at the present day, the country in the world where laws last the shortest time. Almost all the American constitutions have been amended within the course of thirty years: there is therefore not a single American State which has not modified the principles of its legislation in that lapse of time. As for the laws themselves, a single glance upon the archives of the different States of the Union suffices to convince one that in America the activity of the legislator never slackens. Not that the American democracy is naturally less stable than any other, but that it is allowed to follow its capricious propensities in the formation of the laws.[2]

• • •

I do not think that it is possible to combine several principles in the same government, so as at the same time to maintain freedom, and really to oppose them to one another. The form of government which is usually termed mixed has always appeared to me to be a mere chimera. Accurately speaking there is no such thing as a mixed government (with the meaning usually given to that word), because in all communities some one principle of action may be discovered which preponderates over the others. England in the last century, which has been more especially cited as an example of this form of Government, was in point of fact an essentially aristocratic State, although it comprised very powerful elements of democracy; for the laws and customs of the country were such that the aristocracy could not but preponderate in the end, and subject the direction of public affairs to its own will. The error arose from too much attention being paid to the actual struggle which was going on between the nobles and the people, without considering the probable issue of the contest, which was in reality the important point. When a community really has a mixed government, that is to say, when it is equally divided between two adverse principles, it must either pass through a revolution or fall into complete dissolution.

I am therefore of opinion that some one social power must always be made to predominate over the others; but I think that liberty is endangered when this power is checked by no obstacles which may retard its course, and force it to moderate its own vehemence.

Unlimited power is in itself a bad and dangerous thing; human beings are not competent to exercise it with discretion, and God alone can be omnipotent, because His wisdom and His justice are always equal to His power. But no power upon earth is so worthy of honor for itself, or of reverential obedience to the rights which it represents, that I would consent to admit its uncontrolled and all-predominant authority. When I see that the right and the means of absolute command are conferred on a people or upon a king, upon an aristocracy or a democracy, a monarchy or a republic, I recognize the germ of tyranny, and I journey onward to a land of more hopeful institutions.

In my opinion the main evil of the present democratic institutions of the United States does not arise, as is often asserted in Europe, from their weakness, but from their overpowering strength; and I am not so much alarmed at the excessive liberty which reigns in that country as at the very inadequate securities which exist against tyranny.

When an individual or a party is wronged in the United States, to whom can he apply for redress? If to public opinion, public opinion constitutes the majority; if to the legislature, it represents the majority, and implicitly obeys its injunctions; if to the executive power, it is appointed by the majority, and remains a passive tool in its hands; the public troops consist of the majority under arms; the jury is the majority invested with the right of hearing judicial cases; and in certain States even the judges are elected by the majority. However iniquitous or absurd the evil of which you complain may be, you must submit to it as well as you can.[3]

If, on the other hand, a legislative power could be so constituted as to represent the majority without necessarily being the slave of its passions; an executive, so as to retain a certain degree of uncontrolled authority; and a judiciary, so as to remain independent of the two other powers; a government would be formed which would still be democratic without incurring any risk of tyrannical abuse.

• • •

If ever these lines are read in America, I am well assured of two things: in the first place, that all who peruse them will raise their voices to condemn me; and in the second place, that very many of them will acquit me at the bottom of their conscience.

I have heard of patriotism in the United States, and it is a virtue which may be found among the people, but never among the leaders of the people. This may be explained by analogy; despotism debases the oppressed much more than the oppressor: in absolute monarchies the king has often great virtues, but the courtiers are invariably servile. It is true that the American courtiers do not say "Sire," or "Your Majesty"—a distinction without a difference. They are forever talking of the natural intelligence of the populace they serve; they do not debate the question as to which of the virtues of their master is preeminently worthy of admiration, for they assure him that he possesses all the virtues under heaven without having acquired them, or without caring to acquire them; they do not give him their daughters and their wives to be raised at his pleasure to the rank of his concubines, but, by sacrificing their opinions, they prostitute themselves. Moralists and philosophers in America are not obliged to conceal their opinions under the veil of allegory; but, before they venture upon a harsh truth, they say, "We are aware that the people which we are addressing is too superior to all the weaknesses of human nature to lose the command of its temper for an instant; and we should not hold this language if we were not speaking to men whom their virtues and their intelligence render more worthy of freedom than all the rest of the world." It would have been impossible for the sycophants of Louis XIV to flatter more dexterously. For my part, I am persuaded that in all governments, whatever their nature may be, servility will cower to force, and adulation will cling to power. The only means of preventing men from degrading themselves is to invest no one with that unlimited authority which is the surest method of debasing them.

## The Greatest Dangers of the American Republics Proceed from the Unlimited Power of the Majority

**Democratic republics liable to perish from a misuse of their power, and not by impotence—The Governments of the American republics are more centralized and more energetic than those of the monarchies of Europe—Dangers resulting from this—Opinions of Hamilton and Jefferson upon this point.**

Governments usually fall a sacrifice to impotence or to tyranny. In the former case their power escapes from them; it is wrested from their grasp in the latter. Many observers, who have witnessed the anarchy of democratic States, have imagined that the government of those States was naturally weak and impotent. The truth is, that when once hostilities are begun between parties, the government loses its control over society. But I do not think that a democratic power is naturally without force or without resources: say, rather, that it is almost always by the abuse of its force and the misemployment of its resources that a democratic government fails. Anarchy is almost always produced by its tyranny or its mistakes, but not by its want of strength.

It is important not to confound stability with force, or the greatness of a thing with its duration. In democratic republics, the power which directs[4] society is not stable; for it often changes hands and assumes a new direction. But whichever way it turns, its force is almost irresistible. The Governments of the American republics appear to me to be as much centralized as those of the absolute monarchies of Europe, and more energetic than they are. I do not, therefore, imagine that they will perish from weakness.[5]

If ever the free institutions of America are destroyed, that event may be attributed to the unlimited authority of the majority, which may at some future time urge the minorities to desperation, and oblige them to have recourse to physical force. Anarchy will then be the result, but it will have been brought about by despotism.

Mr. Hamilton expresses the same opinion in the "Federalist," No. 51. "It is of great importance in a republic not only to guard the society against the oppression of its rulers, but to guard one part of the society against the injustice of the other part. Justice is the end of government. It is the end of civil society. It ever has been, and ever will be, pursued until it be obtained, or until liberty be lost in the pursuit. In a society, under the forms of which the stronger faction can readily unite and oppress the weaker, anarchy may as truly be said to reign as in a state of nature, where the weaker individual is not secured against the violence of the stronger: and as in the latter state even the stronger individuals are prompted by the uncertainty of their condition to submit to a government which may protect the weak as well as themselves, so in the former state will the more powerful factions be gradually induced by a like motive to wish for a government which will protect all parties, the weaker as well as the more powerful. It can be little doubted that, if the State of Rhode Island was separated from the Confederacy and left to itself, the insecurity of right under the popular form of government within such narrow limits would be displayed by such reiterated oppressions of the factious majorities, that some power altogether independent of the people would soon be called for by the voice of the very factions whose misrule had proved the necessity of it."

Jefferson has also thus expressed himself in a letter to Madison:[6] "The executive power in our Government is not the only, perhaps not even the principal, object of my solicitude. The tyranny of the Legislature is really the danger most to be feared, and will continue to be so for many years to come. The tyranny of the executive power will come in its turn, but at a more distant period." I am glad to cite the opinion of Jefferson upon this subject rather than that of another, because I consider him to be the most powerful advocate democracy has ever sent forth.

## Notes

[1]    We observed, in examining the Federal Constitution, that the efforts of the legislators of the Union had been diametrically opposed to the present ten-

dency. The consequence has been that the Federal Government is more independent in its sphere than that of the States. But the Federal Government scarcely ever interferes in any but external affairs; and the governments of the States are in reality the authorities which direct society in America.

2    The legislative acts promulgated by the State of Massachusetts alone, from the year 1780 to the present time, already fill three stout volumes; and it must not he forgotten that the collection to which I allude was published in 1823, when many old laws which had fallen into disuse were omitted. The State of Massachusetts, which is not more populous than a department of France, may be considered as the most stable, the most consistent, and the most sagacious in its undertakings of the whole Union.

3    A striking instance of the excesses which may be occasioned by the despotism of the majority occurred at Baltimore in the year 1812. At that time the war was very popular in Baltimore. A journal which had taken the other side of the question excited the indignation of the inhabitants by its opposition. The populace assembled, broke the printing-presses, and attacked the houses of the newspaper editors. The militia was called out, but no one obeyed the call; and the only means of saving the poor wretches who were threatened by the frenzy of the mob was to throw them into prison as common malefactors. But even this precaution was ineffectual; the mob collected again during the night, the magistrates again made a vain attempt to call out the militia, the prison was forced, one of the newspaper editors was killed upon the spot, and the others were left for dead; the guilty parties were acquitted by the jury when they were brought to trial. I said one day to an inhabitant of Pennsylvania, "Be so good as to explain to me how it happens that in a State founded by Quakers, and celebrated for its toleration, freed blacks are not allowed to exercise civil rights. They pay the taxes; is it not fair that they should have a vote?"

"You insult us," replied my informant, "if you imagine that our legislators could have committed so gross an act of injustice and intolerance."

"What! then the blacks possess the right of voting in this country?"

"Without the smallest doubt."

"How comes it, then, that at the polling-booth this morning I did not perceive a single negro in the whole meeting?"

"This is not the fault of the law: the negroes have an undisputed right of voting, but they voluntarily abstain from making their appearance."

"A very pretty piece of modesty on their parts!" rejoined I.

"Why, the truth is, that they are not disinclined to vote, but they are afraid of being maltreated; in this country the law is sometimes unable to maintain its authority without the support of the majority. But in this case the majority entertains very strong prejudices against the blacks, and the magistrates are unable to protect them in the exercise of their legal privileges."

"What! then the majority claims the right not only of making the laws, but of breaking the laws it has made?"

4    This power may be centred in an assembly, in which case it will be strong without being stable; or it may be centred in an individual, in which case it will be less strong, but more stable.

5    I presume that it is scarcely necessary to remind the reader here, as well as throughout the remainder of this chapter, that I am speaking, not of the Federal Government, but of the several governments of each State, which the majority controls at its pleasure.

6    March 15, 1789.

# *from* On Liberty

## *John Stuart Mill*

*John Stuart Mill (1806–1873) was the son of a utilitarian political economist, James Mill. In 1859 he published* On Liberty, *a defense of the social utility of allowing the greatest possible freedom to individual expression. Mill argued that only the unrestricted access of all viewpoints to the marketplace of ideas could ensure that the best ideas would be considered and eventually win out over less worthy ones.*

Few persons, out of Germany, even comprehend the meaning of the doctrine which Wilhelm von Humboldt, so eminent both as a savant and as a politician, made the text of a treatise—that "the end of man, or that which is prescribed by the eternal or immutable dictates of reason, and not suggested by vague and transient desires, is the highest and most harmonious development of his powers to a complete and consistent whole"; that, therefore, the object "towards which every human being must ceaselessly direct his efforts, and on which especially those who design to influence their fellow men must ever keep their eyes, is the individuality of power and development"; that for "this there are two requisites, freedom, and variety of situations"; and that from the union of these arise "individual vigor and manifold diversity," which combine themselves in "originality."[1]

Little, however, as people are accustomed to a doctrine like that of Von Humboldt, and surprising as it may be to them to find so high a value attached to individuality, the question, one must nevertheless think, can only be one of degree. No one's idea of excellence in conduct is that people should do absolutely nothing but copy one another. No one would assert that people ought not to put into their mode of life, and into the conduct of their concerns, any impress whatever of their own judgment, or of their own individual character. On the other hand, it would be absurd to pretend that people ought to live as if nothing whatever had been known in the world before they came into it; as if experience had as yet done nothing towards showing that one mode of existence, or conduct, is preferable to another. Nobody denies that people should be so taught and trained in youth, as to know and benefit by the ascertained results of human experience. But it is the privilege and proper condition of a human being, arrived at the maturity of his faculties, to use and interpret experience in his own way. It is for him to find out what part of recorded experience is properly applicable to his own circumstances and character. The traditions and customs of other people are, to a certain extent, evidence of what their experience has taught *them*; presumptive evidence, and as such, have a claim to his deference: but, in the first place, their experience may be too narrow; or they may not have interpreted it rightly. Secondly, their interpretation of experience may be correct, but unsuitable to him. Customs are made for customary circumstances, and customary characters; and his circumstances or his character may be uncustomary. Thirdly, though the customs be both good as customs, and suitable to him, yet to conform to custom, merely as custom, does not educate or develop in him any of the qualities which are the distinctive endowment of a human being. The human faculties of perception, judgment, discriminative feeling, mental activity, and even moral preference are exercised only in making a choice. He who does anything because it is the custom makes no choice. He gains no practice either in discerning or in desiring what is best. The mental and moral, like the muscular powers, are improved only by being used. The faculties are called into no exercise by doing a thing merely because others do it, no more than by believing a thing only because others believe it. If the grounds of an opinion are not conclusive to the person's own reason, his reason cannot be strengthened, but is likely to be weakened, by his adopting it: and if the inducements to an act are not such as are consentaneous[2] to his own feelings and character (where affection, or the rights of others, are not concerned) it is so much done towards rendering his feelings and character inert and torpid, instead of active and energetic.

He who lets the world, or his own portion of it, choose his plan of life for him has no need of any other faculty than the apelike one of imitation. He who chooses his plan for himself employs all his faculties. He must use observation to see, reasoning and judgment to foresee, activity to gather materials for decision, discrimination to decide, and when he has decided, firmness and self-control to hold to his deliberate decision. And these qualities he requires and exercises exactly in proportion as the part of his conduct which he determines according to his own judgment and feelings is a large one. It is possible that he might be guided in some good path, and kept out of harm's way, without any of these things. But what will be his comparative worth as a human being? It really is of importance, not only what men do, but also what manner of men they are that do it. Among the works of man, which human life is rightly employed in perfecting and beautifying, the first in importance surely is man himself. Supposing it were possible to get houses built, corn grown, battles fought, causes tried, and even churches erected and prayers said, by machinery—by automatons in human form—it would be a considerable loss to exchange for these automatons even the men and women who at present inhabit the more civilized parts of the world, and who assuredly are but starved specimens of what nature can and will produce. Human nature is not a machine to be built after a model, and set to do exactly the work prescribed for it, but a tree which requires to grow and develop itself on all sides, according to the tendency of the inward forces which make it a living thing.

It will probably be conceded that it is desirable people should exercise their understandings, and that an intelligent following of custom, or even occasionally an intelligent deviation from custom, is better than a blind and simply mechanical adhesion to it. To a certain extent it is admitted that our understanding should be our own: but there is not the same willingness to admit that our desires and impulses should be our own likewise; or that to possess impulses of our own, and of any strength, is anything but a peril and a snare. Yet desires and impulses are as much a part of a perfect human being, as beliefs and restraints: and strong impulses are only perilous when not properly balanced; when one set of aims and inclinations is developed into strength, while others, which ought to coexist with them, remain weak and inactive. It is not because men's desires are strong that they act ill; it is because their consciences are weak. There is no natural connection between strong impulses and a weak conscience. The natural connection is the other way. To say that one person's desires and feelings are stronger and more various than those of another is merely to say that he has more of the raw material of human nature, and is therefore capable, perhaps of more evil, but certainly of more good. Strong impulses are but another name for energy. Energy may be turned to bad uses; but more good may always be made of an energetic nature than of an indolent and impassive one. Those who have most natural feeling are always those whose cultivated feelings may be made the strongest. The same strong susceptibilities which make the personal impulses vivid and powerful are also the source from whence are generated the most passionate love of virtue, and the sternest self-control. It is through the cultivation of these that society both does its duty and protects its interests: not by rejecting the stuff of which heroes are made, because it knows not how to make them. A person whose desires and impulses are his own—are the expression of his own nature, as it has been developed and modified by his own culture—is said to have a character. One whose desires and impulses are not his own, has no character, no more than a steam engine has a character. If, in addition to being his own, his impulses are strong, and are under the government of a strong will, he has an energetic character. Whoever thinks that individuality of desires and impulses should not be encouraged to unfold itself must maintain that society has no need of strong natures—is not the better for containing many persons who have much character—and that a high general average of energy is not desirable.

In some early states of society, these forces might be, and were, too much ahead of the power which society then possessed of disciplining and controlling them. There has been a time when the element of spontaneity and individuality was in excess, and the social principle had a hard struggle with it. The difficulty then was to induce men of strong bodies or minds to pay obedience to any rules which require them to control their impulses. To overcome this difficulty, law and discipline, like the Popes struggling against the Emperors, asserted a power over the whole man, claiming to control all his life in order to control his character—which society had not found any other sufficient means of binding. But society has now fairly got the better of individuality; and the danger which threatens human nature is not the excess, but the deficiency, of personal impulses and preferences. Things are vastly changed, since the passions of those who were strong by station or by personal endowment were in a state of habitual rebellion against laws and ordinances, and required to be rigorously chained up to enable the persons within their reach to enjoy any particle of security. In our times, from the highest class of society down to the lowest, everyone lives as under the eye of a hostile and dreaded censorship. Not only in what concerns others, but in what concerns only themselves, the individual or the family do not ask themselves—what do I prefer? or, what would suit my character and disposition? or, what would allow the best and highest in me to have fair play, and enable it to grow and thrive? They ask themselves, what is suitable to my position? what is usually done by persons of my station and pecuniary circumstances? or (worse still) what is usually done by persons of a station and circumstances superior to mine? I do not mean that they choose what is customary, in preference to what suits their own inclination. It does not occur to them to have any inclination, except for what is customary. Thus the mind itself is bowed to the yoke: even in what people do for pleasure, conformity is the first thing thought of; they like in crowds; they exercise choice only among things commonly done: peculiarity of taste, eccentricity of conduct, are shunned equally with crimes: until by dint of not following their own nature, they have no nature to follow: their human capacities are withered and starved: they become incapable of any strong wishes or native pleasures, and are generally without either opinions or feelings of home growth, or properly their own. Now is this, or is it not, the desirable condition of human nature?

It is so, on the Calvinistic theory. According to that, the one great offense of man is self-will. All the good of which humanity is capable is comprised in obedience. You have no choice; thus you must do, and no otherwise: "whatever is not a duty is a sin." Human nature being radically corrupt, there is no redemption for anyone until human nature is killed within him. To one holding this theory of life, crushing out any of the human faculties, capacities, and susceptibilities is no evil: man needs no capacity but that of surrendering himself to the will of God: and if he uses any of his faculties for any other purpose but to do that supposed will more effectually, he is better without them. This is the theory of Calvinism; and it is held, in a mitigated form, by many who do not consider themselves Calvinists; the mitigation consisting in giving a less ascetic interpretation to the alleged will of God; asserting it to be his will that mankind should gratify some of their inclinations; of course not in the manner they themselves prefer, but in the way of obedience, that is, in a way prescribed to them by authority; and, therefore, by the necessary conditions of the case, the same for all.

In some such insidious form there is at present a strong tendency to this narrow theory of life, and to the pinched and hidebound type of human character which it patronizes. Many persons, no doubt, sincerely think that human beings thus cramped and dwarfed are as their Maker designed them to be; just as many have thought that trees are a much finer thing when clipped into pollards,[3] or cut out into figures of animals, than as nature made them. But if it be any part of religion to believe that man was made by a good Being, it is more consistent with that faith to believe that this Being gave all human faculties that they might be cultivated and unfolded, not rooted out and consumed, and that he takes delight in every nearer approach made by his creatures to the ideal conception embodied in them, every increase in any of their capabilities of comprehension, of action, or of enjoyment. There is a different type of human excellence from the Calvinistic; a conception of humanity as having its nature bestowed on it for other purposes than merely to be abnegated. "Pagan self-assertion" is one of the elements of human worth, as well as "Christian self-denial."[4] There is a Greek ideal of self-development, which the Platonic and Christian ideal of self-government blends with, but does not supersede. It may be better to be a John Knox than an Alcibiades, but it is better to be a Pericles than either,[5] nor would a Pericles, if we had one in these days, be without anything good which belonged to John Knox.

It is not by wearing down into uniformity all that is individual in themselves, but by cultivating it and calling it forth, within the limits imposed by the rights and interests of others, that human beings become a noble and beautiful object of contemplation; and as the works partake the character of those who do them, by the same process human life also becomes rich, diversified, and animating, furnishing more abundant aliment to high thoughts and elevating feelings, and strengthening the tie which binds every individual to the race, by making the race infinitely better worth belonging to. In proportion to the development of his individuality, each person becomes more valuable to himself, and is therefore capable of being more valuable to others. There is a greater fullness of life about his own existence, and when there is more life in the units there is more in the mass which is composed of them. As much compression as is necessary to prevent the stronger specimens of human nature from encroaching on the rights of others cannot be dispensed with; but for this there is ample compensation even in the point of view of human development. The means of development which the individual loses by being prevented from gratifying his inclinations to the injury of others are chiefly obtained at the expense of the development of other people. And even to himself there is a full equivalent in the better development of the social part of his nature, rendered possible by the restraint put upon the selfish part. To be held to rigid rules of justice for the sake of others develops the feelings and capacities which have the good of others for their object. But to be restrained in things not affecting their good, by their mere displeasure, develops nothing valuable, except such force of character as may unfold itself in resisting the restraint. If acquiesced in, it dulls and blunts the whole nature. To give any fair play to the nature of each, it is essential that different persons should be allowed to lead different lives. In proportion as this latitude has been exercised in any age, has that age been noteworthy to posterity. Even despotism does not produce its worst effects, so long as individuality exists under it; and whatever crushes individuality is despotism, by whatever name it may be called, and whether it professes to be enforcing the will of God or the injunctions of men.

Having said that Individuality is the same thing with development, and that it is only the cultivation of individuality which produces, or can produce, well-developed human beings, I might here close the argument: for what more or better can be said of any condition of human affairs than that it brings human beings themselves nearer to the best thing they can be? or what worse can be said of any obstruction to good than that it prevents this? Doubtless, however, these considerations will not suffice to convince those who most need convincing; and it is necessary further to show that these developed human beings are of some use to the undeveloped—to point out to those who do not desire liberty, and would not avail themselves of it, that they may be in some intelligible manner rewarded for allowing other people to make use of it without hindrance.

In the first place, then, I would suggest that they might possibly learn something from them. It will not be denied by anybody, that originality is a valuable element in human affairs. There is always need of persons not only to discover new truths, and point out when what were once truths are true no longer, but also to commence new practices, and set the example of more enlightened conduct, and better taste and sense in human life. This cannot well be gainsaid by anybody who does not believe that the world has already attained perfection in all its ways and practices. It is true that this benefit is not capable of being rendered by everybody alike: there are but few persons, in comparison with the whole of mankind, whose experiments, if adopted by others, would be likely to be any improvement on established practice. But these few are the salt of the earth; without them, human life would become a stagnant pool. Not only is it they who introduce good things which did not before exist; it is they who keep the life in those which already existed. If there were nothing new to be done, would human intellect cease to be necessary? Would it be a reason why those who do the old things should forget why they are done, and do them like cattle, not like human beings? There is only too great a tendency in the best beliefs and practices to degenerate into the mechanical; and unless there were a succession of persons whose ever-recurring originality prevents the grounds of those beliefs and practices from becoming merely traditional, such dead matter would not resist the smallest shock from anything really alive, and there would be no reason why civilization should not die out, as in the Byzantine Empire. Persons of genius, it is true, are, and are always likely to be, a small minority; but in order to have them, it is necessary to preserve the soil in which they grow. Genius can only breathe freely in an *atmosphere* of freedom. Persons of genius are, *ex vi termini*,[6] more individual than any other people—less capable, consequently, of fitting themselves, without hurtful compression, into any of the small number of molds which society provides in order to save its members the trouble of forming their own character. If from timidity they consent to be forced into one of these molds, and to let all that part of themselves which cannot expand under the pressure remain unexpanded, society will be little the better for their genius. If they are of a strong character, and break their fetters, they become a mark for the society which has not succeeded in reducing them to commonplace, to point at with solemn warning as "wild," "erratic," and the like; much as if one should complain of the Niagara River for not flowing smoothly between its banks like a Dutch canal.

I insist thus emphatically on the importance of genius, and the necessity of allowing it to unfold itself freely both in thought and in practice, being well aware that no one will deny the position in theory, but knowing also that almost everyone, in reality, is totally indifferent to it. People think genius a fine thing if it enables a man to write an exciting poem, or paint a picture. But in its true sense, that of originality in thought and action, though no one says that it is not a thing to be admired, nearly all, at heart, think that they can do very well without it. Unhappily this is too natural to be wondered at. Originality is the one thing which unoriginal minds cannot feel the use of. They cannot see what it is to do for them: how should they? If they could see what it would do for them, it would not be originality. The first service which originality has to render them is that of opening their eyes: which being once fully done, they would have a chance of being themselves original. Meanwhile, recollecting that nothing was ever yet done which someone was not the first to do, and that all good things which exist are the fruits of originality, let them be modest enough to believe that there is something still left for it to accomplish, and assure themselves that they are more in need of originality, the less they are conscious of the want.

In sober truth, whatever homage may be professed, or even paid, to real or supposed mental superiority, the general tendency of things throughout the world is to render mediocrity the ascendant power among mankind. In ancient history, in the middle ages, and in a diminishing degree through the long transition from feudality to the present time, the individual was power in himself; and if he had either great talents or a high social position, he was a considerable power. At present individuals are lost in the crowd. In politics it is almost a triviality to say that public opinion now rules the world. The only power deserving the name is that of masses, and of governments while they make themselves the organ of the tendencies and instincts of masses. This is as true in the moral and social relations of private life as in public transactions. Those whose opinions go by the name of public opinion, are not always the same sort of public: in America they are the whole white population; in England, chiefly the middle class. But they are always a mass, that is to say, collective mediocrity. And what is a still greater novelty, the mass do not now take their opinions from dignitaries in Church or State, from ostensible leaders, or from books. Their thinking is done for them by men much like themselves, addressing them or speaking in their name, on the spur of the moment, through the newspapers. I am not complaining of all this. I do not assert that anything better is compatible, as a general rule, with the present low state of the human mind. But that does not hinder the government of mediocrity from being mediocre government. No government by a democracy or a numerous aristocracy, either in its political acts or in the opinions, qualities, and tone of mind which it fosters, ever did or could rise above mediocrity, except in so far as the sovereign. Many have let themselves be guided (which in their best times they always have done) by the counsels and influence of a more highly gifted and instructed One or Few. The initiation of all wise or noble things, comes and must come from individuals; generally at first from some one individual. The honor and glory of the average man is that he is capable of following that initiative; that he can respond internally to wise and noble things, and be led to them with his eyes open. I am not countenancing the sort of "hero worship" which applauds the strong man of genius for forcibly seizing on the government of the world and making it do his bidding in spite of itself. All he can claim is freedom to point out the way. The power of compelling others into it is not only inconsistent with the freedom and development of all the rest, but corrupting to the strong man himself. It does seem, however, that when the opinions of masses of merely average men are everywhere become or becoming the dominant power, the counterpoise and corrective to that tendency would be the more and more pronounced individuality of those who stand on the higher eminences of thought. It is in these circumstances most especially that exceptional individuals, instead of being deterred, should be encouraged in acting differently from the mass. In other times there was no advantage in their doing so, unless they acted not only differently, but better. In this age, the mere example of nonconformity, the mere refusal to bend the knee to custom, is itself a service. Precisely because the tyranny of opinion is such as to make eccentricity a reproach, it is desirable, in order to break through that tyranny, that people should be eccentric. Eccentricity has always abounded when and where strength of character has abounded; and the amount of eccentricity in a society has generally been proportional to the amount of genius, mental vigor, and moral courage which it contained. That so few now dare to be eccentric marks the chief danger of the time.

• • •

There is one characteristic of the present direction of public opinion, peculiarly calculated to make it intolerant of any marked demonstration of individuality. The general average of mankind are not only moderate in intellect, but also moderate in inclinations: they have no tastes or wishes strong enough to incline them to do anything unusual, and they consequently do not understand those who have, and class all such with the wild and intemperate whom they are accustomed to look down upon. Now, in addition to this fact which is general, we have only to suppose that a strong movement has set in towards the improvement of morals, and it is evident what we have to expect. In these days such a movement has set in; much has actually been effected in the way of increased regularity of conduct, and discouragement of excesses; and there is a philanthropic spirit abroad, for the exercise of which there is no more inviting field than the moral and prudential improvement of our fellow creatures. These tendencies of the times cause the public to be more disposed than at most former periods to prescribe general rules of conduct, and endeavor to make everyone conform to the approved standard. And that standard, express or tacit, is to desire nothing strongly. Its ideal of character is to be without any marked character; to maim by compression, like a Chinese lady's foot, every part of human nature which stands out prominently, and tends to make the person markedly dissimilar in outline to commonplace humanity.

As is usually the case with ideals which exclude one half of what is desirable, the present standard of approbation produces only an inferior imitation of the other half. Instead of great energies guided by vigorous reason, and strong feelings strongly controlled by a conscientious will, its result is weak feelings and weak energies, which therefore can be kept in outward conformity to rule without any strength either of will or reason. Already energetic characters on any large scale are becoming merely traditional. There is now scarcely any outlet for energy in this country except business. The energy expended in this may still be regarded as considerable. What little is left from that employment, is expended on some hobby; which may be a useful, even a philanthropic hobby, but is always some one thing, and generally a thing of small dimensions. The greatness of England is now all collective: individually small, we only appear capable of anything great by our habit of combining; and with this our moral and religious philanthropies are perfectly contended. But it was men of another stamp than this that made England what it has been; and men of another stamp will be needed to prevent its decline.

The despotism of custom is everywhere the standing hindrance to human advancement, being in unceasing antagonism to that disposition to aim at something better than customary, which is called, according to circumstances, the spirit of liberty, or that of progress or improvement. The spirit of improvement is not always a spirit of liberty, for it may aim at forcing improvements on an unwilling people; and the spirit of liberty, in so far as it resists such attempts, may ally itself locally and temporarily with the opponents of improvement; but the only unfailing and permanent source of improvement is liberty, since by it there are as many possible independent centers of improvement as there are individuals. The progressive principle, however, in either shape, whether as the love of liberty or of improvement, is antagonistic to the sway of Custom, involving at least emancipation from that yoke; and the contest between the two constitutes the chief interest of the history of mankind. The greater part of the world has, properly speaking, no history, because the depotism of Custom is complete. This is the case over the whole East. Custom is there, in all things, the final appeal; justice and right mean conformity to custom; the argument of custom no one, unless some tyrant intoxicated with power, thinks of resisting. And we see the result. Those nations must once have had originality; they did not start out of the ground populous, lettered, and versed in many of the arts of life; they made themselves all this, and were then the greatest and most powerful nations of the world. What are they now? The subjects or dependents of tribes whose forefathers wandered in the forests when theirs had magnificent palaces and gorgeous temples, but over whom custom exercised only a divided rule with liberty and progress. A people, it appears, may be progressive for a certain length of time, and then stop: when does it stop? When it ceases to possess individuality. If a similar change should befall the nations of Europe, it will not be in exactly the same shape: the despotism of custom with which these nations are threatened is not precisely stationariness. It proscribes singularity, but it does not preclude change, provided all change together. We have discarded the fixed costumes of our forefathers; everyone must still dress like other people, but the fashion may change once or twice a year. We thus take care that when there is change it shall be for change's sake, and not from any idea of beauty or convenience; for the same idea of beauty or convenience would not strike all the world at the same moment, and be simultaneously thrown aside by all at another moment. But we are progressive as well as changeable: we continually make new inventions in mechanical things, and keep them until they are again superseded by better; we are eager for improvement in politics, in education, even in morals, though in this last our idea of improvement chiefly consists in persuading or forcing other people to be as good as ourselves. It is not progress that we object to; on the contrary, we flatter ourselves that we are the most progressive people who ever lived. It is individuality that we war against: we should think we had done wonders if we had made ourselves all alike; forgetting that the unlikeness of one person to another is generally the first thing which draws the attention of either to the imperfection of his own type, and the superiority of another, or the possibility, by combining the advantages of both, of producing something better than either. We have a warning example in China—a nation of much talent, and, in some respects, even wisdom, owing to the rare good fortune of having been provided at an early period with a particularly good set of customs, the work, in some measure, of men to whom even the most enlightened European must accord, under certain limitations, the title of sages and philosophers. They are remarkable, too, in the excellence of their apparatus for impressing, as far as possible, the best wisdom they possess upon mind in the community, and securing that those who have appropriated most of all shall occupy the posts of honor and power. Surely the people who did this have discovered the secret of human progressiveness, and must have kept themselves steadily at the head of the movement of the world. On the contrary, they have become stationary—have remained so for thousands of years; and if they are ever to be farther improved, it must be by foreigners. They have succeeded beyond all hope in what English philanthropists are so industriously working at—in making people all alike, all governing their thoughts and conduct by the same maxims and rules; and these are the fruits. The modern regime of public opinion is, in an unorganized form, what the Chinese educational and political systems are in an organized; and unless individuality shall be able successfully to assert itself against this yoke, Europe, notwithstanding its noble antecedents and its professed Christianity, will tend to become another China. . . .

## Notes

1   From *The Sphere and Duties of Government,* by Baron Wilhelm von Humboldt (1767–1835), Prussian statesman and man of letters. Originally written 1791, this treatise was first published in Germany in 1852 and was translated into English in 1854.

2   Agreeable.

3   Trees that acquire an artificial shape by being cut back so as to produce a mass of dense foliage.

4   From the *Essays* (1848) of John Sterling a minor writer and friend of Thomas Carlyle's.

5   John Knox (1505–1572) was the stern Scottish Calvinist reformer, Alcibaides (450–404 B.C.) was a dissolute Athenian commander, and Percles (500–429 B.C.) was a model statesman in Athens.

6   Latin for "by force of of the term," i.e. by definition.

# *from* A Vindication of the Rights of Woman

## Mary Wollstonecraft

*Mary Wollstonecraft Godwin (1759–1797) witnessed the French Revolution and applied current ideas on the "rights of man" to the rights of women. She writes to refute the dominant view of her time, that women are inherently inferior to men in physical and mental capacity and should therefore be subject to male tutelage and control. The idea that women lack the capacity for full moral responsibility is deep seated in the Western tradition.*

## Introduction

After considering the historic page, and viewing the living world with anxious solicitude, the most melancholy emotions of sorrowful indignation have depressed my spirits, and I have sighed when obliged to confess, that either nature has made a great difference between man and man, or that the civilization which has hitherto taken place in the world has been very partial. I have turned over various books written on the subject of education, and patiently observed the conduct of parents and the management of schools; but what has been the result?—a profound conviction that the neglected education of my fellow-creatures is the grand source of the misery I deplore; and that women, in particular, are rendered weak and wretched by a variety of concurring causes, originating from one hasty conclusion. The conduct and manners of women, in fact, evidently prove that their minds are not in a healthy state; for, like the flowers which are planted in too rich a soil, strength and usefulness are sacrificed to beauty; and the flaunting leaves, after having pleased a fastidious eye, fade, disregarded on the stalk, long before the season when they ought to have arrived at maturity.—One cause of this barren blooming I attribute to a false system of education, gathered from the books written on this subject by men who, considering females rather as women than human creatures, have been more anxious to make them alluring mistresses than affectionate wives and rational mothers; and the understanding of the sex has been so bubbled by this specious homage, that the civilized women of the present century, with a few exceptions, are only anxious to inspire love, when they ought to cherish a nobler ambition, and by their abilities and virtues exact respect.

In a treatise, therefore, on female rights and manners, the works which have been particularly written for their improvement must not be over-looked; especially when it is asserted, in direct terms, that the minds of women are enfeebled by false refinement; that the books of instruction, written by men of genius, have had the same tendency as more frivolous productions; and that, in the true style of Mahometanism, they are treated as a kind of subordinate beings, and not as a part of the human species, when improvable reason is allowed to be the dignified distinc-tion which raises men above the brute creation, and puts a natural scep-tre in a feeble hand.

Yet, because I am a woman, I would not lead my readers to suppose that I mean violently to agitate the contested question respecting the equality or inferiority of the sex; but as the subject lies in my way, and I cannot pass it over without subjecting the main tendency of my reasoning to misconstruction, I shall stop a moment to deliver, in a few words, my opinion.—In the government of the physical world it is observable that the female in point of strength is, in general, inferior to the male. This is the law of nature; and it does not appear to be suspended or abrogated in favour of woman. A degree of physical superiority cannot, therefore, be denied—and it is a noble prerogative! But not content with this natural pre-eminence, men endeavour to sink us still lower, merely to render us alluring objects for a moment; and women, intoxicated by the adoration which men, under the influence of their senses, pay them, do not seek to obtain a durable interest in their hearts, or to become the friends of the fellow creatures who find amusement in their society.

I am aware of an obvious inference:—from every quarter have I heard exclamations against masculine women; but where are they to be found? If by this appellation men mean to inveigh against their ardour in hunt-ing, shooting, and gaming, I shall most cordially join in the cry; but if it be against the imitation of many virtues, or, more properly speaking, the attainment of those talents and virtues, the exercise of which ennobles the human character, and which raise females in the scale of animal being, when they are comprehensively termed mankind;—all those who view them with a philosophic eye must, I should think, wish with me, that they may every day grow more and more masculine.

This discussion naturally divides the subject. I shall first consider women in the grand light of human creatures, who, in common with men, are placed on this earth to unfold their faculties; and afterwards I shall more particularly point out their peculiar designation.

I wish also to steer clear of an error which many respectable writers have fallen into; for the instruction which has hitherto been addressed to women, has rather been applicable to ladies, if the little indirect advice, that is scattered through Sandford and Merton, be excepted; but, addressing my sex in a firmer tone, I pay particular attention to those in the middle class, because they appear to be in the most natural state. Perhaps the seeds of false refinement, immorality, and vanity, have ever been shed by the great. Weak, artificial beings, raised above the common wants and affections of their race, in a premature unnatural manner, undermine the very foundation of virtue, and spread corruption through the whole mass of society! As a class of mankind they have the strongest claim to pity; the education of the rich tends to render them vain and helpless, and the unfolding mind is not strengthened by the practice of those duties which dignify the human character.—They only live to amuse themselves, and by the same law which in nature invariably produces certain effects, they soon only afford barren amusement.

But as I purpose taking a separate view of the different ranks of society, and of the moral character of women, in each, this hint is, for the present, sufficient, and I have only alluded to the subject, because it appears to me to be the very essence of an introduction to give a cursory account of the contents of the work it introduces.

My own sex, I hope, will excuse me, if I treat them like rational creatures, instead of flattering their *fascinating* graces, and viewing them as if they were in a state of perpetual childhood, unable to stand alone. I earnestly wish to point out in what true dignity and human happiness consists—I wish to persuade women to endeavour to acquire strength, both of mind and body, and to convince them that the soft phrases, susceptibility of heart, delicacy of sentiment, and refinement of taste, are almost synonymous with epithets of weakness, and that those beings who are only the objects of pity and that kind of love, which has been termed its sister, will soon become objects of contempt.

Dismissing then those pretty feminine phrases, which the men condescendingly use to soften our slavish dependence, and despising that weak elegancy of mind, exquisite sensibility, and sweet docility of manners, supposed to be the sexual characteristics of the weaker vessel, I wish to shew that elegance is inferior to virtue, that the first object of laudable ambition is to obtain a character as a human being, regardless of the distinction of sex; and that secondary views should be brought to this simple touchstone.

This is a rough sketch of my plan; and should I express my conviction with the energetic emotions that I feel whenever I think of the subject, the dictates of experience and reflection will be felt by some of my readers. Animated by this important object, I shall disdain to cull my phrases or polish my style;—I aim at being useful, and sincerity will render me unaffected; for, wishing rather to persuade by the force of my arguments, than dazzle by the elegance of my language, I shall not waste my time in rounding periods, or in fabricating the turgid bombast of artificial feelings, which, coming from the head, never reach the heart. I shall be employed about things, not words!—and, anxious to render my sex more respectable members of society, I shall try to avoid that flowery diction which has slided from essays into novels, and from novels into familiar letters and conversation.

These pretty superlatives, dropping glibly from the tongue, vitiate the taste, and create a kind of sickly delicacy that turns away from simple unadorned truth; and a deluge of false sentiments and over-stretched feelings, stifling the natural emotions of the heart, render the domestic pleasures insipid, that ought to sweeten the exercise of those severe duties, which educate a rational and immortal being for a nobler field of action.

The education of women has, of late, been more attended to than formerly; yet they are still reckoned a frivolous sex, and ridiculed or pitied by the writers who endeavour by satire or instruction to improve them. It is acknowledged that they spend many of the first years of their lives in acquiring a smattering of accomplishments; meanwhile strength of body and mind are sacrificed to libertine notions of beauty, to the desire of establishing themselves,—the only way women can rise in the world,—by marriage. And this desire making mere animals of them, when they marry they act as such children may be expected to act:—they dress; they paint, and nickname God's creatures.—Surely these weak beings are only fit for a seraglio!—Can they be expected to govern a family with judgment, or take care of the poor babes whom they bring into the world?

If then it can be fairly deduced from the present conduct of the sex, from the prevalent fondness for pleasure which takes place of ambition and those nobler passions that open and enlarge the soul; that the instruction which women have hitherto received has only tended, with the constitution of civil society, to render them insignificant objects of desire—mere propagators of fools!—if it can be proved that in aiming to accomplish them, without cultivating their understandings, they are taken out of their sphere of duties, and made ridiculous and useless when the short-lived bloom of beauty is over, I presume that *rational* men will excuse me for endeavouring to persuade them to become more masculine and respectable.

Indeed the word masculine is only a bugbear: there is little reason to fear that women will acquire too much courage or fortitude; for their apparent inferiority with respect to bodily strength, must render them, in some degree, dependent on men in the various relations of life; but why should it be increased by prejudices that give a sex to virtue, and confound simple truths with sensual reveries?

Women are, in fact, so much degraded by mistaken notions of female excellence, that I do not mean to add a paradox when I assert, that this artificial weakness produces a propensity to tyrannize, and gives birth to cunning, the natural opponent of strength, which leads them to play off those contemptible infantine airs that undermine esteem even whilst they excite desire. Let men become more chaste and modest, and if women do not grow wiser in the same ratio it will be clear that they have weaker understandings. It seems scarcely necessary to say, that I now speak of the sex in general. Many individuals have more sense than their male relatives; and, as nothing preponderates where there is a constant struggle for an equilibrium, without it has naturally more gravity, some women govern their husbands without degrading themselves, because intellect will always govern.

# *from* Civil Disobedience

## Henry David Thoreau

*Henry David Thoreau was a contemporary of J. S. Mill. He lived in Concord, Massachusetts. These thoughts on civil disobedience were published in 1849 at a time when Thoreau was refusing to pay taxes to what he believed was an immoral government. Thoreau's ideas on civil disobedience were influential in the thinking of Gandhi and Martin Luther King, Jr.*

I heartily accept the motto, "That government is best which governs least;" and I should like to see it acted up to more rapidly and systematically. Carried out, it finally amounts to this, which also I believe,— "That government is best which governs not at all;" and when men are prepared for it, that will be the kind of government which they will have. Government is at best but an expedient; but most governments are usually, and all governments are sometimes, inexpedient. . . .

This American government,—what is it but a tradition, though a recent one, endeavoring to transmit itself unimpaired to posterity, but each instant losing some of its integrity? It has not the vitality and force of a single living man; for a single man can bend it to his will. It is a sort of wooden gun to the people themselves. But it is not the less necessary for this; for the people must have some complicated machinery or other, and hear its din, to satisfy that idea of government which they have. Governments show thus how successfully men can be imposed on, even impose on themselves, for their own advantage. It is excellent, we must all allow. Yet this government never of itself furthered any enterprise, but by the alacrity with which it got out of its way. *It* does not keep the country free. *It* does not settle the West. *It* does not educate. The character inherent in the American people has done all that has been accomplished; and it would have done somewhat more, if the government had not sometimes got in its way. For government is an expedient by which men would fain succeed in letting one another alone; and as has been said, when it is most expedient, the governed are most let alone by it. . . .

But, to speak practically and as a citizen, unlike those who call themselves no-government men, I ask for, not at once no government, but *at once* a better government. Let every man make known what kind of government would command his respect, and that will be one step toward obtaining it.

After all, the practical reason why, when the power is once in the hands of the people, a majority are permitted, and for a long period continue, to rule is not because they are most likely to be in the right, nor because this seems fairest to the minority, but because they are physically the strongest. But a government in which the majority rule in all cases cannot be based on justice, even as far as men understand it. Can there not be a government in which majorities do not virtually decide right and wrong, but conscience?—in which majorities decide only those questions to which the rule of expediency is applicable? Must the citizen ever for a moment, or in the least degree, resign his conscience to the legislator? Why has every man a conscience, then? I think that we should be men first, and subjects afterward. It is not desirable to cultivate a respect for the law, so much as for the right. The only obligation which I have a right to assume is to do at any time what I think right. It is truly enough said that a corporation has no conscience; but a corporation of conscientious men is a corporation *with* a conscience. Law never made men a whit more just; and, by means of their respect for it, even the well-disposed are daily made the agents of injustice. A common and natural result of an undue respect for law is, that you may see a file of soldiers, colonel, captain, corporal, privates, powder-monkeys, and all, marching in admirable order over hill and dale to the wars, against their wills, ay, against their common sense and consciences, which makes it very steep marching indeed, and produces a palpitation of the heart. They have no doubt that it is a damnable business in which they are concerned; they are all peaceably inclined. Now, what are they? Men at all? or small movable forts and magazines, at the service of some unscrupulous man in power? Visit the Navy Yard, and behold a marine, such a man as an American government can make, or such as it can make a man with its black arts,—a mere shadow and reminiscence of humanity, a man laid out alive and standing, and already, as one may say, buried under arms with funeral accompaniments, though it may be,—

> "Not a drum was heard, not a funeral note,
>  As his corse to the rampart we hurried;
> Not a soldier discharged his farewell shot
>  O'er the grave where our hero we buried."

The mass of men serve the state thus, not as men mainly, but as machines, with their bodies. They are the standing army, and the militia, jailers, constables, *posse comitatus*, etc. In most cases there is no free exercise whatever of the judgment or of the moral sense; but they put themselves on a level with wood and earth and stones; and wooden men can perhaps be manufactured that will serve the purpose as well. Such command no more respect than men of straw or a lump of dirt. They have the same sort of worth only as horses and dogs. Yet such as these even are commonly esteemed good citizens. Others—as most legislators, politicians, lawyers, ministers, and office-holders—serve the state chiefly with their heads; and, as they rarely make any moral distinctions, they are as likely to serve the devil, without *intending* it, as God. A very few—as heroes, patriots, martyrs, reformers in the great sense, and *men*—serve the state with their consciences also, and so necessarily resist it for the most part; and they are commonly treated as enemies by it. . . .

How does it become a man to behave toward this American government to-day? I answer, that he cannot without disgrace be associated with it. I cannot for an instant recognize that political organization as *my* government which is the *slave's* government also.

. . . All machines have their friction; and possibly this does enough good to counterbalance the evil. At any rate, it is a great evil to make a stir about it. But when the friction comes to have its machine, and oppression and robbery are organized, I say, let us not have such a machine any longer. In other words, when a sixth of the population of a nation which has undertaken to be the refuge of liberty are slaves, and a whole country is unjustly overrun and conquered by a foreign army, and subjected to military law, I think that it is not too soon for honest men to rebel and revolutionize. What makes this duty the more urgent is the fact that the country so overrun is not our own, but ours is the invading army.

Paley, a common authority with many on moral questions, in his chapter on the "Duty of Submission to Civil Government," resolves all civil obligation into expediency; and he proceeds to say that "so long as the interest of the whole society requires it, that is, so long as the established government cannot be resisted or changed without public inconveniency, it is the will of God . . . that the established government be obeyed—and no longer. This principle being admitted, the justice of every particular case of resistance is reduced to a computation of the quantity of the danger and grievance on the one side, and of the probability and expense of redressing it on the other." Of this, he says, every man shall judge for himself. But Paley appears never to have contemplated those cases to which the rule of expediency does not apply, in which a people, as well as an individual, must do justice, cost what it may. If I have unjustly wrested a plank from a drowning man, I must restore it to him though I drown myself. This, according to Paley, would be inconvenient. But he that would save his life, in such a case, shall lose it. This people must cease to hold slaves, and to make war on Mexico, though it cost them their existence as a people.

. . . I quarrel not with far-off foes, but with those who, near at home, cooperate with, and do the bidding of, those far away, and without whom the latter would be harmless. We are accustomed to say, that the mass of men are unprepared; but improvement is slow, because the few are not materially wiser or better than the many. It is not so important that many should be as good as you, as that there be some absolute goodness somewhere; for that will leaven the whole lump. There are thousands who are *in opinion* opposed to slavery and to the war, who yet in effect do nothing to put an end to them; who, esteeming themselves children of Washington and Franklin, sit down with their hands in their pockets, and say that they know not what to do, and do nothing; who even postpone the question of freedom to the question of free trade, and quietly read the prices-current along with the latest advices from Mexico, after dinner, and, it may be, fall asleep over them both. What is the price-current of an honest man and patriot to-day? They hesitate, and they regret, and sometimes they petition; but they do nothing in earnest and with effect. They will wait, well disposed, for others to remedy the evil, that they may no longer have it to regret. At most, they give only a cheap vote, and a feeble countenance and God-speed, to the right, as it goes by them. There are nine hundred and ninety-nine patrons of virtue to one virtuous man. But it is easier to deal with the real possessor of a thing than with the temporary guardian of it.

All voting is a sort of gaming, like checkers or backgammon, with a slight moral tinge to it, a playing with right and wrong, with moral questions; and betting naturally accompanies it. The character of the voters is not staked. I cast my vote, perchance, as I think right; but I am not vitally concerned that that right should prevail. I am willing to leave it to the majority. Its obligation, therefore, never exceeds that of expediency. Even voting *for the right* is *doing* nothing for it. It is only expressing to men feebly your desire that it should prevail. A wise man will not leave the right to the mercy of chance, nor wish it to prevail through the power of the majority. There is but little virtue in the action of masses of men. When the majority shall at length vote for the abolition of slavery, it will be because they are indifferent to slavery, or because there is but little slavery left to be abolished by their vote. *They* will then be the only slaves. Only *his* vote can hasten the abolition of slavery who asserts his own freedom by his vote. . . .

It is not a man's duty, as a matter of course, to devote himself to the eradication of any, even the most enormous, wrong; he may still properly have other concerns to engage him; but it is his duty, at least, to wash his hands of it, and, if he gives it no thought longer, not to give it practically his support. If I devote myself to other pursuits and contemplations, I must first see, at least, that I do not pursue them sitting upon another man's shoulders. I must get off him first, that he may pursue his contemplations too. See what gross inconsistency is tolerated. I have heard some of my townsmen say, "I should like to have them order me out to help put down an insurrection of the slaves, or to march to Mexico;—see if I would go;" and yet these very men have each, directly by their allegiance, and so indirectly, at least, by their money, furnished a substitute. The soldier is applauded who refuses to serve in an unjust war by those who do not refuse to sustain the unjust government which makes the war; is applauded by those whose own act and authority he disregards and sets at naught; as if the state were penitent to that degree that it hired one to scourge it while it sinned, but not to that degree that it left off sinning for a moment. Thus, under the name of Order and Civil Government, we are all made at last to pay homage to and support our own meanness. After the first blush of sin comes its indifference; and from immoral it becomes, as it were unmoral, and not quite unnecessary to that life which we have made. . . .

How can a man be satisfied to entertain an opinion merely, and enjoy *it*? Is there any enjoyment in it, if his opinion is that he is aggrieved? If you are cheated out of a single dollar by your neighbor, you do not rest satisfied with knowing that you are cheated, or with saying that you are cheated, or even with petitioning him to pay you your due; but you take effectual steps at once to obtain the full amount, and see that you are never cheated again. Action from principle, the perception and the performance of right, changes things and relations; it is essentially revolutionary, and does not consist wholly with anything which was. It not only divides States and churches, it divides families; ay, it divides the *individual*, separating the diabolical in him from the divine.

Unjust laws exist: shall we be content to obey them, or shall we endeavor to amend them, and obey them until we have succeeded, or shall we transgress them at once? Men generally, under such a government as this, think that they ought to wait until they have persuaded the majority to alter them. They think that, if they should resist, the remedy would be worse than the evil. But it is the fault of the government itself that the remedy is worse than the evil. *It* makes it worse. Why is it not more apt to anticipate and provide for reform? Why does it not cherish its wise minority? Why does it cry and resist before it is hurt? Why does it not encourage its citizens to be on alert to point out its faults, and *do* better than it would have them? Why does it always crucify Christ, and excommunicate Copernicus and Luther, and pronounce Washington and Franklin rebels? . . .

If the injustice is part of the necessary friction of the machine of government, let it go, let it go: perchance it will wear smooth,—certainly the machine will wear out. If the injustice has a spring, or a pulley, or a rope, or a crank, exclusively for itself, then perhaps you may consider whether the remedy will not be worse than the evil; but if it is of such a nature that it requires you to be the agent of injustice to another, then, I say, break the law. Let your life be a counter-friction to stop the machine. What I have to do is to see, at any rate, that I do not lend myself to the wrong which I condemn.

As for adopting the ways which the State has provided for remedying the evil, I know not of such ways. They take too much time, and a man's life will be gone. I have other affairs to attend to. I came into this world, not chiefly to make this a good place to live in, but to live in it, be it good or bad. A man has not everything to do, but something; and because he cannot do *everything*, it is not necessary that he should do *something* wrong. It is not my business to be petitioning the Governor or the Legislature any more than it is theirs to petition me; and if they should not hear my petition, what should I do then? But in this case the State has provided no way: its very Constitution is the evil. This may seem to be harsh and stubborn and unconciliatory; but it is to treat with the utmost kindness and consideration the only spirit that can appreciate or deserves it. So is all change for the better, like birth and death, which convulse the body.

I do not hesitate to say, that those who call themselves Abolitionists should at once effectually withdraw their support, both in person and property, from the government of Massachusetts, and not wait till they constitute a majority of one, before they suffer the right to prevail through them. I think that it is enough if they have God on their side, without waiting for that other one. Moreover, any man more right than his neighbors constitutes a majority of one already.

I meet this American government, or its representative, the State government, directly, and face to face, once a year—no more—in the person of its tax-gatherer; this is the only mode in which a man situated as I am necessarily meets it; and it then says distinctly, Recognize me; and the simplest, the most effectual, and, in the present posture of affairs, the indispensablest mode of treating with it on this head, of expressing your little satisfaction with and love for it, is to deny it then. My civil neighbor, the tax-gatherer, is the very man I have to deal with,—for it is, after all, with men and not with parchment that I quarrel,—and he has voluntarily chosen to be an agent of the government. How shall he ever know well what he is and does as an officer of the government, or as a man, until he is obliged to consider whether he shall treat me, his neighbor, for whom he has respect, as a neighbor and well-disposed man, or as a maniac and disturber of the peace, and see if he can get over this obstruction to his neighborliness without a ruder and more impetuous thought or speech corresponding with his action. I know this well, that if one thousand, if one hundred, if ten men whom I could name,—if ten *honest* men only,— ay, if *one* HONEST man, in this State of Massachusetts, *ceasing to hold slaves*, were actually to withdraw from this copartnership, and be locked up in the county jail therefor, it would be the abolition of slavery in America. For it matters not how small the beginning may seem to be: what is once well done is done forever. But we love better to talk about it: that we say is our mission. Reform keeps many scores of newspapers in its service, but not one man. . . .

Under a government which imprisons any unjustly, the true place for a just man is also a prison. The proper place to-day, the only place which Massachusetts has provided for her freer and less desponding spirits, is in her prisons, to be put out and locked out of the State by her own act, as they have already put themselves out by their principles. It is there that the fugitive slave, and the Mexican prisoner on parole, and the Indian come to plead the wrongs of his race should find them; on that separate, but more free and honorable, ground, where the State places those who are not *with* her, but *against* her,—the only house in a slave State in which a free man can abide with honor. If any think that their influence would be lost there, and their voices no longer afflict the ear of the State, that they would not be as an enemy within its wall, they do not know by how much truth is stronger than error, nor how much more eloquently and effectively he can combat injustice who has experienced a little in his own person. Cast your whole vote, not a strip of paper merely, but your whole influence. A minority is powerless while it conforms to the majority; it is not even a minority then; but it is irresistible when it clogs by its whole weight. If the alternative is to keep all just men in prison, or give up war and slavery, the State will not hesitate which to choose. If a thousand men were not to pay their tax-bills this year, that would not be a violent and bloody measure, as it would be to pay them, and enable the State to commit violence and shed innocent blood. This is, in fact, the definition of a peaceable revolution, if any such is possible. If the tax-gatherer, or any other public officer, asks me, as one has done, "But what shall I do?" my answer is, "If you really wish to do anything, resign your office." When the subject has refused allegiance, and the officer has resigned his office, then the revolution is accomplished. But even suppose blood should flow. Is there not a sort of blood shed when the conscience is wounded? Through this would a man's real manhood and immortality flow out, and he bleeds to an everlasting death. I see this blood flowing now.

I have contemplated the imprisonment of the offender, rather than the seizure of his goods,—though both will serve the same purpose,—because they who assert the purest right, and consequently are most dangerous to a corrupt State, commonly have not spent much time in accumulating property. To such the State renders comparatively small service, and a slight tax is wont to appear exorbitant, particularly if they are obliged to earn it by special labor with their hands. If there were one who lived wholly without the use of money, the State itself would hesitate to demand it of him. But the rich man—not to make any invidious comparison—is always sold to the institution which makes him rich. Absolutely speaking, the more money, the less virtue; for money comes between a man and his objects, and obtains them for him; and it was certainly no great virtue to obtain it. It puts to rest many questions which he would otherwise be taxed to answer; while the only new question which it puts is the hard but superfluous one, how to spend it. Thus his moral ground is taken from under his feet. The opportunities of living are diminished in proportion as what are called the "means" are increased.

The best thing a man can do for his culture when he is rich is to endeavor to carry out those schemes which he entertained when he was poor. Christ answered the Herodians according to their condition. "Show me the tribute-money," said he;—and one took a penny out of his pocket;—if you use money which has the image of Ceasar on it, and which he has made current and valuable, that is, *if you are men of the State*, and gladly enjoy the advantages of Caesar's government, then pay him back some of his own when he demands it. "Render therefore to Caesar that which is Caesar's and to God those things which are God's,"—leaving them no wiser than before as to which was which; for they did not wish to know.

When I converse with the freest of my neighbors, I perceive that, whatever they may say about the magnitude and seriousness of the question, and their regard for the public tranquillity, the long and the short of the matter is, that they cannot spare the protection of the existing government, and they dread the consequences to their property and families of disobedience to it. For my own part, I should not like to think that I ever rely on the protection of the State. But, if I deny the authority of the State when it presents its taxbill, it will soon take and waste all my property, and so harass me and my children without end. This is hard. This makes it impossible for a man to live honestly, and at the same time comfortably, in outward respects. It will not be worth the while to accumulate property; that would be sure to go again. You must hire or squat somewhere, and raise but a small crop, and eat that soon. You must live within yourself, and depend upon yourself always tucked up and ready for a start, and not have many affairs. A man may grow rich in Turkey even, if he will be in all respects a good subject of the Turkish government. Confucius said: "If a state is governed by the principles of reason, poverty and misery are subjects of shame; if a state is not governed by the principles of reason, riches and honors are the subjects of shame." No: until I want the protection of Massachusetts to be extended to me in some distant Southern port, where my liberty is endangered, or until I am bent solely on building up an estate at home by peaceful enterprise, I can afford to refuse allegiance to Massachusetts, and her right to my property and life. It costs me less in every sense to incur the penalty of disobedience to the State than it would be to obey. I should feel as if I were worth less in that case. . . .

I have paid no poll-tax for six years. I was put into a jail once on this account, for one night; and, as I stood considering the walls of solid stone, two or three feet thick, the door of wood and iron, a foot thick, and the iron grating which strained the light, I could not help being struck by the foolishness of that institution which treated me as if I were mere flesh and blood and bones, to be locked up. I wondered that it should have concluded at length that this was the best use it could put me to, and had never thought to avail itself of my services in some way. I saw that, if there was a wall of stone between me and my townsmen, there was a still more difficult one to climb or break through before they could get to be as free as I was. I did not for a moment feel confined, and the walls seemed a great waste of stone and mortar. I felt as if I alone of all my townsmen had paid my tax. They plainly did not know how to treat me, but behaved like persons who are underbred. In every threat and in every compliment there was a blunder; for they thought that my chief desire was to stand the other side of that stone wall. I could not but smile to see how industriously they locked the door on my meditations, which followed them out again without let or hindrance, and *they* were really all that was dangerous. As they could not reach me, they had resolved to punish my body; just as boys, if they cannot come at some person against whom they have a spite, will abuse his dog. I saw that the State was half-witted, that it was timid as a lone woman with her silver spoons, and that it did not know its friends from its foes, and I lost all my remaining respect for it, and pitied it.

Thus the State never intentionally confronts a man's sense, intellectual or moral, but only his body, his senses. It is not armed with superior wit or honesty, but with superior physical strength. I was not born to be forced. I will breathe after my own fashion. Let us see who is the strongest. What force has a multitude? They only can force me who obey a higher law than I. They force me to become like themselves. I do not hear of *men* being *forced* to live this way or that by masses of men. What sort of life were that to live? When I meet a government which says to me, "Your money or your life," why should I be in haste to give it my money? It may be in a great strait, and not know what to do: I cannot help that. It must help itself; do as I do. It is not worth the while to snivel about it. I am not responsible for the successful working of the machinery of society. I am not the son of the engineer. I perceive that, when an acorn and a chestnut fall side by side, the one does not remain inert to make way for the other, but both obey their own laws, and spring and grow and flourish as best they can, till one, perchance, overshadows and destroys the other. If a plant cannot live according to its nature, it dies; and so a man. . . .

When I came out of prison,—for some one interfered, and paid that tax,— I did not perceive that great changes had taken place on the common, such as he observed who went in a youth and emerged a tottering and gray-headed man; and yet a change had to my eyes come over the scene,—the town, and State, and country,—greater than any that mere time could effect. I saw yet more distinctly the State in which I lived. I saw to what extent the people among whom I lived could be trusted as good neighbors and friends; that their friendship was for summer weather only; that they did not greatly propose to do right; that they were a distinct race from me by their prejudices and superstitions, as the Chinamen and Malays are; that in their sacrifices to humanity they ran no risks, not even to their property; that after all they were not so noble but they treated the thief as he had treated them, and hoped, by a certain outward observance and a few prayers, and by walking in a particular straight though useless path from time to time, to save their souls. This may be to judge my neighbors harshly; for I believe that many of them are not aware that they have such an institution as the jail in their village.

It was formerly the custom in our village, when a poor debtor came out of jail, for his acquaintances to salute him, looking through their fingers, which were crossed to represent the grating of a jail window, "How do ye do?" My neighbors did not thus salute me, but first looked at me, and then at one another, as if I had returned from a long journey. I was put into jail as I was going to the shoemaker's to get a shoe which was mended. When I was let out the next morning, I proceeded to finish my errand, and, having put on my mended shoe, joined a huckleberry party, who were impatient to put themselves under my conduct; and in half an hour,—for the horse was soon tackled,—was in the midst of a huckleberry field, on one of our highest hills, two miles off, and then the State was nowhere to be seen.

This is the whole history of "My Prisons."

I have never declined paying the highway tax, because I am as desirous of being a good neighbor as I am of being a bad subject; and as for supporting schools, I am doing my part to educate my fellow-countrymen now. It is for no particular item in the tax-bill that I refuse to pay it. I simply wish to refuse allegiance to the State, to withdraw and stand aloof from it effectually. I do not care to trace the course of my dollar, if I could, till it buys a man or a musket to shoot one with,—the dollar is innocent,— but I am concerned to trace the effects of my allegiance. In fact, I quietly declare war with the State, after my fashion, though I will still make what use and get what advantage of her I can, as is usual in such cases.

If others pay the tax which is demanded of me, from a sympathy with the State, they do but what they have already done in their own case, or rather they abet injustice to a greater extent than the State requires. If they pay the tax from a mistaken interest in the individual taxed, to save his property, or prevent his going to jail, it is because they have not considered wisely how far they let their private feelings interfere with the public good.

This, then, is my position at present. But one cannot be too much on his guard in such a case, lest his action be biased by obstinacy or an undue regard for the opinions of men. Let him see that he does only what belongs to himself and to the hour.

I think sometimes, Why, this people mean well, they are only ignorant; they would do better if they knew how: why give your neighbors this pain to treat you as they are not inclined to? But I think again, This is no reason why I should do as they do, or permit others to suffer much greater pain of a different kind. Again, I sometimes say to myself, When many millions of men, without heat, without ill will, without personal feeling of any kind, demand of you a few shillings only, without the possibility, such is their constitution, of retracting or altering their present demand, and without the possibility, on your side, of appeal to any other millions, why expose yourself to this overwhelming brute force? You do not resist cold and hunger, the winds and the waves, thus obstinately; you quietly submit to a thousand similar necessities. You do not put your head into the fire. But just in proportion as I regard this as not wholly a brute force, but partly a human force, and consider that I have relations to those millions as to so many millions of men, and not of mere brute or inanimate things, I see that appeal is possible, first and instantaneously, from them to the Maker of them, and, secondly, from them to themselves. But if I put my head deliberately into the fire, there is no appeal to fire or to the Maker of fire, and I have only myself to blame. If I could convince myself that I have any right to be satisfied with men as they are, and to treat them accordingly, and not according, in some respects, to my requisitions and expectations of what they and I ought to be, then, like a good Mussulman and fatalist, I should endeavor to be satisfied with things as they are, and say it is the will of God. And, above all, there is this difference between resisting this and a purely brute or natural force, that I can resist this with some effect; but I cannot expect, like Orpheus, to change the nature of the rocks and trees and beasts.

I do not wish to quarrel with any man or nation. I do not wish to split hairs, to make fine distinctions, or set myself up as better than my neighbors. I seek rather, I may say, even an excuse for conforming to the laws of the land. I am but too ready to conform to them. Indeed, I have reason to suspect myself on this head; and each year, as the tax-gatherer comes round, I find myself disposed to review the acts and position of the general and State governments, and the spirit of the people, to discover a pretext for conformity.

> "We must affect our country as our parents,
> And if at any time we alienate
> Our love or industry from doing it honor,
> We must respect effects and teach the soul
> Matter of conscience and religion,
> And not desire of rule or benefit."

I believe that the State will soon be able to take all my work of this sort out of my hands, and then I shall be no better a patriot than my fellow-countrymen. Seen from a lower point of view, the Constitution, with all its faults, is very good; the law and the courts are very respectable; even this State and this American government are, in many respects, very admirable, and rare things, to be thankful for, such as a great many have described them; but seen from a point of view a little higher, they are what I have described them; seen from a higher still, and the highest, who shall say what they are, or that they are worth looking at or thinking of at all?

However, the government does not concern me much, and I shall bestow the fewest possible thoughts on it. It is not many moments that I live under a government, even in this world. If a man is thought-free, fancy-free, imagination-free, that which *is not* never for a long time appearing *to be* to him, unwise rulers or reformers cannot fatally interrupt him. . . .

They who know of no purer sources of truth, who have traced up its stream no higher, stand, and wisely stand, by the Bible and the Constitution, and drink at it there with reverence and humility; but they who behold where it comes trickling into this lake or that pool, gird up their loins once more, and continue their pilgrimage toward its fountain-head.

No man with a genius for legislation has appeared in America. They are rare in the history of the world. . . . If we were left solely to the wordy wit of legislators in Congress for our guidance, uncorrected by the seasonable experience and the effectual complaints of the people, America would not long retain her rank among the nations. For eighteen hundred years, though perchance I have no right to say it, the New Testament has been written; yet where is the legislator who has wisdom and practical talent enough to avail himself of the light which it sheds on the science of legislation?

The authority of government, even such as I am willing to submit to,— for I will cheerfully obey those who know and can do better than I, and in many things even those who neither know nor can do so well,—is still an impure one: to be strictly just, it must have the sanction and consent of the governed. It can have no pure right over my person and property but what I concede to it. The progress from an absolute to a limited monarchy, from a limited monarchy to a democracy, is a progress toward a true respect for the individual. Even the Chinese philosopher was wise enough to regard the individual as the basis of the empire. Is a democracy, such as we know it, the last improvement possible in government? Is it not possible to take a step further towards recognizing and organizing the rights of man? There will never be a really free and enlightened State until the State comes to recognize the individual as a higher and independent power, from which all its own power and authority are derived, and treats him accordingly. I please myself with imagining a State at last which can afford to be just to all men, and to treat the individual with respect as a neighbor; which even would not think it inconsistent with its own repose if a few were to live aloof from it, not meddling with it, nor embraced by it, who fulfilled all the duties of neighbors and fellow-men. A State which bore this kind of fruit, and suffered it to drop off as fast as it ripened, would prepare the way for a still more perfect and glorious State, which also I have imagined, but not yet anywhere seen.

# *from* Gandhi's Message to All Men

## *Mahatma Gandhi*

*Mohandas Gandhi (1869–1948) began to develop his techniques of civil disobedience in South Africa, where he led the Indian community in its resistance to the Pass Law. A lawyer, he eventually returned to India where he organized resistance to the British government using tactics of noncooperation and passive resistance. These included the refusal to wear British-made cloth and Gandhi's famous walk to the sea, where he made his own salt in defiance of the British tax on salt. Gandhi was frequently jailed by the British. On occasion the British went so far as to strafe a crowd of protesters with Royal Air Force planes.*

The more efficient a force is, the more silent and the more subtle it is. Love is the subtlest force in the world.

[The] force of love . . . truly comes into play only when it meets with causes of hatred. True Non-violence does not ignore or blind itself to causes of hatred, but in spite of the knowledge of their existence, operates upon the person setting those causes in motion. . . . The law of Non-violence—returning good for evil, loving one's enemy—involves a knowledge of the blemishes of the "enemy." Hence do the Scriptures say . . . "Forgiveness is an attribute of the brave."

. . . I can no more preach Non-violence to a coward than I can tempt a blind man to enjoy healthy scenes. Non-violence is the summit of bravery. . . .

. . . Suffering in one's own person is . . . the essence of non-violence and is the chosen substitute for violence to others. It is not because I value life low that I can countenance with joy thousands voluntarily losing their lives for Satyagraha, but because I know that it results in the long run in the least loss of life, and what is more, it ennobles those who lose their lives . . . [Unless] Europe is to commit suicide, some nation will have to dare to disarm herself and take large risks. The level of non-violence in that nation . . . will naturally have risen so high as to command universal respect. Her judgments will be unerring, her decisions will be firm, her capacity for heroic self-sacrifice will be great, and she will want to live as much for other nations as for herself. . . .

. . . They say "means are after all [just] means." I would say "means are after all everything." As the means, so the end. Violent means will give violent Swaraj. . . . There is no wall of separation between means and end. . . . I have been endeavoring to keep the country to means that are purely peaceful and legitimate.

. . . If we take care of the means we are bound to reach the end sooner or later. . . .

. . . Truth is my God. Non-violence is the means of realizing Him. . . .

I am not a "statesman in the garb of a saint." But since Truth is the highest wisdom, sometimes my acts appear to be consistent with the highest statesmanship. But I hope I have no policy in me save the policy of Truth and Non-violence. . . .

[To] me . . . there is no way to find Truth except the way of Non-violence. . . . For I know that a man who forsakes Truth can forsake his country and his nearest and dearest ones. . . .

. . . I will not sacrifice Truth and Non-violence even for the deliverance of my country or religion. . . .

. . . The movement of non-violent non-cooperation has nothing in common with the historical struggles for freedom in the West. It is not based on brute force or hatred. It does not aim at destroying the tyrant. It is a movement of self-purification. It therefore seeks to convert the tyrant. . . .

. . . A revolutionary murders or robs not for the good of his victims, whom he often considers to be fit only to be injured, but for the supposed good of society.

. . . Conscience is the ripe fruit of strictest discipline. . . . There is no such thing, therefore, as mass conscience.

. . . The introduction of conscience into our public life is welcome . . . if it has taught a few of us to stand up for human dignity and rights in the face of the heaviest odds. . . .

. . . I have no secret methods. I know no diplomacy save that of truth. I have no weapon but non-violence. I may be unconsciously led astray for a while but not for all time. I have therefore well-defined limitations. . . .

I am yet ignorant of what exactly Bolshevism is. I have not been able to study it. I do not know whether it is for the good of Russia in the long run. But I do know that in so far as it is based on violence and denial of God, it repels me. I do not believe in short-violent-cuts to success. Those Bolshevik friends who are bestowing their attention on me should realize that however much I may sympathize with and admire worthy motives, I am an uncompromising opponent of violent methods even to serve the noblest of causes. . . . [Experience] convinces me that permanent good can never be the outcome of untruth and violence. Even if my belief is a fond delusion, it will be admitted that it is a fascinating delusion.

There is no principle worth the name if it is not wholly good. I swear by non-violence because I know that it alone conduces to the highest good of mankind, not merely in the next world, but in this also. I object to violence because, when it appears to do good, the good is only temporary, the evil it does is permanent. . . .

. . . Terrorism set up by reformers may be just as bad as Government terrorism, and it is often worse because it draws a certain amount of false sympathy. . . .

. . . I invite the revolutionaries not to commit suicide and drag with them unwilling victims. India's way is not Europe's. India is not Calcutta and Bombay. India lives in her seven hundred thousand villages. If the revolutionaries are as many let them spread out into these villages and try to bring sunshine into the dark dungeons of the millions of their countrymen. That would be worthier of their ambition and love of the land than the exciting and unquenchable thirst for the blood of English officials and those who are assisting them. It is nobler to try to change their spirit than to take their lives.

[A friend] says that non-violence cannot be attained by the mass of people. And yet, we find the general work of mankind is being carried on from day to day by the mass of people acting in harmony as if by instinct. If they were instinctively violent, the world would end in no time. They remain peaceful. . . . It is when the mass mind is unnaturally influenced by wicked men that the mass of mankind commit violence. But they forget it as quickly as they commit it because they return to their peaceful nature immediately after the evil influence of the directing mind has been removed.

... I hope to demonstrate that real Swaraj [Self Rule] will come not by the acquisition of authority by a few but by the acquisition of the capacity by all to resist authority when abused. In other words, Swaraj is to be attained by educating the masses to a sense of their capacity to regulate and control authority.

... If we all discharge our duties, rights will not be far to seek. If leaving duties unperformed, we run after rights, they will escape us like a will o' the wisp. . . . The same teaching has been embodied by Krishna in the immortal words: "Action alone is thine. Leave thou the fruit severely alone." Action is duty, fruit is the right.

... He who understands the doctrine of self-help blames himself for failure. It is on this ground that I object to violence. If we blame others where we should blame ourselves, and wish for or bring about their destruction, [it] does not remove the root cause of the disease, which, on the contrary sinks all the deeper for. . . ignorance. . . .

[It] is necessary for workers to become self-reliant and dare to prosecute their plans if they so desire, without hankering after the backing of . . . persons supposed to be great and influential. Let them rely upon the strength of their own conviction and the cause they seek to espouse. Mistakes there will be. Suffering, even avoidable, there must be. But nations are not easily made. . . .

... The way of peace insures internal growth and stability. We reject it because we fancy that it involves submission to the will of the ruler who has imposed himself upon us. . . . The suffering to be undergone . . . will be nothing compared to the physical suffering and the moral loss we must incur in trying the way of war. And the suffering in following the way of peace must benefit both. It will be like the pleasurable travail of a new birth.

[He] alone is truly non-violent who remains non-violent even though he has the ability to strike. . . . I have had in my life many an opportunity of shooting my opponents and earning the crown of martyrdom but I had not the heart to shoot any of them. For I did not want them to shoot me, however much they disliked my methods. I wanted them to convince me of my error as I was trying to convince them of theirs. "Do unto others as you would that they should do unto you."

Most people do not understand the complicated machinery of the government. They do not realize every citizen silently but none the less certainly sustains the government of the day in ways of which he has no knowledge. Every citizen therefore renders himself responsible for every act of his government. And it is quite proper to support it so long as the actions of the government are bearable. But when they hurt him and his nation it becomes his duty to withdraw his support.

. . . I cannot satisfy myself with false coöperation—anything inferior to twenty-four carats gold. . . . [My non-coöperation] harms no one, it is non-coöperation with evil, with an evil system, and not with the evil-doer. My religion teaches me to love even an evil-doer. . . .

What are . . . our countrymen in South Africa to do [in the way of preventing further oppressive legislation]? There is nothing in the world like self-help. . . . Self-help in this case, as perhaps in every other, means self-suffering, self-suffering means Satyagraha. When their honor is at stake, when their rights are being taken away, when their livelihood is threatened, they have the right and it becomes their duty to offer Satyagraha. . . .

. . . We may be justly entitled to many things but Satyagraha is offered for things without which self-respect, or which is the same thing, honorable existence, is impossible.

They must count the cost. Satyagraha cannot be offered in bravado or as a mere trial. It is therefore offered because it becomes irresistible. No price is too dear to pay for it—truth. . . .

Bravery and self-sacrifice need not kill. . . .

. . . Civil Disobedience means capacity for unlimited suffering without the intoxicating excitement of killing.

The hardest heart and the grossest ignorance must disappear before the rising sun of suffering without anger and without malice.

. . . A slave is a slave because he consents to slavery. If training in physical resistance is possible, why should that in spiritual resistance be impossible? . . .

The acquisition of the spirit of non-resistance is a matter of long training in self-denial and appreciation of the hidden forces within ourselves. It changes one's outlook upon life. It puts different values upon things and upsets previous calculations. And when once it is set in motion its effect. . . can overtake the whole universe. It is the greatest force because it is the highest expression of the soul. All need not possess the same measure of conscious non-resistance for its full operation. It is enough for one person only to possess it, even as one general is enough to regulate and dispose of the energy of millions of soldiers who enlist under his banner, even though they know not the why and wherefor of his dispositions. . . .

Those who can suffer for one to three years will find themselves inured to suffering for thirty years.

. . . Man is superior to the brute in as much as he is capable of self-restraint and sacrifice, of which the brute is incapable.

. . . If every young man found himself in plenty and never knew what it was to go without . . . he may be found wanting when the trial comes. Sacrifice is joy.

. . . No sacrifice is worth the name unless it is a joy. Sacrifice and a long face go ill together.

Do you think anything on earth can be done without trouble?

[With] me, the safety of the cause has not lain in numbers. . . . A general with a large army cannot march as swiftly as he would like to. He has to take note of all the different units in his army. My position is not unlike such a general's. . . . If it often means strength, it sometimes means a positive hindrance. . . . I am not without hope that I shall not be found wanting if I am left with but two human comrades or without any. . . .

Strength of numbers is the delight of the timid. The valiant of spirit glory in fighting alone. . . .

. . . I suggest the following prescription of Civil Disobedience, which even one man can offer . . . Let a batch, or only one person . . . march on foot to the Government House . . . and walk on to the point where he or she is stopped. There let him or her stop and demand the release of detenues or his or her own arrest. To preserve intact the civil nature of this disobedience, the Satyagrahi must be wholly unarmed, and in spite of insults, kicks or worse, must meekly stand the ground and be arrested without the slightest opposition. He may carry his own food in his pocket, a bottle full of water, take his Gita, the Koran, the Bible . . . as the case may be, and his [spinning device]. If there are many such real Satya-grahis they will certainly transform the atmosphere in an immensely short time, even as one gentle shower transforms the plains of India into a beautiful green carpet in one single day.

Love is the strongest force the world possesses and yet it is the humblest imaginable.

. . . Who has not seen strong-bodied bullies surrendering helplessly to their mothers? Love conquers the brute in the son. . . .

[We] think it impossible to evoke the hidden powers of the soul. Well, I am engaged in trying to show, if I have any of these powers, that I am as frail a mortal as any of us and I never had anything extraordinary about me nor have any now. I claim to be a simple individual liable to err like any other fellow mortal. I own, however, that I have humility enough in me to confess my errors and to retrace my steps. I own that I have an immovable faith in God and His goodness and unconsumable passion for truth and love. But is that not what every person has latent in him? If we are to make progress, we must not repeat history but make new history. . . . If we may make new discoveries and inventions in the phe-nomenal world, must we declare our bankruptcy in the spiritual domain? Is it impossible to multiply the exceptions so as to make them the rule? Must man always be brute first and man after, if at all?

[When] I was passing through a severe crisis of scepticism and doubt . . . I came across Tolstoy's book *The Kingdom of God Is Within You*, and was deeply impressed by it. I was at that time a believer in violence. Its reading cured me of my scepticism and made me a firm believer in [non-violence]. What has appealed to me most in Tolstoy's life is that he practiced what he preached and reckoned no cost too great in his pursuit of truth. . . .

He was the greatest apostle of non-violence the present age has pro-duced. No one in the West before him or since has written and spoken on non-violence so fully or insistently and with such penetration and insight . . . [His] remarkable development of this doctrine puts to shame the pre-sent-day narrow and lop-sided interpretation put upon it by the votaries of Ahimsa in this land of ours. . . . True Ahimsa should mean a complete freedom from ill will and anger and hate and an overflowing love for all. For inculcating this true and higher type of Ahimsa amongst us, Tolstoy's life with its oceanlike love should serve as a beacon light and a never-failing source of inspiration. . . .

Life is governed by a multitude of forces. It would be smooth sailing if one could determine the course of one's actions only by one general principle . . . But I cannot recall a single act which could be so easily determined.

Let me take an illustration. I am a member of an institution which holds a few acres of land whose crops are in imminent perils from monkeys. I believe in the sacredness of all life and hence I regard it as a breach of non-violence to inflict any injury on the monkeys. But I do not hesitate to instigate and direct an attack on the monkeys in order to save the crops. . . .

Even so did I participate in three acts of War [the Boer War, the Zulu Rebellion, World War I]. I could not—it would be madness for me—to sever my connection with the society to which I belong. And on those occasions I had no thought of non-coöperating with the British Government. My position regarding that Government is totally different today and hence I should not participate voluntarily in its wars and I should risk imprisonment and even the gallows if I was forced to take up arms or otherwise take part in its military operations.

I can conceive occasions when it would be my duty to vote for the military training of those who wish to take it. For I know [everyone] does not believe in non-violence to the extent I do. It is not possible to make a person or a society non-violent by compulsion.

[War] is wrong, is an unmitigated evil. I know, too, that it has got to go. I firmly believe that freedom won through bloodshed or fraud is no freedom. . . .

# Public Statement by Eight Alabama Clergymen

*April 12, 1963*

We the undersigned clergymen are among those who, in January, issued "An Appeal for Law and Order and Common Sense," in dealing with racial problems in Alabama. We expressed understanding that honest convictions in racial matters could properly be pursued in the courts, but urged that decisions of those courts should in the meantime be peacefully obeyed.

Since that time there had been some evidence of increased forebearance and a willingness to face facts. Responsible citizens have undertaken to work on various problems which cause racial friction and unrest. In Birmingham, recent public events have given indication that we all have opportunity for a new constructive and realistic approach to racial problems.

However, we are now confronted by a series of demonstrations by some of our Negro citizens, directed and led in part by outsiders. We recognize the natural impatience of people who feel that their hopes are slow in being realized. But we are convinced that these demonstrations are unwise and untimely.

We agree rather with certain local Negro leadership which has called for honest and open negotiation of racial issues in our area. And we believe this kind of facing of issues can best be accomplished by citizens of our own metropolitan area, white and Negro, meeting with their knowledge and experience of the local situation. All of us need to face that responsibility and find proper channels for its accomplishment.

Just as we formerly pointed out that "hatred and violence have no sanction in our religious and political traditions," we also point out that such actions as incite to hatred and violence, however technically peaceful those actions may be, have not contributed to the resolution of our local problems. We do not believe that these days of new hope are days when extreme measures are justified in Birmingham.

We commend the community as a whole, and the local news media and law enforcement officials in particular, on the calm manner in which these demonstrations have been handled. We urge the public to continue to show restraint should the demonstrations continue, and the law enforcement officials to remain calm and continue to protect our city from violence.

We further strongly urge our own Negro community to withdraw support from these demonstrations, and to unite locally in working peacefully for a better Birmingham. When rights are consistently denied, a cause should be pressed in the courts and in negotiations among local leaders, and not in the streets. We appeal to both our white and Negro citizenry to observe the principles of law and order and common sense.

*Signed by:*

C.C.J. Carpenter, D.D., LL.D., *Bishop of Alabama;* Joseph A. Durick, D.D., *Auxiliary Bishop, Diocese of Mobile-Birmingham;* Rabbi Milton L. Grafman, *Temple Emanu-El, Birmingham, Alabama;* Bishop Paul Hardin, *Bishop of the Alabama-West Florida Conference of the Methodist Church;* Bishop Nolan B. Harmon, *Bishop of the North Alabama Conference of the Methodist Church;* George M. Murray, D.D., LL.D., *Bishop Coadjutor, Episcopal Diocese of Alabama;* Edward V. Ramage, *Moderator, Synod of the Alabama Presbyterian Church in the United States;* Earl Stallings, *Pastor, First Baptist Church, Birmingham, Alabama.*

# *from* Letter from Birmingham Jail

*Martin Luther King, Jr.*

We know through painful experience that freedom is never voluntarily given by the oppressor; it must be demanded by the oppressed. Frankly, I have yet to engage in a direct-action campaign that was "well timed" in the view of those who have not suffered unduly from the disease of segregation. For years now I have heard the word "Wait!" It rings in the ear of every Negro with piercing familiarity. This "Wait" has almost always meant "Never." We must come to see, with one of our distinguished jurists, that "justice too long delayed is justice denied."

We have waited for more than 340 years for our constitutional and God-given rights. The nations of Asia and Africa are moving with jetlike speed toward gaining political independence, but we still creep at horse-and-buggy pace toward gaining a cup of coffee at a lunch counter.

. . . There comes a time when the cup of endurance runs over, and men are no longer willing to be plunged into the abyss of despair. I hope, sirs, you can understand our legitimate and unavoidable impatience.

. . . A just law is a man-made code that squares with the moral law or the law of God. An unjust law is a code that is out of harmony with the moral law. To put it in the terms of St. Thomas Aquinas: An unjust law is a human law that is not rooted in eternal law and natural law. Any law that uplifts human personality is just. Any law that degrades human personality is unjust. All segregation statutes are unjust because segregation distorts the soul and damages the personality. It gives the segregator a false sense of superiority and the segregated a false sense of inferiority. Segregation, to use the terminology of the Jewish philosopher Martin Buber, substitutes an "I-it" relationship for an "I-thou" relationship and ends up relegating persons to the status of things. Hence segregation is not only politically, economically, and sociologically unsound, it is morally wrong and sinful. Paul Tillich has said that sin is separation. Is not segregation an existential expression of man's tragic separation, his awful estrangement, his terrible sinfulness? Thus it is that I can urge men to obey the 1954 decision of the Supreme Court, for it is morally right; and I can urge them to disobey segregation ordinances, for they are morally wrong. . . .

I hope you are able to see the distinction I am trying to point out. In no sense do I advocate evading or defying the law, as would the rabid segregationist. That would lead to anarchy. One who breaks an unjust law must do so openly, lovingly, and with a willingness to accept the penalty. I submit that an individual who breaks a law that conscience tells him is unjust, and who willingly accepts the penalty of imprisonment in order to arouse the conscience of the community over its injustice, is in reality expressing the highest respect for law. . . .

I had hoped that the white moderate would understand that law and order exist for the purpose of establishing justice and that when they fail in this purpose they become the dangerously structured dams that block the flow of social progress. I had hoped that the white moderate would understand that the present tension in the South is a necessary phase of the transition from an obnoxious negative peace, in which the Negro passively accepted his unjust plight, to a substantive and positive peace, in which all men will respect the dignity and worth of human personality. Actually, we who engage in nonviolent direct action are not the creators of tension. We merely bring to the surface the hidden tension that is already alive. We bring it out in the open, where it can be seen and dealt with. Like a boil that can never be cured so long as it is covered up but must be opened with all its ugliness to the natural medicines of air and light, injustice must be exposed, with all the tension its exposure creates, to the light of human conscience and the air of national opinion before it can be cured.

In your statement you assert that our actions, even though peaceful, must be condemned because they precipitate violence. But is this a logical assertion? Isn't this like condemning a robbed man because his possession of money precipitated the evil act of robbery? Isn't this like condemning Socrates because his unswerving commitment to truth and his philosophical inquiries precipitated the act by the misguided populace in which they made him drink hemlock? Isn't this like condemning Jesus because his unique God-consciousness and never-ceasing devotion to God's will precipitated the evil act of crucifixion? We must come to see that, as the federal courts have consistently affirmed, it is wrong to urge an individual to cease his efforts to gain his basic constitutional rights because the quest may precipitate violence. Society must protect the robbed and punish the robber.

I had also hoped that the white moderate would reject the myth concerning time in relation to the struggle for freedom. I have just received a letter from a white brother in Texas. He writes: "All Christians know that the colored people will receive equal rights eventually, but it is possible that you are in too great a religious hurry. It has taken Christianity almost two thousand years to accomplish what it has. The teachings of Christ take time to come to earth." Such an attitude stems from a tragic misconception of time, from the strangely irrational notion that there is something in the very flow of time that will inevitably cure all ills. Actually, time itself is neutral; it can be used either destructively or constructively. More and more I feel that the people of ill will have used time much more effectively than have the people of good will. We will have to repent in this generation not merely for the hateful words and actions of the bad people but for the appalling silence of the good people. Human progress never rolls in on wheels of inevitability; it comes through the tireless efforts of men willing to be co-workers with God, and without this hard work, time itself becomes an ally of the forces of social stagnation.

We must use time creatively, in the knowledge that the time is always ripe to do right. Now is the time to make real the promise of democracy and transform our pending national elegy into a creative psalm of brotherhood. Now is the time to lift our national policy from the quicksand of racial injustice to the solid rock of human dignity.

You speak of our activity in Birmingham as extreme. At first I was rather disappointed that fellow clergymen would see my nonviolent efforts as those of an extremist. I began thinking about the fact that I stand in the middle of two opposing forces in the Negro community. One is a force of complacency, made up in part of Negroes who, as a result of long years of oppression, are so drained of self-respect and a sense of "somebodiness" that they have adjusted to segregation; and in part of a few middle-class Negroes who, because of a degree of academic and economic security and because in some ways they profit by segregation, have become insensitive to the problems of the masses. The other force is one of bitterness and hatred, and it comes perilously close to advocating violence. . . .

Oppressed people cannot remain oppressed forever. The yearning for freedom eventually manifests itself, and that is what has happened to the American Negro. Something within has reminded him of his birthright of freedom, and something without has reminded him that it can be gained.

Consciously or unconsciously, he has been caught up by the Zeitgeist, and with his black brothers of Africa and his brown and yellow brothers of Asia, South America, and the Caribbean, the United States Negro is moving with a sense of great urgency toward the promised land of racial justice. If one recognizes this vital urge that has engulfed the Negro community, one should readily understand why public demonstrations are taking place. The Negro has many pent-up resentments and latent frustrations, and he must release them. So let him march; let him make prayer pilgrimages to the city hall; let him go on freedom rides—and try to understand why he must do so. If his repressed emotions are not released in nonviolent ways, they will seek expression through violence; this is not a threat but a fact of history. So I have not said to my people: "Get rid of your discontent." Rather, I have tried to say that this normal and healthy discontent can be channeled into the creative outlet of non-violent direct action. And now this approach is being termed extremist. . . .

But . . . as I continued to think about the matter I gradually gained a measure of satisfaction from being considered an extremist. Was not Jesus an extremist for love: "Love your enemies, bless them that curse you, do good to them that hate you, and pray for them which despitefully use you, and persecute you." Was not Amos an extremist for justice: "Let justice roll down like waters and righteousness like an ever-flowing stream." Was not Paul an extremist for the Christian gospel: "I bear in my body the marks of the Lord Jesus." Was not Martin Luther an extremist: "Here I stand; I cannot do otherwise, so help me God." And John Bunyan: "I will stay in jail to the end of my days before I make a butchery of my conscience." And Abraham Lincoln: "This nation cannot survive half slave and half free." And Thomas Jefferson: "We hold these truths to be self-evident, that all men are created equal . . ." So the question is not whether we will be extremists, but what kind of extremists we will be. Will we be extremists for hate or for love? Will we be extremists for the preservation of injustice or for the extension of justice? In that dramatic scene on Calvary's hill three men were crucified. We must never forget that all three were crucified for the same crime—the crime of extremism. Two were extremists for immorality, and thus fell below their environment. The other, Jesus Christ, was an extremist for love, truth and goodness, and thereby rose above his environment. Perhaps the South, the nation, and the world are in dire need of creative extremists. . . .

I hope this letter finds you strong in the faith. I also hope that circumstances will soon make it possible for me to meet each of you, not as an integrationist or a civil-rights leader, but as a fellow clergyman and a Christian brother. Let us all hope that the dark clouds of racial prejudice will soon pass away and the deep fog of misunderstanding will be lifted from our fear-drenched communities, and in some not too distant tomorrow the radiant stars of love and brotherhood will shine over our great nation with all their scintillating beauty. . . .

# *from* The Wealth of Nations

## *Adam Smith*

*Adam Smith (1723–1790) was a Scottish political economist who lived through the "take-off" period which led to the Industrial Revolution. His* Wealth of Nations, *published in 1776, provided a systematic statement of the essential ideas of economic liberalism. Writing at the end of a period in which states tried to use economic controls to maximize the wealth of the nation, Smith argued that the most efficient economy would emerge naturally if free competition were permitted.*

Every individual is continually exerting himself to find out the most advantageous employment for whatever capital he can command. It is his own advantage, indeed, and not that of the society, which he has in view. But the study of his own advantage, naturally, or rather necessarily, leads him to prefer that employment which is most advantageous to the society. . . .

. . . As every individual, therefore, endeavours as much as he can both to employ his capital in the support of domestic industry, and so to direct that industry that its produce may be of the greatest value, every individual necessarily labours to render the annual revenue of the society as great as he can. He generally, indeed, neither intends to promote the public interest, nor knows how much he is promoting it. By preferring the support of domestic to that of foreign industry, he intends only his own security; and by directing that industry in such a manner as its produce may be of the greatest value, he intends only his own gain, and he is in this, as in many other cases, led by an invisible hand to promote an end which was no part of his intention. Nor is it always the worse for the society that it was no part of it. By pursuing his own interest he frequently promotes that of the society more effectually than when he really intends to promote it. I have never known much good done by those who affected to trade for the public good. . . .

. . . The statesman who should attempt to direct private people in what manner they ought to employ their capitals, would not only load himself with a most unnecessary attention, but assume an authority which could safely be trusted, not only to no single person, but to no council or senate whatever, and which would nowhere be so dangerous as in the hands of a man who had folly and presumption enough to fancy himself fit to exercise it. . . .

It is thus that every system which endeavours, either by extraordinary encouragements to draw towards a particular species of industry a greater share of the capital of the society than would naturally go to it, or, by extraordinary restraints, force from a particular species of industry some share of the capital which would otherwise be employed in it, is in reality subversive to the great purpose which it means to promote. It retards, instead of accelerating, the progress of the society towards real wealth and greatness; and diminishes, instead of increasing, the real value of the annual produce of its land and labour.

All systems either of preference or of restraint, therefore, being thus completely taken away, the obvious and simple system of natural liberty establishes itself of its own accord. Every man, as long as he does not violate the laws of justice, is left perfectly free to pursue his own interest his own way, and to bring both his industry and capital into competition with those of any other man, or order of men. The sovereign is completely discharged from a duty, in the attempting to perform which he must always be exposed to innumerable delusions, and for the proper performance of which no human wisdom or knowledge could ever be sufficient; the duty of superintending the industry of private people, and of directing it towards the employments most suitable to the interest of the society. According to the system of natural liberty, the sovereign has only three duties to attend to; three duties of great importance, indeed, but plain and intelligible to common understandings: first, the duty of protecting the society from the violence and invasion of other independent societies; secondly, the duty of protecting, as far as possible, every member of the society from the injustice or oppression of every other member of it, or the duty of establishing an exact administration of justice; and, thirdly, the duty of erecting and maintaining certain public works and certain public institutions which it can never be for the interest of any individual, or small number of individuals, to erect and maintain; because the profit could never repay the expense to any individual or small number of individuals, though it may frequently do much more than repay it to a great society.

# *from* The Communist Manifesto

## Karl Marx and Friedrich Engels

*Karl Marx and Friedrich Engels collaborated in the development of theories of communism and revolution. They viewed the emergence of capitalist industrialism as a necessary stage of history in which the economic progress brought by the factory system was accompanied by the exploitation of most of humanity for the wealth of a few owners of the means of production (the bourgeoisie). They believed that the capitalist period would end in a violent revolution resulting in the victory of the proletariat and the end of class struggles. The state would wither away as an ideal communist society emerged in which each human would be able to reach his or her full potential. The* Communist Manifesto *was published in 1848 as the call to arms of the working class.*

A specter is haunting Europe—the specter of communism. All the powers of old Europe have entered into a holy alliance to exorcise this specter: Pope and Czar, Metternich and Guizot, French radicals and German police spies.

Where is the party in opposition that has not been decried as communistic by its opponents in power? Where the opposition that has not hurled back the branding reproach of communism against the more advanced opposition parties, as well as against its reactionary adversaries?

Two things result from this fact:

I. Communism is already acknowledged by all European powers to be itself a power.

II. It is high time that communists should openly, in the face of the whole world, publish their views, their aims, their tendencies, and meet this nursery tale of the specter of communism with a Manifesto of the party itself.

To this end, communists of various nationalities have assembled in London and sketched the following manifesto, to be published in the English, French, German, Italian, Flemish, and Danish languages.

# I. Bourgeois and Proletarians

The history of all hitherto existing society is the history of class struggles.

Free man and slave, patrician and plebeian, lord and serf, guild master and journeyman, in a word, oppressor and oppressed, stood in constant opposition to one another, carried on an uninterrupted, now hidden, now open fight, a fight that each time ended either in a revolutionary re-constitution of society at large or in the common ruin of the contending classes.

In the earlier epochs of history we find almost everywhere a complicated arrangement of society into various orders, a manifold gradation of social rank. In ancient Rome we have patricians, knights, plebeians, slaves; in the Middle Ages, feudal lords, vassals, guild masters, journeymen, apprentices, serfs; in almost all of these classes, again, subordinate gradations.

The modern bourgeois society that has sprouted from the ruins of feudal society has not done away with class antagonisms. It has but established new classes, new conditions of oppression, new forms of struggle in place of the old ones.

Our epoch, the epoch of the bourgeoisie, possesses, however, this distinctive feature: it has simplified the class antagonisms. Society as a whole is more and more splitting up into two great hostile camps, into two great classes directly facing each other: bourgeoisie and proletariat.

From the serfs of the Middle Ages sprang the chartered burghers of the earliest towns. From these burgesses the first elements of the bourgeoisie were developed.

The discovery of America, the rounding of the Cape, opened up fresh ground for the rising bourgeoisie. The East Indian and Chinese markets, the colonization of America, trade with the colonies, the increase in the means of exchange and in commodities generally, gave to commerce, to navigation, to industry an impulse never before known, and thereby, to the revolutionary element in the tottering feudal society, a rapid development.

The feudal system of industry, under which industrial production was monopolized by closed guilds, now no longer sufficed for the growing wants of the new markets. The manufacturing system took its place. The guild masters were pushed on one side by the manufacturing middle class; division of labor between the different corporate guilds vanished in the face of division of labor in each single workshop.

Meantime the markets kept ever growing, the demand ever rising. Even manufacture no longer sufficed. Thereupon steam and machinery revolutionized industrial production. The place of manufacture was taken by the giant, modern industry, the place of the industrial middle class by industrial millionaires, the leaders of whole industrial armies, the modern bourgeois.

Modern industry has established the world market, for which the discovery of America paved the way. This market has given an immense development to commerce, to navigation, to communication by land. This development has, in its turn, reacted on the extension of industry; and in proportion as industry, commerce, navigation, railways extended, in the same proportion the bourgeoisie developed, increased its capital, and pushed into the background every class handed down from the Middle Ages.

We see, therefore, how the modern bourgeoisie is itself the product of a long course of development, of a series of revolutions in the modes of production and of exchange.

Each step in the development of the bourgeoisie was accompanied by a corresponding political advance of that class. An oppressed class under the sway of the feudal nobility, an armed and self-governing association in the medieval commune; here independent urban republic (as in Italy and Germany), there taxable "third estate" of the monarchy (as in France), afterwards, in the period of manufacture proper, serving either the semi-feudal or the absolute monarchy as a counterpoise against the nobility, and, in fact, cornerstone of the great monarchies in general, the bourgeoisie has at last, since the establishment of modern industry and of the world market, conquered for itself, in the modern representative state, exclusive political sway. The executive of the modern state is but a committee for managing the common affairs of the whole bourgeoisie.

The bourgeoisie, historically, has played a most revolutionary part.

The bourgeoisie, wherever it has got the upper hand, has put an end to all feudal, patriarchal, idyllic relations. It has pitilessly torn asunder the motley feudal ties that bound man to his "natural superiors," and has left remaining no other nexus between man and man than naked self-interest, than callous "cash payment." It has drowned the most heavenly ecstasies of religious fervor, of chivalrous enthusiasm, of Philistine senti-mentalism in the icy water of egotistical calculation. It has resolved personal worth into exchange value and, in place of the numberless indefeasible chartered freedoms, has set up that single, unconscionable freedom—free trade. In one word, for exploitation, veiled by religious and political illusions, it has substituted naked, shameless, direct, brutal exploitation.

The bourgeoisie has stripped of its halo every occupation hitherto honored and looked up to with reverent awe. It has converted the physician, the lawyer, the priest, the poet, the man of science into its paid wage laborers.

The bourgeoisie has torn away from the family its sentimental veil, and has reduced the family relation to a mere money relation.

The bourgeoisie has disclosed how it came to pass that the brutal display of vigor in the Middle Ages, which reactionists so much admire, found its fitting complement in the most slothful indolence. It has been the first to show what man's activity can bring about. It has accomplished wonders far surpassing Egyptian pyramids, Roman aqueducts, and Gothic cathedrals; it has conducted expeditions that put in the shade all former exoduses of nations and crusades.

The bourgeoisie cannot exist without constantly revolutionizing the instruments of production, and thereby the relations of production, and with them the whole relations of society. Conservation of the old modes of production in unaltered form was, on the contrary, the first condition of existence for all earlier industrial classes. Constant revolutionizing of production, uninterrupted disturbances of all social conditions, everlasting uncertainty and agitation distinguish the bourgeois epoch from all earlier ones. All fixed, fast-frozen relations, with their train of ancient and venerable prejudices and opinions, are swept away, all newformed ones become antiquated before they can ossify. All that is solid melts into air, all that is holy is profaned, and man is at last compelled to face with sober senses his real conditions of life and his relations with his kind.

The need of a constantly expanding market for its products chases the bourgeoisie over the whole surface of the globe. It must nestle everywhere, settle everywhere, establish connections everywhere.

The bourgeoisie has through its exploitation of the world market given a cosmopolitan character to production and consumption in every country.

To the great chagrin of reactionists, it has drawn from under the feet of industry the national ground on which it stood. All old-established national industries have been destroyed or are daily being destroyed. They are dislodged by new industries, whose introduction becomes a life and death question for all civilized nations, by industries that no longer work up indigenous raw material, but raw material drawn from the remotest zones; industries whose products are consumed not only at home, but in every quarter of the globe. In place of the old wants, satisfied by the productions of the country, we find new wants, requiring for their satisfaction the products of distant lands and climes. In place of the old local and national seclusion and self-sufficiency we have intercourse in every direction, universal interdependence of nations. And as in material, so also in intellectual production. The intellectual creations of individual nations become common property. National one-sidedness and narrow-mindedness become more and more impossible, and from the numerous national and local literatures there arises a world literature.

The bourgeoisie, by the rapid improvement of all instruments of production, by the immensely facilitated means of communication, draws all, even the most barbarian, nations into civilization. The cheap prices of its commodities are the heavy artillery with which it batters down all Chinese walls, with which it forces the barbarians' intensely obstinate hatred of foreigners to capitulate. It compels all nations, on pain of extinction, to adopt the bourgeois mode of production; it compels them to introduce what it calls civilization into their midst, i.e., to become bourgeois themselves. In one word, it creates a world after its own image.

The bourgeoisie has subjected the country to the rule of the towns. It has created enormous cities, has greatly increased the urban population as compared with the rural, and has thus rescued a considerable part of the population from the idiocy of rural life. Just as it has made the country dependent on the towns, so it has made barbarian and semi-barbarian countries dependent on the civilized ones, nations of peasants on nations of bourgeois, the East on the West.

The bourgeoisie keeps more and more doing away with the scattered state of the population, of the means of production, and of property. It has agglomerated population, centralized means of production, and has concentrated property in a few hands. The necessary consequence of this was political centralization. Independent, or but loosely connected provinces, with separate interests, laws, governments and systems of taxation, became lumped together into one nation, with one government, one code of laws, one national class interest, one frontier, and one customs tariff.

The bourgeoisie, during its rule of scarce one hundred years, has created more massive and more colossal productive forces than have all preceding generations together. Subjection of nature's forces to man, machinery, application of chemistry to industry and agriculture, steam navigation, railways, electric telegraphs, clearing of whole continents for cultivation, canalization of rivers, whole populations conjured out of the ground—what earlier century had even a presentiment that such productive forces slumbered in the lap of social labor?

We see then: the means of production and of exchange, on whose foundation the bourgeoisie built itself up, were generated in feudal society. At a certain stage in the development of these means of production and of exchange, the conditions under which feudal society produced and exchanged, the feudal organization of agriculture and manufacturing industry, in one word, the feudal relations of property, became no longer compatible with the already developed productive forces; they became so many fetters. They had to be burst asunder; they were burst asunder.

Into their place stepped free competition, accompanied by a social and political constitution adapted to it, and by the economic and political sway of the bourgeois class.

A similar movement is going on before our own eyes. Modern bourgeois society with its relations of production, of exchange, and of property, a society that has conjured up such gigantic means of production and of exchange, is like the sorcerer who is no longer able to control the powers of the nether world whom he has called up by his spells. For many a decade past, the history of industry and commerce is but the history of the revolt of modern productive forces against modern conditions of production, against the property relations that are the conditions for the existence of the bourgeoisie and of its rule. It is enough to mention the commercial crises that by their periodic return put on its trial, each time more threateningly, the existence of the entire bourgeois society. In these crises a great part not only of the existing products but also of the previously created productive forces are periodically destroyed. In these crises there breaks out an epidemic that in all earlier epochs would have seemed an absurdity—the epidemic of overproduction. Society suddenly finds itself put back into a state of momentary barbarism; it appears as if a famine, a universal war of devastation had cut off the supply of every means of subsistence; industry and commerce seem to be destroyed; and why? Because there is too much civilization, too much means of subsistence, too much industry, too much commerce. The productive forces at the disposal of society no longer tend to further the development of the conditions of bourgeois property; on the contrary, they have become too powerful for these conditions, by which they are fettered, and as soon as they overcome these fetters they bring disorder into the whole of bourgeois society, endanger the existence of bourgeois property. The conditions of bourgeois society are too narrow to comprise the wealth created by them. And how does the bourgeoisie get over these crises? On the one hand, by enforced destruction of a mass of productive forces; on the other, by the conquest of new markets, and by the more thorough exploitation of the old ones. That is to say, by paving the way for more extensive and more destructive crises, and by diminishing the means whereby crises are prevented.

The weapons with which the bourgeoisie felled feudalism to the ground are now turned against the bourgeoisie itself.

But not only has the bourgeoisie forged the weapons that bring death to itself; it has also called into existence the men who are to wield those weapons—the modern working class—the proletarians.

In proportion as the bourgeoisie, i.e., capital, is developed, in the same proportion is the proletariat, the modern working class, developed—a class of laborers, who live only so long as they find work, and who find work only so long as their labor increases capital. These laborers, who must sell themselves piecemeal, are a commodity, like every other article of commerce, and are consequently exposed to all the vicissitudes of competition, to all the fluctuations of the market.

Owing to the extensive use of machinery and to division of labor, the work of the proletarians has lost all individual character and, consequently, all charm for the workman. He becomes an appendage of the machine, and it is only the simplest, most monotonous, and most easily acquired knack that is required of him. Hence the cost of production of a workman is restricted, almost entirely, to the means of subsistence that he requires for his maintenance and for the propagation of his race. But the price of a commodity, and therefore also of labor, is equal to its cost of production. In proportion, therefore, as the repulsiveness of the work increases, the wage decreases. Nay, more, in proportion as the use of machinery and division of labor increases, in the same proportion the burden of toil also increases, whether by prolongation of the working hours, by increase of the work exacted in a given time, or by increased speed of the machinery, etc.

Modern industry has converted the little workshop of the patriarchal master into the great factory of the industrial capitalist. Masses of laborers, crowded into the factory, are organized like soldiers. As privates of the industrial army they are placed under the command of a perfect hierarchy of officers and sergeants. Not only are they slaves of the bourgeois class, and of the bourgeois state; they are daily and hourly enslaved by the machine, by the overlooker, and, above all, by the individual bourgeois manufacturer himself. The more openly this despotism proclaims gain to be its end and aim, the more petty, the more hateful, and the more embittering it is.

The less the skill and exertion of strength implied in manual labor, in other words, the more modern industry becomes developed, the more is the labor of men superseded by that of women. Differences of age and sex have no longer any distinctive social validity for the working class. All are instruments of labor, more or less expensive to use, according to their age and sex.

No sooner is the exploitation of the laborer by the manufacturer over, to the extent that he receives his wages in cash, than he is set upon by the other portions of the bourgeoisie, the landlord, the shopkeeper, the pawnbroker, etc.

The lower strata of the middle class—the small tradespeople, shopkeepers, and retired tradesmen generally, the handicraftsmen and peasants— all these sink gradually into the proletariat, partly because their diminutive capital does not suffice for the scale on which modern industry is carried on, and is swamped in the competition with the large capitalists, partly because their specialized skill is rendered worthless by new methods of production. Thus the proletariat is recruited from all classes of the population.

The proletariat goes through various stages of development. With its birth begins its struggle with the bourgeoisie. At first the contest is carried on by individual laborers, then by the workpeople of a factory, then by the operatives of one trade, in one locality, against the individual bourgeois who directly exploits them. They direct their attacks not against the bourgeois conditions of production, but against the instruments of production themselves; they destroy imported wares that compete with their labor, they smash to pieces machinery, they set factories ablaze, they seek to restore by force the vanished status of the workman of the Middle Ages.

At this stage the laborers still form an incoherent mass scattered over the whole country and broken up by their mutual competition. If anywhere they unite to form more compact bodies, this is not yet the consequence of their own active union, but of the union of the bourgeoisie, which class, in order to attain its own political ends, is compelled to set the whole proletariat in motion, and is moreover yet, for a time, able to do so. At this stage, therefore, the proletarians do not fight their enemies, but the enemies of their enemies, the remnants of absolute monarchy, the landowners, the non-industrial bourgeois, the petty bourgeoisie. Thus the whole historical movement is concentrated in the hands of the bourgeoisie; every victory so obtained is a victory for the bourgeoisie.

But with the development of industry the proletariat not only increases in number; it becomes concentrated in greater masses, its strength grows, and it feels that strength more. The various interests and conditions of life within the ranks of the proletariat are more and more equalized, in proportion as machinery obliterates all distinctions of labor and nearly everywhere reduces wages to the same low level. The growing competition among the bourgeois and the resulting commercial crises make the wages of the workers ever more fluctuating. The unceasing improvement of machinery, ever more rapidly developing, makes their livelihood more and more precarious; the collisions between individual workmen and individual bourgeois take more and more the character of collisions between two classes. Thereupon the workers begin to form combinations (trade unions) against the bourgeois; they club together in order to keep up the rate of wages; they found permanent associations in order to make provision beforehand for these occasional revolts. Here and there the contest breaks out into riots.

Now and then the workers are victorious, but only for a time. The real fruit of their battles lies not in the immediate result, but in the ever expanding union of the workers. This union is helped on by the improved means of communication that are created by modern industry and that place the workers of different localities in contact with one another. It was just this contact that was needed to centralize the numerous local struggles, all of the same character, into one national struggle between classes. But every class struggle is a political struggle. And that union, to attain which the burghers of the Middle Ages, with their miserable highways, required centuries, the modern proletarians, thanks to railways, achieve in a few years.

This organization of the proletarians into a class, and consequently into a political party, is continually being upset again by the competition between the workers themselves. But it ever rises up again, stronger, firmer, mightier. It compels legislative recognition of particular interests of the workers by taking advantage of the divisions among the bourgeoisie itself. Thus the ten-hour bill in England was carried.

Altogether collisions between the classes of the old society further, in many ways, the course of development of the proletariat. The bourgeoisie finds itself involved in a constant battle. At first with the aristocracy; later on, with those portions of the bourgeoisie itself whose interests have become antagonistic to the progress of industry; at all times, with the bourgeoisie of foreign countries. In all these battles it sees itself compelled to appeal to the proletariat, to ask for its help, and thus to drag it into the political arena. The bourgeoisie itself, therefore, supplies the proletariat with its own elements of political and general education: in other words, it furnishes the proletariat with weapons for fighting the bourgeoisie.

Further, as we have already seen, entire sections of the ruling classes are, by the advance of industry, precipitated into the proletariat, or are at least threatened in their conditions of existence. These also supply the proletariat with fresh elements of enlightenment and progress.

Finally, in times when the class struggle nears the decisive hour, the process of dissolution going on within the ruling class, in fact within the whole range of old society, assumes such a violent, glaring character that a small section of the ruling class cuts itself adrift and joins the revolutionary class, the class that holds the future in its hands. Just as, therefore, at an earlier period, a section of the nobility went over to the bourgeoisie, so now a portion of the bourgeoisie goes over to the proletariat, and in particular a portion of the bourgeois ideologists, who have raised themselves to the level of comprehending theoretically the historical movement as a whole.

Of all the classes that stand face to face with the bourgeoisie today, the proletariat alone is a really revolutionary class. The other classes decay and finally disappear in the face of modern industry; the proletariat is its special and essential product.

The lower-middle class, the small manufacturer, the shopkeeper, the artisan, the peasant, all these fight against the bourgeoisie, to save from extinction their existence as fractions of the middle class. They are therefore not revolutionary, but conservative. Nay, more, they are reactionary, for they try to roll back the wheel of history. If by chance they are revolutionary they are so only in view of their impending transfer into the proletariat; they thus defend not their present but their future interests, they desert their own standpoint to place themselves at that of the proletariat.

The "dangerous class," the social scum, that passively rotting mass thrown off by the lowest layers of old society, may, here and there, be swept into the movement by a proletarian revolution; its conditions of life, however, prepare it far more for the part of a bribed tool of reactionary intrigue.

In the conditions of the proletariat those of old society at large are already virtually swamped. The proletarian is without property; his relation to his wife and children has no longer anything in common with the bourgeois family relations; modern industrial labor, modern subjection to capital, the same in England as in France, in America as in Germany, has stripped him of every trace of national character. Law, morality, religion are to him so many bourgeois prejudices, behind which lurk in ambush just as many bourgeois interests.

All the preceding classes that got the upper hand sought to fortify their already acquired status by subjecting society at large to their conditions of appropriation. The proletarians cannot become masters of the productive forces of society, except by abolishing their own previous mode of appropriation, and thereby also every other previous mode of appropriation. They have nothing of their own to secure and to fortify; their mission is to destroy all previous securities for, and insurances of, individual property.

All previous historical movements were movements of minorities, or in the interest of minorities. The proletarian movement is the self-conscious, independent movement of the immense majority, in the interests of the immense majority. The proletariat, the lowest stratum of our present society, cannot stir, cannot raise itself up, without the whole superincumbent strata of official society being sprung into the air.

Though not in substance, yet in form, the struggle of the proletariat with the bourgeoisie is at first a national struggle. The proletariat of each country must, of course, first of all settle matters with its own bourgeoisie.

In depicting the most general phases of the development of the proletariat, we traced the more or less veiled civil war, raging within existing society, up to the point where that war breaks out into open revolution, and where the violent overthrow of the bourgeoisie lays the foundation for the sway of the proletariat.

Hitherto every form of society has been based, as we have already seen, on the antagonism of oppressing and oppressed classes. But in order to oppress a class certain conditions must be assured to it under which it can, at least, continue its slavish existence. The serf, in the period of serfdom, raised himself to membership in the commune, just as the petty bourgeois, under the yoke of feudal absolutism, managed to develop into a bourgeois. The modern laborer, on the contrary, instead of rising with the progress of industry, sinks deeper and deeper below the conditions of existence of his own class. He becomes a pauper, and pauperism develops more rapidly than population and wealth. And here it becomes evident that the bourgeoisie is unfit any longer to be the ruling class in society, and to impose its conditions of existence upon society as an overriding law. It is unfit to rule because it is incompetent to assure an existence to its slave within his slavery, because it cannot help letting him sink into such a state that it has to feed him instead of being fed by him. Society can no longer live under this bourgeoisie: in other words, its existence is no longer compatible with society.

The essential condition for the existence, and for the sway of the bourgeois class, is the formation and augmentation of capital; the condition for capital is wage labor. Wage labor rests exclusively on competition between the laborers. The advance of industry, whose involuntary promoter is the bourgeoisie, replaces the isolation of the laborers, due to competition, by their revolutionary combination, due to association. The development of modern industry, therefore, cuts from under its feet the very foundation on which the bourgeoisie produces and appropriates products. What the bourgeoisie, therefore, produces, above all, is its own gravediggers. Its fall and the victory of the proletariat are equally inevitable.

## II. Proletarians and Communists

In what relation do the communists stand to the proletarians as a whole?

The communists do not form a separate party opposed to other working-class parties.

They have no interests separate and apart from those of the proletariat as a whole.

They do not set up any sectarian principles of their own, by which to shape and mold the proletarian movement.

The communists are distinguished from the other working-class parties by this only: 1. In the national struggles of the proletarians of the different countries they point out and bring to the front the common interests of the entire proletariat, independent of all nationality. 2. In the various stages of development which the struggle of the working class against the bourgeoisie has to pass through, they always and everywhere represent the interests of the movement as a whole.

The communists, therefore, are on the one hand, practically, the most advanced and resolute section of the working-class parties of every country, that section which pushes forward all others; on the other hand, theoretically, they have over the great mass of the proletariat the advantage of clearly understanding the line of march, the conditions, and the ultimate general results of the proletarian movement.

The immediate aim of the communists is the same as that of all the other proletarian parties: formation of the proletariat into a class, overthrow of the bourgeois supremacy, conquest of political power by the proletariat.

The theoretical conclusions of the communists are in no way based on ideas or principles that have been invented, or discovered, by this or that would-be universal reformer.

They merely express, in general terms, actual relations springing from an existing class struggle, from a historical movement going on under our very eyes. The abolition of existing property relations is not at all a distinctive feature of communism.

All property relations in the past have continually been subject to historical change consequent upon the change in historical conditions.

The French Revolution, for example, abolished feudal property in favor of bourgeois property.

The distinguishing feature of communism is not the abolition of property generally, but the abolition of bourgeois property. But modern bourgeois private property is the final and most complete expression of the system of producing and appropriating products that is based on class antagonisms, on the exploitation of the many by the few.

In this sense the theory of the communists may be summed up in the single sentence: Abolition of private property.

We communists have been reproached with the desire of abolishing the right of personally acquiring property as the fruit of a man's own labor, which property is alleged to be the groundwork of all personal freedom, activity, and independence.

Hard-won, self-acquired, self-earned property! Do you mean the property of the petty artisan and of the small peasant, a form of property that preceded the bourgeois form? There is no need to abolish that; the development of industry has to a great extent already destroyed it, and is still destroying it daily.

Or do you mean modern bourgeois private property?

But does wage labor create any property for the laborer? Not a bit. It creates capital, i.e., that kind of property which exploits wage labor, and which cannot increase except upon condition of begetting a new supply of wage labor for fresh exploitation. Property, in its present form, is based on the antagonism of capital and wage labor. Let us examine both sides of this antagonism.

To be a capitalist is to have not only a purely personal but a social *status* in production. Capital is a collective product, and only by the united action of many members, nay, in the last resort only by the united action of all members of society, can it be set in motion.

Capital is, therefore, not a personal, it is a social power.

When, therefore, capital is converted into common property, into the property of all members of society, personal property is not thereby transformed into social property. It is only the social character of the property that is changed. It loses its class character.

Let us now take wage labor.

The average price of wage labor is the minimum wage, i.e., that quantum of the means of subsistence which is absolutely requisite to keep the laborer in bare existence as a laborer. What, therefore, the wage laborer appropriates by means of his labor merely suffices to prolong and re-produce a bare existence. We by no means intend to abolish this personal appropriation of the products of labor, an appropriation that is made for the maintenance and reproduction of human life, and that leaves no sur-plus wherewith to command the labor of others. All that we want to do away with is the miserable character of this appropriation, under which the laborer lives merely to increase capital, and is allowed to live only in so far as the interest of the ruling class requires it.

In bourgeois society living labor is but a means to increase accumulated labor. In communist society accumulated labor is but a means to widen, to enrich, to promote the existence of the laborer.

In bourgeois society, therefore, the past dominates the present; in com-munist society the present dominates the past. In bourgeois society capi-tal is independent and has individuality, while the living person is dependent and has no individuality.

And the abolition of this state of things is called by the bourgeois aboli-tion of individuality and freedom! And rightly so. The abolition of bour-geois individuality, bourgeois independence, and bourgeois freedom is undoubtedly aimed at.

By freedom is meant, under the present bourgeois conditions of produc-tion, free trade, free selling and buying.

But if selling and buying disappear, free selling and buying disappear also. This talk about free selling and buying, and all the other "brave words" of our bourgeoisie about freedom in general, have a meaning, if any, only in contrast with restricted selling and buying, with the fettered traders of the Middle Ages, but have no meaning when opposed to the communistic abolition of buying and selling, of the bourgeois conditions of production, and of the bourgeoisie itself.

You are horrified at our intending to do away with private property. But in your existing society private property is already done away with for nine tenths of the population; its existence for the few is solely due to its nonexistence in the hands of those nine tenths. You reproach us, there-fore, with intending to do away with a form of property the necessary condition for whose existence is the non-existence of any property for the immense majority of society.

In one word, you reproach us with intending to do away with your property. Precisely so; that is just what we intend.

From the moment when labor can no longer be converted into capital, money, or rent, into a social power capable of being monopolized, i.e., from the moment when individual property can no longer be transformed into bourgeois property, into capital, from that moment, you say, individuality vanishes.

You must, therefore, confess that by "individual" you mean no other person than the bourgeois, than the middleclass owner of property. This person must, indeed, be swept out of the way and made impossible.

Communism deprives no man of the power to appropriate the products of society; all that it does is to deprive him of the power to subjugate the labor of others by means of such appropriation.

It has been objected that upon the abolition of private property all work will cease and universal laziness will overtake us.

According to this, bourgeois society ought long ago have gone to the dogs through sheer idleness, for those of its members who work acquire nothing and those who acquire anything do not work. The whole of this objection is but another expression of the tautology that there can no longer be any wage labor when there is no longer any capital.

All objections urged against the communistic mode of producing and appropriating material products have, in the same way, been urged against the communistic modes of producing and appropriating intellectual products. Just as, to the bourgeois, the disappearance of class property is the disappearance of production itself, so the disappearance of class culture is to him identical with the disappearance of all culture.

That culture, the loss of which he laments, is, for the enormous majority, a mere training to act as a machine.

But don't wrangle with us so long as you apply, to our intended abolition of bourgeois property, the standard of your bourgeois notions of freedom, culture, law, etc. Your very ideas are but the outgrowth of the conditions of your bourgeois production and bourgeois property, just as your jurisprudence is but the will of your class made into a law for all, a will whose essential character and direction are determined by the economic conditions of existence of your class.

The selfish misconception that induces you to transform into eternal laws of nature and of reason the social forms springing from your present mode of production and form of property—historical relations that rise and disappear in the progress of production—this misconception you share with every ruling class that has preceded you. What you see clearly in the case of ancient property, what you admit in the case of feudal property you are of course forbidden to admit in the case of your own bourgeois form of property.

Abolition of the family! Even the most radical flare up at this infamous proposal of the communists.

On what foundation is the present family, the bourgeois family, based? On capital, on private gain. In its completely developed form this family exists only among the bourgeoisie. But this state of things finds its complement in the practical absence of the family among the proletarians, and in public prostitution.

The bourgeois family will vanish as a matter of course when its complement vanishes, and both will vanish with the vanishing of capital.

Do you charge us with wanting to stop the exploitation of children by their parents? To this crime we plead guilty.

But, you will say, we destroy the most hallowed of relations when we replace home education by social.

And your education! Is not that also social, and determined by the social conditions under which you educate, by the intervention, direct or indirect, of society, by means of schools, etc.? The communists have not invented the intervention of society in education; they do but seek to alter the character of that intervention, and to rescue education from the influence of the ruling class.

The bourgeois claptrap about the family and education, about the hallowed co-relation of parent and child, becomes all the more disgusting, the more, by the action of modern industry, all family ties among the proletarians are torn asunder and their children transformed into simple articles of commerce and instruments of labor.

"But you communists would introduce community of women," screams the whole bourgeoisie in chorus.

The bourgeois sees in his wife a mere instrument of production. He hears that the instruments of production are to be exploited in common and, naturally, can come to no other conclusion than that the lot of being common to all will likewise fall to the women.

He has not even a suspicion that the real point aimed at is to do away with the status of women as mere instruments of production.

For the rest, nothing is more ridiculous than the virtuous indignation of our bourgeois at the community of women which, they pretend, is to be openly and officially established by the communists. The communists have no need to introduce community of women; it has existed almost from time immemorial.

Our bourgeois, not content with having the wives and daughters of their proletarians at their disposal, not to speak of common prostitutes, take the greatest pleasure in seducing each other's wives.

Bourgeois marriage is in reality a system of wives in common and thus, at the most, what the communists might possibly be reproached with is that they desire to introduce, in substitution for a hypocritically concealed, an openly legalized community of women. For the rest, it is self-evident that the abolition of the present system of production must bring with it the abolition of the community of women springing from that system, i.e., of prostitution, both public and private.

The communists are further reproached with desiring to abolish countries and nationality.

The workingmen have no country. We cannot take from them what they have not got. Since the proletariat must first of all acquire political supremacy, must rise to be the leading class of the nation, must constitute itself *the* nation, it is, so far, itself national, though not in the bourgeois sense of the word.

National differences and antagonisms between peoples are daily more and more vanishing, owing to the development of the bourgeoisie, to freedom of commerce, to the world market, to uniformity in the mode of production and in the conditions of life corresponding thereto.

The supremacy of the proletariat will cause them to vanish still faster. United action, of the leading civilized countries at least, is one of the first conditions for the emancipation of the proletariat.

In proportion as the exploitation of one individual by another is put to an end, the exploitation of one nation by another will also be put to an end. In proportion as the antagonism between classes within the nation vanishes, the hostility of one nation to another will come to an end.

The charges against communism made from a religious, a philosophical, and, generally, from an ideological standpoint are not deserving of serious examination.

Does it require deep intuition to comprehend that man's ideas, views, and conceptions, in one word, man's consciousness, change with every change in the conditions of his material existence, in his social relations, and in his social life?

What else does the history of ideas prove than that intellectual production changes its character in proportion as material production is changed? The ruling ideas of each age have ever been the ideas of its ruling class.

When people speak of ideas that revolutionize society they do but express the fact that within the old society the elements of a new one have been created, and that the dissolution of the old ideas keeps even pace with the dissolution of the old conditions of existence.

When the ancient world was in its last throes, the ancient religions were overcome by Christianity. When Christian ideas succumbed in the eighteenth century to rationalist ideas, feudal society fought its death battle with the then revolutionary bourgeoisie. The ideas of religious liberty and freedom of conscience merely gave expression to the sway of free competition within the domain of knowledge.

"Undoubtedly," it will be said, "religious, moral, philosophical, and juridical ideas have been modified in the course of historical development. But religion, morality, philosophy, political science, and law constantly survived this change.

"There are, besides, eternal truths, such as freedom, justice, etc., that are common to all states of society. But communism abolishes eternal truths, it abolishes all religion, and all morality, instead of constituting them on a new basis; it therefore acts in contradiction to all past historical experience."

What does this accusation reduce itself to? The history of all past society has consisted in the development of class antagonisms, antagonisms that assumed different forms at different epochs.

But whatever form they may have taken, one fact is common to all past ages, viz., the exploitation of one part of society by the other. No wonder then that the social consciousness of past ages, despite all the multiplicity and variety it displays, moves within certain common forms, or general ideas, which cannot completely vanish except with the total disappearance of class antagonisms.

The communist revolution is the most radical rupture with traditional property relations; no wonder that its development involves the most radical rupture with traditional ideas.

But let us have done with the bourgeois objections to communism.

We have seen above that the first step in the revolution by the working class is to raise the proletariat to the position of ruling class, to win the battle of democracy.

The proletariat will use its political supremacy to wrest, by degrees, all capital from the bourgeoisie, to centralize all instruments of production in the hands of the state, i.e., of the proletariat organized as the ruling class, and to increase the total of productive forces as rapidly as possible.

Of course, in the beginning this cannot be effected except by means of despotic inroads on the rights of property and on the conditions of bourgeois production; by means of measures, therefore, which appear economically insufficient and untenable, but which, in the course of the movement, outstrip themselves, necessitate further inroads upon the old social order, and are unavoidable as a means of entirely revolutionizing the mode of production.

These measures will of course be different in different countries.

Nevertheless, in the most advanced countries the following will be pretty generally applicable:

   1. Abolition of property in land and application of all rents of land to public purposes.

2. A heavy progressive or graduated income tax.

3. Abolition of all right of inheritance.

4. Confiscation of the property of all emigrants and rebels.

5. Centralization of credit in the hands of the state, by means of a national bank with state capital and an exclusive monopoly.

6. Centralization of the means of communication and transport in the hands of the state.

7. Extension of factories and instruments of production owned by the state; the bringing into cultivation of wastelands, and the improvement of the soil generally in accordance with a common plan.

8. Equal liability of all to labor. Establishment of industrial armies, especially for agriculture.

9. Combination of agriculture with manufacturing industries; gradual abolition of the distinction between town and country, by a more equable distribution of the population over the country.

10. Free education for all children in public schools. Abolition of children's factory labor in its present form. Combination of education with industrial production, etc.

When, in the course of development, class distinctions have disappeared and all production has been concentrated in the hands of a vast association of the whole nation, the public power will lose its political character. Political power, properly so called, is merely the organized power of one class for oppressing another. If the proletariat during its contest with the bourgeoisie is compelled, by the force of circumstances, to organize itself as a class, if, by means of a revolution, it makes itself the ruling class and, as such, sweeps away by force the old conditions of production, then it will, along with these conditions, have swept away the conditions for the existence of class antagonisms and of classes generally, and will thereby have abolished its own supremacy as a class.

In place of the old bourgeois society, with its classes and class antagonisms, we shall have an association in which the free development of each is the condition for the free development of all.

• • •

## IV. Positions of the Communists in Relation to the Various Existing Opposition Parties

The communists fight for the attainment of the immediate aims, for the enforcement of the momentary interests of the working class, but in the movement of the present they also represent and take care of the future of that movement. In France the communists ally themselves with the social democrats against the conservative and radical bourgeoisie, reserving, however, the right to take up a critical position in regard to phrases and illusions traditionally handed down from the Great Revolution.

In Switzerland they support the radicals, without losing sight of the fact that this party consists of antagonistic elements, partly of democratic socialists, in the French sense, partly of radical bourgeois.

In Poland they support the party that insists on an agrarian revolution as the prime condition for national emancipation, that party which fomented the insurrection of Cracow in 1846.

In Germany they fight with the bourgeoisie whenever it acts in a revolutionary way, against the absolute monarchy, the feudal squirearchy and the petty bourgeoisie.

But they never cease, for a single instant, to instill into the working class the clearest possible recognition of the hostile antagonism between bourgeoisie and proletariat, in order that the German workers may straightway use, as so many weapons against the bourgeoisie, the social and political conditions that the bourgeoisie must necessarily introduce along with its supremacy, and in order that, after the fall of the reactionary classes in Germany, the fight against the bourgeoisie itself may immediatly begin.

The communists turn their attention chiefly to Germany, because that country is on the eve of a bourgeois revolution that is bound to be carried out under more advanced conditions of European civilization, and with a much more developed proletariat, than that of England was in the seventeenth and of France in the eighteenth century, and because the bourgeois revolution in Germany will be but the prelude to an immediately following proletarian revolution.

In short, the communists everywhere support every revolutionary movement against the existing social and political order of things.

In all these movements they bring to the front, as the leading question in each, the property question, no matter what its degree of development at the time.

Finally, they labor everywhere for the union and agreement of the democratic parties of all countries.

The communists disdain to conceal their views and aims. They openly declare that their ends can be attained only by the forcible overthrow of all existing social conditions. Let the ruling classes tremble at a communistic revolution.

The proletarians have nothing to lose but their chains. They have a world to win.

WORKINGMEN OF ALL COUNTRIES, UNITE!

# Women's Rights: Declaration of Sentiments (1848)

*The quest by women for equal rights with men was early reflected in a* Declaration of Sentiments *produced at a convention called by several leaders of the women's movement, among them Elizabeth Cady Stanton and Lucretia Mott. It met in Seneca Falls, New York, July 19–20, 1848.*

When, in the course of human events, it becomes necessary for one portion of the family of man to assume among the people of the earth a position different from that which they have hitherto occupied, but one to which the laws of nature and of nature's God entitle them, a decent respect to the opinions of mankind requires that they should declare the causes that impel them to such a course.

We hold these truths to be self-evident: that all men and women are created equal; that they are endowed by their Creator with certain inalienable rights; that among these are life, liberty, and the pursuit of happiness; that to secure these rights governments are instituted, deriving their just powers from the consent of the governed. Whenever any for of government becomes destructive of these ends, it is the right of those who suffer from it to refuse allegiance to it, and to insist upon the institution of a new government, laying its foundation on such principles, and organizing its powers to such form, as to them shall seem most likely to effect their safety and happiness. . . .

Now, in view of this entire disfranchisement of one-half of the people of this country, we insist that they have immediate admission to all the rights and privileges which belong to them as citizens of the United States. . . .

The following resolutions were discussed by Lucretia Mott, . . .

WHEREAS, The great precept of nature is conceded to be, that "man shall pursue his own true and substantial happiness." Blackstone in his Commentaries remarks, that this law of Nature being coeval with mankind, and dictated by God himself, is of course superior in obligation to any other. It is binding over all the globe, in all countries and at all times, no human laws are of any validity if contrary to this, and such of them as are valid, derive all their force, and all their validity, and all their authority, mediately and immediately, for this original; therefore,

172

*Resolved,* That such laws as conflict, in any way, with the true and substantial happiness of woman, are contrary to the great precept of nature and of no validity, for this is "superior in obligation to any other."

*Resolved,* That all laws which prevent woman from occupying such a station in society as her conscience shall dictate, or which place her in a position inferior to that of man, are contrary to the great precept of nature, and therefore of no force or authority.

*Resolved,* That woman is man's equal—was intended to be so by the Creator, and the highest good of the race demands that she should be recognized as such.

*Resolved,* That the women of this country ought to be enlightened in regard to the laws under which they live, that they may no longer publish their degradation by declaring themselves satisfied with their present position, not their ignorance, by asserting that they have all the rights they want.

*Resolved,* That inasmuch as man, while claiming for himself intellectual superiority, does accord to woman moral superiority, it is pre-eminently his duty to encourage her to speak and teach, as she has an opportunity, in all religious assemblies.

*Resolved,* That the same amount of virtue, delicacy, and refinement of behavior that is required of woman in the social state, should also be required of man, and the same transgressions should be visited with equal severity on both man and woman.

*Resolved,* That the objection of indelicacy and impropriety, which is so often brought against woman when she addresses a public audience, comes with a very ill-grace from those who encourage, by their attendance, her appearance on the stage, in the concert, or in feats of the circus.

*Resolved,* That woman has too long rested satisfied in the circumscribed limits which corrupt customs and a perverted application of the Scriptures have marked out for her, and that it is time she should move in the enlarged sphere which her great Creator has assigned her.

*Resolved,* That it is the duty of the women of this country to secure to themselves their sacred right to the elective franchise.

*Resolved*, That the equality of human rights results necessarily from the fact of the identity of the race in capabilities and responsibilities.

*Resolved*, therefore, That, being invested by the Creator with the same capabilities, and the same consciousness of responsibility for their exercise, it is demonstrably the right and duty of woman, equally with man, to promote every righteous cause by every righteous means; and especially in regard to the great subjects of morals and religion, it is self-evidently her right to participate with her brother in teaching them, both in private and in public, by writing and by speaking, by any instrumentalities proper to be used, and in any assemblies proper to be held; and this being a self-evident truth growing out of the divinely implanted principles of human nature, any custom or authority adverse to it, whether modern or wearing the hoary sanction of antiquity, is to be regarded as self-evident falsehood, and at war with mankind.

At the last session Lucretia Mott offered and spoke to the following resolution:

*Resolved*, That the speedy success of our cause depends upon the zealous and untiring efforts of both men and women, for the overthrow of the monopoly of the pulpit, and for the securing to woman an equal participation with men in the various trades, professions, and commerce.

The only resolution that was not unanimously adopted was the ninth, urging the women of the country to secure to themselves the elective franchise. Those who took part in the debate feared a demand for the right to vote would defeat others they deemed more rational, and make the whole movement ridiculous. . . .

# *from* Joseph Mazzini: His Life, Writings, and Political Principles

## *Joseph Mazzini*

*Joseph Mazzini (1805–1872) was an Italian nationalist who organized Young Italy in 1832 to bring into being an Italian republic. At the time, Italy was only a geographical area containing several political entities. Mazzini was an idealist who believed that human potential could best be realized in a world of sovereign nations.*

Young Italy is a brotherhood of Italians who believe in a law of Progress and Duty, and are convinced that Italy is destined to become one nation—convinced also that she possesses sufficient strength within herself to become one, and that the ill success of her former efforts is to be attributed not to the weakness, but to the misdirection of the revolutionary elements within her—that the secret of force lies in constancy and unity of effort. They join this association in the firm intent of consecrating both thought and action to the great aim of reconstituting Italy as one independent sovereign nation of free men and equals. . . .

Young Italy is Republican. . . . Republican—Because theoretically every nation is destined, by the law of God and humanity, to form a free and equal community of brothers; and the republican is the only form of government that insures this future. . . .

The means by which Young Italy proposes to reach its aim are education and insurrection, to be adopted simultaneously, and made to harmonize with each other. Education must ever be directed to reach by example, word, and pen the necessity of insurrection. Insurrection, whenever it can be realized, must be so conducted as to render it a means of national education. . . .

Insurrection—by means of guerrilla bands—is the true method of warfare for all nations desirous of emancipating themselves from a foreign yoke. This method of warfare supplies the want—inevitable at the commencement of the insurrection—of a regular army; it calls the greatest number of elements into the field, and yet may be sustained by the smallest number. It forms the military education of the people, and consecrates every foot of the native soil by the memory of some warlike deed. . . .

Each member will, upon his initiation into the association of Young Italy, pronounce the following form of oath, in the presence of the initiator:

In the name of God and of Italy;

In the name of all the martyrs of the holy Italian cause who have fallen beneath foreign and domestic tyranny;

By the duties which bind me to the land wherein God has placed me, and to the brothers whom God has given me;

By the love—innate in all men—I bear to the country that gave my mother birth, and will be the home of my children;

By the hatred—innate in all men—I bear to evil, injustice, usurpation and arbitrary rule;

By the blush that rises to my brow when I stand before the citizens of other lands, to know that I have no rights of citizenship, no country, and no national flag;

By the aspiration that thrills my soul towards that liberty for which it was created, and is impotent to exert; towards the good it was created to strive after, and is impotent to achieve in the silence and isolation of slavery;

By the memory of our former greatness, and the sense of our present degradation;

By the tears of Italian mothers for their sons dead on the scaffold, in prison, or in exile;

By the sufferings of the millions—

I, . . . believing in the mission intrusted by God to Italy, and the duty of every Italian to strive to attempt its fulfillment; convinced that where God has ordained that a nation shall be, He has given the requisite power to create it; that the people are the depositaries of that power, and that in its right direction for the people, and by the people, lies the secret of victory; convinced that virtue consists in action and sacrifice, and strength in union and constancy of purpose: I give my name to Young Italy, an association of men holding the same faith, and swear:

To dedicate myself wholly and forever to the endeavor with them to constitute Italy one free, independent, republican nation; to promote by every means in my power—whether by written or spoken word, or by action—the education of my Italian brothers towards the aim of Young Italy; towards association, the sole means of its accomplishment, and to virtue, which alone can render the conquest lasting; to abstain from enrolling myself in any other association from this time forth; to obey all the instructions, in conformity with the spirit of Young Italy, given me by those who represent with me the union of my Italian brothers; and to keep the secret of these instructions, even at the cost of my life; to assist my brothers of the association both by action and counsel—

NOW AND FOREVER.

This do I swear, invoking upon my head the wrath of God, the abhorrence of man, and the infamy of the perjurer, if I ever betray the whole or a part of this my oath.

# *from* The Jewish State

## Theodor Herzl

*From the time of the Roman Empire, Jewish people had been widely dispersed throughout the Mediterranean area. As cities developed in northern Europe, Jews were among the early inhabitants. However, as non-Christians they were subject to various restrictions and to occasional pogroms, or campaigns of annihilation. In the late nineteenth century there were Jewish ghettos throughout Europe, where Jews were subject to continuing and even increasing hostility and disabilities even as they took a leading role in the growing industrial societies. Jewish culture was held together through thousands of years of dispersal by a strong tradition of education, the continuity of a common religious language (Hebrew), endogamy (marriage within the group), and a sense of separateness from surrounding communities. Palestine, the area of the original Jewish homeland, was part of the disintegrating Ottoman Empire and was peopled by Jews, Muslims, and Christians. As persecution of Jews increased in Europe and nationalism became a driving political force, a movement to return to the original Jewish homeland and reconstitute a Jewish state gathered momentum, led by thinkers such as Theodor Herzl (1860–1904). The first Zionist general congress met in Switzerland in 1897, with small-scale emigration to Palestine beginning soon after.*

We are a people—one people.

We have honestly endeavored everywhere to merge ourselves in the social life of surrounding communities and to preserve the faith of our fathers. We are not permitted to do so. In vain are we loyal patriots, our loyalty in some places running to extremes; in vain do we make the same sacrifices of life and property as our fellow-citizens; in vain do we strive to increase the fame of our native land in science and art, or her wealth by trade and commerce. In countries where we have lived for centuries we are still cried down as strangers, and often by those whose ancestors were not yet domiciled in the land where Jews had already had experience of suffering. . . .

But I think we shall not be left in peace.

Oppression and persecution cannot exterminate us. No nation on earth has survived such struggles and sufferings as we have gone through. Jew-baiting has merely stripped off our weaklings; the strong among us were invariably true to their race when persecution broke out against them. . . .

. . . [O]ld prejudices against us still lie deep in the hearts of the people. He who would have proofs of this need only listen to the people where they speak with frankness and simplicity: proverb and fairy-tale are both Anti-Semitic. . . .

No one can deny the gravity of the situation of the Jews. Wherever they live in perceptible numbers, they are more or less persecuted. Their equality before the law, granted by statute, has become practically a dead letter. They are debarred from filling even moderately high positions, either in the army, or in any public or private capacity. And attempts are made to thrust them out of business also: "Don't buy from Jews!"

Attacks in Parliaments, in assemblies, in the press, in the pulpit, in the street, on journeys—for example, their exclusion from certain hotels— even in places of recreation, become daily more numerous. The forms of persecutions varying according to the countries and social circles in which they occur. In Russia, imposts are levied on Jewish villages; in Ru- mania, a few persons are put to death; in Germany, they get a good beat- ing occasionally; in Austria, Anti-Semites exercise terrorism over all public life; in Algeria, there are travelling agitators; in Paris, the Jews are shut out of the so-called best social circles and excluded from clubs. Shades of anti-Jewish feeling are innumerable. But this is not to be an attempt to make out a doleful category of Jewish hardships.

I do not intend to arouse sympathetic emotions on our behalf. That would be foolish, futile, and undignified proceeding. I shall content myself with putting the following questions to the Jews: Is it not true that, in countries where we live in perceptible numbers, the position of Jewish lawyers, doctors, technicians, teachers, and employees of all descriptions becomes daily more intolerable? Is it not true, that the Jewish middle classes are seriously threatened? Is it not true, that the passions of the mob are incited against our wealthy people? Is it not true, that our poor endure greater sufferings than any other proletariat? I think that this external pressure makes itself felt everywhere. In our economically upper classes it causes discomfort, in our middle classes continual and grave anxieties, in our lower classes absolute despair.

Everything tends, in fact, to one and the same conclusion, which is clearly enunciated in that classic Berlin phrase: *"Juden Raus!"* (Out with the Jews!)

I shall now put the Question in the briefest possible form: Are we to "get out" now and where to?

Or, may we yet remain? And, how long?

Let us first settle the point of staying where we are. Can we hope for better days, can we possess our souls in patience, can we wait in pious resignation till the princes and peoples of this earth are more mercifully disposed towards us? I say that we cannot hope for a change in the current of feeling. . . . The nations in whose midst Jews live are all either covertly or openly Anti-Semitic. . . .

. . . We might perhaps be able to merge ourselves entirely into surrounding races, if these were to leave us in peace for a period of two generations. But they will not leave us in peace. For a little period they manage to tolerate us, and then their hostility breaks out again and again. . . .

Thus, whether we like it or not, we are now, and shall henceforth remain, a historic group with unmistakable characteristics common to us all.

We are one people—our enemies have made us one without our consent, as repeatedly happens in history. Distress binds us together, and, thus united, we suddenly discover our strength. Yes, we are strong enough to form a State, and, indeed, a model State. We possess all human and material resources necessary for the purpose. . . .

Let the sovereignty be granted us over a portion of the globe large enough to satisfy the rightful requirements of a nation; the rest we shall manage for ourselves. . . .

The creation of a new State is neither ridiculous nor impossible. We have in our day witnessed the process in connection with nations which were not largely members of the middle class, but poorer, less educated, and consequently weaker than ourselves. . . .

Palestine is our ever-memorable historic home. The very name of Palestine would attract our people with a force of marvelous potency. If His Majesty the Sultan were to give us Palestine, we could in return undertake to regulate the whole finances of Turkey. We should there form a portion of a rampart of Europe against Asia, an outpost of civilization as opposed to barbarism. We should as a neutral State remain in contact with all Europe, which would have to guarantee our existence. The sanctuaries of Christendom would be safeguarded by assigning to them an extra-territorial status such as is well-known to the law of nations. We should form a guard of honor about these sanctuaries, answering for the fulfillment of this duty with our existence. This guard of honor would be the great symbol of the solution of the Jewish Question after eighteen centuries of Jewish suffering.

# By-Laws of the Organization: Union or Death

*This document enunciates the principles espoused by Serbian nationalists, one of many ethnic groups in southeastern Europe trying to assert a right to nationhood during the disintegration of the Austro-Hungarian and Ottoman empires. The nature of the document reveals much about the political climate in which Serbian nationalism operated early in the twentieth century and perhaps sheds light on political conditions which surround the breakup of Yugoslavia into warring ethnic factions pursuing policies of "ethnic cleansing."*

*Article 1.* This organization is created for the purpose of realizing the national ideal: the union of all Serbs. Membership is open to every Serb, without distinction of sex, religion, or place of birth, and to all those who are sincerely devoted to this cause.

*Article 2.* This organization prefers terrorist action to intellectual propaganda and for this reason it must remain absolutely secret.

*Article 3.* The organization bears the name *Ujedinjenje ili Smirt* (Union or Death).

*Article 4.* To fulfill its purpose, the organization will do the following:

1. Exercise influence on government circles, on the various social classes, and on the entire social life of the kingdom of Serbia, which is considered the Piedmont of the Serbian nation;

2. Organize revolutionary action in all territories inhabited by Serbs;

3. Beyond the frontiers of Serbia, fight with all means the enemies of the Serbian national idea;

4. Maintain amicable relations with all states, peoples, organizations, and individuals who support Serbia and the Serbian element;

5. Assist those nations and organizations that are fighting for their own national liberation and unification. . . .

*Article 24.* Every member has a duty to recruit new members, but the member shall guarantee with his life those whom he introduces into the organization.

*Article 25.* Members of the organization are forbidden to know each other personally. Only members of the central committee are known to each other.

*Article 26.* In the organization itself, the members are designated by numbers. Only the central committee in Belgrade knows their names.

*Article 27.* Members of the organization must obey absolutely the commands given to them by their superiors.

*Article 28.* Each member has a duty to communicate to the central committee at Belgrade all information that may be of interest to the organization.

*Article 29.* The interests of the organization stand above all other interests.

*Article 30.* On entering the organization, each member must know that he loses his own personality, that he can expect neither personal glory nor personal profit, material or moral. Consequently, any member who endeavors to exploit the organization for personal, social, or party motives, will be punished. If by his acts he harms the organization itself, his punishment will be death.

*Article 31.* Those who enter the organization may never leave it, and no one has the authority to accept a member's resignation.

*Article 32.* Each member must aid the organization, with weekly contributions. If need be, the organization may procure funds through coercion. . . .

*Article 33.* When the central committee of Belgrade pronounces a death sentence the only thing that matters is that the execution is carried out unfailingly. The method of execution is of little importance.

*Article 34.* The organization's seal is composed as follows. On the center of the seal a powerful arm holds in its hand an unfurled flag. On the flag, as a coat of arms, are a skull and crossed bones; by the side of the flag are a knife, a bomb and poison. Around, in a circle, are inscribed the following words reading from left to right: "Unification or Death," and at the base "The Supreme Central Directorate."

*Article 35.* On joining the organization, the recruit takes the following oath:

"I (name), in becoming a member of the organization, 'Unification or Death,' do swear by the sun that shines on me, by the earth that nourishes me, by God, by the blood of my ancestors, on my honor and my life that from this moment until my death, I shall be faithful to the regulations of the organization and that I will be prepared to make any sacrifice for it. I swear before God, on my honor and on my life, that I shall carry with me to the grave the organization's secrets. May God condemn me and my comrades judge me if I violate or do not respect, consciously or not, my oath."

*Article 36.* These regulations come into force immediately.

*Article 37.* These regulations must not be changed.

*Belgrade, 9 May 1911.*

# *from* Search and Find the East

## *Imam Khomeini*

*Modern Iran, cultural successor to the ancient empires of Persia, was ruled from 1941 to 1979 by the Pahlavi dynasty, which had been given the throne by British and Russian agreement. The Pahlavis pursued a policy of close collaboration with the United States, as the threat of the Soviet Union on their northern border shaped their foreign policy. In terms of domestic policy, the Pahlavis opened Iran to Western influences, creating a growing gap between city and countryside and incurring the opposition of Iran's conservative Shiite Muslim clergy, whose leader, the Ayatollah Khomeini, was exiled in 1963. The fundamentalist and puritanical ideas of the Imams, or religious leaders, contrasted sharply with the cosmopolitan worldliness and rampant corruption of the Pahlavi regime. The Shah retained power by strict and brutal repression of political dissent until he was driven out of the country in 1979. The Pahlavi regime was replaced by a government dominated by Islamic clergy and socially conservative forces dedicated to returning Iran to the bosom of Islam. Khomeini's views exemplify the ideology of the Islamic clergymen who spearheaded the drive to oust the Shah.*

September 8, 1979. Imam Khomeini's message in the Faiziyeh School in Qom, to mark the massacre of the 17th of Shahrivar (September 8) of the previous year.

> *In the Name of God*
> *the Merciful, the Compassionate*
>
> *And indeed sent We Moses with Our signs saying:*
> *'Lead thou out thy people from the darkness into the light*
> *and remind them of the days of God;*
> *verily in this are signs for the patient, the grateful' (14:5)*
>
> *God is the Guardian of those who believe*
> *He taketh them out of darkness into light*
> *and those who disbelieve, tyrants are their guardians and*
> *they take them out from the light into darkness*
> *They are the companions of the fire,*
> *therein shall they abide. (2:257)*

These are two subjects which oppose each other, "the taking out of darkness into light" and "the taking out of light into darkness," the doing away with darkness and the taking of people to the light and opposing this, doing away with light and taking people to darkness. This latter is the profession of the tyrants. All disharmony is darkness, all backwardness is darkness, all 'westoxication' is darkness, those who turn their attention to the West and foreigners, have taken the West to be their direction of prayer and their attention is directed to the West. They have moved into darkness and their saints are idols.

Eastern societies which, by means of internal and external propaganda, by means of the orders of the internal and external agents, have turned to the West and have the direction of their prayers, the West, have lost themselves. They do not know themselves. They have lost their gloriousness and honor and in place of that sits a western mind. Their saints are idols. They have entered darkness from the light.

All of the problems of Easterners and, among them, our problems and miseries, are the very cause of our losing ourselves and someone is sitting in place of us. Thus, you see that, in Iran, until something does not have a Western name, it is not accepted. Even a drug store must have a Western name. The material woven in our factories must have something in the latin script in its selvedges and a Western name is put on it.

Our streets must have Western names. Everything must have a Western color to it. Some of these writers and intellectuals either put a Western name on the books they write or, when they express an idea, they do so on behalf of a Westerner. The defect is that they are also 'westoxicated' and so are we. If our books did not have these titles, or our material did not contain that script and if our drug stores did not have that name, we would pay less attention to it. When we turn to a book, a great deal of attention is paid to finding foreign words. They forget their own phrases and the word itself.

Easterners have completely forgotten their honor. They have buried it. In place of it they have put others. These are all darknesses to which a tyrant transforms us from light. It is these very tyrants—of the past and present—who have reached out towards 'westoxication'. They relate everything to the West. They take all their subjects and sources from the West and have given them to us. Our universities were at that time Western universities. Our economy, our culture were Western. We completely forgot ourselves and in place of us we put a Westerner.

I recall that a member of the family of the deposed, accursed Mohammad Reza got tonsillitis and they brought a surgeon from Europe while, for the doctors here it is a simple operation, and this was only so that the world would know that someone who is forcibly at the head of a country and that they recognize to be the king of that country, believes that there is no doctor in Iran to operate on the tonsils. You know what damage this does to Iranian medicine. This is traitorous to the people of Iran that they are introduced to the belief that in all of its country, there is no doctor to operate on someone's tonsils. How much this helps colonialism and the West! How much self-respect of our country is lost with this way of thinking!

When I was young, I remember my eyes weakened—they are still weak—and at that time, Amin ol-Molk, God's Mercy be upon him, was an eye doctor. I went to Tehran to have him treat my eyes. A person who knew he and I, suggested I go to see Dr. Amin ol-Molk. He said, 'One of the Daulahs [of the court] had become near-sighted. He had gone to Europe to see a doctor. That doctor asked him, 'Where are you from?' In answer, he said, 'I am from Iran.' The doctor had asked, 'Isn't Amin ol-Molk there?' He had answered, 'He may be, but I do not know him.' That professor had then said, 'Amin ol-Molk is better than we are.'

We have good doctors, but our minds have become Western brains. The same is true of the doctors. When you go to see them, they themselves say, 'You have to go to Europe,' because their minds think this way. They have lost themselves. They have lost their strength. We and they have both lost our self-respect and our sense of nationality. Until this nation does not come out of this 'westoxication', it will never find independence. As long as our writers—whose books are as they are, who, for every subject which we have, want to express according to such and such a foreigner and Westerner—do not leave aside these dependencies, you will not find independence.

The attention of some of our women is turned to the idea that such and such a mode must come from the West and such and such an ornamentation must move from there to here, so that whenever something is found there, it is imitated here. As long as you do not put aside these imitations, you cannot be a human being and independent. If you want to be independent and have them recognize you as a nation, you must desist from imitating the West.

As long as you are in this state of imitating, do not wish for independence. As long as all of the words of our writers are Western, do not hope to have your nation be independent. As long as these names appear on your streets and your drug stores and your books, and your parks and in all your things, you will not become independent. It is only the mosques which do not have Western names and that is because the clergymen, until now, because of their type, are this way. Otherwise, everything must have a Western name—both those who write use Western names and those who want to read, unless there is a Western name, do not accept it.

'And those who disbelieve,' disbelieve in God's blessings and realities are dark and covered in them. Their saints are idols. 'They take them from light into darkness,—from absolute light, from guidance, from independence, from nationalism, from Islam—they take these out and put them into darkness. We have now lost ourselves. Until the lost be not found, you will not become independent. Search and find it. Search for and find the East.

As long as we are as we are, as long as our writers are as they are, as long as our intellectuals think that way, as long as our freedom-seekers seek that kind of Western freedom, it will remain as it is. They cry out that there is suffocation, there is no freedom. What has happened that there is no freedom?

They say, 'These clergymen do not allow men and women to turn somersaults together in the water. These clergymen do not let our young people go to bars or gambling houses and seek out prostitutes. They do not allow our radio and television to show naked women and that type of ugly lewdness. They do not allow our children and young people to be entertained.' This is an imported kind of freedom which has come from the West. It is a colonialistic freedom, that is, colonialist countries dictate to those who are traitors to their own countries so that they can promote these freedoms. They are free to take heroin. They are free to smoke hashish. They are free to go to gambling houses. They are free to go to houses of entertainment and, as a result, our young people, who must be active in relation to the fate and destiny of their country, become indifferent.

An indifferent person cannot think for a country. Those who are and have been deceived from abroad are foreign agents and they promote prostitution. The promotion of these actions pulls our young people towards corruption. The result of their work is this that a country which gets its strength from its young people and the young people must manage it, they take this strength away from our young people. As a result, thoughts about what goes on in this country and what the ruling bodies are doing to the country or the fact that they brought Mohammad Reza to this country is put out of their heads. In place of serious minds, silly minds appear. As a result, the person who should be a human being, who thinks about his own destiny, this thought is taken away from him. This is a type of freedom which we have to call colonialist freedom. This is other than freedom which must be amidst a people. This is a type of freedom which has come from abroad. They brought us and our young people up like this.

A young person who forms a habit with these kinds of things and no longer thinks about who takes our oil, our steel, our gas. He says, 'What's it to me! Leave me alone to my pleasures. Do I have time to waste, putting efforts into those things?' This is how they brought us up.

Until these unjust writers do not save our young people from these kinds of thoughts and do not promote a healthy kind of freedom and do not prevent their steps and their pens from writing about these corrupt freedoms, there is no hope that we will have an independent and free country. This hope must be taken to the grave.

Moses ( ع ) was appointed to take his tribe from darkness to light. The assignment of all of the prophets was this, that they take people away from darkness and from these things which oppose the way of humanity and oppose the way of a nation and enter them into the light.

An enlightened heart cannot stand by silently and watch while their traditions and honor are trampled upon. An enlightened heart cannot see its people being drawn towards this baseness of spirit or watch in silence while individuals around Tehran live in slums. They want to bring you up in such a way that you remain indifferent in all of your affairs. They do not ask why these poverty-stricken people have remained in poverty and why others take our oil. It never appears in your mind that we have such problems. Look at how your hearts were fifteen, twenty years ago when there was no perseverance. There were only a few people opposing this who occasionally protested and there was neither protest in our mosques nor in our universities—no place.

The second command which God gave to Moses ( ع ) was to 'remind people of the Days of God'. All days belong to God but some days have a particularity and because of that particularity, it is called the Day of God. The day that the great Prophet of Islam migrated to Medina is one of the days that is called the Day of God. The day that he conquered Mecca is one of the days called the Day of God. It is the day that God showed His strength as when an orphan who everyone rejected and who could not live in his home, after a short time, conquered Mecca. He brought the tyrants, the wealthy and the powerful under his influence and he said to them, 'You are free.' Thus such a day is one of the Days of God. The day of Khawareh is a day when Hazrat Ali ( ع )unsheathed his sword and did away with these corrupt and cancerous tumors. This was also one of the Days of God.

These so-called sacred people whose foreheads showed the mark of prayer but do not know God, these were the people that Amir al-mu'minin killed. He arose against them and there were even men in his army who arose against them. But because of the course of the Battle of Siffin, the Imam saw that if they remained, they would corrupt people, he killed all of them except those who had escaped. Thus, this day is among the Days of God. The days which God, the Most High and Exalted, brings something to punish the people, he sends an earthquake, a flood, a thunderstorm, in other words, he whips people so that they will become human beings.

These are all Days of God and they are things which relate to God. One of the days of God is the 15th of Khordad (June 5, 1963) when a people stood against a force and they did something which caused almost five months of martial law. But because the people had no power, they were not consolidated, they were not awake, they were defeated. Of course, they were defeated on the surface, but actually, that was a point of victory for the people. The 17th of Shahrivar (September 8, 1978) was another one of the Days of God when a people, men, women, young people and older people, all stood up and, in order to get their rights, were martyred.

You must recall these Days of God as you have and you must not forget them. It is these days which build human beings. It is on these days that our young people leave their places of entertainment and enter the battlefield. These are the Divine Days. These Days awoke our people. God commands that you enter the Days of God into the minds of people.

Do not forget this great Day which passed for our people and were Days of God like the 15th of Khordad, the 17th of Shahrivar and the Day that that wicked man [the shah] left, was one of the Days of God. A nation which had nothing, broke a force in such a way that nothing remained of it, not only was that power opposing you, but all of the powers of the world, as well. I was aware that the whole world had supported him. The army and Bakhtiar supported him and tried to keep him here.

America was holding him up with both hands. When he fled, they held up Bakhtiar with both hands. They sent people to us saying, 'This is from us. This belongs to us.' They were servants. Do not be surprised that they kept someone for 10, 15, 20 years in the false form of a nationalist for the day when it will serve their purposes. It is possible that a person pray in a mosque for 20 years and worship God and then one day work for them. It is possible that a person claim honesty and claim to be a nationalist and swear at foreigners, write articles against them so that they influence the hearts of the people for the day when they want to come to power.

That day was the day when he [the shah] left and this man [Bakhtiar] replaced him to protect the interests of foreigners. Do not discount this. It happened. You saw how they told us, 'It is too soon. Do not go to Iran now.' They wanted to consolidate their powers and end the troubles so that there would no longer be a possibility of going. That was also one of the Days of God.

One of the great Days of God, the Most High and Exalted, was the night when they had planned a coup d'etat when we were in Tehran. They announced a 24 hour martial law so that even in the daytime people should not come out. Later they informed us that they had intended that night to kill the leaders of Qom and whoever opposed them, finish them off and end the job. God did not want it to be so. That was an enlightened insurrection of a responsible nation which took place and the power of that side joined this side and we were victorious. This was the Divine Will and one of the Days of God.

Do not forget this that all of the conspiracies were fixed so that on one night they would fall into place and have a coup d'etat and all the people who could do something would be destroyed and the nation returned to the way it was. God did not want it to be so. This was one of the Days of God which you, the enlightened and noble people of Iran, with your hearts filled with faith, should not fear. Even though they had announced martial law that day, you went into the streets and did away with that which they had wanted. They had wanted the streets to be empty so that they could bring in tanks and place them everywhere and at night be busy with their crime. God, the Most High and Exalted, answered the cries of this nation. That day is one of the great Days of God.

All powers supported them, not just the super-powers but other powers as well. Those who work for the rate of that day and according to the idea that whoever pays more is better, eat according to the rates of that day. Everyone supported them that day. In spite of this, God the Most High and Exalted, blessed you and made you victorious over these great powers and curtailed the hands of foreigners. With the Will of God, their hands will remain curtailed. This is a great Day of God.

Do not forget that we had a 15th of Khordad and this is the beginning of the Islamic movement of Iran. Do not forget that we had a 17th of Shahrivar and we must not forget that on that day, we gave so many martyrs and so much blood and the nation arose against foreigners and their agents. Blood was spilt, but it was victorious and also all the other innumerable days.

Recall days that they attacked us with complete cruelty and you, with complete courage, your men and women, stood against them. Someone told me, 'I saw, with my own eyes, that a child of 10 or 12 was riding a motorcycle and went towards the tanks. The tank ran over and killed him.' A spirit was born which prompted a child to do such an act. Empty handed, a monarchial empire of 2500 years, 2500 years of criminals was done away with. If a person studies history perhaps there is not one person among them who was more or less distant from their crimes. Those who were like them called themselves 'people of paradise'. They were also criminals.

One of the shahs blinded his own courageous son so that the day would not come when he would gain power but the principal crime and the person who was a genius at crime was this Mohammad Reza. His father was not a criminal to the same extent because this Mohammad Reza both inherited criminal tendencies and he himself was a criminal. He was a genius in crime and kept everything we had backwards in the name of 'The Great Civilization'. He wanted to obliterate our Islam in the name of Islam. He wanted to take away our honor. He wanted to destroy our great history. He was more original in his crimes—that very person who is wandering over the world at the moment.

Do not forget your honor. Our intellectuals and writers and all of our groups of scholars should turn their attention to their own honor and glory. They should not prostrate themselves so much towards the West and writers of books. You yourselves have things to say. What difference does it make to you what so and so from the West said? Why do you quote from a foreigner so that the spirit of our young people becomes melancoly and show them to be out of their framework. You people must protest and not buy anything from a drug store with a foreign name until they change its name. These beloved university students of ours should pay attention to the fact that when a writer quotes from a foreigner, do not buy that book and do not read it. If you do this and buyers pull back, they will stop doing it. They want customers. When a commodity has no customers, it is discontinued.

Push away and turn your backs on things which pull you to the West and trample upon your honor and in place of it, they put Western things. With the Will of God, if there is time, I will speak more about this. I cannot now express the whole situation. I pray for you. May God continue His Mercy upon this nation in the way that He Blessed this nation and showed it Mercy and saved us from foreigners and their agents so that foreigners will no longer penetrate. May God give you all happiness, health, greatness, strength and seriousness.

# *from* Social Statics

## *Herbert Spencer*

*Herbert Spencer (1820–1903) was one of the leading proponents of the theory of evolution. Spencer argued that the essential principles of natural selection applied to human society (that is, to culture) as well as to the genetic development of humans and other creatures. Spencer's ideas became the foundation for Social Darwinism, one of the most influential social theories from the late nineteenth century to the present.*

The expediency-philosophy of which this general state-superintendence is a practical expression, embodies the belief that government ought not only to guarantee men in the unmolested pursuit of happiness, but should provide the happiness for them and deliver it at their doors. Now no scheme could be more self-defeating, for no scheme could be more completely at variance with the constitution of things. Man, as briefly delineated at the outset, consists of a congeries of faculties, qualifying him for surrounding conditions. Each of these faculties, if normally developed, yields to him, when exercised, a gratification constituting part of his happiness; whilst, in the act of exercising it, some deed is done subserving the wants of the man as a whole, and affording to the other faculties the opportunity of performing in turn their respective functions, and of producing every one its peculiar pleasure: so that, when healthily balanced, each subserves all, and all subserve each. We cannot live at all unless this mechanism works with tolerable efficiency; and we can live entirely—that is, can have entire happiness—only when the reciprocity between capacities and requirements is perfect. As before said, the complete man is the self-sufficing man—the man who is in every point fitted to his circumstances—the man in whom there are desires corresponding, not only to all the acts which are immediately advantageous, but to those which are remotely so. Evidently, one who is thus rightly constituted cannot be helped. To do any thing for him by some artificial agency, is to supersede certain of his powers—is to leave them unexercised, and therefore to diminish his happiness. To healthily-developed citizens, therefore, state aid is doubly detrimental. It injures them both by that it takes and by that it does. By the revenues required to support its agencies it absorbs the means on which certain of the faculties depend for their exercise; and by the agencies themselves it shuts out other faculties from their spheres of action.

"But men are *not* complete; they are *not* healthily developed; they have *not* capacities in harmony with their wants; and therefore, as matters stand, a government does *not* by its interpositions preoccupy offices which there are faculties to fill." Very true; but next to being what we ought to be, the most desirable thing is that we should become what we ought to be as fast as possible. We are undergoing the process of adaptation. We have to lose the characteristics which fitted us for our original state, and to gain those which will fit us for our present state; and the question to be asked, respecting these mechanical remedies for our deficiencies, is—do they facilitate the change? Certainly not. A moment's thought will convince us that they retard it. No one can need reminding that demand and supply is the law of life as well as the law of trade—that strength will show itself only where strength is called for—that an undeveloped capability can be developed only under the stern discipline of necessity. Would you draw out and increase some too feeble sentiment? Then you must set it to do, as well as it can, the work required of it. It must be kept ever active, ever strained, ever inconvenienced by its incompetency. Under this treatment it will, in the slow lapse of generations, attain to efficiency; and what was once its impossible task will become the source of a healthy, pleasurable, and desired excitement. But let a state-instrumentality be thrust between such faculty and its work, and the process of adaptation is at once suspended. Growth ceases; and in its place commences retrogression. The embryo agency now superseded by some commission—some board and staff of officers, straightway dwindles; for power is as inevitably lost by inactivity as it is gained by activity. Hence, humanity no longer goes on moulding itself into harmony with the natural requirements of the social state; but begins, instead, to assume a form fitting these artificial requirements. It is consequently stopped in its progress toward that self-sufficingness characteristic of the complete man; or, in other words, is prevented from fulfilling the conditions essential to complete happiness. And thus, as before said, not only does a government reverse its function by taking away more property than is needful for protective purposes, but even what it gives, in return for the excess so taken, is in essence a loss.

• • •

For when government fulfils the function here assigned it, of retaining men in the circumstances to which they are to be adapted, it fulfils the function which we on other hand assigned it—that of protector. To administer justice—to mount guard over men's rights—to prevent aggression—is simply to render society possible, to enable men to live together—to keep them in contact with their new conditions. And seeing that the two definitions are thus at root the same, we shall be prepared for the fact that, in whichever way we specify its duty, the state cannot exceed that duty without defeating itself. For, if regarded as a protector, we find that the moment it does any thing more than protect, it becomes an aggressor instead of a protector; and if regarded as a help to adaptation, we find that when it does any thing more than sustain the social state, it retards adaptation instead of hastening it.

Thus much for the positive evidence: let us now enter upon the negative. The expediency-philosophers say that government has other functions to fulfil besides that of upholding men's rights. If so, what are they? To the assertion that the boundary line of state-duty as above drawn is at the wrong place, the obvious rejoinder is—show us where it should be drawn. This appeal the expediency-philosophers have never yet been able to answer. Their alleged definitions are no definitions—managed by commissioners, boards, clerks, and collectors, who perform their respective functions as tasks—and kept a-going by money forcibly taken from all classes indiscriminately. In place of the music breathed by feelings attuned to kind deeds, we have the harsh creaking and jarring of a thing that cannot stir without creating discord—a thing whose every act, from the gathering of its funds to their final distribution, is prolific of grumblings, discontent, anger—a thing that breeds squabbles about authority, disputes as to claims, brow-beatings, jealousies, litigations, corruption, trickery, lying, ingratitude—a thing that supplants, and therefore makes dormant, men's nobler feelings, whilst it stimulates their baser ones.

And now mark how we find illustrated in detail the truth elsewhere expressed in the abstract, that whenever a government oversteps its duty—the maintaining of men's rights—it inevitably retards the process of adaptation. For what faculty is it whose work a poor-law so officiously undertakes? Sympathy. The very faculty above all others needing to be exercised. The faculty which distinguishes the social man from the savage. The faculty which originates the idea of justice—which makes men regardful of each other's claims—which renders society possible. The faculty of whose growth civilization is a history—on whose increased strength the future ameliorations of man's state mainly depend—and by whose ultimate supremacy, human morality, freedom, and happiness will be secured. Of this faculty poor-laws partially supply the place. By doing which they diminish the demands made upon it, limit its exercise, check its development, and therefore retard the process of adaptation.

Pervading all nature we may see at work a stern discipline, which is a little cruel that it may be very kind. That state of universal warfare maintained throughout the lower creation, to the great perplexity of many worthy people, is at bottom the most merciful provision which the circumstances admit of. It is much better that the ruminant animal, when deprived by age of the vigour which made its existence a pleasure, should be killed by some beast of prey, than that it should linger out a life made painful by infirmities, and eventually die of starvation. By the destruction of all such, not only is existence ended before it becomes burdensome, but room is made for a younger generation capable of the fullest enjoyment; and, moreover, out of the very act of substitution happiness is derived for a tribe of predatory creatures. Note further, that their carnivorous enemies not only remove from herbivorous herds individuals past their prime, but also weed out the sickly, the malformed, and the least fleet or powerful. By the aid of which purifying process, as well as by the fighting, so universal in the pairing season, all vitiation of the race through the multiplication of its inferior samples is prevented; and the maintenance of a constitution completely adapted to surrounding conditions, and therefore most productive of happiness, is ensured.

The development of the higher creation is a progress toward a form of being capable of a happiness undiminished by these drawbacks. It is in the human race that the consummation is to be accomplished. Civilization is the last stage of its accomplishment. And the ideal man is the man in whom all the conditions of that accomplishment are fulfilled. Meanwhile the well-being of existing humanity, and the unfolding of it into this ultimate perfection, are both secured by that same beneficent, though severe discipline, to which the animate creation at large is subject: a discipline which is pitiless in the working out of good: a felicity-pursuing law which never swerves for the avoidance of partial and temporary suffering. The poverty of the incapable, the distresses that come upon the imprudent, the starvation of the idle, and those shouldering aside of the weak by the strong, which leave so many "in shallows and in miseries," are the decrees of a large, far-seeing benevolence. It seems hard that an unskillfulness which with all his efforts he cannot overcome, should entail hunger upon the artisan. It seems hard that a labourer incapacitated by sickness from competing with his stronger fellows, should have to bear the resulting privations. It seems hard that widows and orphans should be left to struggle for life or death. Nevertheless, when regarded not separately, but in connection with the interests of universal humanity, these harsh fatalities are seen to be full of the highest beneficence—the same beneficence which brings to early graves the children of diseased parents, and singles out the low-spirited, the intemperate, and the debilitated as the victims of an epidemic.

There are many very amiable people—people over whom in so far as their feelings are concerned we may fitly rejoice—who have not the nerve to look this matter fairly in the face. Disabled as they are by their sympathies with present suffering, from duly regarding ultimate consequences, they pursue a course which is very injudicious, and in the end even cruel. We do not consider it true kindness in a mother to gratify her child with sweetmeats that are certain to make it ill. We should think it a very foolish sort of benevolence which led a surgeon to let his patient's disease progress to a fatal issue, rather than inflict pain by an operation. Similarly, we must call those spurious philanthropists, who, to prevent present misery, would entail greater misery upon future generations. All defenders of a poor-law must, however, be classed amongst such. That rigorous necessity which, when allowed to act on them, becomes so sharp a spur to the lazy, and so strong a bridle to the random, these paupers' friends would repeal, because of the wailings it here and there produces. Blind to the fact, that under the natural order of things society is constantly excreting its unhealthy, imbecile, slow, vacillating, faithless members, these unthinking, though well-meaning, men advocate an interference which not only stops the purifying process, but even increases the vitiation—absolutely encourages the multiplication of the reckless and incompetent by offering them an unfailing provision, and discourages the multiplication of the competent and provident by heightening the prospective difficulty of maintaining a family. And thus, in their eagerness to prevent the really salutary sufferings that surround us, these sigh-wise and groan-foolish people bequeath to posterity a continually increasing curse.

Returning again to the highest point of view, we find that there is a second and still more injurious mode in which law-enforced charity checks the process of adaptation. To become fit for the social state, man has not only to lose his savageness, but he has to acquire the capacities needful for civilized life. Power of application must be developed; such modification of the intellect as shall qualify it for its new tasks must take place; and, above all, there must be gained the ability to sacrifice a small immediate gratification for a future great one. The state of transition will of course be an unhappy state. Misery inevitably results from incongruity between constitution and conditions. All these evils, which afflict us, and seem to the uninitiated the obvious consequences of this or that removable cause, are unavoidable attendants on the adaptation now in progress. Humanity is being pressed against the inexorable necessities of its new position—is being moulded into harmony with them, and has to bear the resulting unhappiness as best it can. The process *must* be undergone, and the sufferings *must* be endured. No power on earth, no cunningly-devised laws of statesmen, no world-rectifying schemes of the humane, no communist panaceas, no reforms that men ever did broach or ever will broach, can diminish them one jot. Intensified they may be, and are; and in preventing their intensification, the philanthropic will find ample scope for exertion. But there is bound up with the change a *normal* amount of suffering, which cannot be lessened without altering the very laws of life. Every attempt at mitigation of this eventuates in exacerbation of it. All that a poor-law, or any kindred institution can do, is to partially suspend the transition—to take off for awhile, from certain members of society, the painful pressure which is effecting their transformation. At best this is merely to postpone what must ultimately be borne. But it is more than this: it is to undo what has already been done. For the circumstances to which adaptation is taking place cannot be superseded without causing a retrogression—a partial loss of the adaptation previously effected; and as the whole process must some time or other be passed through, the lost ground must be gone over again, and the attendant pain borne afresh. Thus, besides retarding adaptation, a poor-law adds to the distresses inevitably attending it.

At first sight these considerations seem conclusive against *all* relief to the poor—voluntary as well as compulsory; and it is no doubt true that they imply a condemnation of whatever private charity enables the recipients to elude the necessities of our social existence. With this condemnation, however, no rational man will quarrel. That careless squandering of pence which has fostered into perfection a system of organized begging—which has made skilful mendicancy more profitable than ordinary manual labour—which induces the simulation of palsy, epilepsy, cholera, and no end of diseases and deformities—which has called into existence warehouses for the sale and hire of impostor's dresses—which has given to pity-inspiring babes a market value of 9*d*. per day—the unthinking benevolence which has generated all this, cannot but be disapproved by every one. Now it is only against this injudicious charity that the foregoing argument tells. To that charity which may be described as helping men to help themselves, it makes no objection—countenances it rather. And in helping men to help themselves, there remains abundant scope for the exercise of a people's sympathies. Accidents will still supply victims on whom generosity may be legitimately expended. Men thrown upon their backs by unforeseen events, men who have failed for want of knowledge inaccessible to them, men ruined by the dishonesty of others, and men in whom hope long delayed has made the heart sick, may, with advantage to all parties, be assisted. Even the prodigal, after severe hardship has branded his memory with the unbending conditions of social life to which he must submit, may properly have another trial afforded him. And, although by these ameliorations the process of adaptation must be remotely interfered with, yet in the majority of cases, it will not be so much retarded in one direction as it will be advanced in another.

# *from* National Life from the Standpoint of Science

*Karl Pearson*

What I have said about bad stock seems to me to hold for the lower races of man. How many centuries, how many thousands of years, have the Kaffir [a tribe in southern Africa] or the negro held large districts in Africa undisturbed by the white man? Yet their intertribal struggles have not yet produced a civilization in the least comparable with the Aryan [western European]. Educate and nurture them as you will, I do not believe that you will succeed in modifying the stock. History shows me one way, and one way only, in which a high state of civilization has been produced, namely, the struggle of race with race, and the survival of the physically and mentally fitter race. . . .

. . . Let us suppose we could prevent the white man, if we liked, from going to lands of which the agricultural and mineral resources are not worked to the full; then I should say a thousand times better for him that he should not go than that he should settle down and live alongside the inferior race. The only healthy alternative is that he should go and completely drive out the inferior race. That is practically what the white man has done in North America. . . . But I venture to say that no man calmly judging will wish either that the whites had never gone to America, or would desire that whites and Red Indians were to-day living alongside each other as negro and white in the Southern States, as Kaffir and European in South Africa, still less that they had mixed their blood as Spaniard and Indian in South America. . . . I venture to assert, then, that the struggle for existence between white and red man, painful and even terrible as it was in its details, has given us a good far outbalancing its immediate evil. In place of the red man, contributing practically nothing to the work and thought of the world, we have a great nation, mistress of many arts, and able, with its youthful imagination and fresh, untrammelled impulses, to contribute much to the common stock of civilized man. . . .

But America is but one case in which we have to mark a masterful human progress following an inter-racial struggle. The Australian nation is another case of great civilization supplanting a lower race unable to work to the full the land and its resources. . . . The struggle means suffering, intense suffering, while it is in progress; but that struggle and that suffering have been the stages by which the white man has reached his present stage of development, and they account for the fact that he no longer lives in caves and feeds on roots and nuts. This dependence of progress on the survival of the fitter race, terribly black as it may seem to some of you, gives the struggle for existence its redeeming features; it is the fiery crucible out of which comes the finer metal. You may hope for a time when the sword shall be turned into the ploughshare, when American and German and English traders shall no longer compete in the markets of the world for their raw material and for their food supply, when the white man and the dark shall share the soil between them, and each till it as he lists [pleases]. But, believe me, when that day comes mankind will no longer progress; there will be nothing to check the fertility of inferior stock; the relentless law of heredity will not be controlled and guided by natural selection. Man will stagnate. . . .

The . . . great function of science in national life . . . is to show us what national life means, and how the nation is a vast organism subject. . . to the great forces of evolution. . . . There is a struggle of race against race and of nation against nation. In the early days of that struggle it was a blind, unconscious struggle of barbaric tribes. At the present day, in the case of the civilized white man, it has become more and more the conscious, carefully directed attempt of the nation to fit itself to a continuously changing environment. The nation has to foresee how and where the struggle will be carried on; the maintenance of national position is becoming more and more a conscious preparation for changing conditions, an insight into the needs of coming environments. . . .

. . . If a nation is to maintain its position in this struggle, it must be fully provided with trained brains in every department of national activity, from the government to the factory, and have, if possible, *a reserve of brain and physique* to fall back upon in times of national crisis. . . .

You will see that my view—and I think it may be called the scientific view of a nation—is that of an organized whole, kept up to a high pitch of internal efficiency by insuring that its numbers are substantially recruited from the better stocks, and kept up to a high pitch of external efficiency by contest, chiefly by way of war with inferior races, and with equal races by the struggle for trade-routes and for the sources of raw material and of food supply. This is the natural history view of mankind, and I do not think you can in its main features subvert it. . . .

. . . Is it not a fact that the daily bread of our millions of workers depends on their having somebody to work for? That if we give up the contest for trade-routes and for free markets and for waste lands, we indirectly give up our food supply? Is it not a fact that our strength depends on these and upon our colonies, and that our colonies have been won by the ejection of inferior races, and are maintained against equal races only by respect for the present power of our empire? . . .

. . . We find that the law of the survival of the fitter is true of mankind, but that the struggle is that of the gregarious animal. A community not knit together by strong social instincts, by sympathy between man and man, and class and class, cannot face the external contest, the competition with other nations, by peace or by war, for the raw material of production and for its food supply. This struggle of tribe with tribe, and nation with nation, may have its mournful side; but we see as a result of it the gradual progress of mankind to higher intellectual and physical efficiency. It is idle to condemn it; we can only see that it exists and recognise what we have gained by it—civilization and social sympathy. But while the statesman has to watch this external struggle, . . . he must be very cautious that the nation is not silently rotting at its core. He must insure that the fertility of the inferior stocks is checked, and that of the superior stocks encouraged; he must regard with suspicion anything that tempts the physically and mentally fitter men and women to remain childless. . . .

. . . The path of progress is strewn with the wrecks of nations; traces are everywhere to be seen of the hecatombs (slaughtered remains) of inferior races, and of victims who found not the narrow way to perfection. Yet these dead people are, in very truth, the stepping stones on which mankind has arisen to the higher intellectual and deeper emotional life of today.

# Shooting an Elephant

*George Orwell*

In Moulmein, in lower Burma, I was hated by large numbers of people—the only time in my life that I have been important enough for this to happen to me. I was sub-divisional police officer of the town, and in an aimless, petty kind of way anti-European feeling was very bitter. No one had the guts to raise a riot, but if a European woman went through the bazaars alone somebody would probably spit betel juice over her dress. As a police officer I was an obvious target and was baited whenever it seemed safe to do so. When a nimble Burman tripped me up on the football field and the referee (another Burman) looked the other way, the crowd yelled with hideous laughter. This happened more than once. In the end the sneering yellow faces of young men that met me everywhere, the insults hooted after me when I was at a safe distance, got badly on my nerves. The young Buddhist priests were the worst of all. There were several thousands of them in the town and none of them seemed to have anything to do except stand on street corners and jeer at Europeans.

All this was perplexing and upsetting. For at that time I had already made up my mind that imperialism was an evil thing and the sooner I chucked up my job and got out of it the better. Theoretically—and secretly, of course—I was all for the Burmese and all against their oppressors, the British. As for the job I was doing, I hated it more bitterly than I can perhaps make clear. In a job like that you see the dirty work of Empire at close quarters. The wretched prisoners huddling in the stinking cages of the lock-ups, the gray, cowed faces of the long-term convicts, the scarred buttocks of the men who had been flogged with bamboos—all these oppressed me with an intolerable sense of guilt. But I could get nothing into perspective. I was young and ill educated and I had had to think out my problems in the utter silence that is imposed on every Englishman in the East. I did not even know that the British Empire is dying, still less did I know that it is a great deal better than the younger empires that are going to supplant it. All I knew was that I was stuck between my hatred of the empire I served and my rage against the evil-spirited little beasts who tried to make my job impossible. With one part of my mind I thought of the British Raj as an unbreakable tyranny, as something clamped down, in *saecula saeculorum*, upon the will of prostrate peoples; with another part I thought that the greatest joy in the world would be to drive a bayonet into a Buddhist priest's guts. Feelings like these are the normal by-products of imperialism; ask any Anglo-Indian official, if you can catch him off duty.

One day something happened which in a roundabout way was enlightening. It was a tiny incident in itself, but it gave me a better glimpse than I had had before of the real nature of imperialism—the real motives for which despotic governments act. Early one morning the sub-inspector at a police station the other end of the town rang me up on the 'phone and said that an elephant was ravaging the bazaar. Would I please come and do something about it? I did not know what I could do, but I wanted to see what was happening and I got on to a pony and started out. I took my rifle, an old .44 Winchester and much too small to kill an elephant, but I thought the noise might be useful *in terrorem*. Various Burmans stopped me on the way and told me about the elephant's doings. It was not, of course, a wild elephant, but a tame one which had gone "must." It had been chained up, as tame elephants always are when their attack of "must" is due, but on the previous night it had broken its chain and escaped. Its mahout, the only person who could manage it when it was in that state, had set out in pursuit, but had taken the wrong direction and was now twelve hours' journey away, and in the morning the elephant had suddenly reappeared in the town. The Burmese population had no weapons and were quite helpless against it. It had already destroyed somebody's bamboo hut, killed a cow and raided some fruit-stalls and devoured the stock; also it had met the municipal rubbish van and, when the driver jumped out and took to his heels, had turned the van over and inflicted violences upon it.

The Burmese sub-inspector and some Indian constables were waiting for me in the quarter where the elephant had been seen. It was a very poor quarter, a labyrinth of squalid bamboo huts, thatched with palm-leaf, winding all over a steep hillside. I remember that it was a cloudy, stuffy morning at the beginning of the rains. We began questioning the people as to where the elephant had gone and, as usual, failed to get any definite information. That is invariably the case in the East; a story always sounds clear enough at a distance, but the nearer you get to the scene of events the vaguer it becomes. Some of the people said that the elephant had gone in one direction, some said that he had gone in another, some professed not even to have heard of any elephant. I had almost made up my mind that the whole story was a pack of lies, when we heard yells a little distance away. There was a loud, scandalized cry of "Go away, child! Go away this instant!" and an old woman with a switch in her hand came round the corner of a hut, violently shooing away a crowd of naked children. Some more women followed, clicking their tongues and exclaiming; evidently there was something that the children ought not to have seen. I rounded the hut and saw a man's dead body sprawling in the mud. He was an Indian, a black Dravidian coolie, almost naked, and he could not have been dead many minutes. The people said that the elephant had come suddenly upon him round the corner of the hut, caught him with its trunk, put its foot on his back and ground him into the earth. This was the rainy season and the ground was soft, and his face had scored a trench a foot deep and a couple of yards long. He was lying on his belly with arms crucified and head sharply twisted to one side. His face was coated with mud, the eyes wide open, the teeth bared and grinning with an expression of unendurable agony. (Never tell me, by the way, that the dead look peaceful. Most of the corpses I have seen looked devilish.) The friction of the great beast's foot had stripped the skin from his back as neatly as one skins a rabbit. As soon as I saw the dead man I sent an orderly to a friend's house nearby to borrow an elephant rifle. I had already sent back the pony, not wanting it to go mad with fright and throw me if it smelt the elephant.

The orderly came back in a few minutes with a rifle and five cartridges, and meanwhile some Burmans had arrived and told us that the elephant was in the paddy fields below, only a few hundred yards away. As I started forward practically the whole population of the quarter flocked out of the houses and followed me. They had seen the rifle and were all shouting excitedly that I was going to shoot the elephant. They had not shown much interest in the elephant when he was merely ravaging their homes, but it was different now that he was going to be shot. It was a bit of fun to them, as it would be to an English crowd; besides they wanted the meat. It made me vaguely uneasy. I had no intention of shooting the elephant—I had merely sent for the rifle to defend myself if necessary—and it is always unnerving to have a crowd following you. I marched down the hill, looking and feeling a fool, with the rifle over my shoulder and an ever-growing army of people jostling at my heels. At the bottom, when you got away from the huts, there was a metalled road and beyond that a miry waste of paddy fields a thousand yards across, not yet ploughed but soggy from the first rains and dotted with coarse grass. The elephant was standing eight yards from the road, his left side toward us. He took not the slightest notice of the crowd's approach. He was tearing up bunches of grass, beating them against his knees to clean them, and stuffing them into his mouth.

I had halted on the road. As soon as I saw the elephant I knew with perfect certainty that I ought not to shoot him. It is a serious matter to shoot a working elephant—it is comparable to destroying a huge and costly piece of machinery—and obviously one ought not to do it if it can possibly be avoided. And at that distance, peacefully eating, the elephant looked no more dangerous than a cow. I thought then and I think now that his attack of "must" was already passing off; in which case he would merely wander harmlessly about until the mahout came back and caught him. Moreover, I did not in the least want to shoot him. I decided that I would watch him for a little while to make sure that he did not turn savage again, and then go home.

But at that moment I glanced round at the crowd that had followed me. It was an immense crowd, two thousand at the least and growing every minute. It blocked the road for a long distance on either side. I looked at the sea of yellow faces above the garish clothes—faces all happy and excited over this bit of fun, all certain that the elephant was going to be shot. They were watching me as they would watch a conjurer about to perform a trick. They did not like me, but with the magical rifle in my hands I was momentarily worth watching. And suddenly I realized that I should have to shoot the elephant after all. The people expected it of me and I had got to do it; I could feel their two thousand wills pressing me forward, irresistibly. And it was at this moment, as I stood there with the rifle in my hands, that I first grasped the hollowness, the futility of the white man's dominion in the East. Here was I, the white man with his gun, standing in front of the unarmed native crowd—seemingly the leading actor of the piece; but in reality I was only an absurd puppet pushed to and fro by the will of those yellow faces behind. I perceived in this moment that when the white man turns tyrant it is his own freedom that he destroys. He becomes a sort of hollow, posing dummy, the conventionalized figure of a sahib. For it is the condition of his rule that he shall spend his life in trying to impress the "natives," and so in every crisis he has got to do what the "natives" expect of him. He wears a mask, and his face grows to fit it. I had got to shoot the elephant. I had committed myself to doing it when I sent for the rifle. A sahib has got to act like a sahib; he has got to appear resolute, to know his own mind and do definite things. To come all that way, rifle in hand, with two thousand people marching at my heels, and then to trail feebly away, having done nothing—no, that was impossible. The crowd would laugh at me. And my whole life, every white man's life in the East, was one long struggle not to be laughed at.

But I did not want to shoot the elephant. I watched him beating his bunch of grass against his knees with that preoccupied grandmotherly air that elephants have. It seemed to me that it would be murder to shoot him. At that age I was not squeamish about killing animals, but I had never shot an elephant and never wanted to. (Somehow it always seems worse to kill a large animal.) Besides, there was the beast's owner to be considered. Alive, the elephant was worth at least a hundred pounds; dead, he would only be worth the value of his tusks, five pounds, possibly. But I had got to act quickly. I turned to some experienced-looking Burmans who had been there when we arrived. and asked them how the elephant had been behaving. They all said the same thing: he took no notice of you if you left him alone, but he might charge if you went too close to him.

It was perfectly clear to me what I ought to do. I ought to walk up to within, say, twenty-five yards of the elephant and test his behavior. If he charged, I could shoot; if he took no notice of me, it would be safe to leave him until the mahout came back. But also I knew that I was going to do no such thing. I was a poor shot with a rifle and the ground was soft mud into which one would sink at every step. If the elephant charged and I missed him, I should have about as much chance as a toad under a steam-roller. But even then I was not thinking particularly of my own skin, only of the watchful yellow faces behind. For at that moment, with the crowd watching me, I was not afraid in the ordinary sense, as I would have been if I had been alone. A white man mustn't be frightened in front of "natives"; and so, in general, he isn't frightened. The sole thought in my mind was that if anything went wrong those two thousand Burmans would see me pursued, caught, trampled on, and reduced to a grinning corpse like that Indian up the hill. And if that happened it was quite probable that some of them would laugh. That would never do. There was only one alternative. I shoved the cartridges into the magazine and lay down on the road to get a better aim.

The crowd grew very still, and a deep, low, happy sigh, as of people who see the theater curtain go up at last, breathed from innumerable throats. They were going to have their bit of fun after all. The rifle was a beautiful German thing with cross-hair sights. I did not then know that in shooting an elephant one would shoot to cut an imaginary bar running from ear-hole to ear-hole. I ought, therefore, as the elephant was sideways on, to have aimed straight at his ear-hole; actually I aimed several inches in front of this, thinking the brain would be further forward.

When I pulled the trigger I did not hear the bang, or feel the kick—one never does when a shot goes home—but I heard the devilish roar of glee that went up from the crowd. In that instant, in too short a time, one would have thought, even for the bullet to get there a mysterious, terrible change had come over the elephant. He neither stirred nor fell, but every line of his body had altered. He looked suddenly stricken, shrunken immensely old, as though the frightful impact of the bullet had paralyzed him, without knocking him down. At last, after what seemed a long time—it might have been five seconds, I dare say—he sagged flabbily to his knees. His mouth slobbered. An enormous senility seemed to have settled upon him. One could have imagined him thousands of years old. I fired again into the same spot. At the second shot he did not collapse but climbed with desperate slowness to his feet and stood weakly upright, with legs sagging and head drooping. I fired a third time. That was the shot that did for him. You could see the agony of it jolt his whole body and knock the last remnant of strength from his legs. But in falling he seemed for a moment to rise, for as his hind legs collapsed beneath him he seemed to tower upward like a huge rock toppling, his trunk reaching skyward like a tree. He trumpeted, for the first and only time. And then down he came, his belly toward me, with a crash that seemed to shake the ground even where I lay.

I got up. The Burmans were already racing past me across the mud. It was obvious that the elephant would never rise again, but he was not dead. He was breathing very rhythmically with long rattling gasps, his great mound of a side painfully rising and falling. His mouth was wide open— I could see far down into caverns of pale pink throat. I waited a long time for him to die but his breathing did not weaken. Finally I fired my two remaining shots into the spot where I thought his heart must be. The thick blood welled out of him like red velvet but still he did not die. His body did not even jerk when the shots hit him, the tortured breathing continued without a pause. He was dying, very slowly and in great agony, but in some world remote from me where not even a bullet could damage him further. I felt that I had got to put an end to that dreadful noise. It seemed dreadful to see the great beast lying there, powerless to move and yet powerless to die, and not even to be able to finish him. I sent back for my small rifle and poured shot after shot into his heart and down his throat. They seemed to make no impression. The tortured gasps continued as steadily as the ticking of a clock.

In the end I could not stand it any longer and went away. I heard later that it took him half an hour to die. Burmans were bringing dahs and baskets even before I left, and I was told they had stripped his body almost to the bones by the afternoon.

Afterward, of course, there were endless discussions about the shooting of the elephant. The owner was furious, but he was only an Indian and could do nothing. Besides, legally I had done the right thing, for a mad elephant has to be killed, like a mad dog, if its owner fails to control it. Among the Europeans opinion was divided. The older men said I was right, the younger men said it was a damn shame to shoot an elephant for killing a coolie, because an elephant was worth more than any damn Coringhee coolie. And afterward I was very glad that the coolie had been killed; it put me legally in the right and it gave me a sufficient pretext for shooting the elephant. I often wondered whether any of the others grasped that I had done it solely to avoid looking a fool.

# Excerpts from the Works of Nietzsche

*Friedrich Nietzsche*

*Friedrich Nietzsche (1844–1900) was one of the most controversial philosophers in European history. In many respects he can be thought of as a radical critic of precisely those aspects of the Western tradition that Enlightenment thinkers had pointed to as evidence of progress, ideas such as reason, justice, and democracy. He was a virulent critic of Christianity and Christian moral values, as well as of the emergent industrial society in which he lived. In works such as* The Birth of Tragedy, The Genealogy of Morals, *and* The Will to Power *he struck out at prevailing European values, arguing for unleashing the will to power of the great creative individuals and recognizing the poverty of culture based on the common people.*

## The Birth of Tragedy

Once we have fully realized how, after Socrates, the mystagogue [a teacher who initiates followers into the mysteries of his discipline of science], one school of philosophers after another came upon the scene and departed; how generation after generation of inquirers, spurred by an insatiable thirst for knowledge, explored every aspect of the universe; and how by that ecumenical concern a common net of knowledge was spread over the whole globe, affording glimpses into the workings of an entire solar system—once we have realized all this, and the monumental pyramid of present-day knowledge, we cannot help viewing Socrates as the vortex and turning point of Western civilization. . . .

. . . Socrates represents the archetype of the theoretical optimist, who, strong in the belief that nature can be fathomed, considers knowledge to be the true panacea and error to be radical evil. To Socratic man the one noble and truly human occupation was that of laying bare the workings of nature, of separating true knowledge from illusion and error. So it happened that ever since Socrates the mechanism of concepts, judgments, and syllogisms [logical arguments] has come to be regarded as the highest exercise of man's powers, nature's most admirable gift. Socrates and his successors, down to our own day, have considered all moral and sentimental accomplishments—noble deeds, compassion, self-sacrifice,

211

heroism, even that spiritual calm, so difficult of attainment, which the Apollonian Greek called *sophrosyne*—to be ultimately derived from the dialectic of knowledge, and therefore teachable. Whoever has tasted the delight of a Socratic perception, experienced how it moves to encompass the whole world of phenomena in ever widening circles, knows no sharper incentive to life than his desire to complete the conquest, to weave the net absolutely tight. . . .

Our whole modern world is caught in the net of Alexandrian culture and recognizes as its ideal the man of theory, equipped with the highest cognitive powers, working in the service of science, and whose archetype and progenitor is Socrates. All our pedagogic devices are oriented toward this ideal. Any type of existence that deviates from this model has a hard struggle and lives, at best, on sufferance. It is a rather frightening thought that for centuries the only form of educated man to be found was the scholar. Even our literary arts have been forced to develop out of learned imitations, and the important role rhyme plays in our poetry still betokens the derivation of our poetic forms from artificial experiments with a language not vernacular but properly learned. To any true Greek, that product of modern culture, *Faust*, would have seemed quite unintelligible, though we ourselves understand it well enough. We have only to place Faust, who storms unsatisfied through all the provinces of knowledge and is driven to make a bargain with the powers of darkness, beside Socrates in order to realize that modern man has begun to be aware of the limits of Socratic curiosity and to long, in the wide, waste ocean of knowledge, for a shore. Goethe once said to Eckermann, referring to Napoleon: "Yes indeed, my friend, there is also a productivity of actions." This *aperçu* [insight] suggests that for us moderns the man of action is something amazing and incredible, so that the wisdom of a Goethe was needed to find such a strange mode of existence comprehensible, even excusable.

We should acknowledge, then, that Socratic culture is rooted in an optimism which believes itself omnipotent. . . .

The blight which threatens theoretical culture has only begun to frighten modern man, and he is groping uneasily for remedies out of the storehouse of his experience, without having any real conviction that these remedies will prevail against disaster. In the meantime, there have arisen certain men of genius who, with admirable circumspection and consequence, have used the arsenal of science to demonstrate the limitations of science and of the cognitive faculty itself. They have authoritatively rejected science's claim to universal validity and to the attainment of universal goals and exploded for the first time the belief that man may plumb the universe by means of the law of causation. The extraordinary courage and wisdom of Kant and Schopenhauer have won the most difficult victory, that over the optimistic foundations of logic, which form the underpinnings of our culture. Whereas the current optimism had treated the universe as knowable, in the presumption of eternal truths, and space, time, and causality as absolute and universally valid laws, Kant showed how these supposed laws serve only to raise appearance . . . to the status of true reality, thereby rendering impossible a genuine understanding of that reality: in the words of Schopenhauer, binding the dreamer even faster in sleep. . . .

. . . Socratic culture has been shaken and has begun to doubt its own infallibility. . . . The man of theory, having begun to dread the consequences of his views, no longer dares commit himself freely to the icy flood of existence but runs nervously up and down the bank.

## The Will to Power

720 (*1886–1887*)

The most fearful and fundamental desire in man, his drive for power—this drive is called "freedom"—must be held in check the longest. This is why ethics . . . has hitherto aimed at holding the desire for power in check: it disparages the tyrannical individual and with its glorification of social welfare and patriotism emphasizes the power-instinct of the herd.

728 (*March–June 1888*)

. . . A society that definitely and *instinctively* gives up war and conquest is in decline: it is ripe for democracy and the rule of shopkeepers—In most cases, to be sure, assurances of peace are merely narcotics.

751 (*March–June 1880*)

"The will to power" is so hated in democratic ages that their entire psychology seems directed toward belittling and defaming it. . . .

752 (*1884*)

. . . Democracy represents the disbelief in great human beings and an elite society: "Everyone is equal to everyone else." "At bottom we are one and all self-seeking cattle and mob."

753 (*1885*)

I am opposed to 1. socialism, because it dreams quite naively of "the good, true, and beautiful" and of "equal rights" (—anarchism also desires the same ideal, but in a more brutal fashion); 2. parliamentary government and the press, because these are the means by which the herd animal becomes master.

762 (*1885*)

European democracy represents a release of forces only to a very small degree. It is above all a release of laziness, of weariness, of *weakness*.

765 (*Jan.–Fall 1888*)

. . . Another Christian concept, no less crazy, has passed even more deeply into the tissue of modernity: the concept of the "equality of souls before God." This concept furnishes the prototype of all theories of equal rights: mankind was first taught to stammer the proposition of equality in a religious context, and only later was it made into morality: no wonder that man ended by taking it seriously, taking it practically!—that is to say, politically, democratically, socialistically, in the spirit of the pessimism of indignation.

854 (*1884*)

In the age of *suffrage universel*, i.e., when everyone may sit in judgment on everyone and everything, I feel impelled to reestablish *order of rank*.

855 (*Spring–Fall 1887*)

What determines rank, sets off rank, is only quanta of power, and nothing else.

857 (*Jan.–Fall 1888*)

I distinguish between a type of ascending life and another type of decay, disintegration, weakness. Is it credible that the question of the relative rank of these two types still needs to be posed?

858 (*Nov. 1887–March 1888*)

What determines your rank is the quantum of power you are: the rest is cowardice.

861 (*1884*)

A declaration of war on the masses by *higher men* is needed! Everywhere the mediocre are combining in order to make themselves master! Everything that makes soft and effeminate, that serves the ends of the "people" or the "feminine," works in favor of *suffrage universel*, i.e., the dominion of *inferior* men. But we should take reprisal and bring this whole affair (which in Europe commenced with Christianity) to light and to the bar of judgment.

862 (*1884*)

A doctrine is needed powerful enough to work as a breeding agent: strengthening the strong, paralyzing and destructive for the world-weary.

The annihilation of the decaying races. Decay of Europe.—The annihilation of slavish evaluations.—Dominion over the earth as a means of producing a higher type.—The annihilation of the tartuffery [hypocrisy] called "morality." . . . The annihilation of *suffrage universel*; i.e., the system through which the lowest natures prescribe themselves as laws for the higher.—The annihilation of mediocrity and its acceptance. (The onesided, individuals—peoples; to strive for fullness of nature through the pairing of opposites: race mixture to this end).—The new courage— no *a priori* [innate and universal] truths (such truths were sought by those accustomed to faith!), but a *free* subordination to a ruling idea that has its time: e.g., time as a property of space, etc.

870 (*1884*)

*The root of all evil*: that the slavish morality of meekness, chastity, selflessness, absolute obedience, has triumphed—ruling natures were thus condemned (1) to hypocrisy, (2) to torments of conscience—creative natures felt like rebels against God, uncertain and inhibited by eternal values. . . .

*In summa*: the best things have been slandered because the weak or the immoderate swine have cast a bad light on them—and the best men have remained hidden—and have often misunderstood themselves.

874 (*1884*)

The degeneration of the rulers and the ruling classes has been the cause of the greatest mischief in history! Without the Roman Caesars and Roman society, the insanity of Christianity would never have come to power.

When lesser men begin to doubt whether higher men exist, then the danger is great! And one ends by discovering that there is *virtue* also among the lowly and subjugated, the poor in spirit, and that *before God* men are equal—which has so far been the . . . [height] of nonsense on earth! For ultimately, the higher men measured themselves according to the standard of virtue of slaves—found they were "proud," etc., found all their higher qualities reprehensible.

997 (*1884*)

I teach: that there are higher and lower men, and that a single individual can under certain circumstances justify the existence of whole millennia—that is, a full, rich, great, whole human being in relation to countless incomplete fragmentary men.

998 (*1884*)

The highest men live beyond the rulers, freed from all bonds; and in the rulers they have their instruments.

999 (*1884*)

*Order of rank*: He who *determines* values and directs the will of millennia by giving direction to the highest natures is the *highest* man.

1001 (*1884*)

Not "mankind" but *overman* is the goal!

1067 (*1885*)

. . . *This world is the will to power—and nothing besides!* And you yourselves are also this will to power—and nothing besides!

# *from* Mein Kampf

## *Adolf Hitler*

*After World War I Europe experienced international tensions fueled by unful-filled nationalist aspirations and by economic instability, featuring weak mar-kets, uncontrolled inflation, and high unemployment. In Italy widespread discontent led to the rise of Mussolini and the establishment of a fascist state in 1922. Mussolini offered the working class badly needed jobs and social services in return for their support of total state power. In Germany, also, public despair led in the direction of extreme nationalism. Germany was particularly hard-hit by European economic problems and bore the additional burden of national humiliation and heavy economic reparations. In this environment socialists and extreme nationalists battled in the streets for political power. The victor was Adolf Hitler (1889–1945), founder of the Nazi Party. Son of a minor Austrian bureaucrat, Hitler failed at various pursuits in life, fought in the German army in World War I, and was arrested after a failed Nazi (National Socialist) putsch in 1923. While in jail he wrote* Mein Kampf, *which would serve as the theoret-ical enunciation of Nazi doctrines. Hitler was appointed Chancellor of Germany in 1933 and proceeded to build the Nazi state.*

## [The Primacy of Race]

No more than Nature desires the mating of weaker with stronger indi-viduals, even less does she desire the blending of a higher with a lower race, since, if she did, her whole work of higher breeding, over per-haps hundreds of thousands of years, might be ruined with one blow.

Historical experience offers countless proofs of this. It shows with terri-fying clarity that in every mingling of Aryan blood with that of lower peoples the result was the end of the cultured people. North America, whose population consists in by far the largest part of Germanic elements who mixed but little with the lower colored peoples, shows a different humanity and culture from Central and South America, where the pre-dominantly Latin immigrants often mixed with the aborigines on a large scale. By this one example, we can clearly and distinctly recognize the effect of racial mixture. The Germanic inhabitant of the American conti-nent, who has remained racially pure and unmixed, rose to be master of

217

the continent; he will remain the master as long as he does not fall a victim to defilement of the blood.

The result of all racial crossing is therefore in brief always the following:

(a) Lowering of the level of the higher race;

(b) Physical and intellectual regression and hence the beginning of a slowly but surely progressing sickness.

To bring about such a development is, then, nothing else but to sin against the will of the eternal creator.

Everything we admire on this earth today—science and art, technology and inventions—is only the creative product of a few peoples and originally perhaps of *one* race. On them depends the existence of this whole culture. If they perish, the beauty of this earth will sink into the grave with them. . . .

All great cultures of the past perished only because the originally creative race died out from blood poisoning.

The ultimate cause of such a decline was their forgetting that all culture depends on men and not conversely; hence that to preserve a certain culture the man who creates it must be preserved. This preservation is bound up with the rigid law of necessity and the right to victory of the best and stronger in this world. . . .

If we were to divide mankind into three groups, the founders of culture, the bearers of culture, the destroyers of culture, only the Aryan could be considered as the representative of the first group. From him originate the foundations and walls of all human creation. . . .

Blood mixture and the resultant drop in the racial level is the sole cause of the dying out of old cultures; for men do not perish as a result of lost wars, but by the loss of that force of resistance which is contained only in pure blood.

All who are not of good race in this world are chaff. . . .

A state which in this age of racial poisoning dedicates itself to the care of its best racial elements must some day become lord of the earth.

## [Anti-Semitism]

The mightiest counterpart to the Aryan is represented by the Jews. . . .

. . . The Jewish people, despite all apparent intellectual qualities, is without any true culture, and especially without any culture of its own. For what sham culture the Jew today possesses is the property of other peoples, and for the most part it is ruined in his hands.

In judging the Jewish people's attitude on the question of human culture, the most essential characteristic we must always bear in mind is that there has never been a Jewish art and accordingly there is none today either; that above all the two queens of all the arts, architecture and music, owe nothing original to the Jews. What they do accomplish in the field of art is either patchwork or intellectual theft. Thus, the Jew lacks those qualities which distinguish the races that are creative and hence culturally blessed. . . .

On this first and greatest lie, that the Jews are not a race but a religion, more and more lies are based in necessary consequence. Among them is the lie with regard to the language of the Jew. For him it is not a means for expressing his thoughts, but a means for concealing them. When he speaks French, he thinks Jewish, and while he turns out German verses, in his life he only expresses the nature of his nationality. As long as the Jew has not become the master of the other peoples, he must speak their languages whether he likes it or not, but as soon as they became his slaves, they would all have to learn a universal language. . . .

With satanic joy in his face, the black-haired Jewish youth lurks in wait for the unsuspecting girl whom he defiles with his blood, thus stealing her from her people. With every means he tries to destroy the racial foundations of the people he has set out to subjugate. . . .

For a racially pure people which is conscious of its blood can never be enslaved by the Jew. In this world he will forever be master over bastards and bastards alone.

And so he tries systematically to lower the racial level by a continuous poisoning of individuals.

And in politics he begins to replace the idea of democracy by the dictatorship of the proletariat.

In the organized mass of Marxism he has found the weapon which lets him dispense with democracy and in its stead allows him to subjugate and govern the peoples with a dictatorial and brutal fist.

He works systematically for revolutionization in a twofold sense: economic and political.

Around peoples who offer too violent a resistance to attack from within he weaves a net of enemies, thanks to his international influence, incites them to war, and finally, if necessary, plants the flag of revolution on the very battlefields.

In economics he undermines the states until the social enterprises which have become unprofitable are taken from the state and subjected to his financial control.

In the political field he refuses the state the means for its self-preservation, destroys the foundations of all national self-maintenance and defense, destroys faith in the leadership, scoffs at its history and past, and drags everything that is truly great into the gutter.

Culturally he contaminates art, literature, the theater, makes a mockery of natural feeling, overthrows all concepts of beauty and sublimity, of the noble and the good, and instead drags men down into the sphere of his own base nature.

Religion is ridiculed, ethics and morality represented as outmoded, until the last props of a nation in its struggle for existence in this world have fallen. . . .

*And so the Jew today is the great agitator for the complete destruction of Germany. Wherever in the world we read of attacks against Germany, Jews are their fabricators, just as in peacetime and during the War the press of the Jewish stock exchange and Marxists systematically stirred up hatred against Germany until state after state abandoned neutrality and, renouncing the true interests of the peoples, entered the service of the World War coalition.*

The Jewish train of thought in all this is clear. The Bolshevization of Germany—that is, . . . to make possible the sweating of the German working class under the yoke of Jewish world finance [which] is conceived only as a preliminary to the further extension of this Jewish tendency of world conquest. As often in history, Germany is the great pivot in the mighty struggle. If our people and our state become the victim of these blood-thirsty and avaricious Jewish tyrants of nations, the whole earth will sink into the snares of this octopus; if Germany frees herself from this embrace, this greatest of dangers to nations may be regarded as broken for the whole world. . . .

## [Propaganda and Mass Rallies]

The function of propaganda does not lie in the scientific training of the individual, but in calling the masses' attention to certain facts, processes, necessities, etc., whose significance is thus for the first time placed within their field of vision.

The whole art consists in doing this so skillfully that everyone will be convinced that the fact is real, the process necessary, the necessity correct, etc. . . . Its effect for the most part must be aimed at the emotions and only to a very limited degree at the so-called intellect.

All propaganda must be popular and its intellectual level must be adjusted to the most limited intelligence among those it is addressed to. Consequently, the greater the mass it is intended to reach, the lower its purely intellectual level will have to be. . . .

The art of propaganda lies in understanding the emotional ideas of the great masses and finding, through a psychologically correct form, the way to the attention and thence to the heart of the broad masses. . . .

The receptivity of the great masses is very limited, their intelligence is small, but their power of forgetting is enormous. In consequence of these facts, all effective propaganda must be limited to a very few points and must harp on these in slogans until the last member of the public understands what you want him to understand by your slogans. As soon as you sacrifice this slogan and try to be many-sided, the effect will piddle away, for the crowd can neither digest nor retain the material offered. In this way the result is weakened and in the end entirely cancelled out.

Thus we see that propaganda must follow a simple line and correspondingly the basic tactics must be psychologically sound. . . .

The function of propaganda is, for example, not to weigh and ponder the rights of different people, but exclusively to emphasize the one right which it has set out to argue for. Its task is not to make an objective study of the truth, in so far as it favors the enemy, and then set it before the masses with academic fairness; its task is to serve our own right, always and unflinchingly. . . .

But the most brilliant propagandist technique will yield no success unless one fundamental principle is borne in mind constantly and with unflagging attention. It must confine itself to a few points and repeat them over and over. Here, as so often in this world, persistence is the first and most important requirement for success. . . .

The purpose of propaganda is not to provide interesting distraction for blasé young gentlemen, but to convince, and what I mean is to convince the masses. But the masses are slow-moving, and they always require a certain time before they are ready even to notice a thing, and only after the simplest ideas are repeated thousands of times will the masses finally remember them.

When there is a change, it must not alter the content of what the propaganda is driving at, but in the end must always say the same thing. For instance, a slogan must be presented from different angles, but the end of all remarks must always and immutably be the slogan itself. Only in this way can the propaganda have a unified and complete effect. . . .

All advertising, whether in the field of business or politics, achieves success through the continuity and sustained uniformity of its application. . . .

*The mass meeting is . . . necessary for the reason that in it the individual, who at first, while becoming a supporter of a young movement, feels lonely and easily succumbs to the fear of being alone, for the first time gets the picture of a larger community, which in most people has a strengthening, encouraging effect.* The same man, within a company or a battalion, surrounded by all his comrades, would set out on an attack with a lighter heart than if left entirely on his own. In the crowd he always feels somewhat sheltered, even if a thousand reasons actually argue against it.

But the community of the great demonstration not only strengthens the individual, it also unites and helps to create an *esprit de corps*. The man who is exposed to grave tribulations, as the first advocate of a new doctrine in his factory or workshop, absolutely needs that strengthening which lies in the conviction of being a member and fighter in a great comprehensive body. And he obtains an impression of this body for the first time in the mass demonstration. When from his little workshop or big factory, in which he feels very small, he steps for the first time into a mass meeting and has thousands and thousands of people of the same opinions around him, when, as a seeker, he is swept away by three or four thousand others into the mighty effect of suggestive intoxication and enthusiasm, when the visible success and agreement of thousands confirm to him the rightness of the new doctrine and for the first time arouse doubt in the truth of his previous conviction—then he himself has succumbed to the magic influence of what we designate as "mass suggestion." The will, the longing, and also the power of thousands are accumulated in every individual. The man who enters such a meeting doubting and wavering leaves it inwardly reinforced: he has become a link in the community. . . .

## [Lebensraum]

*Only an adequately large space on this earth assures a nation of freedom of existence. . . .*

*If the National Socialist movement really wants to be consecrated by history with a great mission for our nation, it must be permeated by knowledge and filled with pain at our true situation in this world; boldly and conscious of its goal, it must take up the struggle against the aimlessness and incompetence which have hitherto guided our German nation in the line of foreign affairs. Then, without consideration of "traditions" and prejudices, it must find the courage to gather our people and their strength for an advance along the road that will lead this people from its present restricted living space to new land and soil, and hence also free it from the danger of vanishing from the earth or of serving others as a slave nation.*

*The National Socialist movement must strive to eliminate the disproportion between our population and our area—viewing this latter as a source of food as well as a basis for power politics—between our historical past and the hopelessness of our present impotence. . . .*

*. . . The demand for restoration of the frontiers of 1914 is a political absurdity of such proportions and consequences as to make it seem a crime. Quite aside from the fact that the Reich's frontiers in 1914 were anything but logical. For in reality they were neither complete in the sense of embracing the people of German nationality, nor sensible with regard to geomilitary expediency. . . .*

As opposed to this, we National Socialists must hold unflinchingly to our aim in foreign policy, namely, *to secure for the German people the land and soil to which they are entitled on this earth.* And this action is the only one which, before God and our German posterity, would make any sacrifice of blood seem justified. . . .

. . . Just as our ancestors did not receive the soil on which we live today as a gift from Heaven, but had to fight for it at the risk of their lives, in the future no folkish grace will win soil for us and hence life for our people, but only the might of a victorious sword.

Much as all of us today recognize the necessity of a reckoning with France, it would remain ineffectual in the long run if it represented the whole of our aim in foreign policy. It can and will achieve meaning only if it offers the rear cover for an enlargement of our people's living space in Europe. . . .

If we speak of soil in Europe today, we can primarily have in mind only *Russia* and her vassal border states. . . .

# The Slaughter of Jews in the Ukraine

*Hermann Graebe*

*Just as the victory of the Bolsheviks in Russia in 1917 had raised the "specter of Communism" around the globe as a real alternative to capitalism rather than merely theoretical speculation, so the application of Nazi policies of Aryan racial superiority demonstrated to the world the consequences of the racial ideas which had been widely supported in nineteenth and twentieth-century Europe. In this selection, we see a concrete example of the application of Hitler's ideas.*

On October 5, 1942, when I visited the building office at Dubno, my foreman told me that in the vicinity of the site, Jews from Dubno had been shot in three large pits, each about 30 metres long and 3 metres deep. About 1,500 persons had been killed daily. All the 5,000 Jews who had still been living in Dubno before the pogrom were to be liquidated. As the shooting had taken place in his presence, he was still much upset.

Thereupon, I drove to the site accompanied by my foreman and saw near it great mounds of earth, about 30 metres long and 2 metres high. Several trucks stood in front of the mounds. Armed Ukrainian militia drove the people off the trucks under the supervision of an S.S. man. The militiamen acted as guards on the trucks and drove them to and from the pit. All these people had the regulation yellow patches on the front and back of their clothes, and thus could be recognized as Jews.

My foreman and I went directly to the pits. Nobody bothered us. Now I heard rifle shots in quick succession from behind one of the earth mounds. The people who had got off the trucks—men, women and children of all ages—had to undress upon the orders of an S.S. man, who carried a riding or dog whip. They had to put down their clothes in fixed places, sorted according to shoes, top clothing and underclothing. I saw a heap of shoes of about 800 to 1,000 pairs, great piles of underlinen and clothing.

Without screaming or weeping, these people undressed, stood around in family groups, kissed each other, said farewells, and waited for a sign from another S.S. man, who stood near the pit, also with a whip in his hand. During the fifteen minutes that I stood near I heard no complaint or plea for mercy. I watched a family of about eight persons, a man and a woman both about fifty with their children of about one, eight and ten, and two grown-up daughters of about twenty to twenty-nine. An old woman with snow-white hair was holding the one-year-old child in her arms and singing to it and tickling it. The child was cooing with delight. The couple were looking on with tears in their eyes. The father was holding the hand of a boy about ten years old and speaking to him softly; the boy was fighting his tears. The father pointed to the sky, stroked his head, and seemed to explain something to him.

At that moment the S.S. man at the pit shouted something to his comrade. The latter counted off about twenty persons and instructed them to go behind the earth mound. Among them was the family which I have mentioned. I well remember a girl, slim and with black hair, who, as she passed close to me, pointed to herself and said "23." I walked around the mound and found myself confronted by a tremendous grave. People were closely wedged together and lying on top of each other so that only their heads were visible. Nearly all had blood running over their shoulders from their heads. Some of the people shot were still moving. Some were lifting their arms and turning their heads to show that they were still alive. The pit was already two-thirds full. I estimated that it already contained about 1,000 people.

I looked for the man who did the shooting. He was an S.S. man, who sat at the edge of the narrow end of the pit, his feet dangling into the pit. He had a tommy-gun on his knees and was smoking a cigarette. The people, completely naked, went down some steps which were cut in the clay wall of the pit and clambered over the heads of the people lying there, to the place to which the S.S. man directed them. They lay down in front of the dead or injured people; some caressed those who were still alive and spoke to them in a low voice.

Then I heard a series of shots. I looked into the pit and saw that the bodies were twitching or the heads lying motionless on top of the bodies which lay before them. Blood was running from their necks. I was surprised that I was not ordered away, but I saw that there were two or three postmen in uniform nearby. The next batch was approaching already. They went down into the pit, lined themselves up against the previous victims and were shot.

When I walked back round the mound, I noticed another truckload of people which had just arrived. This time it included sick and infirm persons. An old, very thin woman with terribly thin legs was undressed by others who were already naked, while two people held her up. The woman appeared to be paralyzed. The naked people carried the woman around the mound. I left with my foreman and drove in my car back to Dubno.

On the morning of the next day, when I again visited the site, I saw about thirty naked people lying near the pit—about 30 to 50 metres away from it. Some of them were still alive; they looked straight in front of them with a fixed stare and seemed to notice neither the chilliness of the morning nor the workers of my firm who stood around. A girl of about twenty spoke to me and asked me to give her clothes and help her escape. At that moment we heard a fast car approach and I noticed that it was an S.S. detail. I moved away to my site. Ten minutes later we heard shots from the vicinity of the pit. The Jews alive had been ordered to throw the corpses into the pit, then they had themselves to lie down in it to be shot in the neck.

# A German Perspective on the Holocaust

## Richard von Weizsäcker

*Many societies, like the Germans, have to live in the present with shameful rec-
ollections of the past. Great Britain, for example, committed mass atrocities in
the South African War, India, and in other parts of its Empire. The U.S. looks
back with shame upon slavery and its aftermath of enduring racial discrimination against people of African ancestry. Germany must struggle with its own
memories, which today are complicated by widespread unemployment following
the collapse of many industries in former East Germany and by the presence of
many non-German foreign workers (who are granted the right to reside and
work in Germany, but usually not citizenship). In this environment, anti-Semi-
tism is one of a number of forms of racism which have reemerged in German
political life.*

May 8th is a day of remembrance. Remembering means recalling an
occurrence honestly and undistortedly so that it becomes a part of
our very beings. This places high demands on our truthfulness.

Today we mourn all the dead of the war and tyranny. In particular we
commemorate the six million Jews who were murdered in German concentration camps. . . .

At the root of the tyranny was Hitler's immeasurable hatred of our Jewish
compatriots. Hitler had never concealed this hatred from the public, and
made the entire nation a tool of it. Only a day before his death, on April
30, 1945, he concluded his so-called "will" with the words: "Above all, I
call upon the leaders of the nation and their followers to observe painstakingly the race laws and to oppose ruthlessly the poisoners of all nations:
international Jewry." Hardly any country has in its history always
remained free from blame for war or violence. The genocide of the Jews is,
however, unparalleled in history.

The perpetration of this crime was in the hands of a few people. It was
concealed from the eyes of the public, but every German was able to
experience what his Jewish compatriots had to suffer, ranging from plain
apathy and hidden intolerance to outright hatred. Who could remain
unsuspecting after the burning of the synagogues, the plundering, the

228

stigmatization with the Star of David, the deprivation of rights, the cease-less violation of human dignity? Whoever opened his eyes and ears and sought information could not fail to notice that Jews were being deported. The nature and scope of the destruction may have exceeded human imagination, but in reality there was, apart from the crime itself, the attempt by too many people, including those of my generation, who were young and were not involved in planning the events and carrying them out, not to take note of what was happening. There were many ways of not burdening one's conscience, of shunning responsibility, look-ing away, keeping mum. When the unspeakable truth of the Holocaust then became known at the end of the war, all too many of us claimed that they had not known anything about it or even suspected anything.

There is no such thing as the guilt or innocence of an entire nation. Guilt is, like innocence, not collective, but personal. There is discovered or con-cealed individual guilt. There is guilt which people acknowledge or deny. Everyone who directly experienced that era should today quietly ask himself about his involvement then.

The vast majority of today's population were either children then or had not been born. They cannot profess a guilt of their own for crimes that they did not commit. No discerning person can expect them to wear a penitential robe simply because they are Germans. But their forefathers have left them a grave legacy. All of us, whether guilty or not, whether old or young, must accept the past. We are all affected by its conse-quences and liable for it. The young and old generations must and can help each other to understand why it is vital to keep alive the memories. It is not a case of coming to terms with the past. That is not possible. It cannot be subsequently modified or made undone. However, anyone who closes his eyes to the past is blind to the present. Whoever refuses to remember the inhumanity is prone to new risks of infection.

The Jewish nation remembers and will always remember. We seek recon-ciliation. Precisely for this reason we must understand that there can be no reconciliation without remembrance. The experience of millionfold death is part of the very being of every Jew in the world, not only because people cannot forget such atrocities, but also because remembrance is part of the Jewish faith.

"Seeking to forget makes exile all the longer; the secret of redemption lies in remembrance." This oft quoted Jewish adage surely expresses the idea that faith in God is faith in the work of God in history. Remembrance is experience of the work of God in history. It is the source of faith in redemption. This experience creates hope, creates faith in redemption, in reunification of the divided, in reconciliation. Whoever forgets this experience loses his faith.

If we for our part sought to forget what has occurred, instead of remembering it, this would not only be inhuman. We would also impinge upon the faith of the Jews who survived and destroy the basis of reconciliation. We must erect a memorial to thoughts and feelings in our own hearts.

# *from* What Is to Be Done?

## *Vladimir Lenin*

*Vladimir Ilyich Ulyanov (1870–1924), or Lenin, as history knows him, was one of many in his generation whose opposition to the repressive policies of the Tsar led to his own arrest and eventual exile. In exile the young Russian idealists, many of them drawn to Marxism, plotted and planned revolutionary overthrow of the regime of Nicholas ll. Lenin emerged as a leader of the group, editing* Iskra (The Spark), *and eventually returning to enunciate the program of the revolution and lead the Bolsheviks to victory.*

Without revolutionary theory there can be no revolutionary movement. This idea cannot be insisted upon too strongly. . . . Yet, for Russian Social-Democrats the importance of theory is enhanced by three other circumstances, which are often forgotten: first, by the fact that our Party is only in process of formation, its features are only just becoming defined, and it has as yet far from settled accounts with the other trends of revolutionary thought that threaten to divert the movement from the correct path. . . .

Secondly, the Social-Democratic movement is in its very essence an international movement. This means, not only that we must combat national chauvinism, but that an incipient movement in a young country can be successful only if it makes use of the experiences of other countries. In order to make use of these experiences it is not enough merely to be acquainted with them, or simply to copy out the latest resolutions. What is required is the ability to treat these experiences critically and to test them independently. He who realises how enormously the modern working-class movement has grown and branched out will understand what a reserve of theoretical forces and political (as well as revolutionary) experience is required to carry out this task.

[T]he national tasks of Russian Social-Democracy are such as have never confronted any other socialist party in the world. We shall have occasion further on to deal with the political and organisational duties which the task of emancipating the whole people from the yoke of autocracy imposes upon us. At this point, we wish to state only that the *role of van-*

*guard fighter can be fulfilled only by a party that is guided by the most advanced theory. . . .*

We have said that there *could not have been* Social-Democratic consciousness among the workers. It would have to be brought to them from without. The history of all countries shows that the working class, exclusively by its own effort, is able to develop only trade-union consciousness, i.e., the conviction that it is necessary to combine in unions, fight the employers, and strive to compel the government to pass necessary labor legislation, etc. The theory of socialism, however, grew out of the philosophic, historical, and economic theories elaborated by educated representatives of the propertied classes, by intellectuals. By their social status, the founders of modern scientific socialism, Marx and Engels, themselves belonged to the bourgeois intelligentsia. In the very same way, in Russia, the theoretical doctrine of Social-Democracy arose altogether independently of the spontaneous growth of the working-class movement; it arose as a natural and inevitable outcome of the development of thought among the revolutionary socialist intelligentsia. . . .

. . . I assert: (1) that no revolutionary movement can endure without a stable organisation of leaders maintaining continuity; (2) that the broader the popular mass drawn spontaneously into the struggle, which forms the basis of the movement and participates in it, the more urgent the need for such an organisation, and the more solid this organisation must be (for it is much easier for all sorts of demagogues to sidetrack the more backward sections of the masses); (3) that such an organisation must consist chiefly of people professionally engaged in revolutionary activity; (4) that in an autocratic state, the more we *confine* the membership of such an organisation to people who are professionally engaged in revolutionary activity and who have been professionally trained in the art of combating the political police, the more difficult will it be to unearth the organisation; and (5) the *greater* will be the number of people from the working class and from the other social classes who will be able to join the movement and perform active work in it. . . .

. . . Social-Democracy leads the struggle of the working class, not only for better terms for the sale of labour-power, but for the abolition of the social system that compels the propertyless to sell themselves to the rich. Social-Democracy represents the working class, not in its relation to a given group of employers alone, but in its relation to all classes of modern society and to the state as an organized political force. Hence, it follows that not only must Social-Democrats not confine themselves exclusively to the economic struggle, but that they must not allow [investigating mismanagement of the economy] to become the predominant part of their activities. We must take up actively the political education of the working class and the development of its political consciousness.

. . . We can never give a mass organisation that degree of secrecy without which there can be no question of persistent and continuous struggle against the government. To concentrate all secret functions in the hands of as small a number of professional revolutionaries as possible does not mean that the latter will "do the thinking for all" and that the rank and file will not take an active part in the *movement*. On the contrary, the membership will promote increasing numbers of the professional revolutionaries from its ranks; for it will know that it is not enough for a few students and for a few working men waging the economic struggle to gather in order to form a "committee," but that it takes years to train oneself to be a professional revolutionary. . . . Centralization of the most secret functions in an organisation of revolutionaries will not diminish, but rather increase the extent and enhance the quality of the activity of a large number of other organisations, that are intended for a broad public and are therefore as loose and as non-secret as possible, such as workers' trade unions; workers' self-education circles and circles for reading illegal literature; and socialist, as well as democratic, circles among *all* other sections of the population; etc., etc. We must have such circles, trade unions, and organisations everywhere in *as large a number as possible* and with the widest variety of functions. . . .

. . . The only serious organisational principle for the active workers of our movement should be the strictest secrecy, the strictest selection of members, and the training of professional revolutionaries. Given these qualities, something even more than "democratism" would be guaranteed to us, namely, complete, comradely, mutual confidence among revolutionaries. . . . They have a lively sense of their *responsibility*, knowing as they do from experience that an organisation of real revolutionaries will stop at nothing to rid itself of an unworthy member. . . .

. . . Our worst sin with regard to organisation consists in the fact that *by our primitiveness we have lowered the prestige of revolutionaries in Russia*. A person who is flabby and shaky on questions of theory, who has a narrow outlook, who pleads the spontaneity of the masses as an excuse for his own sluggishness, who resembles a trade-union secretary more than a spokesman of the people, who is unable to conceive of a broad and bold plan that would command the respect even of opponents, and who is inexperienced and clumsy in his own professional art—the art of combating the political police—such a man is not a revolutionary, but a wretched amateur!

# Quotations from Chairman Mao Tse-Tung

## Mao Tse-Tung

*Mao Tse-Tung (also spelled Mao Zedong) was the central leader of Chinese Communism. Though basing his ideas in Marxism, Mao fit Communism into the Chinese context, with its long history of suffering under both Western and Japanese Imperialism, its small industrial base, its huge peasant population, and its ancient philosophical tradition. Chairman Mao's thoughts were condensed into a "Little Red Book" that became the Bible of Chinese Communists. The following quotations come from the "Little Red Book."*

## 1. The Communist Party

The force at the core leading our cause forward is the Chinese Communist Party.

The theoretical basis guiding our thinking is Marxism-Leninism.

> Opening address at the First Session of the First National People's Congress of the People's Republic of China (September 15, 1954).

If there is to be revolution, there must be a revolutionary party. Without a revolutionary party, without a party built on the Marxist-Leninist revolutionary theory and in the Marxist-Leninist revolutionary style, it is impossible to lead the working class and the broad masses of the people in defeating imperialism and its running dogs.

> "Revolutionary Forces of the World Unite, Fight Against Imperialist Aggression!" (November 1948), *Selected Works*, Vol. IV, p. 284.

## 6. Imperialism and All Reactionaries Are Paper Tigers

All reactionaries are paper tigers. In appearance, the reactionaries are terrifying, but in reality they are not so powerful. From a long-term point of view, it is not the reactionaries but the people who are really powerful.

> "Talk with the American Correspondent Anna Louise Strong" (August 1946), *Selected Works*, Vol. IV, p. 100.

Just as there is not a single thing in the world without a dual nature (this is the law of the unity of opposites), so imperialism and all reactionaries have a dual nature—they are real tigers and paper tigers at the same time. In past history, before they won state power and for some time afterwards, the slave-owning class, the feudal landlord class and the bourgeoisie were vigorous, revolutionary and progressive; they were real tigers. But with the lapse of time, because their opposites—the slave class, the peasant class and the proletariat—grew in strength step by step, struggled against them more and more fiercely, these ruling classes changed step by step into the reverse, changed into reactionaries, changed into backward people, changed into paper tigers. And eventually they were overthrown, or will be overthrown, by the people. The reactionary, backward, decaying classes retained this dual nature even in their last life-and-death struggles against the people. On the one hand, they were real tigers; they devoured people, devoured people by the millions and tens of millions. The cause of the people's struggle went through a period of difficulties and hardships, and along the path there were many twists and turns. To destroy the rule of imperialism, feudalism and bureaucrat-capitalism in China took the Chinese people more than a hundred years and cost them tens of millions of lives before the victory in 1949. Look! Were these not living tigers, iron tigers, real tigers? But in the end they changed into paper tigers; dead tigers, bean-curd tigers. These are historical facts. Have people not seen or heard about these facts? There have indeed been thousands and tens of thousands of them! Thousands and tens of thousands! Hence, imperialism and all reactionaries, looked at in essence, from a long-term point of view, from a strategic point of view, must be seen for what they are—paper tigers. On this we should build our strategic thinking. On the other hand, they are also living tigers, iron tigers, real tigers which can devour people. On this we should build our tactical thinking.

> Speech at the Wuchang Meeting of the Political Bureau of the Central Committee of the Communist Party of China (December 1, 1958), quoted in the explanatory note to "Talk with the American Correspondent Anna Louise Strong," *Selected Works*, Vol. IV, pp. 98–99.

Imperialism will not last long because it always does evil things. It persists in grooming and supporting reactionaries in all countries who are against the people, it has forcibly seized many colonies and semi-colonies and many military bases, and it threatens the peace with atomic war. Thus, forced by imperialism to do so, more than 90 per cent of the people of the world are rising or will rise up in struggle against it. Yet imperialism is still alive, still running amuck in Asia, Africa and Latin America. In the West imperialism is still oppressing the people at home. This situation must change. It is the task of the people of the whole world to put an end to the aggression and oppression perpetrated by imperialism, and chiefly by U.S. imperialism.

> Interview with a Hsinhua News Agency correspondent (September 29, 1958).

Riding roughshod everywhere, U.S. imperialism has made itself the enemy of the people of the world and has increasingly isolated itself. Those who refuse to be enslaved will never be cowed by the atom bombs and hydrogen bombs in the hands of the U.S. imperialists. The raging tide of the people of the world against the U.S. aggressors is irresistible. Their struggle against U.S. imperialism and its lackeys will assuredly win still greater victories.

> "Statement Supporting the Panamanian People's Just Patriotic Struggle Against U.S. *People of the World, Unite and Defeat the U.S. Aggressors and All Their Lackeys*, 2nd ed., pp. 9–10.

If the U.S. monopoly capitalist groups persist in pushing their policies of aggression and war, the day is bound to come when they will be hanged by the people of the whole world. The same fate awaits the accomplices of the United States.

> Speech at the Supreme State Conference (September 8, 1958).

Over a long period we have developed this concept for the struggle against the enemy: strategically we should despise all our enemies, but tactically we should take them all seriously. This also means that we must despise the enemy with respect to the whole, but that we must take him seriously with respect to each and every concrete question. If we do not despise the enemy with respect to the whole, we shall be committing the error of opportunism. Marx and Engels were only two individuals, and yet in those early days they already declared that capitalism would be overthrown throughout the world. But in dealing with concrete problems and particular enemies we shall be committing the error of adventurism unless we take them seriously. In war, battles can only be fought one by one and the enemy forces can only be destroyed one by one. Factories can only be built one by one. The peasants can only plough the land plot by plot. The same is even true of eating a meal. Strategically, we take the eating of a meal lightly—we know we can finish it. But actually we eat it mouthful by mouthful. It is impossible to swallow an entire banquet in one gulp. This is known as a piecemeal solution. In military parlance, it is called wiping out the enemy forces one by one.

Speech at the Moscow Meeting of Communist and Workers' Parties (November 18, 1957).

It is my opinion that the international situation has now reached a new turning point. There are two winds in the world today, the East Wind and the West Wind. There is a Chinese saying, "Either the East Wind prevails over the West Wind or the West Wind prevails over the East Wind." I believe it is characteristic of the situation today that the East Wind is prevailing over the West Wind. That is to say, the forces of socialism have become overwhelmingly superior to the forces of imperialism.

Ibid.

# *from* The Gulag Archipelago

## *Aleksandr Solzhenitsyn*

*Stalinist Russia moved from crisis to crisis. Some of them, such as the rise of Nazi Germany and the subsequent German invasion of Russia in 1941, were beyond Russia's control. Others, such as the rapid industrialization and collectivization of Russia between the wars, were generated partly by the need to develop military power and partly by the desire to move quickly to a socialist state. Often Stalin implemented state programs against overwhelming popular opposition by the use of terror which cost millions of lives and made any form of political expression extremely hazardous. At times Stalin seems to have been motivated more by paranoid delusions than by responses to actual threats to his power. There also was a method to his madness, however, as nearly all the "old Bolsheviks" who had come through the revolution of 1917 and had a claim to power were eliminated in successive purges. Aleksandr Solzhenitsyn (1918–) captured the mood of the Stalin era in his 1973 novel,* The Gulag Archipelago.

The life of the natives consists of work, work, work; of starvation, cold, and cunning. This work, for those who are unable to push others out of the way and set themselves up in a soft spot, is that selfsame *general work* which raises socialism up out of the earth, and drives us down into the earth.

One cannot enumerate nor cover all the different aspects of this work, nor wrap your tongue about them. To push a wheelbarrow. . . . To carry hand barrows. To unload bricks barehanded (the skin quickly wears off the fingers). To haul bricks on one's own body by "goat" (in a shoulder barrow). To break up stone and coal in quarry and mine, to dig clay and sand. To hack out eight cubic yards of goldbearing ore with a pick and haul them to the screening apparatus. Yes, and just to dig in the earth, just to "chew" up earth (flinty soil and in winter). To cut coal underground. And there are ores there too—lead and copper. Yes, and one can also . . . pulverize copper ore (a sweet taste in the mouth, and one waters at the nose). One can impregnate [railroad] ties with creosote (and one's whole body at the same time too). One can carve out tunnels for railroads. And build roadbeds. One can dig peat in the bog up to one's waist in the mud. One can smelt ores. One can cast metal. One can cut hay on hummocks in swampy meadows (sinking up to one's ankles in water). One can be a stableman or a drayman [cart driver] (yes, and steal oats from the horse's bag for one's own pot, but the horse is government-issue, the old grass-bag, and she'll last it out, most likely, but you can drop dead). Yes, and generally at the "*selkhozy*"—the Agricultural Camps—you can do every kind of peasant work (and there is no work better than that: you'll grab something from the ground for yourself).

But the father of all is our Russian forest with its genuinely golden tree trunks. . . . And the oldest of all the kinds of work in the Archipelago is logging. It summons everyone to itself and has room for everyone, and it is not even out of bounds for cripples (they will send out a three-man gang of armless men to stamp down the foot-and-a-half snow). Snow comes up to your chest. You are a lumberjack. First you yourself stamp it down next to the tree trunk. You cut down the tree. Then, hardly able to make your way through the snow, you cut off all the branches (and you have to feel them out in the snow and get to them with your ax). Still dragging your way through the same loose snow, you have to carry off all the branches and make piles of them and burn them. (They smoke. They don't burn.) And now you have to saw up the wood to size and stack it. And the work norm for you and your brother for the day is six and a half cubic yards each, or thirteen cubic yards for two men working together. (In Burepolom the norm was nine cubic yards, but the thick pieces also had to be split into blocks.) By then your arms would not be capable of lifting an ax nor your feet of moving.

During the war years (on war rations), the camp inmates called three weeks at logging "*dry execution.*" . . .

. . . [T]heir summer workday was sometimes sixteen hours long! I don't know how it was with sixteen, but for many it was thirteen hours long—on earth-moving work in Karlag and at the northern logging operations—and these were hours on the job itself, over and above the three miles' walk to the forest and three back. And anyway, why should we argue about the length of the day? After all, the *work norm* was senior in rank to the length of the workday, and when the brigade didn't fulfill the norm, the only thing that was changed at the end of the shift was the convoy, and the work sloggers were left in the woods by the light of searchlights until midnight—so that they got back to the camp just before morning in time to eat their dinner along with their breakfast and go out into the woods again.

There is no one to tell about it either. They all died.

And then here's another way they raised the norms and proved it was possible to fulfill them: In cold lower than 60 degrees below zero, workdays were written off; in other words, on such days the records showed that the workers had not gone out to work; but they chased them out anyway, and whatever they squeezed out of them on those days was added to the other days, thereby raising the percentages. . . .

And how did they feed them in return? They poured water into a pot, and the best one might expect was that they would drop unscrubbed small potatoes into it, but otherwise black cabbage, beet tops, all kinds of trash. Or else vetch or bran, they didn't begrudge these. (And wherever there was a water shortage, as there was at the Samarka Camp near Karaganda, only one bowl of gruel was cooked a day, and they also gave out a ration of two cups of turbid salty water.) Everything any good was always and without fail stolen for the chiefs, for the trustees, and for the thieves—the cooks were all terrorized, and it was only by submissiveness that they kept their jobs. Certain amounts of fat and meat "subproducts" (in other words, not real food) were signed out from the warehouses, as were fish, peas, and cereals. But not much of that ever found its way into the mouth of the pot. And in remote places the chiefs even took all the *salt* for themselves for their own pickling. (In 1940, on the Kotlas-Vorkuta Railroad, both the bread and the gruel were unsalted.) The worse the food, the more of it they gave the zeks. They used to give them horse meat from exhausted horses driven to death at work, and, even though it was quite impossible to chew it, it was a feast. . . .

It was impossible to try to keep nourished on Gulag norms anyone who worked out in the bitter cold for thirteen or even ten hours. And it was completely impossible once the basic ration had been plundered. . . .

. . . [N]o matter how many hours there are in the working day—sooner or later sloggers will return to the barracks.

Their barracks? Sometimes it is a dugout, dug into the ground. And in the North more often . . . *a tent*—true, with earth banked and reinforced hit or miss with boards. Often there are kerosene lamps in place of electricity, but sometimes there are the ancient Russian "splinter lamps" or else cotton-wool wicks. (In Ust-Vym for two years they saw no kerosene, and even in headquarters barracks they got light from oil from the food store.) It is by this pitiful light that we will survey this ruined world.

Sleeping shelves in two stories, sleeping shelves in three stories, or, as a sign of luxury, "vagonki"—multiple bunks—the boards most often bare and nothing at all on them; on some of the work parties they steal so thoroughly (and then sell the spoils through the free employees) that nothing government-issue is given out and no one keeps anything of his own in the barracks; they take both their mess tins and their mugs to work with them (and even tote the bags containing their belongings— and thus laden they dig in the earth); those who have them put their blankets around their necks. . . or else lug their things to trusty friends in a guarded barracks. During the day the barracks are as empty as if uninhabited. At night they might turn over their wet work clothes to be dried in the drier (if there is a drier!)—but undressed like that you are going to freeze on the bare boards! And so they dry their clothes on themselves. At night their caps may freeze to the wall of the tent—or, in a woman's case, her hair. They even hide their bast sandals under their heads so they won't be stolen off their feet. . . . In the middle of the barracks there is an oil drum with holes in it which has been converted into a stove, and it is good when it gets red-hot—then the steamy odor of drying footcloths permeates the entire barracks—but it sometimes happens that the wet firewood in it doesn't burn. Some of the barracks are so infested with insects that even four days' fumigation with burning sulphur doesn't help and when in the summer the zeks go out to sleep on the ground in the camp compound the bedbugs crawl after them and find them even there. And the zeks boil the lice off their underwear in their mess tins after dining from them. . . .

And later there was that constant, clinging (and, for an intellectual, torturing) *lack of privacy*, the condition of not being an individual but a member of a brigade instead, and the necessity of acting for whole days and whole years not as you yourself have decided but as the brigade requires. . . .

Now that is the way of life of my Archipelago.

# *from* New Year's Address, 1990

## *Vaclav Havel*

*Vaclav Havel became the president of Czechoslovakia in 1989 after the collapse of the Soviet empire in eastern Europe. His election marked the renewed independence of a society which for over forty years had had to fear the roar of Soviet tanks if it moved too far in the direction of autonomy.*

## The Truth, Unvarnished

For 40 years you have heard on this day from the mouths of my predecessors, in a number of variations, the same thing: how our country is flourishing, how many more millions of tons of steel we have produced, how we are all happy, how we believe in our Government and what beautiful prospects are opening ahead of us. I assume you have not named me to this office so that I, too, should lie to you.

Our country is not flourishing. The great creative and spiritual potential of our nations is not being applied meaningfully. Entire branches of industry are producing things for which there is no demand while we are short of things we need.

The state, which calls itself a state of workers, is humiliating and exploiting them instead. Outmoded economy wastes energy, which we have in short supply. The country, which could once be proud of the education of its people, is spending so little on education that today, in that respect, we rank 72nd in the world. We have spoiled our land, rivers and forests, inherited from our ancestors, and we have, today, the worst environment in the whole of Europe. Adults die here earlier than in the majority of European countries. . . .

## Learning to Believe Again

The worst of it is that we live in a spoiled moral environment. We have become morally ill because we are used to saying one thing and thinking another. We have learned not to believe in anything, not to care about each other, to worry only about ourselves. The concepts of love, friendship, mercy, humility or forgiveness have lost their depths and dimension, and for many of us they represent only some sort of psychological curiosity or they appear as long-lost wanderers from faraway times, somewhat ludicrous in the era of computers and space ships. . . .

## Cogs No Longer

The previous regime, armed with a proud and intolerant ideology, reduced people into the means of production, and nature into its tools. So it attacked their very essence, and their mutual relations. . . . Out of talented and responsible people, ingeniously husbanding their land, it made cogs of some sort of great, monstrous, thudding, smelly machine, with an unclear purpose. All it can do is slowly but irresistibly, wear itself out, with all its cogs.

If I speak about a spoiled moral atmosphere I don't refer only to our masters. . . . I'm speaking about all of us. For all of us have grown used to the totalitarian system and accepted it as an immutable fact, and thereby actually helped keep it going. None of us are only its victims; we are all also responsible for it.

It would be very unwise to think of the sad heritage of the last 40 years only as something foreign; something inherited from a distant relative. On the contrary, we must accept this heritage as something we have inflicted on ourselves. If we accept it in such a way, we shall come to understand it is up to all of us to do something about it.

Let us make no mistake: even the best Government, the best Parliament and the best President cannot do much by themselves. Freedom and democracy, after all, mean joint participation and shared responsibility. If we realize this, then all the horrors that the new Czechoslovak democracy inherited cease to be so horrific. If we realize this, then hope will return to our hearts.

Everywhere in the world, people were surprised how these malleable, humiliated, cynical citizens of Czechoslovakia, who seemingly believed in nothing, found the tremendous strength within a few weeks to cast off the totalitarian system, in an entirely peaceful and dignified manner. We ourselves are surprised at it.

And we ask: Where did young people who had never known another system get their longing for truth, their love of freedom, their political imagination, their civic courage and civic responsibility? How did their parents, precisely the generation thought to have been lost, join them?

How is it possible that so many people immediately understood what to do and that none of them needed any advice or instructions? . . .

## Recalling Ruined Lives

Naturally we too had to pay for our present-day freedom. Many of our citizens died in prison in the 1950's. Many were executed. Thousands of human lives were destroyed. Hundreds of thousands of talented people were driven abroad. . . . Those who fought against totalitarianism during the war were also persecuted. . . . Nobody who paid in one way or another for our freedom could be forgotten.

Independent courts should justly evaluate the possible guilt of those responsible, so that the full truth about our recent past should be exposed.

But we should also not forget that other nations paid an even harsher price for their present freedom, and paid indirectly for ours as well. All human suffering concerns each human being. . . . Without changes in the Soviet Union, Poland, Hungary, and the German Democratic Republic, what happened here could hardly have taken place, and certainly not in such a calm and peaceful way.

Now it depends only on us whether this hope will be fulfilled, whether our civic, national and political self-respect will be revived. Only a man or nation with self-respect, in the best sense of the word, is capable of listening to the voices of others, while accepting them as equals, of forgiving enemies and of expiating sins. . . .

## [A Humane Republic]

Perhaps you are asking what kind of republic I am dreaming about. I will answer you: a republic that is independent, free, democratic, a republic with economic prosperity and also social justice, a humane republic that serves man and that for that reason also has the hope that man will serve it. . . .

## The People Hold Sway

My most important predecessor started his first speech by quoting from Comenius. Permit me to end my own first speech by my own paraphrase. Your Government, my people, has returned to you.

*Section Three*

# Belief and Thought

# *from* Lives of the Artists

## *Giorgio Vasari*

The distinguished artists described in the second part of these *Lives* made an important contribution to architecture, sculpture, and painting, adding to what had been achieved by those of the first period the qualities of good rule, order, proportion, design, and style. Their work was in many ways imperfect, but they showed the way to the artists of the third period (whom I am now going to discuss) and made it possible for them, by following and improving on their example, to reach the perfection evident in the finest and most celebrated modern works.

But to clarify the nature of the progress that these artists made, I would like to define briefly the five qualities that I mentioned above and discuss the origins of the excellence that has made modern art even more glorious than that of the ancient world.

By rule in architecture we mean the method used of measuring antiques and basing modern works on the plans of ancient buildings. Order is the distinction made between one kind of architectural style and another, so that each has the parts appropriate to it and there is no confusion between Doric, Ionic, Corinthian, and Tuscan. Proportion is a universal law of architecture and sculpture (and also of painting) which stipulates that all bodies must be correctly aligned, with their parts properly arranged. Design is the imitation of the most beautiful things in nature, used for the creation of all figures whether in sculpture or painting; and this quality depends on the ability of the artist's hand and mind to reproduce what he sees with his eyes accurately and correctly on to paper or a panel or whatever flat surface he may be using. The same applies to works of relief in sculpture. And then the artist achieves the highest perfection of style by copying the most beautiful things in nature and combining the most perfect members, hands, head, torso, and legs, to produce the finest possible figure as a model for use in all his works; this is how he achieves what we know as fine style.

Now the work of Giotto and the other early craftsmen did not possess these qualities, although they did discover the right principles for solving artistic problems and they applied them as best they could. Their drawing, for example, was more correct and truer to nature than anything done before, as was the way they blended their colours, composed their figures, and made the other advances I have already discussed. However, although the artists of the second period made further progress still, they in turn fell short of complete perfection, since their work lacked that spontaneity which, although based on correct measurement, goes beyond it without conflicting with order and stylistic purity. This spontaneity enables the artist to enhance his work by adding innumerable inventive details and, as it were, a pervasive beauty to what is merely artistically correct. Again, when it came to proportion the early craftsmen lacked that visual judgement which, disregarding measurement, gives the artist's figures, in due relation to their dimensions, a grace that simply cannot be measured. They also failed to realize the full potentialities of design; for example, although their arms were rounded and their legs straight, they missed the finer points when they depicted the muscles, ignoring the charming and graceful facility which is suggested rather than revealed in living subjects. In this respect their figures appeared crude and excoriated, offensive to the eye and harsh in style. Their style lacked the lightness of touch that makes an artist's figures slender and graceful, and particularly those of his women and children, which should be as realistic as the male figures and yet possess a roundness and fullness derived from good judgement and design rather than the coarseness of living bodies. Their works also lacked the abundance of beautiful clothes, the imaginative details, charming colours, many kinds of building and various landscapes in depth that we see depicted today.

• • •

Success came to the artists who followed, after they had seen some of the finest works of art mentioned by Pliny dug out of the earth: namely, the Laocoon, the Hercules, the great torso of Belvedere, as well as the Venus, the Cleopatra, the Apollo, and countless others, all possessing the appeal and vigour of living flesh and derived from the finest features of living models. Their attitudes were entirely natural and free, exquisitely graceful and full of movement. And these statues caused the disappearance of the dry, hard, harsh style that art had acquired through the excessive study of Piero della Francesca, Lazzaro Vasari, Alesso Baldovinetti, Andrea del Castagno, Pesello, Ercole Ferrarese, Giovanni Bellini, Cosimo Rosselli, the abbot of San Clemente, Domenico Ghirlandaio, Sandro Botticelli, Andrea Mantegna, Filippino Lippi, and Luca Signorelli. These artists forced themselves to try and do the impossible through their exertions, especially in their ugly foreshortenings and perspectives which were as disagreeable to look at as they were difficult to do. Although the greater part of their work was well designed and free from error, it still lacked any sense of liveliness as well as the harmonious blending of colours which was first seen in the works of Francia of Bologna and Piero Perugino (and which made the people run like mad to gaze on this new, realistic beauty, as if they would never see the like again).

But how wrong they were was then demonstrated for all to see in the work of Leonardo da Vinci. It was Leonardo who originated the third style or period, which we like to call the modern age; for in addition to the force and robustness of his draughtsmanship and his subtle and exact reproduction of every detail in nature, he showed in his works an understanding of rule, a better knowledge of order, correct proportion, perfect design, and an inspired grace. An artist of great vision and skill and abundant resources, Leonardo may be said to have painted figures that moved and breathed.

•   •   •

## Life of Leonardo Da Vinci

### Florentine painter and sculptor, 1452–1519

In the normal course of events many men and women are born with various remarkable qualities and talents; but occasionally, in a way that transcends nature, a single person is marvellously endowed by heaven with beauty, grace, and talent in such abundance that he leaves other men far behind, all his actions seem inspired, and indeed everything he does clearly comes from God rather than from human art.

Everyone acknowledged that this was true of Leonardo da Vinci, an artist of outstanding physical beauty who displayed infinite grace in everything he did and who cultivated his genius so brilliantly that all problems he studied he solved with ease. He possessed great strength and dexterity; he was a man of regal spirit and tremendous breadth of mind; and his name became so famous that not only was he esteemed during his lifetime but his reputation endured and became even greater after his death.

This marvellous and divinely inspired Leonardo was the son of Piero da Vinci. He would have been very proficient at his early lessons if he had not been so volatile and unstable; for he was always setting himself to learn many things only to abandon them almost immediately. Thus he began to learn arithmetic, and after a few months he had made so much progress that he used to baffle his master with the questions and problems that he raised. For a little while he attended to music, and then he very soon resolved to learn to play the lyre, for he was naturally of an elevated and refined disposition; and with this instrument he accompanied his own charming improvised singing. All the same, for all his other enterprises Leonardo never ceased drawing and working in relief, pursuits which best suited his temperament.

Realizing this, and considering the quality of his son's intelligence, Piero one day took some of Leonardo's drawings along to Andrea del Verrocchio (who was a close friend of his) and earnestly begged him to say whether it would be profitable for the boy to study design.[1] Andrea was amazed to see what extraordinary beginnings Leonardo had made and he urged Piero to make him study the subject. So Piero arranged for Leonardo to enter Andrea's workshop. The boy was delighted with this decision, and he began to practice not only one branch of the arts but all the branches in which design plays a part. He was marvellously gifted, and he proved himself to be a first-class geometrician in his work as a sculptor and architect. In his youth Leonardo made in clay several heads of women, with smiling faces, of which plaster casts are still being made, as well as some children's heads executed as if by a mature artist. He also did many architectural drawings both of ground plans and of other elevations, and, while still young, he was the first to propose reducing the Arno to a navigable canal between Pisa and Florence. He made designs for mills, fulling machines, and engines that could be driven by water-power; and as he intended to be a painter by profession he carefully studied drawing from life. Sometimes he made clay models, draping the figures with rags dipped in plaster, and then drawing them painstakingly on fine Rheims cloth or prepared linen. These drawings were done in black and white with the point of the brush, and the results were marvellous, as one can see from the examples I have in my book of drawings. Besides this, Leonardo did beautiful and detailed drawings on paper which are unrivalled for the perfection of their finish. (I have an example of these in a superb head in coloured silverpoint.) Altogether, his genius was so wonderfully inspired by the grace of God, his powers of expression were so powerfully fed by a willing memory and intellect, and his writing conveyed his ideas so precisely, that his arguments and reasonings confounded the most formidable critics. In addition, he used to make models and plans showing how to excavate and tunnel through mountains without difficulty, so as to pass from one level to another; and he demonstrated how to lift and draw great weights by means of levers, hoists, and winches, and ways of cleansing harbours and using pumps to suck up water from great depths. His brain was always busy on such devices, and one can find drawings of his ideas and experiments scattered among our craftsmen today; I myself have seen many of them. He also spent a great deal of time in making a pattern of a series of knots, so arranged that the connecting thread can be traced from one end to the other and the complete design fills a round space. There exists a splendid engraving of one of these fine and intricate designs, with these words in the centre: *Leonardos Vinci Academia.*

Among his models and plans there was one which Leonardo would often put before the citizens who were then governing Florence—many of them men of great discernment—showing how he proposed to raise and place steps under the church of San Giovanni without damaging the fabric. His arguments were so cogent that they would allow themselves to be convinced, although when they all went their several ways each of them would realize the impossibility of what Leonardo suggested.

Leonardo's disposition was so lovable that he commanded everyone's affection. He owned, one might say, nothing and he worked very little, yet he always kept servants as well as horses. These gave him great pleasure as indeed did all the animal creation which he treated with wonderful love and patience. For example, often when he was walking past the places where birds were sold he would pay the price asked, take them from their cages, and let them fly off into the air, giving them back their lost freedom. In return he was so favoured by nature that to whatever he turned his mind or thoughts the results were always inspired and perfect; and his lively and delightful works were incomparably graceful and realistic.

Clearly, it was because of his profound knowledge of painting that Leonardo started so many things without finishing them; for he was convinced that his hands, for all their skill, could never perfectly express the subtle and wonderful ideas of his imagination. Among his many interests was included the study of nature; he investigated the properties of plants and then observed the motion of the heavens, the path of the moon, and the course of the sun.

I mentioned earlier that when he was still young Leonardo entered the workshop of Andrea del Verrocchio. Now at that time Verrocchio was working on a panel picture showing the Baptism of Christ by St. John, for which Leonardo painted an angel who was holding some garments; and despite his youth, he executed it in such a manner that his angel was far better than the figures painted by Andrea. This was the reason why Andrea would never touch colours again, he was so ashamed that a boy understood their use better than he did. Leonardo was then commissioned to make a cartoon (for a tapestry to be woven of gold and silk in Flanders and sent to the king of Portugal) showing the sin of Adam and Eve in the Garden of Paradise. For this he drew with the brush in chiaroscuro, with the lights in lead-white, a luxuriant meadow full of different kinds of animals; and it can truthfully be said that for diligence and faithfulness to nature nothing could be more inspired or perfect. There is a fig tree, for example, with its leaves foreshortened and its branches drawn from various aspects, depicted with such loving care that the brain reels at the thought that a man could have such patience. And there is a palm tree, the radiating crown of which is drawn with such marvellous skill that no one without Leonardo's understanding and patience could have done it.

While he was engaged on this work Leonardo proposed to the duke that he should make a huge equestrian statue in bronze as a memorial to his father; then he started and carried the work forward on such a scale that it was impossible to finish it. There have even been some to say (men's opinions are so various and, often enough, so envious and spiteful) that Leonardo had no intention of finishing it when he started. This was because it was so large that it proved an insoluble problem to cast it in one piece; and one can realize why, the outcome being what it was, many came to the conclusion they did, seeing that so many of his works remained unfinished. The truth, however, is surely that Leonardo's profound and discerning mind was so ambitious that this was itself an impediment; and the reason he failed was because he endeavoured to add excellence to excellence and perfection to perfection. As our Petrarch has said, the desire outran the performance. In fact, those who saw the great clay model that Leonardo made considered that they had never seen a finer or more magnificent piece of work. It was preserved until the French came to Milan under King Louis and smashed it to pieces. Also lost is a little wax model which was held to be perfect, together with a reference book which Leonardo composed on the anatomy, of horses.

Leonardo then applied himself, even more assiduously, to the study of human anatomy, in which he collaborated with that excellent philosopher Marc Antonio della Torre, who was then lecturing at Pavia and who wrote on the subject. Della Torre, I have heard, was one of the first to illustrate the problems of medicine by the teachings of Galen and to throw true light on anatomy, which up to then had been obscured by the shadows of ignorance. In this he was wonderfully served by the intelligence, work, and hand of Leonardo, who composed a book annotated in pen and ink in which he did meticulous drawings in red chalk of bodies he had dissected himself. He showed all the bone structure, adding in order all the nerves and covering them with the muscles: the first attached to the skeleton, the second that hold it firm and the third that move it. In the various sections he wrote his observations in puzzling characters (written in reverse with the left hand) which cannot be deciphered by anyone who does not know the trick of reading them in a mirror.

## Note

1    Andrea del Verrocchio, painter and goldsmith, and the chief sculptor in Florence after Donatello's death.

# The Indulgence Controversy *and* Proposals for Practical Reform

## *Martin Luther*

*Luther was drawn into the arena of reform by his objection to the practice of indulgences. The particular instance lay in the instructions of Albert of Mainz to the vendors of indulgences in his territories. Albert's pretensions on behalf of the indulgence were the most extravagant ever made. Luther's Ninety-Five Theses were an attack upon this document. They can be found in English translation in full in many places, among others in the* Works of Martin Luther *(A. J. Holman Co., Philadelphia, 1915), vol. 1, pp. 25–38. The reply to Luther by Sylvester Prierias lifted the controversy to a new level by its assertion of papal authority, and Luther in his two replies dwarfed the indulgence question by a flat denial of papal and also of conciliar infallibility. In the summer of 1520, three years after the outbreak of the controversy, Luther issued several great manifestoes of reform, of which one was* The Address to the Nobility of the German Nation. *This deals largely with the moral and financial abuses of the Church. The appeal is addressed in medieval fashion to the civil arm of a Christian society to redress the offenses of the spiritual. Luther's doctrine of the priesthood of all believers supports his appeal to the lay rulers. This work is translated in full in the work referred to above.*

*Both the* Theses *and the* Address *are translated in Bertram Lee Woolf,* Reformation Writings of Martin Luther, *vol. 1 (London, 1952).*

## I. The *Instructions* of Albert of Mainz to the Indulgence Preachers, 1517

Inasmuch as the Church of Peter and Paul, the head of all the churches, was razed by the order of Pope Julius II of pious memory, we intend to construct a new edifice surpassing every other. Since the bones of Peter and Paul and innumerable saints on this spot are subject to constant desecration of rain and hail and since the entire resources of the Roman See are inadequate to finish this magnificent project, his Holiness has been prompted by God to stir up the faithful to this end by offering them these indulgences which are the peculiar treasury of Saint Peter.

Four graces are conceded in this indulgence. The first is the plenary remission of all sins and that the pains of purgatory are completely remitted. In order the more readily to induce contributions the preachers should propose a graduated scale. Kings, queens, and their sons, archbishops and bishops, and other great magnates should give at least twenty-five gold Rhenish florins. Abbots, prelates of cathedral churches, counts, barons and other great nobles and their wives should give ten (and so on). . . . Those who have no money may contribute by prayers and fasting, for the kingdom of heaven belongs no less to the poor than to the rich. The second grace is that once later in life and in the hour of death there is granted a plenary indulgence of even the gravest sins. The third is participation in all the benefits of the Church, that is, in the benefits accruing from all the prayers, fasts, pilgrimages and alms in the universal holy Church militant. The fourth is that a plenary remission of all sins is given to souls in purgatory. This the Pope grants by way of intercession. There is no need that those who contribute on behalf of these souls should themselves be contrite and confessed.

## II. Luther's *Ninety-five Theses*, October 31, 1517

(5)    The Pope does not wish and cannot remit any penalties save those which he has himself imposed.

(8)    The penitential canons are imposed only on the living.

(21)   Those indulgence preachers are wrong who say that the Pope can remit every penalty.

(27–28) They say, "As soon as the coin in the coffer rings the soul from purgatory springs." What "springs" out is the spirit of avarice.

(29)   Who knows whether the souls in purgatory wish to be released?

(30)   No one is certain as to his contrition.

(40)   Genuine contrition seeks and loves penalties.

(45)   Christians should be taught that he who neglects the needy in order to secure pardons earns not the indulgence of the Pope but the indignation of God.

(50)   If the Pope knew the exactions of the venal preachers, he would prefer that the Basilica of St. Peter should lie in ashes rather than

that it should be built out of the hide, flesh and bones of his sheep.

(56) The treasury of the Church from which the Pope grants indulgences (58) is not the merits of Christ and the saints because these always and without the Pope bring grace to the inward man and the cross, death and hell to the outward man.

(62) The true treasury of the Church is the most holy gospel of the glory and grace of God.

(66) The treasury of indulgences is a net for catching the riches of men.

(82) If the Pope is willing to release infinite souls from purgatory on account of filthy gain, for the trivial purpose of building a basilica, why does he not empty the place out of most holy love and the most just of all purposes, namely the supreme need of souls?

(86) Why doesn't he build the Basilica of St. Peter out of his own money seeing that he is richer than Croesus?

(94) Christians should be taught to seek Christ, their head, through mortification, death and hell.

## III. The Reply of Prierias

*The Pope commissioned the Dominican, Sylvester Prierias, to reply to Luther. In December, 1517 he brought out his* Dialogue Concerning the Power of the Pope.

The universal Church is essentially the gathering in divine worship of all those believing in Christ. The universal Church indeed is virtually the Roman Church, the head of all the churches and the Pope. The Roman Church consists representatively in the college of cardinals, virtually however in the Pope, who is the head of the Church, in a different sense however than Christ. As the universal Church is not able to err in determining faith and morals, so also a true council . . . is not able to err. . . . Likewise neither is the Roman church nor the Pope able to err when acting in his official capacity as Pope. . . . He who does not accept the doctrine of the Roman Church and of the Roman pontiff as the infallible rule of faith from which sacred Scripture draws its strength and authority is a heretic. The Roman Church is able to determine not only in word but also in deed concerning faith and morals. . . . Wherefore, just as he is a heretic who thinks incorrectly concerning the truth of the Scriptures, so also is he who thinks wrongly concerning the doctrine and the deeds of the Church in matters of faith and morals. The corollary is that whoever says that the Roman Church is not able to do in the matter of indulgences what actually she does is a heretic.

## IV. Luther's Two *Replies to Prierias,* 1518 and 1520

A. *The Reply of 1518*: The Roman Church, you say, is representatively the cardinals and virtually the Pope. I reply that the Pope can err and a council can err. . . . I would say that the Church is virtually Christ and representatively a council. If you are right that what the Pope does the Church does, I ask you what abomination will you not have to regard as deeds of the Church? Look at the ghastly bloodshed of Julius II, the abominable tyrannies of Boniface VIII, of whom it was said that he entered as a wolf, ran as a lion and died as a dog. You will not persuade us that such atrocious abuses are deeds of the most holy Church. We Germans suspect that you have written not so much to refute Martin as to adulate the Pope and the cardinals. If the Pope is the virtual Church and the cardinals the representative Church what do you make of a council? . . . I reject your view that Peter can loose what God has bound. . . . I marvel that you make no appeal to Scripture. For me Augustine is greater than St. Thomas and Paul is my foundation. I marvel that you call the Roman Church the rule of faith. I always supposed that faith is the rule of the Roman Church and of all the churches. . . . Our basilicas are of more use to us than St. Peter's which we cannot attend. Better that St. Peter's should never be built than that our parochial churches should be wrecked. We regret that all the revenues of the churches are sucked into the insatiable Basilica of St. Peter's. . . . You alleged that if the Pope would give me a bishopric endowed with a plenary indulgence for the repair of my church I would abound in sweet words. If I aspired to a bishopric I would not say what you hear with such impatience. Don't you think I know that the very boys in the streets sing about the way bishoprics are obtained at Rome? . . . I know we have an excellent Pope, Leo X [*The Lion*]. He is like Daniel at Babylon [*in the den of lions*] by his innocence in danger of his very life [*referring to a plot among the cardinals to assassinate the Pope*].

B. *The Second Reply*: If what you say is held and taught with the knowledge of the Pope and the cardinals, which I hope is not the case, then I say flatly that in these writings the very Anti-Christ sits in the temple of God and the Roman Curia is the synagogue of Satan. What shall I say? Prierias makes even an impious Pope into a god and derives the authority of Holy Scripture from that man however unworthy, whereas all agree that the authority of the Pope is derived from Christ. . . . And now this Satan fortifies Scripture through a man. What is Anti-Christ if such a Pope is not? . . . Weep, reader, that the glory of Rome is so far fallen that such heretical, blasphemous, diabolical and hellish poison is not only nurtured but propagated at Rome. If this is what Rome believes, blessed are the Greeks, the Bohemians and those separated from this Babylon. And if this is what the Pope and the cardinals teach, then I confess that I dissent from the Roman Church and reject it together with the Pope and the cardinals as the abomination standing in the holy place.

## V. The *Address to the Christian Nobility of the German Nation*, August, 1520

[*Luther begins by suggesting that a new Joshua is about to blow down the walls of the Jericho at Rome.*] The First wall is that the spiritual is above the civil power, the second is that only the Pope is able to interpret the Scripture, and the third is that no one can call a council except the Pope. . . . As for the first, all Christians are truly of the spiritual estate and there is no difference among them except as to their office. . . . Through baptism we are all ordained to the priesthood. . . . When a bishop ordains it is simply that one person is selected to exercise for the rest the power in which all share. To illustrate, if a little group of Christians were taken into exile where there was no ordained priest and if they were to elect one of their number, married or unmarried, they could confer on him authority to baptize, say mass, absolve, and preach, and he would be as true a priest as if ordained by all the bishops and popes. . . . And since the civil rulers have the same baptism as we, the same faith in the Gospel, we must regard them as priests and bishops. But although we are all priests, we are not to assume the office without the commission of the congregation, and if anyone is deposed, he is in the same status as he was before because a priest in a Christian church is nothing but an office-holder.

Since the civil power is ordained of God, it should not be impeded throughout Christendom in the exercise of its office though it apply to pope, bishop, priest, monk, or nun. . . . If a priest is killed the land is laid under an interdict [*an excommunication applying to an entire area*] and why not if a peasant is murdered? Whence arises such a difference among Christians, if not from the laws of men?

The second wall is even more flimsy that the papists claim to be the sole interpreters of the Holy Scriptures. . . . If that were so, what need would there be for the Holy Scriptures? Let us burn them and rely on the un-learned lords at Rome who have the Holy Spirit. . . . The clause in the creed would have to be altered "I believe in one Holy Christian Church" to read "I believe in the Pope at Rome," and thus reduce the Church to one single man. . . . If God through Balaam's ass spoke against the prophet, should He not be able to speak through a godly man against the Pope?

The third wall falls because the council referred to in the Book of Acts in the fifteenth chapter was called not by Peter but by all the apostles and elders. Consequently if necessity demands and the Pope is an offense to Christendom, then the first who can, should try as a true member of the whole body to bring together a truly free council which none can better do than the civil rulers because they too with us are fellow Christians, fellow priests, and fellow "spirituals."

We may now look at the matters which may properly be taken up in a council. . . . To begin with, it is shocking to see the head of Christendom, who boasts himself as the vicar of Christ and successor of Peter, living in such worldly pomp that no king or emperor can touch him. He has a three-layer crown whereas the highest king has but one. If that is like Christ and Peter, it is a new kind of likeness. [There follows an account of the extravagance of the cardinals.] The cardinals have sucked Italy dry and now turn to Germany. . . . I propose that the number of cardinals be reduced or that the Pope be forced to maintain them himself. . . . If the Pope's court were reduced, ninety-nine per cent, it would still be large enough to give decisions in matters of faith. Annates [a tax of one half of the first year's income of a newly appointed bishop] are levied ostensibly for crusades against the Turks which never come off. The money goes into a bottomless bag. When the Pope rides out he is accompanied by three or four thousand mule riders beyond any emperor or king. Christ and Peter had to go on foot in order that their vicar might the better swagger. . . . The overweening, lying, reservation [the reserving of appeals to Rome] of the popes has made Rome unspeakable. . . . The reign of Anti-Christ could not be worse.

Recommendations: Every prince, noble, and city should strictly forbid their subjects to pay annates to Rome. . . . No civil case should be appealed to Rome. . . . Ecclesiastical cases should be referred to the Primate of Germany. The Pope has no authority over the Emperor who should not yield to devilish arrogance and kiss the Pope's toe. Pilgrimages should be abolished. The money might much better be given to the poor. But if anybody wishes simply to see the world, let him go. Priests should be free to marry. There is many a worthy priest against whom there is nothing except that he has come to shame with a woman when both of them desire in their hearts to live faithfully in holy wedlock, if only they could do so in good conscience. All holy days should be given up and Sunday alone observed. . . . By what authority does the Pope canonize the saints? Let them canonize themselves. Public begging should be forbidden throughout Christendom. Let each town support its own poor. I will not pass judgment on the writings of John Hus [a Bohemian heretic executed in 1415] though so far I have found in them no errors. In any case heretics should be overcome with writings, not with fire. If fire were the way, the executioners would be the greatest doctors on earth. There would be no need to study, but he who could overcome another by force might burn him. The Pope should permit the Bohemians to choose for themselves an Archbishop of Prague.

# Luther's Revision of the Sacraments

## Roland Bainton

The Babylonian Captivity *which followed by one month the* Address to Nobility *was at once deemed the most radical of all Luther's utterances because it largely demolished the Church's sacramental system on which rested so much else. One may plausibly assume that the examiner of Luther at the Diet of Worms was giving him an opportunity to disclaim this work. First he was asked whether he had actually written all of the books which had appeared under his name. When he acknowledged them all he was asked whether he would defend all that he had said in them. If he had renounced what he had said on the sacraments the other points of his attack would have been open to discussion. This tract is translated in full in the* Works of Martin Luther *(A. J. Holman Co., Philadelphia, 1915), vol. II, pp. 170–293.* The Freedom of the Christian Man *is pp. 301–348.*

*Though Luther's attack on the sacraments was considered the most drastic he was popularly charged with demolishing also the Christian ethic by eliminating the motive of reward. In* The Freedom of the Christian Man *he rebuilt ethics on the basis of gratitude and devotion. Both of the works in this section are translated in Bertram Lee Woolf,* Reformation Writings of Martin Luther, *vol. I (London, 1952).*

## I. *The Babylonian Captivity,* September, 1520

To begin with, I must deny that there are seven sacraments. For the moment I would assume three: baptism, penance and the bread and all of these have been carried by the Roman Church into dire captivity.

**The Sacrament of the Bread.** *Communion in both kinds*: If the Church is able to withhold the wine from the laity, she might also withhold the bread and thus completely abnegate the institution of Christ. . . . The most important evidence to my mind is that Christ said, "This is my blood which is shed for you and for many for the remission of sins." Here you see most clearly that the blood is to be given to those for whose sins it has been shed. *Transubstantiation*: Years ago I was impressed by the statement of Cardinal Pierre D'Ailly that it would be much simpler and more probable to assume that real bread and real wine were on the altar and not mere accidents had not the Church ruled otherwise. When I came to see that the Church which so ruled was the Thomistic, that is the Aristotelian church, I became bolder because I saw that Thomistic opinions, even though approved by the Pope or a council, remained only opinions and not articles of faith, for what is asserted without the authority of Scripture or an approved revelation may be opined but need not be believed. . . . The Church believed correctly for more than twelve hundred years and during that time the holy fathers never once mentioned the preposterous word for a monstrous idea, transubstantiation, introduced only when the pseudo-philosophy of Aristotle ran riot in the Church. . . . Why should not Christ contain his body in the substance as well as in the accidents of the bread? Just as fire and iron, two substances, are so mingled when red hot that each is iron and fire. Let us not meddle too much with philosophy. If I cannot grasp how the bread is the body of Christ, I will subject my understanding to obedience to Christ and hold simply to his word. I believe firmly not only that the body of Christ is in the bread but that the bread is the body of Christ. . . . For the godhead to be incarnated in him, it was not necessary that his human nature be transubstantiated. . . . Likewise in the sacrament it is not necessary that bread and wine be transubstantiated in order to be the true body and the true blood. What we call the Mass is a promise of the forgiveness of sins made to us by God and confirmed by the death of His son. A faith holding faithfully to this promise is all that is needed in order to hold the Mass worthily. There follows unprompted from this state a most sweet welling of the heart, whereby the spirit of man is enlarged and waxes fat. He is drawn to Christ and becomes utterly a new man. Who would not weep sweetly and almost faint for joy in Christ if he really believed that this inestimable promise actually applied to him? . . . But our theologians have become immersed in infinite metaphysical quibbles.

*A Good Work*: The doctrines of impious men have converted the Mass into a good work. . . . It cannot possibly be a good work. There is nothing to be worked. It operates only by faith and faith is not a work but the lord and life of all works. The Mass is a divine promise which can profit none, apply to none, intercede for none, and be communicated to none unless he believes with his own faith. How can the promise of God which demands faith individually of everyone be accepted or applied by one on behalf of another? Am I able to give the promise of God to another if he does not believe? Can I believe for another? Can I make him believe? . . . This invincible truth must stand. Where there is a divine promise, there each must stand for himself, believe for himself and answer for himself. . . . But you say, would you undercut the very basis of so many churches and monasteries for they base their anniversaries, intercessions, etc., that is, their fat intake on the Mass? Precisely! That is what I call the Babylonian Captivity. . . . I readily concede that the prayers which those congregated for the Mass say on behalf of each other are good works in the sense of benefits . . . but does any priest when he sacrifices think that he is offering nothing more than prayers? . . . God alone gives the Mass to those men who accept it in faith, in faith alone, without works and without merits.

*A Sacrifice*: The Mass is held to be a sacrifice offered to God. . . . To this we must oppose the words and the example of Christ, for unless we hold the Mass to be a promise we shall lose the whole Gospel and our solace. A promise is simply accepted. A sacrifice has to be offered, and it is not possible at the same moment both to give and receive the Mass. The testament or promise of Christ is the only cure for the sad, afflicted, perturbed, confused and erring consciences. He who does not believe will never by any works or effort be able to appease his conscience. Faith alone brings peace.

*Baptism*: The first point in Baptism is the divine promise, "He who believes and is baptized shall be saved.". . . Unless one believes, Baptism is of no avail. . . . One must begin with the faith of the sacraments without any works whatsoever. . . . The efficacy of baptism resides not in him who confers it but in him who receives in faith and use. . . . Baptism signifies death and resurrection, that is full and complete justification. . . . Not that sin completely dies before the body of sin which we carry in this life is destroyed but as soon as we believe we begin to die to this world. . . . Sacramentally we are baptized only once, but in faith constantly because we must always die and always live. . . . Baptism must occupy us body and soul all our lives until we are clothed in the robe of immortality.

*Infant Baptism*: In view of the above some may object that infants should not be baptized because they cannot grasp the promise, cannot have faith, and therefore either faith is not required or else babies should not be baptized. I reply that they are sustained by the faith of the sponsors through the prayers of the faithful in the church. The child is changed, cleansed, and renewed through an infused faith.

*Vows*: One more point. I should like to abolish all vows completely, whether vows to become monks, to go on pilgrimages or anything else.

... We have vowed enough in our baptism and more than we can fulfill. ... We fill the world with priests, monks, and nuns and lock them up in perpetual vows. Some even say that to enter a religious order constitutes a new baptism. ... Not that I would go so far as to impede a free and private vow, but I absolutely disapprove of institutionalizing vows into a public way of life. ... There is no example in Scripture of a perpetual vow of poverty, chastity, and obedience. I would not persuade and would vehemently dissuade anyone from entering an order or becoming a priest unless he recognizes that what he does, however rugged, counts no more in the eyes of God than the work of a farmer in the field or a *Hausfrau* in the home, because the eyes of the Lord look only onto faith.

*Penance*: The trouble with this sacrament is that there is not a shred of it left. It has been divided into three parts: contrition, confession, and satisfaction. Contrition is held to precede faith and thereby it becomes a merit. ... A contrite heart is a great thing, but it is found only where there is a burning faith in God's promises and menaces. Yet contrition has been less subject to tyranny and exploitation than to impiety. ... But confession and satisfaction are a veritable minting house of wealth and power. There is no doubt that confession of sins is necessary and commended of God ... and secret confession, even though not commended in Scripture, is nevertheless highly useful and necessary, but I detest the prostitution of confession to gain. Secret sins and minor sins are reserved for absolution by the ministers of the Golden Calf, but I believe that anyone is absolved of secret sins who confesses, seeks pardon and amendment of life privately from any brother. The doctrine of satisfaction has been so perverted that people do not realize that satisfaction is simply amendment of life, not pilgrimages, flagellation, mortifications, etc. To the woman taken in adultery Christ said only, "Go and sin no more."

*Confirmation*: I marvel that anyone ever got it into his head to make a sacrament out of the laying on of hands. It is enough to regard confirmation as a rite of the Church or as a sacramental ceremony.

*Marriage*: There is no Scripture for regarding marriage as a sacrament because in every sacrament there is a promise and a sign, but marriage is not instituted of God as a sign of anything. Moreover, marriage was instituted from the beginning of the world and applied to non-Christians. Therefore it cannot be specifically a sacrament of the Church. With regard to *spiritual consanguinity*, what but the superstition of men invented this? Is not every baptized man a brother to every baptized woman and could

Paul not have married a girl in Corinth because he boasted that he had begotten all in Christ? . . . Between a priest and his wife there is an indissoluble marriage approved by the ordinance of God. . . . What earthly sense is there in the rule that no man can marry a widow of a deceased relative to the fourth degree? . . . As for divorce I so hate it that I would prefer bigamy.

*Ordination*: Of this sacrament the Church of Christ knows nothing. The strongest buttress adduced is that Christ said, "Do this in remembrance of me." Christ is claimed by these words to have ordained the disciples as priests, but who of the fathers ever interpreted his saying in this way? This forced exegesis has sown impossible enmity and divided the clergy and the laity as far as heaven and earth . . . to the point that those who are anointed, tonsured and vestured not only exalt themselves above lay Christians anointed by the Holy Spirit but treat them actually as dogs not fit to be counted with them in the Church. . . . If they were brought to admit that all who are baptized are equally priests, as truly we are, and that they have received their ministry solely through our consent, they would realize that they had no authority over us, save in so far as we confer it upon them. . . . We are all priests and those we call priests are ministers chosen by us to act in our name. The priesthood is nothing but a ministry and the sacrament of ordination is nothing other than a rite of choosing a preacher in the Church. . . . No one, however, is to assume this office without the consent of the community or the call of a superior.

*Extreme Unction*: If ever there were delirium, this is it.

One might include among the sacraments prayer, the word and the cross whereas strictly the term is used of promises with signs annexed and in this sense there are really but two, baptism and the bread. The sacrament of penance lacks the visible and divinely instituted sign, and as I said is only a return to baptism.

## II. On the Freedom of the Christian Man, November, 1520

The soul which with a firm faith cleaves to the promises of God is united with them, absorbed by them, penetrated, saturated, inebriated by their power. If the touch of Christ was healing, how much more does that most tender touch in the spirit, that absorption in the Word convey to the soul all the qualities of the Word so that it becomes trustworthy, peaceable, free, full of every good, a true child of God. From this we see very easily why faith can do so much and no good work is like unto it, for no good work comes from God's Word like faith. No good work can be within the soul, but the Word and faith reign there. What the Word is that the soul is, as iron becomes fire-red through union with the flame. Plainly then faith is enough for the Christian man. He has no need for works to be made just. Then is he free from the law.

But he is not therefore to be lazy or loose. Good works do not make a man good, but a good man does good works. A bishop is not a bishop because he consecrates a church, but he consecrates a church because he is a bishop. Unless a man is already a believer and a Christian, his works have no value at all. They are foolish, idle, damnable sins, because when good works are brought forward as ground for justification, they are no longer good. Understand that we do not reject good works, but praise them highly. The apostle Paul said, "Let this mind be in you which was also in Christ Jesus, who being on an equality with God emptied himself, taking the form of a servant, and becoming obedient unto death." Paul means that when Christ was fully in the form of God, abounding in all things, so that he had no need of any work or any suffering to be saved, he was not puffed up, did not arrogate to himself power, but rather in suffering, working, enduring, and dying made himself like other men, as if he needed all things and were not in the form of God. All this he did to serve us. When God in his sheer mercy and without any merit of mine has given me such unspeakable riches, shall I not then freely, joyously, wholeheartedly, unprompted do everything that I know will please him? I will give myself as a sort of Christ to my neighbor as Christ gave himself for me. . . .

I must even take to myself the sins of others as Christ took mine to himself. Thus we see that the Christian man lives not to himself but to Christ and his neighbor through love. By faith he rises above himself to God and from God goes below himself in love and remains always in God and in love.

# The Catholic Reformation

## Roland Bainton

*The two documents following illustrate some of the divergent strains within the Catholic reformatory movement. There were the liberals who desired to reform morals and attenuate or accommodate doctrine and to do all by persuasion, and there were the intransigents, who wished to eradicate laxity in conduct and heresy or even fuzziness of belief, by stringent measures. The first document outlines the moral reforms on which both parties were agreed. Space has precluded an excerpt from the liberal point of view. The writings of Erasmus, easily available in English, afford many examples. The founding of the Jesuits looked in the direction of a victory for the sterner party, because, although the Jesuits were dedicated to education and were lenient toward offenders, yet their utter obedience to their general and to the Pope did not encourage a spirit of free inquiry. The founding of the Inquisition marks the triumph of the tougher policy.*

## I. The Reforms Proposed by the Cardinals Addressed to Pope Paul III in 1538

Most blessed Father, we cannot express the gratitude which Christendom should feel toward God for having raised you up in these times as a shepherd to His flock, for the spirit of God has determined through you to restore the falling Church to her pristine sublimity. You have instructed us to declare, without regard for the feelings of yourself or anyone else, those abuses and grievous ailments from which the Church suffers and particularly the Roman Curia. The trouble is that your predecessors surrounded themselves with sychophants, dextrous in proving that whatever they liked was licit. From this Trojan horse issued such ills upon the Church that she is like not to recover. Her ill repute occasions derision among the infidels so that through us the name of Christ is blasphemed among the Gentiles. Since you, most holy Father and truly most holy, are so genuinely concerned to cure these ills, we are laying before you such remedies as our feeble powers can devise. We touch only upon that which affects the Church universal.

To begin with laws should be observed. Nothing is more subversive of laws than dispensations. Nor should the vicar of Christ in exercising the power of the keys have any eye to gain. One abuse is the ordination of priests, even mere lads, utterly unqualified reprobates. No one should be ordained save by a bishop who should have a teacher in his see for clerics in minor orders. Benefices should be conferred only on learned, upright men who will be in residence. An Italian should not be appointed to a post in Spain or Britain. A great abuse is the reservation of revenues designed for the indigent but consigned to the wealthy. The permutation of benefices for gain is simony. By no subterfuge should benefices be treated as legacies. The granting of expectations on benefices engenders the wish that somebody will die. Pluralities, especially in bishoprics, should be abolished and as for the combining of benefices, is not that an evasion of the law? The holding of bishoprics and sometimes several by cardinals is incompatible with their office, because they should assist Your Holiness in the governance of the Church universal, whereas a bishop should look after his flock. How is the Holy See to correct the abuses of others if there be so many in the chief members? Nothing is more important, blessed Father, than that bishops should reside in their sees. What more grievous sight could afflict a traveler throughout Christendom than to view so many neglected churches? Equally is it an abuse that the cardinals should reside in their provinces rather than here at Rome. By the blood of Christ we beseech Your Holiness not to suborn the authority of the bishops by suffering priests under discipline to escape through appeal. Confessors should be appointed not by friars but by bishops. A most pernicious abuse is the teaching of impiety by professors in the universities and especially in Italy. The *Colloquies* of Erasmus should not be used for the instruction of youth. Apostate monks, who have abandoned their habits, should not be given dispensations for money. Dispensations should not be given to those in holy orders to marry unless it be to retain an entire people in the faith, especially in these days when the Lutherans so insistently demand clerical marriage. Dispensations for marriage should not be given in the second degree and in the other degrees only for good cause and without money. Absolution should not be given for simony. There are those who having committed it, then buy absolution and retain the benefice purchased. Portable confessionals are not approved. Indulgences should not be allowed in a given territory more than once a year. Commutation of vows is not approved. Testaments are not to be altered unless some grave change has occurred in the fortunes of the family. Since Rome is the mother of the churches it is scandalous that the priests officiating in St. Peter's are ignorant and filthy. In this city prostitutes are conveyed like matrons by mules followed by cardinals and clerics. This shameful abuse must be ended. The cardinals should endeavor to compose feuds between Roman citizens. There are in this city hospitals and widows who should be your especial care.

Blessed Father, these are our modest proposals to be tempered by your goodness and wisdom. You have taken the name of Paul. May you imitate the love of Paul that you may make the Church a washed and spotless dove.

## II. The Founding of the Jesuits, 1539

*Ten young men including Ignatius Loyola and Francis Xavier, the best known in the group, applied to the Pope for recognition as a religious order. The Pope reviewed their worthy record and then gave his approval to the oath which Loyola had proposed, namely:*

Whoever wishes to be a warrior of God under the banner of the cross in our society, which bears the name of Jesus, to serve God alone and His vicar on earth, the Roman Pontiff, must after taking the solemn vow of perpetual chastity dedicate himself to propagate the faith through public preaching and ministry of the Word of God, spiritual exercises and works of piety and particularly the religious education of children, by affording spiritual consolation through the hearing of confessions. He must keep constantly God before his eyes, striving to attain the goal set him by God and to fulfill those rules which are in a sense a way to God. Lest any behave with excessive zeal let each member place himself entirely under the direction of the general or prelates chosen by us. This general shall have authority to establish a constitution in conclave where the decision of the majority shall prevail. In major matters a majority of the entire membership must be present; in minor affairs those who happen to be at hand. Let every member recognize that not only when he makes his profession, but throughout his life, he is subject to the present Pope and to his successors. We are bound beyond the ordinary by a particular vow in this regard. If then the present Pope or his successors should send us for the improvement of souls or the propagation of the faith to the Turks or other infidels even in India or to heretics, schismatics or some of the faithful, we are to obey without evasion or excuse. Wherefore, those who would join us should consider long before taking this load upon their shoulders and should well count the cost whether they have sufficient spiritual wealth to build the tower. In everything touching the rule, let obedience be given to the general. He in turn is always to be mindful of the goodness, gentleness, and love of Christ. All should be concerned for the instruction of youth in Christian doctrine and the Ten Commandments. Since we have discovered a life of poverty to be more conducive to happiness, purity and edification, we vow ourselves to perpetual poverty not only singly but as an order in the sense that there is to be no legal holding but rather contentment with gifts covering necessities, except that in schools it is permissible to have whatever is necessary for students.

# A Discourse on Witchcraft

## Cotton Mather

*In the winter of 1688–1689, after Goodwife Glover of Boston was hanged for bewitching John Goodwin's children, Cotton Mather preached a sermon on witchcraft, describing the crime and discussing the problems it forced on the people. This sermon presents, as well as any single work could present, the orthodox Puritan's attitude toward witchcraft in the last decade of the seventeenth century. Cotton published this sermon in his* Memorable Providences, Relating to Witchcrafts and Possessions, *Boston, 1689.*

## I. Sam. XV. 23.
## Rebellion is as the Sin of Witchcraft.

### Prop. I.

Such an Hellish thing there is as *Witchcraft* in the World. There are Two things which will be desired for the advantage of this Assertion. It should *first* be showed,

WHAT *Witchcraft* is.

My Hearers will not expect from me an *accurate* definition of the *vile Thing;* since the Grace of God has given me the Happiness to speak without *Experience* of it. But from Accounts both by *Reading* and *Hearing* I have learn'd to describe it so.

WITCHCRAFT is the doing of *strange* (and for the most part *ill*) things by the help of *evil Spirits, covenanting* with (and usually *Representing* of) the woeful Children of Men.

This is the *Diabolical Art* that *Witches* are notorious for.

First, *Witches* are the Doers of *strange* Things. They cannot indeed perform any proper *Miracles;* those are things to be done only by the *Favorites* and *Ambassadors* of the LORD. But *Wonders* are often produced by them, though chiefly such Wonders as the Apostle calls in 2 *Thes.* 2.9. *Lying Wonders.* There are *wonderful Storms* in the *great* World, and *wonderful Wounds* in the *little* World, often effected by these *evil Causes.* They do

272

things which transcend the ordinary *course* of Nature, and which puzzle the ordinary *Sense* of Mankind. Some *strange* things are done by them in a way of *Real Production*. They do really *Torment*, they do really *Afflict* those that their Spite shall extend unto. Other *strange* things are done by them in a way of *Crafty Illusion*. They do craftily make of the *Air*, the *Figures* and *Colors* of things that never can be truly created by them. All men might *see*, but, I believe, no man could *feel* some of the Things which the *Magicians* of *Egypt*, exhibited of old.

*Secondly,* They are not only *strange* things, but *ill* things, that *Witches* are the Doers of. In this regard also they are not the Authors of *Miracles*: those are things *commonly* done for the *good* of Man, *always* done for the *praise* of GOD. But of these *Hell-hounds* it may in a special manner be said, as in *Psal. 52. 3. Thou lovest evil more than good.* For the most part they labor to rob *Man* of his *Ease* or his *Wealth*; they labor to wrong *God* of his *Glory*. There is mention of Creatures that they call *White Witches*, which do only *Good-Turns* for their Neighbors. I suspect that there are none of that sort; but rather think, *There is none that doeth good no, not one.* If they *do good,* it is only that they *may do hurt.*

*Thirdly,* It is by virtue of *evil Spirits* that *Witches* do what they do. We read in *Ephes. 22.* about the *Prince of the power of the Air.* There is confined unto the *Atmosphere* of our *Air* a vast *Power,* or *Army* of *Evil Spirits,* under the Government of a Prince who employs them in a continual Opposition to the Designs of GOD: The Name of that *Leviathan* who is the *Grand Seignior of Hell,* we find in the Scripture to be *Beelzebub.* Under the Command of that mighty Tyrant, there are vast *Legions* and *Myriads* of *Devils,* whose *businesses* and *accomplishments* are not all the same. Every one has his *Post,* and his *Work;* and they are all glad of an opportunity to be *mischievous* in the World. These are they by whom *Witches* do exert their devilish and malignant rage upon their *Neighbors:* And especially Two Acts concur hereunto. The *First* is, Their *Covenanting* with the *Witches.* There is a most hellish *League* made between them, with various *Rites* and *Ceremonies.* The *Witches* promise to serve the *Devils,* and the *Devils* promise to *help* the Witches; *how?* It is not convenient to be related. The *Second* is, Their *Representing* of the Witches. And hereby indeed these are drawn into *Snares* and *Cords* of Death. The *Devils,* when they go upon the Errands of the *Witches,* do bear their Names; and hence do *Harms* too come to be carried from the *Devils* to the *Witches.* We need not suppose such a wild thing as the *Transforming* of those Wretches into *Brutes* or *Birds,* as we too often do.

It should next be proved THAT Witchcraft *is*.

The *Being* of such a thing is denied by many that place a *great part* of their *small wit* in deriding the Stories that are told of it. Their chief Argument is, that they never *saw* any Witches, therefore there are *none*. Just as if you or I should say, we never met with any *Robbers* on the Road, therefore there was never any *Padding* there.

Indeed the *Devils* are loath to have true Notions of *Witches* entertained with us. I have beheld them to put out the Eyes of an Enchanted Child, when a Book that proves, *There is Witchcraft*, was laid before her. But there are especially two Demonstrations that Evince the Being of that Infernal mysterious thing.

First, We have the Testimony of *Scripture* for it. We find *Witchcrafts* often mentioned, sometimes by way of *Assertion*, sometimes by way of *Allusion*, in the Oracles of God. Besides that, We have there the History of divers *Witches* in these infallible and inspired Writings. Particularly, the Instance of the *Witch* at *Endor*, in I *Sam.* 28. 7. is so plain and full that *Witchcraft* itself is not a more amazing thing than any *Dispute* about the Being of it, after this. The Advocates of *Witches* must use more *Tricks* to make Nonsense of the *Bible*, than ever the *Witch* of *Endor* used in her Magical Incantations, if they would Evade the Force of that Famous History. They that will believe no *Witches*, do imagine that *Jugglers* only are meant by them whom the Sacred Writ calleth so. But what do they think of that Law in *Exod.* 22. 18. *Thou shalt not suffer a Witch to live*? Methinks 'tis a little too hard to punish every silly *Juggler* with so great severity.

*Secondly*, We have the *Testimony of Experience* for it. What will those *Incredulous*, who must be the only *Ingenious* Men say to this? Many *Witches* have like those in *Acts* 19. 18. *Confessed and showed their Deeds*. We see these things done, that it is impossible any *Disease* or any *Deceit* should procure. We see some hideous *Wretches* in hideous *Horrors* confessing, *That they did the Mischiefs*. This Confession is often made by them that are owners of as much Reason as the people that laugh at all *Conceit* of *Witchcraft*: The Exactest Scrutiny of Skillful Physicians cannot find any distraction in their minds. This *Confession* is often made by them that are apart one from another, and yet they *agree* in all the Circumstances of it. This *Confession* is often made by them that at the same time will produce the *Engines* and *Ensigns* of their *Hellish Trade*, and give the standers-by an *Ocular Conviction* of what they do, and how. There can be no Judgment left of any *Human Affairs*, if such *Confessions* must be Ridiculed: all the *Murders*, yea, and all the *Bargains* in the World must be mere *Imaginations* if such *Confessions* are of no Account.

## *Prop. II.*

WITCHCRAFT is a most Monstrous and Horrid *Evil*. Indeed there is a vast Heap of Bloody Roaring Impieties contained in the *Bowels* of it. *Witchcraft*, is a Renouncing of *God*, and Advancing of a filthy *Devil* into the Throne of the Most High; 'tis the most nefandous *High-Treason* against the MAJESTY on High. *Witchcraft*, is a Renouncing of *Christ*, and preferring the Communion of a loathesome lying *Devil* before all the Salvation of the Lord Redeemer; 'tis a Trampling under foot that *Blood* which is more precious than *Hills* of *Silver*, or whole *Mountains* of *Gold*. There is in *Witchcraft*, a most explicit *Renouncing* of all that is *Holy*, and *Just* and *Good*. The *Law* given by *God*, the *Prayer* taught by *Christ*, the *Creed* left by the *Apostles*, is become *Abominable* where *Witchcraft* is Embraced: The very Reciting of those blessed things is commonly burdensome where *Witchcraft* is. All the *sure Mercies* of the *New Covenant*, and all the *just Duties* of it, are utterly abdicated by that *cursed Covenant* which *Witchcraft* is Constituted with. *Witchcraft* is a Siding with *Hell* against *Heaven* and *Earth*; and therefore a *Witch* is not to be endured in either of them. 'Tis a *Capital* Crime; and it is to be prosecuted as a piece of *Devilism* that would not only deprive *God* and *Christ* of all His Honor, but also plunder Man of all his Comfort. *Witchcraft*, it's an impotent, but an impudent *Essay* to make an *Hell* of the Universe, and to allow Nothing but a *Tophet* in the World. *Witchcraft—What* shall I say of it! It is the furthest Effort of our *Original Sin*; and all that can make any Practice or Persons odious, is here in the *Exalt[at]ion* of it.

It was the speech of *Jehu* to *Joram*, in 2 *King*. 9. 22. *What peace, so long as the* Witchcrafts *of thy Mother are so many?* Truly, as *Witchcraft* would break the *Peace* of all Mankind, so 'tis a thing that should enjoy no *Peace* among the Children of *Adam*. Nothing too *vile* can be said of, nothing too hard can be done to such an horrible Iniquity as *Witchcraft* is.

# *from* The Birthmark

## *Nathaniel Hawthorne*

In the latter part of the last century there lived a man of science, an eminent proficient in every branch of natural philosophy, who not long
before our story opens had made experience of a spiritual affinity more
attractive than any chemical one. He had left his laboratory to the care of
an assistant, cleared his fine countenance from the furnace smoke,
washed the stain of acids from his fingers, and persuaded a beautiful
woman to become his wife. In those days, when the comparatively recent
discovery of electricity, and other kindred mysteries of Nature seemed to
open paths into the region of miracle, it was not unusual for the love of
science to rival the love of woman in its depth and absorbing energy. The
higher intellect, the imagination, the spirit, and even the heart might all
find their congenial aliment in pursuits, which, as some, of their ardent
votaries believed, would ascend from one step of powerful intelligence to
another, until the philosopher should lay his hand on the secret of creative force and perhaps make new worlds for himself. We know not
whether Aylmer possessed this degree of faith in man's ultimate control
over Nature. He had devoted himself, however, too unreservedly to scientific studies ever to be weaned from them by any second passion. His
love for his young wife might prove the stronger of the two; but it could
only be by intertwining itself with his love of science and uniting the
strength of the latter to his own.

Such a union accordingly took place, and was attended with truly
remarkable consequences and a deeply impressive moral. One day, very
soon after their marriage, Aylmer sat gazing at his wife with a trouble in
his countenance that grew stronger until he spoke.

"Georgiana," said he, "has it never occurred to you that the mark upon
your cheek might be removed?"

"No, indeed," said she, smiling; but, perceiving the seriousness of his
manner, she blushed deeply. "To tell you the truth, it has been so often
called a charm that I was simple enough to imagine it might be so."

"Ah, upon another face perhaps it might," replied her husband; "but
never on yours. No, dearest Georgiana, you came so nearly perfect from

the hand of Nature that this slightest possible defect, which we hesitate whether to term a defect or a beauty, shocks me, as being the visible mark of earthly imperfection."

"Shocks you, my husband!" cried Georgiana, deeply hurt; at first reddening with momentary anger, but then bursting into tears. "Then why did you take me from my mother's side? You cannot love what shocks you!"

# *from* The Western Intellectual Tradition: From Leonardo to Hegel

*Jacob Bronowski and Bruce Mazlish*

## Calvin

### I

Calvin, born in 1509, was of a different generation from Luther. He was also of a very different character. Luther, the son of a miner, had been prepared for the law, but became a monk after a deep, personal experience during a thunderstorm. Calvin, on the other hand, came from petty-bourgeois townspeople, was destined for the church, and left theology for the law.[1] Unlike Luther, there was nothing mystical about Calvin; indeed, his character tended to the judicial and the narrow.

His early education was acquired in a family of local gentry near Paris. The family's most honored member was a bishop, and here Calvin imbibed good manners and a taste for the humanities. From 1523 to 1528, he studied theology at the University of Paris. In the latter year, he left to study law at Orléans, and then Greek at Bourges. His becoming a lawyer was in tune with the lay rather than clerical nature of the Calvinist reform. Luther drew most of his early reformers from the ranks of the Augustinian and Franciscan monks, but Calvin's followers seem to have come mainly from the humanists.

Calvin himself received his initial impetus from the works of the humanists, and his first book, a commentary on Seneca's *De Clementia* (1532), relates to the classical Renaissance rather than to the Lutheran Reformation. From this study of Roman Stoicism may well have come Calvin's emphasis on stern ethical qualities.

By 1533, however, the influence upon Calvin of Erasmus' New Testament and certain writings of Luther can be perceived. Calvin had been caught up in the religious question. On All Saints' Day of that year his friend, Nicholas Cop, as new rector of the University of Paris, delivered an address clearly defending the doctrine of justification by faith; the address may have been largely written by Calvin. Both Cop and Calvin had to flee Paris.

Renouncing Catholicism, Calvin settled after a while at Basel and wrote the first sketch of his *Institutes of the Christian Religion*, in 1536. The *Institutes* is a remarkable work for a man of 26; at one blow it placed the young Calvin at the head of the reforming forces. Luther's writings had been passionate outbursts, expressive of his inner feelings but giving little in the way of definite, codified, external dogma. Calvin made up for this lack; in six chapters, slowly to grow by the last edition of 1559–1560 to eighty chapters, he set forth a tightly reasoned, logically arranged system of morals, polity, and dogma.[2]

The core of Calvin's dogma was that man was a helpless being before an omnipotent God. Calvin pushed Luther's arguments against Free Will to their absolute, logical conclusion, and emphasized that man could do nothing to alter his fate: he was predestined either for hell or to be saved. If he were saved, i.e., one of the "Elect," he would probably show this by his exemplary behavior on earth. This was a sign of God's favor; but it was only a sign, not a guarantee.

Instead of Luther's discursive outpourings on these matters, Calvin offered fixed laws. By providing a dogmatic creed, he gave to the Swiss and French reformers of his time a rallying point. Thus, it was only natural that Guillaume Farel, who was attempting to convert Geneva to the reformed doctrine, should prevail upon Calvin to turn his hand to the work there.

## II

Geneva was ripe for Calvin's experiment. It had just revolted against its bishop, who had ruled for the Duke of Savoy over the city; nevertheless, it had a tradition of being an ecclesiastical state. This fitted in perfectly with Calvin's belief that the state was subordinate to the church and that obedience to God came before that to the state.

At first, Calvin's power in Geneva was a moral power. Indeed, he was appointed on his arrival in Geneva a "Reader in Holy Scriptures," and never held a post higher than pastor. The Genevans, however, were proud to have as a minister the author of the *Institutes* and the leader of the Reformed Church. They groaned under his harsh standard (and at one point they turned him out of the city for about three years) but felt, like Americans under Prohibition, that it was good for them and their children.

When Calvin returned to Geneva, he did so only on the condition that the citizens accept his terms. These terms he embodied in the *Ordonnances ecclésiastiques* and the *Ordonnances sur le régime du peuple*, under which the people of Geneva henceforth lived; those who objected to Calvin's terms simply left, or were jailed or executed. This time, Calvin's power was not only moral but legal and political.

The Ordinances show Calvin's prowess as a legislator. He set up two main organs of government: the Ministry and the Consistory. The Ministry established, for the first time, instead of chance recruits, a disciplined army of Protestant preachers who adhered to a definite program and way of life. Candidates for the Calvinist ministry had to run the gauntlet of examination by the existing ministers (Calvin as one, of course) and approval by the city council. Then they were made to preach before the people, without whose approval they could not be called to a post. The latter condition, at least in theory (it became, in practice, a mere formality), introduced a democratic leavening into the theocratic government of Geneva.

This Ministry handled religious doctrine; questions of morality were dealt with by the Consistory, which consisted of six ministers and twelve elected elders. The Consistory examined charges and passed sentences and, eventually, even had the power to excommunicate. A decision by the Consistory was enforced by the civil officials. Thus questions of morality were turned into questions of law, and made subject to the power of the state.

Between the Consistory and the Ministry, which together met every three months in a Synod to review discipline, Calvin had at his disposal sufficient tools with which to create a "new man" as well as a Calvinist Church. Indeed, as A. M. Fairbairn phrases it, the Church was "not simply an institution for the worship of God, but an agency for the making of men fit to worship Him."[3] It is this idea of a civic church power creating its own citizens that was so strongly to attract and influence Rousseau later on.

The regimen Calvin imposed on Geneva was in many ways similar to that in More's *Utopia*—a regimen which included getting up very early, working very hard, and being always concerned with good morals and good reading. The virtues of thrift and abstinence were omnipresent.

Behind them, we must remember, stands what we have described earlier: the protest against the luxury of the church; the failure of the papal court to be close to the simple needs of the members of the church; and, above all, the feeling that, at bottom, religion is a matter of personal conviction and conscience. The result of these feelings is most familiar to us in the type of character produced by Calvin's regimen: the Puritan.

Calvin enforced his regimen with great vigor and, frequently, with outright ferocity.[4] One of his "citizens" was beheaded for writing a set of what Calvin called obscene verses. A card player was pilloried, and an adulterer whipped through the streets and then banished.

Among these, the persecution of Servetus was the gravest incident of Calvin's rule in Geneva. Servetus, who was a doctor and scientist living in France, wrote a book attacking the orthodox doctrine of the Trinity. Thereupon, he and Calvin became engaged, by letter, in a violent theological polemic. Calvin's anger mounted to the point where, himself a heretic from the Catholic Church, he secretly accused Servetus of heresy to the Catholic Inquisition in France. Servetus was forced to flee; and, as bad luck would have it, his escape route took him through Geneva. Although his book had been neither written nor printed at Geneva, Calvin had Servetus seized and burned at the stake.[5]

Calvin's violent action in burning an early adherent of more or less Unitarian doctrines, who was also a scientist, suggests an important note about the Reformation. Both Luther and Calvin opposed not only the new art but the developing science of their time as well. In many ways, they were more fiercely antiscientific in their attitude than was the Church of Rome, and it has often been pointed out that Galileo, although he was badly treated by the Inquisition in Rome, would have suffered more severely if he had been unfortunate enough to live in the Geneva of Calvin's regime. Later, the twists and turns of history were to make the Puritans stanch supporters of the new science; but none of this was intended by Calvin's doctrine and discipline.

## III

In all essentials, Calvin's state was a theocratic dictatorship.[6] Yet, as in the case of Luther, Calvin's movement, as it worked itself out in history, led to a greater independence of the individual. It contributed, intentionally and unintentionally, to personal, economic, and political individualism.

For one thing, Calvin realized that an enlightened, trained ministry which controlled its flock by preaching instead of by sacraments implied an enlightened citizenry; and the Calvinist stress on Bible reading meant a literate populace. Thus, Calvin set up a system of education which had more to offer to the ordinary person than had earlier systems. In his schools all children had equal educational opportunities, regardless of birth or wealth.

Further, Calvin accepted (although he did not always approve of) the New Economics. He assumed the existence of a capitalist economic system for society and set up his ethics on that basis. According to R. H. Tawney, Calvin openly accepted the main features of a "commercial" civilization and "broke with the tradition which, regarding a preoccupation with economic interests 'beyond what is necessary for subsistence' as reprehensible, had stigmatized the middleman as a parasite and the usurer as a thief."[7] The self-indulgent and ostentatious use of riches was abhorrent to Calvin; but he was not opposed to the accumulation of riches. The excessive exaction of usury from the poor was roundly condemned by Calvin; but he accepted the fact that the merchant ought to pay interest on the borrowed capital which made his profits possible. It should be little surprise, therefore, to discover that Calvinism appealed greatly to the rising bourgeoisie and, as Arnold Toynbee asserts, braced it for the coming struggle for power in the same way that Marxism later served the proletariat.

The movement which Calvin had set going also contributed to the development of political individualism; but this was no part of Calvin's conscious intention. It came about accidentally, as a result of particular, historical pressures, and not in Geneva which the Calvinists dominated but in countries like France and England where they were a minority.

In Geneva, Calvin rejected both religious and political individualism, i.e., the freedom of the individual to make his own choice in these matters. Geneva was a Calvinist theocracy, and no deviation was tolerated. It was in this spirit that Calvin, at his university, trained men, such as John Knox and the English reformers, who returned to their own countries and tried to introduce the Calvinist reform.[8]

However, in their own countries—at least in France and England—these reformers were for long in a minority. They could not impose their will on others; hence, they were, initially, in the position of having to ask religious toleration for themselves. As it became dear that religious toleration was dependent on the disposition of political power, the Calvinists sought to achieve political power. Once again, their minority position frequently forced them onto the side of tolerance. The Calvinists became "anti-absolutists," and, occasionally, vaguely akin to democrats.

Thus, by historical accident more than by doctrinal tendency (although this did exist), Calvinism became related to "free" government and associated not only with economic but with political individualism. We can see this clearly if we study the French Huguenots.

## Notes

1  The monumental work on Calvin's life is Emile Doumergue, *Jean Calvin, les hommes et les choses de son temps* (Lausanne, 1899–1927), 7 vols. J'ean-Daniel Benôit, *Jean Calvin: La Vie, l'homme, la pensee* (Neuilly, 1933), presents what he calls "the quintessence of the seven big volumes of my old master, dear Emile Doumergue," in 275 pages. James MacKinnon, *Calvin and the Reformation* (London, 1936), as the author says, "is not a biography, but primarily a critical survey of the Reformer's work and influence, into which the biographical element into enters as far as it is relevant." In English, there is also R. N. C. Hunt, *Calvin* (London, 1933). John T. McNeill, "Thirty Years of Calvin Study," *Church History* (Sept., 1948), is a basic and exhaustive bibliographical article. See, too, Roland H. Bainton, *Bibliography of the Continental Reformation; Materials Available in English* (Chicago, 1935). For a good treatment of Calvin by a Catholic, see Pierre Imbart de la Tour's work, which forms Vol. IV of that author's *Les Origines de la Réforme* with the title, *Jean Calvin: L'Institution chrétienne* (Paris, 1935). In his *Thought and Expression in the Sixteenth Century*, 2 vols. (New York, 1920), Vol. I, Chap. 17, Henry Osborn Taylor has 35 vivid pages on the thought, style, and personality of Calvin. André Fauvé-Dorsaz, *Calvin et Loyola: Deux réformes* (Paris, 1951), is a very interesting work of comparative psychology and theology.

2  John T. McNeill has edited Calvin's *Institutes of the Christian Religion* for the Library of Christian Classics. In this same Library is Calvin's *Theological Treatises*, tr. with introduction and notes by the Rev. J. K. S. Reid (Philadelphia, 1954), which presents aspects of Calvin's work as a teacher, administrator, and controversialist as well as theologian which might not be found in the *Institutes*; of especial interest is "The Genevan Confession of 1536," one of the best short statements of Calvinist beliefs. *Calvin: Textes choisis*, par Charles Gagnebin, préface de Karl Barth (Paris, 1948), offers a brief view of Calvin's

writings in the original (mainly from his sermons and the *Institutes*) and permits us to see why his influence on French language and literature is considered to have been so strong.

3    *Cambridge Modern History*, Vol. II, p. 364.

4    Blame for these incidents is hardly mitigated by the fact that the citizens had the choice of accepting the Confession of Faith or departing, and that only those who elected to remain were expected to conform. Nor is it softened by the fact that this rigor was a reaction against the relaxed moral standards of the Renaissance Church of Rome.

5    This gave rise to a prolonged controversy about religious tolerance in which Calvin's defense of his action was challenged by Sébastien Castellion in 1554, and redefined by Calvin's disciple Théodore Beza. It might be added that Castellion's plea for freedom of religious opinion from persecution strongly influenced the development of Arminianism in Holland, whence the notion of tolerance spread to England. Cf. J. W. Allen, *Political Thought in the Sixteenth Century* (London, 1928). An interesting but somewhat novelized, emotional, and extremely anti-Calvin account of the burning of Servetus and of the resultant controversy between Calvin and Castellion is Stefan Zweig, *The Right to Heresy: Castellio Against Calvin*, tr. by Eden and Cedar Paul (New York, 1936).

6    R. N. Carew Hunt, "Calvin's Theory of Church and State," *The Church Quarterly Review* (April, 1929), p. 71, denies this when he writes, "Did Calvin then establish a theocracy at Geneva? If by a theocracy we mean clerical domination he certainly did not." However, he finally admits, "But in strict definition Calvin not only aimed at a theocracy but by the end of his life he had come very near to creating one."

7    Tawney, op. cit., p. 93. However, André-E. Sayous. who has studied the question of capitalism in Calvin's Geneva, in "Calvinisme et capitalisme: L'Expérience génevoise," *Annales d'histoire economiques et sociale*, Vol. VII (1935), pp. 225–244, finds that the Calvinist discipline so restricted capitalism as to keep it in a primitive form.

A fascinating debate has raged in recent times over the exact relationship of the reformers and the Reformation to the development of our modern economic system. The starting point is Max Weber's *The Protestant Ethic and the Spirit of Capitalism*, which, although first published in 1904 and now much outdated, opened up a whole new avenue of inquiry for many historians. Weber's thesis is that the material conditions for capitalism were present at many times in the past and in many places. However, it only came into existence in the West, in modern times, because "of the development of the spirit of capitalism." What Weber calls the "rationalistic economic ethic" was prepared by Luther's notion of the "calling" (which might very well be commercial) and by the Calvinist-Puritan idea of "worldly asceticism."

The Weber thesis was developed and partially modified by R. H. Tawney, who stressed the Calvinist rather than Lutheran teachings as being more sympathetic to capitalism and claimed, indeed, that the real acceptance and glorification of the New Economics was the work of seventeenth-century Puritanism. In Tawney's view, "To think of the abdication of religion from its theoretical primacy over economic activity and social institutions as synchronizing with the revolt from Rome is to antedate a movement which was not finally accomplished for another century and a half" (Tawney, op. cit., p. 77). According to Tawney's analysis, other religions or sects might gradually and grudgingly make their agreement with the mundane necessities of the emerging economic world (the Jesuits, for example, tried to adapt Catholicism to the New Economics). Puritanism alone clasped that world to its breast.

The Weber-Tawney thesis, as it has come to be called, has been attacked and supported from many sides. A good account of the debate is given 1 in the preface to the 1937 edition of Tawney's own book, *Religion and the Rise of Capitalism*, and n. 1 on p. 237 gives a good bibliography. We cite one attack on the Weber-Tawney thesis as a mere sample: Weber had emphasized the "spirit of capitalism" molding the material circumstances. H. M. Robertson, in his *Aspects of the Rise of Economic Individualism* (Cambridge, 1935), denounced Weber's "sociological method" and claimed that the opposite was true. Robertson insisted that the rising capitalism changed the religious ethic. He claimed that the "spirit of capitalism rose not from religious impulses but from the "material conditions of civilization." Similarly, in the preface to Robertson's book, the economic historian J. H. Clapham asserts that "We see . . . the Puritan spirit not begetting capitalism but coming to terms with it."

What is our view in this lively controversy? Although it has become fashionable today in some academic circles to decry the Weber-Tawney thesis as either naive or malicious, our opinion is that this is to miss the point of Weber's and Tawney's work and to overlook the limitations they themselves imposed on the application of their theories. As Weber pointed out, his own work was exploratory; he did not wish "to substitute for a one-sided 'materialistic' an equally one-sided 'spiritual' interpretation of civilization and history."

Our position is balanced in the same way. We believe that what men think and feel is of the utmost importance; but thoughts and feelings must always be related to the circumstances surrounding them. Thus, changes in a religious ethos are complementary to and go hand in hand with developments in other areas of men's lives. Cause and effect in such matters are interwoven and hard to distinguish, and the specific nature of the religious-economic link in the seventeenth century is a subject for empirical investigation.

But that some such connection existed seems beyond rational doubt. We find support for this in the fact that seventeenth-century thinkers—contemporaries of the twin developments of the reformed religious groups and of capitalism—linked the two movements closely. As Sir William Petty remarked, "Trade is most vigorously carried on, in every State and Government, by the Heterodox part of the same." By historical circumstances, the "Heterodox" in seventeenth-century England, for example, were generally Puritans; it was their heterodoxy, in our view, rather than specific Calvinist doctrine which linked them to the new economic activity. (In the same way, Parsees in India or Jews in various countries have played an economic role out of proportion to their members) Weber and Tawney perhaps overemphasized the Calvinist doctrinal affiliation with capitalism; but at least they were on the right track. We prefer to emphasize the sense of isolation and of mission which inspires a group, as being a key value of heterodox. (The issue is complex, however; heterodoxy, almost by definition, closes off certain positions and employments but opens others; in some cases, the openings might be military rather than economic. Also, the past traditions and culture of the heterodox must be taken into account: Irish Catholics in nineteenth-century New England were heterodox; but they went into the police force rather than into business. To go further into this intriguing subject, however, would require a book in itself; we must rest content here with a mere glance at the subject.) It is also interesting to note that a significant by-product of the link between heterodoxy and economic development was the growth of tolerance. Sir William Petty went so far as to suggest that, from the economic point of view, schismatics had a positive value. In the seventeenth century, it seemed obvious that persecution was incompatible with prosperity, since it was the nonconformists who were in the forefront of economic progress. One result of this belief, in western and central Europe, was greater toleration for the Jews; especially was this a result of the Dutch example. See further Eli Heckscher, *Mercantilism*, tr. by Mendel Schapiro, 2 vols. (London, 1935), Vol. II, pp. 304–305. See, too, G. P. Gooch, *Political Thought in England from Bacon to Halifax* (Oxford, 1950), pp. 174–177, for the poet Andrew Marvell's defense of toleration as an economic measure. Emphasis on the commercial arguments for toleration may also be found in the thought of William Penn. This economic motivation for religious tolerance is overlooked by some historians, who assume that tolerance emerged largely from the inconclusive wars of religion, or was a result of the triumph of altruism and humanitarianism in the eighteenth century.

8   Lutheranism had been too tied to German institutions (for example, the territorial princedoms) and nationalism to appeal fully, for example, to Frenchmen or Englishmen. Part of Calvin's accomplishment was to fashion a reformed theology which suited other than German conditions.

# *from* The Spiritual Exercises

## *Ignatius of Loyola*

**IHS**

**Introductory Explanations, to Gain Some Understanding of the Spiritual Exercises Which Follow, And to Aid Both the One Who Gives Them And the One Who Receives Them.**

*The First Explanation.* By the term Spiritual Exercises we mean every method of examination of conscience, meditation, contemplation, vocal or mental prayer, and other spiritual activities, such as will be mentioned later. For, just as taking a walk, traveling on foot, and running are physical exercises, so is the name of spiritual exercises given to any means of preparing and disposing our soul to rid itself of all its disordered affections and then, after their removal, of seeking and finding God's will in the ordering of our life for the salvation of our soul.

*The Second.* The person who gives to another the method and procedure for meditating or contemplating should accurately narrate the history contained in the contemplation or meditation, going over the points with only a brief or summary explanation. For in this way the person who is contemplating, by taking this history as the authentic foundation, and by going over it and reasoning about it for oneself, can thus discover something that will bring better understanding or a more personalized concept of the history—either through one's own reasoning or to the extent that the understanding is enlightened by God's grace. This brings more spiritual relish and spiritual fruit than if the one giving the Exercises had lengthily explained and amplified the meaning of the history. For, what fills and satisfies the soul consists, not in knowing much, but in our understanding the realities profoundly and in savoring them interiorly.

*The Third.* In all the following Spiritual Exercises we use the acts of the intellect in reasoning and of the will in eliciting acts of the affections. In regard to the affective acts which spring from the will we should note that when we are conversing with God our Lord or his saints vocally or mentally, greater reverence is demanded of us than when we are using the intellect to understand.

*The Fourth.* Four Weeks are taken for the following Exercises, corresponding to the four parts into which they are divided. That is, the First Week is devoted to the consideration and contemplation of sins; the Second, to the life of Christ our Lord up to and including Palm Sunday; the Third, to the Passion of Christ our Lord; and the Fourth, to the Resurrection and Ascension. To this week are appended the Three Methods of Praying. However, this does not mean that each week must necessarily consist of seven or eight days. For during the First Week some persons happen to be slower in finding what they are seeking, that is, contrition, sorrow, and tears for their sins. Similarly, some persons work more diligently than others, and are more pushed back and forth and probed by different spirits. In some cases, therefore, the week needs to be shortened, and in others lengthened. This holds as well for all the following weeks, while the retreatant is seeking for what corresponds to their subject matter. But the Exercises ought to be completed in thirty days, more or less.

*The Fifth.* The persons who receive the Exercises will benefit greatly by entering upon them with great spirit and generosity toward their Creator and Lord, and by offering all their desires and freedom to him so that his Divine Majesty can make use of their persons and of all they possess in whatsoever way is according to his most holy will.

*The Sixth.* When the one giving the Exercises notices that the person making them is not experiencing any spiritual motions in his or her soul, such as consolations or desolations, or is not being moved one way or another by different spirits, the director should question the exercitant much about the Exercises: Whether the exercitant is making them at the appointed times, how they are being made, and whether the Additional Directives are being diligently observed. The director should ask about each of these items in particular. Consolation and desolation are treated in [316–324], the Additional Directives in [73–90].

*The Seventh.* When the giver of the Exercises sees that the recipient is experiencing desolation and temptation, he or she should not treat the retreatant severely or harshly, but gently and kindly. The director should encourage and strengthen the exercitant for the future, unmask the deceptive tactics of the enemy of our human nature, and help the retreatant to prepare and dispose himself or herself for the consolation which will come.

## The First Week

### Principle and Foundation

Human beings are created to praise, reverence, and serve God our Lord, and by means of this to save their souls.

The other things on the face of the earth are created for the human beings, to help them in working toward the end for which they are created.

From this it follows that I should use these things to the extent that they help me toward my end, and rid myself of them to the extent that they hinder me.

To do this, I must make myself indifferent to all created things, in regard to everything which is left to my freedom of will and is not forbidden. Consequently, on my own part I ought not to seek health rather than sickness, wealth rather than poverty, honor rather than dishonor, a long life rather than a short one, and so on in all other matters.

I ought to desire and elect only the thing which is more conducive to the end for which I am created.

## Daily Particular Examination of Conscience

*It comprises three times in the day and two examinations of conscience.*

*The First Time* is in the morning. Upon arising the person should resolve to guard carefully against the particular sin or fault he or she wants to correct or amend.

*The Second Time* is after the noon meal. One should ask God our Lord for what one desires, namely, grace to recall how often one has fallen into the particular sin or fault, in order to correct it in the future. Then one should make the first examination, exacting an account of oneself with regard to the particular matter one has decided to take for correction and improvement. One should run through the time, hour by hour or period by period, from the moment of rising until the present examination. On the upper line of the G⹀ one should enter a dot for each time one fell into the particular sin or fault. Then one should renew one's resolution to do better during the time until the second examination which will be made later.

*The Third Time* is after supper. The person should make the second examination, likewise hour by hour starting from the previous examination down to the present one. For each time he or she fell into the particular sin or fault, a dot should be entered on the lower line of the g══.

## Four Additional Directives
*to help toward quicker riddance of the*
*particular sin or fault.*

*The First Directive.* Each time one falls into the particular sin or fault, one should touch one's hand to one's breast in sorrow for having fallen. This can be done even in public without its being noticed by others.

*The Second.* Since the upper line of the G══ represents the first examination and the lower line the second, the person should look at night to see if there was any improvement from the first line to the second, that is, from the first examination to the second.

*The Third.* The person should compare the second day with the first, that is, the two examinations of each day with those of the previous day, to see whether any improvement has been made from one day to the next.

*The Fourth.* The person should compare this week with the previous one, to see if any improvement has been made during the present week in comparison with the one before.

It should be noted that the first large G══ on the top line indicates Sunday, the second and smaller g══ Monday, the third Tuesday, and so on.

G════════.
g════════.
g════════.
g════════.

## The First Exercise Is a Meditation By Using the Three Powers of the Soul About the First, Second, and Third Sins.
*It contains, after a preparatory prayer and two preludes, three main points and a colloquy.*

*The Preparatory Prayer* is to ask God our Lord for the grace that all my intentions, actions, and operations may be ordered purely to the service and praise of his Divine Majesty.

*The First Prelude* is a composition made by imagining the place. Here we should take notice of the following. When a contemplation or meditation is about something that can be gazed on, for example, a contemplation of Christ our Lord, who is visible, the composition consists of seeing in imagination the physical place where that which I want to contemplate is taking place. By physical place I mean, for instance, a temple or a mountain where Jesus Christ or Our Lady happens to be, in accordance with the topic I desire to contemplate.

When a contemplation or meditation is about something abstract and invisible, as in the present case about the sins, the composition will be to see in imagination and to consider my soul as imprisoned in this corruptible body, and my whole compound self as an exile in this valley [of tears] among brute animals. I mean, my whole self as composed of soul and body.

*The Second Prelude* is to ask God our Lord for what I want and desire. What I ask for should be in accordance with the subject matter. For example, in a contemplation on the Resurrection, I will ask for joy with Christ in joy; in a contemplation on the Passion, I will ask for pain, tears, and suffering with Christ suffering.

In the present meditation it will be to ask for shame and confusion about myself, when I see how many people have been damned for committing a single mortal sin, and how many times I have deserved eternal damnation for my many sins.

*Note.* All the contemplations or meditations ought to be preceded by this same preparatory prayer, which is never changed, and also by the two preludes, which are sometimes changed in accordance with the subject matter.

*The First Point* will be to use my memory, by going over the first sin, that of the angels; next, to use my understanding, by reasoning about it; and then my will. My aim in remembering and reasoning about all these matters is to bring myself to greater shame and confusion, by comparing the one sin of the angels with all my own many sins. For one sin they went to hell; then how often have I deserved hell for my many sins!

In other words, I will call to memory the sin of the angels: How they were created in grace and then, not wanting to better themselves by using their freedom to reverence and obey their Creator and Lord, they fell into pride, were changed from grace to malice, and were hurled from heaven into hell. Next I will use my intellect to ruminate about this in greater detail, and then move myself to deeper affections by means of my will.

*The Second Point* will be meditated in the same way. That is, I will apply the three faculties to the sin of Adam and Eve. I will recall to memory how they did long penance for their sin, and the enormous corruption it brought to the human race, with so many people going to hell.

Again in other words, I will call to memory the second sin, that of our first parents: How Adam was created in the plain of Damascus and placed in the earthly paradise; and how Eve was created from his rib; how they were forbidden to eat of the tree of knowledge, but did eat, and thus sinned; and then, clothed in garments of skin and expelled from paradise, they lived out their whole lives in great hardship and penance, deprived of the original justice which they had lost. Next I will use my intellect to reason about this in greater detail, and then use the will, as is described just above.

*The Third Point* will likewise be to use the same method on the third sin, the particular sin of anyone who has gone to hell because of one mortal sin; and further, of innumerable other persons who went there for fewer sins than I have committed.

That is, about this third particular sin too I will follow the same procedure as above. I will call to memory the gravity and malice of the sin against my Creator and Lord; then I will use my intellect to reason about it—how by sinning and acting against the Infinite Goodness the person has been justly condemned forever. Then I will finish by using the will, as was described above.

*Colloquy.* Imagine Christ our Lord suspended on the cross before you, and converse with him in a colloquy: How is it that he, although he is the Creator, has come to make himself a human being? How is it that he has passed from eternal life to death here in time, and to die in this way for my sins?

In a similar way, reflect on yourself and ask: What have I done for Christ? What am I doing for Christ? What ought I to do for Christ?

In this way, too, gazing on him in so pitiful a state as he hangs on the cross, speak out whatever comes to your mind.

A colloquy is made, properly speaking, in the way one friend speaks to another, or a servant to one in authority—now begging a favor, now accusing oneself of some misdeed, now telling one's concerns and asking counsel about them. Close with an Our Father.

# Dark Night of the Soul

## San Juan de la Cruz

*This famous mystic, one of the finest poets of Spain's Golden Age, attended the University of Salamanca where Fray Luis de León was a professor. Like Santa Teresa, whom he admired, San Juan was a member of the Carmelite order and was of Jewish descent. Because of a violent jurisdictional dispute within the religious order, he was imprisoned in a cell in Toledo, and it was here that he wrote his passionate religious lyrics. To him, "the dark night of the soul" was a final stage of soul-suffering that precedes the union of the human soul with God, called by the poet "the mystical marriage."*

*San Juan wrote an incandescent lyric poetry that joined the limpid simplicity of his country's ballads and folk songs, the polished and refined language of the Renaissance, and the religious exaltation of the Old Testament prophets, who carried on personal conversations with their God. Garcilaso and the Bible's Song of Songs furnish much of his rhythm and imagery. Saint John's poems invariably describe the allegorical search of the beloved (the soul) for the lover (God). The flowing lines rise on spirals of increasing tension and beauty, for San Juan de la Cruz has, above all, written love poems of the most passionate, tender, and perfect kind. An English critic remarked, "Such poetry has never been written in Spain to women."*

## Dark Night of the Soul

In the dark of night,
eager for love, impassioned and aroused,
ah the sweet delight!
I stole, still as a mouse,
from the peace and quiet of my house.

Secure, though it was night,
through the secret stairway in disguise,
Ah, the sweet delight!
hidden from all eyes,
knowing my house was left at peace behind.

Over the happy ground,
in secret, where nobody else had spied,
I did not look around,
and I had no light or guide
except what in my heart was burning bright.

And that light guided me
more surely than the light of noonday sun
to where awaited he—
the one I knew, the one
who waited in the darkness all alone.

Oh night that led so true!
Oh night, more generous than the breaking dawn!
Oh night that joined the two,
the beloved with her lover,
the beloved into the lover then transformed!

Upon my flowered breast
that wholly and for him alone I kept,
there I let him rest,
there he sweetly slept,
and the air of the cedar grove cooled him with its
     breath.

The air through the turrets stirred;
and as I ran my fingers through his hair,
his hand brought my face toward his,
my neck was pierced by bliss,

## Noche Oscura Del Alma

En una noche oscura,
con ansias en amores inflamada.
¡oh dichosa ventura!,
salí sin ser notada,
estando ya mi casa sosegada:

a escuras y segura,
por la secreta escala disfrazada,
¡oh dichosa ventura!
a escuras y en celada,
estando ya mi casa sosegada;

en la noche díchosa,
en secreto, que nadie me veía,
ni yo miraba cosa,
sin otra luz y guía
sino la que en el corazón ardía.

Aquésta me guiaba
más cierto que la luz del mediodía,
a donde me esperaba
quien yo bien me sabía,
en parte donde nadie parecía.

¡Oh noche que guiaste!,
¡oh noche amable más que el alborada!
¡oh noche que juntaste
amado con amada,
amada en el amado transformada!

En mi pecho florido,
que entero para él solo se guardaba,
allí quedó dormido,
y yo le regalaba;
y el ventalle de cedros aire daba.

El aire de la almena,
cuando yo sus cabellos esparcía,
con su mano serena
en mi cuello hería,

and my senses were suspended I knew not
    where.

I lost all sense of time;
my face leaned over my lover still to yield,
the world had stopped and I
left my cares to heal
forgotten among the lilies of the field.

y todos mis sentidos suspendía.

Quedéme y olvidéme,
el rostro recliné sobre el amado,
cesó todo, y dejéme,
dejando mi cuidado
entre las azucenas olvidado.

*translation by Ruth K. Crispin*

# *from* Selected Essays

*Michel de Montaigne*

## *Apology for Raimond Sebond*

### MAN'S PRESUMPTION AND LITTLENESS

What does Truth preach to us, when she preaches to us to fly worldly philosophy, when she so often impresses upon us. That our wisdom is folly in the sight of God; That of all vain things the most vain is man; That man, who presumes on his learning, does not yet know what it is to know; and That if man, who is nothing, thinks himself something, he deceives and beguiles himself? These sayings of the Holy Spirit so clearly and vividly express what I wish to maintain, that I should need no other proof against men who would bow with all submission and obedience to its authority. But the others would rather be whipped to their own cost, and will not suffer their reason to combated except by itself.

Let us then for the nonce consider man alone, without outside assistance, armed only with his own weapons, and destitute of the divine grace and knowledge, which comprise all his honour, his strength and the foundation of his being. Let us see how he will hold out in this fine equipment. Let him explain to me, by the force of his reason, on what foundation he has built those great advantages he thinks he has over the other creatures. What has induced him to believe that that wonderful motion of the heavenly vault, the eternal light of those torches rolling so proudly over his head, the awe-inspiring agitations of that infinite sea, were established and endure through so many centuries for his service and convenience?

Is it possible to imagine anything more ridiculous than that this miserable and puny creature, who is not so much as master of himself, exposed to shocks on all sides should call himself Master and Emperor of the universe, of which it is not in his power to know the smallest part, much less to command it? And that privilege which he assumes of being the only creature in this great edifice that has the capacity to know the beauty and the several parts of it, the only one who is able to give thanks to the architect, and to keep an account of the receipts and outlay of the world: who has sealed him this privilege? Let him show us his letters-patent for this great and noble charge.

Have they been granted in favour of the wise only? Then few people would be concerned. Are the fools and the wicked deserving of so extra-ordinary a favour, and, being the worst lot in the world, of being pre-ferred to all the rest?

Shall we believe the man who says this. *For whose sake shall we then say that the world has been made? Undoubtedly for those creatures that have the use of reason: these are gods and men, to whom assuredly nothing is superior?* (Balbus the Stoic, according to Cicero). We could never sufficiently deride the impudence of this coupling of gods and men.

But, poor devil, what is there in him deserving of such a privilege? When we consider the incorruptible life of the heavenly bodies, their beauty, their grandeur, their continual motion by so exact a rule:

> *When we gaze aloft*
> *Upon the skiey vaults of yon great world*
> *The ether, fixt high over twinkling stars,*
> *And into our thought there come the journeyings*
> *Of sun and moon; (Lucretius.)*

when we consider the dominion and power those bodies have, not only over our lives and the conditions of our fortune,

> *Our lives and actions on the stars depend, (Manilius.)*

but even over our dispositions, our judgment, our will, which they gov-ern, impel and stir at the mercy of their influence, as our reason discov-ers and tells us:

> *This we learn; the far, far distant stars*
> *Govern by silent laws; the world is ruled*
> *By periodic causes, and the turns of destiny*
> *Observed by certain signs; (Manilius.)*

when we see that not only a man, not only a king but kingdoms, empires, and all this world here below are moved according to the lightest swing of the heavenly motions:

> *How great a change each little motion brings!*
> *So great this kingdom that it governs kings; (Manilius.)*

if our virtue, our vices, our talents and our knowledge, if even this dissertation of mine on the power of the stars, this comparison between them and ourselves, comes, as our reason supposes, by their means and their favour;

> Maddened by love, Leander swims the strait.
> A Grecian king o'erturns the walls of Troy.
> 'Tis this man's lot to give his country laws.
> Sons kill their fathers, fathers kill their sons,
> And brothers arm themselves in mutual strife.
> Not we have made these wars; tis Fate compels
> To bear such pains with lacerated limbs.
> And Fate it is that makes me ponder Fate; (Manilius.)

if this little portion of reason we possess has been allotted to us by heaven, how can reason make us the equal of heaven? How can it subject its essence and conditions to our knowledge? All that we see in those bodies fills us with amazement. *What apparatus, what instruments, what levers, what engines, what craftsmen were employed about so mighty a work?* (Cicero).

Why do we deny them a soul, and life and reason? Have we discovered in them any stubborn, senseless stupidity, we who have no concern with them but to obey them? Shall we say that we have seen no other creature but man in possession of a reasoning mind? Why! have we not seen anything comparable to the sun? Does it exist the less for our not having seen its like? Does it move the less because no other movement is to be compared with it? If what we have not seen does not exist, our knowledge is marvelously shortsighted: *How close the confines of our mind!* (Cicero).

Is it not a delusion of human vanity to make the moon a celestial earth, and to imagine that there are mountains and valleys upon it, as did Anaxagoras; to set up human habitations and dwellings and establish colonies upon it for our convenience, as do Plato and Plutarch, and to make our earth a bright and shining star? *Amongst other infirmities of human nature is that mental blindness which not only forces man to err, but makes him hug his errors* (Seneca). *The corruptible body weighs down the soul, and this earthly habitation prevents it from pondering on many things* (The Book of Wisdom, quoted by Saint Augustine).

Presumption is our natural and original infirmity. The frailest and most vulnerable of all creatures is man, and at the same time the most arrogant.

He sees and feels himself lodged here in the mud and filth of the world, nailed and riveted to the worst, the deadest and most stagnant part of the universe, at the lowest story of the house and the most remote from the vault of heaven, with the animals of the worst condition of the three; and he goes and sets himself in imagination above the circle of the moon, and brings heaven under his feet.

With this same vanity of imagination he makes himself the equal of God, assumes to himself divine qualities, selects and separates himself from among the multitude of other creatures, carves out their shares to each of his fellows and comrades, the animals, and allots to them their portion of faculties and powers according as it seems good to him. How can he know by the force of his understanding, the secret and internal motions of the animals? By what comparison between them and himself does he suppose them to be as stupid as he thinks?

When I play with my cat, who knows but that she regards me more as a plaything than I do her? (We amuse each other with our respective monkey-tricks; if I have my moments for beginning and refusing, so she has hers.)

Plato, in his picture of the golden age under Saturn, numbers, among the chief advantages of the man of that time, his communion with the beasts, of whom inquiring and learning he knew the real attributes and differences of each of them; whereby he acquired a very perfect understanding and wisdom, and in consequence passed his life very much more happily than we are able to do. Do we need a better proof of the impudence of man where the beasts are concerned? That great author opined that, in giving them their bodily shape, Nature for the most part only considered the use they could be put to in the prognostications which were drawn from them in his time.

That defect which hinders communication between us and them, why may it not as well be in ourselves as in them? It is a matter of conjecture with whom the fault lies that we do not understand one another: for we understand them no more than they do us. By the same reasoning they may regard us as beasts, as we do them.

It is no great wonder if we do not understand them for neither do we understand the Basques and the Troglodytes. Yet some have boasted of understanding them, as Apollonius of Tyana, Melampus, Tiresias, Thales, and others. And since it is the case that, as the cosmographers tell, there are nations that receive a dog for their king, they must needs in some way interpret its voice and actions.

We must observe the parity there is between us. We have some halfway understanding of their meaning, as the animals have of ours, in about the same degree. They cajole us, they threaten us, they entreat us, as we do them. Moreover, it is very evident to us that they are able fully and completely to communicate with one another, that they understand one another, and not only those of the same species, but also those of different species.

> *Since even the speechless herds, aye, since*
> *The very generations of wild beasts*
> *Are wont dissimilar and diverse sounds*
> *To rouse from in them, when there's fear or pain,*
> *And when they burst with joys. (Lucretius.)*

A horse knows that a dog is angry when it barks in a certain way, but is not afraid when it gives voice in another way. Even in those creatures that have no voice we may easily infer, from the mutual services we see them rendering each other, that they have some other means of communication; their movements speak and negotiate:

> *In much the same way as the lack-speech years*
> *Compel young children into gesturings. (Lucretius.)*

Why not? just as well as our deaf-mutes dispute, argue and tell stories by means of signs? I have seen some so skilful and practised in that language, that in truth they did not fall short of perfection in making themselves understood. Lovers use their eyes to express anger, reconciliation, entreaty, thanks, to make appointments, in short for every purpose;

> *Silence too our thought and wish betrays. (Tasso.)*

What of the hands? We beg, we promise, we call, we send away, threaten, pray, entreat, deny, refuse, question, wonder, count, confess, repent, we express fear and shame, we doubt, inform, command, incite, encourage, swear, testify, abuse, condemn, absolve, instill, despise, challenge, we show vexation, we flatter, applaud, bless, humiliate, mock, reconcile, recommend, exalt, welcome, rejoice, complain, we express grief, dejection, despair, astonishment, protestation, silence, and what not, in such varied and numerous ways, in rivalry with the tongue.

With the head we invite, we dismiss, admit, disclaim, give the lie, welcome, honour, reverence, disdain, demand, show the door, we cheer, lament, caress, chide, submit, defy, exhort, threaten, assure, and inquire. What of the eye-brows? What of the shoulders? There is no movement that does not speak an intelligible, untaught language, that is understood by all. Which shows that, seeing the variety that distinguishes the spoken languages in use, this one must rather be considered the proper and natural speech of humankind. I pass over that which a particular necessity teaches one who is taken unawares; and the finger-alphabet; and grammar and the sciences which are only practised and expressed by gestures; and the nations that Pliny tells of, who have no other language.

An ambassador of the city of Abdera, after speaking at great length to King Agis of Sparta, said to him, 'Well, Sire, what answer do you wish me to carry back to our citizens?' 'That I allowed you to say all that you would and as much as you would, without ever a word.' Was not that a very speaking and intelligible silence?

After all, which of our arts do we not see in the activities of animals? Is there any organization regulated with more order, with a better distribution of charges and functions, and more consistently maintained, than that of the bees? Can we imagine that so well-ordered a disposition of activities and occupations could be carried on without reason and foresight?

> *Following signs and instances like these,*
> *Some testify that bees possess a share*
> *Of the world-spirit and the mind divine. (Virgil.)*

Do the swallows that we see at the return of spring, ferreting out all the corners of the houses, conduct their search without judgment? Do they choose without discrimination, out of a thousand places, that which is most commodious for their lodging? Are the birds, when they weave those beautiful and wonderful habitations of theirs, able to use a square figure rather than a round, an obtuse rather than a right angle, without knowing their properties and effects? Do they fetch, now water, now clay without having concluded that hardness is softened by moisture? Do they line the floors of their palaces with moss or down unless they have foreseen that the tender limbs of their young will lie more softly and comfortably? Do they shelter themselves from the rainy wind and build their cabins to the east, without knowing the different properties of the winds, and without considering that one is more healthy for them than the other?

Why does the spider thicken her web in one place and slacken it in another? Why does she use now one kind of knot, now another, unless she possesses thought, deliberation and the power of inference?

We may see well enough, in most of their works, how much the animals surpass us, and how much we fall short in the art of imitating them. And yet, in our ruder performances, we are sensible of what faculties we employ, and we know that our mind applies to them its utmost powers; why do we not conclude the same of the animals? Why do we ascribe to I know not what slavish instinct of nature those works that excel anything we can do by nature or art? Herein we unconsciously give them a very great advantage over ourselves, in making Nature, with a maternal kindness, to accompany and lead them as it were by the hand, to all the activities and conveniences of their life; whilst us she abandons to chance and fortune, and forces us to seek by art the things necessary for our preservation, at the same time denying us the means of attaining, by any education or mental effort, to the natural skill of the animals. So that their brutish stupidity surpasses in all their contrivances everything we are able to do with our divine intelligence.

Truly, by this reckoning, we might with great reason call her a very unjust stepmother; but that is not so. Our organization is not so formless and unregulated. Nature has been universally kind to all her creatures, and there is none that she has not very amply furnished with all means necessary for the preservation of its being. For those common complaints that I hear men uttering (as the licence of their opinions now lifts them up above the clouds, now brings them down to the antipodes), that we are the only outcast animal, bare on the bare earth, bound and tied down, with no means of arming or covering ourselves but with others spoils; whereas all the other creatures have been clothed by Nature with shells, husks, bark, hair, wool, spikes, leather, down, feathers, scales, fleece, bristles, according to the need of their being; armed with claws, teeth, horns for attack and defence, and has herself instructed them in what is requisite to each, to swim, run, fly, sing, whilst man cannot even walk or speak, nor eat, nor do anything but weep, without an apprenticeship:

> *Then again the babe,*
> *Like to the castaway of the raging surf,*
> *Lies naked on the ground, speechless, in want*

> *Of every help for life, when Nature first*
> *Hath poured him forth upon the shores of light*
> *With birth-pangs from within the mother's womb,*
> *And with a plaintive wail he fills the place,—*
> *As well befitting one for whom remains*
> *In life a journey through so many ills.*
> *But all the flocks and herds and all wild beasts*
> *Come forth and grow, nor need the little rattles,*
> *Nor must be treated to the humouring nurse's*
> *Dear broken chatter, nor seek they divers clothes*
> *To suit the changing skies; nor need, in fine,*
> *Nor arms, nor lofty ramparts, wherewithal*
> *Their own to guard—because the earth herself*
> *And Nature, artificer of the world, bring forth*
> *Aboundingly all things for all. (Lucretius.)*

These complaints are unfounded, there is in the governance of the world a much greater equality and a more uniform relationship. Our skin is provided as abundantly as theirs with power to resist the inclemency of the weather. Witness the many nations that have not yet tried the use of clothes. Our ancient Gauls wore hardly any clothes, like our neighbours the Irish of the present day, in spite of their cold climate.

But we may judge better by ourselves: for all those parts of our person which we are pleased to expose to the wind and air are adapted to endure it, the feet, the face, the hands, the legs, the shoulders, the head, according to the demands of usage. For if there is in us a tender spot, in which we should seem to fear the cold, it should be the stomach, where digestion takes place; our fathers used to leave it uncovered, and our ladies, soft and delicate as they are, sometimes go half-covered down to the navel.

Nor are the bindings and swaddlings of infants any more necessary. The Lacedemonian mothers reared their children in all freedom to move their limbs, without any wrappings or fastenings.

Our weeping we have in common with most of the other animals; there are hardly any that do not wail and whine long after their birth seeing that it is a natural effect of their helplessness at that age. As to the habit of eating, it is natural to us as well as to them, and comes without instruction:

> *For each creature feels*
> *By instinct to what use to put its powers.*
> *(Lucretius.)*

Who doubts but that a child, having acquired the strength to feed himself, is able to seek his food? And the earth yields and offers him enough for his needs, without any cultivation and artifice; and if not at all times, no more does she do it for the animals. Witness the provision we see made by the ants and other creatures, in view of the barren season of the year. Those nations we have lately discovered, so abundantly provided with meat and a natural drink, without care or trouble on their part, have now made us realize that bread is not our only sustenance, and that, without any tilling, our Mother Nature has plentifully provided us with all that we need. Nay, as seems very probable, more amply and richly than she does now that we have taken to meddling with it by our contrivances:

> *She first, the Earth, of own accord*
> *The shining grains and vineyards of all joy*
> *Created for mortality; herself*
> *Gave the sweet fruitage and the pastures glad,*
> *Which now to-day yet scarcely wax in size,*
> *Even when, aided by our toiling arms,*
> *We break the ox, and wear away the strength*
> *Of sturdy farm-hands; (Lucretius.)*

the excess and unruliness of our appetite outstripping all the inventions wherewith we seek to satisfy it.

With regard to weapons, we are better provided by Nature than most other animals; we are more able to move our limbs about and to extract service from them, naturally and without being taught. Those who are trained to fight naked are seen to rush into dangers just like our own soldiers. If some of the beasts surpass us in this advantage, we surpass many others in the same. We possess by a natural instinct and teaching the skill to fortify our bodies and protect them by acquired means. That this is so is proved by the example of the elephant who sharpens and grinds the teeth which he makes use of in warfare (for he has special teeth which he saves and employs for this purpose only). When bulls go to battle they throw up and scatter the dust around them, the boars whet their tusks; the ichneumon, when it is about to grapple with a crocodile, fortifies its body by coating it all over with a crust of mud, well kneaded and compressed, as with a cuirass. Why shall we not say that it is as natural to us to arm ourselves with wood and iron?

As to speech, it is certain that, if it is not natural neither is it necessary. Nevertheless I believe that a child brought up in complete solitude, far from all intercourse (which would be a difficult experiment to make), would have some kind of speech to express his ideas. And it is not to be believed that Nature has denied us this power which she has given to many other animals; for what else but speech is that faculty we observe in them of complaining, rejoicing, calling to one another for succour, inviting to love, which they do by the use of their voice?

Why should they not speak with one another? They speak to us, and we to them: in how many different tones do we not speak to our dogs? and they answer us. We use another language with them, than we do in talking to birds, pigs, oxen and horses, and give them other names; we change the idiom according to the kind.

> *So ants amidst their sable-coloured band*
> *One with another mouth to mouth confer,*
> *Haply their way or state to understand. (Dante.)*

Lactantius seems to attribute to beasts not only the power of speech but also of laughter. And the same difference of tongues which, according to the differences of countries, is found in human beings, is also found in animals of the same species. Aristotle, writing on this subject, instances the various calls of partridges, according to locality:

> *The dappled birds*
> *Utter at other times far other cries*
> *Than when they fight for food, or with their prey*
> *Struggle and strain. And birds there are which change*
> *With changing weather their own raucous songs.*
> *(Lucretius.)*

But it is yet to be known what language the supposed child would speak; and what has been conjectured about it has no great probability. If any one declares to me, in opposition to this belief, that those deaf by nature do not speak, I reply that it is not only because they have not been taught to speak by ear, but more because the sense of hearing, of which they are deprived, is related to that of speech, and that they hold together by a natural tie; in such a way that the words we speak must in the first place be spoken to ourselves, and be made to strike upon our own inward ears, before being sent out to others' ears.

I have said all this to establish the resemblance to human conditions, and to bring us back and join us to the majority. We are neither superior nor inferior to the rest. All that is under heaven, says the sage, is subject to one law and one fate:

> Enshackled in the gruesome bonds of doom. (Lucretius.)

Some difference there is; there are orders and degrees, but under the aspect of one same Nature:

> But each sole thing
> Proceeds according to its proper wont,
> And all conserve their own distinctions, based
> In Nature's fixed decree. (Lucretius.)

Man must be forced and lined up within the barriers of this organization. The poor wretch has no mind really to step over them. He is shackled and entangled, he is subjected to the same obligation as the other creatures of his order, and is of a very mediocre condition, without any real and essential prerogative and preeminence. That which he thinks and imagines himself to possess, neither has body nor can it be perceived. And if it be so that he alone of all the animals has this freedom of imagination, this licence of thought, which represents to him that which is, that which is not, that which he wills, the false and the true; it is an advantage sold to him very dearly, and of which he has very little cause to boast. For from it springs the principal source of all the ills that press upon him, sin, sickness, irresolution, affliction, despair.

## Of Repentance

### "THESE TESTIMONIES OF A GOOD CONSCIENCE"

Others form man: I describe him, and portray a particular, very ill-made one, who, if I had to fashion him anew, should indeed be very different from what he is. But now it is done.

Now the features of my painting do not err, although they change and vary. The world is but a perennial see-saw. All things in it are incessantly on the swing, the earth, the rocks of the Caucasus, the Egyptian pyramids, both with the common movement and their own particular movement. Even fixedness is nothing but a more sluggish motion.

I cannot fix my object: it is befogged and reels with a natural intoxication. I seize it at this point as it is at the moment when I beguile myself with it. I do not portray the thing in itself. I portray the passage; not a passing from one age to another or, as the people put it, from seven years to seven years, but from day to day, from minute to minute. I must adapt my history to the moment. I may presently change, not only by chance, but also by intention. It is a record of diverse and changeable events, of undecided, and when the occasion arises, contradictory ideas; whether it be that I am another self, or that I grasp a subject in different circumstances and see it from a different point of view. So it may be that I contradict myself, but, as Demades said, the truth I never contradict. If my mind could find a firm footing, I should not speak tentatively, I should decide; it is always in a state of apprenticeship, and on trial.

I am holding up to view a humble and lustreless life; that is all one. Moral philosophy, in any degree, may apply to an ordinary and secluded life as well as to one of richer stuff; every man carries within him the entire form of the human constitution.

Authors communicate themselves to the world by some special extrinsic mark; I am the first to do so by my general being, as Michel de Montaigne, not as a grammarian or a poet or a lawyer. If the world finds fault with me for speaking too much of myself, I find fault with the world for not even thinking of itself.

But is it reasonable that I, who am so retired in actual life, should aspire to make myself known to the public? And is it reasonable that I should show up to the world, where artifice and ceremony enjoy so much credit and authority, the crude and simple results of nature, and of a nature besides very feeble? Is it not like making a wall without stone or a similar material, thus to build a book without learning or art? The ideas of music are guided by art, mine by chance. This I have at least in conformity with rules, that no man ever treated of a subject that he knew and understood better than I do this that I have taken up; and that in this I am the most learned man alive. Secondly, that no man ever penetrated more deeply into his matter, nor more minutely analysed its parts and consequences, nor more fully and exactly reached the goal he had made it his business to set up. To accomplish it I need only bring fidelity to it; and that is here, as pure and sincere as may be found.

I speak the truth, not enough to satisfy myself, but as much as I dare to speak. And I become a little more daring as I grow older; for it would seem that custom allows this age more freedom to prate, and more indiscretion in speaking of oneself. It cannot be the case here, as I often see elsewhere, that the craftsman and his work contradict each other. 'How could a man who shows to such advantage in company write so foolish a book?' or, 'Are these learned writings the work of a man of such feeble conversation?'

When a man of ordinary conversation writes uncommon things, it means that his talent lies in the place from which he borrows them, and not in himself. A learned man is not learned at all things; but the accomplished man is accomplished in all things, even in ignorance.

Here, my book and I go hand in hand together, and keep one pace. In other cases we may commend or censure the work apart from the workman; not so here. Who touches the one touches the other. He who judges the one without knowing the other will wrong himself more than he does me; he who has come to know the work will completely satisfy me. Happy beyond my deserts if I have only this share of public approval, that intelligent persons will be made to feel that I was capable of profiting by learning, if I had any; and that I deserved more assistance from my memory!

In this place let me offer an excuse for what I often repeat, that I seldom repent, and that my conscience is satisfied with itself, not as the conscience of an angel or a horse, but as the conscience of a man; always with the addition of this refrain, not a formal or conventional refrain, but prompted by a real and natural modesty, 'that I speak as an inquirer and an ignoramus, leaving the decision purely and simply to the common and authorized beliefs.' I do not teach, I relate.

There is no vice, that is really a vice, which is not hurtful and which a sound judgment does not condemn; for its ugliness and evil consequences are so apparent that they are perhaps right who say that it is chiefly begotten of stupidity and ignorance. So hard it is to imagine that a man may know it and not hate it!

Wickedness sucks in the greater part of its own venom, and poisons itself with it.

Vice, like an ulcer in the flesh, leaves a repentance in the soul, which is always scratching itself and drawing blood. For Reason blots out all other grief and sorrow, but begets that of repentance, which is the more hard to bear since it is born from within; as the chill and heat of a fever are more acutely felt than those which are external. I regard as vices (but each according to it measure), not only those which are condemned by reason and Nature, but those too which have been created by human opinion, even false and erroneous opinion, if it is authorized by laws and custom.

There is likewise no goodness in which a well-born nature does not delight. We feel indeed a certain self-congratulation when we do a good deed, which gives us inward satisfaction, and that generous pride which accompanies a good conscience. A boldly wicked soul may perhaps arm itself with assurance; but with that complacency and satisfaction it cannot provide itself.

There is no small pleasure in feeling oneself preserved from the contagion of so corrupt an age, and saying to oneself, 'Should any one look into my very soul, he would yet not find me guilty of the affliction or ruin of any man, or of revenge or envy, of publicly offending against the laws, of innovation or disturbance, or of failing to keep my word. And whatever the licence of the times may permit or suggest to any man, I have laid hands on no Frenchman's property nor dived into his purse. I have never lived but on what is my own, either in war or peace time; and have never used another man's labour without hire.' These testimonies of a good conscience please; and this natural satisfaction is a great boon to us, and the only payment that will never fail us.

# *from* Hamlet, Prince of Denmark

*William Shakespeare*

*Hamlet.* A goodly one; in which there are many confines, wards, and dungeons, Denmark being one o' the worst.

*Rosencrantz.* We think not so, my lord.

*Hamlet.* Why, then 't is none to you; for there is nothing either good or bad, but thinking makes it so: to me it is a prison.

*Rosencrantz.* Why, then your ambition makes it one; 't is too narrow for your mind.

*Hamlet.* O God, I could be bounded in a nut-shell, and count myself a king of infinite space, were it not that I have bad dreams.

*Guildenstern.* Which dreams indeed are ambition, for the very substance of the ambitious is merely the shadow of a dream.

*Hamlet.* A dream itself is but a shadow.

*Rosencrantz.* Truly, and I hold ambition of so airy and light a quality that it is but a shadow's shadow.

*Hamlet.* Then are our beggars bodies, and our monarchs and outstretched heroes the beggars' shadows. Shall we to the court? for, by my fay, I cannot reason.

*Rosencrantz & Guildenstern.* We'll wait upon you.

*Hamlet.* No such matter: I will not sort you with the rest of my servants; for, to speak to you like an honest man, I am most dreadfully attended. But, in the beaten way of friendship, what make you at Elsinore?

*Rosencrantz.* To visit you, my lord; no other occasion.

*Hamlet.* Beggar that I am, I am even poor in thanks; but I thank you: and sure, dear friends, my thanks are too dear a halfpenny. Were you not sent for? Is it your own inclining? Is it a free visitation? Come, deal justly with me: come, come; nay, speak.

*Guildenstern.* What should we say, my lord?

314

*Hamlet.* Why, any thing, but to the purpose. You were sent for; and there is a kind of confession in your looks which your modesties have not craft enough to colour. I know the good king and queen have sent for you.

*Rosencrantz.* To what end, my lord?

*Hamlet.* That you must teach me. But let me conjure you, by the rights of our fellowship, by the consonancy of our youth, by the obligation of our ever-preserved love, and by what more dear a better proposer could charge you withal, be even and direct with me, whether you were sent for, or no?

*Rosencrantz.* [*Aside to Guildenstern*] What say you?

*Hamlet.* [*Aside*] Nay, then I have an eye of you.—If you love me, hold not off.

*Guildenstern.* My lord, we were sent for.

*Hamlet.* I will tell you why; so shall my anticipation prevent your discovery, and your secrecy to the king and queen moult no feather. I have of late—but wherefore I know not—lost all my mirth, forgone all custom of exercises; and indeed it goes so heavily with my disposition that this goodly frame, the earth, seems to me a sterile promontory; this most excellent canopy, the air, look you, this brave o'erhanging firmament, this majestical roof fretted with golden fire,—why, it appears no other thing to me than a foul and pestilent congregation of vapours. What a piece of work is man! how noble in reason! how infinite in faculty! in form and moving how express and admirable! in action how like an angel! in apprehension how like a god! the beauty of the world! the paragon of animals! And yet, to me, what is this quintessence of dust? man delights not me; no, nor woman neither, though by your smiling you seem to say so.

*Rosencrantz.* My lord, there was no such stuff in my thoughts.

*Hamlet.* Why did you laugh then, when I said 'man delights not me?'

*Rosencrantz.* To think my lord, if you delight not in man, what lenten entertainment the players shall receive from you; we coted them on the way, and hither are they coming to offer you service.

*Hamlet.* He that plays the king shall be welcome; his majesty shall have tribute of me; the adventurous knight shall use his foil and target; the lover shall not sigh gratis; the humorous man shall end his part in peace; the clown shall make those laugh whose lungs are tickle o' the sere; and the lady shall say her mind freely, or the blank verse shall halt for 't. What players are they?

*Rosencrantz.* Even those you were wont to take delight in, the tragedians of the city.

*Hamlet.* How chances it they travel? their residence, both in reputation and profit, was better both ways.

*Rosencrantz.* I think their inhibition comes by the means of the late innovation.

*Hamlet.* Do they hold the same estimation they did when I was in the city? are they so followed?

*Rosencrantz.* No, indeed, are they not.

*Hamlet.* How comes it? do they grow rusty?

*Rosencrantz.* Nay, their endeavour keeps in the wonted pace; but there is, sir, an aery of children, little eyases, that cry out on the top of question, and are most tyrannically clapped for 't: these are now the fashion, and so berattle the common stages—so they call them—that many wearing rapiers are afraid of goose-quills, and dare scarce come thither.

*Hamlet.* What, are they children? who maintains 'em? how are they escorted? Will they pursue the quality no longer than they can sing? will they not say afterwards, if they should grow themselves to common players—as it is most like, if their means are no better—their writers do them wrong, to make them exclaim against their own succession?

*Rosencrantz.* Faith, there has been much to-do on both sides, and the nation holds it no sin to tarre them to controversy; there was for a while no money bid for argument, unless the poet and the player went to cuffs in the question.

*Hamlet.* Is 't possible?

*Guildenstern.* O, there has been much throwing about of brains.

*Hamlet.* Do the boys carry it away?

*Rosencrantz.* Ay, that they do, my lord; Hercules and his load too.

*Hamlet.* It is not very strange; for mine uncle is king of Denmark, and those that would make mows at him while my father lived give twenty, forty, fifty, an hundred ducats apiece for his picture in little. 'Sblood, there is something in this more than natural, if philosophy could find it out.

[*Flourish of trumpets within.*

*Enter* HAMLET.

*Hamlet.* To be, or not to be,—that is the question:
Whether 't is nobler in the mind to suffer
The slings and arrows of outrageous fortune,
Or to take arms against a sea of troubles,
And by opposing end them? To die,—to sleep,—
No more; and by a sleep to say we end
The heart-ache and the thousand natural shocks
That flesh is heir to,—'t is a consummation
Devoutly to be wish'd. To die,—to sleep,—
To sleep! perchance to dream! ay, there's the rub;
For in that sleep of death what dreams may come
When we have shuffled off this mortal coil,
Must give us pause: there's the respect
That makes calamity of so long life;
For who would bear the whips and scorns of time,
The oppressor's wrong, the proud man's contumely,
The pangs of dispriz'd love, the law's delay,
The insolence of office, and the spurns
That patient merit of the unworthy takes,
When he himself might his quietus make
With a bare bodkin? who would fardels bear,
To grunt and sweat under a weary life,
But that the dread of something after death,
The undiscover'd country from whose bourn
No traveller returns, puzzles the will,
And makes us rather bear those ills we have
Than fly to others that we know not of?
Thus conscience does make cowards of us all;
And thus the native hue of resolution
Is sicklied o'er with the pale cast of thought,
And enterprises of great pith and moment
With this regard their currents turn awry,
And lose the name of action.—Soft you now!

The fair Ophelia!—Nymph, in thy orisons
Be all my sins remember'd.

*Ophelia.* Good my lord,
How does your honour for this many a day?

*Hamlet.* I humbly thank you; well, well, well.

*Ophelia.* My lord, I have remembrances of yours,
That I have longed long to re-deliver;
I pray you, now receive them.

*Hamlet.* No, not I;
I never gave you aught.

*Ophelia.* My honour'd lord, I know right well you did;
And with them words of so sweet breath compos'd
As made the things more rich: their perfume lost,
Take these again; for to the noble mind
Rich gifts wax poor when givers prove unkind.
There, my lord.

*Hamlet.* Ha, ha! are you honest?

*Ophelia.* My lord?

*Hamlet.* Are you fair?

*Ophelia.* What means your lordship?

*Hamlet.* That if you be honest and fair, your honesty should admit no discourse to your beauty.

*Ophelia.* Could beauty, my lord, have better commerce than with honesty?

*Hamlet.* Ay, truly; for the power of beauty will sooner transform honesty from what it is to a bawd than the force of honesty can translate beauty into his likeness: this was sometime a paradox, but now the time gives it proof. I did love you once.

*Ophelia.* Indeed, my lord, you made me believe so.

*Hamlet.* You should not have believed me; for virtue cannot so inoculate our old stock but we shall relish of it: I loved you not.

*Ophelia.* I was the more deceived.

*Hamlet.* Get thee to a nunnery; why wouldst thou be a breeder of sinners? I am myself indifferent honest; but yet I could accuse me of such things that it were better my mother had not borne me: I am very proud, revengeful, ambitious, with more offences at my beck than I have thoughts to put them in, imagination to give them shape, or time to act them in. What should such fellows as I do crawling between earth and heaven? We are arrant knaves all; believe none of us. Go thy ways to a nunnery. Where's your father?

*Ophelia.* At home, my lord.

*Hamlet.* Let the doors be shut upon him, that he may play the fool no where but in 's own house. Farewell.

*Ophelia.* [*Aside*] O, help him, you sweet heavens!

*Hamlet.* If thou dost marry, I'll give thee this plague for thy dowry: be thou as chaste as ice, as pure as snow, thou shalt not escape calumny. Get thee to a nunnery, go; farewell. Or, if thou wilt needs marry, marry a fool; for wise men know well enough what monsters you make of them. To a nunnery, go; and quickly too. Farewell.

*Ophelia.* [*Aside*] O heavenly powers, restore him!

*Hamlet.* I have heard of your paintings too, well enough; God has given you one face, and you make yourselves another: you jig, you amble, and you lisp, and nickname God's creatures, and make your wantonness your ignorance. Go to, I'll no more on 't; it hath made me mad. I say, we will have no marriages: those that are married already, all but one, shall live; the rest shall keep as they are. To a nunnery, go.                    [*Exit.*

*Ophelia.* O, what a noble mind is here o'erthrown!
The courtier's, scholar's, soldier's, eye, tongue, sword;
The expectancy and rose of the fair state,
The glass of fashion and the mould of form,
The observ'd of all observers, quite, quite down!
And I, of ladies most deject and wretched,
That suck'd the honey of his music vows,
Now see that noble and most sovereign reason,
Like sweet bells jangled out of tune, and harsh;
That unmatch'd form and feature of blown youth
Blasted with ecstasy: O, woe is me,
To have seen what I have seen, see what I see!

*Enter* KING *and* POLONIUS.

*King.* Love! his affections do not that way tend;
Nor what he spake, though it lack'd form a little,
Was not like madness. There 's something in his soul
O'er which his melancholy sits on brood,
And I do doubt the hatch and the disclose
Will be some danger; which for to prevent,
I have in quick determination
Thus set it down: he shall with speed to England,
For the demand of our neglected tribute.
Haply the seas and countries different
With variable objects shall expel
This something-settled matter in his heart,
Whereon his brains still beating puts him thus
From fashion of himself. What think you on 't?

*Polonius.* It shall do well; but yet do I believe
The origin and commencement of his grief
Sprung from neglected love.—How now, Ophelia!
You need not tell us what Lord Hamlet said;
We heard it all.—My lord, do as you please;
But, if you hold it fit, after the play
Let his queen mother all alone entreat him
To show his grief: let her be round with him;
And I'll be plac'd, so please you, in the ear
Of all their conference. If she find him not,
To England send him, or confine him where
Your wisdom best shall think.

*King.* It shall be so;
Madness in great ones must not unwatch'd go.

[*Exeunt.*

Scene II. *A Hall in the Castle.*

*Enter* HAMLET *and* PLAYERS

*Hamlet.* Speak the speech, I pray you, as I pronounced it to you, trip-
pingly on the tongue; but if you mouth it, as many of your players do, I
had as lief the town-crier spoke my lines. Nor do not saw the air too
much with your hand, thus, but use all gently; for in the very torrent,

tempest, and, as I may say, the whirlwind of passion, you must acquire and beget a temperance that may give it smoothness. O, it offend me to the soul to hear a robustious periwig-pated fellow tear a passion to tatters, to very rags, to split the ears of the groundlings, who for the most part are capable of nothing but inexplicable dumb-shows and noise. I could have such a fellow whipped for o'erdoing Termagant; it out-herods Herod: pray you avoid it.

*I Player*. I warrant your honour.

*Hamlet*. Be not too tame neither, but let your own discretion be your tutor: suit the action to the word, the word to the action; with this special observance, that you o'erstep not the modesty of nature; for any thing so overdone is from the purpose of playing, whose end, both at the first and now, was and is, to hold, as 't were, the mirror up to nature; to show virtue her own feature, scorn her own image, and the very age and body of the time his form and pressure. Now this overdone, or come tardy off, though it make the unskilful laugh, cannot but make the judicious grieve; the censure of the which one must in your allowance o'erweigh a whole theatre of others. O, there be players that I have seen play, and heard others praise, and that highly, not to speak it profanely, that, neither having the accent of Christians nor the gait of Christian, pagan, nor man, have so strutted and bellowed that I have thought some of nature's journeymen had made men and not made them well, they imitated humanity so abominably.

*I Player*. I hope we have reformed that indifferently with us, sir.

*Hamlet*. O, reform it altogether. And let those that play your clowns speak no more than is set down for them; for there be of them that will themselves laugh, to set on some quantity of barren spectators to laugh too, though in the mean time some necessary question of the play be then to be considered: that 's villanous and shows a most pitiful ambition in the fool that uses it. Go, make you ready.　　　　　　　　[*Exeunt Players.*

*Enter* POLONIUS, ROSENCRANTZ, *and* GUILDENSTERN.

How now, my lord! will the king hear this piece of work?

*Polonius*. And the queen too, and that presently.

*Hamlet*. Bid the players make haste—　　　　　　　[*Exit Polonius.*]
Will you two help hasten them?

*Rosencrantz & Guildenstern.* We will, my lord.

> [*Exeunt Rosencrantz and Guildenstern.*

*Hamlet.* What ho! Horatio!

*Enter* HORATIO.

*Horatio.* Here, sweet lord, at your service.

*Hamlet.* Horatio, thou art e'en as just a man
As e'er my conversation cop'd withal.

*Horatio.* O, my dear lord,—

*Hamlet.* Nay, do not think I flatter;
For what advancement may I hope from thee
That no revenue hast but thy good spirits,
To feed and clothe thee? Why should the poor be flatter'd?
No, let the candied tongue lick absurd pomp,
And crook the pregnant hinges of the knee
Where thrift may follow fawning. Dost thou hear?
Since my dear soul was mistress of her choice
And could of men distinguish, her election
Hath seal'd thee for herself; for thou hast been
As one, in suffering all, that suffers nothing,
A man that fortune's buffets and rewards
Hath ta'en with equal thanks: and blest are those
Whose blood and judgment are so well commingled
That they are not a pipe for Fortune's finger
To sound what stop she please. Give me that man
That is not passion's slave, and I will wear him
In my heart's core, ay, in my heart of heart,
As I do thee.—Something too much of this.—

*Enter* HAMLET.

*Hamlet.* Now might I do it pat, now he is praying;
And now I'll do 't—And so he goes to heaven;
And so am I reveng'd. That would be scann'd:
A villain kills my father; and for that,
I, his sole son, do this same villain send
To heaven.

O, this is hire and salary, not revenge.
He took my father grossly, full of bread,
With all his crimes broad blown, as flush as May;
And how his audit stands who knows save heaven?
But in our circumstance and course of thought,
'T is heavy with him; and am I then reveng'd,
To take him in the purging of his soul,
When he is fit and season'd for his passage?
No!
Up, sword, and know thou a more horrid hent:
When he is drunk asleep, or in his rage,
Or in the incestuous pleasure of his bed;
At gaming, swearing, or about some act
That has no relish of salvation in 't;
Then trip him, that his heels may kick at heaven,
And that his soul may be as damn'd and black
As hell, whereto it goes. My mother stays.—
This physic but prolongs thy sickly days.                    [*Exit.*

*King.* [*Rising*] My words fly up, my thoughts remain below;
Words without thoughts never to heaven go.                    [*Exit.*

# *from* The Adventures of Don Quixote

## Miguel de Cervantes

*Chapter I. Which treats of the quality and way of life of the famous knight Don Quixote de la Mancha.*

In a certain village in La Mancha, which I do not wish to name, there lived not long ago a gentleman—one of those who have always a lance in the rack, an ancient shield, a lean hack and a greyhound for coursing. His habitual diet consisted of a stew, more beef than mutton, of hash most nights, boiled bones on Saturdays, lentils on Fridays, and a young pigeon as a Sunday treat; and on this he spent three-quarters of his income. The rest of it went on a fine cloth doublet, velvet breeches and slippers for holidays, and a homespun suit of the best in which he decked himself on weekdays. His household consisted of a housekeeper of rather more than forty, a niece not yet twenty, and a lad for the field and market, who saddled his horse and wielded the pruning-hook.

Our gentleman was verging on fifty, of tough constitution, lean-bodied, thin-faced, a great early riser and a lover of hunting. They say that his surname was Quixada or Quesada—for there is some difference of opinion amongst authors on this point. However, by very reasonable conjecture we may take it that he was called Quexana. But this does not much concern our story; enough that we do not depart by so much as an inch from the truth in the telling of it.

The reader must know, then, that this gentleman, in the times when he had nothing to do—as was the case for most of the year—gave himself up to the reading of books of knight errantry; which he loved and enjoyed so much that he almost entirely forgot his hunting, and even the care of his estate. So odd and foolish, indeed, did he grow on this subject that he sold many acres of cornland to buy these books of chivalry to read, and in this way brought home every one he could get. And of them all he considered none so good as the works of the famous Feliciano de Silva. For his brilliant style and those complicated sentences seemed to him very pearls, especially when he came upon those love-passages and challenges frequently written in the manner of: 'The reason for the unreason with which you treat my reason, so weakens my reason that with reason I complain of your beauty'; and also when he read: 'The high heavens that with their stars divinely fortify you in your divinity and make you deserving of the desert that your greatness deserves.'

These writings drove the poor knight out of his wits; and he passed sleepless nights trying to understand them and disentangle their meaning, though Aristotle himself would never have unravelled or understood them, even if he had been resurrected for that sole purpose. He did not much like the wounds that Sir Belianis gave and received, for he imagined that his face and his whole body must have been covered with scars and marks, however skilful the surgeons who tended him. But, for all that, he admired the author for ending his book with the promise to continue with that interminable adventure, and often the desire seized him to take up the pen himself, and write the promised sequel for him. No doubt he would have done so, and perhaps successfully, if other greater and more persistent preoccupations had not prevented him.

Often he had arguments with the priest of his village, who was a scholar and a graduate of Siguenza, as to which was the better knight—Palmerin of England or Amadis of Gaul. But Master Nicholas, the barber of that village, said that no one could compare with the Knight of the Sun. Though if anyone could, it was Sir Galaor, brother of Amadis of Gaul. For he had a very accommodating nature, and was not so affected nor such a sniveller as his brother, though he was not a bit behind him in the matter of bravery.

In short, he so buried himself in his books that he spent the nights reading from twilight till daybreak and the days from dawn till dark; and so from little sleep and much reading, his brain dried up and he lost his wits. He filled his mind with all that he read in them, with enchantments, quarrels, battles, challenges, wounds, wooings, loves, torments and other impossible nonsense; and so deeply did he steep his imagination in the belief that all the fanciful stuff he read was true, that to his mind no history in the world was more authentic. He used to say that the Cid Ruy Diaz must have been a very good knight, but that he could not be compared to the Knight of the Burning Sword, who with a single backstroke had cleft a pair of fierce and monstrous giants in two. And he had an even better opinion of Bernardo del Carpio for slaying the enchanted Roland at Roncesvalles, by making use of Hercules' trick when he throttled the Titan Antaeus in his arms.

He spoke very well of the giant Morgante; for, though one of that giant brood who are all proud and insolent, he alone was affable and well-mannered. But he admired most of all Reynald of Montalban, particularly when he saw him sally forth from his castle and rob everyone he met, and when in heathen lands overseas he stole that idol of Mahomet, which history says was of pure gold. But he would have given his housekeeper and his niece into the bargain, to deal the traitor Galaon a good kicking.

In fact, now that he had utterly wrecked his reason he fell into the strangest fancy that ever a madman had in the whole world. He thought it fit and proper, both in order to increase his renown and to serve the state, to turn knight errant and travel through the world with horse and armour in search of adventures, following in every way the practice of the knights errant he had read of, redressing all manner of wrongs, and exposing himself to chances and dangers, by the overcoming of which he might win eternal honour and renown. Already the poor man fancied himself crowned by the valour of his arm, at least with the empire of Trebizond; and so, carried away by the strange pleasure he derived from these agreeable thoughts, he hastened to translate his desires into action.

The first thing that he did was to clean some armour which had belonged to his ancestors, and had lain for ages forgotten in a corner, eaten with rust and covered with mould. But when he had cleaned and repaired it as best he could, he found that there was one great defect: the helmet was a simple head-piece without a visor. So he ingeniously made good this deficiency by fashioning out of pieces of pasteboard a kind of half-visor which, fitted to the helmet, gave the appearance of a complete head-piece. However, to see if it was strong enough to stand up to the risk of a sword-cut, he took out his sword and gave it two strokes, the first of which demolished in a moment what had taken him a week to make. He was not too pleased at the ease with which he had destroyed it, and to safeguard himself against this danger, reconstructed the visor, putting some strips of iron inside, in such a way as to satisfy himself of his protection; and, not caring to make another trial of it, he accepted it as a fine jointed head-piece and put it into commission.

Next he went to inspect his hack, but though, through leanness, he had more quarters than there are pence in a groat, and more blemishes than Gonella's horse, which was nothing but skin and bone, he appeared to our knight more than the equal of Alexander's Bucephalus and the Cid's Babieca. He spent four days pondering what name to give him; for, he reflected, it would be wrong for the horse of so famous a knight, a horse so good in himself, to be without a famous name. Therefore he tried to fit him with one that would signify what he had been before his master turned knight errant, and what he now was; for it was only right that as his master changed his profession, the horse should change his name for a sublime and high-sounding one, befitting the new order and the new calling he professed. So, after many names invented, struck out and rejected, amended, cancelled and remade in his fanciful mind, he finally decided to call him Rocinante, a name which seemed to him grand and sonorous, and to express the common horse he had been before arriving at his present state: the first and foremost of all hacks in the world.

Having found so pleasing a name for his horse, he next decided to do the same for himself, and spent another eight days thinking about it. Finally he resolved to call himself Don Quixote. And that is no doubt why the authors of this true history, as we have said, assumed that his name must have been Quixada and not Quesada, as other authorities would have it. Yet he remembered that the valorous Amadis had not been content with his bare name, but had added the name of his kingdom and native country in order to make it famous, and styled himself Amadis of Gaul. So, like a good knight, he decided to add the name of his country to his own and call himself Don Quixote de la Mancha. Thus, he thought, he very clearly proclaimed his parentage and native land and honoured it by taking his surname from it.

Now that his armour was clean, his helmet made into a complete headpiece, a name found for his horse, and he confirmed in his new title, it struck him that there was only one more thing to do: to find a lady to be enamoured of. For a knight errant without a lady is like a tree without leaves or fruit and a body without a soul. He said to himself again and again: 'If I for my sins or by good luck were to meet with some giant hereabouts, as generally happens to knights errant, and if I were to overthrow him in the encounter, or cut him down the middle or, in short, conquer him and make him surrender, would it not be well to have someone to whom I could send him as a present, so that he could enter and kneel down before my sweet lady and say in tones of humble submission: "Lady, I am the giant Caraculiambro, lord of the island of Malindrania, whom the never-sufficiently-to-be-praised knight, Don Quixote de la Mancha, conquered in single combat and ordered to appear before your Grace, so that your Highness might dispose of me according to your will"?' Oh, how pleased our knight was when he had made up this speech, and even gladder when he found someone whom he could call his lady. It happened, it is believed, in this way: in a village near his there was a very good-looking farm girl, whom he had been taken with at one time, although she it supposed not to have known it or had proof of it. Her name was Aldonza Lorenzo, and she it was he thought fit to call the lady of his fancies; and, casting around for a name which should not be too far away from her own, yet suggest and imply a princess and great lady, he resolved to call her Dulcinea del Toboso— for she was a native of El Toboso—, a name which seemed to him as musical, strange and significant as those others that he had devised for himself and his possessions.

*Chapter II. Which treats of the First Expedition which the ingenious Don Quixote made from his village.*

Once these preparations were completed, he was anxious to wait no longer before putting his ideas into effect, impelled to this by the thought of the loss the world suffered by his delay, seeing the grievances there were to redress, the wrongs to right, the injuries to amend, the abuses to correct, and the debts to discharge. So, telling nobody of his intention, and quite unobserved, one morning before dawn—it was on one of those sweltering July days—he armed himself completely, mounted Rocinante, put on his badly-mended head-piece, slung on his shield, seized his lance and went out into the plain through the back gate of his yard, pleased and delighted to see with what ease he had started on his fair design. But scarcely was he in open country when he was assailed by a thought so terrible that it almost made him abandon the enterprise he had just begun. For he suddenly remembered that he had never received the honour of knighthood, and so, according to the laws of chivalry, he neither could nor should take arms against any knight, and even if he had been knighted he was bound, as a novice, to wear plain armour without a device on his shield until he should gain one by his prowess. These reflections made him waver in his resolve, but as his madness outweighed any other argument, he made up his mind to have himself knighted by the first man he met, in imitation of many who had done the same, as he had read in the books which had so influenced him. As to plain armour, he decided to clean his own, when he had time, till it was whiter than ermine. With this he quieted his mind and went on his way, taking whatever road his horse chose, in the belief that in this lay the essence of adventure.

As our brand-new adventurer journeyed along, he talked to himself, saying: 'Who can doubt that in ages to come, when the authentic story of my famous deeds comes to light, the sage who writes of them will say, when he comes to tell of my first expedition so early in the morning: "Scarce had the ruddy Apollo spread the golden threads of his lovely hair over the broad and spacious face of the earth, and scarcely had the forked tongues of the little painted birds greeted with mellifluous harmony the coming of the rosy Aurora who, leaving the soft bed of her jealous husband, showed herself at the doors and balconies of the Manchegan horizon, when the famous knight, Don Quixote de la Mancha, quitting the slothful down, mounted his famous steed Rocinante and began to journey across the ancient and celebrated plain of Montiel"?' That was, in fact, the road that our knight actually took, as he went on: 'Fortunate the age and fortunate the times in which my famous deeds shall come to light, deeds worthy to be engraved in bronze, carved in marble and painted on wood, as a memorial for posterity. And you, sage enchanter, whoever you may be, to whose lot it falls to be the chronicler of this strange history, I beg you not to forget my good Rocinante, my constant companion on all my rides and journeys!' And presently he cried again, as if he had really been in love: 'O Princess Dulcinea, mistress of this captive heart! You did me great injury in dismissing me and inflicting on me the cruel rigour of your command not to appear in your beauteous presence. Deign, lady, to be mindful of your captive heart, which suffers such griefs for love of you.'

He went on stringing other nonsense on to this, all after the fashion he had learnt in his reading, and imitating the language of his books as best he could. And all the while he rode so slowly and the sun's heat increased so fast that it would have been enough to turn his brain, if he had had any. Almost all that day he rode without encountering anything of note, which reduced him to despair, for he longed to meet straightway someone against whom he could try the strength of his strong arm.

There are authors who say that the first adventure he met was that of the pass of Lapice. Others say it was the windmills. But what I have been able to discover of the matter and what I have found written in the annals of La Mancha, is that he rode all that day, and that at nightfall his horse and he were weary and dying of hunger. Looking in all directions to see if he could discover any castle or shepherd's hut where he could take shelter and supply his urgent needs, he saw, not far from the road he was travelling on, an inn, which seemed to him like a star to guide him to the gates, if not to the palace, of his redemption. So he hurried on, and reached it just as night was falling. Now there chanced to be standing at the inn door two young women of *easy virtue*, as they are called, who were on the way to Seville with some carriers who happened to have taken up their quarters at the inn that evening. As everything that our adventurer thought, saw or imagined seemed to follow the fashion of his reading, as soon as he saw the inn he convinced himself that it was a fortress with its four towers and pinnacles of shining silver, complete with a drawbridge, a deep moat and all those appurtenances with which such castles are painted. So he approached the inn, which to his mind was a castle, and when still a short distance away reined Rocinante in, expecting some dwarf to mount the battlements and sound a trumpet to announce that a knight was approaching the fortress. But when he saw that there was some delay, and that Rocinante was in a hurry to get to the stable, he went up to the inn door and, seeing the two young women standing there, took them for two beauteous maidens or graceful ladies taking the air at the castle gate. Now at that very moment, as chance would have it, a swineherd was collecting from the stubble a drove of hogs—pardon me for naming them—and blew his horn to call them together. But Don Quixote immediately interpreted this in his own way, as some dwarf giving notice of his approach. So with rare pleasure he rode up, whereupon those ladies, thoroughly frightened at seeing a man come towards them dressed in armour with lance and shield, turned to go back into the inn. But Don Quixote, gathering from their flight that they were afraid, raised his pasteboard visor, partly revealing his lean and dusty face, and addressed them with a charming expression and in a calm voice: 'I beg you, ladies, not to fly, nor to fear any outrage; for it ill fits or suits the order of chivalry which I profess to injure anyone, least of all maidens of such rank as your appearance proclaims you to be.'

The girls stared at him, trying to get a look at his face, which was almost covered by the badly made visor. But when they heard themselves called maidens—a title ill-suited to their profession—they could not help laughing, which stung Don Quixote into replying: 'Civility befits the fair; and laughter arising from trivial causes is, moreover, great folly. I do not say this to offend you nor to incur your displeasure, for I have no other wish than to serve you.'

His language, which was unintelligible to them, and the uncouth figure our knight cut, made the ladies laugh the more. Whereat he flew into a rage, and things would have gone much farther, had not the innkeeper, a very fat man and therefore very peaceable, emerged at this moment. Now when he saw this grotesque figure in his equipment of lance, shield and coat of armour, which sorted so ill with his manner of riding, he was on the point of joining the young women in their demonstrations of amusement. But, fearing such a collection of armaments, he decided to speak politely, and addressed him thus: 'If your worship is looking for lodging, Sir Knight, except for a bed—we have none in this inn—you will find plenty of everything.'

And Don Quixote replied, seeing the humility of the warden of the fortress—for such he took the innkeeper to be: 'For me, Sir Castellan, whatever you have is enough. My ornaments are arms, my rest the bloody fray.'

The host thought that he had called him castellan because he took him for a safe man from Castile, though he was an Andalusian from the Strand of San Lucar, as thievish as Cacus and as tricky as a student or a page. So he replied: 'At that rate, your bed shall be the cruel rock, your sleep to watch till day, and that being so, you can safely dismount here in the certainty that you will find in this house ample reason for lying awake not only for one night but for a whole year.'

As he spoke he went to take Don Quixote's stirrup, and our knight dismounted with great labour and difficulty, as he had fasted all day. He then bade the host take good care of his steed, saying that no better piece of horseflesh munched oats in all the world. The innkeeper stared at the beast, which did not seem as good as Don Quixote said, not by a half. However, he put him up in the stable and, when he came back for his guest's orders, he found that the maidens had made it up with him and were taking off his armour. But although they had got off his breast-plate and back-piece, they had no idea how to get him out of his gorget, nor how to take off his counterfeit head-piece, which was tied with green ribbons that would have to be cut, as they could not undo the knot. But to this he would on no account agree, and so he stayed all that night with his helmet on, cutting the strangest and most ridiculous figure imaginable. And whilst he was being disarmed, imagining that these draggled and loose creatures were illustrious ladies and the mistresses of that castle, he addressed them most gracefully:

> *'Never was there knight*
> *By ladies so attended*
> *As was Don Quixote*

*When he left his village.*
*Maidens waited on him,*
*On his horse, princesses—*

or Rocinante, which, dear ladies, is the name of my horse, and Don Quixote de la Mancha is mine. For, although I did not wish to reveal myself till deeds done in your service and for your benefit do so for me, the need to adapt this old ballad of Lancelot to the present occasion has betrayed my name to you before the due season. But the time will come when your ladyships may command me and I shall obey; and the valour of my arms will then disclose the desire I have to serve you.'

The girls, who were not used to hearing such highflown language, did not say a word in reply, but only asked whether he would like anything to eat.

'I would gladly take some food,' replied Don Quixote, 'for I think there is nothing that would come more opportunely.'

That day happened to be a Friday, and there was no food in the inn except some portions of a fish that is called pollack in Castile and cod in Andalusia, in some parts ling and in other troutlet. They asked whether his worship would like some troutlet, as there was no other fish to eat.

'So long as there are plenty of troutlet they may serve me for one trout,' replied Don Quixote, 'for I had just as soon be paid eight separate *reals*, as an eight *real* piece. What is more, these troutlet may be like veal, which is better than beef, or kid, which is better than goats' meat. But, however that may be, let me have it now, for the toil and weight of arms cannot be borne without due care for the belly.'

They set the table for him at the inn door for coolness' sake, and the host brought him a portion of badly soaked and worse cooked salt cod with some bread as black and grimy as his armour. It made them laugh a great deal to see him eat because, as he kept his helmet on and his visor up, he could get nothing into his mouth with his own hands, and required someone's assistance to put it in; and so one of those ladies performed this task for him. But to give him anything to drink would have been impossible if the innkeeper had not bored a reed, put one end into his mouth and poured the wine into the other. All this he bore with patience rather than break the ribbons of his helmet.

While they were thus occupied there happened to come to the inn a hog-gelder, and as he arrived he blew his reed whistle four or five times; which finally convinced Don Quixote that he was at some famous castle, that they were entertaining him with music, that the pollack was trout, the black bread of the whitest flour, the whores ladies and the innkeeper warden of the castle. This made him feel that his resolution and his expedition had been to good purpose, but what distressed him most deeply was that he was not yet knighted, for he believed that he could not rightfully embark on any adventure without first receiving the order of knighthood.

# *from* Novum Organum

## *Francis Bacon*

The human understanding, from its peculiar nature, easily supposes a greater degree of order and equality in things than it really finds; and although many things in nature be *sui generis* and most irregular, will yet invent parallels and conjugates and relatives, where no such thing is. Hence the fiction, that all celestial bodies move in perfect circles, thus rejecting entirely spiral and serpentine lines (except as explanatory terms). Hence also the element of fire is introduced with its peculiar orbit, to keep square with those other three which are objects of our senses. The relative rarity of the elements (as they are called) is arbitrarily made to vary in tenfold progression, with many other dreams of the like nature. Nor is this folly confined to theories, but it is to be met with even in simple notions.

46. The human understanding, when any proposition has been once laid down (either from general admission and belief, or from the pleasure it affords), forces everything else to add fresh support and confirmation; and although most cogent and abundant instances may exist to the contrary, yet either does not observe or despises them, or gets rid of and rejects them by some distinction, with violent and injurious prejudice, rather than sacrifice the authority of its first conclusions. It was well answered by him who has shown in a temple the votive tablets suspended by such as had escaped the peril of shipwreck, and was pressed as to whether he would then recognize the power of the gods, by an inquiry. But where are the portraits of those who have perished in spite of their vows? All superstition is much the same, whether it be that of astrology, dreams, omens, retributive judgment, or the like, in all of which the deluded believers observe events which are fulfilled, but neglect and pass over their failure, though it be much more common. But this evil insinuates itself still more craftily in philosophy and the sciences, in which a settled maxim vitiates and governs every other circumstance, though the latter be much more worthy of confidence. Besides, even in the absence of that eagerness and want of thought (which we have mentioned), it is the peculiar and perpetual error of the human understanding to be more moved and excited by affirmatives than negatives,

334

whereas it ought duly and regularly to be impartial; nay, in establishing any true axiom the negative instance is the most powerful.

47. The human understanding is most excited by that which strikes and enters the mind at once and suddenly, and by which the imagination is immediately filled and inflated. It then begins almost imperceptibly to conceive and suppose that everything is similar to the few objects which have taken possession of the mind, whilst it is very slow and unfit for the transition to the remote and heterogeneous instances by which axioms are tried as by fire, unless the office be imposed upon it by severe regulations and a powerful authority.

48. The human understanding is active and cannot halt or rest, but even, though without effect, still presses forward. Thus we cannot conceive of any end or external boundary of the world, and it seems necessarily to occur to us that there must be something beyond. Nor can we imagine how eternity has flowed on down to the present day, since the usually received distinction of an infinity, a *parte ante* and a *parte post* cannot hold good; for it would thence follow that one infinity is greater than another, and also that infinity is wasting away and tending to an end. There is the same difficulty in considering the infinite divisibility of lines arising from the weakness of our minds, which weakness interferes to still greater disadvantage with the discovery of causes; for although the greatest generalities in nature must be positive just as they are found, and in fact not causable, yet the human understanding, incapable of resting, seeks for something more intelligible. Thus, however, whilst aiming at further progress, it falls back to what is actually less advanced, namely, final causes; for they are clearly more allied to man's own nature, than the system of the universe, and from this source they have wonderfully corrupted philosophy. But he would be an unskilful and shallow philosopher who should seek for causes in the greatest generalities, and not be anxious to discover them in subordinate objects.

49. The human understanding resembles not a dry light, but admits a tincture of the will and passions, which generate their own system accordingly; for man always believes more readily that which he prefers. He, therefore, rejects difficulties for want of patience in investigation; sobriety, because it limits his hope; the depths of nature, from superstition; the light of experiment, from arrogance and pride, lest his mind should appear to be occupied with common and varying objects; paradoxes, from a fear of the opinion of the vulgar; in short, his feelings

imbue and corrupt his understanding in innumerable and sometimes imperceptible ways.

50. But by far the greatest impediment and aberration of the human understanding proceeds from the dulness, incompetency, and errors of the senses; since whatever strikes the senses preponderates over everything, however superior, which does not immediately strike them. Hence contemplation mostly ceases with sight, and a very scanty, or perhaps no regard is paid to invisible objects. The entire operation, therefore, of spirits enclosed in tangible bodies is concealed, and escapes us. All that more delicate change of formation in the parts of coarser substances (vulgarly called alteration, but in fact a change of position in the smallest particles) is equally unknown; and yet, unless the two matters we have mentioned be explored and brought to light, no great effect can be produced in nature. Again, the very nature of common air, and all bodies of less density (of which there are many) is almost unknown; for the senses are weak and erring, nor can instruments be of great use in extending their sphere or acuteness—all the better interpretations of nature are worked out by instances, and fit and apt experiments, where the senses only judge of the experiment, the experiment of nature and the thing itself.

51. The human understanding is, by its own nature, prone to abstraction, and supposes that which is fluctuating to be fixed. But it is better to dissect than abstract nature; such was the method employed by the school of Democritus, which made greater progress in penetrating nature than the rest. It is best to consider matter, its conformation, and the changes of that conformation, its own action, and the law of this action or motion; for forms are a mere fiction of the human mind, unless you will call the laws of action by that name.

52. Such are the idols of the tribe, which arise either from the uniformity of the constitution of man's spirit, or its prejudices, or its limited faculties or restless agitation, or from the interference of the passions, or the incompetency of the senses, or the mode of their impressions.

53. The idols of the den derive their origin from the peculiar nature of each individual's mind and body, and also from education, habit, and accident; and although they be various and manifold, yet we will treat of some that require the greatest caution, and exert the greatest power in polluting the understanding.

54. Some men become attached to particular sciences and contemplations, either from supposing themselves the authors and inventors of them, or from having bestowed the greatest pains upon such subjects, and thus become most habituated to them. If men of this description apply themselves to philosophy and contemplations of a universal nature, they wrest and corrupt them by their preconceived fancies, of which Aristotle affords us a signal instance, who made his natural philosophy completely subservient to his logic, and thus rendered it little more than useless and disputatious. The chemists, again, have formed a fanciful philosophy with the most confined views, from a few experiments of the furnace. Gilbert, too, having employed himself most assiduously in the consideration of the magnet, immediately established a system of philosophy to coincide with his favorite pursuit.

55. The greatest and, perhaps, radical distinction between different men's dispositions for philosophy and the sciences is this, that some are more vigorous and active in observing the differences of things, others in observing their resemblances; for a steady and acute disposition can fix its thoughts, and dwell upon and adhere to a point, through all the refinements of differences, but those that are sublime and discursive recognize and compare even the most delicate and general resemblances; each of them readily falls into excess, by catching either at nice distinctions or shadows of resemblance.

56. Some dispositions evince an unbounded admiration of antiquity, others eagerly embrace novelty, and but few can preserve the just medium, so as neither to tear up what the ancients have correctly laid down, nor to despise the just innovations of the moderns. But this is very prejudicial to the sciences and philosophy, and instead of a correct judgment we have but the factions of the ancients and moderns. Truth is not to be sought in the good fortune of any particular conjuncture of time, which is uncertain, but in the light of nature and experience, which is eternal. Such factions, therefore, are to be abjured, and the understanding must not allow them to hurry it on to assent.

57. The contemplation of nature and of bodies in their individual form distracts and weakens the understanding; but the contemplation of nature and of bodies in their general composition and formation stupefies and relaxes it. We have a good instance of this in the school of Leucippus and Democritus compared with others, for they applied themselves so much to particulars as almost to neglect the general struc-

ture of things, whilst the others were so astounded whilst gazing on the structure that they did not penetrate the simplicity of nature. These two species of contemplation must, therefore, be interchanged, and each employed in its turn, in order to render the understanding at once penetrating and capacious, and to avoid the inconveniences we have mentioned, and the idols that result from them.

58. Let such, therefore, be our precautions in contemplation, that we may ward off and expel the idols of the den, which mostly owe their birth either to some predominant pursuit, or, secondly, to an excess in synthesis and analysis, or, thirdly, to a party zeal in favor of certain ages, or, fourthly, to the extent or narrowness of the subject. In general, he who contemplates nature should suspect whatever particularly takes and fixes his understanding, and should use so much the more caution to preserve it equable and unprejudiced.

59. The idols of the market are the most troublesome of all, those namely which have entwined themselves round the understanding from the associations of words and names. For men imagine that their reason governs words, whilst, in fact, words react upon the understanding; and this has rendered philosophy and the sciences sophistical and inactive. Words are generally formed in a popular sense, and define things by those broad lines which are most obvious to the vulgar mind; but when a more acute understanding, or more diligent observation is anxious to vary those lines, and to adapt them more accurately to nature, words oppose it. Hence the great and solemn disputes of learned men often terminate in controversies about words and names, in regard to which it would be better (imitating the caution of mathematicians) to proceed more advisedly in the first instance, and to bring such disputes to a regular issue by definitions. Such definitions, however, cannot remedy the evil in natural and material objects, because they consist themselves of words, and these words produce others; so that we must necessarily have recourse to particular instances, and their regular series and arrangement, as we shall mention when we come to the mode and scheme of determining notions and axioms.

60. The idols imposed upon the understanding by words are of two kinds. They are either the names of things which have no existence (for as some objects are from inattention left without a name, so names are formed by fanciful imaginations which are without an object), or they are the names of actual objects, but confused, badly defined, and hastily and

irregularly abstracted from things. Fortune, the primum mobile, the planetary orbits, the element of fire, and the like fictions, which owe their birth to futile and false theories, are instances of the first kind. And this species of idols is removed with greater facility, because it can be exterminated by the constant refutation or the desuetude of the theories themselves. The others, which are created by vicious and unskilful abstraction, are intricate and deeply rooted. Take some word for instance, as moist, and let us examine how far the different significations of this word are consistent. It will be found that the word moist is nothing but a confused sign of different actions admitted of no settled and defined uniformity. For it means that which easily diffuses itself over another body; that which is indeterminable and cannot be brought to a consistency; that which yields easily in every direction; that which is easily divided and dispersed; that which is easily united and collected; that which easily flows and is put in motion; that which easily adheres to, and wets another body; that which is easily reduced to a liquid state though previously solid. When, therefore, you come to predicate or impose this name, in one sense flame is moist, in another air is not moist, in another fine powder is moist, in another glass is moist; so that it is quite clear that this notion is hastily abstracted from water only, and common ordinary liquors, without any due verification of it.

There are, however, different degrees of distortion and mistake in words. One of the least faulty classes is that of the names of substances, particularly of the less abstract and more defined species (those then of chalk and mud are good, of earth bad); words signifying actions are more faulty, as to generate, to corrupt, to change; but the most faulty are those denoting qualities (except the immediate objects of sense), as heavy, light, rare, dense. Yet in all of these there must be some notions a little better than others, in proportion as a greater or less number of things come before the senses.

61. The idols of the theatre are not innate, nor do they introduce themselves secretly into the understanding, but they are manifestly instilled and cherished by the fictions of theories and depraved rules of demonstration. To attempt, however, or undertake their confutation would not be consistent with our declarations. For since we neither agree in our principles nor our demonstrations, all argument is out of the question. And it is fortunate that the ancients are left in possession of their honors. We detract nothing from them, seeing our whole doctrine relates only to the path to be pursued. The lame (as they say) in the path outstrip the

swift who wander from it, and it is clear that the very skill and swiftness of him who runs not in the right direction must increase his aberration.

Our method of discovering the sciences is such as to leave little to the acuteness and strength of wit, and indeed rather to level wit and intellect. For as in the drawing of a straight line, or accurate circle by the hand, much depends on its steadiness and practice, but if a ruler or compass be employed there is little occasion for either; so it is with our method. Although, however, we enter into no individual confutations, yet a little must be said, first, of the sects and general divisions of these species of theories; secondly, something further to show that there are external signs of their weakness; and, lastly, we must consider the causes of so great a misfortune, and so long and general a unanimity in error, that we may thus render the access to truth less difficult, and that the human understanding may the more readily be purified, and brought to dismiss its idols.

62. The idols of the theatre, or of theories, are numerous, and may, and perhaps will, be still more so. For unless men's minds had been now occupied for many ages in religious and theological considerations, and civil governments (especially monarchies), had been averse to novelties of that nature even in theory (so that men must apply to them with some risk and injury to their own fortunes, and not only without reward, but subject to contumely and envy), there is no doubt that many other sects of philosophers and theorists would have been introduced, like those which formerly flourished in such diversified abundance amongst the Greeks. For as many imaginary theories of the heavens can be deduced from the phenomena of the sky, so it is even more easy to found many dogmas upon the phenomena of philosophy—and the plot of this our theatre resembles those of the poetical, where the plots which are invented for the stage are more consistent, elegant, and pleasurable than those taken from real history.

In general, men take for the groundwork of their philosophy either too much from a few topics, or too little from many; in either case their philosophy is founded on too narrow a basis of experiment and natural history, and decides on too scanty grounds. For the theoretic philosopher seizes various common circumstances by experiment, without reducing them to certainty or examining and frequently considering them, and relies for the rest upon meditation and the activity of his wit.

There are other philosophers who have diligently and accurately attended to a few experiments, and have thence presumed to deduce and invent systems of philosophy, forming everything to conformity with them.

A third set, from their faith and religious veneration, introduce theology and traditions; the absurdity of some among them having proceeded so far as to seek and derive the sciences from spirits and genii. There are, therefore, three sources of error and three species of false philosophy; the sophistic, empiric, and superstitious.

63. Aristotle affords the most eminent instance of the first; for he corrupted natural philosophy by logic—thus he formed the world of categories, assigned to the human soul, the noblest of substances, a genus determined by words of secondary operation, treated of density and rarity (by which bodies occupy a greater or lesser space), by the frigid distinctions of action and power, asserted that there was a peculiar and proper motion in all bodies, and that if they shared in any other motion, it was owing to an external moving cause, and imposed innumerable arbitrary distinctions upon the nature of things; being everywhere more anxious as to definitions in teaching and the accuracy of the wording of his propositions, than the internal truth of things. And this is best shown by a comparison of his philosophy with the others of greatest repute among the Greeks. For the similar parts of Anaxagoras, the atoms of Leucippus and Democritus, the heaven and earth of Parmenides, the discord and concord of Empedocles, the resolution of bodies into the common nature of fire, and their condensation according to Heraclitus, exhibit some sprinkling of natural philosophy, the nature of things, and experiment; whilst Aristotle's physics are mere logical terms, and he remodelled the same subject in his metaphysics under a more imposing title, and more as a realist than a nominalist. Nor is much stress to be laid on his frequent recourse to experiment in his books on animals, his problems, and other treatises; for he had already decided, without having properly consulted experience as the basis of his decisions and axioms, and after having so decided, he drags experiment along as a captive constrained to accommodate herself to his decisions; so that he is even more to be blamed than his modern followers (of the scholastic school) who have deserted her altogether.

64. The empiric school produces dogmas of a more deformed and monstrous nature than the sophistic or theoretic school; not being founded in

the light of common notions (which, however poor and superstitious, is yet in a manner universal, and of a general tendency), but in the confined obscurity of a few experiments. Hence this species of philosophy appears probable, and almost certain to those who are daily practiced in such experiments, and have thus corrupted their imagination, but incredible and futile to others. We have a strong instance of this in the alchemists and their dogmas; it would be difficult to find another in this age, unless perhaps in the philosophy of Gilbert. We could not, however, neglect to caution others against this school, because we already foresee and argue, that if men be hereafter induced by our exhortations to apply seriously to experiments (bidding farewell to the sophistic doctrines), there will then be imminent danger from empirics, owing to the premature and forward haste of the understanding, and its jumping or flying to generalities and the principles of things. We ought, therefore, already to meet the evil.

65. The corruption of philosophy by the mixing of it up with superstition and theology, is of a much wider extent, and is most injurious to it both as a whole and in parts. For the human understanding is no less exposed to the impressions of fancy, than to those of vulgar notions. The disputatious and sophistic school entraps the understanding, whilst the fanciful, bombastic, and, as it were, poetical school, rather flatters it. There is a clear example of this among the Greeks, especially in Pythagoras, where, however, the superstition is coarse and overcharged, but it is more dangerous and refined in Plato and his school. This evil is found also in some branches of other systems of philosophy, where it introduces abstracted forms, final and first causes, omitting frequently the intermediate and the like. Against it we must use the greatest caution; for the apotheosis of error is the greatest evil of all, and when folly is worshipped, it is, as it were, a plague spot upon the understanding. Yet some of the moderns have indulged this folly with such consummate inconsiderateness, that they have endeavored to build a system of natural philosophy on the first chapter of Genesis, the book of Job, and other parts of Scripture; seeking thus the dead amongst the living. And this folly is the more to be prevented and restrained, because not only fantastical philosophy, but heretical religion spring from the absurd mixture of matters divine and human. It is therefore most wise soberly to render unto faith the things that are faith's.

66. Having spoken of the vicious authority of the systems founded either on vulgar notions, or on a few experiments, or on superstition, we must now consider the faulty subjects for contemplation, especially in natural

philosophy. The human understanding is perverted by observing the power of mechanical arts, in which bodies are very materially changed by composition or separation, and is induced to suppose that something similar takes place in the universal nature of things. Hence the fiction of elements, and their co-operation in forming natural bodies. Again, when man reflects upon the entire liberty of nature, he meets with particular species of things, as animals, plants, minerals, and is thence easily led to imagine that there exist in nature certain primary forms which she strives to produce, and that all variation from them arises from some impediment or error which she is exposed to in completing her work, or from the collision or metamorphosis of different species. The first hypothesis has produced the doctrine of elementary properties, the second that of occult properties and specific powers; and both lead to trifling courses of reflection, in which the mind acquiesces, and is thus diverted from more important subjects. But physicians exercise a much more useful labor in the consideration of the secondary qualities of things, and the operations of attraction, repulsion, attenuation, inspissation, dilation, astringency, separation, maturation, and the like; and would do still more if they would not corrupt these proper observations by the two systems I have alluded to, of elementary qualities and specific powers, by which they either reduce the secondary to first qualities, and their subtile and immeasurable composition, or at any rate neglect to advance by greater and more diligent observation to the third and fourth qualities, thus terminating their contemplation prematurely. Nor are these powers (or the like) to be investigated only among the medicines for the human body, but also in all changes of other natural bodies.

A greater evil arises from the contemplation and investigation rather of the stationary principles of things from which, than of the active by which things themselves are created. For the former only serve for discussion, the latter for practice. Nor is any value to be set on those common differences of motion which are observed in the received system of natural philosophy, as generation, corruption, augmentation, diminution, alteration, and translation. For this is their meaning: if a body, unchanged in other respects, is moved from its place, this is translation; if the places and species be given, but the quantity changed, it is alteration; but, if from such a change, the mass and quantity of the body do not continue the same, this is the motion of augmentation and diminution; if the change be continued so as to vary the species and substance, and transfuse them to others, this is generation and corruption. All this is merely popular, and by no means penetrates into nature; and these are but the measures and bounds of motion, and not different species of it; they merely suggest how far, and not how or whence. For they exhibit neither the affections of bodies nor the process of their parts, but merely establish a division of that motion, which coarsely exhibits to the senses matter in its varied form. Even when they wish to point out something relative to the causes of motion, and to establish a division of them, they most absurdly introduce natural and violent motion, which is also a popular notion, since every violent motion is also in fact natural, that is to say, the external efficient puts nature in action in a different manner to that which she had previously employed.

But if, neglecting these, any one were for instance to observe that there is in bodies a tendency of adhesion, so as not to suffer the unity of nature to be completely separated or broken, and a vacuum to be formed, or that they have a tendency to return to their natural dimensions or tension, so that, if compressed or extended within or beyond it, they immediately strive to recover themselves, and resume their former volume and extent; or that they have a tendency to congregate into masses with similar bodies—the dense, for instance, towards the circumference of the earth, the thin and rare towards that of the heavens. These and the like are true physical genera of motions, but the others are clearly logical and scholastic, as appears plainly from a comparison of the two.

Another considerable evil is, that men in their systems and contemplations bestow their labor upon the investigation and discussion of the principles of things and the extreme limits of nature, although all utility and means of action consist in the intermediate objects. Hence men cease not to abstract nature till they arrive at potential and shapeless matter, and still persist in their dissection, till they arrive at atoms; and yet were all this true, it would be of little use to advance man's estate.

67. The understanding must also be cautioned against the intemperance of systems, so far as regards its giving or withholding its assent; for such intemperance appears to fix and perpetuate idols, so as to leave no means of removing them.

These excesses are of two kinds. The first is seen in those who decide hastily, and render the sciences positive and dictatorial. The other in those who have introduced scepticism, and vague unbounded inquiry. The former subdues, the latter enervates the understanding. The Aristotelian philosophy, after destroying other systems (as the Ottomans do their brethren) by its disputatious confutations, decided upon every-thing, and Aristotle himself then raises up questions at will, in order to settle them; so that everything should be certain and decided, a method now in use among his successors.

The school of Plato introduced scepticism, first, as it were in joke and irony, from their dislike to Protagoras, Hippias, and others, who were ashamed of appearing not to doubt upon any subject. But the new acad-emy dogmatized in their scepticism, and held it as their tenet. Although this method be more honest than arbitrary decision (for its followers allege that they by no means confound all inquiry, like Pyrrho and his disciples, but hold doctrines which they can follow as probable, though they cannot maintain them to be true), yet when the human mind has once despaired of discovering truth, everything begins to languish. Hence men turn aside into pleasant controversies and discussions, and into a sort of wandering over subjects rather than sustain any rigorous investigation. But as we observed at first, we are not to deny the author-ity of the human senses and understanding, although weak, but rather to furnish them with assistance.

68. We have now treated of each kind of idols, and their qualities, all of which must be abjured and renounced with firm and solemn resolution, and the understanding must be completely freed and cleared of them, so that the access to the kingdom of man, which is founded on the sciences, may resemble that to the kingdom of heaven, where no admission is con-ceded except to children.

69. Vicious demonstrations are the muniments and support of idols, and those which we possess in logic, merely subject and enslave the world to human thoughts, and thoughts to words. But demonstrations are in some manner themselves systems of philosophy and science; for such as they are, and accordingly as they are regularly or improperly established, such will be the resulting systems of philosophy and contemplation. But those which we employ in the whole process leading from the senses and things to axioms and conclusions, are fallacious and incompetent. This process is fourfold, and the errors are in equal number. In the first place the impressions of the senses are erroneous, for they fail and deceive us. We must supply defects by substitutions, and fallacies by their correction. Secondly, notions are improperly abstracted from the senses, and inde-terminate and confused when they ought to be the reverse. Thirdly, the induction that is employed is improper, for it determines the principles of

sciences by simple enumeration, without adopting exclusions and resolutions, or just separations of nature. Lastly, the usual method of discovery and proof, by first establishing the most general propositions, then applying and proving the intermediate axioms according to them, is the parent of error and the calamity of every science. But we will treat more fully of that which we now slightly touch upon, when we come to lay down the true way of interpreting nature, after having gone through the above expiatory process and purification of the mind.

# *from* Discourse on Method

### *René Descartes*

I do not know whether I ought to touch upon my first meditations here, for they are so metaphysical and out (558) of the ordinary that they might not be interesting to most people. Nevertheless, in order to show whether my fundamental notions are sufficiently sound, I find myself more or less constrained to speak of them. I had noticed for a long time that in practice it is sometimes necessary to follow opinions which we know to be very uncertain, just as though they were indubitable, as I stated before; but inasmuch as I desired to devote myself wholly to the search for truth, I thought that I should take a course precisely contrary, and reject as absolutely false anything of which I could have the least doubt, in order to see whether anything would be left after this procedure which could be called wholly certain. Thus, [32] as our senses deceive us at times, I was ready to suppose that nothing was at all the way our senses represented them to be. As there are men who make mistakes in reasoning even on the simplest topics in geometry, I judged that I was as liable to error as any other, and rejected as false all the reasoning which I had previously accepted as valid demonstration. Finally, as the same percepts which we have when awake may come to us when asleep without their being true, I decided to suppose that nothing that had ever entered my mind was more real than the illusions of my dreams. But I soon noticed that while I thus wished to think everything false, it was necessarily true that I who thought so was something. Since this truth, *I think, therefore I am, (or exist,)* was so firm and assured that all the most extravagant suppositions of the sceptics were unable to shake it, I judged that I could safely accept it as the first principle of the philosophy I was seeking.

I then examined closely what I was, and saw that I could imagine that I had no body, and that there was no world nor any place that I occupied, but that I could not imagine for a moment that I did not exist. On the contrary, from the very fact that I doubted the truth of other things, (or had any other thought,) it followed [very] evidently (and very certainly that I existed.) On the other hand, if I had [33] ceased to think while (my body and the world and) all the rest of what I had ever imagined remained

347

true, I would have had no reason to believe that I existed (during that time); therefore I concluded that I was a (thing or) substance whose whole essence or nature was only to think, and which, to exist, has no need of space nor of any material thing (or body). Thus it follows that this ego, (this mind,) [this soul,] by which I am what I am, (559) is entirely distinct from the body and is easier to know than the latter, and that even if the body were not, the soul would not cease to be all that it now is.

Next, I considered in general what is required of a proposition for it to be true and certain, for since I had just discovered one to be such, I thought I ought also to know of what that certitude consisted. I saw that there was nothing at all in this statement, "I think, therefore I am," to assure me that I was saying the truth, unless it was that I saw very clearly that to think one must exist. So I judged that I could accept as a general rule that the things which we conceive very clearly and [very] distinctly are always true, but that there may well be some difficulty in deciding which are those which we conceive distinctly.

After that I reflected [upon the fact] that I doubted (many things), and that, in consequence, my spirit was not wholly perfect, for I saw clearly that it was a greater perfection to know than to doubt. I decided to ascertain from what source I had learned to think of something more perfect than myself, and it appeared evident that it must have been [34] from some nature which was in fact more perfect. As for my ideas about many other things outside of me, as the sky, earth, light, heat, and thousands of other things, I was not so much troubled to discover where they came from, because I found nothing in them superior to my own nature. If they really existed, I could believe that whatever perfection they possessed might be derived from my own nature; if they did not exist, I could believe that they were derived from nothingness, that is, that they were derived from my own defects. But this could not be the explanation of my (thought or) idea of a being more perfect than my own. To derive it from nothingness was manifestly impossible, and it is no less repugnant to good sense to assume what is more perfect comes from and depends on the less perfect than it is to assume that something comes from nothing, so that I could not assume that it came from myself. Thus the only hypothesis left was that this idea was put in my mind by a nature that was really more perfect than I was, which had all the perfections that I could imagine, and which was, in a word, God. To this I added that since I knew some perfections which I did not possess, I was not the only being in existence—I will here use freely, if you will pardon me, the terms of the school—and that it followed of necessity that there was someone else more perfect upon whom I depended and from whom I had acquired all that I possessed. For if I had been alone and independent of anything else, so that I had (560) bestowed [35] upon myself all that limited quantity of value which I shared with the perfect Being, I would have been able to get from myself, in the same way, all the surplus which I recognize as lacking in me, and so would have been myself infinite, eternal, immutable, omniscient, omnipotent, and, in sum, I would possess all the perfections that I could discover in God.

For to know the nature of God, (whose existence has been proved), following the reasoning which I have just explained, as far as I was capable of such knowledge, I had only to consider each quality of which I had an idea, and decide whether it was or was not a perfection to possess that quality. I would then be certain that none of those which had some imperfection were in him, but that all the others were. I saw that doubt, inconstancy, sorrow and similar things could not be part of God's nature, since I would be happy to be without them myself. In addition, I had ideas of many sensible and corporeal entities, for although I might suppose that I was dreaming and that all that I saw or imagined was false, I could not at any rate deny that the ideas were truly in my consciousness. [Since] I had already recognized very clearly that intelligent nature is distinct from corporeal nature, (and that in every composite one part depended upon another, and the whole upon its parts, and that whatever depends upon something else is not perfect), [I considered that composition is an evidence of dependency and that dependency is manifestly a defect]. From this I judged that it could not be a perfection in God to be composed of these two natures, and that consequently he was not so composed. But if there were in the world bodies, or even intelligences or other natures that were not wholly [36] perfect, their being must depend on God's power in such a way that they could not subsist without him for a single moment.

At this point I wished to seek for other truths, and proposed for consideration the object of the geometricians. This I conceived as a continuous body, or a space infinitely extended in length, breadth, and [height or] depth; divisible into various parts which can have different shapes and sizes and can be moved or transposed in any way: all of which is presumed by geometricians to be true of their object. I went through some of their simplest demonstrations and noticed that the great certainty which everyone attributes to them is only based on the fact that they are (clearly

and) evidently conceived, following the rule previously established. I
noticed also that there was nothing at all in them to assure me of the existence of their object; it was clear, for example, that if we posit a triangle,
its three angles must be (561) equal to two right angles, but there was
nothing in that to assure me that there was a single triangle in the world.
When I turned back to my idea of a perfect Being, on the other hand, I
(immediately) discovered that existence was included in that idea in the
same way that the idea of a triangle contains the equality of its angles to
two right angles, or that the idea of a [sphere (or] circle) includes the
equidistance of all its parts from its center. Perhaps, in fact, the existence
of the perfect Being is even more evident. Consequently, it is at least as
certain that God, who is this perfect Being, exists, as any theorem of
geometry could possibly be. [37]

What makes many people feel that it is difficult to know of the existence
of God, or even of the nature of their own souls, is that they never withdraw their minds from their senses and consider things higher than corporeal objects. They are so accustomed never to think of anything
without picturing it, that is, without picturing in their imagination some
image, as though of a corporeal thing, [—a method of thinking suitable
only for material objects—] that everything which is not picturable seems
to them unintelligible. This is also manifest in the fact that even philosophers hold it as a maxim in the schools that there is nothing in the understanding which was not first in the senses, a location where it is clearly
evident that the ideas of God and of the soul have never been. It seems to
me that those who wish to use imagery to understand these matters are
doing precisely the same thing that they would be doing if they tried to
use their eyes to hear sounds or smell odors. There is even this difference:
that the sense of sight gives us no less certainty of the truth of objects than
do those of smell and hearing, while neither our imagery nor our senses
could assure us of anything without the cooperation of our understanding (or reason).

Finally, if there are still some men who are not sufficiently persuaded of
the existence of God and of their souls (as really existing things considered apart from the body,) by the reasons which I have given, I want them
to understand that all the other things of which they might think themselves more certain, such as their having a body, or the existence of stars
and of an earth, and other such things are less certain. For even though
we have a moral assurance (, as philosophers say,) of these things, such
that it seems [38] we cannot doubt them without extravagance, yet with-

out being unreasonable we cannot deny that, as far as metaphysical certainty goes, there is sufficient room for doubt. For we can imagine, when asleep, that we have another body and see other stars and another earth without there being any such. How could one know that the thoughts which come to us in dreams are false rather than the others (which we have when awake), since they are often no less vivid and detailed? (562) Let the best minds study this question as long as they wish, I do not believe they can find any reason good enough to remove this doubt unless they presuppose the existence of God. The very principle which I took as a rule to start with, namely, that all those things which we conceived very clearly and very distinctly are true, is known to be true only because God exists, and because he is a (supreme and) perfect Being, and because everything in us (necessarily) comes from him. From this it follows that our ideas or notions, being real things which come from God insofar as they are clear and distinct, cannot to that extent fail to be true. Consequently, though we often have ideas which contain falsity, they can only be those ideas which contain some confusions and obscurity, in which respect they (do not come from the supreme Being, but proceed from [or] participate in] nothingness. That is to say, they are (obscure and) confused in us only because we (lack something or) are not wholly perfect. It is evident that it is no less (impossible [and] repugnant to good sense] to assume that falsity or [39] imperfection as such is derived from God, as that truth or perfection is derived from nothingness. But if we did not know that all reality and truth within us came from a perfect and infinite Being, however clear and distinct our ideas might be, we would have no reason to be certain that they were [endowed with the perfection of being] true.

After the knowledge of God and the soul has thus made us certain of our rule, it is easy to see that the (errors of our) dreams [which we have when asleep] do not in any way cast doubt upon the truth of our waking thoughts. For if it happened that we had some very distinct idea, even while sleeping, as for example when a geometrician dreams of some new proof, his sleep does not keep the proof from being good. As for the most common error of dreams, which is to picture various objects in the same way as our external senses represent them to us (when awake), it does not matter if this gives us a reason to distrust the truth of the impressions we receive (or think we receive,) from the senses, because we can also be mistaken in them frequently without being asleep, as when jaundiced persons see everything yellow, or as the stars and other distant objects appear much smaller than they really are. For in truth, whether we are asleep or awake, we should never allow ourselves to be convinced except on the evidence of our reason. Note that I say of our reason, and not of our imagination or of our senses; for even though we see the [40] sun very clearly, we must not judge thereby that its size is such as we see it, and we can well imagine distinctly the head of a lion (563) mounted on the body of a goat, without concluding that a chimera exists in this world. For reason does not insist that all we see or visualize in this way is true, but it does insist that all our ideas or notions must have some foundation in truth, for it would not be possible that God, who is all-perfect and wholly truthful, would otherwise have given them to us. Since our reasonings (or judgments) are never as (clear and distinct [, as) evident or as complete] in sleep as in waking life, although sometimes our imaginations are then [as] lively and detailed [as when awake, or even more so], and since reason tells us also that all our thoughts cannot be true, as we are not wholly perfect; whatever of truth is to be found in our ideas will [inevitably] occur in those which we have when awake rather than in our dreams.

# The Assayer

*Galileo Galilei*

In accordance with the promise which I made to Your Excellency, I shall certainly state my ideas concerning the proposition "Motion is the cause of heat," explaining in what way it appears to me to be true. But first it will be necessary for me to say a few words concerning that which we call "heat," for I strongly suspect that the commonly held conception of the matter is very far from the truth, inasmuch as heat is generally believed to be a true accident, affection, or quality which actually resides in the material which we feel to be heated.

Now, whenever I conceive of any material or corporeal substance, I am necessarily constrained to conceive of that substance as bounded and as possessing this or that shape, as large or small in relationship to some other body, as in this or that place during this or that time, as in motion or at rest, as in contact or not in contact with some other body, as being one, many, or few—and by no stretch of imagination can I conceive of any corporeal body apart from these conditions. But I do not at all feel myself compelled to conceive of bodies as necessarily conjoined with such further conditions as being red or white, bitter or sweet, having sound or being mute, or possessing a pleasant or unpleasant fragrance. On the contrary, were they not escorted by our physical senses, perhaps neither reason nor understanding would ever, by themselves, arrive at such notions. I think, therefore, that these tastes, odors, colors, etc., so far as their objective existence is concerned, are nothing but mere names for something which resides exclusively in our sensitive body (*corpo sensitivo*), so that if the perceiving creatures were removed, all of these qualities would be annihilated and abolished from existence. But just because we have given special names to these qualities, different from the names we have given to the primary and real properties, we are tempted into believing that the former really and truly exist as well as the latter.

An example, I believe, will clearly explain my concept. Suppose I pass my hand, first over a marble statue, then over a living man. So far as the hand, considered in itself, is concerned, it will act in an identical way upon each of these objects; that is, the primary qualities of motion and contact will similarly affect the two objects, and we would use identical language to describe this in each case. But the living body, which I subject to this experiment, will feel itself affected in various ways, depending upon the part of the body I happen to touch; for example, should it be touched on the sole of the foot or the kneecap, or under the armpit, it will feel, in addition to simple contact, a further affection to which we have given a special name: we call it "tickling." This latter affection is altogether our own, and is not at all a property of the hand itself. And it seems to me that he would be gravely in error who would assert that the hand, in addition to movement and contact, intrinsically posesses another and different faculty which we might call the "tickling faculty," as though tickling were a resident property of the hand per se. Again, a piece of paper or a feather, when gently rubbed over any part of our body whatsoever, will in itself act everywhere in an identical way; it will, namely, move and contact. But we, should we be touched between the eyes, on the tip of the nose, or under the nostrils, will feel an almost intolerable titillation—while if touched in other places, we will scarcely feel anything at all. Now this titillation is completely ours and not the feather's, so that if the living, sensing body were removed, nothing would remain of the titillation but an empty name. And I believe that many other qualities, such as taste, odor, color, and so on, often predicated of natural bodies, have a similar and no greater existence than this.

A solid body and, so to speak, one that is sufficiently heavy, when moved and applied against any part of my body whatsoever, will produce in me the sensation which we call "touch." Although this sense is to be found in every part of the body, it appears principally to reside in the palm of the hand, and even more so in the fingertips, with which we can feel the minutest differences of roughness, texture, and softness and hardness—differences which the other parts of the body are less capable of distinguishing. Some amongst these tactile sensations are more pleasing than others, depending upon the differences of configuration of tangible bodies; that is to say, in accordance with whether they are smooth or irregular, sharp or dull, flexible or rigid. And the sense of touch, being more material than the other senses and being produced by the mass of the material itself, seems to correspond to the element of earth.

Since certain material bodies are continually resolving themselves into tiny particles, some of the particles, because they are heavier than air, will descend; and some of them, because they are lighter than air, will ascend. From this, perhaps, two further senses are born, for certain of the particles penetrate two parts of our body which are effectively more sensitive than the skin, which is incapable of feeling the incursion of materials which are too fine, subtle, or flexible. The descending particles are received by the upper surface of the tongue, and penetrating, they blend with its substance and moisture. Thus our tastes are caused, pleasant or harsh in accordance with variations in the contact of diversely shaped particles, and depending upon whether they are few or many, and whether they have high or low velocity. Other particles ascend, and entering the nostrils they penetrate the various nodes (*mammilule*) which are the instruments of smell; and these particles, in like manner through contact and motion, produce savoriness or unsavoriness—again depending upon whether the particles have this or that shape, high or low velocity, and whether they are many or few. It is remarkable how providently the tongue and nasal passages are situated and disposed, the former stretched beneath to receive the ingression of descending particles, and the latter so arranged as to receive those which ascend. The arrangement whereby the sense of taste is excited in us is perhaps analogous to the way in which fluids descend through the air, and the stimulation of the sense of smell may be compared to the manner in which flames ascend in it.

There remains the element of air, which corresponds to the sense of sound. Sounds come to us indiscriminately, from above and below and from either side, since we are so constituted as to be equally disposed to every direction of the air's movement; and the ear is so situated as to accommodate itself in the highest possible degree to any position in space. Sounds, then, are produced in us and felt when (without any special quality of harmoniousness or dissonance) there is a rapid vibration of air, forming minutely small waves, which move certain cartilages of a certain drum which is in our ear. The various external ways in which this wave-motion of the air is produced are manifold, but can in large part be reduced to the vibrating of bodies which strike the air and form the waves which spread out with great velocity. High frequencies give rise to high tones; low frequencies give rise to low tones, but I cannot believe that there exists in external bodies anything, other than their size, shape, or motion (slow or rapid), which could excite in us our tastes, sounds, and odors. And indeed I should judge that, if ears, tongues, and noses be taken away, the number, shape, and motion of bodies would remain, but not their tastes, sounds, and odors. The latter, external to the living creature, I believe to be nothing but mere names, just as (a few lines back) I asserted tickling and titillation to be, if the armpit or the sensitve skin inside the nose were removed. As to the comparison between the four senses which we have mentioned and the four elements, I believe that the sense of sight, most excellent and noble of all the senses, is like light itself. It stands to the others in the same measure of comparative excellence as the finite stands to the infinite, the gradual to the instantaneous, the divisible to the indivisible, the darkness to the light. Of this sense, and all that pertains to it, I can pretend to understand but little; yet a great deal of time would not suffice for me to set forth even this little bit that I know, or (to put it more exactly) for me to sketch it out on paper. Therefore I shall ponder it in silence.

I return to my first proposition, having now shown how some affections, often reputed to be indwelling properties of some external body, have really no existence save in us, and apart from us are mere names. I confess myself to be very much inclined to believe that heat, too, is of this sort, and that those materials which produce and make felt in us the sense of heat and to which we give the general name "fire" consist of a multitude of tiny particles of such and such a shape, and having such and such a velocity. These, when they encounter our body, penetrate it by means of their extreme subtlety; and it is their contact, felt by us in their passage through our substance, which is the affection we call "heat." It will be pleasantly warm or unpleasantly hot depending upon the number and the velocity (greater or lesser) of these pricking, penetrating particles— pleasant if by their penetration our necessary perspiring is facilitated, unpleasant if their penetrating effects too great a division and dissolution of our substance. In sum, the operation of fire, considered in itself, is nothing but movement, or the penetration of bodies by its extreme subtlety, quickly or slowly, depending upon the number and velocity of tiny corpuscles of flame (*ignicoli*) and upon the greater or lesser density of the bodies concerned. Many bodies dissolve in such a manner that the major part of them becomes transformed into further corpuscles of flame; and this dissolution continues as further dissolvable material is encountered. But that there exists in fire, apart from shape, number, movement, penetration, and contact, some further quality which we call "heat," I cannot believe. And I again judge that heat is altogether subjective, so that if the living, sensitive body be removed, what we call heat would be nothing but a simple word. Since it is the case that this affection is produced in us by passage of tiny corpuscles of flame through our substance and their contact with it, it is obvious that once this motion ceases, their operation upon us will be null. It is thus that we perceive that a quantity of fire, retained in the pores and pits of a piece of calcified stone, does not heat—even if we hold it in the palm of our hand—because the flame remains stationary in the stone. But should we swish the stone in water where, because of its weight, it has greater propensity for movement and where the pits of the stone open somewhat, the corpuscles of flame will escape and, encountering our hand, will penetrate it, so that we will feel heat. Since, in order for heat to be stimulated in us, the mere presence of corpuscles of flame is not by itself sufficient, and since movement is required in addition, it is with considerable reason that I declare motion to be the cause of heat.

This or that movement by which a scantling or other piece of wood is burned up or by which lead and other metals are melted will continue so long as the corpuscles of flame, moved either by their own velocity or (if this be insufficient) aided by a strong blast from a bellows, continue to penetrate the body in question; the former will resolve itself into further corpuscles of flame or into ash; the latter will liquify and be rendered fluid like water. From a common-sense point of view, to assert that that which moves a stone, piece of iron, or a stick, is what heats it, seems like an extreme vanity. But the friction produced when two hard bodies are rubbed together, which either reduces them to fine flying particles or permits the corpuscles of flame contained in them to escape, can finally be analyzed as motion. And the particles, when they encounter our body and penetrate and tear through it, are felt, in their motion and contact, by the living creature, who thus feels those pleasant or unpleasant affections which we call "heat," "burning," or "scorching."

Perhaps while this pulverizing and attrition continue, and remain confined to the particles themselves, their motion will be temporary and their operation will be merely that of heating. But once we arrive at the point of ultimate and maximum dissolution into truly indivisible atoms, light itself may be created, with an instantaneous motion or (I should rather say) an instantaneous diffusion and expansion, capable—I do not know if by the atoms' subtlety, rarity, immateriality, or by different and as yet unspecifiable conditions—capable, I say, of filling vast spaces.

But I should not like, Your Excellency, inadvertently to engulf myself in an infinite ocean without the means to find my way back to port. Nor should I like, while removing one doubt, to give birth to a hundred more, as I fear might in part be the case even in this timid venture from shore. Therefore, I shall await a more opportune moment to re-embark.

# *from* Principia Mathematica

## *Isaac Newton*

### Rules of Reasoning in Philosophy

*Rule 1. We are to admit no more causes of natural things than such as are both true and sufficient to explain their appearances.*

To this purpose the philosophers say that Nature does nothing in vain, and more is in vain when less will serve; for Nature is pleased with simplicity, and affects not the pomp of superfluous causes.

*Rule II. Therefore to the same natural effects we must, as far as possible, assign the same causes.*

As to respiration in a man and in a beast; the descent of stones [meteorites] in *Europe* and in *America*; the light of our culinary fire and of the sun; the reflection of light in the earth, and in the planets.

*Rule III. The qualities of bodies, which admit neither* [intensification] *nor remission of degrees, and which are found to belong to all bodies within the reach of our experiments, are to be esteemed the universal qualities of all bodies whatsoever.*

For since the qualities of bodies are only known to us by experiments, we are to hold for universal all such as universally agree with experiments; and such as are not liable to diminution can never be quite taken away. We are certainly not to relinquish the evidence of experiments for the sake of dreams and vain fictions of our own devising; nor are we to recede from the analogy of Nature, which [is] . . . simple, and always consonant to itself. We no other way know the extension of bodies than by our senses, nor do these reach it in all bodies; but because we perceive extension in all that are sensible, therefore, we ascribe it universally to all others also. That abundance of bodies are hard, we learn by experience; and because the hardness of the whole arises from the hardness of the parts, we, therefore, justly infer the hardness of the undivided particles not only of the bodies we feel but of all others. That all bodies are impenetrable, we gather not from reason, but from sensation. The bodies which we handle we find impenetrable, and thence, conclude impenetrability to be a universal property of all bodies whatsoever. That all bodies are moveable, and endowed with certain powers (which we call . . . {*inertia*}) of persevering in their motion, or in their rest, we only infer from the like properties observed in the bodies which we have seen. The extension, hardness, impenetrability, mobility, . . . of the whole, result from the extension, hardness, impenetrability, mobility, . . . of the parts; and thence we conclude the least particles of all bodies to be also all extended, and hard and impenetrable, and moveable, . . . And this is the foundation of all philosophy. . . .

Lastly, if it universally appears, by experiments and astronomical observations, that all bodies about the earth gravitate towards the earth, and that in proportion to the quantity of matter which they severally contain; that the moon likewise, according to the quantity of its matter, gravitates towards the earth; that, on the other hand, our sea gravitates towards the moon; and all the planets mutually one towards another; and the comets in like manner towards the sun; we must, in consequence of this rule, universally allow that all bodies whatsoever are endowed with a principle of mutual gravitation. . . .

*Rule IV. In experimental philosophy we are to look upon propositions collected by general induction from phenomena as accurately or very nearly true, notwithstanding any contrary hypotheses that may be imagined, till such time as other phenomena occur, by which they may either be made more accurate, or liable to exceptions.*

This rule we must follow, that the argument of induction may not be evaded by hypotheses.

## [Gravity]

Hitherto, we have explained the phenomena of the heavens and of our sea by the power of gravity, but have not yet assigned the cause of this power. This is certain, that it must proceed from a cause that penetrates to the very centres of the sun and planets, without suffering the least diminution of its force; that operates not according to the quantity of the surfaces of the particles upon which it acts (as mechanical causes used to do) but according to the quantity of the solid matter which they contain, and propagates its virtue on all sides to immense distances, decreasing always in the duplicate portion of the distances. . . .

Hitherto I have not been able to discover the cause of those properties of gravity from the phenomena, and I frame no hypothesis; for whatever is not deduced from the phenomena is to be called an hypothesis; and hypotheses, whether metaphysical or physical, whether of occult qualities or mechanical, have no place in experimental philosophy. In this philosophy particular propositions are inferred from the phenomena, and afterward rendered general by induction. Thus it was the impenetrability, the mobility, and the impulsive forces of bodies, and the laws of motion and of gravitation were discovered. And to us it is enough that gravity does really exist, and acts according to the laws which we have explained, and abundantly serves to account for all the motions of the celestial bodies, and of our sea.

## [God and the Universe]

This most beautiful system of the sun, planets, and comets could only proceed from the counsel and dominion of an intelligent and powerful Being. And if the fixed stars are the centers of other like systems, these, being formed by the like wise counsel, must be all subject to the dominion of One, especially since the light of the fixed stars is of the same nature with the light of the sun and from every system light passes into all the other systems; and lest the systems of the fixed stars should, by their gravity, fall on each other mutually, he hath placed those systems at immense distances from one another.

This Being governs all things not as the soul of the world, but as Lord over all; and on account of his dominion he is wont to be called "Lord God" . . . or "Universal Ruler." . . . It is the dominion of a spiritual being which constitutes a God. . . . And from his true dominion it follows that the true God is a living, intelligent and powerful Being. . . . he governs all things, and knows all things that are or can be done. . . . He endures for ever, and is every where present; and by existing always and every where, he constitutes duration and space. . . . In him are all things contained and moved; yet neither affects the other: God suffers nothing from the motion of bodies; bodies find no resistance from the omnipresence of God. . . . As a blind man has no idea of colors so we have no idea of the manner by which the all-wise God preserves and understands all things. He is utterly void of all body and bodily figure, and can therefore neither be seen, nor heard, nor touched; nor ought to be worshipped under the representation of any corporeal thing. We have ideas of his attributes, but what the real substance of any thing is we know not. . . . Much less, then, have we any idea of the substance of God. We know him only by his most wise and excellent contrivances of things. . . . [W]e reverence and adore him as his servants; and a god without dominion, providence, and final causes, is nothing else but Fate and Nature. Blind metaphysical necessity, which is certainly the same always and everywhere, could produce no variety of things. All that diversity of natural things which we find suited to different times and places could arise from nothing but the ideas and will of a Being necessarily existing. . . . And thus much concerning God; to discourse of whom from the appearances of things does certainly belong to Natural Philosophy.

# The Agents of Enlightenment

*Crane Brinton*

Nature became to some of the true believers of the Enlightenment wholly a benign concept. To the Christian, even to the Thomist Christian, Nature had been always somewhat suspect, and certainly always inadequate without the help of the divine. From the time of the Enlightenment on, however, those who used the term Nature to try to influence human beings enjoyed to the full the benefits of the ambiguity exploited in the natural law of the Romans. Nature, to the man of the Enlightenment, was the external world he lived in, a world that clearly existed but in which by no means everything that happened was "natural." In fact, to the really ardent eighteenth-century partisan of the Enlightenment almost everything that happens, that exists at the moment, almost everything in the *actual* external world of Nature—or at any rate, of *human* nature as organized in society—was *unnatural*. Class distinctions, the etiquette of society, the privileges of clergy and nobles, the contrast of slum and palace—these did exist, but they were unnatural. Of course our partisan was thinking of *natural* in the sense of "good," or "normal," *unnatural* as "bad" or "abnormal." The point is that the Nature of Newton as the concept of it filtered down into the educated and half-educated was the orderly, untroubled, beautifully simple working of the universe *properly understood*. Once we understand this Nature in human affairs, all we have to do is to regulate our actions accordingly, and there will be no more unnatural behavior.

We understand the workings of this immanent (but not to the *untrained* obvious or indeed perceptible) Nature by what the Enlightenment loved to call Reason—often, as here, with a capital R. Reason is at its clearest, and indeed first showed itself among men, as mathematics. Reason, argued the agents of Enlightenment, enables us to penetrate from appearances to reality. Without Reason, or even with the faulty kind of Reason that, as common sense, men got along with for so many centuries, we should believe that the sun actually "rises" and "sets"; with Reason, we know the true relation of earth and sun. Similarly, Reason applied to human relations will show us that kings are not fathers of their people, that if meat is good to eat on Thursdays it is good to eat on Fridays, that if pork is nourishing to a Gentile it is nourishing to a Jew. Reason will enable us to find human institutions, human relations that are "natural"; once we find such institutions, we shall conform to them and be happy. Reason will clear up the mess that superstition, revelation, faith (the devils of the rationalists) have piled up here on earth.

With the validity of this leap, or series of leaps, from the law of gravity to human relations we are not at the moment concerned. The point is that the generation that read Newton and Locke made the leap. Neither Newton nor Locke went as far as the men of the next two or three generations who appealed to their authority. Outside his own work as a natural scientist, Newton was no innovator, and indeed is best known in such fields for a most unmodern and unenlightened excursion into Biblical literature. Locke, whose main concern was indeed psychology, ethics, and political theory, was a cautious person, a middle-of-the-roader, for whom the new methods served in part at least to confirm ancient wisdom.

Nor is the first generation to spread the new gospel of Reason radical in a simplifying, extremist fashion. This generation did indeed popularize and make available for ordinary educated men—and very definitely by this time, women—the ideas of the seventeenth century, which Alfred Whitehead has called the "century of genius." They are mostly Frenchmen, and indeed if on the whole England had rather more than her share of the seminal minds that produced the ideas of the Enlightenment, it was above all the French who transmitted these ideas throughout Europe and into Russia, even into the growing outposts of Western society all over the world. The greatest of these Frenchmen is Voltaire, in whose ninety-odd volumes you will find neatly and often wittily expressed almost all the ideas with which the Enlightenment started.

Started, not finished. For Voltaire, with Montesquieu, Pope, the English deists, belongs to the first or moderate generation of the Enlightenment. They are still greatly influenced by the current of taste we analyzed as that of the "spare humanists" of the Age of Louis XIV. They still believe in restraint, in decorum, in those "rules of old discovered, not devised" which preserve a social as well as an aesthetic equilibrium. They don't like the stuffy old ways, especially when the stuffiness is applied with compulsion, and in particular they dislike the old churches, Roman Catholic and Anglican. They make fun of what they don't like. The next generation will find the old ways much too objectionable to joke about.

Montesquieu's *Spirit of the Laws* (1748), the great sociological work of the moderate first generation, marks a kind of turning point. Though Voltaire lived until 1778, an object of hero worship in his final years, the new men after 1750 are mostly radicals. Like most radicals, they tend to be one-sided, to push a particular idea into the ground, to be, in short, sectarian. If their main interest is in religion, they go on from a mild deism to outright materialism and atheism. This atheism is not in any sense a form of skepticism, but a positive belief that the universe is a great machine. If they are psychologists, they go on from Locke's innocent distinction between primary and secondary qualities to construct a whole man on the basis of sensations impinging on an automatically recording psyche; that is, they have already the essence of twentieth-century notions of behaviorism, conditioned reflexes, and the like. Holbach and others are already at the point of view neatly summarized in the title of a book by a lesser colleague, La Mettrie's *L'homme machine*, "Man the Machine." If they are economists, they go on with the French physiocrats to coin one of the great simplicities of our world—and a powerful one—*laissez-faire, laissez-passer*—or to such long-popular slogans as "that government governs best which governs least, and least expensively." Adam Smith, whose *Wealth of Nations* was first published in 1776, and the Scottish group generally are exceptions to our rule. Smith is a moderate, a man temperamentally of the first generation of the Enlightenment, by no means a doctrinaire believer in absolutely free economic competition; it was his followers who simplified his doctrines into "rugged individualism." Or finally, with the followers of Rousseau this second generation could plunge into complete emotional rejection of their social and cultural environment and seek to make it over wholly in accord with the dictates of the Nature that spoke so clearly to simple peasants, primitive savages, children, and literary men like themselves.

By the time a third generation had grown up, the two elements of the later Enlightenment, the rationalist-classical and the sentimental-romantic, had been fully developed. In the critical years before the French Revolution, these two attitudes, these two clusters of ideas, worked together at least to the discredit of the old regime. We shall attempt in a later chapter a more detailed analysis of the importance of the Romantic Movement, which exists almost full-blown in Rousseau himself. Here we may note that rationalism and romanticism are inseparably woven together in the minds of most eighteenth-century Western men of the Enlightenment. Reason and sentiment not merely agreed to condemn the old ways of nobles, priests, and the unenlightened generally; in many minds, they combined to approve the new, the rule of the *intelligent and kind-hearted* majority of unspoiled men. Indeed, the natural man of the simpler followers of the Enlightenment was *both* naturally virtuous and naturally reasonable; his heart and his head were both sound.

It is not here maintained that differences between Rousseau and the rationalists did not exist. They were real, they were picturesquely expressed, and they are worth studying. Romanticism was a *revolt* from rationalism. But it is much more important for us to note that the revolt was the revolt of a child from its parent—a child that greatly resembled the parent. The resemblance lay in a fundamental: Both rejected the doctrine of original sin, and both held that man's life on earth can be almost indefinitely improved—that he can lead the good life—if certain environmental changes are made.

A third generation listened to both rationalist and romantic and made the American and the French revolutions, remade Britain without a "revolution, and set the foundations for the developed cosmology of the nineteenth century. These men were of varied kinds, by no means in agreement. Indeed, at the height of the French Revolution they set a classic example of quarrels to the death—for power, no doubt, but power embodied in ideas. To seek a least common denominator among John Adams, Sam Adams, Thomas Jefferson, Tom Paine, La Fayette, Danton, Robespierre, Francis Place, Lord Grey, and the other leaders of this movement would be difficult and unprofitable. We shall here attempt only to indicate the broad lines of the attitude toward human relations, toward society in the broadest sense of the word, which might be that of an ordinary, educated, forward-looking young person of the later eighteenth century in the Western world.

He must of necessity be a fictitious person. Even in the cosmopolitan eighteenth century there would be firm national and regional imprints; the young Westernizing Russian aristocrat reading Voltaire in French was not much like the Yankee lad discovering in Locke and the English deists how wrong his Congregational minister was about hell-fire. The young German, especially, was even by 1780 the soulful, deep, questing German never content with the shallow rationalism of his French neighbors and enemies. He was already on his German way to something more, something greater, something immeasurable, something impossible. We shall, however, have much to do later with nationalism. Here we must attempt frankly a process of simplification and abstraction.

One further word is needed before we attempt to see what the new cosmology was. With the eighteenth century we are in many ways in modern times. Certainly we have no longer any serious question about the *fact* of the spread of ideas in some form among many thousands, indeed millions, who cannot be numbered among the intellectuals, nor among the ruling classes in any restricted sense of the term. There are many and unresolved problems regarding the nature of their spread, indeed there are in essence all the problems that face us today in the study of public opinion. But at least we know there *was* a public opinion, and we have some clues to what it believed.

The newspaper was in its infancy at the beginning of the century, though by the end it had attained something like its modern form, especially in England, the United States, and France. Throughout the century, however, the cheap pamphlet or broadside meant that the printed word could circulate very widely. Books remained relatively expensive, but there were the beginnings of the circulating library in many social clubs and other voluntary groups. Literacy now began to extend to a considerable part of the population in the West. The masses did not yet read, though by the end of the century the skilled workers in the more advanced countries could and did read. Only the rural masses were still completely illiterate, and the French Revolution made a beginning of literacy even for them. The important thing, however, is the existence in all these countries of a strong, literate middle class, numbering all told several millions, and devoted to the ideas of the Enlightenment.

Finally, the eighteenth century saw the ripening of those characteristically modern agents of the spread of ideas for which we really have no good single name—they were voluntary groups organized sometimes for a specific goal, like the later Anti-Saloon League in the United States, sometimes for social ritual and insurance, like the many fraternal societies, sometimes purely for amusement, like the informal conversation groups the French call *salons*. Western society in the eighteenth century had a very rich group life indeed. As the century wore on, especially in France, all these groups, even those that seem as remote from the history of ideas as a *tabagie* (i.e., smoking club, from *tabac*, tobacco) became in fact agents for the spread of the new, and by then actually revolutionary ideas. Of course, these bourgeois flirted, danced, played cards, and indulged in small talk; but they probably mixed in more serious intellectual effort than is usual in such circles. Even their pleasures took on a tinge of what they fashionably called *patriotisme,* which is not what we call patriotism, but rather loyalty toward the Enlightenment. The French have a game of cards, a variant of whist, which they call *le boston,* after the town that stood up so valiantly in the 1770's for the new ideas.

## The Faith of the Enlightened

In the widest terms the change in the attitude of Western men toward the universe and everything in it was the change from the Christian supernatural heaven after death to the rationalist natural heaven on this earth, now—or at least very shortly. But the clearest way of realizing the greatness of that change is to start off with a very basic modern doctrine that is unquestionably new—the doctrine of progress. Belief in progress, in spite of the two world wars of our generation, the constant threat of a third and worse one, and the grave economic crisis of the thirties, is still so much a part of the way young Americans are brought up that very few Americans realize how unprecedented that belief is. Of course, men have long felt that one way of doing something is "better" than another; they have known specific improvements in techniques; above all, they have been aware as members of a group that their particular group was in a flourishing state, or the reverse.

But remember fifth-century Athens. Here were men in the flush of a very great corporate achievement, men who were quite aware of the fact that they were doing many things better than their ancestors had done them. Thucydides almost calls his Peloponnesian War a "bigger and better" war than any that had been fought before. There is in the funeral speech of Pericles a touch of the Chamber of Commerce of today. Yet you can find no clear notion of progress as a part of the cosmos, as a process of development from lower to higher, in these confident years of Athenian culture. And you find even less that resembles the doctrine of progress if you look at other phases of ancient and medieval history.

You find, indeed, several organized schemes of man's destiny as seen in history. The popular pagan legends of the Mediterranean put the happiest and best age of mankind in the distant past, in a Golden Age, an age of heroes, an age of which the Hebrew version is our familiar Garden of Eden. Among the intellectuals of the Graeco-Roman world there were various sophisticated ideas about the course of history, and notably a series of cyclical theories. Such for instance is the most widely accepted one of a Golden Age followed by a Silver Age in turn followed by an Iron Age, after which there was to be a catastrophe, a new Golden Age, and then the cycle all over again, world without end. It seems quite likely that some of these ideas are related to Hindu ideas about transmigration of souls, eternal recurrences, and the like, and that they mark an otherwise unrecorded meeting of the East and West. They are, of course, quite unlike our ideas of progress. And notably, they are held by men who usually think of themselves as living in an Iron Age. They are, in short, for those holding them, like the notions of a past Golden Age, based on a belief in *regression* or decadence, not on a belief in progress.

We have already noted that traditional Christianity did not have a theory of progress in nature on this earth—certainly not in the clear form this theory took in the Enlightenment. We shall return at the end of this chapter to the subtle and difficult problem of the relations between traditional Christian belief and the Enlightenment. We may note here in passing that the relation is a very close one indeed, that in fact the Enlightenment is a child of Christianity—which may explain for our Freudian times why the Enlightenment was so hostile to traditional Christianity. There is even in Christianity a certain emotional basis not at all incongruous with belief in progress. The formal cosmology of traditional Christianity is, however, clearly closer to pagan notions of man's course on earth than to those of the Enlightenment. The best was first—the state of innocence before the Fall; man has *lapsed*; he cannot reconstitute Eden on earth; he can better himself, it is true, but not actually by any *process*, not even by actions that are properly speaking historical, but only by a transcendental miracle, that of salvation through grace; heaven is quite definitely not to be achieved on earth.

We noted in the *quérelle des anciens et des modernes* of the late seventeenth century the beginnings of public debate among intellectuals on these matters. The doctrine, in broad lines much like our own American folk notions of progress, gets itself very quickly accepted in Western culture of the eighteenth century, though by no means unanimously, and by no means without opposition. You can get from Voltaire, for instance, as much evidence for the thesis that he believed in cycles, with 1750 *lower* in a cycle than the Age of Louis XIV, as for the theory that he believed in progress, and in his own Age of Enlightenment. At the very end of the century, however, Condorcet's *Progres de l'esprit humain* gives a complete, full-dress account of the ten stages by which men had lifted themselves from primitive savagery to the brink of perfection on earth. Fifteen hundred years after St. Augustine comes this philosophy of history in which the *civitas Dei* and the *civitas terrena* are melted indistinguishably together.

Condorcet is rather vague about the way in which all this happens, about the moving force that pushes humanity from one stage to a higher one, and in general it can be said that until in the next century Darwinian ideas of organic evolution were drawn upon in the social sciences, there is hardly a satisfactory general theory of progress that attempts to explain why and how detailed progressive changes are made. The favorite explanation among the intellectuals in the eighteenth century was that progress is due to the spread of reason, to the increasing enlightenment (*les lumieres*) that enables men to control their environment better.

Here is already seen most clearly the historic association of scientific and technological improvement with the idea of progress in the moral and cultural sense. By the eighteenth century the work of scientists from Copernicus through Newton had produced a very broad set of generalizations about the behavior of the material universe—generalizations by 1750 known to laymen at least as well as we know those of relativity and quantum mechanics. Moreover, it was clear that these Newtonian generalizations were better, truer, than those of his medieval predecessors. Still more, by mid-century there was evident the kind of material progress that is with the unreflective perhaps a much firmer source of belief in progress than is pure science. There were better roads along which coaches traveled each year a bit faster; there were obvious, homely improvements such as water closets; there was even, at the end of the century, the beginning of the conquest of the air. The conquest was an imperfect one in balloons, it is true, but even so, in 1787 a Frenchman achieved a very modern death attempting to cross the English Channel in the air. In short, a very old man in the eighteenth century might look back to his childhood as a time when men had fewer conveniences, a simpler material environment, fewer and less efficient tools and machines, a lower standard of living.

The theory of progress, however much it owes to the growth of cumulative knowledge and to the increasing ability of men to produce material wealth from their natural environment, is a theory of morals and indeed metaphysics. Men are, according to this theory, becoming better, happier, more nearly what the ideals of the best of our cultures have aimed at. If you try to pursue this notion of moral improvement into concrete details, you will come up against something of the same kind of vagueness that has always clung to Christian notions of heaven—in itself, perhaps, some evidence for the idea that the doctrine of progress is no more than a modern eschatology. Progress will lead us—and in the original, eighteenth-century notion of progress, will lead us very quickly, within a human generation or two—to a state in which men will all be happy, in which there will be no evil. This happiness is by no means just physical comfort. It is not inaccurate to say that in the eighteenth century most of those who talked of progress and the perfectibility of man were thinking in terms close to those of Christian, Greek, and later Hebraic ethics, of peace on earth to men of good will, of the absence of all the traditional vices, of the presence of the traditional virtues.

So much for the broad basis of a belief in progress on this earth. This progress was to be brought about by the spread of reason. Reason, to the ordinary man of the Enlightenment we are attempting here to follow, was the great key word to his new universe. It was reason that would lead men to understand nature (his other great key word) and by understanding nature to mold his conduct in accordance with nature, and thus avoid the vain attempts he had made under the mistaken notions of traditional Christianity and its moral and political allies to go contrary to nature. Now reason was not quite something that came suddenly into existence about 1687 (this is the date of the publication of Newton's *Philosophiae Naturalis Principia Mathematica*). It must be admitted that there were intolerant modernists who came very close to holding that everything prior to about 1700 was one huge series of mistakes, the blundering of an awkward man in a darkened room; but our average enlightened intellectual was inclined to credit the old Greeks and Romans with having done good spade work, and to believe that what we call the Renaissance and Reformation had begun once more the development of reason. It was in the Church, and especially in the medieval Catholic Church and its successors, that the enlightened found the source of darkness, the unnatural suppression of nature—in short, the Satan every religion needs. To this matter we shall return, for it is of great importance.

For the moment, we can register the fact that the man of the Enlightenment believed that reason was something all men, save a few unfortunate defectives, were capable of following; reason had been suppressed, perhaps even atrophied, by the long rule of traditional Christianity. But now, in the eighteenth century, reason could once more resume its sway, and do for all men what it had done for men like Newton and Locke. Reason could show men how to control their environment and themselves.

For reason could show men how nature worked or would work if men ceased impeding that work by their unnatural institutions and habits. Reason could make them aware of natural laws they had in their ignorance been violating. For instance, they had been trying by tariffs, navigation acts, and all sorts of economic regulations to "protect" the trade of their own country, to secure for their country a larger share of wealth. Once they reasoned on these matters, they would see that if each man pursued his own economic interest (that is, acted naturally) to buy most cheaply and sell most dearly there would be established by the free (natural) play of supply and demand a maximum production of wealth. They would see that tariffs, and indeed all attempts to regulate economic activity by political action, made for *less* production, and could benefit only a very few who thereby got an *unnatural* monopoly.

Or again, men had been trying for generations to drive out or exorcise the demons they believed had somehow got into the insane. They whipped the poor insane people, they tied them down, they went through all sorts of ritual performances to drive out the demons. But reason, working on the problems of religion, could show men that there are no such things as demons; and working on the level of medical and psychological research, it could show that insanity was a natural (if regrettable) disturbance of the mind (and perhaps body), a *disease*, in short, which might be cured or at least alleviated by further use of reason.

Or finally, men and women had for centuries joined monastic orders, taken oaths of chastity, obedience, poverty, and lived out their lives as monks and nuns. Reason would show that, though originally monks had perhaps cleared fields and drained swamps, though still perhaps they occasionally did some useful work, on the whole monasticism meant a great waste of human productive power; even more clearly, reason would show that it was most unnatural for healthy human beings to abstain entirely from sexual intercourse, and that theological justification for such unnatural behavior was as much nonsense as was the idea of demons possessing the insane. When reason got through with monasticism, that institution was seen as a typical example of bad beliefs, bad habits, bad ways of doing things; monasticism would disappear in the new society.

All this added up to the enlightened man into a system that explained the universe. For that system we have already noted the useful term "Newtonian world-machine." It was a machine which, especially as it concerned human relations, the enlightened were only beginning to understand. Thanks to Newton and his predecessors, they understood the solar system, gravity, mass, and in fact in its broad lines all natural science; research was needed only to fill in the details. But as to human relations, though they knew enough to know that their unenlightened predecessors, under the influence of traditional Christianity, had been all wrong about human relations, had indeed built up a system of laws and institutions inadequate at best, vicious at worst, they had as yet not quite attained their Newton. He was, however, just around the corner, this Newton of social science, the man who would sum up our enlightened knowledge into a system of social science men had only to follow to ensure the *real* Golden Age, the *real* Eden—the one that lies ahead, not behind.

Traditional Christianity could no longer provide a cosmology for the enlightened. There was beginning to be enough geology so that the date of creation—4004 B.C. according to Archbishop Ussher—and the story of the flood came to seem more and more unlikely. But there was no need to wait for the growth of geological knowledge. Take the Christian doctrine of the Trinity. Mathematics was against that: In no respectable arithmetical system could three be three and at the same time one. As for miracles, why had they stopped? If you could raise the dead in the first century why not in the eighteenth? And so on, in arguments nowadays familiar enough, but then fresh and daring.

Those whose faith in traditional Christianity was shaken, however, did not at once do away with the idea of God. Most of the enlightened in the first half of the century, including such great figures as Voltaire and Pope, were, at least publicly, deists. Now deism is a fairly definite and concrete belief about the universe, and save in some polemics of the time and since, is not a synonym either of atheism or of skepticism (agnosticism). *Deism* needs to be distinguished from *theism*, which involves a more personal God, a God not necessarily anthropomorphic, but at least in some senses immanent, capable of being prayed to; from *pantheism*, which has God penetrate every particle of the universe; and from *philosophical idealism*, which talks of spirit (*Geist*) rather than God. Actually your deist is very firm about the existence of God, remote and chilly though this God be. The deist's belief is the neatest possible reflection of Newton's orderly universe, spiraling around according to law. The deist's God is the person responsible for planning, building, and setting in motion this world-machine: for how can one have a machine without a maker, a result without a cause? In technical terms, the deist proved the existence of his God by two very old arguments, the argument from a First Cause, and the argument from Design. But once this necessary God had got the world-machine to running, he ceased to do anything about it. This clockmaker God had made his clock-universe, wound it up for eternity, and would let it run for eternity, according to the laws Newton had just made clear. Men in this universe are on their own. God has designed them as part of his machine, and has arranged for them to run on, but with the special gift of getting to know by the use of their reason just how they run. Clearly there is no use praying to this clockmaker God, who could not if he would interfere with his own handiwork. Clearly this God never showed himself to Moses on Sinai, never sent his only begotten son to earth to redeem sinful men—couldn't possibly have such a son.

He seemed, in fact, a by no means necessary God, a sort of do-nothing God. That men should have set up so emotionally unsatisfactory a God at all is an interesting example of the way intellectual changes have to, proceed slowly. The jump from a Christian God to no God was simply too great. But deism was one of the unsatisfactory kinds of compromise, as inadequate intellectually as emotionally. Voltaire's own famous epigram about his God—"if God did not exist, he would have to be invented"—betrays a fatal weakness. The radicals of the next generation saw no need to invent him. They were already familiar through mathematics with the concept of infinity. The world-machine had always existed and would always exist, at least as far as mere men could tell. How could anyone possibly know that a God as remote as that of the deists existed? If he was altogether outside the created universe, how could he be inside, even inside our minds as a conception? Clearly he was not necessary. Nature was enough—this great universe we should never have enough time to study in its entirety. Let us stop worrying about God, and make ours a religion of reason, a system of ethics without all the nonsense of theology.

Such at least was the view of the milder rebels, materialists who found God unnecessary. Others went beyond them, and found God a positive evil, especially if he were the God of the Roman Catholic Church. They proudly called themselves atheists, men without a God. Theirs was no longer a doubt. They knew the Christian God did not exist; they knew the universe was a system of "matter" in motion, which could be fully understood by the use of human reason along lines established by the natural sciences. Their materialism, their atheism was a positive belief, not a form of skepticism; it was a definite form of faith, a kind of religion. This positive belief in a knowable universe ultimately composed of particles of matter has remained ever since an element in Western culture. And yet no one knows at all accurately how many people have accepted, and still accept, some form of this belief.

Deist and atheist both rejected the organized Christianity of their day. The eighteenth was the great century of anticlericalism, the century when all kinds of hostilities and grievances against Catholic and Protestant Christianity could come out in the open, thanks to the "spirit of the age" of the Enlightenment, to cheap printing, to lax censorship, to inefficient police, to the amused approval with which the old ruling classes greeted these attacks on the established religion. What was legal in those two amazingly free countries, England and Holland, was readily bootlegged into France and the Germanies. For the first time since the Roman Empire, Christianity felt itself under heavy attack within its own culture. By the time of the French Revolution, that attack was to attain an extraordinary bitterness, especially in continental countries, and Christians were once more to suffer martyrdom for their faith, this time on the guillotine.

All the faithful of the new religion of reason, deist and complete materialist alike, even though they dismissed the Christian God, had to contend with the problem of evil. It was a very knotty problem for them. They postulated a world-machine, of which man is definitely part, which runs according to the laws of nature. They further postulated a faculty in men, which they called reason, by the exercise of which men could understand these laws of nature, orderly and just laws, and by conforming in their conduct to these laws of nature could live together peaceably and happily. Yet as they looked about this world of the eighteenth century they saw strife and misery everywhere, they saw all sorts of evils. Were these evils in accord with the laws of nature, benign nature? Of course not, they were most unnatural, and the enlightened were naturally at work rooting them out. But how did they get there? How did the unnatural get to be the natural? How did the higher become the lower?

This difficulty had already been encountered in Christianity. But Christianity has at least its Satan, however difficult it may be to reconcile Satan's existence with God's goodness and omnipotence. Those who accepted the cosmology of the Newtonian world-machine had still graver difficulties in introducing, or at any rate in justifying, their obvious desire to change, to improve, something that was already perfect, automatic, determined. In fact, in no monistic naturalism is it easy to slip in the unnatural. Rousseau himself was no admirer of the Newtonian world-machine and of reason. The nature he found at the bottom of all things was the spontaneous, outgoing, loving-kindness of the heart as displayed by simple and uncorrupted persons, such as children, savages, and peasants. Above all, he found this state of nature in the past, before civilization brought corruption. In his *Discourse on the Origin of Inequality* Rousseau attempts to describe the origin of evil. The first man who dared to take from the common ownership a plot of ground, fence it in, and say "this is mine!"—he is the villain responsible for the end of the state of nature. Rousseau does not explain why this child of nature acted so unnaturally.

If the enlightened could not solve the problem of the origin of evil, they had very firm ideas about good and evil in their own time. Evil they considered to be a historical growth embodied in customs, laws, institutions—that is to say, in the environment, especially in the social environment, in what man had made of man. The physical environment they realized, especially after Montesquieu's *Spirit of the Laws*, was often harsh and barren, or too easy and luxurious; and they knew that certain diseases were apparently not wholly the result of the social environment. But they hoped they could master the physical environment; indeed they hoped they could master the social environment. The social environment of their own time they thought was almost wholly bad, so bad that perhaps it would have to be destroyed root and branch. They did not, for the most part, believe that this destruction would be violent. They foresaw a French Revolution, but not a Reign of Terror.

In a general view, the "average" enlightened person (not, we repeat, such complex and subtle persons as Voltaire, Diderot, or even Rousseau) equated evil with the environment, and good with something innate in human beings, with human nature. Man is born good; he is made bad by society. The way to make him good again is to protect this natural goodness from the corruption society brings with it. Or more tangibly, the way to reform individuals is to reform society. Reason can show us how; every law, every custom, every institution must be submitted to the test of its reasonableness. Is a hereditary nobility reasonable? If it is not, we must abolish it; if it is, we must retain it. Hereditary nobility when examined by reason as reason worked in the minds of most enlightened men at least by the 1780's turned out not to be reasonable. One of the first acts of the French National Assembly called to remake France was to abolish nobility.

We have come up against one of the great forms in which ethical and political problems present themselves to modern men, the form we all know as environment versus heredity. Occasionally someone will announce firmly that he finds war and its attendant sufferings and cruelty a Good Thing, and someone else will complain that our physical comforts are a Bad Thing. But men in Western society are mostly agreed on the broad lines of what they find good and what they find evil. Where they differ is in their explanation of the persistence of evil. The Enlightenment and we ourselves as heirs of the Enlightenment push the emphasis over onto the side of environment; we tend to believe—most Americans tend to believe—that if we can only work out the proper "arrangements," in laws, institutions, above all education, human beings will get along together in something pretty close to the good life. Christian tradition tends to push the explanation over onto the side of human nature—men are born with something inside them that makes them incline to evil; they are born in sin. It is true that Christianity sees a way out in the possibility of salvation Jesus brought us, but this is not quite environmentalism, not quite faith in the possibility of passing laws and working out educational curricula.

Now it is important to realize that even in its most hopeful early phases modern environmentalism did not usually go to absurd extremes. Only a madman would assert that any infant taken at random from a number of newborn babes could by the manipulation of his environment be made into anything at all—into a heavyweight boxer, a great musician, or a great physicist. Eighteenth-century psychology, taking its cue from Locke, did indeed think of the human mind as a blank receptacle into which experience poured the content of life; but not even the psychology of the *tabula rasa* interpreted human equality as human identity. More characteristic of eighteenth-century environmentalism is a statement by one of its younger sons, the socialist Robert Owen:

> Any general character, from the best to the worst, from the most ignorant to the most enlightened, may be given to any community, even to the world at large, by the application of proper means; which means are to a great extent

at the command and under the control of those who have influence in the affairs of men.

Here the key word is "general." Owen does not think he can achieve certain specific results with each individual; he does think he can do so for large groups. After all, is this very far from the notions that lie behind all efforts to influence and condition peoples today?

In fact, a belief in environmentalism is still essential for all who hope to bring about fairly rapid and *extensive* changes in the actual behavior of human beings on earth. There are few today who believe such changes can be accomplished by the intervention of a supernatural power, by religion in the traditional sense. And only the crank could believe that quick results are possible by any eugenical manipulation of the human organism. We cannot *breed* better men and women fast; we shall have to *make* better men and women from our present materials. Let Owen speak again with the optimism of the Enlightenment, undimmed in him by the horrors of the French Revolution and the Napoleonic world wars:

> These plans must be devised to train children from their earliest infancy in good habits of every description (which will of course prevent them from acquiring those of falsehood and deception). They must afterwards be rationally educated, and their labour be usefuly directed. Such habits and education will impress them with an active and ardent desire to promote the happiness of every individual, and that without the *shadow of exception* for sect, or party, or country, or climate. They will also ensure, with the fewest possible exceptions, health, strength, and vigour of body; for the happiness of man can be erected only on the foundations of health of body and peace of mind.

# *from* An Essay on Criticism

*Alexander Pope*

'Tis hard to say, if greater want of skill
Appear in writing or in judging ill;
But, of the two, less dangerous is the offence
To tire our patience, than mislead our sense.
Some few in that, but numbers err in this,
Ten censure wrong for one who writes amiss;
A fool might once himself alone expose,
Now one in verse makes many more in prose.

'Tis with our judgments as our watches; none
Go just alike, yet each believes his own.
In poets as true genius is but rare,
True taste as seldom is the critic's share;
Both must alike from Heaven derive their light,
These born to judge, as well as those to write.
Let such teach others who themselves excel,
And censure freely who have written well.
Authors are partial to their wit, 'tis true,
But are not critics to their judgment too?

Yet if we look more closely, we shall find
Most have the seeds of judgment in their mind;
Nature affords at least a glimmering light;
The lines, though touched but faintly, are drawn right.
But as the slightest sketch, if justly traced,
Is by ill colouring but the more disgraced,
So by false learning is good sense defaced;
Some are bewildered in the maze of schools,
And some made coxcombs Nature meant but fools.
In search of wit these lose their common sense,
And then turn critics in their own defence.
Each burns alike, who can, or cannot write,
Or with a rival's or an eunuch's spite.
All fools have still an itching to deride,
And fain would be upon the laughing side;

If Maevius scribble in Apollo's spite,
There are who judge still worse than he can write.

Some have at first for wits, then poets past,
Turned critics next, and proved plain fools at last;
Some neither can for wits nor critics pass,
As heavy mules are neither horse nor ass.
Those half-learned witlings, numerous in our isle,
As half-formed insects on the banks of Nile;
Unfinished things, one knows not what to call,
Their generation's so equivocal:
To tell 'em, would a hundred tongues require,
Or one vain wit's, that might a hundred tire.

But you who seek to give and merit fame,
And justly bear a critic's noble name,
Be sure yourself and your own reach to know,
How far your genius, taste, and learning go;
Launch not beyond your depth, but be discreet,
And mark that point where sense and dulness meet.

Nature to all things fixed the limits fit,
And wisely curbed proud man's pretending wit:
As on the land while here the ocean gains,
In other parts it leaves wide sandy plains;
Thus in the soul while memory prevails,
The solid power of understanding fails;
Where beams of warm imagination play,
The memory's soft figures melt away.
One science only will one genius fit,
So vast is art, so narrow human wit;
Not only bounded to peculiar arts,
But oft in those confined to single parts.
Like kings we lose the conquests gained before,
By vain ambition still to make them more;
Each might his several province well command,
Would all but stoop to what they understand.

First follow Nature, and your judgment frame
By her just standard, which is still the same:
Unerring NATURE, still divinely bright,
One clear, unchanged, and universal light,

Life, force, and beauty, must to all impart,
At once the source, and end, and test of art.
Art from that fund each just supply provides,
Works without show, and without pomp presides
In some fair body thus the informing soul
With spirits feeds, with vigour fills the whole,
Each motion guides, and every nerve sustains;
Itself unseen, but in the effects, remains.
Some to whom Heaven in wit has been profuse,
Want as much more to turn it to its use;
For wit and judgment often are at strife,
Though meant each other's aid, like man and wife.
'Tis more to guide than spur the Muse's steed:
Restrain his fury, than provoke his speed;
The wingèd courser, like a generous horse,
Shows most true mettle when you check his course.

Those RULES of old discovered, not devised,
Are Nature still, but Nature methodized;
Nature, like liberty, is but restrained
By the same laws which first herself ordained.

Hear how learnèd Greece her useful rules indites,
When to repress, and when indulge our flights:
High on Parnassus' top her sons she showed,
And pointed out those arduous paths they trod,
Held from afar, aloft, the immortal prize,
And urged the rest by equal steps to rise;
Just precepts thus from great examples given,
She drew from them what they derived from Heaven.
The generous critic fanned the poet's fire,
And taught the world with reason to admire.
Then criticism the Muses' handmaid proved,
To dress her charms, and make her more beloved;
But following wits from that intention strayed,
Who could not win the mistress, wooed the maid;
Against the poets their own arms they turned,
Sure to hate most the men from whom they learned.
So modern 'pothecaries, taught the art
By doctor's bills to play the doctor's part,
Bold in the practice of mistaken rules,

Prescribed, apply, and call their masters fools.
Some on the leaves of ancient authors prey,
Nor time nor moths e'er spoiled so much as they:
Some drily plain, without invention's aid,
Write dull receipts how poems may be made:
These leave the sense, their learning to display,
And those explain the meaning quite away.

You then whose judgment the right course would steer,
Know well each ancient's proper character;
His fable, subject, scope in every page;
Religion, country, genius of his age:
Without all these at once before your eyes,
Cavil you may, but never criticize.
Be Homer's works your study and delight,
Read them by day, and meditate by night;
Thence form your judgment, thence your maxims bring,
And trace the Muses upward to their spring;
Still with itself compared, his text peruse;
And let your comment be the Mantuan Muse.

When first young Maro in his boundless mind
A work to outlast immortal Rome designed,
Perhaps he seemed above the critic's law,
And but from Nature's fountains scorned to draw:
But when to examine every part he came,
Nature and Homer were, he found, the same:
Convinced, amazed, he checks the bold design,
And rules as strict his laboured work confine,
As if the Stagirite o'erlooked each line.
Learn hence for ancient rules a just esteem;
To copy nature is to copy them.

Some beauties yet no precepts can declare,
For there's a happiness as well as care.
Music resembles poetry, in each
Are nameless graces which no methods teach,
And which a master hand alone can reach.
If, where the rules not far enough extend,
(Since rules were made but to promote their end)
Some lucky licence answer to the full

The intent proposed, that licence is a rule.
Thus Pegasus, a nearer way to take,
May boldly deviate from the common track;
From vulgar bounds with brave disorder part,
And snatch a grace beyond the reach of art,
Which, without passing through the judgment, gains
The heart, and all its end at once attains.
In prospects, thus, some objects please our eyes,
Which out of nature's common order rise,
The shapeless rock, or hanging precipice.
Great wits sometimes may gloriously offend,
And rise to faults true critics dare not mend.
But though the ancients thus their rules invade,
(As kings dispense with laws themselves have made)
Moderns, beware! or if you must offend
Against the precept, ne'er transgress its end;
Let it be seldom, and compelled by need,
And have, at least, their precedent to plead.
The critic else proceeds without remorse,
Seizes your fame, and puts his laws in force.

I know there are, to whose presumptuous thoughts
Those freer beauties, even in them, seem faults:
Some figures monstrous and misshaped appear,
Considered singly, or beheld too near,
Which, but proportioned to their light or place,
Due distance reconciles to form and grace.
A prudent chief not always must display
His powers in equal ranks, and fair array,
But with the occasion and the place comply,
Conceal his force, nay seem sometimes to fly.
Those oft are stratagems which error seem,
Nor is it Homer nods, but we that dream.

Still green with bays each ancient altar stands,
Above the reach of sacrilegious hands,
Secure from flames, from envy's fiercer rage,
Destructive war, and all-involving age.
See, from each clime the learned their incense bring!
Hear, in all tongues consenting paeans ring!
In praise so just, let every voice be joined,

And fill the general chorus of mankind!
Hail Bards triumphant! born in happier days;
Immortal heirs of universal praise!
Whose honours with increase of ages grow,
As streams roll down, enlarging as they flow!
Nations unborn your mighty names shall sound,
And worlds applaud that must not yet be found!
Oh may some spark of your celestial fire,
The last, the meanest of your sons inspire,
(That on weak wings, from far, pursues your flights;
Glows while he reads, but trembles as he writes)
To teach vain wits a science little known,
To admire superior sense, and doubt their own!

Of all the causes which conspire to blind
Man's erring judgment, and misguide the mind,
What the weak head with strongest bias rules,
Is *pride*, the never-failing vice of fools.
Whatever Nature has in worth denied,
She gives in large recruits of needful pride;
For as in bodies, thus in souls, we find
What wants in blood and spirits, swelled with wind;
Pride, where wit fails, steps in to our defence,
And fills up all the mighty void of sense.
If once right reason drives that cloud away,
Truth breaks upon us with resistless day;
Trust not yourself; but your defects to know,
Make use of every friend—and every foe.

A *little learning* is a dangerous thing;
Drink deep, or taste not the Pierian spring:
There shallow draughts intoxicate the brain,
And drinking largely sobers us again.
Fired at first sight with what the Muse imparts,
In fearless youth we tempt the heights of arts,
While from the bounded level of our mind,
Short views we take, nor see the lengths behind,
But more advanced, behold with strange surprise
New, distant scenes of endless science rise!
So pleased at first, the towering Alps we try,
Mount o'er the vales, and seem to tread the sky;

The eternal snows appear already past,
And the first clouds and mountains seem the last:
But those attained, we tremble to survey
The growing labours of the lengthened way,
The increasing prospect tires our wandering eyes,
Hills peep o'er hills, and Alps on Alps arise!

A perfect judge will read each work of wit
With the same spirit that its author writ:
Survey the WHOLE, nor seek slight faults to find,
Where nature moves, and rapture warms the mind;
Nor lose, for that malignant dull delight,
The generous pleasure to be charmed with wit.
But in such lays as neither ebb, nor flow,
Correctly cold, and regularly low,
That shunning faults, one quiet tenor keep;
We cannot blame indeed—but we may sleep.
In wit, as nature, what affects our hearts
Is not the exactness of peculiar parts;
'Tis not a lip, or eye, we beauty call,
But the joint force and full result of all.
Thus when we view some well-proportioned dome,
(The world's just wonder, and even thine O Rome!)
No single parts unequally surprise;
All comes united to the admiring eyes;
No monstrous height, or breadth, or length appear;
The whole at once is bold, and regular.

Whoever thinks a faultless piece to see,
Thinks what ne'er was, nor is, nor e'er shall be.
In every work regard the writer's end,
Since none can compass more than they intend;
And if the means be just, the conduct true,
Applause, in spite of trivial faults, is due.
As men of breeding, sometimes men of wit,
To avoid great errors, must the less commit,
Neglect the rules each verbal critic lays,
For not to know some trifles, is a praise.
Most critics, fond of some subservient art,
Still make the whole depend upon a part,

They talk of principles, but notions prize,
And all to one loved folly sacrifice.

Thus critics, of less judgment than caprice,
Curious, not knowing, not exact, but nice,
Form short ideas; and offend in arts
(As most in manners) by a love to parts.

Some to *conceit* alone their taste confine,
And glittering thoughts struck out at every line;
Pleased with a work where nothing's just or fit;
One glaring chaos and wild heap of wit:
Poets like painters, thus, unskilled to trace
The naked nature and the living grace,
With gold and jewels cover every part,
And hide with ornaments their want of art.
True wit is nature to advantage dressed,
What oft was thought, but ne'er so well expressed,
Something, whose truth convinced at sight we find,
That gives us back the image of our mind:
As shades more sweetly recommend the light,
So modest plainness sets off sprightly wit:
For works may have more wit than does 'em good,
As bodies perish through excess of blood.

Others for *language* all their care express.
And value books, as women men, for dress:
Their praise is still—the style is excellent:
The sense, they humbly take upon content.
Words are like leaves; and where they most abound,
Much fruit of sense beneath is rarely found.
False eloquence, like the prismatic glass,
Its gaudy colours spreads on every place;
The face of nature we no more survey,
All glares alike, without distinction gay:
But true expression, like the unchanging sun,
Clears and improves whate'er it shines upon,
It gilds all objects, but it alters none.
Expression is the dress of thought, and still
Appears more decent as more suitable;
A vile conceit in pompous words expressed,

Is like a clown in regal purple dressed;
For different styles with different subjects sort,
As several garbs with country, town, and court.
Some by old words to fame have made pretence;
Ancients in phrase, mere moderns in their sense!
Such laboured nothings, in so strange a style,
Amaze the unlearned, and make the learnèd smile.
Unlucky, as Fungoso in the play,
These sparks with awkward vanity display
What the fine gentleman wore yesterday;
And but so mimic ancient wits at best,
As apes our grandsires in their doublets drest.
In words, as fashions, the same rule will hold;
Alike fantastic, if too new, or old;
Be not the first by whom the new are tried,
Nor yet the last to lay the old aside.

But most by *numbers* judge a poet's song,
And smooth or rough, with them, is right or wrong;
In the bright Muse though thousand charms conspire,
Her voice is all these tuneful fools admire,
Who haunt Parnassus but to please their ear,
Not mend their minds; as some to church repair,
Not for the doctrine but the music there.
These equal syllables alone require,
Though oft the ear the open vowels tire,
While expletives their feeble aid do join,
And ten low words oft creep in one dull line,
While they ring round the same unvaried chimes,
With sure returns of still expected rhymes.
Where'er you find 'the cooling western breeze,'
In the next line, it 'whispers through the trees';
If crystal streams 'with pleasing murmurs creep,'
The reader's threatened (not in vain) with 'sleep.'
Then, at the last and only couplet fraught
With some unmeaning thing they call a thought,
A needless Alexandrine ends the song,
That, like a wounded snake, drags its slow length along.
Leave such to tune their own dull rhymes, and know
What's roundly smooth, or languishingly slow;

And praise the easy vigour of a line
Where Denham's strength, and Waller's sweetness join.
True ease in writing comes from art, not chance,
As those move easiest who have learned to dance.
'Tis not enough no harshness gives offence,
The sound must seem an echo to the sense.
Soft is the strain when Zephyr gently blows,
And the smooth stream in smoother numbers flows;
But when loud surges lash the sounding shore,
The hoarse, rough verse should like the torrent roar.
When Ajax strives, some rock's vast weight to throw,
The line too labours, and the words move slow;
Not so, when swift Camilla scours the plain,
Flies o'er the unbending corn, and skims along the main.
Hear how Timotheus' varied lays surprise,
And bid alternate passions fall and rise!
While, at each change, the son of Libyan Jove
Now burns with glory, and then melts with love;
Now his fierce eyes with sparkling fury glow;
Now sighs steal out, and tears begin to flow:
Persians and Greeks like turns of nature found,
And the world's victor stood subdued by sound!
The power of music all our hearts allow,
And what Timotheus was, is DRYDEN now.

# Progress of the Human Mind

*Marquis de Condorcet*

*Marie Jean Antoine Nicolas Caritat, Marquis de Condorcet (1743–1794), was born in Picardy, and educated at the Jesuit College in Rheims and at the College of Navarre in Paris. A zealous propagandist for the religious and political views of the philosophes, he greeted the outbreak of the French Revolution with enthusiasm, and was one of the first to declare for a republic. His best-known work,* Outlines of an Historical View of the Progress of the Human Mind, *projected the idea of the continuous progress of the human race to perfection, and the equality of civil and political rights for both sexes. He attributed the excesses of the Revolution to bad institutions, from which humanity would ultimately free itself. His book was the ideal expression of the supreme optimism and confidence of the thinkers of the Age of Reason. Imprisoned at Bourg-la-Reine for his political views, he was found dead in his cell, whether from poison or exhaustion is unknown.*

All the causes which contribute to the improvement of the human species . . . must, from their very nature, exercise an influence always active, and acquire an extent forever increasing. The proofs of this have been exhibited, and from their development in the work itself they will derive additional force: accordingly we may already conclude, that the perfectibility of man is indefinite. Meanwhile we have hitherto considered him as possessing only the same natural faculties, as endowed with the same organization. How much greater would be the certainty, how much wider the compass of our hopes, could we prove that these natural faculties themselves, that this very organization, are also susceptible of amelioration? And this is the last question that we shall examine.

The organic perfectibility or deterioration of the classes of the vegetable, or species of the animal kingdom, may be regarded as one of the general laws of nature.

This law extends to the human race; and it cannot be doubted that the progress of the sanitative art [sanitation], that the use of more wholesome food and more comfortable habitations, that a mode of life which shall develop the physical powers by exercise, without at the same time impairing them by excess; in fine, that the destruction of the two most active causes of deterioration, penury and wretchedness on the one hand, and enormous wealth on the other, must necessarily tend to prolong the common duration of man's existence, and secure him a more constant health and a more robust constitution. It is manifest that the improvement of the practice of medicine, become more efficacious in consequence of the progress of reason and the social order, must in the end put a period to transmissible or contagious disorders, as well to those general maladies resulting from climate, ailments, and the nature of certain occupations. Nor would it be difficult to prove that this hope might be extended to almost every other malady, of which it is probable we shall hereafter discover the most remote causes. Would it even be absurd to suppose this quality of melioration in the human species as susceptible of an indefinite advancement; to suppose that a period must one day arrive when death will be nothing more than the effect either of extraordinary accidents, or of the flow and gradual decay of the vital powers; and that the duration of the middle space, of the interval between the birth of man and this decay, will itself have no assignable limit? Certainly man will not become immortal; but may not the distance between the moment in which he draws his first breath and the common term when, in the course of nature, without malady, without accident, he finds it impossible any longer to exist, be necessarily protracted? As we are now speaking of a progress that is capable of being represented with precision, by numerical quantities or by lines, we shall embrace the opportunity of explaining the two meanings that may be affixed to the word *indefinite*.

In reality, this middle term of life, which in proportion as men advance upon the ocean of futurity, we have supposed incessantly to increase, may receive additions either in conformity to a law by which, though approaching continually an illimitable extent, it could never possibly arrive at it; or a law by which, in the immensity of ages, it may acquire a greater extent than any determinate quantity whatever that may be assigned as its limit. In the latter case, this duration of life is indefinite in the strictest sense of the word, since there exist no bounds on this side of which it must necessarily stop. And in the former, it is equally indefinite to us; if we cannot fix the term, it may forever approach, but can never surpass; particularly if, knowing only that it can never stop, we are ignorant in which of the two senses the term indefinite is applicable to it; and this is precisely the state of the knowledge we have as yet acquired relative to the perfectibility of the species.

Thus, in the instance we are considering, we are bound to believe that the mean duration of human life will forever increase, unless its increase can be prevented by the physical revolutions of the system: but we cannot tell what is the bound which the duration of human life can never exceed; we cannot even tell, whether there be any circumstance in the laws of nature which has determined and laid down its limit.

But may not our physical faculties, the force, the sagacity, the acuteness of the senses, be numbered among the qualities, the individual improvement of which it will be practicable to transmit? An attention to the different breeds of animals must lead us to adopt the affirmative of this question, and a direct observation of the human species itself will be found to strengthen the opinion.

Lastly, may we not include in the same circle the intellectual and moral faculties? May not our parents, who transmit to us the advantages or defects of their conformation, and from whom we received our features and shape, as well as our propensities to certain physical affections, transmit to us also that part of organization upon which intellect, strength of understanding, energy of soul or moral sensibility depend? Is it not probable that education, by improving these qualities will at the same time have an influence upon, will modify and improve this organization itself? Analogy, an investigation of the human faculties, and even some facts, appear to authorize these conjectures, and thereby to enlarge the boundary of our hopes.

Such are the questions with which we shall terminate the last division of our work. And how admirably calculated is this view of the human race, emancipated from its chains, released alike from the dominion of chance, as well as from that of the enemies of its progress, and advancing with a firm and indeviate step in the paths of truth, to console the philosopher lamenting the errors, the flagrant acts of injustice, the crimes with which the earth is still polluted? It is the contemplation of this prospect that rewards him for all his efforts to assist the progress of reason and the establishment of liberty. He dares to regard these efforts as a part of the eternal chain of the destiny of mankind; and in this persuasion he finds the true delight of virtue, the pleasure of having performed a durable service, which no vicissitude will ever destroy in a fatal operation calculated to restore the reign of prejudice and slavery. This sentiment is the asylum into which he retires, and to which the memory of his persecutors cannot follow him: he unites himself in imagination with man restored to his rights, delivered from oppression, and proceeding with rapid strides in the path of happiness: he forgets his own misfortunes while his thoughts are thus employed; he lives no longer to adversity, calumny, and malice, but becomes the associate of these wiser and more fortunate beings whose enviable condition he so earnestly contributed to produce.

# *from* The Age of Reason, Part One (1794)

*Thomas Paine*

## The Author's Profession of Faith

It has been my intention, for several years past, to publish my thoughts upon religion. I am well aware of the difficulties that attend the subject, and from that consideration, had reserved it to a more advanced period of life. I intended it to be the last offering I should make to my fellow-citizens of all nations, and that at a time when the purity of the motive that induced me to it could not admit of a question, even by those who might disapprove the work. The circumstance that has now taken place in France of the total abolition of the whole national order of priesthood, and of everything appertaining to compulsive systems of religion, and compulsive articles of faith, has not only precipitated my intention, but rendered a work of this kind exceedingly necessary, lest in the general wreck of superstition, of false systems of government and false theology, we lose sight of morality, of humanity and of the theology that is true.

As several of my colleagues, and others of my fellow-citizens of France, have given me the example of making their voluntary and individual profession of faith, I also will make mine; and I do this with all that sincerity and frankness with which the mind of man communicates with itself.

I believe in one God, and no more; and I hope for happiness beyond this life.

I believe in the equality of man; and I believe that religious duties consist in doing justice, loving mercy, and endeavouring to make our fellow-creatures happy.

But, lest it should be supposed that I believe many other things in addition to these, I shall, in the progress of this work, declare the things I do not believe, and my reasons for not believing them.

I do not believe in the creed professed by the Jewish Church, by the Roman Church, by the Greek Church, by the Turkish Church, by the

Protestant Church, nor by any church that I know of. My own mind is my own church.

All national institutions of churches, whether Jewish, Christian or Turkish, appear to me no other than human inventions, set up to terrify and enslave mankind, and monopolize power and profit.

I do not mean by this declaration to condemn those who believe otherwise; they have the same right to their belief as I have to mine. But it is necessary to the happiness of man that he be mentally faithful to himself. Infidelity does not consist in believing, or in disbelieving; it consists in professing to believe what he does not believe.

It is impossible to calculate the moral mischief, if I may so express it, that mental lying has produced in society. When a man has so far corrupted and prostituted the chastity of his mind as to subscribe his professional belief to things he does not believe he has prepared himself for the commission of every other crime.

He takes up the trade of a priest for the sake of gain, and in order to qualify himself for that trade he begins with a perjury. Can we conceive any thing more destructive to morality than this?

Soon after I had published the pamphlet *Common Sense*, in America, I saw the exceeding probability that a revolution in the system of government would be followed by a revolution in the system of religion. The adulterous connection of church and state, wherever it has taken place, whether Jewish, Christian or Turkish, has so effectually prohibited by pains and penalties every discussion upon established creeds, and upon first principles of religion, that until the system of government should be changed, those subjects could not be brought fairly and openly before the world; but that whenever this should be done, a revolution in the system of religion would follow. Human inventions and priestcraft would be detected; and man would return to the pure, unmixed and unadulterated belief of one God, and no more.

## Concerning Missions and Revelations

Every national church or religion has established itself by pretending some special mission from God, communicated to certain individuals. The Jews have their Moses; the Christians their Jesus Christ, their apostles and saints; and the Turks their Mahomet, as if the way to God was not open to every man alike.

Each of those churches show certain books, which they call *revelation*, or the Word of God. The Jews say that their Word of God was given by God to Moses, face to face; the Christians say that their Word of God came by divine inspiration; and the Turks say that their Word of God (the Koran) was brought by an angel from heaven. Each of those churches accuses the other of unbelief; and for my own part, I disbelieve them all.

As it is necessary to affix right ideas to words, I will, before I proceed further into the subject, offer some observations on the word *revelation*. Revelation, when applied to religion, means something communicated *immediately* from God to man.

No one will deny or dispute the power of the Almighty to make such a communication, if He pleases. But admitting, for the sake of a case, that something has been revealed to a certain person, and not revealed to any other person, it is revelation to that person only. When he tells it to a second person, a second to a third, a third to a fourth, and so on, it ceases to be a revelation to all those persons. It is revelation to the first person only, and *hearsay* to every other, and consequently they are not obliged to believe it.

It is a contradiction in terms and ideas, to call anything a revelation that comes to us at second-hand, either verbally or in writing. Revelation is necessarily limited to the first communication—after this it is only an account of something which that person says was a revelation made to him; and though he may find himself obliged to believe it, it cannot be incumbent on me to believe it in the same manner; for it was not a revelation made to *me*, and I have only his word for it that it was made to him. When Moses told the children of Israel that he received the two tables of the commandments from the hands of God, they were not obliged to believe him, because they had no other authority for it than his telling them so; and I have no other authority for it than some historian telling me so. The commandments carry no internal evidence of divinity with them; they contain some good moral precepts, such as any man qualified to be a lawgiver, or a legislator, could produce himself, without having recourse to supernatural intervention.[1]

When I am told that the Koran was written in heaven and brought to Mahomet by an angel, the account comes too near the same kind of hearsay evidence and second-hand authority as the former. I did not see the angel myself and, therefore, I have a right not to believe it.

When also I am told that a woman called the Virgin Mary, said, or gave out, that she was with child without any cohabitation with a man, and that her betrothed husband, Joseph, said that an angel told him so, I have a right to believe them or not; such a circumstance required a much stronger evidence than their bare word for it; but we have not even this—for neither Joseph nor Mary wrote any such matter themselves; it is only reported by others that *they said so*—it is hearsay upon hearsay, and I do not choose to rest my belief upon such evidence.

It is, however, not difficult to account for the credit that was given to the story of Jesus Christ being the Son of God. He was born at a time when the heathen mythology had still some fashion and repute in the world, and that mythology had prepared the people for the belief of such a story. Almost all the extraordinary men that lived under the heathen mythology were reputed to be the sons of some of their gods. It was not a new thing, at that time, to believe a man to have been celestially begotten; the intercourse of gods with women was then a matter of familiar opinion.

Their Jupiter, according to their accounts, had cohabited with hundreds: the story, therefore, had nothing in it either new, wonderful or obscene; it was conformable to the opinions that then prevailed among the people called Gentiles, or Mythologists, and it was those people only that believed it.

The Jews, who had kept strictly to the belief of one God, and no more, and who had always rejected the heathen mythology, never credited the story.

It is curious to observe how the theory of what is called the Christian Church sprung out of the tail of the heathen mythology. A direct incorporation took place in the first instance, by making the reputed founder to be celestially begotten. The trinity of gods that then followed was no other than a reduction of the former plurality, which was about twenty or thirty thousand. The statue of Mary succeeded the statue of Diana of Ephesus; the deification of heroes changed into the canonization of saints; the Mythologists had gods for everything; the Christian Mythologists had saints for everything; the Church became as crowded with the one as the Pantheon had been with the other, and Rome was the place of both. The Christian theory is little else than the idolatry of the ancient Mythologists, accommodated to the purposes of power and revenue; and it yet remains to reason and philosophy to abolish the amphibious fraud.

## An Appreciation of the Character of Jesus Christ, and His History

Nothing that is here said can apply, even with the most distant disrespect, to the real character of Jesus Christ. He was a virtuous and an amiable man. The morality that he preached and practised was of the most benevolent kind; and though similar systems of morality had been preached by Confucius, and by some of the Greek philosophers, many years before; by the Quakers since; and by many good men in all ages, it has not been exceeded by any.

Jesus Christ wrote no account of himself, of his birth, parentage, or anything else; not a line of what is called the New Testament is of his own writing. The history of him is altogether the work of other people; and as to the account given of his resurrection and ascension, it was the necessary counterpart to the story of his birth. His historians, having brought him into the world in a supernatural manner, were obliged to take him out again in the same manner, or the first part of the story must have fallen to the ground.

The wretched contrivance with which this latter part is told exceeds every thing that went before it. The first part, that of the miraculous conception, was not a thing that admitted of publicity; and therefore the tellers of this part of the story had this advantage, that though they might not be credited, they could not be detected. They could not be expected to prove it, because it was not one of those things that admitted of proof, and it was impossible that the person of whom it was told could prove it himself.

But the resurrection of a dead person from the grave, and his ascension through the air, is a thing very different as to the evidence it admits of, to the invisible conception of a child in the womb. The resurrection and ascension, supposing them to have taken place, admitted of public and ocular demonstration, like that of the ascension of a balloon, or the sun at noon-day, to all Jerusalem at least.

A thing which everybody is required to believe requires that the proof and evidence of it should be equal to all, and universal; and as the public visibility of this last related act was the only evidence that could give sanction to the former part, the whole of it falls to the ground, because that evidence never was given. Instead of this, a small number of persons, not more than eight or nine, are introduced as proxies for the whole world to say they saw it, and all the rest of the world are called upon to believe it. But it appears that Thomas did not believe the resurrection, and, as they say, would not believe without having ocular and manual demonstration himself. *So neither will I,* and the reason is equally as good for me, and for every other person, as for Thomas.

It is in vain to attempt to palliate or disguise this matter. The story, so far as relates to the supernatural part, has every mark of fraud and imposition stamped upon the face of it. Who were the authors of it is as impossible for us now to know, as it is for us to be assured that the books in which the account is related were written by the persons whose names they bear; the best surviving evidence we now have respecting this affair is the Jews. They are regularly descended from the people who lived in the times this resurrection and ascension is said to have happened, and they say, *it is not true.* It has long appeared to me a strange inconsistency to cite the Jews as a proof of the truth of the story. It is just the same as if a man were to say, I will prove the truth of what I have told you by producing the people who say it is false.

That such a person as Jesus existed, and that he was crucified, which was the mode of execution at that day, are historical relations strictly within the limits of probability. He preached most excellent morality and the equality of man; but he preached also against the corruptions and avarice of the Jewish priests, and this brought upon him the hatred and vengeance of the whole order of priesthood.

The accusation which those priests brought against him was that of sedition and conspiracy against the Roman government, to which the Jews were then subject and tributary; and it is not improbable that the Roman government might have some secret apprehensions of the effects of his doctrine, as well as the Jewish priests; neither is it improbable that Jesus Christ had in contemplation the delivery of the Jewish nation from the bondage of the Romans. Between the two, however, this virtuous reformer and revolutionist lost his life.

## Fabulous Bases of Christianity

It is upon this plain narrative of facts, together with another case I am going to mention, that the Christian Mythologists, calling themselves the Christian Church, have erected their fable, which, for absurdity and extravagance, is not exceeded by anything that is to be found in the mythology of the ancients.

The ancient Mythologists tell that the race of Giants made war against Jupiter, and that one of them threw a hundred rocks against him at one throw; that Jupiter defeated him with thunder, and confined him afterwards under Mount Etna, and that every time the giant turns himself Mount Etna belches fire. It is here easy to see that the circumstance of the mountain, that of its being a volcano, suggested the idea of the fable; and that the fable is made to fit and wind itself up with that circumstance.

The Christian Mythologists tell that their Satan made war against the Almighty, who defeated him, and confined him afterwards, not under a mountain, but in a pit. It is here easy to see that the first fable suggested the idea of the second; for the fable of Jupiter and the Giants was told many hundred years before that of Satan.

Thus far the ancient and the Christian Mythologists differ very little from each other. But the latter have contrived to carry the matter much farther.

They have contrived to connect the fabulous part of the story of Jesus Christ with the fable originating from Mount Etna; and in order to make all the parts of the story tie together they have taken to their aid the traditions of the Jews; for the Christian mythology is made up partly from the ancient mythology and partly from the Jewish traditions.

The Christian Mythologists, after having confined Satan in a pit, were obliged to let him out again to bring on the sequel of the fable. He is then introduced into the Garden of Eden, in the shape of a snake or a serpent, and in that shape he enters into familiar conversation with Eve, who is no way surprised to hear a snake talk; and the issue of this *tête-à-tête* is that he persuades her to eat an apple, and the eating of that apple damns all mankind.

After giving Satan this triumph over the whole creation, one would have supposed that the Church Mythologists would have been kind enough to send him back again to the pit: or, if they had not done this, that they would have put a mountain upon him (for they say that their faith can remove a mountain), or have put him *under* a mountain, as the former mythologists had done, to prevent his getting again among the women and doing more mischief. But instead of this they leave him at large, without even obliging him to give his parole—the secret of which is that they could not do without him; and after being at the trouble of making him, they bribed him to stay. They promised him ALL the Jews, ALL the Turks by anticipation, nine-tenths of the world beside, and Mahomet into the bargain. After this, who can doubt the bountifulness of the Christian Mythology?

Having thus made an insurrection and a battle in heaven, in which none of the combatants could be either killed or wounded—put Satan into the pit—let him out again—gave him a triumph over the whole creation—damned all mankind by the eating of an apple, these Christian Mythologists bring the two ends of their fable together. They represent this virtuous and amiable man, Jesus Christ, to be at once both God and Man, and also the Son of God, celestially begotten, on purpose to be sacrificed, because they say that Eve in her longing had eaten an apple.

## Examination of the Preceding Bases

Putting aside everything that might excite laughter by its absurdity, or detestation by its profaneness, and confining ourselves merely to an examination of the parts, it is impossible to conceive a story more derogatory to the Almighty, more inconsistent with His wisdom, more contradictory to His power, than this story is.

In order to make for it a foundation to rise upon, the inventors were under the necessity of giving to the being whom they call Satan, a power equally as great, if not greater than they attribute to the Almighty. They have not only given him the power of liberating himself from the pit, after what they call his fall, but they have made that power increase afterwards to infinity. Before this fall they represent him only as an angel of limited existence, as they represent the rest. After his fall, he becomes, by their account, omnipresent. He exists everywhere, and at the same time. He occupies the whole immensity of space.

Not content with this deification of Satan, they represent him as defeating, by stratagem, in the shape of an animal of the creation, all the power and wisdom of the Almighty. They represent him as having compelled the Almighty to the *direct necessity* either of surrendering the whole of the creation to the government and sovereignty of this Satan, or of capitulating for its redemption by coming down upon earth, and exhibiting Himself upon a cross in the shape of a man.

Had the inventors of this story told it the contrary way, that is, had they represented the Almighty as compelling Satan to exhibit *himself* on a cross, in the shape of a snake, as a punishment for his new transgression, the story would have been less absurd—less contradictory. But instead of this, they make the transgressor triumph, and the Almighty fall.

That many good men have believed this strange fable, and lived very good lives under that belief (for credulity is not a crime), is what I have no doubt of. In the first place, they were educated to believe it, and they would have believed anything else in the same manner.

There are also many who have been so enthusiastically enraptured by what they conceived to be the infinite love of God to man, in making a sacrifice of Himself, that the vehemence of the idea has forbidden and deterred them from examining into the absurdity and profaneness of the story. The more unnatural anything is, the more it is capable of becoming the object of dismal admiration.

## Of the True Theology

But if objects for gratitude and admiration are our desire, do they not present themselves every hour to our eyes? Do we not see a fair creation prepared to receive us the instant we are born—a world furnished to our hands, that cost us nothing? Is it we that light up the sun, that pour down the rain, and fill the earth with abundance? Whether we sleep or wake, the vast machinery of the universe still goes on.

Are these things, and the blessings they indicate in future, nothing to us? Can our gross feelings be excited by no other subjects than tragedy and suicide? Or is the gloomy pride of man become so intolerable, that nothing can flatter it but a sacrifice of the Creator?

I know that this bold investigation will alarm many, but it would be paying too great a compliment to their credulity to forbear it upon that account; the times and the subject demand it to be done. The suspicion that the theory of what is called the Christian Church is fabulous is becoming very extensive in all countries; and it will be a consolation to men staggering under that suspicion, and doubting what to believe and what to disbelieve, to see the object freely investigated. I therefore pass on to an examination of the books called the Old and New Testaments.

## Examination of the Old Testament

These books, beginning with Genesis and ending with Revelation (which, by the bye, is a book of riddles that requires a revelation to explain it), are, we are told, the Word of God. It is, therefore, proper for us to know who told us so, that we may know what credit to give to the report. The answer to this question is that nobody can tell, except that we tell one another so. The case, however, historically appears to be as follows:

When the Church Mythologists established their system, they collected all the writings they could find and managed them as they pleased. It is a matter altogether of uncertainty to us whether such of the writings as now appear under the name of the Old and New Testaments are in the same state in which those collectors say they found them, or whether they added, altered, abridged or dressed them up.

Be this as it may, they decided by *vote* which of the books out of the collection they had made should be the WORD OF GOD, and which should not. They rejected several; they voted others to be doubtful, such as the books called the Apocrypha; and those books which had a majority of votes were voted to be the Word of God. Had they voted otherwise, all the people, since calling themselves Christians, had believed otherwise— for the belief of the one comes from the vote of the other. Who the people were that did all this, we know nothing of; they called themselves by the general name of the Church, and this is all we know of the matter.

As we have no other external evidence or authority for believing these books to be the Word of God than what I have mentioned, which is no evidence or authority at all, I come in the next place to examine the internal evidence contained in the books themselves.

In the former part of this essay, I have spoken of revelation; I now proceed further with that subject for the purpose of applying it to the books in question.

Revelation is a communication of something which the person to whom that thing is revealed did not know before. For if I have done a thing, or seen it done, it needs no revelation to tell me I have done it, or seen it, nor to enable me to tell it, or to write it.

Revelation, therefore, cannot be applied to anything done upon earth, of which man himself is the actor or the witness; and consequently all the historical and anecdotal parts of the Bible, which is almost the whole of it, is not within the meaning and compass of the word revelation, and, therefore, is not the Word of God.

When Samson ran off with the gate-posts of Gaza, if he ever did so (and whether he did or not is nothing to us), or when he visited his Delilah, or caught his foxes, or did anything else, what has revelation to do with these things? If they were facts, he could tell them himself; or his secretary, if he kept one, could write them, if they were worth either telling or writing; and if they were fictions, revelation could not make them true; and whether true or not, we are neither the better nor the wiser for knowing them. When we contemplate the immensity of that Being who directs and governs the incomprehensible WHOLE, of which the utmost ken of human sight can discover but a part, we ought to feel shame at calling such paltry stories the Word of God.

As to the account of the Creation, with which the book of Genesis opens, it has all the appearance of being a tradition which the Israelites had among them before they came into Egypt; and after their departure from that country they put it at the head of their history, without telling (as it is most probable) that they did not know how they came by it. The manner in which the account opens shows it to be traditionary. It begins abruptly; it is nobody that speaks; it is nobody that hears; it is addressed to nobody; it has neither first, second, nor third person; it has every criterion of being a tradition; it has no voucher. Moses does not take it upon himself by introducing it with the formality that he used on other occasions, such as that of saying, *'The Lord spake unto Moses, saying'*.

Why it has been called the Mosaic account of the Creation, I am at a loss to conceive. Moses, I believe, was too good a judge of such subjects to put his name to that account. He had been educated among the Egyptians, who were a people as well skilled in science, and particularly in astronomy, as any people of their day; and the silence and caution that Moses observes in not authenticating the account is a good negative evidence that he neither told it nor believed it.

The case is that every nation of people has been world-makers, and the Israelites had as much right to set up the trade of world-making as any of the rest; and as Moses was not an Israelite, he might not choose to contradict the tradition. The account, however, is harmless; and this is more than can be said for many other parts of the Bible.

Whenever we read the obscene stories, the voluptuous debaucheries, the cruel and torturous executions, the unrelenting vindictiveness, with which more than half the Bible is filled, it would be more consistent that we called it the word of a demon than the Word of God. It is a history of wickedness that has served to corrupt and brutalize mankind; and, for my part, I sincerely detest it as I detest everything that is cruel.[2]

We scarcely meet with anything, a few phrases excepted, but what deserves either our abhorrence or our contempt, till we come to the miscellaneous parts of the Bible. In the anonymous publications, the Psalms, and the book of Job, more particularly in the latter, we find a great deal of elevated sentiment reverentially expressed of the power and benignity of the Almighty; but they stand on no higher rank than many other compositions on similar subjects, as well before that time as since.

The Proverbs which are said to be Solomon's, though most probably a collection (because they discover a knowledge of life which his situation excluded him from knowing), are an instructive table of ethics. They are inferior in keenness to the proverbs of the Spaniards, and not more wise and economical than those of the American Franklin.

All the remaining parts of the Bible, generally known by the name of the Prophets, are the works of the Jewish poets and itinerant preachers, who mixed poetry, anecdote, and devotion together—and those works still retain the air and style of poetry, though in translation.

## Defining the True Revelation

But some, perhaps, will say: Are we to have no Word of God—no revelation? I answer, Yes; there is a Word of God; there is a revelation.

THE WORD OF GOD IS THE CREATION WE BEHOLD and it is in this word, which no human invention can counterfeit or alter, that God speaketh universally to man.

Human language is local and changeable, and is therefore incapable of being used as the means of unchangeable and universal information. The idea that God sent Jesus Christ to publish, as they say, the glad tidings to all nations, from one end of the earth unto the other, is consistent only with the ignorance of those who knew nothing of the extent of the world, and who believed, as those world-saviours believed, and continued to believe for several centuries (and that in contradiction to the discoveries of philosophers and the experience of navigators), that the earth was flat like a trencher, and that man might walk to the end of it.

But how was Jesus Christ to make anything known to all nations? He could speak but one language, which was Hebrew, and there are in the world several hundred languages. Scarcely any two nations speak the same language, or understand each other; and as to translations, every man who knows anything of languages knows that it is impossible to translate from one language into another, not only without losing a great part of the original, but frequently mistaking the sense; and besides all this, the art of printing was wholly unknown at the time Christ lived.

It is always necessary that the means that are to accomplish any end be equal to the accomplishment of that end, or the end cannot be accomplished. It is in this that the difference between finite and infinite power and wisdom discovers itself. Man frequently fails in accomplishing his ends, from a natural inability of the power to the purpose, and frequently from the want of wisdom to apply power properly. But it is impossible for infinite power and wisdom to fail as man faileth. The means it uses are always equal to the end; but human language, more especially as there is not an universal language, is incapable of being used as an universal means of unchangeable and uniform information, and therefore it is not the means that God uses in manifesting himself universally to man.

It is only in the CREATION that all our ideas and conceptions of a *Word of God* can unite. The Creation speaks a universal language, independently of human speech or human language, multiplied and various as they be. It is an ever-existing original, which every man can read. It cannot be forged; it cannot be counterfeited; it cannot be lost; it cannot be altered; it cannot be suppressed. It does not depend upon the will of man whether it shall be published or not; it publishes itself from one end of the earth to the other. It preaches to all nations and to all worlds; and this *Word of God* reveals to man all that is necessary for man to know of God.

Do we want to contemplate His power? We see it in the immensity of the creation. Do we want to contemplate His wisdom? We see it in the unchangeable order by which the incomprehensible whole is governed. Do we want to contemplate His munificence? We see it in the abundance with which He fills the earth. Do we want to contemplate His mercy? We see it in His not withholding that abundance even from the unthankful. In fine, do we want to know that God is? Search not the book called the Scripture, which any human hand might make, but the Scripture called the creation.

## Concerning God, and the Lights Cast on His Existence and Attributes By the Bible

The only idea man can affix to the name of God is that of a *first cause*, the cause of all things. And incomprehensible and difficult as it is for a man to conceive what a first cause is, he arrives at the belief of it from the tenfold greater difficulty of disbelieving it.

It is difficult beyond description to conceive that space can have no end; but it is more difficult to conceive an end. It is difficult beyond the power of man to conceive an eternal duration of what we call time; but it is more impossible to conceive a time when there shall be no time.

In like manner of reasoning, everything we behold carries in itself the internal evidence that it did not make itself. Every man is an evidence to himself that he did not make himself; neither could his father make himself, nor his grandfather, nor any of his race; neither could any tree, plant or animal make itself; and it is the conviction arising from this evidence that carries us on, as it were, by necessity to the belief of a first cause eternally existing, of a nature totally different to any material existence we know of, and by the power of which all things exist; and this first cause man calls God.

It is only by the exercise of reason that man can discover God. Take away that reason, and he would be incapable of understanding anything; and, in this case, it would be just as consistent to read even the book called the Bible to a horse as to a man. How, then, is it that people pretend to reject reason?

Almost the only parts of the book called the Bible that convey to us any idea of God are some chapters in Job and the 19th Psalm; I recollect no other. Those parts are true *deistical* compositions, for they treat of the Deity through His works. They take the book of creation as the Word of God, they refer to no other book, and all the inferences they make are drawn from that volume.

I insert in this place the 19th Psalm, as paraphrased into English verse by Addison. I recollect not the prose, and where I write this I have not the opportunity of seeing it.

> The spacious firmament on high,
> With all the blue ethereal sky,
> And spangled heavens, a shining frame
> Their great original proclaim.
> The unwearied sun, from day to day,
> Does his Creator's power display;
> And publishes to every land
> The work of an Almighty hand.

*Soon as the evening shades prevail,*
*The moon takes up the wondrous tale,*
*And nightly to the list'ning earth*
*Repeats the story of her birth;*
*While all the stars that round her burn,*
*And all the planets in their turn,*
*Confirm the tidings as they roll,*
*And spread the truth from pole to pole.*

*What, though in solemn silence all*
*Move round this dark, terrestrial ball?*
*What though no real voice, nor sound,*
*Amidst their radiant orbs be found?*
*In reason's ear they all rejoice*
*And utter forth a glorious voice,*
*Forever singing, as they shine,*
*THE HAND THAT MADE US IS DIVINE.*

What more does man want to know than that the hand or power that made these things is divine, in omnipotent? Let him believe this with the force it is impossible to repel, if he permits his reason to act, and his rule of moral life will follow of course.

The allusions in Job have, all of them, the same tendency with this Psalm; that of deducing or proving a truth that would be otherwise unknown, from truths already known.

I recollect not enough of the passages in Job to insert them correctly; but there is one occurs to me that is applicable to the subject I am speaking upon. 'Canst thou by searching find out God? Canst thou find out the Almighty to perfection?'

I know not how the printers have pointed this passage, for I keep no Bible; but it contains two distinct questions that admit of distinct answers.

*First,*—Canst thou by searching find out God? Yes; because, in the first place, I know I did not make myself, and yet I have existence; and by *searching* into the nature of other things, I find that no other thing could make itself; and yet millions of other things exist; therefore it is, that I know, by positive conclusion resulting from this search, that there is a power superior to all those things, and that power is God.

*Secondly*,—Canst thou find out the Almighty to *perfection*? No; not only because the power and wisdom He has manifested in the structure of the creation that I behold is to me incomprehensible, but because even this manifestation, great as it is, is probably but a small display of that immensity of power and wisdom by which millions of other worlds, to me invisible by their distance, were created and continue to exist.

It is evident that both these questions were put to the reason of the person to whom they are supposed to have been addressed; and it is only by admitting the first question to be answered affirmatively that the second could follow. It would have been unnecessary, and even absurd, to have put a second question, more difficult than the first, if the first question had been answered negatively.

The two questions have different objects; the first refers to the existence of God; the second to His attributes; reason can discover the one, but it falls infinitely short in discovering the whole of the other.

I recollect not a single passage in all the writings ascribed to the men called apostles that conveys any idea of what God is. Those writings are chiefly controversial; and the subjects they dwell upon, that of a man dying in agony on a cross, is better suited to the gloomy genius of a monk in a cell, by whom it is not impossible they were written, than to any man breathing the open air of the creation.

●　●　●

The setters-up, therefore, and the advocates of the Christian system of faith could not but foresee that the continually progressive knowledge that man would gain, by the aid of science, of the power and wisdom of God, manifested in the structure of the universe and in all the works of creation, would militate against, and call into question, the truth of their system of faith; and therefore it became necessary to their purpose to cut learning down to a size less dangerous to their project, and this they effected by restricting the idea of learning to the dead study of dead languages.

They not only rejected the study of science out of the Christian schools, but they persecuted it, and it is only within about the last two centuries that the study has been revived. So late as 1610, Galileo, a Florentine, discovered and introduced the use of telescopes, and by applying them to observe the motions and appearances of the heavenly bodies afforded additional means for ascertaining the true structure of the universe.

Instead of being esteemed for those discoveries, he was sentenced to renounce them, or the opinions resulting from them, as a damnable heresy. And, prior to that time, Virgilius was condemned to be burned for asserting the antipodes, or in other words that the earth was a globe, and habitable in every part where there was land; yet the truth of this is now too well known even to be told.

If the belief of errors not morally bad did no mischief, it would make no part of the moral duty of man to oppose and remove them. There was no moral ill in believing the earth was flat like a trencher, any more than there was moral virtue in believing it was round like a globe; neither was there any moral ill in believing that the Creator made no other world than this, any more than there was moral virtue in believing that He made millions and that the infinity of space is filled with worlds.

But when a system of religion is made to grow out of a supposed system of creation that is not true, and to unite itself therewith in a manner almost inseparable therefrom, the case assumes an entirely different ground. It is then that errors not morally bad become fraught with the same mischiefs as if they were. It is then that the truth, though otherwise indifferent itself, becomes an essential by becoming the criterion that either confirms by corresponding evidence, or denies by contradictory evidence the reality of the religion itself.

In this view of the case, it is the moral duty of man to obtain every possible evidence that the structure of the heavens or any other part of creation affords, with respect to systems of religion. But this, the supporters or partisans of the Christian system, as if dreading the result, incessantly opposed, and not only rejected the sciences, but persecuted the professors.

Had Newton or Descartes lived three or four hundred years ago and pursued their studies as they did, it is most probable they would not have lived to finish them; and had Franklin drawn lightning from the clouds at the same time, it would have been at the hazard of expiring for it in the flames.

Later times have laid all the blame upon the Goths and the Vandals; but, however unwilling the partisans of the Christian system may be to believe or to acknowledge it, it is nevertheless true that the age of ignorance commenced with the Christian system. There was more knowledge in the world before that period than for many centuries afterwards; and as to religious knowledge, the Christian system, as already said, was only another species of mythology, and the mythology to which it succeeded was a corruption of an ancient system of theism.[3]

It is owing to this long interregnum of science, *and to no other cause*, that we have now to look back through a vast chasm of many hundred years to the respectable characters we call the ancients. Had the progression of knowledge gone on proportionately with that stock that before existed, that chasm would have been filled up with characters rising superior in knowledge to each other; and those ancients we now so much admire would have appeared respectably in the background of the scene. But the Christian system laid all waste; and if we take our stand about the beginning of the sixteenth century, we look back through that long chasm to the times of the ancients, as over a vast sandy desert, in which not a shrub appears to intercept the vision to the fertile hills beyond.

It is an inconsistency scarcely possible to be credited that anything should exist, under the name of a religion, that held it to be *irreligious* to study and contemplate the structure of the universe that God has made. But the fact is too well established to be denied. The event that served more than any other to break the first link in this long chain of despotic ignorance is that known by the name of the Reformation by Luther.

From that time, though it does not appear to have made any part of the intention of Luther, or of those who are called reformers, the sciences began to revive, and liberality, their natural associate, began to appear. This was the only public good the Reformation did; for with respect to religious good it might as well not have taken place. The mythology still continued the same, and a multiplicity of National Popes grew out of the downfall of the Pope of Christendom.

• • •

## Recapitulation

Having now extended the subject to a greater length than I first intended, I shall bring it to a close by abstracting a summary from the whole.

*First*—That the idea or belief of a Word of God existing in print, or in writing, or in speech, is inconsistent in itself for reasons already assigned.

These reasons, among many others, are the want of a universal language; the mutability of language; the errors to which translations are subject; the possibility of totally suppressing such a word; the probability of altering it, or of fabricating the whole, and imposing it upon the world.

*Secondly*—That the creation we behold is the real and ever-existing Word of God, in which we cannot be deceived. It proclaims His power, it demonstrates His wisdom, it manifests His goodness and beneficence.

*Thirdly*—That the moral duty of man consists in imitating the moral goodness and beneficence of God, manifested in the creation towards all His creatures. That seeing, as we daily do, the goodness of God to all men, it is an example calling upon all men to practise the same towards each other; and, consequently, that everything of persecution and revenge between man and man, and everything of cruelty to animals, is a violation of moral duty.

I trouble not myself about the manner of future existence. I content myself with believing, even to positive conviction, that the Power that gave me existence is able to continue it, in any form and manner He pleases, either with or without this body; and it appears more probable to me that I shall continue to exist hereafter, than that I should have had existence, as I now have, before that existence began.

It is certain that, in one point, all the nations of the earth and all religions agree—all believe in a God; the things in which they disagree are the redundancies annexed to that belief; and, therefore, if ever a universal religion should prevail, it will not be by believing anything new, but in getting rid of redundancies and believing as man believed at first. Adam, if ever there were such a man, was created a Deist; but in the meantime, let every man follow, as he has a right to do, the religion and the worship he prefers.

## Notes

1   It is, however, necessary to except the declaration which says that God *visits the sins of the fathers upon the children*; it is contrary to every principle of moral justice.—Paine.

2   Paine's references to the Bible usually denote the Old Testament.—Editors.

3   It is impossible for us now to know at what time the heathen mythology began; but it is certain, from the internal evidence that it carries, that it did not begin in the same state or condition in which it ended. All the gods of that

mythology, except Saturn, were of modern invention. The supposed reign of Saturn was prior to that which is called the heathen mythology, and was so far a species of theism, that it admitted the belief of only one God. Saturn is supposed to have abdicated the government in favour of his three sons and one daughter, Jupiter, Pluto, Neptune and Juno; after this, thousands of other gods and demi-gods were imaginarily created, and the calendar of gods increased as fast as the calendar of saints and the calendars of courts have increased since.

All the corruptions that have taken place in theology and in religion have been produced by admitting of what man calls *revealed religion*. The Mythologists pretended to more revealed religion than the Christians do. They had their oracles and their priests, who were supposed to receive and deliver the word of God verbally, on almost all occasions.

Since then, all corruptions, down from Moloch to modern predestinarianism, and the human sacrifices of the heathens to the Christian sacrifice of the Creator, have been produced by admitting of what is called *revealed religion*. The most effectual means to prevent all such evils and impositions is not to admit of any other revelation than that which is manifested in the book of creation, and to contemplate the creation as the only true and real Word of God that ever did or ever will exist; and that everything else, called the Word of God, is fable and imposition.—Paine.

# *from* An Introduction to the Principles of Morals and Legislation

*Jeremy Bentham*

## Of the Principle of Utility

Nature has placed mankind under the governance of two sovereign masters, *pain* and *pleasure*. It is for them alone to point out what we ought to do, as well as to determine what we shall do. On the one hand the standard of right and wrong, on the other the chain of causes and effects, are fastened to their throne. They govern us in all we do, in all we say, in all we think: every effort we can make to throw off our subjection, will serve but to demonstrate and confirm it. In words a man may pretend to abjure their empire: but in reality he will remain a subject to it all the while. The *principle of utility* recognizes this subjection, and assumes it for the foundation of that system, the object of which is to rear the fabric of felicity by the hands of reason and of law. Systems which attempt to question it, deal in sounds instead of sense, in caprice instead of reason, in darkness instead of light.

But enough of metaphor and declamation: it is not by such means that moral science is to be improved.

II. The principle of utility is the foundation of the present work: it will be proper therefore at the outset to give an explicit and determinate account of what is meant by it. By the principle of utility is meant that principle which approves or disapproves of every action whatsoever, according to the tendency which it appears to have to augment or diminish the happiness of the party whose interest is in question: or, what is the same thing in other words, to promote or to oppose that happiness. I say of every action whatsoever; and therefore not only of every action of a private individual, but of every measure of government.

III. By utility is meant that property in any object, whereby it tends to produce benefit, advantage, pleasure, good, or happiness, (all this in the present case comes to the same thing) or (what comes again to the same thing) to prevent the happening of mischief, pain, evil, or unhappiness to the party whose interest is considered: if that party be the community in general, then the happiness of the community: if a particular individual, then the happiness of that individual.

IV. The interest of the community is one of the most general expressions that can occur in the phraseology of morals: no wonder that the meaning of it is often lost. When it has a meaning, it is this. The community is a fictitious *body*, composed of individual persons who are considered as constituting as it were its *members*. The interest of the community then is, what?—the sum of the interests of the several members who compose it.

V. It is in vain to talk of the interest of the community, without understanding what is the interest of the individual. A thing is said to promote the interest, or to be for the interest, of an individual, when it tends to add to the sum total of his pleasures: or, what comes to the same thing, to diminish the sum total of his pains.

VI. An action then may be said to be conformable to the principle of utility, or, for shortness sake, to utility, (meaning with respect to the community at large) when the tendency it has to augment the happiness of the community is greater than any it has to diminish it. . . .

X. Of an action that is conformable to the principle of utility one may always say either that it is one that ought to be done, or at least that it is not one that ought not to be done. One may say also, that it is right it should be done; at least that it is not wrong it should be done: that it is a right action; at least that it is not a wrong action. When thus interpreted, the words *ought*, and *right* and *wrong*, and others of the stamp, have a meaning: when otherwise, they have none.

XI. Has the rectitude of this principle been ever formally contested? It should seem that it had, by those who have not known what they have been meaning. Is it susceptible of any direct proof? it should seem not: for that which is used to prove every thing else, cannot itself be proved: a chain of proofs must have their commencement somewhere. To give such proof is as impossible as it is needless.

XII. Not that there is or ever has been that human creature breathing, however stupid or perverse, who has not on many, perhaps on most occasions of his life, deferred to it. By the natural constitution of the human frame, on most occasions of their lives men in general embrace this principle, without thinking of it: if not for the ordering of their own actions, yet for the trying of their own actions, as well as those of other men. There have been, at the same time, not many, perhaps, even of the most intelligent, who have been disposed to embrace it purely and without reserve. There are even few who have not taken some occasion or other to quarrel with it, either on account of their not understanding always how to apply it, or on account of some prejudice or other which they were afraid to examine into, or could not bear to part with. For such is the stuff that man is made of: in principle and in practice, in a right track and in a wrong one, the rarest of all human qualities is consistency.

XIII. When a man attempts to combat the principle of utility, it is with reasons drawn, without his being aware of it, from that very principle itself. His arguments, if they prove any thing, prove not that the principle is wrong, but that according to the applications he supposes to be made of it, it is *misapplied*. Is it possible for a man to move the earth? Yes; but he must first find out another earth to stand upon.

# Sonnet—To Science

*Edgar Allan Poe*


Science! true daughter of Old Time thou art!
    Who alterest all things with thy peering eyes.
Why preyest thou thus upon the poet's heart,
    Vulture, whose wings are dull realities?
How should he love thee? or how deem thee wise,
    Who wouldst not leave him in his wandering
To seek for treasure in the jewelled skies,
    Albeit he soared with an undaunted wing?
Hast thou not dragged Diana from her car?
    And driven Hamadryad from the wood
To seek shelter in some happier star?
    Hast thou not torn the Naiad from her flood,
The Elfin from the green grass, and from me
The summer dream beneath the tamarind tree?
                        [1829, 1843]

# *from* Frankenstein

*Mary Wollstonecraft Shelley*

## Chapter IV

From this day natural philosophy, and particularly chemistry, in the most comprehensive sense of the term, became nearly my sole occupation. I read with ardour those works, so full of genius and discrimination, which modern inquirers have written on these subjects. I attended the lectures and cultivated the acquaintance of the men of science of the university, and I found even in M. Krempe a great deal of sound sense and real information, combined, it is true, with a repulsive physiognomy and manners, but not on that account the less valuable. In M. Waldman I found a true friend. His gentleness was never tinged by dogmatism, and his instructions were given with an air of frankness and good nature that banished every idea of pedantry. In a thousand ways he smoothed for me the path of knowledge and made the most abstruse inquiries clear and facile to my apprehension. My application was at first fluctuating and uncertain; it gained strength as I proceeded and soon became so ardent and eager that the stars often disappeared in the light of morning whilst I was yet engaged in my laboratory.

As I applied so closely, it may be easily conceived that my progress was rapid. My ardour was indeed the astonishment of the students and my proficiency that of the masters. Professor Krempe often asked me, with a sly smile, how Cornelius Agrippa went on, whilst M. Waldman expressed the most heartfelt exultation in my progress. Two years passed in this manner, during which I paid no visit to Geneva, but was engaged, heart and soul, in the pursuit of some discoveries which I hoped to make. None but those who have experienced them can conceive of the enticements of science. In other studies you go as far as others have gone before you, and there is nothing more to know; but in a scientific pursuit there is continual food for discovery and wonder. A mind of moderate capacity which closely pursues one study must infallibly arrive at great proficiency in that study; and I, who continually sought the attainment of one object of pursuit and was solely wrapped up in this, improved so rapidly that at the end of two years I made some discoveries in the improvement of some chemical instruments, which procured me great esteem and admiration at the university. When I had arrived at this point and had become as well acquainted with the theory and practice of natural philosophy as depended on the lessons of any of the professors at Ingolstadt, my residence there being no longer conducive to my improvements, I thought of returning to my friends and my native town, when an incident happened that protracted my stay.

One of the phenomena which had peculiarly attracted my attention was the structure of the human frame and, indeed, any animal endued with life.

Whence, I often asked myself, did the principle of life proceed? It was a bold question, and one which has ever been considered as a mystery; yet with how many things are we upon the brink of becoming acquainted, if cowardice or carelessness did not restrain our inquiries. I revolved these circumstances in my mind and determined thenceforth to apply myself more particularly to those branches of natural philosophy which relate to physiology. Unless I had been animated by an almost supernatural enthusiasm, my application to this study would have been irksome and almost intolerable. To examine the causes of life, we must first have recourse to death. I became acquainted with the science of anatomy, but this was not sufficient; I must also observe the natural decay and corruption of the human body. In my education my father had taken the greatest precautions that my mind should be impressed with no supernatural horrors. I do not ever remember to have trembled at a tale of superstition or to have feared the apparition of a spirit. Darkness had no effect upon my fancy, and a churchyard was to me merely the receptacle of bodies deprived of life, which, from being the seat of beauty and strength, had become food for the worm. Now I was led to examine the cause and progress of this decay and forced to spend days and nights in vaults and charnel houses. My attention was fixed upon every object the most insupportable to the delicacy of the human feelings. I saw how the fine form of man was degraded and wasted; I beheld the corruption of death succeed to the blooming cheek of life; I saw how the worm inherited the wonders of the eye and brain. I paused, examining and analyzing all the minutiae of causation, as exemplified in the change from life to death, and death to life, until from the midst of this darkness a sudden light broke in upon me—a light so brilliant and wondrous, yet so simple, that while I became dizzy with the immensity of the prospect which it illustrated, I was surprised that among so many men of genius who had directed their inquiries towards the same science, that I alone should be reserved to discover so astonishing a secret.

Remember, I am not recording the vision of a madman. The sun does not more certainly shine in the heavens than that which I now affirm is true. Some miracle might have produced it, yet the stages of the discovery were distinct and probable. After days and nights of incredible labour and fatigue, I succeeded in discovering the cause of generation and life; nay, more, I became myself capable of bestowing animation upon lifeless matter.

The astonishment which I had at first experienced on this discovery soon gave place to delight and rapture. After so much time spent in painful labour, to arrive at once at the summit of my desires was the most gratifying consummation of my toils. But this discovery was so great and overwhelming that all the steps by which I had been progressively led to it were obliterated, and I beheld only the result. What had been the study and desire of the wisest men since the creation of the world was now within my grasp. Not that, like a magic scene, it all opened upon me at once: the information I had obtained was of a nature rather to direct my endeavours so soon as I should point them towards the object of my search than to exhibit that object already accomplished. I was like the Arabian who had been buried with the dead and found a passage to life, aided only by one glimmering and seemingly ineffectual light.

I see by your eagerness and the wonder and hope which your eyes express, my friend, that you expect to be informed of the secret with which I am acquainted; that cannot be; listen patiently until the end of my story, and you will easily perceive why I am reserved upon that subject. I will not lead you on, unguarded and ardent as I then was, to your destruction and infallible misery. Learn from me, if not by my precepts, at least by my example, how dangerous is the acquirement of knowledge and how much happier that man is who believes his native town to be the world, than he who aspires to become greater than his nature will allow.

When I found so astonishing a power placed within my hands, I hesitated a long time concerning the manner in which I should employ it. Although I possessed the capacity of bestowing animation, yet to prepare a frame for the reception of it, with all its intricacies of fibres, muscles, and veins, still remained a work of inconceivable difficulty and labour. I doubted at first whether I should attempt the creation of a being like myself, or one of simpler organization; but my imagination was too much exalted by my first success to permit me to doubt of my ability to give life to an animal as complex and wonderful as man. The materials at present within my command hardly appeared adequate to so arduous an undertaking, but I doubted not that I should ultimately succeed. I prepared myself for a multitude of reverses; my operations might be incessantly baffled, and at last my work be imperfect, yet when I considered the improvement which every day takes place in science and mechanics, I was encouraged to hope my present attempts would at least lay the foundations of future success. Nor could I consider the magnitude and complexity of my plan as any argument of its impracticability. It was with these feelings that I began the creation of a human being. As the minuteness of the parts formed a great hindrance to my speed, I resolved, contrary to my first intention, to make the being of a gigantic stature, that is to say, about eight feet in height and proportionately large. After having formed this determination and having spent some months in successfully collecting and arranging my materials, I began.

No one can conceive the variety of feelings which bore me onwards, like a hurricane, in the first enthusiasm of success. Life and death appeared to me ideal bounds, which I should first break through and pour a torrent of light into our dark world. A new species would bless me as its creator and source; many happy and excellent natures would owe their being to me. No father could claim the gratitude of his child so completely as I should deserve theirs. Pursuing these reflections, I thought that if I could bestow animation upon lifeless matter, I might in process of time (although I now found it impossible) renew life where death had apparently devoted the body to corruption.

These thoughts supported my spirits, while I pursued my undertaking with unremitting ardour. My cheek had grown pale with study, and my person had become emaciated with confinement. Sometimes, on the very brink of certainty, I failed; yet still I clung to the hope which the next day or the next hour might realize. One secret which I alone possessed was the hope to which I had dedicated myself; and the moon gazed on my midnight labours, while, with unrelaxed and breathless eagerness, I pursued nature to her hiding places. Who shall conceive the horrors of my secret toil as I dabbled among the unhallowed damps of the grave or tortured the living animal to animate the lifeless clay? My limbs now tremble, and my eyes swim with the remembrance; but then a restless and almost frantic impulse urged me forward; I seemed to have lost all soul or sensation but for this one pursuit. It was indeed but a passing trance that only made me feel with renewed acuteness so soon as, the unnatural stimulus ceasing to operate, I had returned to my old habits. I collected bones from charnel houses and disturbed, with profane fingers, the tremendous secrets of the human frame. In a solitary chamber, or rather cell, at the top of the house, and separated from all the other apartments by a gallery and staircase, I kept my workshop of filthy creation; my eyeballs were starting from their sockets in attending to the details of my employment. The dissecting room and the slaughterhouse furnished many of my materials; and often did my human nature turn with loathing from my occupation, whilst, still urged on by an eagerness which perpetually increased, I brought my work near to a conclusion.

The summer months passed while I was thus engaged, heart and soul, in one pursuit. It was a most beautiful season; never did the fields bestow a more plentiful harvest or the vines yield a more luxuriant vintage, but my eyes were insensible to the charms of nature. And the same feelings which made me neglect the scenes around me caused me also to forget those friends who were so many miles absent, and whom I had not seen for so long a time. I knew my silence disquieted them, and I well remembered the words of my father: "I know that while you are pleased with yourself you will think of us with affection, and we shall hear regularly from you. You must pardon me if I regard any interruption in your correspondence as a proof that your other duties are equally neglected."

I knew well therefore what would be my father's feelings; but I could not tear my thoughts from my employment, loathsome in itself, but which had taken an irresistible hold of my imagination. I wished, as it were, to procrastinate all that related to my feelings of affection until the great object, which swallowed up every habit of my nature, should be completed.

I then thought that my father would be unjust if he ascribed my neglect to vice or faultiness on my part, but I am now convinced that he was justified in conceiving that I should not be altogether free from blame. A human being in perfection ought always to preserve a calm and peaceful mind and never to allow passion or a transitory desire to disturb his tranquility. I do not think that the pursuit of knowledge is an exception to this rule. If the study to which you apply yourself has a tendency to weaken your affections and to destroy your taste for those simple pleasures in which no alloy can possibly mix, then that study is certainly unlawful, that is to say, not befitting the human mind. If this rule were always observed, if no man allowed any pursuit whatsoever to interfere with the tranquility of his domestic affections, Greece had not been enslaved, Caesar would have spared his country, America would have been discovered more gradually, and the empires of Mexico and Peru had not been destroyed.

But I forget that I am moralizing in the most interesting part of my tale, and your looks remind me to proceed.

My father made no reproach in his letters and only took notice of my silence by inquiring into my occupations more particularly than before. Winter, spring, and summer passed away during my labours; but I did not watch the blossom or the expanding leaves—sights which before always yielded me supreme delight—so deeply was I engrossed in my occupation. The leaves of that year had withered before my work drew near to a close, and now every day showed me more plainly how well I had succeeded. But my enthusiasm was checked by my anxiety, and I appeared rather like one doomed by slavery to toil in the mines, or any other unwholesome trade, than an artist occupied by his favourite employment. Every night I was oppressed by a slow fever, and I became nervous to a most painful degree; the fall of a leaf startled me, and I shunned my fellow creatures as if I had been guilty of a crime. Sometimes I grew alarmed at the wreck I perceived that I had become; the energy of my purpose alone sustained me: my labours would soon end, and I believed that exercise and amusement would then drive away incipient disease; and I promised myself both of these when my creation should be complete.

## Chapter V

It was on a dreary night of November that I beheld the accomplishment of my toils. With an anxiety that almost amounted to agony, I collected the instruments of life around me, that I might infuse a spark of being into the lifeless thing that lay at my feet. It was already one in the morning; the rain pattered dismally against the panes, and my candle was nearly burnt out, when, by the glimmer of the half-extinguished light, I saw the dull yellow eye of the creature open; it breathed hard, and a convulsive motion agitated its limbs.

How can I describe my emotions at this catastrophe, or how delineate the wretch whom with such infinite pains and care I had endeavoured to form? His limbs were in proportion, and I had selected his features as beautiful. Beautiful! Great God! His yellow skin scarcely covered the work of muscles and arteries beneath; his hair was of a lustrous black, and flowing; his teeth of a pearly whiteness; but these luxuriances only formed a more horrid contrast with his watery eyes, that seemed almost of the same colour as the dun-white sockets in which they were set, his shrivelled complexion, and straight black lips.

The different accidents of life are not so changeable as the feelings of human nature. I had worked hard for nearly two years, for the sole purpose of infusing life into an inanimate body. For this I had deprived myself of rest and health. I had desired it with an ardour that far exceeded moderation; but now that I had finished, the beauty of the dream vanished and breathless horror and disgust filled my heart. Unable to endure the aspect of the being I had created, I rushed out of the room and continued a long time traversing my bedchamber, unable to compose my mind to sleep. At length lassitude succeeded to the tumult I had before endured, and I threw myself on the bed in my clothes, endeavouring to seek a few moments of forgetfulness. But it was in vain; I slept, indeed, but I was disturbed by the wildest dreams. I thought I saw Elizabeth, in the bloom of health, walking in the streets of Ingolstadt. Delighted and surprised, I embraced her, but as I imprinted the first kiss on her lips, they became livid with the hue of death; her features appeared to change, and I thought that I held the corpse of my dead mother in my arms; a shroud enveloped her form, and I saw the grave worms crawling in the folds of the flannel. I started from my sleep with horror, a cold dew covered my forehead, my teeth chattered, and every limb became convulsed; when, by the dim and yellow light of the moon, as it forced its way through the window shutters, I beheld the wretch—the miserable monster whom I had created. He held up the curtain of the bed; and his eyes, if eyes they may be called, were fixed on me. His jaws opened, and he muttered some inarticulate sounds, while a grin wrinkled his cheeks. He might have spoken, but I did not hear; one hand was stretched out, seemingly to detain me, but I escaped and rushed downstairs. I took refuge in the courtyard belonging to the house which I inhabited, where I remained during the rest of the night, walking up and down in the greatest agitation, listening attentively, catching and fearing each sound as if it were to announce the approach of the demoniacal corpse to which I had so miserably given life.

Oh! No mortal could support the horror of that countenance. A mummy again endued with animation could not be so hideous as that wretch. I had gazed on him while unfinished; he was ugly then, but when those muscles and joints were rendered capable of motion, it became a thing such as even Dante could not have conceived.

I passed the night wretchedly. Sometimes my pulse beat so quickly and hardly that I felt the palpitation of every artery; at others, I nearly sank to the ground through languor and extreme weakness. Mingled with this horror, I felt the bitterness of disappointment; dreams that had been my food and pleasant rest for so long a space were now become a hell to me; and the change was so rapid, the overthrow so complete!

Morning, dismal and wet, at length dawned and discovered to my sleepless and aching eyes the church of Ingolstadt, its white steeple and clock, which indicated the sixth hour. The porter opened the gates of the court, which had that night been my asylum, and I issued into the streets, pacing them with quick steps, as if I sought to avoid the wretch whom I feared every turning of the street would present to my view. I did not dare return to the apartment which I inhabited, but felt impelled to hurry on, although drenched by the rain which poured from a black and comfortless sky.

I continued walking in this manner for some time, endeavouring by bodily exercise to ease the load that weighed upon my mind. I traversed the streets without any clear conception of where I was or what I was doing. My heart palpitated in the sickness of fear, and I hurried on with irregular steps, not daring to look about me:

> Like one who, on a lonely road,
>   Doth walk in fear and dread,
> And, having once turned round, walks on,
>   And rums no more his head;
> Because he knows a frightful fiend
>   Doth close behind him tread.

Continuing thus, I came at length opposite to the inn at which the various diligences and carriages usually stopped. Here I paused, I knew not why; but I remained some minutes with my eyes fixed on a coach that was coming towards me from the other end of the street. As it drew nearer, I observed that it was the Swiss diligence; it stopped just where I was standing, and on the door being opened, I perceived Henry Clerval, who, on seeing me, instantly sprang out. "My dear Frankenstein," exclaimed he, "how glad I am to see you! How fortunate that you should be here at the very moment of my alighting!"

Nothing could equal my delight on seeing Clerval; his presence brought back to my thoughts my father, Elizabeth, and all those scenes of home so dear to my recollection. I grasped his hand, and in a moment forgot my horror and misfortune; I felt suddenly, and for the first time during many months, calm and serene joy. I welcomed my friend, therefore, in the most cordial manner, and we walked towards my college. Clerval continued talking for some time about our mutual friends and his own good fortune in being permitted to come to Ingolstadt. "You may easily believe," said he, "how great was the difficulty to persuade my father that all necessary knowledge was not comprised in the noble art of bookkeeping; and, indeed, I believe I left him incredulous to the last, for his constant answer to my unwearied entreaties was the same as that of the Dutch school-master in *The Vicar of Wakefield*: 'I have ten thousand florins a year without Greek, I eat heartily without Greek.' But his affection for me at length overcame his dislike of learning, and he has permitted me to undertake a voyage of discovery to the land of knowledge."

"It gives me the greatest delight to see you; but tell me how you left my father, brothers, and Elizabeth."

"Very well, and very happy, only a little uneasy that they hear from you so seldom. By the by, I mean to lecture you a little upon their account myself. But, my dear Frankenstein," continued he, stopping short and gazing full in my face, "I did not before remark how very ill you appear; so thin and pale; you look as if you had been watching for several nights."

"You have guessed right; I have lately been so deeply engaged in one occupation that I have not allowed myself sufficient rest, as you see; but I hope, I sincerely hope, that all these employments are now at an end and that I am at length free."

I trembled excessively; I could not endure to think of, and far less to allude to, the occurences of the preceding night. I walked with a quick pace, and we soon arrived at my college. I then reflected, and the thought made me shiver, that the creature whom I had left in my apartment might still be there, alive and walking about. I dreaded to behold this monster, but I feared still more that Henry should see him. Entreating him, therefore, to remain a few minutes at the bottom of the stairs, I darted up towards my own room. My hand was already on the lock of the door before I recollected myself. I then paused, and a cold shivering came over me. I threw the door forcibly open, as children are accustomed to do when they expect a spectre to stand in waiting for them on the other side; but nothing appeared. I stepped fearfully in; the apartment was empty, and my bedroom was also freed from its hideous guest. I could hardly believe that so great a good fortune could have befallen me, but when I became assured that my enemy had indeed fled, I clapped my hands for joy and ran down to Clerval.

We ascended into my room, and the servant presently brought breakfast; but I was unable to contain myself. It was not joy only that possessed me; I felt my flesh tingle with excess of sensitiveness, and my pulse beat rapidly. I was unable to remain for a single instant in the same place; I jumped over the chairs, clapped my hands, and laughed aloud. Clerval at first attributed my unusual spirits to joy on his arrival, but when he observed me more attentively, he saw a wildness in my eyes for which he could not account; and my loud, unrestrained, heartless laughter frightened and astonished him.

"My dear Victor," cried he, "what, for God's sake, is the matter? Do not laugh in that manner. How ill you are! What is the cause of all this?"

"Do not ask me," cried I, putting my hands before my eyes, for I thought I saw the dreaded spectre glide into the room. "*He* can tell. Oh, save me! Save me!" I imagined that the monster seized me; I struggled furiously and fell down in a fit.

Poor Clerval! What must have been his feelings? A meeting, which he anticipated with such joy, so strangely turned to bitterness. But I was not the witness of his grief, for I was lifeless and did not recover my senses for a long, long time.

This was the commencement of a nervous fever which confined me for several months. During all that time Henry was my only nurse. I afterwards learned that, knowing my father's advanced age and unfitness for so long a journey, and how wretched my sickness would make Elizabeth, he spared them this grief by concealing the extent of my disorder. He knew that I could not have a more kind and attentive nurse than himself; and, firm in the hope he felt of my recovery, he did not doubt that, instead of doing harm, he performed the kindest action that he could towards them.

But I was in reality very ill, and surely nothing but the unbounded and unremitting attentions of my friend could have restored me to life. The form of the monster on whom I had bestowed existence was forever before my eyes, and I raved incessantly concerning him. Doubtless my words surprised Henry; he at first believed them to be the wanderings of my disturbed imagination, but the pertinacity with which I continually recurred to the same subject persuaded him that my disorder indeed owned its origin to some uncommon and terrible event.

By very slow degrees, and with frequent relapses that alarmed and grieved my friend, I recovered. I remember the first time I became capable of observing outward objects with any kind of pleasure, I perceived that the fallen leaves had disappeared and that the young buds were shooting forth from the trees that shaded my window. It was a divine spring, and the season contributed greatly to my convalescence. I felt also sentiments of joy and affection revive in my bosom; my gloom disappeared, and in a short time I became as cheerful as before I was attacked by the fatal passion.

"Dearest Clerval," exclaimed I, "how kind, how very good you are to me. This whole winter, instead of being spent in study, as you promised yourself, has been consumed in my sickroom. How shall I ever repay you? I feel the greatest remorse for the disappointment of which I have been the occasion, but you will forgive me."

"You will repay me entirely if you do not discompose yourself, but get well as fast as you can; and since you appear in such good spirits, I may speak to you on one subject, may I not?

I trembled. One subject! What could it be? Could he allude to an object on whom I dared not even think?

"Compose yourself," said Clerval, who observed my change of colour, "I will not mention it if it agitates you; but your father and cousin would be very happy if they received a letter from you in your own handwriting. They hardly know how ill you have been and are uneasy at your long silence."

"Is that all, my dear Henry? How could you suppose that my first thought would not fly towards those dear, dear friends whom I love and who are so deserving of my love?"

# The Poison Tree *and* The Sick Rose

*William Blake*

### The Poison Tree

I was angry with my friend;
I told my wrath, my wrath did end.
I was angry with my foe;
I told it not, my wrath did grow.

And I watered it in fears,
Night and morning with my tears;
And I sunned it with my smiles,
And with soft deceitful wiles.

And it grew both day and night,
Till it bore an apple bright;
And my foe beheld it shine,
And he knew that it was mine.

And into my garden stole
When the night had veil'd the pole;
In the morning glad I see
My foe outstretched beneath the tree.

### The Sick Rose

O Rose, thou art sick!
The invisible worm,
That flies in the night
In the howling storm,

Has found out thy bed
Of crimson joy,
And his dark secret love
Does thy life destroy.

# *from* Songs of Innocence and of Experience

*William Blake*

### The Tyger

Tyger Tyger, burning bright,
In the forests of the night;
What immortal hand or eye,
Could frame thy fearful symmetry?

In what distant deeps or skies,
Burnt the fire of thine eyes?
On what wings dare he aspire?
What the hand, dare seize the fire?

And what shoulder, & what art,
Could twist the sinews of thy heart?
And when thy heart began to beat,
What dread hand? & what dread feet?

What the hammer? what the chain,
In what furnace was thy brain?
What the anvil? what dread grasp,
Dare its deadly terrors clasp?

When the stars threw down their spears
And water'd heaven with their tears:
Did he smile his work to see?
Did he who made the Lamb make thee?

Tyger Tyger burning bright,
In the forests of the night:
What immortal hand or eye,
Dare frame thy fearful symmetry?

## A Divine Image

Cruelty has a Human Heart
And Jealousy a Human Face
Terror, the Human Form Divine
And Secrecy, the Human Dress
The Human Dress, is forged Iron
The Human Form, a fiery Forge.
The Human Face, a Furnace seal'd
The Human Heart, its hungry Gorge.

## London

I wander thro' each charter'd street,
Near where the charter'd Thames does flow
And mark in every face I meet
Marks of weakness, marks of woe.

In every cry of every Man,
In every Infants cry of fear,
In every voice; in every ban,
The mind-forg'd manacles I hear

How the Chimney-sweepers cry
Every blackning Church appalls,
And the hapless Soldiers sigh
Runs in blood down Palace walls

But most thro' midnight streets I hear
How the youthful Harlots curse
Blasts the new-born Infants tear
And blights with plagues the Marriage hearse

# The Chimney Sweeper

A little black thing among the snow:
Crying "'weep," "'weep," in notes of woe!
"Where are thy father & mother? say!"
"They are both gone up to the church to pray.

"Because I was happy upon the heath,
And smil'd among the winters snow:
They clothed me in the clothes of death,
And taught me to sing the notes of woe.

"And because I am happy, & dance & sing,
They think they have done me no injury:
And are gone to praise God & his Priest & King
Who make up a heaven of our misery."

# Mock on, Mock on, Voltaire, Rousseau

Mock on, Mock on, Voltaire, Rousseau;
Mock on, Mock on, 'tis all in vain.
You throw the sand against the wind,
And the wind blows it back again.

And every sand becomes a Gem
Reflected in the beams divine;
Blown back, they blind the mocking Eye,
But still in Israel's paths they shine.

The Atoms of Democritus
And Newton's Particles of light
Are sands upon the Red sea shore,
Where Israel's tents do shine so bright.

# Selected Poems

*William Wordsworth*

## The World Is Too Much with Us

The world is too much with us; late and soon,
Getting and spending, we lay waste our powers:
Little we see in Nature that is ours;
We have given our hearts away, a sordid boon!
This Sea that bares her bosom to the moon;
The winds that will be howling at all hours,
And are up-gathered now like sleeping flowers;
For this, for everything, we are out of tune;
It moves us not.  Great God! I'd rather be
A Pagan suckled in a creed outworn;
So might I, standing on this pleasant lea,
Have glimpses that would make me less forlorn;
Have sight of Proteus rising from the sea;
Or hear old Triton blow his wreathed horn.

[1806]

## I Wandered Lonely as a Cloud[1]

I wandered lonely as a cloud
That floats on high o'er vales and hills,
When all at once I saw a crowd,
A host, of golden daffodils;
Beside the lake, beneath the trees,
Fluttering and dancing in the breeze.
Continuous as the stars that shine
And twinkle on the milky way,
They stretched in never-ending line
Along the margin of a bay:
Ten thousand saw I at a glance,
Tossing their heads in sprightly dance.  *[handwritten: PATHETIC FALLACY]*
The waves beside them danced; but they
Out-did the sparkling waves in glee:

A poet could not but be gay,
In such a jocund company;
I gazed—and gazed—but little thought
What wealth the show to me had brought:
For oft, when on my couch I lie
In vacant or in pensive mood,
They flash upon that inward eye
Which is the bliss of solitude;
And then my heart with pleasure fills,
And dances with the daffodils.

[1807]

## My Heart Leaps Up

My heart leaps up when I behold
    A rainbow in the sky:
So was it when my life began;
So is it now I am a man;
So be it when I shall grow old,
    Or let me die!
The Child is father of the Man;
And I could wish my days to be
Bound each to each by natural piety.[2]

March 26, 1802  1807

## Notes

[1]    The last stanza describes the kind of recollection in tranquillity from which
this poem arose, two years after the original experience. This event Dorothy
Wordsworth described in her *Journals* for April 15, 1802; the occasion was a
walk past the shore of Ullswater: "I never saw daffodils so beautiful. They
grew among the mossy stones about and about them; some rested their
heads upon these stones, as on a pillow, for weariness; and the rest tossed
and reeled and danced, and seemed as if they verily laughed with the wind,
that blew upon them over the lake; they looked so gay, every glancing, every
changing."

[2]    As distinguished from piety based on the Scriptures; a continuing respon-
siveness to the miracle of ordinary things is the religious sentiment that binds
Wordsworth's maturity to his childhood.

# On First Looking into Chapman's Homer

*John Keats*

Much have I travell'd in the realms of gold,
And many goodly states and kingdoms seen;
Round many western islands have I been
Which bards in fealty to Apollo hold.
Oft of one wide expanse had I been told
That deep-brow'd Homer ruled as his demesne;
Yet did I never breathe its pure serene
Till I heard Chapman speak out loud and bold.
Then felt I like some watcher of the skies
When a new planet swims into his ken;
Or like stout Cortez when with eagle eyes
He star'd at the Pacific—and all his men
Look'd at each other with a wild surmise—
Silent, upon a peak in Darien.

[1816]

# Ode to a Nightingale

*John Keats*

## I

My heart aches, and a drowsy numbness pains
　　My sense, as though of hemlock I had drunk,
Or emptied some dull opiate to the drains
　　One minute past, and Lethe-wards[1] had sunk:
'T is not through envy of thy happy lot,
　　But being too happy in thine happiness,—
　　　　That thou, light-wingèd Dryad[2] of the trees,
　　　　　　In some melodious plot
　　Of beechen green, and shadows numberless,
　　　　Singest of summer in full-throated ease.

## II

O, for a draught of vintage! that hath been
　　Cooled a long age in the deep-delved earth,
Tasting of Flora[3] and the country-green,
　　Dance, and Provençal song,[4] and sunburnt mirth!
O for a beaker full of the warm South,
　　Full of the true, the blushful Hippocrene,[5]
　　　　With beaded bubbles winking at the brim,
　　　　　　And purple-stainèd mouth;
　　That I might drink, and leave the world unseen,
　　　　And with thee fade away into the forest dim:

## III

Fade far away, dissolve, and quite forget
    What thou among the leaves hast never known,
The weariness, the fever, and the fret
    Here, where men sit and hear each other groan;
Where palsy shakes a few, sad, last gray hairs,
        Where youth grows pale, and spectra-thin, and dies;
            Where but to think is to be full of sorrow
                And leaden-eyed despairs,
        Where Beauty cannot keep her lustrous eyes,
            Or new Love pine at them beyond tomorrow.

## IV

Away! away! for I will fly to thee,
    Not charioted by Bacchus and his pards,[6]
But on the viewless wings of Poesy,
    Though the dull brain perplexes and retards:
Already with thee! tender is the night,
        And haply the Queen-Moon is on her throne,
            Clustered around by all her starry Fays;
                But here there is no light,
    Save what from heaven is with the breezes blown
        Through verdurous glooms and winding mossy
        ways.

## V

I cannot see what flowers are at my feet,
    Nor what soft incense hangs upon the boughs,
But, in embalmed darkness, guess each sweet
    Wherewith the seasonable month endows
The grass, the thicket, and the fruit-tree wild;
        White hawthorn, and the pastoral eglantine;
            Fast fading violets covered up in leaves;
                And mid-May's eldest child,
        The coming musk-rose, full of dewy wine,
            The murmurous haunt of flies on summer eves.

## VI

Darkling[7] I listen; and, for many a time
    I have been half in love with easeful Death,
Called him soft names in many a musèd rhyme,
    To take into the air my quiet breath;
Now more than ever seems it rich to die,
    To cease upon the midnight with no pain,
        While thou art pouring forth thy soul abroad
        In such an ecstasy!
    Still wouldst thou sing, and I have ears in vain—
    To thy high requiem become a sod.

## VII

Thou wast not born for death, immortal Bird!
    No hungry generations tread thee down;
The voice I hear this passing night was heard
    In ancient days by emperor and clown:
Perhaps the self-same song that found a path
    Through the sad heart of Ruth,[8] when, sick for home
        She stood in tears amid the alien corn;
        The same that oft-times hath
    Charmed magic casements, opening on the foam
    Of perilous seas, in faery lands forlorn.

## VIII

Forlorn! the very word is like a bell
    To toll me back from thee to my sole self!
Adieu! the fancy cannot cheat so well
    As she is famed to do, deceiving elf.
Adieu! adieu! thy plaintive anthem fades
    Past the near meadows, over the still stream,

Up the hill-side; and now 't is buried deep
    In the next valley-glades:
Was it a vision, or a waking dream?
    Fled is that music:—do I wake or sleep?

                    [1819]

## Notes

1 Toward Lethe, the river of forgetfulness in the Underworld.

2 Wood nymph.

3 The goddess of flowers.

4 The medieval troubadors of Provence in southern France were famous for their songs.

5 A mythological fountain whose waters bring poetic inspiration.

6 Bacchus, the god of wine, rode in a chariot drawn by leopards.

7 In the dark.

8 A young widow in the Bible, Ruth 2.

# Ozymandias

*Percy Bysshe Shelley*

I met a traveler from an antique land
Who said: Two vast and trunkless legs of stone
Stand in the desert. . . . Near them, on the sand,
Half sunk, a shattered visage lies, whose frown,
And wrinkled lip, and sneer of cold command,
Tell that its sculptor well those passions read
Which yet survive, stamped on these lifeless things,
The hand that mocked them, and the heart that fed:
And on the pedestal these words appear:
"My name is Ozymandias, King of Kings:
Look on my works, ye Mighty, and despair!"
Nothing beside remains. Round the decay
Of that colossal wreck, boundless and bare
The lone and level sands stretch far away.

[1818]

# *from* The Origin of Species

## *Charles Darwin*

When on board H.M.S. 'Beagle,' as naturalist, I was much struck with certain facts in the distribution of the organic beings inhabiting South America, and in the geological relations of the present to the past inhabitants of that continent. These facts, as will be seen in the latter chapters of this volume, seemed to throw some light on the origin of species—that mystery of mysteries, as it has been called by one of our greatest philosophers. On my return home, it occurred to me, in 1837, that something might perhaps be made out on this question by patiently accumulating and reflecting on all sorts of facts which could possibly have any bearing on it. After five years' work I allowed myself to speculate on the subject, and drew up some short notes; these I enlarged in 1844 into a sketch of the conclusions, which then seemed to me probable; from that period to the present day I have steadily pursued the same object. I hope that I may be excused for entering on these personal details, as I give them to show that I have not been hasty in coming to a decision.

My work is now (1859) nearly finished; but as it will take me many more years to complete it, and as my health is far from strong, I have been urged to publish this Abstract. I have more especially been induced to do this, as Mr. Wallace, who is now studying the natural history of the Malay Archipelago, has arrived at almost exactly the same general conclusions that I have on the origin of species. In 1858 he sent me a memoir on this subject, with a request that I would forward it to Sir Charles Lyell, who sent it to the Linnean Society, and it is published in the third volume of the Journal of that Society. Sir C. Lyell and Dr. Hooker, who both knew of my work—the latter having read my sketch of 1844—honoured me by thinking it advisable to publish, with Mr. Wallace's excellent memoir, some brief extracts from my manuscripts.

This Abstract, which I now publish, must necessarily be imperfect. I cannot here give references and authorities for my several statements; and I must trust to the reader reposing some confidence in my accuracy. No doubt errors will have crept in, though I hope I have always been cautious in trusting to good authorities alone. I can here give only the general conclusions at which I have arrived, with a few facts in illustration, but which, I hope, in most cases will suffice. No one can feel more sensible than I do of the necessity of hereafter publishing in detail all the facts, with references, on which my conclusions have been grounded; and I hope in a future work to do this. For I am well aware that scarcely a single point is discussed in this volume on which facts cannot be adduced, often apparently leading to conclusions directly opposite to those at which I have arrived. A fair result can be obtained only by fully stating and balancing the facts and arguments on both sides of each question; and this is here impossible.

I much regret that want of space prevents my having the satisfaction of acknowledging the generous assistance which I have received from very many naturalists, some of them personally unknown to me. I cannot, however, let this opportunity pass without expressing my deep obligations to Dr. Hooker, who, for the last fifteen years, has aided me in every possible way by his large stores of knowledge and his excellent judgment.

In considering the origin of species, it is quite conceivable that a naturalist, reflecting on the mutual affinities of organic beings, on their embryological relations, their geographical distribution, geological succession, and other such facts, might come to the conclusion that species have not been independently created, but had descended, like varieties, from other species. Nevertheless, such a conclusion, even if well founded, would be unsatisfactory, until it could be shown how the innumerable species inhabiting this world have been modified, so as to acquire that perfection of structure and coadaptation which justly excites our admiration. Naturalists continually refer to external conditions, such as climate, food, etc., as the only possible cause of variation. In one limited sense, as we shall hereafter see, this may be true; but it is preposterous to attribute to mere external conditions, the structure, for instance, of the woodpecker, with its feet, tail, beak, and tongue, so admirably adapted to catch insects under the bark of trees. In the case of the mistletoe, which draws its nourishment from certain trees, which has seeds that must be transported by certain birds, and which has flowers with separate sexes absolutely requiring the agency of certain insects to bring pollen from one flower to the other, it is equally preposterous to account for the structure of this parasite, with its relations to several distinct organic beings, by the effects of external conditions, or of habit, or of the volition of the plant itself.

It is, therefore, of the highest importance to gain a clear insight into the means of modification and coadaptation. At the commencement of my observations it seemed to me probable that a careful study of domesticated animals and of cultivated plants would offer the best chance of making out this obscure problem. Nor have I been disappointed; in this and in all other perplexing cases I have invariably found that our knowledge, imperfect though it be, of variation under domestication, afforded the best and safest clue. I may venture to express my conviction of the high value of such studies, although they have been very commonly neglected by naturalists.

From these considerations, I shall devote the first chapter of this Abstract to Variation under Domestication. We shall thus see that a large amount of hereditary modification is at least possible; and, what is equally or more important, we shall see how great is the power of man in accumulating by his Selection successive slight variations. I will then pass on to the variability of species in a state of nature; but I shall, unfortunately, be compelled to treat this subject far too briefly, as it can be treated properly only by giving long catalogues of facts. We shall, however, be enabled to discuss what circumstances are most favourable to variation. In the next chapter the Struggle for Existence amongst all organic beings throughout the world, which inevitably follows from the high geometrical ratio of their increase, will be considered. This is the doctrine of Malthus, applied to the whole animal and vegetable kingdoms. As many more individuals of each species are born than can possibly survive; and as, consequently, there is a frequently recurrent struggle for existence, it follows that any being, if it vary however slightly in any manner profitable to itself, under the complex and sometimes varying conditions of life, will have a better chance of surviving, and thus be *naturally* selected. From the strong principle of inheritance, any selected variety will tend to propagate its new and modified form.

This fundamental subject of Natural Selection will be treated at some length in the fourth chapter; and we shall then see how Natural Selection almost inevitably causes much Extinction of the less improved forms of life, and leads to what I have called Divergence of Character. In the next chapter I shall discuss the complex and little known laws of variation. In the five succeeding chapters, the most apparent and gravest difficulties in accepting the theory will be given: namely, first, the difficulties of transitions, or how a simple being or a simple organ can be changed and perfected into a highly developed being or into an elaborately constructed organ; secondly, the subject of Instinct, or the mental powers of animals; thirdly, Hybridism, or the infertility of species and the fertility of varieties when intercrossed; and fourthly, the imperfection of the Geological Record. In the next chapter I shall consider the geological succession of organic beings throughout time; in the twelfth and thirteenth, their geographical distribution throughout space; in the fourteenth, their classification or mutual affinities, both when mature and in an embryonic condition. In the last chapter I shall give a brief recapitulation of the whole work, and a few concluding remarks.

No one ought to feel surprise at much remaining as yet unexplained in regard to the origin of species and varieties, if he make due allowance for our profound ignorance in regard to the mutual relations of the many beings which live around us. Who can explain why one species ranges widely and is very numerous, and why another allied species has a narrow range and is rare? Yet these relations are of the highest importance, for they determine the present welfare, and, as I believe, the future success and modification of every inhabitant of this world. Still less do we know of the mutual relations of the innumerable inhabitants of the world during the many past geological epochs in its history. Although much remains obscure, and will long remain obscure, I can entertain no doubt, after the most deliberate study and dispassionate judgment of which I am capable, that the view which most naturalists until recently entertained, and which I formerly entertained—namely, that each species has been independently created—is erroneous. I am fully convinced that species are not immutable; but that those belonging to what are called the same genera are lineal descendants of some other and generally extinct species, in the same manner as the acknowledged varieties of any one species are the descendants of that species. Furthermore, I am convinced that Natural Selection has been the most important, but not the exclusive, means of modification.

# Father and Son

*Edmund Gosse*

On the first occasion, I recollect, our Cockney housemaid, enthusiastic young creature that she was, flung herself down upon her knees, and drank of the salt waters. Miss Marks, more instructed in phenomena, refrained, but I, although I was perfectly aware what the taste would be, insisted on sipping a few drops from the palm of my hand. This was a slight recurrence of what I have called my "natural magic" practices, which had passed into the background of my mind, but had not quite disappeared. I recollect that I thought I might secure some power of walking on the sea, if I drank of it—a perfectly irrational movement of mind, like those of savages.

My great desire was to walk out over the sea as far as I could, and then lie flat on it, face downwards, and peer into the depths. I was tormented with this ambition, and, like many grown-up people, was so fully occupied by these vain and ridiculous desires that I neglected the actual natural pleasures around me. The idea was not quite so demented as it may seem, because we were in the habit of singing, as well as reading, of those enraptured beings who spend their days in "flinging down their golden crowns upon the jasper sea." Why, I argued, should I not be able to fling down my straw hat upon the tides of Oddicombe? And, without question, a majestic scene upon the Lake of Gennesaret had also inflamed my fancy. Of all these things, of course, I was careful to speak to no one.

It was not with Miss Marks, however, but with my Father, that I became accustomed to make the laborious and exquisite journeys down to the sea and back again. His work as a naturalist eventually took him, laden with implements, to the rock-pools on the shore, and I was in attendance as an acolyte. But our earliest winter in South Devon was darkened for us both by disappointments, the cause of which lay, at the time, far out of my reach. In the spirit of my Father were then running, with furious velocity, two hostile streams of influence. I was standing, just now, thinking of these things, where the Cascine ends in the wooded point which is carved out sharply by the lion-coloured swirl of the Arno on the one side and by the pure flow of the Mugnone on the other. The rivers meet, and run parallel, but there comes a moment when the one or the other must conquer, and it is the yellow vehemence that drowns the purer tide.

So, through my Father's brain, in that year of scientific crisis, 1857, there rushed two kinds of thought, each absorbing, each convincing, yet totally irreconcilable. There is a peculiar agony in the paradox that truth has two forms, each of them indisputable, yet each antagonistic to the other. It was this discovery, that there were two theories of physical life, each of which was true, but the truth of each incompatible with the truth of the other, which shook the spirit of my Father with perturbation. It was not, really, a paradox, it was a fallacy, if he could only have known it, but he allowed the turbid volume of superstition to drown the delicate stream of reason. He took one step in the service of truth, and then he drew back in an agony, and accepted the servitude of error.

This was the great moment in the history of thought when the theory of the mutability of species was preparing to throw a flood of light upon all departments of human speculation and action. It was becoming necessary to stand emphatically in one army or the other. Lyell was surrounding himself with disciples, who were making strides in the direction of discovery. Darwin had long been collecting facts with regard to the variation of animals and plants. Hooker and Wallace, Asa Gray and even Agassiz, each in his own sphere, were coming closer and closer to a perception of that secret which was first to reveal itself clearly to the patient and humble genius of Darwin. In the year before, in 1856, Darwin, under pressure from Lyell, had begun that modest statement of the new revelation, that "abstract of an essay," which developed so mightily into "The Origin of Species." Wollaston's "Variation of Species" had just appeared, and had been a nine days' wonder in the wilderness.

On the other side, the reactionaries, although never dreaming of the fate which hung over them, had not been idle. In 1857 the astounding question had for the first time been propounded with contumely, "What, then, did we come from an orang-outang?" The famous "Vestiges of Creation" had been supplying a sugar-and-water panacea for those who could not escape from the trend of evidence, and who yet clung to revelation. Owen was encouraging reaction by resisting, with all the strength of his prestige, the theory of the mutability of species.

In this period of intellectual ferment, as when a great political revolution is being planned, many possible adherents were confidentially tested with hints and encouraged to reveal their bias in a whisper. It was the notion of Lyell, himself a great mover of men, that before the doctrine of natural selection was given to a world which would be sure to lift up at it a howl of execration, a certain body-guard of sound and experienced naturalists, expert in the description of species, should be privately made aware of its tenour. Among those who were thus initiated, or approached with a view towards possible illumination, was my Father. He was spoken to by Hooker, and later on by Darwin, after meetings of the Royal Society in the summer of 1857.

My Father's attitude towards the theory of natural selection was critical in his career, and, oddly enough, it exercised an immense influence on my own experience as a child. Let it be admitted at once, mournful as the admission is, that every instinct in his intelligence went out at first to greet the new light. It had hardly done so, when a recollection of the opening chapter of Genesis checked it at the outset. He consulted with Carpenter, a great investigator, but one who was fully as incapable as himself of remodelling his ideas with regard to the old, accepted hypotheses. They both determined, on various grounds, to have nothing to do with the terrible theory, but to hold steadily to the law of the fixity of species. It was exactly at this juncture that we left London, and the slight and occasional, but always extremely salutary personal intercourse with men of scientific leading which my Father had enjoyed at the British Museum and at the Royal Society came to an end. His next act was to burn his ships, down to the last beam and log out of which a raft could have been made. By a strange act of wilfulness, he closed the doors upon himself for ever.

My Father had never admired Sir Charles Lyell. I think that the famous "Lord Chancellor manner" of the geologist intimidated him, and we undervalue the intelligence of those whose conversation puts us at a disadvantage. For Darwin and Hooker, on the other hand, he had a profound esteem, and I know not whether this had anything to do with the fact that he chose, for his impetuous experiment in reaction, the field of geology, rather than that of zoölogy or botany. Lyell had been threatening to publish a book on the geological history of Man, which was to be a bomb-shell flung into the camp of the catastrophists. My Father, after long reflection, prepared a theory of his own, which, as he fondly hoped, would take the wind out of Lyell's sails, and justify geology to godly readers of "Genesis." It was, very briefly, that there had been no gradual modification of the surface of the earth, or slow development of organic forms, but that when the catastrophic act of creation took place, the world presented, instantly, the structural appearance of a planet on which life had long existed.

The theory, coarsely enough, and to my Father's great indignation, was defined by a hasty press as being this—that God hid the fossils in the rocks in order to tempt geologists into infidelity. In truth, it was the logical and inevitable conclusion of accepting, literally, the doctrine of a sudden act of creation; it emphasised the fact that any breach in the circular course of nature could be conceived only on the supposition that the object created bore false witness to past processes, which had never taken place. For instance, Adam would certainly possess hair and teeth and bones in a condition which it must have taken many years to accomplish, yet he was created full-grown yesterday. He would certainly—though Sir Thomas Browne denied it—display an *omphalos*, yet no umbilical cord had ever attached him to a mother.

Never was a book cast upon the waters with greater anticipations of success than was this curious, this obstinate, this fanatical volume. My Father lived in a fever of suspense, waiting for the tremendous issue. This "Omphalos" of his, he thought, was to bring all the turmoil of scientific speculation to a close, fling geology into the arms of Scripture, and make the lion eat grass with the lamb. It was not surprising, he admitted, that there had been experienced an ever-increasing discord between the facts which geology brings to light and the direct statements of the early chapters of "Genesis." Nobody was to blame for that. My Father, and my Father alone, possessed the secret of the enigma; he alone held the key which could smoothly open the lock of geological mystery. He offered it, with a glowing gesture, to atheists and Christians alike. This was to be the universal panacea; this the system of intellectual therapeutics which could not but heal all the maladies of the age. But, alas! atheists and Christians alike looked at it and laughed, and threw it away.

In the course of that dismal winter, as the post began to bring in private letters, few and chilly, and public reviews, many and scornful, my Father looked in vain for the approval of the churches, and in vain for the acquiescence of the scientific societies, and in vain for the gratitude of those "thousands of thinking persons," which he had rashly assured himself of receiving. As his reconciliation of Scripture statements and geological deductions was welcomed nowhere; as Darwin continued silent, and the youthful Huxley was scornful, and even Charles Kingsley, from whom my Father had expected the most instant appreciation, wrote that he could not "give up the painful and slow conclusion of five and twenty years' study of geology, and believe that God has written on the rocks one enormous and superfluous lie,"—as all this happened or failed to happen, a gloom, cold and dismal, descended upon our morning teacups. It was what the poets mean by an "inspissated" gloom; it thickened day by day, as hope and self-confidence evaporated in thin clouds of disappointment. My Father was not prepared for such a fate. He had been the spoiled darling of the public, the constant favourite of the press, and now, like the dark angels of old,

> so huge a rout
> Encumoered him with ruin.

He could not recover from amazement at having offended everybody by an enterprise which had been undertaken in the cause of universal reconciliation.

During that grim season, my Father was no lively companion, and circumstance after circumstance combined to drive him further from humanity. He missed more than ever the sympathetic ear of my Mother; there was present to support him nothing of that artful, female casuistry which insinuates into the wounded consciousness of a man the conviction that, after all, he is right and all the rest of the world is wrong. My Father used to tramp in solitude round and round the red ploughed field which was going to be his lawn, or, sheltering himself from the thin Devonian rain, pace up and down the still-naked verandah where blossoming creepers were to be. And I think that there was added to his chagrin with all his fellow mortals a first tincture of that heresy which was to attack him later on. It was now that, I fancy, he began, in his depression, to be angry with God. How much devotion had he given, how many sacrifices had he made, only to be left storming round this red morass with no one in all the world to care for him except one pale-faced child with its cheek pressed to the window!

After one or two brilliant excursions to the sea, winter, in its dampest, muddiest, most languid form, had fallen upon us and shut us in. It was a dreary winter for the wifeless man and the motherless boy. We had come into the house, in precipitate abandonment to that supposed answer to prayer, a great deal too soon. In order to rake together the lump sum for buying it, my Father had denuded himself of almost everything, and our sticks of chairs and tables filled but two or three rooms. Half the little house, or "villa" as we called it, was not papered, two-thirds were not furnished. The workmen were still finishing the outside when we arrived, and in that connection I recall a little incident which exhibits my Father's morbid delicacy of conscience. He was accustomed, in his brighter moments—and this was before the publication of his "Omphalos"— occasionally to sing loud Dorsetshire songs of his early days, in a strange, broad Wessex lingo that I loved. One October afternoon he and I were sitting on the verandah, and my Father was singing; just round the corner, out of sight, two carpenters were putting up the framework of a greenhouse. In a pause, one of them said to his fellow: "He can zing a zong, zo well's another, though he be a minister." My Father, who was holding my hand loosely, clutched it, and looking up, I saw his eyes darken. He never sang a secular song again during the whole of his life.

Later in the year, and after his literary misfortune, his conscience became more troublesome than ever. I think he considered the failure of his attempt at the reconciliation of science with religion to have been intended by God as a punishment for something he had done or left undone. In those brooding tramps round and round the garden, his soul was on its knees searching the corners of his conscience for some sin of omission or commission, and one by one every pleasure, every recreation, every trifle scraped out of the dust of past experience, was magnified into a huge offence. He thought that the smallest evidence of levity, the least unbending to human instinct, might be seized by those around him as evidence of inconsistency, and might lead the weaker brethren into offence. The incident of the carpenters and the comic song is typical of a condition of mind which now possessed my Father, in which act after act became taboo, not because each was sinful in itself, but because it might lead others into sin.

I have the conviction that Miss Marks was now mightily afraid of my Father. Whenever she could, she withdrew to the room she called her "boudoir," a small, chilly apartment, sparsely furnished, looking over what was in process of becoming the vegetable garden. Very properly, that she might have some sanctuary, Miss Marks forbade me to enter this virginal bower, which, of course, became to me an object of harrowing curiosity. Through the key-hole I could see practically nothing; one day I contrived to slip inside, and discovered that there was nothing to see but a plain bedstead and a toilet-table, void of all attraction. In this "boudoir," on winter afternoons, a fire would be lighted, and Miss Marks would withdraw to it, not seen by us any more between high-tea and the apocalyptic exercise known as "worship"—in less strenuous households much less austerely practised under the name of "family prayers." Left meanwhile to our own devices, my Father would mainly be reading, his book or paper held close up to the candle, while his lips and heavy eye-brows occasionally quivered and palpitated, with literary ardour, in a manner strangely exciting to me. Miss Marks, in a very high cap, and her large teeth shining, would occasionally appear in the doorway, desiring, with spurious geniality, to know how we were "getting on." But on these occasions neither of us replied to Miss Marks.

Sometimes, in the course of this winter, my Father and I had long cosy talks together over the fire. Our favourite subject was murders. I wonder whether little boys of eight, soon to go up-stairs alone at night, often dis-cuss violent crime with a widower-papa? The practice, I cannot help thinking, is unusual; it was, however, consecutive with us. We tried other secular subjects, but we were sure to come round at last to "what do you suppose they really did with the body?" I was told, a thrilled listener, the adventure of Mrs. Manning, who killed a gentleman on the stairs and buried him in quick-lime in the back-kitchen, and it was at this time that I learned the useful historical fact, which abides with me after half a cen-tury, that Mrs. Manning was hanged in black satin, which thereupon went wholly out of fashion in England. I also heard about Burke and Hare, whose story nearly froze me into stone with horror.

These were crimes which appear in the chronicles. But who will tell me what "the Carpetbag Mystery" was, which my Father and I discussed evening after evening? I have never come across a whisper of it since, and I suspect it of having been a hoax. As I recall the details, people in a boat, passing down the Thames, saw a carpet-bag hung high in air, on one of the projections of a pier of Waterloo Bridge. Being with difficulty dragged down—or perhaps up—this bag was found to be full of human remains, dreadful butcher's business of joints and fragments. Persons were missed, were identified, were again denied—the whole is a vapour in my memory which shifts as I try to define it. But clear enough is the picture I hold of myself, in a high chair, on the left-hand side of the sitting-room fire-place, the leaping flames reflected in the glass-case of tropical insects on the opposite wall, and my Father, leaning anxiously forward, with uplifted finger, emphasising to me the pros and cons of the horrible car-pet-bag evidence.

I suppose that my interest in these discussions—and Heaven knows I was animated enough—amused and distracted my Father, whose idea of a suitable theme for childhood's ear now seems to me surprising. I soon found that these subjects were not welcome to everybody, for, starting the Carpet-bag Mystery one morning with Miss Marks, in the hope of delaying my arithmetic lesson, she fairly threw her apron over her ears, and told me, from that vantage, that if I did not desist at once, she should scream.

Occasionally we took winter wallks together, my Father and I, down some lane that led to a sight of the sea, or over the rolling downs. We tried to recapture the charm of those delightful strolls in London, when we used to lean over the bridges and watch the ducks. But we could not recover this pleasure. My Father was deeply enwoven in the chain of his own thoughts, and would stalk on, without a word, buried in angry reverie. If he spoke to me, on these excursions, it was a pain to me to answer him. I could talk on easy terms with him indoors, seated in my high chair, with our heads on a level, but it was intolerably laborious to look up into the firmament and converse with a dark face against the sky. The actual exercise of walking, too, was very exhausting to me; the bright red mud, to the strange colour of which I could not for a long while get accustomed, becoming caked about my little shoes, and wearying me extremely. I would grow petulant and cross, contradict my Father, and oppose his whims. These walks were distressing to us both, yet he did not like to walk alone, and he had no other friend. However, as the winter advanced, they had to be abandoned, and the habit of our taking a "constitutional" together was never resumed.

I look back upon myself at this time as upon a cantankerous, ill-tempered and unobliging child. The only excuse I can offer is that I really was not well. The change to Devonshire had not suited me; my health gave the excellent Miss Marks some anxiety, but she was not ready in resource. The dampness of the house was terrible; indoors and out, the atmosphere seemed soaked in chilly vapours. Under my bed-clothes at night I shook like a jelly unable to sleep for cold, though I was heaped with coverings, while my skin was all puckered with goose-flesh. I could eat nothing solid, without suffering immediately from violent hiccough, so that much of my time was spent lying prone on my back upon the hearth-rug, awakening the echoes like a cuckoo. Miss Marks, therefore, cut off all food but milk-sop, a loathly bowl of which appeared at every meal. In consequence the hiccough lessened, but my strength declined with it. I languished in a perpetual catarrh. I was roused to a consciousness that I was not considered well by the fact that my Father prayed publicly at morning and evening "worship" that if it was the Lord's will to take me to himself there might be no doubt whatever about my being a sealed child of God and an inheritor of glory. I was partly disconcerted by, partly vain of, this open advertisement of my ailments.

Of our dealings with the "Saints," a fresh assortment of whom met us on our arrival in Devonshire, I shall speak presently. My Father's austerity of behaviour was, I think, perpetually accentuated by his fear of doing anything to offend the consciences of these persons, whom he supposed, no doubt, to be more sensitive than they really were. He was fond of saying that "a very little stain upon the conscience makes a wide breach in our communion with God," and he counted possible errors of conduct by hundreds and by thousands. It was in this winter that his attention was particularly drawn to the festival of Christmas, which, apparently, he had scarcely noticed in London.

On the subject of all feasts of the Church he held views of an almost grotesque peculiarity. He looked upon each of them as nugatory and worthless, but the keeping of Christmas appeared to him by far the most hateful, and nothing less than an act of idolatry. "The very word is Popish," he used to exclaim, "Christ's Mass!" pursing up his lips with the gesture of one who tastes assafœtida by accident. Then he would adduce the antiquity of the so-called feast, adapted from horrible heathen rites, and itself a soiled relic of the abominable Yule-Tide. He would denounce the horrors of Christmas until it almost made me blush to look at a holly-berry.

On Christmas Day of this year 1857 our villa saw a very unusual sight. My Father had given strictest charge that no difference whatever was to be made in our meals on that day; the dinner was to be neither more copious than usual nor less so. He was obeyed, but the servants, secretly rebellious, made a small plum-pudding for themselves. (I discovered afterwards, with pain, that Miss Marks received a slice of it in her boudoir.) Early in the afternoon, the maids,—of whom we were now advanced to keeping two,—kindly remarked that "the poor dear child ought to have a bit, anyhow," and wheedled me into the kitchen, where I ate a slice of plum-pudding. Shortly I began to feel that pain inside which in my frail state was inevitable, and my conscience smote me violently. At length I could bear my spiritual anguish no longer, and bursting into the study I called out: "Oh! Papa, Papa, I have eaten of flesh offered to idols!" It took some time, between my sobs, to explain what had happened. Then my Father sternly said: "Where is the accursed thing?" I explained that as much as was left of it was still on the kitchen table. He took me by the hand, and ran with me into the midst of the startled servants, seized what remained of the pudding, and with the plate in one hand and me still tight in the other, ran till we reached the dust-heap, when he flung the idolatrous confectionery on to the middle of the ashes, and then raked it deep down into the mass. The suddenness, the violence, the velocity of this extraordinary act made an impression on my memory which nothing will ever efface.

The key is lost by which I might unlock the perverse malady from which my Father's conscience seemed to suffer during the whole of this melancholy winter. But I think that a dislocation of his intellectual system had a great deal to do with it. Up to this point in his career, he had, as we have seen, nourished the delusion that science and revelation could be mutually justified, that some sort of compromise was possible. With great and ever greater distinctness, his investigations had shown him that in all departments of organic nature there are visible the evidences of slow modification of forms, of the type developed by the pressure and practice of æons. This conviction had been borne in upon him until it was positively irresistible. Where was his place, then, as a sincere and accurate observer? Manifestly, it was with the pioneers of the new truth, it was with Darwin, Wallace and Hooker. But did not the second chapter of "Genesis" say that in six days the heavens and earth were finished, and the host of them, and that on the seventh day God ended his work which he had made?

Here was a dilemma! Geology certainly *seemed* to be true, but the Bible, which was God's word, *was* true. If the Bible said that all things in Heaven and Earth were created in six days, created in six clays they were,—in six literal days of twenty-four hours each. The evidences of spontaneous variation of form, acting, over an immense space of time, upon ever-modifying organic structures, *seemed* overwhelming, but they must either be brought into line with the six-day labour of creation, or they must be rejected. I have already shown how my Father worked out the ingenious "Omphalos" theory in order to justify himself as a strictly scientific observer who was also a humble slave of revelation. But the old convention and the new rebellion would alike have none of his compromise.

To a mind so acute and at the same time so narrow as that of my Father—
a mind which is all logical and positive without breadth, without sup-
pleness and without imagination—to be subjected to a check of this kind
is agony. It has not the relief of a smaller nature, which escapes from the
dilemma by some foggy formula; nor the resolution of a larger nature to
take to it wings and surmount the obstacle. My Father, although half suffocated by the emotion of being lifted, as it were, on the great biological
wave, never dreamed of letting go his clutch of the ancient tradition, but
hung there, strained and buffeted. It is extraordinary that he—an "honest
hodman of science," as Huxley once called him—should not have been
content to allow others, whose horizons were wider than his could be, to
pursue those purely intellectual surveys for which he had no species of
aptitude. As a collector of facts and marshaller of observations, he had
not a rival in that age; his very absence of imagination aided him in his
work. But he was more an attorney than a philosopher, and he lacked that
sublime humility which is the crown of genius. For, this obstinate persuasion that he alone knew the mind of God, that he alone could interpret the designs of the Creator, what did it result from if not from a
congenital lack of that highest modesty which replies "I do not know"
even to the questions which Faith, with menacing finger, insists on having most positively answered?

# Terence, This Is Stupid Stuff

*A. E. Housman*

"Terence, this is stupid stuff:
You eat your victuals fast enough;
There can't be much amiss, 'tis clear,
To see the rate you drink your beer.
But oh, good Lord, the verse you make,
It gives a chap the belly-ache.
The cow, the old cow, she is dead;
It sleeps well the horned head:
We poor lads, 'tis our turn now
To hear such tunes as killed the cow.
Pretty friendship 'tis to rhyme
Your friends to death before their time
Moping melancholy mad:
Come, pipe a tune to dance to, lad."

Why, if 'tis dancing you would be,
There's brisker pipes than poetry.
Say, for what were hop-yards meant,
Or why was Burton built on Trent?

Oh many a peer of England brews
Livelier liquor than the Muse,
And malt does more than Milton can
To justify God's ways to man.
Ale, man, ale's the stuff to drink
For fellows whom it hurts to think:
Look into the pewter pot
To see the world as the world's not.
And faith, 'tis pleasant till 'tis past:
The mischief is that 'twill not last.
Oh I have been to Ludlow fair
And left my necktie God knows where,
And carried half-way home, or near,
Pints and quarts of Ludlow beer:

454

Then the world seemed none so bad,
And I myself a sterling lad;
And down in lovely muck I've lain,
Happy till I woke again.
Then I saw the morning sky:
Heigho, the tale was all a lie;
The world, it was the old world yet,
I was I, my things were wet,
And nothing now remained to do
But begin the game anew.

      Therefore, since the world has still
Much good, but much less good than ill,
And while the sun and moon endure
Luck's a chance, but trouble's sure,
I'd face it as a wise man would,
And train for ill and not for good.
'Tis true, the stuff I bring for sale
Is not so brisk a brew as ale:
Out of a stem that scored the hand
I wrung it in a weary land.
But take it: if the smack is sour,
The better for the embittered hour;
It should do good to heart and head
When your soul is in my soul's stead;
And I will friend you, if I may,
In the dark and cloudy day.

      There was a king reigned in the East.
There, when kings will sit to feast,
They get their fill before they think
With poisoned meat and poisoned drink.
He gathered all that springs to birth
From the many-venomed earth;
First a little, thence to more,
He sampled all her killing store;
And easy, smiling, seasoned sound,
Sate the king when healths went round.
They put arsenic in his meat
And stared aghast to watch him eat;

They poured strychnine in his cup
And shook to see him drink it up:
They shook, they stared as white's their shirt:
Them it was their poison hurt.
—I tell the tale that I heard told.
Mithridates, he died old.

# The Second Coming

*William Butler Yeats*

Turning and turning in the widening gyre
The falcon cannot hear the falconer;
Things fall apart; the center cannot hold;
Mere anarchy is loosed upon the world,
The blood-dimmed tide is loosed, and everywhere
The ceremony of innocence is drowned;
The best lack all conviction, while the worst
Are full of passionate intensity.

Surely some revelation is at hand;
Surely the Second Coming is at hand.
The Second Coming! Hardly are those words out
When a vast image out of *Spiritus Mundi*
Troubles my sight: somewhere in sands of the desert
A shape with lion body and the head of a man,
A gaze blank and pitiless as the sun,
Is moving its slow thighs, while all about it
Reel shadows of the indignant desert birds.
The darkness drops again; but now I know
That twenty centuries of stony sleep
Were vexed to nightmare by a rocking cradle,
And what rough beast, its hour come round at last,
Slouches towards Bethlehem to be born?

January 1919                                         [1920, 1921]

# *from* The Evolution of Physics

*Albert Einstein and Leopold Infeld*

By a continued repetition of this process the whole path of the motion may be traced without further recourse to observational data. This is, in principle, the way mechanics predicts the course of a body in motion, but the method used here is hardly practical. In practice such a step-by-step procedure would be extremely tedious as well as inaccurate. Fortunately, it is quite unnecessary; mathematics furnishes a short cut, and makes possible precise description of the motion in much less ink than we use for a single sentence. The conclusions reached in this way can be proved or disproved by observation.

The same kind of external force is recognized in the motion of a stone falling through the air and in the revolution of the moon in its orbit, namely, that of the earth's attraction for material bodies. Newton recognized that the motions of falling stones, of the moon, and of planets are only very special manifestations of a universal gravitational force acting between any two bodies. In simple cases the motion may be described and predicted by the aid of mathematics. In remote and extremely complicated cases, involving the action of many bodies on each other, a mathematical description is not so simple, but the fundamental principles are the same.

We find the conclusions, at which we arrived by following our initial clews, realized in the motion of a thrown stone, in the motion of the moon, the earth, and the planets.

It is really our whole system of guesses which is to be either proved or disproved by experiment. No one of the assumptions can be isolated for separate testing. In the case of the planets moving around the sun it is found that the system of mechanics works splendidly. Nevertheless we can well imagine that another system, based on different assumptions, might work just as well.

Physical concepts are free creations of the human mind, and are not, however it may seem, uniquely determined by the external world. In our endeavor to understand reality we are somewhat like a man trying to understand the mechanism of a closed watch. He sees the face and the moving hands, even hears its ticking, but he has no way of opening the case. If he is ingenious he may form some picture of a mechanism which could be responsible for all the things he observes, but he may never be quite sure his picture is the only one which could explain his observations. He will never be able to compare his picture with the real mechanism and he cannot even imagine the possibility or the meaning of such a comparison. But he certainly believes that, as his knowledge increases, his picture of reality will become simpler and simpler and will explain a wider and wider range of his sensuous impressions. He may also believe in the existence of the ideal limit of knowledge and that it is approached by the human mind. He may call this ideal limit the objective truth.

# *from* Nausea

## *Jean-Paul Sartre*

"M. de Rollebon was quite ugly. Queen Marie Antoinette called him her 'dear ape.' Yet he had all the ladies of the court, but not by clowning like Voisenon the baboon: but by a magnetism which carried his lovely victims to the worst excesses of passion. He intrigues, plays a fairly suspect role in the affair of the Queen's necklace and disappears in 1790, after having dealings with Mirabeau-Tonneau and Nerciat. He turns up again in Russia where he attempts to assassinate Paul I, and from there, he travels to the farthest countries; the Indies, China, Turkestan. He smuggles, plots, spies. In 1813 he returns to Paris. By 1816, he has become all-powerful: he is the sole confidant of the Duchess d'Angoulême. This capricious old woman, obsessed by horrible childhood memories, grows calm and smiles when she sees him. Through her, he works his will at court. In March 1820, he marries Mlle de Roquelaure, a very beautiful girl of eighteen. M. de Rollebon is seventy; he is at the height of distinction, at the apogee of his life. Seven months later, accused of treason, he is arrested, thrown into a cell, where he dies after five years of imprisonment, without ever being brought to trial."

I re-read with melancholy this note of Germain Berger.[1]

It was by those few lines that I first knew M. de Rollebon. How attractive he seemed and how I loved him after these few words! It is for him, for this mannikin that I am here. When I came back from my trip I could just as well have settled down in Paris or Marseilles. But most of the documents concerning the Marquis' long stays in France are in the municipal library of Bouville. Rollebon was the *Lord of the Manor of Marmommes*. Before the war, you could still find one of his descendants in this little town, an architect named Rollebon-Campouyré, who, at his death in 1912, left an important legacy to the Bouville library: letters of the Marquis, the fragment of a journal, and all sorts of papers. I have not yet gone through it all.

I am glad to have found these notes. I had not read them for ten years. My handwriting has changed, or so it seems to me; I used to write in a smaller hand. How I loved M. de Rollebon that year! I remember one evening—a Tuesday evening: I had worked all day in the Mazarine; I had just gathered, from his correspondence, of 1789–90, in what a magisterial way he duped Nerciat. It was dark, I was going down the Avenue du Maine and I bought some chestnuts at the corner of the Rue de la Gaîté. Was I happy! I laughed all by myself thinking of the face Nerciat must have made when he came back from Germany. The face of the Marquis is like this ink: it has paled considerably since I have worked over it.

In the first place, starting from 1801, I understand nothing more about his conduct. It is not the lack of documents: letters, fragments of memoirs, secret reports, police records. On the contrary I have almost too many of them. What is lacking in all this testimony is firmness and consistency. They do not contradict each other, neither do they agree with each other; they do not seem to be about the same person. And yet other historians work from the same sources of information. How do they do it? Am I more scrupulous or less intelligent? In any case, the question leaves me completely cold. In truth, what am I looking for? I don't know. For a long time, Rollebon the man has interested me more than the book to be written. But now, the man . . . the man begins to bore me. It is the book which attracts me. I feel more and more need to write—in the same proportion as I grow old, you might say.

Evidently it must be admitted that Rollebon took an active part in the assassination of Paul I, that he then accepted an extremely important espionage mission to the Orient from the Czar and constantly betrayed Alexander to the advantage of Napoleon. At the same time he was able to carry on an active correspondence with the Comte d'Artois and send him unimportant information in order to convince him of his fidelity: none of all that is improbable; Fouché, at the same time, was playing a comedy much more dangerous and complex. Perhaps the Marquis also carried on a rifle-supplying business with the Asiatic principalities for his own profit.

Well, yes: he could have done all that, but it is not proved: I am beginning to believe that nothing can ever be proved. These are honest hypotheses which take the facts into account: but I sense so definitely that they come from me, and that they are simply a way of unifying my own knowledge. Not a glimmer comes from Rollebon's side. Slow, lazy, sulky, the facts adapt themselves to the rigour of the order I wish to give them; but it remains outside of them. I have the feeling of doing a work of pure imagination. And I am certain that the characters in a novel would have a more genuine appearance, or, in any case, would be more agreeable.

•  •  •

This is what I thought: for the most banal even to become an adventure, you must (and this is enough) begin to recount it. This is what fools people: a man is always a teller of tales, he lives surrounded by his stories and the stories of others, he sees everything that happens to him through them; and he tries to live his own life as if he were telling a story.

But you have to choose: live or tell. For example, when I was in Hamburg, with that Erna girl I didn't trust and who was afraid of me, I led a funny sort of life. But I was in the middle of it, I didn't think about it. And then one evening, in a little cafe in San Pauli, she left me to go to the ladies' room. I stayed alone, there was a phonograph playing "Blue Skies." I began to tell myself what had happened since I landed. I told myself, "The third evening, as I was going into a dance hall called *La Grotte Bleue*, I noticed a large woman, half seas over. And that woman is the one I am waiting for now, listening to 'Blue Skies,' the woman who is going to come back and sit down at my right and put her arms around my neck." Then I felt violently that I was having an adventure. But Erna came back and sat down beside me, she wound her arms around my neck and I hated her without knowing why. I understand now: one had to begin living again and the adventure was fading out.

Nothing happens while you live. The scenery changes, people come in and go out, that's all. There are no beginnings. Days are tacked on to days without rhyme or reason, an interminable, monotonous addition. From time to time you make a semi-total: you say: I've been travelling for three years, I've been in Bouville for three years. Neither is there any end: you never leave a woman, a friend, a city in one go. And then everything looks alike: Shanghai, Moscow, Algiers, everything is the same after two weeks. There are moments—rarely—when you make a landmark, you realize that you're going with a woman, in some messy business. The time of a flash. After that, the procession starts again, you begin to add up hours and days: Monday, Tuesday, Wednesday. April, May, June. 1924, 1925, 1926.

That's living. But everything changes when you tell about life; it's a change no one notices: the proof is that people talk about true stories. As if there could possibly be true stories; things happen one way and we tell about them in the opposite sense. You seem to start at the beginning: "It was a fine autumn evening in 1922. I was a notary's clerk in Marommes." And in reality you have started at the end. It was there, invisible and present, it is the one which gives to words the pomp and value of a beginning. "I was out walking, I had left the town without realizing it, I was thinking about my money troubles." This sentence, taken simply for what it is, means that the man was absorbed, morose, a hundred leagues from an adventure, exactly in the mood to let things happen without noticing them. But the end is there, transforming everything. For us, the man is already the hero of the story. His moroseness, his money troubles are much more precious than ours, they are all gilded by the light of future passions. And the story goes on in the reverse: instants have stopped piling themselves in a lighthearted way one on top of the other, they are snapped up by the end of the story which draws them and each one of them in turn, draws out the preceding instant: "It was night, the street was deserted." The phrase is cast out negligently, it seems superfluous; but we do not let ourselves be caught and we put it aside: this is a piece of information whose value we shall subsequently appreciate. And we feel that the hero has lived all the details of this night like annunciations, promises, or even that he lived only those that were promises, blind and deaf to all that did not herald adventure. We forget that the future was not yet there; the man was walking in a night without forethought, a night which offered him a choice of dull rich prizes, and he did not make his choice.

I wanted the moments of my life to follow and order themselves like those of a life remembered. You might as well try and catch time by the tail.

• • •

I lean my hand on the seat but pull it back hurriedly: it exists. This thing I'm sitting on, leaning my hand on, is called a seat. They made it purposely for people to sit on, they took leather, springs and cloth, they went to work with the idea of making a seat and when they finished, that was what they had made. They carried it here, into this car and the car is now rolling and jolting with its rattling windows, carrying this red thing in its bosom. I murmur: "It's a seat," a little like an exorcism. But the word stays on my lips: it refuses to go and put itself on the thing. It stays what it is, with its red plush, thousands of little red paws in the air, all still, little dead paws. This enormous belly turned upward, bleeding, inflated—

bloated with all its dead paws, this belly floating in this car, in this grey sky, is not a seat. It could just as well be a dead donkey tossed about in the water, floating with the current, belly in the air in a great grey river, a river of floods; and I could be sitting on the donkey's belly, my feet dangling in the clear water. Things are divorced from their names. They are there, grotesque, headstrong, gigantic and it seems ridiculous to call them seats or say anything at all about them: I am in the midst of things, nameless things. Alone, without words, defenceless, they surround me, are beneath me, behind me, above me. They demand nothing, they don't impose themselves: they are there.

• • •

And suddenly, suddenly, the veil is torn away, I have understood, I have seen.

*6.00 p.m.*

I can't say I feel relieved or satisfied; just the opposite, I am crushed. Only my goal is reached: I know what I wanted to know; I have understood all that has happened to me since January. The Nausea has not left me and I don't believe it will leave me so soon; but I no longer have to bear it, it is no longer an illness or a passing fit: it is I.

So I was in the park just now. The roots of the chestnut tree were sunk in the ground just under my bench. I couldn't remember it was a root any more. The words had vanished and with them the significance of things, their methods of use, and the feeble points of reference which men have traced on their surface. I was sitting, stooping forward, head bowed, alone in front of this black, knotty mass, entirely beastly, which frightened me. Then I had this vision.

It left me breathless. Never, until these last few days, had I understood the meaning of "existence." I was like the others, like the ones walking along the seashore, all dressed in their spring finery. I said, like them, "The ocean is green; that white speck up there is a seagull," but I didn't feel that it existed or that the seagull was an "existing seagull"; usually existence hides itself. It is there, around us, in us, it is us, you can't say two words without mentioning it, but you can never touch it. When I believed I was thinking about it, I must believe that I was thinking nothing, my head was empty, or there was just one word in my head, the word "to be." Or else I was thinking . . . how can I explain it? I was thinking of *belonging*, I was telling myself that the sea belonged to the class of green objects, or that the green was a part of the quality of the sea. Even when I looked at things, I was miles from dreaming that they existed: they looked like scenery to me. I picked them up in my hands, they served me as tools, I foresaw their resistance. But that all happened on the surface. If anyone had asked me what existence was, I would have answered, in good faith, that it was nothing, simply an empty form which was added to external things without changing anything in their nature. And then all of a sudden, there it was, clear as day: existence had suddenly unveiled itself. It had lost the harmless look of an abstract category: it was the very paste of things, this root was kneaded into existence. Or rather the root, the park gates, the bench, the sparse grass, all that had vanished: the diversity of things, their individuality, were only an appearance, a veneer. This veneer had melted, leaving soft, monstrous masses, all in disorder—naked, in a frightful, obscene nakedness.

I kept myself from making the slightest movement, but I didn't need to move in order to see, behind the trees, the blue columns and the lamp posts of the bandstand and the Velleda, in the midst of a mountain of laurel. All these objects . . . how can I explain? They inconvenienced me; I would have liked them to exist less strongly, more dryly, in a more abstract way, with more reserve. The chestnut tree pressed itself against my eyes. Green rust covered it half-way up; the bark, black and swollen, looked like boiled leather. The sound of the water in the Masqueret Fountain sounded in my ears, made a nest there, filled them with signs; my nostrils overflowed with a green, putrid odour. All things, gently, tenderly, were letting themselves drift into existence like those relaxed women who burst out laughing and say: "It's good to laugh," in a wet voice; they were parading, one in front of the other, exchanging abject secrets about their existence. I realized that there was no half-way house between non-existence and this flaunting abundance. If you existed, you had to *exist all the way*, as far as mouldiness, bloatedness, obscenity were concerned. In another world, circles, bars of music keep their pure and rigid lines. But existence is a deflection. Trees, night-blue pillars, the happy bubbling of a fountain, vital smells, little heat-mists floating in the cold air, a red-haired man digesting on a bench: all this somnolence, all these meals digested together, had its comic side. . . . Comic . . . no: it didn't go as far as that, nothing that exists can be comic; it was like a floating analogy, almost entirely elusive, with certain aspects of vaudeville. We were a heap of living creatures, irritated, embarrassed at ourselves, we hadn't the slightest reason to be there, none of us, each one, confused, vaguely alarmed, felt in the way in relation to the others. *In the way*: it was the only relationship I could establish between these trees, these gates, these stones. In vain I tried to count the chestnut trees, to *locate* them by their relationship to the Velleda, to compare their height with the height of the plane trees: each of them escaped the relationship in which I tried to enclose it, isolated itself, and overflowed. Of these relations (which I insisted on maintaining in order to delay the crumbling of the human world, measures, quantities, and directions)—I felt myself to be the arbitrator; they no longer had their teeth into things.

• • •

The word absurdity is coming to life under my pen; a little while ago, in the garden, I couldn't find it, but neither was I looking for it, I didn't need it: I thought without words, on things, with things. Absurdity was not an idea in my head, or the sound of a voice, only this long serpent dead at my feet, this wooden serpent. Serpent or claw or root or vulture's talon, what difference does it make. And without formulating anything clearly, I understood that I had found the key to Existence, the key to my Nauseas, to my own life. In fact, all that I could grasp beyond that returns to this fundamental absurdity. Absurdity: another word; I struggle against words; down there I touched the thing. But I wanted to fix the absolute character of this absurdity here. A movement, an event in the tiny coloured world of men is only relatively absurd: by relation to the accompanying circumstances. A madman's ravings, for example, are absurd in relation to the situation in which he finds himself, but not in relation to his delirium. But a little while ago I made an experiment with the absolute or the absurd. This root—there was nothing in relation to which it was absurd. Oh, how can I put it in words? Absurd: in relation to the stones, the tufts of yellow grass, the dry mud, the tree, the sky, the green benches. Absurd, irreducible; nothing—not even a profound, secret upheaval of nature—could explain it. Evidently I did not know everything, I had not seen the seeds sprout, or the tree grow. But faced with this great wrinkled paw, neither ignorance nor knowledge was important: the world of explanations and reasons is not the world of existence. A circle is not absurd, it is clearly explained by the rotation of a straight segment around one of its extremities. But neither does a circle exist. This root, on the other hand, existed in such a way that I could not explain it. Knotty, inert, nameless, it fascinated me, filled my eyes, brought me back unceasingly to its own existence. In vain to repeat: "This is a root"—it didn't work any more. I saw clearly that you could not pass from its function as a root, as a breathing pump, *to that*, to this hard and compact skin of a sea lion, to this oily, callous, headstrong look. The function explained nothing: it allowed you to understand generally that it was a root, but not *that one* at all. This root, with its colour, shape, its congealed movement, was . . . below all explanation. Each of its qualities escaped it a little, flowed out of it, half solidified, almost became a thing; each one was *In the way* in the root and the whole stump now gave me the impression of unwinding itself a little, denying its existence to lose itself in a frenzied excess. I scraped my heel against this black claw: I wanted to peel off some of the bark. For no reason at all, out of defiance, to make the bare pink appear absurd on the tanned leather: to *play* with the absurdity of the world. But, when I drew my heel back, I saw that the bark was still black.

Black? I felt the word deflating, emptied of meaning with extraordinary rapidity. Black? The root was not black, there was no black on this piece of wood—there was . . . something else: black, like the circle, did not exist.

## Note

1    Editor's Footnote: Germain Berger: Mirabeau-Tonneau et ses amis, page 406, note 2. Champion 1906.

# *from* Waiting for Godot

*Samuel Beckett*

| | |
|---|---|
| ESTRAGON: | You're sure it was this evening? |
| VLADIMIR: | What? |
| ESTRAGON: | That we were to wait. |
| VLADIMIR: | He said Saturday. (*Pause.*) I think. |
| ESTRAGON: | You think. |
| VLADIMIR: | I must have made a note of it. (*He fumbles in his pockets, bursting with miscellaneous rubbish.*) |
| ESTRAGON: | (*very insidious*). But what Satur-day? And is it Saturday? Is it not rather Sunday? (*Pause.*) Or Monday? (*Pause.*) Or Friday? |
| VLADIMIR: | (*looking wildly about him, as though the date was inscribed in the landscape*). It's not possible! |
| ESTRAGON: | Or Thursday? |
| VLADIMIR: | What'll we do? |
| ESTRAGON: | If he came yesterday and we weren't here you may be sure he won't come again to-day. |
| VLADIMIR: | But you say we were here yesterday. |
| ESTRAGON: | I may be mistaken. (*Pause.*) Let's stop talking for a minute, do you mind? |
| VLADIMIR: | (*feebly*). All right. (*Estragon sits down on the mound. Vladimir paces agitatedly to and fro, halting from time to time to gaze into distance off. Estragon falls asleep. Vladimir halts finally before Estragon.*) Gogo! . . . Gogo! . . . GOGO! *Estragon wakes with a start.* |
| ESTRAGON: | (*restored to the horror of his situation*). I was asleep! (*Despairingly.*) Why will you never let me sleep? |
| VLADIMIR: | I felt lonely. |
| ESTRAGON: | I had a dream. |
| VLADIMIR: | Don't tell me! |
| ESTRAGON: | I dreamt that— |
| VLADIMIR: | DON'T TELL ME! |
| ESTRAGON: | (*gesture towards the universe*). This one is enough for you? (*Silence.*) It's not nice of you, Didi. Who am I to tell my private nightmares to if I can't tell them to you? |

| | |
|---|---|
| VLADIMIR: | Let them remain private. You know I can't bear that. |
| ESTRAGON: | *(coldly)*. There are times when I wonder if it wouldn't be better for us to part. |
| VLADIMIR: | You wouldn't go far. |
| ESTRAGON: | That would be too bad, really too bad. (*Pause.*) Wouldn't it, Didi, be really too bad? (*Pause.*) When you think of the beauty of the way. (*Pause.*) And the goodness of the wayfarers. (*Pause. Wheedling.*) Wouldn't it, Didi? |
| VLADIMIR: | Calm yourself. |
| ESTRAGON: | *(voluptuously)*. Calm . . . calm . . . The English say cawm. (*Pause.*) You know the story of the English-man in the brothel? |
| VLADIMIR: | Yes. |
| ESTRAGON: | Tell it to me. |
| VLADIMIR: | Ah stop it! |
| ESTRAGON: | An Englishman having drunk a little more than usual proceeds to a brothel. The bawd asks him if he wants a fair one, a dark one or a red-haired one. Go on. |
| VLADIMIR: | STOP IT! |
| | *Exit Vladimir hurriedly. Estragon gets up and follows him as far as the limit of the stage. Gestures of Estragon like those of a spectator encouraging a pugilist. Enter Vladimir. He brushes past Estragon, crosses the stage with bowed head. Estragon takes a step towards him, halts.* |
| POZZO: | Help! |
| ESTRAGON: | And suppose we gave him a good beating the two of us? |
| VLADIMIR: | You mean if we fell on him in his sleep? |
| ESTRAGON: | Yes. |
| VLADIMIR: | That seems a good idea all right. But could we do it? Is he really asleep? (*Pause.*) No, the best would be to take advantage of Pozzo's calling for help— |
| POZZO: | Help! |
| VLADIMIR: | To help him— |
| ESTRAGON: | *We* help *him*? |
| VLADIMIR: | In anticipation of some tangible return. |
| ESTRAGON: | And suppose he— |
| VLADIMIR: | Let us not waste our time in idle discourse! (*Pause. Vehemently.*) Let us do something, while we have the chance! It is not every day that we are needed. Not indeed that we personally are needed. Others would meet the case |

equally well, if not better. To all mankind they were addressed, those cries for help still ringing in our ears! But at this place, at this moment of time, all mankind is us, whether we like it or not. Let us make the most of it, before it is too late! Let us represent worthily for once the foul brood to which a cruel fate consigned us! What do you say? (*Estragon says nothing.*) It is true that when with folded arms we weigh the pros and cons we are no less a credit to our species. The tiger bounds to the help of his congeners without the least reflexion, or else he slinks away into the depths of the thickets. But that is not the question. What are we doing here, *that* is the question. And we are blessed in this, that we happen to know the answer. Yes, in this immense confusion one thing alone is clear. We are waiting for Godot to come—

ESTRAGON:    Ah!

POZZO:    Help!

VLADIMIR:    Or for night to fall. (*Pause.*) We have kept our appointment and that's an end to that. We are not saints, but we have kept our appointment. How many people can boast as much?

ESTRAGON:    Billions.

VLADIMIR:    You think so?

ESTRAGON:    I don't know.

VLADIMIR:    You may be right.

POZZO:    Help!

VLADIMIR:    All I know is that the hours are long, under these conditions, and constrain us to beguile them with proceedings which—how shall I say—which may at first sight seem reasonable, until they become a habit. You may say it is to prevent our reason from foundering. No doubt. But has it not long been straying in the night without end of the abyssal depths? That's what I sometimes wonder. You follow my reasoning?

ESTRAGON:    (*aphoristic for once*). We are all born mad.

VLADIMIR:    But—

POZZO:    Enough! Up pig!

VLADIMIR:    You were bringing him to the fair to sell him. You spoke to us. He danced. He thought. You had your sight.

POZZO:    As you please. Let me go! (*Vladimir moves away.*)

Up!
*Lucky gets up, gathers up his burdens.*

VLADIMIR: Where do you go from here?

POZZO: On. (*Lucky, laden down, takes his place before Pozzo.*) Whip! (*Lucky puts everything down, looks for whip, finds it, puts it into Pozzo's hand, takes up everything again.*) Rope! (*Lucky puts everything down, puts end of rope into Pozzo's hand, takes up everything again.*)

VLADIMIR: What is there in the bag?

POZZO: Sand. (*He jerks the rope.*) On!

VLADIMIR: Don't go yet.

POZZO: I'm going.

VLADIMIR: What do you do when you fall far from help?

POZZO: We wait till we can get up. Then we go on. On!

VLADIMIR: Before you go tell him to sing.

POZZO: Who?

VLADIMIR: Lucky.

POZZO: To sing?

VLADIMIR: Yes. Or to think. Or to recite.

POZZO: But he is dumb.

VLADIMIR: Dumb!

POZZO: Dumb. He can't even groan.

VLADIMIR: Dumb! Since when?

POZZO: (*suddenly furious*). Have you not done tormenting me with your accursed time! It's abominable! When! When! One day, is that not enough for you, one day he went dumb, one day I went blind, one day we'll go deaf, one day we were born, one day we shall die, the same day, the same second, is that not enough for you? (*Calmer.*) They give birth astride of a grave, the light gleams an instant, then it's night once more. (*He jerks the rope.*) On! *Exeunt Pozzo and Lucky. Vladimir follows them to the edge of the stage, looks after them. The noise of falling, reinforced by mimic of Vladimir, announces that they are down again. Silence. Vladimir goes towards Estragon, contemplates him a moment, then shakes him awake.*

ESTRAGON: (*wild gestures, incoherent words. Finally.*) Why will you never let me sleep?

VLADIMIR: I felt lonely.

ESTRAGON: I was dreaming I was happy.

| | |
|---|---|
| VLADIMIR: | That passed the time. |
| ESTRAGON: | I was dreaming that— |
| VLADIMIR: | (*violently*). Don't tell me! (*Silence.*) I wonder is he really blind. |
| ESTRAGON: | Blind? Who? |
| VLADIMIR: | Pozzo. |
| ESTRAGON: | Blind? |
| VLADIMIR: | He told us he was blind. |
| ESTRAGON: | Well what about it? |
| VLADIMIR: | It seemed to me he saw us. |
| ESTRAGON: | You dreamt it. (*Pause.*) Let's go. We can't. Ah! (*Pause.*) Are you sure it wasn't him? |
| VLADIMIR: | Who? |
| ESTRAGON: | Godot. |
| VLADIMIR: | But who? |
| ESTRAGON: | Pozzo. |
| VLADIMIR: | Not at all! (*Less sure.*) Not at all! (*Still less sure.*) Not at all! |
| ESTRAGON: | I suppose I might as well get up. (*He gets up painfully.*) Ow! Didi! |
| VLADIMIR: | I don't know what to think any more. |
| ESTRAGON: | My feet! (*He sits down again and tries to take off his boots.*) Help me! |
| VLADIMIR: | Was I sleeping, while the others suffered? Am I sleeping now? To-morrow, when I wake, or think I do, what shall I say of to-day? That with Estragon my friend, at this place, until the fall of night, I waited for Godot? That Pozzo passed, with his carrier, and that he spoke to us? Probably. But in all that what truth will there be? (*Estragon, having struggled with his boots in vain, is dozing off again. Vladimir looks at him.*) He'll know nothing. He'll tell me about the blows he received and I'll give him a carrot. (*Pause.*) Astride of a grave and a difficult birth. Down in the hole, lingeringly, the grave-digger puts on the forceps. We have time to grow old. The air is full of our cries. (*He listens.*) But habit is a great deadener. (*He looks again at Estragon.*) At me too someone is looking, of me too someone is saying, He is sleeping, he knows nothing, let him sleep on. (*Pause.*) I can't go on! (*Pause.*) What have I said? *He goes feverishly to and fro, halts finally at extreme left, broods. Enter Boy right. He halts. Silence.* |

| | |
|---|---|
| BOY: | Mister . . . (*Vladimir turns.*) Mister Albert . . . |
| VLADIMIR: | Off we go again. (*Pause.*) Do you not recognize me? |
| BOY: | No Sir. |
| VLADIMIR: | It wasn't you came yesterday. |
| BOY: | No Sir. |
| VLADIMIR: | This is your first time. |
| BOY: | Yes Sir. |
| | *Silence.* |
| VLADIMIR: | You have a message from Mr. Godot. |
| BOY: | Yes Sir. |
| VLADIMIR: | He won't come this evening. |
| BOY: | No Sir. |
| VLADIMIR: | But he'll come to-morrow. |
| BOY: | Yes Sir. |
| VLADIMIR: | Without fail. |
| BOY: | Yes Sir. |
| | *Silence.* |
| VLADIMIR: | Did you meet anyone? |
| BOY: | No Sir. |
| VLADIMIR: | Two other . . . (*he hesitates*) <br> . . . men? |
| BOY: | I didn't see anyone, Sir. (*Silence.*) |
| VLADIMIR: | What does he do, Mr. Godot? (*Silence.*) Do you hear me? |
| BOY: | Yes Sir. |
| VLADIMIR: | Well? |
| BOY: | He does nothing, Sir. |
| | *Silence.* |
| VLADIMIR: | How is your brother? |
| BOY: | He's sick, Sir. |
| VLADIMIR: | Perhaps it was he came yesterday. |
| BOY: | I don't know, Sir. |
| | *Silence.* |
| VLADIMIR: | (*softly*). Has he a beard, Mr. Godot? |
| BOY: | Yes Sir. |
| VLADIMIR: | Fair or . . . (*he hesitates*) . . . or black? |
| BOY: | I think it's white, Sir. |
| | *Silence.* |
| VLADIMIR: | Christ have mercy on us! |
| | *Silence.* |
| BOY: | What am I to tell Mr. Godot, Sir? |

| | |
|---|---|
| VLADIMIR: | Tell him . . . (he hesitates) . . . tell him you saw me and that . . .(he hesitates) . . . that you saw me. (Pause. Vladimir advances, the Boy recoils. Vladimir halts, the Boy halts. With sudden violence.) You're sure you saw me, you won't come and tell me to-morrow that you never saw me!<br>*Silence. Vladimir makes a sudden spring forward, the Boy avoids him and exits running. Silence. The sun sets, the moon rises. As in Act I. Vladimir stands motionless and bowed. Estragon wakes, takes off his boots, gets up with one in each hand and goes and puts them down center front, then goes towards Vladimir.* |
| ESTRAGON: | What's wrong with you? |
| VLADIMIR: | Nothing. |
| ESTRAGON: | I'm going. |
| VLADIMIR: | So am I. |
| ESTRAGON: | Was I long asleep? |
| VLADIMIR: | I don't know.<br>*Silence.* |
| ESTRAGON: | Where shall we go? |
| VLADIMIR: | Not far. |
| ESTRAGON: | Oh yes, let's go far away from here. |
| VLADIMIR: | We can't. |
| ESTRAGON: | Why not? |
| VLADIMIR: | We have to come back to-morrow. |
| ESTRAGON: | What for? |
| VLADIMIR: | To wait for Godot. |
| ESTRAGON: | Ah! (*Silence.*) He didn't come? |
| VLADIMIR: | No. |
| ESTRAGON: | And now it's too late. |
| VLADIMIR: | Yes, now it's night. |
| ESTRAGON: | And if we dropped him? (*Pause.*) If we dropped him? |
| VLADIMIR: | He'd punish us. (*Silence. He looks at the tree.*) Everything's dead but the tree. |
| ESTRAGON: | (*looking at the tree*). What is it? |
| VLADIMIR: | It's the tree. |
| ESTRAGON: | Yes, but what kind? |
| VLADIMIR: | I don't know. A willow. |

*Estragon draws Vladimir towards the tree. They stand motionless before it. Silence.*

ESTRAGON:   Why don't we hang ourselves?

VLADIMIR:   With what?

ESTRAGON:   You haven't got a bit of rope?

VLADIMIR:   No.

ESTRAGON:   Then we can't.
*Silence.*

VLADIMIR:   Let's go.

ESTRAGON:   Wait, there's my belt.

VLADIMIR:   It's too short.

ESTRAGON:   You could hang on to my legs.

VLADIMIR:   And who'd hang on to mine?

ESTRAGON:   True.

VLADIMIR:   Show all the same. (*Estragon loosens the cord that holds up his trousers which, much too big for him, fall about his ankles. They look at the cord.*) It might do at a pinch. But is it strong enough?

ESTRAGON:   We'll soon see. Here.
*They each take an end of the cord and pull. It breaks. They almost fall.*

VLADIMIR:   Not worth a curse.
*Silence.*

ESTRAGON:   You say we have to come back to-morrow?

VLADIMIR:   Yes.

ESTRAGON:   Then we can bring a good bit of rope.

VLADIMIR:   Yes.
*Silence.*

ESTRAGON:   Didi.

VLADIMIR:   Yes.

ESTRAGON:   I can't go on like this.

VLADIMIR:   That's what you think.

ESTRAGON:   If we parted? That might be better for us.

VLADIMIR:   We'll hang ourselves to-morrow. (*Pause.*) Unless Godot comes.

ESTRAGON:   And if he comes?

VLADIMIR:   We'll be saved.
*Vladimir takes off his hat (Lucky's), peers inside it, feels about inside it, shakes it, knocks on the crown, puts it on again.*

ESTRAGON:   Well? Shall we go?

VLADIMIR:        Pull on your trousers.
ESTRAGON:        What?
VLADIMIR:        Pull on your trousers.
ESTRAGON:        You want me to pull off my trousers?
VLADIMIR:        Pull ON your trousers.
ESTRAGON:        (*realizing his trousers are down*). True.
                 *He pulls up his trousers.*
VLADIMIR:        Well? Shall we go?
ESTRAGON:        Yes, let's go.
                 *They do not move.*

### Curtain

# *from* The Social Construction of Reality

*Peter L. Berger and Thomas Luckmann*

Reification is the apprehension of human phenomena as if they were things, that is, in non-human or possibly supra-human terms. Another way of saying this is that reification is the apprehension of the products of human activity *as if* they were something else than human products—such as facts of nature, results of cosmic laws, or manifestations of divine will. Reification implies that man is capable of forgetting his own authorship of the human world, and further, that the dialectic between man, the producer, and his products is lost to consciousness. The reified world is, by definition, a dehumanized world. It is experienced by man as a strange facticity, an *opus alienum* over which he has no control rather than as the *opus proprium* of his own productive activity.

It will be clear from our previous discussion of objectivation that, as soon as an objective social world is established, the possibility of reification is never far away. The objectivity of the social world means that it confronts man as something outside of himself. The decisive question is whether he still retains the awareness that, however objectivated, the social world was made by men—and, therefore, can be remade by them. In other words, reification can be described as an extreme step in the process of objectivation, whereby the objectivated world loses its comprehensibility as a human enterprise and becomes fixated as a non-human, non-humanizable, inert facticity. Typically, the real relationship between man and his world is reversed in consciousness. Man, the producer of a world, is apprehended as its product, and human activity as an epiphenomenon of non-human processes. Human meanings are no longer understood as world-producing but as being, in their turn, products of the "nature of things." It must be emphasized that reification is a modality of consciousness, more precisely, a modality of man's objectification of the human world. Even while apprehending the world in reified terms, man continues to produce it. That is, man is capable paradoxically of producing a reality that denies him.

Reification is possible on both the pretheoretical and theoretical levels of consciousness. Complex theoretical systems can be described as reifications, though presumably they have their roots in pretheoretical reifica-

477

tions established in this or that social situation. Thus it would be an error to limit the concept of reification to the mental constructions of intellectuals. Reification exists in the consciousness of the man in the street and, indeed, the latter presence is more practically significant. It would also be a mistake to look at reification as a perversion of an originally non-reified apprehension of the social world, a sort of cognitive fall from grace. On the contrary, the available ethnological and psychological evidence seems to indicate the opposite, namely, that the original apprehension of the social world is highly reified both phylogenetically and ontogenetically. This implies that an apprehension of reification as a modality of consciousness is dependent upon an at least relative *de*reification of consciousness, which is a comparatively late development in history and in any individual biography.

Both the institutional order as a whole and segments of it may be apprehended in reified terms. For example, the entire order of society may be conceived of as a microcosm reflecting the macrocosm of the total universe as made by the gods. Whatever happens "here below" is but a pale reflection of what takes place "up above." Particular institutions may be apprehended in similar ways. The basic "recipe" for the reification of institutions is to bestow on them an ontological status independent of human activity and signification. Specific reifications are variations on this general theme. Marriage, for instance, may be reified as an imitation of divine acts of creativity, as a universal mandate of natural law, as the necessary consequence of biological or psychological forces, or, for that matter, as a functional imperative of the social system. What all these reifications have in common is their obfuscation of marriage as an ongoing human production. As can be readily seen in this example, the reification may occur both theoretically and pretheoretically. Thus the mystagogue can concoct a highly sophisticated theory reaching out from the concrete human event to the farthest corners of the divine cosmos, but an illiterate peasant couple being married may apprehend the event with a similarly reifying shudder of metaphysical dread. Through reification, the world of institutions appears to merge with the world of nature. It becomes necessity and fate, and is lived through as such, happily or unhappily as the case may be.

Roles may be reified in the same manner as institutions. The sector of self-consciousness that has been objectified in the role is then also apprehended as an inevitable fate, for which the individual may disclaim responsibility. The paradigmatic formula for this kind of reification is the statement "I have no choice in the matter, I have to act this way because of my position"—as husband, father, general, archbishop, chairman of the board, gangster, or hangman, as the case may be. This means that the reification of roles narrows the subjective distance that the individual may establish between himself and his role-playing. The distance implied in all objectification remains, of course, but the distance brought about by disidentification shrinks to the vanishing point. Finally, identity itself (the total self, if one prefers) may be reified, both one's own and that of others. There is then a total identification of the individual with his socially assigned typifications. He is apprehended as *nothing but* that type. This apprehension may be positively or negatively accented in terms of values or emotions. The identification of "Jew" may be equally reifying for the anti-Semite and the Jew himself, except that the latter will accent the identification positively and the former negatively. Both reifications bestow an ontological and total status on a typification that is humanly produced and that, even as it is internalized, objectifies but a segment of the self. Once more, such reifications may range from the pretheoretical level of "what everybody knows about Jews" to the most complex theories of Jewishness as a manifestation of biology ("Jewish blood"), psychology ("the Jewish soul") or metaphysics ("the mystery of Israel").

*Section Four*

# Nature

# *from* The Book of Genesis

## Chapter 1

In the beginning God created the heaven and the earth.

2 And the earth was without form, and void and darkness *was* upon the face of the deep. And the Spirit of God moved upon the face of the waters.

3 And God said, Let there be light: and there was light.

4 And God saw the light, that *it was* good: and God divided the light from the darkness.

5 And God called the light Day, and the darkness he called Night. And the evening and the morning were the first day.

6 ¶ And God said, Let there be a firmament in the midst of the waters, and let it divide the waters from the waters.

7 And God made the firmament, and divided the waters which *were* under the firmament from the waters which *were* above the firmament: and it was so.

8 And God called the firmament Heaven. And the evening and the morning were the second day

9 ¶ And God said, Let the waters under the heaven be gathered together unto one place, and let the dry *land* appear: and it was so.

10 And God called the dry *land* Earth; and the gathering together of the waters called he Seas: and God saw that *it was* good.

11 And God said, Let the earth bring forth grass, the herb yielding seed *and* the fruit tree yielding fruit after his kind, whose seed *is* in itself, upon the earth: and it was so.

12 And the earth brought forth grass, *and* herb yielding seed after his kind, and the tree yielding fruit, whose seed *was* in itself, after his kind: and God saw that *it was* good.

13 And the evening and the morning were the third day.

14 ¶ And God said, Let there be lights in the firmament of the heaven to divide the day from the night; and let them be for signs, and for seasons, and for days, and years:

15 And let them be for lights in the firmament of the heaven to give light upon the earth: and it was so.

16 And God made two great lights; the greater light to rule the day, and the lesser light to rule the night: *he made* the stars also.

17 And God set them in the firmament of the heaven to give light upon the earth,

18 And to rule over the day and over the night, and to divide the light from the darkness: and God saw that *it was* good.

19 And the evening and the morning were the fourth day.

20 And God said, Let the waters bring forth abundantly the moving creature that hath life, and fowl *that* may fly above the earth in the open firmament of heaven.

21 And God created great whales, and every living creature that moveth, which the waters brought forth abundantly after their kind, and every winged fowl after his kind: and God saw that *it was* good.

22 And God blessed them, saying, Be fruitful, and multiply, and fill the waters in the seas, and let fowl multiply in the earth.

23 And the evening and the morning were the fifth day.

24 ¶ And God said, Let the earth bring forth the living creature after his kind, cattle, and creeping thing, and beast of the earth after his kind: and it was so.

25 And God made the beast of the earth after his kind, and cattle after their kind, and every thing that creepeth upon the earth after his kind: and God saw that *it was* good.

26 ¶ And God said, Let us make man in our image, after our likeness: and let them have dominion over the fish of the sea, and over the fowl of the air, and over the cattle, and over all the earth, and over every creeping thing that creepeth upon the earth.

27 So God created man in his *own* image in the image of God created he him; male and female created he them.

28 And God blessed them, and God said unto them, Be fruitful, and multiply, and replenish the earth, and subdue it: and have dominion over the fish of the sea, and over the fowl of the air, and over every living thing that moveth upon the earth.

29 ¶ And God said, Behold, I have given you every herb bearing seed, which is upon the face of all the earth, and every tree, in the which *is* the fruit of a tree yielding seed; to you it shall be for meat.

30 And to every beast of the earth, and to every fowl of the air, and to every thing that creepeth upon the earth, wherein *there is* life, *I have given* every green herb for meat: and it was so.

31 And God saw every thing that he had made, and, behold, *it was* very good. And the evening and the morning were the sixth day.

## Chapter 2

1 Thus the heavens and the earth were finished, and all the host of them.

2 And on the seventh day God ended his work which he had made; and he rested on the seventh day from all his work which he had made.

3 And God blessed the seventh day and sanctified it: because that in it he had rested from all his work which God created and made.

4 ¶ These *are* the generations of the heavens and of the earth when they were created, in the day that the LORD God made the earth and the heavens,

5 And every plant of the field before it was in the earth, and every herb of the field before it grew: for the LORD God had not caused it to rain upon the earth, and *there was* not a man to till the ground.

6 But there went up a mist from the earth, and watered the whole face of the ground.

7 And the LORD God formed man *of* the dust of the ground, and breathed into his nostrils the breath of life; and man became a living soul.

8 ¶ And the LORD God planted a garden eastward in Ē-dĕn; and there he put the man whom he had formed.

9 And out of the ground made the LORD God to grow every tree that is pleasant to the sight, and good for food; the tree of life also in the midst of the garden, and the tree of knowledge of good and evil.

10 And a river went out of Ē-dĕn to water the garden; and from thence it was parted, and became into four heads.

11 The name of the first is Pi'-sŏn: that is it which compasseth the whole land of Hăv'-i-läh, where *there is* gold;

12 And the gold of that land *is* good: there *is* bdellium and the onyx stone.

13 And the name of the second river is Gi'-hon: the same is it that compasseth the whole land of Ē-thi-ō-pi-ă.

14 And the name of the third river is Hid'-dĕ-kĕl: that is it which goeth toward the east of Ăs-syr'-i-a. And the fourth river is Eu-phrā'-tēs.

15 And the LORD God took the man, and put him into the garden of Ē-dĕn to dress it and to keep it.

16 And the LORD God commanded the man, saying, Of every tree of the garden thou mayest freely eat:

17 But of the tree of the knowledge of good and evil, thou shalt not eat of it: for in the day that thou eatest thereof thou shalt surely die.

18 ¶ And the LORD God said, *It is* not good that the man should be alone; I will make him an help meet for him.

19 And out of the ground the LORD God formed every beast of the field, and every fowl of the air; and brought them unto Ăd'-ăm to see what he would call them: and whatsoever Ăd'-ăm called every living creature, that *was* the name thereof.

20 And Ăd'-ăm gave names to all cattle, and to the fowl of the air, and to every beast of the field, but for Ăd'-ăm there was not found an help meet for him.

21 And the LORD God caused a deep sleep to fall upon Ăd'-ăm, and he slept: and he took one of his ribs, and closed up the flesh instead thereof;

22 And the rib, which the LORD God had taken from man, made he a woman, and brought her unto the man.

23 And Ăd'-ăm said, This is now bone of my bones, and flesh of my flesh: she shall be called Woman, because she was taken out of Man.

24 Therefore shall a man leave his father and his mother and shall cleave to his wife: and they shall be one flesh.

25 And they were both naked, the man and his wife, and were not ashamed.

## Chapter 3

1 Now the serpent was more subtil than any beast of the field which the Lord God had made. And he said unto the woman, Yea, hath God said, Ye shall not eat of every tree of the garden?

2 And the woman said unto the serpent, We may eat of the fruit of the trees of the garden:

3 But of the fruit of the tree which *is* in the midst of the garden, God hath said Ye shall not eat of it, neither shall ye touch it, lest ye die.

4 And the serpent said unto the woman, Ye shall not surely die:

5 For God cloth know that in the day ye eat thereof, then your eyes shall be opened, and ye shall be as gods, knowing good and evil.

6 And when the woman saw that the tree *was* good for food, and that it was pleasant to the eyes, and a tree to be desired to make *one* wise, she took of the fruit thereof, and did eat, and gave also unto her husband with her, and he did eat.

7 And the eyes of them both were opened, and they knew that they were naked; and they sewed fig leaves together, and made themselves aprons.

8 And they heard the voice of the Lord God walking in the garden in the cool of the day: and Ăd'-ăm and his wife hid themselves from the presence of the Lord God amongst the trees of the garden.

9 And the Lord God called unto Ăd'-ăm, and said unto him, Where art thou?

10 And he said, I heard thy voice in the garden, and I was afraid, because I *was* naked; and I hid myself.

11 And he said, Who told thee that thou *wast* naked? Hast thou eaten of the tree, whereof I commanded thee that thou shouldest not eat?

12 And the man said, The woman whom thou gavest *to be* with me, she gave me of the tree, and I did eat.

13 And the LORD God said unto the woman, What *is* this *that* thou hast done? And the woman said, The serpent beguiled me, and I did eat.

14 And the LORD God said unto the serpent, Because thou hast done this thou art cursed above all cattle, and above every beast of the field, upon thy belly shalt thou go, and dust shalt thou eat all the days of thy life:

15 And I will put enmity between thee and the woman, and between thy seed and her seed; it shall bruise thy head, and thou shalt bruise his heel.

16 Unto the woman he said, I will greatly multiply thy sorrow and thy conception, in sorrow thou shalt bring forth children; and thy desire *shall be* to thy husband, and he shall rule over thee.

17 And unto Ăd'-ăm he said, Because thou has heartened unto the voice of thy wife, and hast eaten of the tree, of which I commanded thee, saying, Thou shalt not eat of it: cursed *is* the ground for thy sake, in sorrow shalt thou eat *of* it all the days of thy life.

18 Thorns also and thistles shall it bring forth to thee, and thou shalt eat the herb of the field.

19 In the sweat of thy face shalt thou eat bread, till thou return unto the ground; for out of it wast thou taken: for dust thou *art*, and unto dust shalt thou return.

20 And Ăd'-ăm called his wife's name Ēve; because she was the mother of all living.

21 Unto Ăd'-ăm also and to his wife did the LORD God make coats of skins, and clothed them.

22 ¶ And the LORD God said, Behold, the man is become as one of us, to know good and evil: and now, lest he put forth his hand, and take also of the tree of life, and eat, and live for ever:

23 Therefore the LORD God sent him forth from the Garden of Ē-děn, to till the ground from whence he was taken.

24 So ho drove out the man, and he placed at the east of the garden of Ē-děn Chĕr-ū-bims, and a flaming sword which turned every way. to keep the way of the tree of life.

## Chapter 4

And Ăd'-ăm knew Ēve his wife; and she conceived, and bare C<u>ai</u>n, and said, I have gotten a man from the LORD.

2 And she again bare his brother Ā'-bĕl. And Ā'-bĕl was a keeper of sheep, but C<u>ai</u>n was a tiller of the ground.

3 And in process of time it came to pass, that C<u>ai</u>n brought of the fruit of the ground an offering unto the LORD.

4 And Ā'-bĕl, he also brought of the firstlings of his flock and of the fat thereof. And the LORD had respect unto Ā'-bĕl and to his offering:

5 But unto C<u>ai</u>n and to his offering he had not respect. And C<u>ai</u>n was very wroth, and his countenance fell.

6 And the LORD said unto C<u>ai</u>n, Why art thou wroth? and why is thy countenance fallen?

7 If thou doest well, shalt thou not be accepted? and if thou doest not well, sin lieth at the door. And unto thee *shall be* his desire, and thou shalt rule over him.

8 And C<u>ai</u>n talked with Ā'-bĕl his brother: and it came to pass, when they were in the field, that C<u>ai</u>n rose up against Ā'-bĕl his brother, and slew him.

9 ¶ And the LORD said unto C<u>ai</u>n, Where is Ā'-bĕl thy brother? And he said, I know not: Am I my brother's keeper?

10 And he said, What hast thou done? the voice of thy brother's blood crieth unto me from the ground.

11 And now art thou cursed from the earth, which hath opened her mouth to receive thy brother's blood from thy hand.

12 When thou tillest the ground, it shall not henceforth yield unto thee her strength; a fugitive and a vagabond shalt thou be in the earth.

13 And C<u>ai</u>n said unto the LORD, My punishment is greater than I can bear.

14 Behold, thou hast driven me out this day from the face of the earth; and from thy face shall I be hid and I shall be a fugitive and a vagabond in the earth; and it shall come to pass, *that* every one that findeth me shall slay me.

15 And the LORD said unto him, Therefore whosoever slayeth Cain, vengeance shall be taken on him sevenfold. And the LORD set a mark upon Cain, lest any finding him should kill him.

16 ¶ And Cain went out from the presence of the LORD, and dwelt in the land of Nod, on the east of Ē-dĕn.

17 And Cain knew his wife; and she conceived, and bare Ē'-nŏch: and he builded a city, and called the name of the city, after the name of his son, Ē'-nŏch.

18 And unto Ē'-nŏch was born Í'-răd: and Í'-răd begat Mĕ-hū-ja'-ĕl: and Mĕ-hū-ja'-ĕl begat Mĕ-thū-sā-ĕl: and Mĕ-thū-sā-ĕl begat Lā'-mĕch.

19 And Lā'-mĕch took unto him two wives: the name of the one *was* Ā-dăh, and the name of the other Zil'-lăh.

20 And Ā-dăh bare Jā'-băl: he was the father of such as dwell in tents, and *of such as have* cattle.

21 And his brother's name *was* Jā'-băl: he was the father of all such as handle the harp and organ.

22 And Zil'-lăh, she also bare Tū'-băl-cain, an instructor of every artificer in brass and iron: and the sister of Tū'-băl-cain *was* Nā'-ă-măh.

23 And Lā'-mĕch said unto his wives Ā-dăh and Zil'-lăh, Hear my voice. ye wives of Lā'-mĕch, hearken unto my speech: for I have slain a man to my wounding, and a young man to my hurt.

24 If Cain shall be avenged sevenfold, truly Lā'-mĕch seventy and sevenfold.

25 And Ad'-am knew his wife again and she bare a son, and called his name Sĕth: For God, *said she*, hath appointed me another seed instead of Ā'-bĕl, whom Cain slew.

26 And to Sĕth, to him also there was born a son; and he called his name Ē'-nŏs: then began men to call upon the name of the LORD.

## Chapter 5

1 This *is* the book of the generations of Ăd'-ăm. In the day that God created man in the likeness of God made he him;

2 Male and female created he them, and blessed them, and called their name Ăd'-ăm, in the day when they were created.

3 ¶ And Ăd'-ăm lived an hundred and thirty years, and begat *a son* in his own likeness, after his image, and called his name Sĕth:

4 And the days of Ăd'-ăm after he had begotten Sĕth were eight hundred years: and he begat sons and daughters:

5 And all the days that Ăd'-ăm lived were nine hundred and thirty years: and he died.

6 And Sĕth lived an hundred and five years, and begat Ē'-nŏs:

7 And Sĕth lived after he begat Ē'-nŏs eight hundred and seven years, and begat sons and daughters:

8 And all the days of Sĕth were nine hundred and twelve years: and he died.

9 ¶ And Ē'-nŏs lived ninety years, and begat Cā-ī'-năn:

10 And Ē'-nŏs lived after he begat Cā-ī'-năn eight hundred and fifteen years, and begat sons and daughters:

11 And all the days of Ē'-nŏs were nine hundred and five years: and he died.

12  And Cā-ī'-năn lived seventy years, and begat Mă-hăl'-ă-leel:

13 And Cā-ī'-năn lived after he begat Mă-hăl'-ă-leel eight hundred and forty years, and begat sons and daughters:

14 And all the days of Cā-ī'-năn were nine hundred and ten years: and he died.

15 ¶ And Mă-hăl'-ă-leel lived sixty and five years, and begat Jâr'-ĕd:

16 And Mă-hăl'-ă-leel lived after he begat Jâr'-ĕd eight hundred and thirty years and begat sons and daughters:

17 And all the days of Mă-hăl'-ă-leel were eight hundred ninety and five years: and he died.

18 ¶ And Jâr'-ĕd lived an hundred sixty and two years, and he begat Ē'-nŏch:

19 And Jâr′-ĕd lived after he begat Ē′-nŏch eight hundred years, and begat sons and daughters:

20 And all the days of Jâr′-ĕd were nine hundred sixty and two years: and he died.

21 And Ē′-nŏch lived sixty and five years, and begat Mĕ-thū′-sĕ-lăh:

22 And Ē′-nŏch walked with God after he begat Mĕ-thū′-sĕ-lăh three hundred years and begat sons and daughters:

23 And all the days of Ē′-nŏch were three hundred sixty and five Years:

24 And Ē′-nŏch walked with God: and he *was* not, for God took him.

25 And Mĕ-thū′-sĕ-lăh lived an hundred eighty and seven years, and begat Lā′-mĕ<u>ch</u>.

26 And Mĕ-thū′-sĕ-lăh lived after he begat Lā′-mĕ<u>ch</u> seven hundred eighty and two years, and begat sons and daughters:

27 And all the days of Mĕ-thū′-sĕ-lăh were nine hundred sixty and nine years: and he died.

28 ¶ And Lā′-mĕ<u>ch</u> lived an hundred eighty and two years, and begat a son:

29 And he called his name Nō′-ăh, saying, This *same* shall comfort us concerning our work and toil of our hands, because of the ground which the Lord hath cursed.

30 And Lā′-mĕ<u>ch</u> lived after he begat Nō′-ăh five hundred ninety and five years, and begat sons and daughters:

31 And all the days of Lā′-mĕ<u>ch</u> were seven hundred seventy and seven years and he died.

32 And Nō′-ăh was five hundred years old: and Nō′-ăh begat Shĕm, Hăm and Jā′-phĕth.

# Chapter 6

1 And it came to pass, when men began to multiply on the face of the earth, and daughters were born unto them,

2 That the sons of God saw the daughters of men that they *were* fair; and they took them wives of all which they chose.

3 And the LORD said, My spirit shall not always strive with man, for that he also is flesh: yet his days shall be an hundred and twenty years.

4 There were giants in the earth in those days; and also after that, when the sons of God came in unto the daughters of men, and they bare *children* to them, the same *became* mighty men which were of *old*, men of renown.

5 ¶ And GOD saw that the wickedness of man was great in the earth, and that every imagination of the thoughts of his heart was only evil continually.

6 And it repented the LORD that he had made man on the earth, and it grieved him at his heart.

7 And the LORD said, I will destroy man whom I have created from the face of the earth, both man, and beast, and the creeping thing, and the fowls of the air; for it repenteth me that I have made them.

8 But Nō′-ăh found grace in the eyes of the LORD.

9 ¶ These are the generations of Nō′-ăh: Nō′-ăh was a just man and perfect in his generations, and Nō′-ăh walked with God.

10 And Nō′-ăh begat three sons, Shĕm, Hăm and Jā′-phĕth.

11 The earth also was corrupt before God, and the earth was filled with violence.

12 And God looked upon the earth and, behold, it was corrupt; for all flesh had corrupted his way upon the earth.

13 And God said unto Nō′-ăh, The end of all flesh is come before me, for the earth is filled with violence through them and, behold, I will destroy them with the earth.

14 ¶ Make thee an ark of gō′-phĕr wood, rooms shalt thou make in the ark and shalt pitch it within and without with pitch.

15 And this *is the fashion* which thou shalt make it *of*: The length of the ark *shall* be three hundred cubits, the breadth of it fifty cubits, and the height of it thirty cubits.

16 A window shalt thou make to the ark, and in a cubit shalt thou finish it above; and the door of the ark shalt thou set in the side thereof; *with* lower, second *and* third *stories* shalt thou make it.

17 And, behold. I, even I, do bring a flood of waters upon the earth, to destroy all flesh, wherein *is* the breath of life, from under heaven; *and* every thing that *is* in the earth shelf die.

# *from* Mummies: Death and Life in Ancient Egypt

*James Hamilton-Paterson and Carol Andrews*

## The People

By the time of the Old Kingdom the Egyptians' was a flourishing civilization with well-developed literary, artistic and scientific abilities. It also had a highly sophisticated governmental and legal system based on careful codification and libraries of written records. Nothing could have been further removed from the tribesmen who roamed Europe at this time, dressed in skins, living in caves and with weapons no more sophisticated than flint axes. In its bureaucratic and legal aspects ancient Egypt was much like any modern state run by civil servants in accordance with the law of the land. Its body of statutes and precedents was carved, inscribed, painted and memorized, and these laws both reflected and bolstered the central strength of Egypt's philosophy: a belief in the importance of changelessness.

The countryside of Egypt was peculiarly suitable for the growth of such a philosophy. The climate was more or less uniform and there were no cataclysms like volcanoes—and only the occasional earth tremor—to contend with. There was too much inhospitable desert to be crossed to make the country irresistibly attractive to invaders on either side. Life flowed on undisturbed like the Nile in its immemorial bed. The seasons came round with strict punctuality, the Nile flooded, crops sprang up. It is small wonder that, unaffected by outside contacts and with an orderly and stable society apparently as old as creation itself, the Egyptians believed that the world was static. If there were ever any changes to be seen, they were of a recurrent variety: the cyclical changes of nature. Any other events were nothings, momentary ripples on the surface of the great stream of eternity which soon effaced themselves and were lost. As a result the Egyptians, being almost entirely an agricultural people, closely identified themselves with the natural world; and out of this identification sprang a characteristic aspect of their religious beliefs.

## Animal Cults

For the Egyptians the animal world possessed a peculiar, and to us elusive, significance. They worshipped an enormous variety of animals from millipedes to bulls, some of which were only sacred locally while others were sacred throughout Egypt. It is tempting to try and make sense of this phenomenon by proposing such theories as 1) the animals each had a different characteristic which made them worthy to be worshipped, or 2) animals peculiar to a particular locality were used for political reasons to hold a tribe together around a common god.

Unfortunately, such theories never quite meet all the facts and are true only some of the time. Many of the animals the Egyptians worshipped had nothing obvious about them to make them divine. It is quite true that a good many of the wilder animals were gods, and it may look as though the more terrifying ones such as crocodiles were worshipped to keep them happy and placate their anger. For example, lionesses were connected with savage heat and desert winds and were symbols of pestilence and plague. Yet the Egyptians 'tamed' them by turning them into the lioness-headed Sekhmet, the patron goddess of doctors. Likewise the jackal, which scavenged graves and devoured corpses, was very much feared by the Egyptians who above all wanted their bodies to be undamaged. So they changed it from being an attacker into the protector of the dead, Anubis, the jackal-headed god of embalming. (This principle of 'placation' is well established in other cultures, too. The Greeks' name for the Furies who hounded people mercilessly was the 'Eumenides' or the 'favourably-disposed ones', and they named the Black Sea—infamous for its violent storms—the 'Euxine' or 'good to strangers').

But such a theory would not explain what the Egyptians found sacred about a frog or a baboon. Too literal an interpretation is misleading; in fact they acknowledged something sacred about *all* animals, because in animals they recognized a radical difference from themselves. Animals were not like human beings: they were not individuals who did stupid and wilful things to upset the flow of life. On the contrary, they represented the very continuity of nature—something which, as we have seen, the Egyptians revered above all else but from which, being human, they felt apart.

They therefore saw nature in terms of gods. Their everyday experience of the natural phenomena around them (birth, death, water, the seasons, their crops, the stars, etc.) turned their lives into a continuous relationship with their gods. It was this mystical and practical harmony of man and nature which gave the Egyptians their idea of divinity.

## The Pharaoh

The person who ruled over this unchanging agricultural society was a god. The pharaoh's divinity was no mere metaphor: he had supernatural status since he was the successor of the creator himself who had been the first pharaoh of Egypt. In this way Egypt was not really a state or a country at all; it was the world itself, ordained by the creator and continuing to be ruled by him as part of the natural order. Everything came from the pharaoh: all power and wealth and authority, and there was no way of describing the land he ruled except as defined by the exercise of that power and wealth and authority. Remove the pharaoh (inconceivable thought!) and Egypt would vanish, lock, stock and barrel, together with all creation. 'What is the king of Upper and Lower Egypt? He is a god by whose dealing one lives, the father and mother of all men, alone by himself without an equal,' says Alan Gardiner in his translation of *The Autobiography of Rekhmire*.

Yet the pharaoh was no despot drunk with absolute power. He wielded justice or truth (*maat*) and it is most unlikely that the pharaonic system, had it led to arbitrariness and casual cruelty on a mass scale, would have lasted three thousand years without being overthrown. Indeed, the very stability of the system was both created and fulfilled by the Egyptians' expectation of changelessness. In this way the pharaoh was as much a part of the natural order as the animals they worshipped.

It has to be said, though, that after the chaos of the 1st Intermediate Period had been resolved and the Middle Kingdom had become established, the pharaoh's godlike status was never again quite what it had been in the Old Kingdom. From being quite literally untouchable by anybody other than close relatives (even accidental contact merited instant death) he gradually became 'humanized' so that by the New Kingdom he was a man among men enough to lead his troops on the battlefield or go hunting with his court. However, he retained his divine aspect at all times because mythology and the theory of the pharaonic system demanded it.

## Death

As we said earlier, if the Egyptians acknowledged change at all it was only in the form of recurrent change like the seasons. Any other kind of change did not matter and could safely be ignored since it was only temporary. Even the death of a pharaoh was less than devastating because he never really died: he was born again in his own successor. However, this left the Egyptians with the awkward problem of how to accommodate their own deaths. As individuals they knew they were not going to recur like the seasons, and as commoners they knew they were not everlasting gods like the pharaoh.

They got round this problem by seeing death as an interruption to life which afterwards would continue 'elsewhere'. This way of dealing with death has been common among many different societies and at all times in history. But seldom has such emphasis been laid on taking the right number and variety of goods into the tomb in order to ensure survival after death. The burial treasures of the pharaohs are justly famous, and even the merely well-to-do took an extraordinary clutter of objects with them to their graves.

To judge from what they took it looks as though they were expecting life to go on exactly as before. But on closer examination this may be making too easy an assumption. A great part of their grave-goods were concerned directly or indirectly with providing themselves with food and drink, i.e. the means to go on living. Their tombs thus became intensive care units to keep their bodies going. This enabled that part of them which was not their bodies to live in an afterworld which, according to different myths, was by no means always identical to the world they had just left.

## The KA

The Egyptians divided their 'spirit' (or whatever was not their physical bodies) into three separate entities. Firstly there was the *ka*, which was perhaps the nearest to what Protestant Christians would mean by the word 'spirit', and denoted a person's vital force or what made him a conscious being. In the plural, the word *ka* meant 'sustenance', clearly linking the spirit with its dependence on food. A dead man could be described as having gone 'to his *ka*'. Since his spirit had left his body but was presumed alive elsewhere it must obviously be getting nourishment from somewhere. Sustaining the *ka* after death was of prime importance to the Egyptians, which is why so many of their funerary rites were devoted to offerings of provisions. But all this was only a means to an end; the end was survival rather than the act of *ensuring* survival.

The *ka* did not have an individual existence of its own until after a person's death. It was then expected to inhabit the *ka*-statue in a chapel to which the offerings would be made rather than live in the burial chamber itself, which might in any case be some distance away or deep underground.

## The BA

Yet a man could not survive without a body. The idea of a person's disembodied *ka* living any sort of comprehensible life was alien to the Egyptians. The dead body had therefore to be well protected against the twin threats of decay and tomb-robbers. His *ka* and his preserved body were united into a new physical state which was able to leave the tomb and step out into the world of the living and was called the *ba*.

*Ba* means 'manifestation', and a dead person as represented by his *ba* could take on any shape he chose when leaving his tomb. Normally, however, the Egyptians pictured the *ba* as a bird with a human head. A translation of a text from the cenotaph of Seti I by Henri Frankfort in *Ancient Egyptian Religion* reads:

> These birds have faces like men, but their nature is that of birds. One of them speaks to the other with words of weeping. Now after they come to eat vegetables and green-stuff in Egypt, they flutter under the rays of heaven and then their shapes become bird-like.

The Egyptians were always acutely conscious of the link between the *ba*, which was privileged to be free to leave the body, and the body itself which was home to the *ka*. The ba did not have complete independence: the *ka* had first to be fed and sustained, otherwise there could be no *ba*. At all events the *ba* always returned to the tomb at night.

## The AKH

The Egyptians held that the dead were dependent on their tombs in order to live again as *bas* in a world which—if not precisely like the one they had left—was nevertheless full of everyday things and familiar to them from myth and legend. But they also had a third concept, one which made the dead person far more remote. This was the *akh*. It was a rarefied idea to describe how the dead could be made part of the universe, and thus immortal. The dead person's *akh* was that part of him which dwelt among the stars rather than in an afterworld. There, in deep and glacial purity far removed from earth, the *akh* revolved slowly and majestically for ever around the North star Polaris.

It was with this idea of eternal life that the Egyptians managed to come to terms with the paradox of death. This paradox was that although death only ever came once to a person, it could hardly be dismissed as trivial along with everything else which did not recur. However, in the form of *akhu* they could, once dead, become part of the cosmos, endlessly and predictably revolving with the universe.

This spiritual trinity of *ka, ba* and *akh* which everyone possessed was quite a sophisticated solution to the common human difficulty of reconciling bodily death with the desire for an eternal life of some sort. By this means the Egyptians could have their cake and eat it: they could carry on living in a world directly linked to the one they had left (it was not only food that formed a link—people would write letters to their dead relatives asking for assistance) and at the same time they were assured of becoming part of the eternal universe. Yet this unfortunately led them straight into another awkward paradox. If a man in the form of his *akh* became an immortal part of the cosmos, and the pharaoh—being a god—was also part of the same everlasting order, did not that mean there was something in common between the pharaoh and the man? How could an Egyptian peasant have anything in common with a god? If such a thing could be, it would need a very convincing explanation.

Not surprisingly, the Egyptians found one. The solution lay in their legend of Osiris, probably the most famous piece of mythology ever to come from the ancient Near East.

## The Osiris Myth

The myth of Osiris existed in various versions, depending on the period. Osiris gained in importance from the Old Kingdom and was pre-eminent by the Middle Kingdom. The legend itself, though, dates back in one form or another to pre-dynastic times. Unfortunately, the complete legend has never been found in an Egyptian source. There are numerous allusions to it throughout dynastic history, but it was evidently a tale too well known to have needed re-telling. It was up to the much later Greek writer Plutarch to piece together a full version.

According to the legend, Osiris was a just and good king who lived in the Nile Delta from where he ruled over all Egypt. For some reason his brother Set became insanely jealous of him and finally invited Osiris to a banquet given by his cronies. During the feast Set brought out a large and beautiful box which, he said, would be presented to whoever in the room fitted into it. One by one they all tried it, but it was not until Osiris lay down in it that the perfect fit was revealed. Promptly, Set's gang slammed the lid on him, fastened the catch, lugged him down to the Nile and threw him in. Thus Osiris was drowned.

His body was retrieved by his wife Isis but Set, on learning this, took it away from her and cut it up into fourteen pieces (or sixteen, depending on the version). He then scattered the pieces throughout Egypt. The grieving Isis, accompanied by her sister Nephthys, then trudged round Egypt looking for them, at last finding every bit except for her husband's penis.

This was no problem to someone with Isis's magic skills. She put Osiris together again so well that she conceived a son by him even though he was still technically dead. The son was named Horus and was kept hidden away in the Delta until he was old enough to take the throne and avenge his father's murder. It took a long time and many battles, but eventually Horus won and Set was soundly defeated.

The Osiris legend, like many including the Arthurian legend in Britain, was probably founded on fact. Many Egyptologists believe that there really was a king who, in pre-dynastic times, had ruled all Egypt from his capital in the Delta. The story of his violent death by drowning at the hands of his brother Set was probably an allegory to describe a rebellion from the southern city of Ombos which was later identified as the seat of Set's worship. Osiris was presumably killed in this rebellion, and a war began which divided the country into two parts, Upper and Lower Egypt. When eventually Egypt was reunited, following a victory by the north, this was reflected in the Osiris legend by the account of Horus's victory over Set. The dead Osiris was then turned into a god. Seen in this way, the story is an allegory both of real historical events and of the age-old tale of good triumphing over evil. Isis was merely the personification of the throne (her name means 'seat'), and Nephthys represented Osiris's palace (her name means 'lady of the castle').

Legends arise not just because they are good stories but because they can be used to explain a culture's history or philosophy in a simple way. The Egyptians used Osiris himself to personify many things. From his drowning he became a vegetation god re-born after the annual Nile floods, and he also came to symbolize resurrection after his magical mending by his wife. This aspect of Osiris has special significance where the Egyptians' beliefs about death are concerned.

There was another side to Osiris, too, which gave this legend such power. Although he was pharaoh he was human. He was betrayed by his brother, murdered by his enemies, lamented by his wife and dependent on his son for revenge. He was therefore not the all-powerful, triumphant and immortal king but a betrayed and suffering figure. In this way the ordinary Egyptian could easily identify with him and hope that, if his own son could prove as reliable to him after death as Horus had to Osiris, he too could be re-born. (It is not difficult at this point to see common elements in the Osiris legend and Christian mythology). Thus bit by bit the Egyptians identified so closely with Osiris that they would refer to dead people as 'the Osiris so-and-so' or 'the Osiris x' just as we might talk about 'the late Mr Brown'.

But the Osiris myth was of still further use to the Egyptians since they could also employ it to describe and explain the pharaonic system. When a pharaoh died he became one with Osiris, and his son Horus took the throne. The dead pharaoh, as Osiris, went back into the earth and became alive again with the Nile floods, the growing crops and the rising moon. Thus the long chain of pharaohs was nothing but the unchanging succession of Osiris and Horus endlessly repeated.

The Old Kingdom, which had seen the pyramid-building pharaohs at the greatest power they were ever to reach, was abruptly ended by the First Intermediate Period which temporarily plunged Egypt into anarchy. By the time unity was restored with the Middle Kingdom, Osiris had become useful once again. The system appeared to have broken down for a while, and the Egyptians badly needed a theory to explain how the great stream of Egyptian history was nevertheless still flowing as it always had despite a seeming interruption. They found one quite easily. In his role as a vegetation god, Osiris could be seen by all to be alive and well in the waving corn. In his role as a resurrection god, he was already identified with the imperishable dead pharaohs of olden days. The Egyptians had only to look at their crops to know that nothing had really changed. The new pharaohs of the Middle Kingdom were still one with the old: the system continued.

In this way the Osiris legend helped them make sense of the political turmoil from which they were emerging. It was typical that they should have looked backwards to an already ancient legend for an explanation rather than working out a new philosophy which could account for how their 'static' system had undeniably been given a bad shaking. In times of trouble, however, they reached for Osiris and with their extraordinary conservatism once more pressed him into service. He now became even more closely linked with resurrection and re-birth by guaranteeing the 'State's' immortality. Osiris was proved triumphant: the cosmic order was unshaken, Egypt's *akhu* were immortal; and since he was re-born as the current pharaoh, that same pharaoh's very existence guaranteed that the cosmic order was intact.

The Egyptians were thus employing a system of belief based, like any religion, on a logical fallacy. In effect they were saying 'Egypt exists because Osiris exists, which proves Osiris must exist since Egypt does.' Given a philosophy as flexible as this, solving the problem of how ordinary mortals could have anything in common with a god was child's play. The Egyptians simply worked out that the Osiris x's *akh* could share the same universe with the pharaoh since both the universe and the pharaoh were also part of Osiris. It was a very neat solution.

In consequence Abydos, where Osiris's body was reputed to lie, became a popular place to be buried. And because of Osiris's oneness with the pharaohs the fashion grew for commoners to be buried with pictures of crowns, sceptres and other royal equipment on their coffins, a piece of democratization which would have been impossible in the grand old days of the Old Kingdom. But this identification with Osiris guaranteed the dead person's incorporation into the cosmic order. Whether his *akh*—according to his belief—went round with the stars, followed the sun, rose with the moon or, like Osiris, became one with the Nile and the crops, the ordinary Egyptian was assured of an eternal place in the cosmos. It was a triumph for mythology, theology, and sheer ingenuity.

## The Universe

The Osiris myth explained well enough how Egypt was the universe (and therefore how the universe was Egypt), and it also explained the relationship between the universe, the pharaoh and the common people. However, like any ancient—or, indeed, modern—civilization, the Egyptians had their own version of how that universe had itself been created. They also had little stories to explain recurrent phenomena such as night and day and the appearance of the stars at evening.

Their story of creation was that the earth, Geb, and the sky, Nut, had given birth to the sun, Re. Each night Re was swallowed up again by Nut, passed through her body and was reborn again at dawn the next day. Geb, the earth, was thus the father of the gods, the most ancient of them all. This explanation of night was also adapted to account for the disappearance of the stars at dawn. The stars were in fact little piglets which a heavenly sow gobbled up when the sun rose and then gave birth to once again at sunset. The Egyptians' word for evening, *mesut*, actually means 'time of birth'.

But how had Geb and Nut themselves been created? This account of the birth of Re made a nice enough story of the day-night-day cycle, but it was much more of an illustration than an explanation. So the Egyptians devised a separate theory of creation. Awkwardly for us this theory never existed in a single form but was found in three main versions. These versions depended on where the story came from, since the three cities of Heliopolis, Hermopolis and Memphis each had its own tradition and each tradition was jealously guarded by its priests. Somewhat simplified, the different versions ran like this:

## The Heliopolitan system

The world started with a chaos of shapeless masses of water called Nun. Out of Nun, self-created, emerged the sun Re (also at this point known as Atum), perched on a mound called a *benben*. This creator god Re/Atum then produced Shu (air) and Tefnut (moisture) by a process of masturbation or spitting. Shu and Tefnut in turn produced Geb and Nut who themselves eventually created Osiris, Isis, Nephthys and Set. These nine (known to Egyptologists as 'the ennead') then governed Egypt by turn.

## The Hermopolitan system

This theory also held that the world began with chaos, but it was a chaos made up of four constituents: water, space, darkness and invisibility, each of which had a male/female pair of gods. These eight gods (or 'the ogdoad') were represented as four couples of serpents and frogs, and together they created an egg on a mound which emerged from Nun at Hermopolis. Nun was thus the creator of Re/Atum, the sun.

## The Memphite system

This system developed when Memphis became the Early Dynastic capital. Since Memphis was the seat of the god Ptah his priests insisted that he should play the leading role in the story of creation. Accordingly, Ptah took Re/Atum's place; but in order to avoid a direct confrontation with the priests at Heliopolis the Memphites compromised slightly. Ptah was still the great creator god but alongside him were eight other gods: Tatenen, the god of the earth emerging from chaos; Nun and Naunet (the first pair of the Hermopolitan ogdoad); Atum the great; and four others who were probably Horus, Thoth, Nefertum and some kind of a snake-god. Atum represented the creator god Ptah's intelligence and also his will. The intelligence was further personified by Horus, while the will was personified by Thoth.

According to this Memphite system Ptah first conceived the world intellectually before creating it. He then went on to the more mundane task of organizing civilization.

## The Different Religions

Originally, there were two main branches of Egyptian religion: divine (the theology which accounted for the different gods and creation) and funerary, which was more concerned with death and the after life. However, the more the Egyptians' civilization developed, the more they found they had to take into account the ancient popular beliefs which dated from way back before the priesthoods were formed. The divine and the funerary religions were understood only by the priests and the educated classes. The huge majority of Egyptians had their own beliefs superstitions and local gods, depending on where they happened to live.

# A Myth of the Deluge from Ancient India

*('Shatapatha-Brāhmana,' 1, 8, 1–6)*

1. In the morning they brought to Manu water for washing, just as now also they (are wont to) bring (water) for washing the hands. When he was washing himself, a fish came into his hands.

2. It spake to him the word, 'Rear me, I will save thee!' 'Wherefrom wilt thou save me?' 'A flood will carry away all these creatures: from that I will save thee!' 'How am I to rear thee?'

3. It said, 'As long as we are small, there is great destruction for us: fish devours fish. Thou wilt first keep me in a jar. When I outgrow that, thou wilt dig a pit and keep me in it. When I outgrow that, thou wilt take me down to the sea, for then I shall be beyond destruction.'

4. It soon became a *ghasha* (a great fish); for that grows largest (of all fish). Thereupon it said, 'In such and such a year that flood will come. Thou shalt then attend to me (i.e. to my advice) by preparing a ship; and when the flood has risen thou shalt enter into the ship, and I will save thee from it.'

5. After he had reared it in this way, he took it down to the sea. And in the same year which the fish had indicated to him, he attended to (the advice of the fish) by preparing a ship; and when the flood had risen, he entered into the ship. The fish then swam up to him, and to its horn he tied the rope of the ship, and by that means he passed swiftly up to yonder northern mountain.

6. It then said, 'I have saved thee. Fasten the ship to a tree; but let not the water cut thee off whilst thou art on the mountain. As the water subsides, thou mayest gradually descend!' Accordingly he gradually descended and hence that (slope) of the northern mountain is called 'Manu's descent.' The flood then swept away all these creatures, and Manu alone remained here.

# *from* African Folkfales

*Paul Radin*

## The Wonder-Worker of the Plains

Once there was a man and a woman to whom were born first a boy and then a girl. When the bride-price had been paid for the girl and she was married, the parents said to the son, "We have a herd for you to dispose of. It is now time for you to take a wife. We will choose you a pretty wife, one whose parents are honest people."

The son, however, firmly refused. "No," he said. "do not bother. I do not like any of the girls who are here. If I absolutely have to marry, I shall choose for myself what I want."

"Do as you will," said the parents, "but if you are unhappy later on, it will not be our fault."

Then the boy set out, left the country, and travelled far, very far, into an unknown region. Finally, he came to a village where he saw some young girls, some of them crushing corn and others cooking. Secretly he made his choice, and said to himself, "That one there is the one I like." Then he went to the men of the village and said, "Good day, fathers!"

"Good day, young man!" they answered. "What is it that you wish?"

"I want to look at your daughters, for I want to take a wife."

"Well, well," they said, "we shall show them to you, and then you can choose."

So they led all of their daughters past him and he indicated the one he wanted. She gave her consent right away.

"Your parents, we expect, will pay us a visit and bring us the bride-price, is that right?" asked the young girl's parents.

"No, not at all," answered the young man, "I have my bride-price with me. Take it, here it is!"

"Then," they added, "they will, we trust, come later in order to conduct your wife to you?'

506

'No, no, I fear they would only pain you with the hard admonitions they would give the girl. Let me, myself, take her along right away."

The parents of the young girl gave their consent to this request, but they took her aside in the hut once more to give her advice on how to conduct herself. "Be good to your parents-in-law and take diligent care of your husband!" Then they offered the young couple a younger daughter who could help with the housework. But the woman refused. Two, ten, twenty were then offered for her to choose from. All the girls were first examined before being offered to her.

"No," she insisted, "I do not want them. Give me instead the buffalo of the country, our buffalo, the Wonder-Worker of the Plains. Let him serve me."

"How can you ask for him?" they said. "You know that our life depends on him. Here he is well taken care of, but what would you do with him in a strange country? He will starve, die, and then all of us will die with him."

Before she left her parents, she took with her a pot containing a package of medicinal roots, a horn for bleeding, a little knife for making incisions, and a gourd full of fat.

Then she set out with her husband. The buffalo followed them, but he was visible to her alone. The man did not see him. He did not suspect that the Wonder-Worker of the Plains was the servant accompanying his wife.

As soon as they had come to the husband's village, they were received with joyful cries: "*Hoyo, hoyo!*"

"Now look at him!" said the old ones. "So you have found a wife after all! You did not want one of those whom we suggested to you, but that makes no difference. It is well as it is. You have acted according to your own will. If, however, at some time, you have enemies, you will have no right to complain. "

The man then took his wife into the fields and showed her which were his and which were his mother's. The girl noted everything carefully and returned with him to the village. On the way she said, "I have lost my pearls in the field; I must return to look for them at once." In reality, however, she wanted to see the buffalo. She said to him, "Here is the boundary of the fields. Stay here! And there, too, is the forest in which you can hide."

"You are right," he replied.

Now whenever the wife wanted any water, she merely went to the cultivated fields and set the pitcher down in front of the buffalo. He ran with
it to the lake, filled it, and brought the vessel back to his mistress. Whenever she wanted wood, he would go into the brush, break trees with his
horns, and bring her as much as she needed.

The people in the village were surprised at all these things. "What
strength she has!" they said. "She is always back from the well right
away; in the twinkling of an eye she has gathered a bundle of dry wood."
But no one suspected that a buffalo assisted her as a servant.

The wife did not, however, bring the buffalo anything to eat, for she had
only one plate for herself and her husband. At home, of course, they had
had a separate plate for the Wonder-Worker and fed him carefully. Here,
therefore, the buffalo was hungry. She would bring him her pitcher and
send him to fetch water. This he did willingly, but he felt great pangs of
hunger.

One day she showed him a corner in the brush which he was to clear.
During the night the buffalo took a hoe and prepared a vast acreage.
Everyone commented, "How clever she is! And how fast she has done
her work!"

One evening the buffalo said to his mistress, "I am hungry and you give
me nothing to eat. Soon I shall not be able to work any more!"

"*Aie*," said she, "what shall I do? We have only one plate at the house.
The people at home were right when they said that you would have to
start stealing. So, steal! Go into my field and take a bean here and there.
Then, again, go farther. Do not, however, take them all from the same
spot, thus the owners may not be too much aware of it and will not fall
over in terror right away."

That night, accordingly, the buffalo went to the field. He devoured a bean
here and a bean there, jumped from one corner to the other, and finally
fled back to his hiding place. When the women came into the fields the
next morning, they could not believe their eyes. "Hey, hey, what is going
on here? We have never seen anything like this! A wild beast has
destroyed our plants! One can even follow his spoor. Ho, the poor land!"
So they ran back and told the story in the village.

In the evening, the young woman said to the buffalo, "To be sure, they
were very much terrified, but not too much, nevertheless. They did not

fall on their backs. So keep on stealing tonight!" And so it continued. The owners of the devastated fields cried out loud and then turned to the men and asked them to summon the watchmen with their guns.

Now, the husband of the young woman was a very good marksman. He, therefore, hid in an ambush in his field and waited. The buffalo, however, thought that someone might be lying in wait for him where he had stolen the night before, so he went to his mistress's beans, the place where he had pastured the first time.

"Say," cried the man, "this is a buffalo! One has never seen any like him here. This is a strange animal, indeed." He fired. The bullet entered the temple of the buffalo, close to the ear, and came out exactly opposite on the other side. The Wonder-Worker of the Plains turned one somersault and fell dead.

"That was a good shot!" exclaimed the hunter and announced it to the village.

But the woman now began to cry out in pain and writhe. "Oh, I have stomach-aches, oh, oh!"

"Calm yourself," she was told. She seemed sick, but in reality she only wanted to explain why she was crying thus, and why she was so terrified when she heard of the buffalo's death. She was given medicine, but she poured it out when nobody else saw her.

Now everyone set out, women with baskets, and men with weapons, in order to cut up the buffalo. The young wife alone remained in the village. Soon, however, she followed them, holding her belly, whimpering and crying.

"What is wrong with you, that you come here," said her husband. "If you are sick, stay at home!"

"No, I did not want to stay in the village all by myself."

Her mother-in-law scolded her, saying that she could not understand what she was doing and that she would kill herself by this. When they had filled the baskets with meat, she said, "Let me carry the head!"

"But no, you are sick, it is much too heavy for you."

"No," said she, "let me do it!" So she shouldered it and carried it.

After they had arrived at the village, however, instead of stepping into the house, she went into the shed where the cooking-pots were kept and set down the buffalo's head. Obstinately, she refused to move. Her husband looked for her in order to bring her into the hut. He said she would be much better off there, but she only replied to him harshly, "Do not disturb me!"

Then her mother-in-law came and admonished her gently. "Why do you torture yourself?"

And she replied crossly, "Will you not let me sleep even a little?"

Then they brought her some food, but she pushed it away. Night came. Her husband went to rest. He did not sleep, however, but listened.

The woman now fetched fire, cooked some water in her little pot, and poured into it the package of medicine which she had brought with her from her home. Then she took the buffalo's head and, with the knife, made incisions in front of the ear, at the temple, where the bullet had struck the animal. There she set the bleeding horn and sucked, sucked with all the force of her body, and succeeded in drawing first a few lumps of clotted blood, and then liquid blood. Thereupon she exposed the place to the steam which rose from the cooking-pot after having, however, smeared it completely with the fat that she had saved in the gourd. That soothed the spot. Then she sang as follows:

*"Ah, my father, Wonder-Worker of the Plains,*

*They told me: You would go through the deep darkness; that in all directions you would stumble through the night, Wonder-Worker of the Plains;*

*You are the young wonder-tree plant, grown out of ruins, which dies before its time, consumed by a gnawing worm. . . .*

*You made flowers and fruit fall upon your road, Wonder-Worker of the Plains!"*

When she had finished her invocation formula, the head moved, the limbs grew again, the buffalo came to life once more, shook his ears and horns, rose up, and stretched his limbs. . . .

But at this point the man, who could not sleep in the hut, stepped out and said, "Why does my wife have to cry so long? I must see why she pours out all these sighs!" He entered the shed and called for her, but in great anger she replied, "Leave me alone!" Thereupon, however, the buffalo's head fell to the ground again, dead, pierced as before.

The man returned to the hut; he had understood nothing of all this and had seen nothing. Once again the woman took the pot, cooked the medicine, made the incisions, placed the bleeding horn in the proper spot, exposed the wound to the steam, and sang as before:

*"Ah, my father, Wonder-Worker of the Plains,*

*Indeed they have told me: You would go through the deep darkness; that in all directions you would stumble through the night, Wonder-Worker of the Plains;*

*You are the young wonder-tree plant, grown out of ruins, which dies before its time, consumed by a gnawing worm. . . .*

*You made flowers and fruit fall upon your road, Wonder-Worker of the Plains!"*

Once again, the buffalo rose up, his limbs grew together again, he felt himself coming to life, shook his ears and horns, stretched himself—but then again came the man, disquieted, in order to see what his wife was doing. Then she became very angry with him, but he settled down in the shed in order to watch what was going on. Now she took her fire, her cooking pot and all the other things and went out. She pulled up grass to kindle the embers and began for the third time to resuscitate the buffalo.

Morning had already broken when her mother-in-law came—and once more the head fell to the ground. Day came, and the buffalo's wound began to grow worse.

Finally, she said to all of them, "I would like to go bathing in the lake all alone."

They answered her, "But how will you get there since you are sick?"

She went on her way anyhow and then came back and said, "On my way I came upon someone from home. He told me that my mother is very, very sick. I told him to come here to the village but he refused and said, 'They would offer me food and that would only delay me.' He went on right away and added that I should hurry lest my mother die before my arrival. Therefore, good-bye, I am going away!"

Of course, all this was a lie. She had thought of the idea of going to the lake so that she could invent this story and have a reason for carrying the news of the buffalo's death to her people.

She went off, carrying the basket on her head and singing all along the road the end of the song about the Wonder-Worker of the Plains. Wherever she passed, the people would band together behind her to accompany her into her village. Arrived there, she announced to them that the buffalo no longer lived.

Then they sent out messengers in all directions in order to gather together the inhabitants of the country. They reproached the young woman earnestly, saying, "Do you see now? We told you so. But you refused all the young girls and wanted absolutely to have the buffalo. Now you have killed all of us!"

Things had advanced thus far when the man, who had followed his wife into the village, also arrived. He rested his gun against a tree trunk and sat down. They greeted him by shouting, "Be saluted, criminal, be saluted! You have killed us all!" He did not understand this and wondered how one could call him a murderer and a criminal.

"To be sure, I have killed a buffalo," said he, "but that is all."

"Yes, but this buffalo was your wife's assistant. He drew water for her, cut wood, worked in the field."

Completely stunned, the man said, "Why did you not let me know that? I would not have killed him then."

"That is how it is," they added. "The lives of all of us depended on him." Thereupon all of the people began to cut their own throats. First, the young woman, who, as she did it, called out:

"Ah, my father, Wonder-Worker of the Plains!"

Then came her parents, brothers, sisters, one after the other.

The first one said:

"You shall go through darkness! "

The next:

"You shall stumble through the night in all directions!"

The next:

"You are the young wonder-tree plant which dies before its time."

The next:

"You made flowers and fruit fall upon your road!"

All cut their throats and they even slew the little children who were still being carried in skins upon the back. "Why should we let them live," they said, "since they would only lose their minds!"

The man returned home and told his people how, by shooting the buffalo, he had killed them all. His parents said to him, "Do you see now? Did we not tell you that misfortune would come to you? When we offered a fitting and wise woman for you, you wanted to act according to your own desire. Now you have lost your fortune. Who will give it back to you, since they are all dead, all of your wife's relatives, to whom you have given your money!"

This is the end.

[ BARONGA ]

## The Origin of Death

The Moon, it is said, once sent an insect to men, saying, "Go to men and tell them, 'As I die, and dying live; so you shall also die, and dying live.'"

The insect started with the message, but, while on his way, was overtaken by the hare, who asked, "On what errand are you bound?"

The insect answered, "I am sent by the Moon to men, to tell them that as she dies and dying lives, so shall they also die and dying live."

The hare said, "As you are an awkward runner, let me go." With these words he ran off, and when he reached men, he said, "I am sent by the Moon to tell you, 'As I die and dying perish, in the same manner you also shall die and come wholly to an end.'"

The hare then returned to the Moon and told her what he had said to men. The Moon reproached him angrily, saying, "Do you dare tell the people a thing which I have not said?"

With these words the moon took up a piece of wood and struck the hare on the nose. Since that day the hare's nose has been slit, but men believe what Hare had told them.

[ HOTTENTOT ]

## The Elephant and the Tortoise

Two beings, Elephant and Rain, had a dispute. Elephant said, "If you say that you nourish me, in what way is it that you do so?" Rain answered, "If you say that I do not nourish you, when I go away, will you not die?" And Rain then departed.

Elephant said, "Vulture! Cast lots to make rain for me!" Vulture said, "I will not cast lots."

Then Elephant said to Crow, "Cast lots!" and Crow answered, "Give the things with which I may cast lots." Crow cast lots and rain fell. It rained at the lagoons, but then they dried up, and only one lagoon remained.

Elephant went hunting. There was, however, Tortoise, to whom Elephant said, "Tortoise, remain at the water!" Thus Tortoise was left behind when Elephant went hunting.

There came Giraffe, and said to Tortoise, "Give me water!" Tortoise answered, "The water belongs to Elephant."

There came Zebra, who said to Tortoise, "Give me water!" Tortoise answered, "The water belongs to Elephant."

There came Gemsbok, and said to Tortoise, "Give me water!" Tortoise answered, "The water belongs to Elephant."

There came Wildebeest, and said, "Give me water!" Tortoise said, "The water belongs to Elephant."

There came Roodebok, and said to Tortoise, "Give me water!" Tortoise answered, "The water belongs to Elephant."

There came Springbok, and said to Tortoise, "Give me water!" Tortoise said, "The water belongs to Elephant."

There came Jackal, and said to Tortoise, "Give me water!" Tortoise said, "The water belongs to Elephant."

There came Lion, and said, "Little Tortoise, give me water!" When little Tortoise was about to say something, Lion got hold of it and beat it. Lion drank of the water, and since then all the animals drink water.

When Elephant came back from the hunting, he said, "Little Tortoise, where is the water?" Tortoise answered, "The animals have drunk the water." Elephant asked, "Little Tortoise, shall I chew you or swallow you down?" Little Tortoise said, "Swallow me, if you please," and Elephant swallowed it whole.

After Elephant had swallowed little Tortoise, and it had entered his body, it tore off his liver, heart, and kidneys. Elephant said, "Little Tortoise, you kill me."

So Elephant died. But little Tortoise came out of his dead body and went wherever it liked.

[ HOTTENTOT ]

# *from* The Portable North American Reader

## Cherokee

Before smallpox, wars, and removal the Cherokee numbered upward of twenty thousand people ranged through a vast and sprawling territory which covered essentially the entire Allegheny region—about forty thousand square miles. Their proper tribal name is Yûñ' wiyǎ', signifying the "real people." and the fall of this empire is one of the darkest blots on our national escutcheon, for the Cherokee made every attempt to accommodate themselves to the white life-style that surrounded them. They built schools, libraries, mills; they farmed and owned livestock. It was not enough; their land was too valuable, and Andrew Jackson sent them west with the other tribes. These myths and stories, however, were gathered on the old home grounds of the tribe in North Carolina where a few of them still live, separated by several hundred miles from their brothers and sisters in Oklahoma. There are several excellent studies of Cherokee culture and history, the most recent of which is Thurman Wilkins' *Cherokee Tragedy*.

## *How the World Was Made*

The earth is a great island floating in a sea of water, and suspended at each of the four cardinal points by a cord hanging down from the sky vault, which is of solid rock. When the world grows old and worn out, the people will die and the cords will break and let the earth sink down into the ocean, and all will be water again. The Indians are afraid of this.

When all was water, the animals were above in Gălûñ'lătĭ, beyond the arch; but it was very much crowded, and they were wanting more room. They wondered what was below the water. and at last Dâyuni'sĭ, "Beaver's Grandchild," the little Waterbeetle, offered to go and see if it could learn. It darted in every direction over the surface of the water, but could find no firm place to rest. Then it dived to the bottom and came up with some soft mud, which began to grow and spread on every side until it became the island which we call the earth. It was afterward fastened to the sky with four cords, but no one remembers who did this.

At first the earth was flat and very soft and wet. The animals were anxious to get down, and sent out different birds to see if it was yet dry, but they found no place to alight and came back again to Gălûñ'lătĭ. At last it seemed to be time, and they sent out the Buzzard and told him to go and make ready for them. This was the Great Buzzard, the father of all the buzzards we see now. He flew all over the earth, low down near the ground, and it was still soft. When he reached the Cherokee country, he was very tired, and his wings began to flap and strike the ground, and wherever they struck the earth there was a valley, and where they turned up again there was a mountain. When the animals above saw this, they were afraid that the whole world would be mountains, so they called him back, but the Cherokee country remains full of mountains to this day.

When the earth was dry and the animals came down, it was still dark, so they got the sun and set it in a track to go every day across the island from east to west, just overhead. It was too hot this way, and Tsiska'gĭlĭ', the Red Crawfish, had his shell scorched a bright red, so that his meat was spoiled; and the Cherokee do not eat it. The conjurers put the sun another handbreadth higher in the air, but it was still too hot. They raised it another time, and another, until it was seven handbreadths high and just under the sky arch. Then it was right, and they left it so. This is why the conjurers call the highest place Gûlkwâ'gine Di'gălûñ'lătiyûñ', "the seventh height," because it is seven handbreadths above the earth. Every day the sun goes along under this arch, and returns at night on the upper side to the starting place.

There is another world under this, and it is like ours in everything—animals, plants, and people—save that the seasons are different. The streams that come down from the mountains are the trails by which we reach this underworld, and the springs at their heads are the doorways by which we enter it, but to do this one must fast and go to water and have one of the underground people for a guide. We know that the seasons in the underworld are different from ours, because the water in the springs is always warmer in winter and cooler in summer than the outer air.

When the animals and plants were first made—we do not know by whom—they were told to watch and keep awake for seven nights, just as young men now fast and keep awake when they pray to their medicine. They tried to do this, and nearly all were awake through the first night, but the next night several dropped off to sleep, and the third night others were asleep, and then others, until, on the seventh night, of all the animals only the owl, the panther, and one or two more were still awake. To these were given the power to see and to go about in the dark, and to make prey of the birds and animals which must sleep at night. Of the trees only the cedar, the pine, the spruce, the holly, and the laurel were awake to the end, and to them it was given to be always green and to be greatest for medicine, but to the others it was said: "Because you have not endured to the end you shall lose your hair every winter."

Men came after the animals and plants. At first there were only a brother and sister until he struck her with a fish and told her to multiply, and so it was. In seven days a child was born to her, and thereafter every seven days another, and they increased very fast until there was danger that the world could not keep them. Then it was made that a woman should have only one child in a year, and it has been so ever since.

## The First Fire

In the beginning there was no fire, and the world was cold, until the Thunders (Ani'-Hyûñ'tĭkwălâ'skĭ), who lived up in Gălûñ'lătĭ, sent their lightning and put fire into the bottom of a hollow sycamore tree which grew on an island. The animals knew it was there, because they could see the smoke coming out at the top, but they could not get to it on account of the water, so they held a council to decide what to do. This was a long time ago.

Every animal that could fly or swim was anxious to go after the fire. The Raven offered, and because he was so large and strong they thought he could surely do the work, so he was sent first. He flew high and far across the water and alighted on the sycamore tree, but while he was wondering what to do next, the heat had scorched all his feathers black, and he was frightened and came back without the fire. The little Screech-owl (Wa'huhu') volunteered to go, and reached the place safely, but while he was looking down into the hollow tree a blast of hot air came up and nearly burned out his eyes. He managed to fly home as best he could, but it was a long time before he could see well, and his eyes are red to this day. Then the Hooting Owl (U'guku') and the Horned Owl ( Tskĭlĭ') went, but by the time they got to the hollow tree the fire was burning so fiercely that the smoke nearly blinded them, and the ashes carried up by the wind made white rings about their eyes. They had to come home again without the fire, but with all their rubbing they were never able to get rid of the white rings.

Now no more of the birds would venture, and so the little Uksu'hĭ snake, the black racer, said he would go through the water and bring back some fire. He swam across to the island and crawled through the grass to the tree, and went in by a small hole at the bottom. The heat and smoke were too much for him, too, and after dodging about blindly over the hot ashes until he was almost on fire himself he managed by good luck to get out again at the same hole, but his body had been scorched black, and he has ever since had the habit of darting and doubling on his track as if trying to escape from close quarters. He came back, and the great blacksnake, Gûle'gĭ, "The Climber," offered to go for fire. He swam over to the island and climbed up the tree on the outside, as the blacksnake always does, but when he put his head down into the hole the smoke choked him so that he fell into the burning stump, and before he could climb out again he was as black as the Uksu'hĭ.

Now they held another council, for still there was no fire, and the world was cold, but birds, snakes, and four-footed animals all had some excuse for not going, because they were all afraid to venture near the burning sycamore, until at last Kănăne'skĭ Amai'yĕhĭ (the Water Spider) said she would go. This is not the water spider that looks like a mosquito, but the other one, with black downy hair and red stripes on her body. She can run on top of the water or dive to the bottom, so there would be no trouble to get over to the island, but the question was, How could she bring back the fire? "I'll manage that," said the Water Spider; so she spun a thread from her body and wove it into a *tusti* bowl, which she fastened on her back. Then she crossed over to the island and through the grass to where the fire was still burning. She put one little coal of fire into her bowl, and came back with it, and ever since we have had fire, and the Water Spider still keeps her *tusti* bowl.

• • •

## Senachwine

POTOWATOMI

*Senachwine, venerable Potawatomi, spoke at a council fire at Indiantown in Illinois in June 1830, when Black Hawk tried to induce them to join forces to rout the whites. His dissenting speech caused Black Hawk to rise and stalk from the meeting with his band.*

For more than seventy years I have hunted in this grove and fished in this stream, and for many years I have worshiped on this ground. Through these groves and over these prairies in pursuit of game our fathers roamed, and by them this land was left unto us as a heritage forever. No one is more attached to his home than myself, and none among you is so grieved to leave it. But the time is near at hand, when the red men of the forest will have to leave the land of their nativity, and find a home toward the setting sun. The white men of the east, whose numbers are like the sands of the sea, will overrun and take possession of this country. They will build wigwams and villages all over the land, and their domain will extend from sea to sea.

In my boyhood days I have chased the buffalo across the prairies, and hunted the elk in the groves; but where are they now? Long since they have left us; the near approach of the white man has frightened them away. The deer and the turkey will go next, and with them the sons of the forest.

Resistance to the aggression of the whites is useless; war is wicked and must result in our ruin. Therefore, let us submit to our fate, return not evil for evil, as this would offend the Great Spirit and bring ruin upon us. The time is near when our race will become extinct, and nothing left to show the world that we ever did exist . . . but this I do know, the monitor within my breast has taught me the will of the Great Spirit, and now tells me good Indians will be rewarded, and bad ones punished. My friends, do not listen to the words of Black Hawk for he is trying to lead you astray. Do not imbrue your hands in human blood; for such is the work of the evil one, and will only lead to retribution upon our heads.

## Seattle

*DWAMISH*

*Seattle (Seathl), Dwamish chief, spoke to Isaac Stevens, Governor of Washington Territory, in 1854.*

Yonder sky that has wept tears of compassion upon my people for centuries untold, and which to us appears changeless and eternal, may change. Today is fair. Tomorrow it may be overcast with clouds. My words are like the stars that never change. Whatever Seattle says the great chief at Washington can rely upon with as much certainty as he can upon the return of the sun or the seasons. The White Chief says that Big Chief at Washington sends us greetings of friendship and goodwill. That is kind of him for we know he has little need of our friendship in return.

His people are many. They are like the grass that covers vast prairies. My people are few. They resemble the scattering trees of a storm-swept plain. . . . I will not dwell on, nor mourn over, our untimely decay, nor reproach our paleface brothers with hastening it, as we too may have been somewhat to blame. . . .

Your God is not our God. Your God loves your people and hates mine. He folds his strong and protecting arms lovingly about the paleface and leads him by the hand as a father leads his infant son—but He has forsaken His red children—if they really are His. Our God, the Great Spirit, seems also to have forsaken us. Your God makes your people strong every day. Soon they will fill the land. Our people are ebbing away like a rapidly receding tide that will never return. The white man's God cannot love our people or He would protect them. They seem to be orphans who can look nowhere for help. How then can we be brothers? . . . We are two distinct races with separate origins and separate destinies. There is little in common between us.

To us the ashes of our ancestors are sacred and their resting place is hallowed ground. You wander far from the graves of your ancestors and seemingly without regret. Your religion was written upon tables of stone by the iron finger of your God so that you could not forget. The Red Man could never comprehend nor remember it. Our religion is the traditions of our ancestors—the dreams of our old men, given them in solemn hours of night by the Great Spirit; and the visions of our sachems; and it is written in the hearts of our people.

Your dead cease to love you and the land of their nativity as soon as they pass the portals of the tomb and wander way beyond the stars. They are soon forgotten and never return. Our dead never forget the beautiful world that gave them being.

Day and night cannot dwell together. The Red Man has ever fled the approach of the While Man, as the morning mist flees before the morning sun. However, your proposition seems fair and I think that my people will accept it and will retire to the reservation you offer them. Then we will dwell apart in peace. . . . It matters little where we pass the remnant of our days. They will not be many. A few more moons; a few more winters—and not one of the descendants of the mighty hosts that once moved over this broad land or lived in happy homes, protected by the Great Spirit, will remain to mourn over the graves of a people once more powerful and hopeful than yours. But why should I mourn at the untimely fate of my people? Tribe follows tribe, and nation follows nation, like the waves of the sea. It is the order of nature, and regret is useless. Your time of decay may be distant, but it will surely come, for even the White Man whose God walked and talked with him as friend with friend, cannot be exempt from the common destiny. We may be brothers after all. We will see. . . .

Every part of this soil is sacred in the estimation of my people. Every hillside, every valley, every plain and grove, has been hallowed by some sad or happy event in days long vanished. The very dust upon which you now stand responds more lovingly to their footsteps than to yours, because it is rich with the blood of our ancestors and our bare feet are conscious of the sympathetic touch. Even the little children who lived here and rejoiced here for a brief season will love these somber solitudes and at eventide they greet shadowy returning spirits. And when the last Red Man shall have perished, and the memory of my tribe shall have become a myth among the White Men, these shores will swarm with the invisible dead of my tribe, and when your children's children think themselves alone in the field, the store, the shop, upon the highway, or in the silence of the pathless woods, they will not be alone. At night when the streets of your cities and villages are silent and you think them deserted, they will throng with the returning hosts that once filled and still love this beautiful land. The White Man will never be alone.

Let him be just and deal kindly with my people, for the dead are not powerless. Dead, did I say? There is no death, only a change of worlds.

# *from* On Population

*Thomas Robert Malthus*

## Chapter I

The great and unlooked for discoveries that have taken place of late years in natural philosophy, the increasing diffusion of general knowledge from the extension of the art of printing, the ardent and unshackled spirit of inquiry that prevails throughout the lettered and even unlettered world, the new and extraordinary lights that have been thrown on political subjects which dazzle and astonish the understanding, and particularly that tremendous phenomenon in the political horizon, the French revolution, which, like a blazing comet, seems destined either to inspire with fresh life and vigour, or to scorch up and destroy the shrinking inhabitants of the earth, have all concurred to lead able men into the opinion that we were touching on a period big with the most important changes, changes that would in some measure be decisive of the future fate of mankind.

It has been said that the great question is now at issue, whether man shall henceforth start forwards with accelerated velocity towards illimitable, and hitherto unconceived improvement, or be condemned to a perpetual oscillation between happiness and misery, and after every effort remain still at an immeasurable distance from the wished-for goal.

Yet, anxiously as every friend of mankind must look forwards to the termination of this painful suspense, and eagerly as the inquiring mind would hail every ray of light that might assist its view into futurity, it is much to be lamented that the writers on each side of this momentous question still keep aloof from each other. Their mutual arguments do not meet with a candid examination. The question is not brought to rest on fewer points, and even in theory scarcely seems to be approaching to a decision.

The advocate for the present order of things is apt to treat the sect of speculative philosophers either as a set of artful and designing knaves who preach up ardent benevolence and draw captivating pictures of a happier state of society only the better to enable them to destroy the present establishments and to forward their own deep-laid schemes of ambition, or as wild and mad-headed enthusiasts whose silly speculations and absurd paradoxes are not worthy the attention of any reasonable man.

The advocate for the perfectibility of man, and of society, retorts on the defender of establishments a more than equal contempt. He brands him as the slave of the most miserable and narrow prejudices; or, as the defender of the abuses of civil society, only because he profits by them. He paints him either as a character who prostitutes his understanding to his interest, or as one whose powers of mind are not of a size to grasp any thing great and noble, who cannot see above five yards before him, and who must therefore be utterly unable to take in the views of the enlightened benefactor of mankind.

In this unamicable contest the cause of truth cannot but suffer. The really good arguments on each side of the question are not allowed to have their proper weight. Each pursues his own theory, little solicitous to correct or improve it by an attention to what is advanced by his opponents.

The friend of the present order of things condemns all political speculations in the gross. He will not even condescend to examine the grounds from which the perfectibility of society is inferred. Much less will he give himself the trouble in a fair and candid manner to attempt an exposition of their fallacy.

The speculative philosopher equally offends against the cause of truth. With eyes fixed on a happier state of society, the blessings of which he paints in the most captivating colours, he allows himself to indulge in the most bitter invectives against every present establishment, without applying his talents to consider the best and safest means of removing abuses and without seeming to be aware of the tremendous obstacles that threaten, even in theory, to oppose the progress of man towards perfection.

It is an acknowledged truth in philosophy that a just theory will always be confirmed by experiment. Yet so much friction, and so many minute circumstances occur in practice, which it is next to impossible for the most enlarged and penetrating mind to foresee, that on few subjects can any theory be pronounced just, that has not stood the test of experience. But an untried theory cannot fairly be advanced as probable, much less as just, till all the arguments against it have been maturely weighed and clearly and consistently refuted.

I have read some of the speculations on the perfectibility of man and of society with great pleasure. I have been warmed and delighted with the enchanting picture which they hold forth. I ardently wish for such happy improvements. But I see great, and, to my understanding, unconquerable difficulties in the way to them. These difficulties it is my present purpose to state, declaring, at the same time, that so far from exulting in them, as a cause of triumph over the friends of innovation, nothing would give me greater pleasure than to see them completely removed.

The most important argument that I shall adduce is certainly not new. The principles on which it depends have been explained in part by Hume, and more at large by Dr. Adam Smith. It has been advanced and applied to the present subject, though not with its proper weight, or in the most forcible point of view, by Mr. Wallace, and it may probably have been stated by many writers that I have never met with. I should certainly therefore not think of advancing it again, though I mean to place it in a point of view in some degree different from any that I have hitherto seen, if it had ever been fairly and satisfactorily answered.

The cause of this neglect on the part of the advocates for the perfectibility of mankind is not easily accounted for. I cannot doubt the talents of such men as Godwin and Condorcet. I am unwilling to doubt their candour. To my understanding, and probably to that of most others, the difficulty appears insurmountable. Yet these men of acknowledged ability and penetration, scarcely deign to notice it, and hold on their course in such speculations, with unabated ardour and undiminished confidence. I have certainly no right to say that they purposely shut their eyes to such arguments. I ought rather to doubt the validity of them, when neglected by such men, however forcibly their truth may strike my own mind. Yet in this respect it must be acknowledged that we are all of us too prone to err. If I saw a glass of wine repeatedly presented to a man, and he took no notice of it, I should be apt to think that he was blind or uncivil. A juster philosophy might teach me rather to think that my eyes deceived me and that the offer was not really what I conceived it to be.

In entering upon the argument I must premise that I put out of the question, at present, all mere conjectures, that is, all suppositions, the probable realization of which cannot be inferred upon any just philosophical grounds. A writer may tell me that he thinks man will ultimately become an ostrich. I cannot properly contradict him. But before he can expect to bring any reasonable person over to his opinion, he ought to shew, that the necks of mankind have been gradually elongating, that the lips have grown harder and more prominent, that the legs and feet are daily altering their shape, and that the hair is beginning to change into stubs of feathers. And till the probability of so wonderful a conversion can be shewn, it is surely lost time and lost eloquence to expatiate on the happiness of man in such a state; to describe his powers, both of running and flying, to paint him in a condition where all narrow luxuries would be contemned, where he would be employed only in collecting the necessaries of life, and where, consequently, each man's share of labour would be light, and his portion of leisure ample.

I think I may fairly make two postulata.

First, That food is necessary to the existence of man.

Secondly, That the passion between the sexes is necessary and will remain nearly in its present state.

These two laws, ever since we have had any knowledge of mankind, appear to have been fixed laws of our nature, and, as we have not hitherto seen any alteration in them, we have no right to conclude that they will ever cease to be what they now are, without an immediate act of power in that Being who first arranged the system of the universe, and for the advantage of his creatures, still executes, according to fixed laws, all its various operations.

I do not know that any writer has supposed that on this earth man will ultimately be able to live without food. But Mr. Godwin has conjectured that the passion between the sexes may in time be extinguished. As, however, he calls this part of his work a deviation into the land of conjecture, I will not dwell longer upon it at present than to say that the best arguments for the perfectibility of man are drawn from a contemplation of the great progress that has already made from the savage state and the difficulty of saying where he is to stop. But towards the extinction of the passion between the sexes, no progress whatever has hitherto been made. It appears to exist in as much force at present as it did two thousand or four thousand years ago. There are individual exceptions now as there always have been. But, as these exceptions do not appear to increase in number, it would surely be a very unphilosophical mode of arguing, to infer merely from the existence of an exception, that the exception would, in time, become the rule, and the rule the exception.

Assuming then, my postulata as granted, I say, that the power of population is indefinitely greater than the power in the earth to produce subsistence for man.

Population, when unchecked, increases in a geometrical ratio. Subsistence increases only in an arithmetical ratio. A slight acquaintance with numbers will shew the immensity of the first power in comparison of the second.

By that law of our nature which makes food necessary to the life of man, the effects of these two unequal powers must be kept equal.

This implies a strong and constantly operating check on population from the difficulty of subsistence. This difficulty must fall some where and must necessarily be severely felt by a large portion of mankind.

Through the animal and vegetable kingdoms, nature has scattered the seeds of life abroad with the most profuse and liberal hand. She has been comparatively sparing in the room and the nourishment necessary to rear them. The germs of existence contained in this spot of earth, with ample food, and ample room to expand in, would fill millions of worlds in the course of a few thousand years. Necessity, that imperious all pervading law of nature, restrains them within the prescribed bounds. The race of plants, and the race of animals shrink under this great restrictive law. And the race of man cannot, by any efforts of reason, escape from it. Among plants and animals its effects are waste of seed, sickness, and premature death. Among mankind, misery and vice. The former, misery, is an absolutely necessary consequence of it. Vice is a highly probable consequence, and we therefore see it abundantly prevail, but it ought not, perhaps, to be called an absolutely necessary consequence. The ordeal of virtue is to resist all temptation to evil.

This natural inequality of the two powers of population and of production in the earth and that great law of our nature which must constantly keep their effects equal form the great difficulty that to me appears insurmountable in the way to the perfectibility of society. All other arguments are of slight and subordinate consideration in comparison of this. I see no way by which man can escape from the weight of this law which pervades all animated nature. No fancied equality, no agrarian regulations in their utmost extent, could remove the pressure of it even for a single century. And it appears, therefore, to be decisive against the possible existence of a society, all the members of which should live in ease, happiness, and comparative leisure; and feel no anxiety about providing the means of subsistence for themselves and families.

Consequently, if the premises are just, the argument is conclusive against the perfectibility of the mass of mankind.

I have thus sketched the general outline of the argument, but I will examine it more particularly, and I think it will be found that experience, the true source and foundation of all knowledge, invariably confirms its truth.

## Chapter II

I said that population, when unchecked, increased in a geometrical ratio, and subsistence for man in an arithmetical ratio.

Let us examine whether this position be just.

I think it will be allowed, that no state has hitherto existed (at least that we have any account of) where the manners were so pure and simple, and the means of subsistence so abundant, that no check whatever has existed to early marriages, among the lower classes, from a fear of not providing well for their families, or among the higher classes, from a fear of lowering their condition in life. Consequently in no state that we have yet known has the power of population been left to exert itself with perfect freedom.

Whether the law of marriage be instituted or not, the dictate of nature and virtue seems to be an early attachment to one woman. Supposing a liberty of changing in the case of an unfortunate choice, this liberty would not affect population till it arose to a height greatly vicious; and we are now supposing the existence of a society where vice is scarcely known.

In a state therefore of great equality and virtue, where pure and simple manners prevailed, and where the means of subsistence were so abundant that no part of the society could have any fears about providing amply for a family, the power of population being left to exert itself unchecked, the increase of the human species would evidently be much greater than any increase that has been hitherto known.

In the United States of America, where the means of subsistence have been more ample, the manners of the people more pure, and consequently the checks to early marriages fewer than in any of the modern states of Europe, the population has been found to double itself in twenty-five years.

This ratio of increase, though short of the utmost power of population, yet as the result of actual experience, we will take as our rule, and say, that population, when unchecked, goes on doubling itself every twenty-five years or increases in a geometrical ratio.

Let us now take any spot of earth, this Island for instance, and see in what ratio the subsistence it affords can be supposed to increase. We will begin with it under its present state of cultivation.

If I allow that by the best possible policy, by breaking up more land and by great encouragements to agriculture, the produce of this Island may be doubled in the first twenty-five years, I think it will be allowing as much as any person can well demand.

In the next twenty-five years, it is impossible to suppose that the produce could be quadrupled. It would be contrary to all our knowledge of the qualities of land. The very utmost that we can conceive, is, that the increase in the second twenty-five years might equal the present produce. Let us then take this for our rule, though certainly far beyond the truth, and allow that by great exertion, the whole produce of the Island might be increased every twenty-five years, by a quantity of subsistence equal to what it at present produces. The most enthusiastic speculator cannot suppose a greater increase than this. In a few centuries it would make every acre of land in the Island like a garden.

Yet this ratio of increase is evidently arithmetical.

It may be fairly said, therefore, that the means of subsistence increase in an arithmetical ratio. Let us now bring the effects of these two ratios together.

The population of the Island is computed to be about seven millions, and we will suppose the present produce equal to the support of such a number. In the first twenty-five years the population would be fourteen millions, and the food being also doubled, the means of subsistence would be equal to this increase. In the next twenty-five years the population would be twenty-eight millions, and the means of subsistence only equal to the support of twenty-one millions. In the next period, the population would be fifty-six millions, and the means of subsistence just sufficient for half that number. And at the conclusion of the first century the population would be one hundred and twelve millions and the means of subsistence only equal to the support of thirty-five millions, which would leave a population of seventy-seven millions totally unprovided for.

A great emigration necessarily implies unhappiness of some kind or other in the country that is deserted. For few persons will leave their families, connections, friends, and native land, to seek a settlement in untried foreign climes, without some strong subsisting causes of uneasiness where they are, or the hope of some great advantages in the place to which they are going.

But to make the argument more general and less interrupted by the partial views of emigration, let us take the whole earth, instead of one spot, and suppose that the restraints to population were universally removed. If the subsistence for man that the earth affords was to be increased every twenty-five years by a quantity equal to what the whole world at present produces, this would allow the power of production in the earth to be absolutely unlimited, and its ratio of increase much greater than we can conceive that any possible exertions of mankind could make it.

Taking the population of the world at any number, a thousand millions, for instance, the human species would increase in the ratio of—1, 2, 4, 8, 16, 32, 64, 128, 256, 512, &c. and subsistence as—1, 2, 3, 4, 5, 6, 7, 8, 9, 10, &c. In two centuries and a quarter, the population would be to the means of subsistence as 512 to 10: in three centuries as 4096 to 13, and in two thousand years the difference would be almost incalculable, though the produce in that time would have increased to an immense extent.

No limits whatever are placed to the productions of the earth; they may increase for ever and be greater than any assignable quantity; yet still the power of population being a power of a superior order, the increase of the human species can only be kept commensurate to the increase of the means of subsistence, by the constant operation of the strong law of necessity acting as a check upon the greater power.

The effects of this check remain now to be considered.

Among plants and animals the view of the subject is simple. They are all impelled by a powerful instinct to the increase of their species, and this instinct is interrupted by no reasoning or doubts about providing for their offspring. Wherever therefore there is liberty, the power of increase is exerted, and the superabundant effects are repressed afterwards by want of room and nourishment, which is common to animals and plants, and among animals, by becoming the prey of others.

The effects of this check on man are more complicated. Impelled to the increase of his species by an equally powerful instinct, reason interrupts his career and asks him whether he may not bring beings into the world, for whom he cannot provide the means of subsistence. In a state of equality, this would be the simple question. In the present state of society, other considerations occur. Will he not lower his rank in life? Will he not subject himself to greater difficulties than he at present feels? Will he not be obliged to labour harder? and if he has a large family, will his utmost exertions enable him to support them? May he not see his offspring in rags and misery, and clamouring for bread that he cannot give them? And may he not be reduced to the grating necessity of forfeiting his independence, and of being obliged to the sparing hand of charity for support?

These considerations are calculated to prevent, and certainly do prevent, a very great number in all civilized nations from pursuing the dictate of nature in an early attachment to one woman. And this restraint almost necessarily, though not absolutely so, produces vice. Yet in all societies, even those that are most vicious, the tendency to a virtuous attachment is so strong that there is a constant effort towards an increase of population. This constant effort as constantly tends to subject the lower classes of the society to distress and to prevent any great permanent amelioration of their condition.

The way in which these effects are produced seems to be this.

We will suppose the means of subsistence in any country just equal to the easy support of its inhabitants. The constant effort towards population, which is found to act even in the most vicious societies, increases the number of people before the means of subsistence are increased. The food therefore which before supported seven millions must now be divided among seven millions and a half or eight millions. The poor consequently must live much worse, and many of them be reduced to severe distress. The number of labourers also being above the proportion of the work in the market, the price of labour must tend toward a decrease, while the price of provisions would at the same time tend to rise. The labourer therefore must work harder to earn the same time as he did before. During this season of distress, the discouragements to marriage, and the difficulty of rearing a family are so great that population is at a stand. In the mean time the cheapness of labour, the plenty of labourers, and the necessity of an increased industry amongst them, encourage cultivators to employ more labour upon their land, to turn up fresh soil, and to manure and improve more completely what is already in tillage, till ultimately the means of subsistence become in the same proportion to the population as at the period from which we set out. The situation of the labourer being then again tolerably comfortable, the restraints to population are in some degree loosened, and the same retrograde and progressive movements with respect to happiness are repeated.

This sort of oscillation will not be remarked by superficial observers, and it may be difficult even for the most penetrating mind to calculate its periods. Yet that in all old states some such vibration does exist, though from various transverse causes, in a much less marked, and in a much more irregular manner than I have described it, no reflecting man who considers the subject deeply can well doubt.

Many reasons occur why this oscillation has been less obvious, and less decidedly confirmed by experience, than might naturally be expected.

One principal reason is that the histories of mankind that we possess are histories only of the higher classes. We have but few accounts that can be depended upon of the manners and customs of that part of mankind, where these retrograde and progressive movements chiefly take place. A satisfactory history of this kind, of one people, and of one period, would require the constant and minute attention of an observing mind during a long life. Some of the objects of enquiry would be, in what proportion to the number of adults was the number of marriages, to what extent vicious customs prevailed in consequence of the restraints upon matrimony, what was the comparative mortality among the children of the most distressed part of the community and those who lived rather more at their ease, what were the variations in the real price of labour, and what were the observable differences in the state of the lower classes of society with respect to ease and happiness, at different times during a certain period.

Such a history would tend greatly to elucidate the manner in which the constant check upon population acts and would probably prove the existence of the retrograde and progressive movements that have been mentioned, though the times of their vibration must necessarily be rendered irregular, from the operation of many interrupting causes, such as the introduction or failure of certain manufactures, a greater or less prevalent spirit of agricultural enterprize, years of plenty, or years of scarcity, wars and pestilence, poor laws, the invention of processes for shortening labour without the proportional extension of the market for the commodity, and, particularly, the difference between the nominal and real price of labour, a circumstance which has perhaps more than any other contributed to conceal this oscillation from common view.

It very rarely happens that the nominal price of labour universally falls, but we well know that it frequently remains the same, while the nominal price of provisions has been gradually increasing. This is, in effect, a real fall in the price of labour, and during this period the condition of the lower orders of the community must gradually grow worse and worse. But the farmers and capitalists are growing rich from the real cheapness of labour. Their increased capitals enable them to employ a greater number of men. Work therefore may be plentiful, and the price of labour would consequently rise. But the want of freedom in the market of labour, which occurs more or less in all communities, either from parish laws, or the more general cause of the facility of combination among the rich, and its difficulty among the poor, operates to prevent the price of labour from rising at the natural period, and keeps it down some time longer; perhaps, till a year of scarcity, when the clamour is too loud, and the necessity too apparent to be resisted.

The true cause of the advance in the price of labour is thus concealed, and the rich affect to grant it as an act of compassion and favour to the poor, in consideration of a year of scarcity, and, when plenty returns, indulge themselves in the most unreasonable of all complaints, that the price does not again fall, when a little reflection would shew them that it must have risen long before but from an unjust conspiracy of their own.

But though the rich by unfair combinations contribute frequently to prolong a season of distress among the poor, yet no possible form of society could prevent the almost constant action of misery upon a great part of mankind, if in a state of inequality, and upon all, if all were equal.

The theory on which the truth of this position depends appears to me so extremely clear that I feel at a loss to conjecture what part of it can be denied.

That population cannot increase without the means of subsistence is a proposition so evident that it needs no illustration.

That population does invariably increase where there are the means of subsistence, the history of every people that have ever existed will abundantly prove.

And that the superior power of population cannot be checked without producing misery or vice, the ample portion of these too bitter ingredients in the cup of human life and the continuance of the physical causes that seem to have produced them bear too convincing a testimony.

But in order more fully to ascertain the validity of these three propositions, let us examine the different states in which mankind have been known to exist. Even a cursory review will, I think, be sufficient to convince us that these propositions are incontrovertible truths.

# *from* The Voyage of the Beagle

## *Charles Darwin*

The natural history of these islands is eminently curious, and well deserves attention. Most of the organic productions are aboriginal creations, found nowhere else; there is even a difference between the inhabitants of the different islands; yet all show a marked relationship with those of America, though separated from that continent by an open space of ocean, between 500 and 600 miles in width. The archipelago is a little world within itself, or rather a satellite attached to America, whence it has derived a few stray colonists, and has received the general character of its indigenous productions. Considering the small size of the islands, we feel the more astonished at the number of their aboriginal beings, and at their confined range. Seeing every height crowned with its crater, and the boundaries of most of the lava-streams still distinct, we are led to believe that within a period geologically recent the unbroken ocean was here spread out. Hence, both in space and time, we seem to be brought somewhat near to that great fact—that mystery of mysteries—the first appearance of new beings on this earth.

Of terrestrial mammals, there is only one which must be considered as indigenous, namely, a mouse (Mus Galapagoensis), and this is confined, as far as I could ascertain, to Chatham Island, the most easterly island of the group. It belongs, as I am informed by Mr. Waterhouse, to a division of the family of mice characteristic of America. At James Island, there is a rat sufficiently distinct from the common kind to have been named and described by Mr. Waterhouse; but as it belongs to the old-world division of the family, and as this island has been frequented by ships for the last hundred and fifty years, I can hardly doubt that this rat is merely a variety produced by the new and peculiar climate, food, and soil, to which it has been subjected. Although no one has a right to speculate without distinct facts, yet even with respect to the Chatham Island mouse, it should be borne in mind, that it may possibly be an American species imported here; for I have seen, in a most unfrequented part of the Pampas, a native mouse living in the roof of a newly built hovel, and therefore its transportation in a vessel is not improbable: analogous facts have been observed by Dr. Richardson in North America.

Of landbirds I obtained twenty-six kinds, all peculiar to the group and found nowhere else, with the exception of one lark-like finch from North America (Dolichonyx oryzivorus), which ranges on that continent as far north as 54°, and generally frequents marshes. The other twenty-five birds consist, firstly, of a hawk, curiously intermediate in structure between a buzzard and the American group of carrion-feeding Polybori; and with these latter birds it agrees most closely in every habit and even tone of voice. Secondly, there are two owls, representing the short-eared and white barn-owls of Europe. Thirdly, a wren, three tyrant-flycatchers (two of them species of Pyrocephalus, one or both of which would be ranked by some ornithologists as only varieties), and a dove—all analogous to, but distinct from, American species. Fourthly, a swallow, which though differing from the Progne purpurea of both Americas, only in being rather duller colored, smaller, and slenderer, is considered by Mr. Gould as specifically distinct. Fifthly, there are three species of mocking thrush—a form highly characteristic of America. The remaining landbirds form a most singular group of finches, related to each other in the structure of their beaks, short tails, form of body and plumage: there are thirteen species, which Mr. Gould has divided into four subgroups. All these species are peculiar to this archipelago; and so is the whole group, with the exception of one species of the sub-group Cactornis, lately brought from Bow Island, in the Low Archipelago. Of Cactornis, the two species may be often seen climbing about the flowers of the great cactus-trees; but all the other species of this group of finches, mingled together in flocks, feed on the dry and sterile ground of the lower districts. The males of all, or certainly of the greater number, are jet black; and the females (with perhaps one or two exceptions) are brown. The most curious fact is the perfect gradation in the size of the beaks in the different species of Geospiza, from one as large as that of a hawfinch to that of a chaffinch, and (if Mr. Gould is right in including his sub-group, Certhidea, in the main group) even to that of a warbler. The largest beak in the genus Geospiza is shown in Fig. 1, and the smallest in Fig. 3; but instead of there being only one intermediate species, with a beak of the size shown in Fig. 2, there are no less than six species with insensibly graduated beaks. The beak of the sub-group Certhidea, is shown in Fig. 4. The beak of Cactornis is somewhat like that of a starling and that of the fourth sub-group, Camarhynchus, is slightly parrot-shaped. Seeing this gradation and diversity of structure in one small, intimately related group of birds, one might really fancy that from an original paucity of birds in this archipelago, one species had been taken and modified for different ends. In a like manner it might be fancied that a bird originally a buzzard, had been induced here to undertake the office of the carrion-feeding Polybori of the American continent.

1. Geospiza magnirostris.          2. Geospiza fortis

3. Geospiza parvula.                4. Certhidea olivasea.

Of waders and water-birds I was able to get only eleven kinds, and of these only three (including a rail confined to the damp summits of the islands) are new species. Considering the wandering habits of the gulls, I was surprised to find that the species inhabiting these islands is peculiar, but allied to one from the southern parts of South America. The far greater peculiarity of the landbirds, namely, twenty-five out of twenty-six, being new species, or at least new races, compared with the waders and web-footed birds, is in accordance with the greater range which these latter orders have in all parts of the world. We shall hereafter see this law of aquatic forms, whether marine or fresh-water, being less peculiar at any given point of the earth's surface than the terrestrial forms of the same classes, strikingly illustrated in the shells, and in a lesser degree in the insects of this archipelago.

Two of the waders are rather smaller than the same species brought from other places: the swallow is also smaller, though it is doubtful whether or not it is distinct from its analogue. The two owls, the two tyrant-catchers (Pyrocephalus) and the dove, are also smaller than the analogous but distinct species, to which they are most nearly related; on the other hand, the gull is rather larger. The two owls, the swallow, all three species of mocking-thrush, the dove in its separate colours though not in its whole plumage, the Totanus, and the gull, are likewise duskier coloured than their analogous species; and in the case of the mocking-thrush and Totanus, than any other species of the two genera. With the exception of a wren with a fine yellow breast, and of a tyrant-flycatcher with a scarlet tuft and breast, none of the birds are brilliantly coloured, as might have been expected in an equatorial district. Hence it would appear probable, that the same causes which here make the immigrants of some peculiar species smaller, make most of the peculiar Galapageian species also smaller, as well as very generally more dusky coloured. All the plants have a wretched, weedy appearance, and I did not see one beautiful flower. The insects, again, are small-sized and dull-coloured, and, as Mr. Waterhouse informs me, there is nothing in their general appearance which would have led him to imagine that they had come from under the equator.[1] The birds, plants, and insects have a desert character, and are not more brilliantly coloured than those from southern Patagonia; we may, therefore, conclude that the usual gaudy colouring of the inter-tropical productions, is not related either to the heat or light of those zones, but to some other cause, perhaps to the conditions of existence being generally favourable to life.

• • •

To finish with the zoology: the fifteen kinds of sea-fish which I procured here are all new species; they belong to twelve genera, all widely distributed, with the exception of Prionotus, of which, the four previously known species live on the eastern side of America. Of land-shells I collected sixteen kinds (and two marked varieties), of which, with the exception of one Helix found at Tahiti, all are peculiar to this archipelago: a single fresh-water shell (Paludina) is common to Tahiti and Van Diemen's Land. Mr. Cuming, before our voyage, procured here ninety species of sea-shells, and this does not include several species not yet specifically examined, of Trochus, Turbo, Monodonta, and Nassa. He has been kind enough to give me the following interesting results: Of the ninety shells, no less than forty-seven are unknown elsewhere—a wonderful fact, considering how widely distributed sea-shells generally are. Of the forty-three shells found in other parts of the world, twenty-five inhabit the western coast of America, and of these eight are distinguishable as varieties; the remaining eighteen (including one variety) were found by Mr. Cuming in the Low

Archipelago, and some of them also at the Philippines. This fact of shells from islands in the central parts of the Pacific occurring here, deserves notice, for not one single sea-shell is known to be common to the islands of that ocean and to the west coast of America. The space of open sea running north and south off the west coast, separates two quite distinct conchological provinces; but at the Galapagos Archipelago we have a halting-place, where many new forms have been created, and whither these two great conchological provinces have each sent up several colonists. The American province has also sent here representative species; for there is a Galapageian species of Monoceros, a genus only found on the west coast of America; and there are Galapageian species of Fissurella and Cancellaria, genera common on the west coast, but not found (as I am informed by Mr. Cuming) in the central islands of the Pacific. On the other hand, there are Galapageian species of Oniscia and Stylifer, genera common to the West Indies and to the Chinese and Indian seas, but not found either on the west coast of America or in the central Pacific. I may here add, that after the comparison by Messrs. Cuming and Hinds of about 2000 shells from the eastern and western coasts of America, only one single shell was found in common, namely, the Purpura patula, which inhabits the West Indies, the coast of Panama, and the Galapagos. We have, therefore, in this quarter of the world, three great conchological sea-provinces, quite distinct, though surprisingly near each other, being separated by long north and south spaces either of land or of open sea.

I took great pains in collecting the insects, but excepting Tierra del Fuego, I never saw in this respect so poor a country. Even in the upper and damp region I procured very few, excepting some minute Diptera and Hymenoptera, mostly of common mundane forms. As before remarked, the insects, for a tropical region, are of very small size and dull colours. Of beetles I collected twenty-five species (excluding a Dermestes and Corynetes imported, wherever a ship touches); of these, two belong to the Harpalidae, two to the Hydrophilidae, nine to three families of the Heteromera, and the remaining twelve to as many different families. This circumstance of insects (and I may add plants), where few in number, belonging to many different families, is, I believe, very general. Mr. Waterhouse, who has published[2] an account of the insects of this archipelago, and to whom I am indebted for the above details, informs me that there are several new genera: and that of the genera not new, one or two are American, and the rest of mundane distribution. With the exception of a wood-feeding Apate, and of one or probably two water-beetles from the American continent, all the species appear to be new.

The botany of this group is fully as interesting as the zoology. Dr. J. Hooker will soon publish in the "Linnean Transactions" a full account of the Flora, and I am much indebted to him for the following details. Of flowering plants there are, as far as at present is known, 185 species, and 40 cryptogamic species, making altogether 225; of this number I was fortunate enough to bring home 193. Of the flowering plants, 100 are new species, and are probably confined to this archipelago. Dr. Hooker conceives that, of the plants not so confined, at least 10 species found near the cultivated ground at Charles Island, have been imported. It is, I think, surprising that more American species have not been introduced naturally, considering that the distance is only between 500 and 600 miles from the continent; and that (according to Collnet, p. 58) drift-wood, bamboos, canes, and the nuts of a palm, are often washed on the south-eastern shores. The proportion of 100 flowering plants out of 185 (or 175 excluding the imported weeds) being new, is sufficient, I conceive, to make the Galapagos Archipelago a distinct botanical province; but this Flora is not nearly so peculiar as that of St. Helena, nor, as I am informed by Dr. Hooker, of Juan Fernandez. The peculiarity of the Galapageian Flora is best shown in certain families;—thus there are 21 species of Compositae, of which 20 are peculiar to this archipelago; these belong to twelve genera, and of these genera no less than ten are confined to the archipelago! Dr. Hooker informs me that the Flora has an undoubtedly Western American character; nor can he detect in it any affinity with that of the Pacific. If, therefore, we except the eighteen marine, the one fresh-water, and one land-shell, which have apparently come here as colonists from the central islands of the Pacific, and likewise the one distinct Pacific species of the Galapageian group of finches, we see that this archipelago, though standing in the Pacific Ocean, is zoologically part of America.

If this character were owing merely to immigrants from America, there would be little remarkable in it; but we see that a vast majority of all the land animals, and that more than half of the flowering plants, are aboriginal productions. It was most striking to be surrounded by new birds, new reptiles, new shells, new insects, new plants, and yet by innumerable trifling details of structure, and even by the tones of voice and plumage of the birds, to have the temperate plains of Patagonia, or rather the hot dry deserts of Northern Chile, vividly brought before my eyes. Why, on these small points of land, which within a late geological period must have been covered by the ocean, which are formed by basaltic lava, and therefore differ in geological character from the American continent, and which are placed under a peculiar climate,—why were their aboriginal inhabitants, associated, I may add, in different proportions both in kind and number from those on the continent, and therefore acting on each other in a different manner—why were they created on American types of organization? It is probable that the islands of the Cape de Verd group resemble, in all their physical conditions, far more closely the Galapagos Islands, than these latter physically resemble the coast of America, yet the aboriginal inhabitants of the two groups are totally unlike; those of the Cape de Verd Islands bearing the impress of Africa, as the inhabitants of the Galapagos Archipelago are stamped with that of America.

I have not as yet noticed by far the most remarkable feature in the natural history of this archipelago; it is, that the different islands to a considerable extent are inhabited by a different set of beings. My attention was first called to this fact by the Vice-Governor, Mr. Lawson, declaring that the tortoises differed from the different islands, and that he could with certainty tell from which island any one was brought. I did not for some time pay sufficient attention to this statement, and I had already partially mingled together the collections from two of the islands. I never dreamed that islands, about 50 or 60 miles apart, and most of them in sight of each other, formed of precisely the same rocks, placed under a quite similar climate, rising to a nearly equal height, would have been differently tenanted; but we shall soon see that this is the case. It is the fate of most voyagers, no sooner to discover what is most interesting in any locality, than they are hurried from it; but I ought, perhaps, to be thankful that I obtained sufficient materials to establish this most remarkable fact in the distribution of organic beings.

The inhabitants, as I have said, state that they can distinguish the tortoises from the different islands; and that they differ not only in size, but in other characters. Captain Porter has described[3] those from Charles and from the nearest island to it, namely, Hood Island, as having their shells in front thick and turned up like a Spanish saddle, whilst the tortoises from James Island are rounder, blacker, and have a better taste when cooked. M. Bibron, moreover, informs me that he has seen what he considers two distinct species of tortoise from the Galapagos, but he does not know from which islands. The specimens that I brought from three islands were young ones: and probably owing to this cause neither Mr. Gray nor myself could find in them any specific differences. I have remarked that the marine Amblyrhynchus was larger at Albemarle Island than elsewhere; and M. Bibron informs me that he has seen two distinct aquatic species of this genus; so that the different islands probably have their representative species or races of the Amblyrhynchus, as well as of the tortoise. My attention was first thoroughly aroused, by comparing together the numerous specimens, shot by myself and several other parties on board, of the mocking-thrushes, when, to my astonishment, I discovered that all those from Charles Island belonged to one species (Mimus trifasciatus); all from Albemarle Island to M. parvulus; and all from James and Chatham Islands (between which two other islands are situated, as connecting links) belonged to M. melanotis. These two latter species are closely allied, and would by some ornithologists be considered as only well-marked races or varieties; but the Mimus trifasciatus is very distinct. Unfortunately most of the specimens of the finch tribe were mingled together; but I have strong reasons to suspect that some of the species of the sub-group Geospiza are confined to separate islands. If the different islands have their representatives of Geospiza, it may help to explain the singularly large number of the species of this sub-group in this one small archipelago, and as a probable consequence of their numbers, the perfectly graduated series in the size of their beaks. Two species of the sub-group Cactornis, and two of the Camarhynchus, were procured in the archipelago; and of the numerous specimens of these two subgroups shot by four collectors at James Island, all were found to belong to one species of each; whereas the numerous specimens shot either on Chatham or Charles Island (for the two sets were mingled together) all belonged to the two other species: hence we may feel almost sure that these islands possess their respective species of these two sub-groups. In land-shells this law of distribution does not appear to hold good. In my very small collection of insects, Mr. Waterhouse remarks, that of those which were ticketed with their locality, not one was common to any two of the islands.

If we now turn to the Flora, we shall find the aboriginal plants of the different islands wonderfully different. I give all the following results on the high authority of my friend Dr. J. Hooker. I may premise that I indiscriminately collected everything in flower on the different islands, and fortunately kept my collections separate. Too much confidence, however, must not be placed in the proportional results, as the small collections brought home by some other naturalists, though in some respects confirming the results, plainly show that much remains to be done in the botany of this group: the Leguminosæ, moreover, has as yet been only approximately worked out:—

| Name of Island. | Total No. of Species. | No. of Species found in other parts of the world. | No. of Species confined to the Galapagos Archipelago. | No. confined to the one Island. | No. of Species confined to the Galapagos Archipelago, but found on more than the one Island. |
|---|---|---|---|---|---|
| James Island | 71 | 33 | 38 | 30 | 8 |
| Albermarle Island | 44 | 18 | 26 | 22 | 4 |
| Chatham Island | 32 | 16 | 16 | 12 | 4 |
| Charles Island | 68 | 39 (or 29, if the probably imported plants be subtracted) | 29 | 21 | 8 |

Hence we have the truly wonderful fact, that in James Island, of the thirty-eight Galapageian plants, or those found in no other part of the world, thirty are exclusively confined to this one island; and in Albemarle Island, of the twenty-six aboriginal Galapageian plants, twenty-two are confined to this one island, that is, only four are at present known to grow in the other islands of the archipelago; and so on, as shown in the above table, with the plants from Chatham and Charles Islands. This fact will, perhaps, be rendered even more striking, by giving a few illustrations:— thus, Scalesia, a remarkable arborescent genus of the Compositæ, is confined to the archipelago: it has six species: one from Chatham, one from Albemarle, one from Charles Island, two from James Island, and the sixth from one of the three latter islands, but it is not known from which: not one of these six species grows on any two islands. Again, Euphorbia, a mundane or widely distributed genus, has here eight species, of which seven are confined to the archipelago, and not one found on any two islands: Acalypha and Borreria, both mundane genera, have respectively six and seven species, none of which have the same species on two islands, with the exception of one Borreria, which does occur on two islands. The species of the Compositæ are particularly local; and Dr. Hooker has furnished me with several other most striking illustrations of the difference of the species on the different islands. He remarks that this law of distribution holds good both with those genera confined to the archipelago, and those distributed in other quarters of the world: in like manner we have seen that the different islands have their proper species of the mundane genus of tortoise, and of the widely distributed American genus of the mocking-thrush, as well as of two of the Galapageian sub-groups of finches, and almost certainly of the Galapageian genus Amblyrhynchus.

# Notes

1    The progress of research has shown that some of these birds, which were then thought to be confined to the islands, occur on the American continent. The eminent ornithologist, Mr. Sclater, informs me that this is the case with the Strix punctatissima and Pyrocephalus nanus; and probably with the Otus Galapagoensis and Zenaida Galapagoensis: so that the number of endemic birds is reduced to twenty-three, or probably to twenty-one. Mr. Sclater thinks that one or two of these endemic forms should be ranked rather as varieties than species, which always seemed to me probable.

2    Ann. and Mag. of Nat. Hist., vol. xvi. p. 19.

3    Voyage in the U. S. ship Essex, vol. i. p. 215.

# *from* Nature

### Ralph Waldo Emerson

## I

To go into solitude, a man needs to retire as much from his chamber as from society. I am not solitary whilst I read and write, though nobody is with me. But if a man would be alone, let him look at the stars. The rays that come from those heavenly worlds will separate between him and what he touches. One might think the atmosphere was made transparent with this design, to give man, in the heavenly bodies, the perpetual presence of the sublime. Seen in the streets of cities, how great they are! If the stars should appear one night in a thousand years, how would men believe and adore; and preserve for many generations the remembrance of the city of God which had been shown! But every night come out these envoys of beauty, and light the universe with their admonishing smile.

The stars awaken a certain reverence, because though always present, they are inaccessible; but all natural objects make a kindred impression, when the mind is open to their influence. Nature never wears a mean appearance. Neither does the wisest man extort her secret, and lose his curiosity by finding out all her perfection. Nature never became a toy to a wise spirit. The flowers, the animals, the mountains, reflected the wisdom of his best hour, as much as they had delighted the simplicity of his childhood.

When we speak of nature in this manner, we have a distinct but most poetical sense in the mind. We mean the integrity of impression made by manifold natural objects. It is this which distinguishes the stick of timber of the wood-cutter from the tree of the poet. The charming landscape which I saw this morning is indubitably made up of some twenty or thirty farms. Miller owns this field, Locke that, and Manning the woodland beyond. But none of them owns the landscape. There is a property in the horizon which no man has but he whose eve can integrate all the parts, that is, the poet. This is the best part of these men's farms, yet to this their warranty-deeds give no title.

To speak truly, few adult persons can see nature. Most persons do not see the sun. At least they have a very superficial seeing. The sun illuminates only the eye of the man, but shines into the eye and the heart of the child. The lover of nature is he whose inward and outward senses are still truly adjusted to each other; who has retained the spirit of infancy even into the era of manhood. His intercourse with heaven and earth becomes part of his daily food. In the presence of nature a wild delight runs through the man, in spite of real sorrows. Nature says,—he is my creature, and maugre all his impertinent griefs, he shall be glad with me. Not the sun or the summer alone, but every hour and season yields its tribute of delight; for every hour and change corresponds to and authorizes a different state of the mind, from breathless noon to grimmest midnight. Nature is a setting that fits equally well a comic or a mourning piece. In good health, the air is a cordial of incredible virtue. Crossing a bare common, in snow puddles, at twilight, under a clouded sky, without having in my thoughts any occurrence of special good fortune, I have enjoyed a perfect exhilaration. I am glad to the brink of fear. In the woods, too, a man casts off his years, as the snake his slough, and at what period soever of life is always a child. In the woods is perpetual youth. Within these plantations of God, a decorum and sanctity reign, a perennial festival is dressed, and the guest sees not how he should tire of them in a thousand years. In the woods, we return to reason and faith. There I feel that nothing can befall me in life,—no disgrace, no calamity (leaving me my eyes), which nature cannot repair. Standing on the bare ground,—my head bathed by the blithe air and uplifted into infinite space,—all mean egotism vanishes. I become a transparent eyeball; I am nothing; I see all; the currents of the Universal Being circulate through me; I am part or parcel of God. The name of the nearest friend sounds then foreign and accidental: to be brothers, to be acquaintances, master or servant, is then a trifle and a disturbance. I am the lover of uncontained and immortal beauty. In the wilderness, I find something more dear and connate than in streets or villages. In the tranquil landscape, and especially in the distant line of the horizon, man beholds somewhat as beautiful as his own nature.

The greatest delight which the fields and woods minister is the suggestion of an occult relation between man and the vegetable. I am not alone and unacknowledged. They nod to me, and I to them. The waving of the boughs in the storm is new to me and old. It takes me by surprise, and yet is not unknown. Its effect is like that of a higher thought or a better emotion coming over me, when I deemed I was thinking justly or doing right.

Yet it is certain that the power to produce this delight does not reside in nature, but in man, or in a harmony of both. It is necessary to use these pleasures with great temperance. For nature is not always tricked in holiday attire, but the same scene which yesterday breathed perfume and glittered as for the frolic of the nymphs is overspread with melancholy to-day. Nature always wears the colors of the spirit. To a man laboring under calamity, the heat of his own fire hath sadness in it. Then there is a kind of contempt of the landscape felt by him who has just lost by death a dear friend. The sky is less grand as it shuts down over less worth in the population.

## II

## Commodity

WHOEVER considers the final cause of the world will discern a multitude of uses that enter as parts into that result. They all admit of being thrown into one of the following classes: Commodity; Beauty; Language; and Discipline.

Under the general name of commodity, I rank all those advantages which our senses owe to nature. This, of course, is a benefit which is temporary and mediate, not ultimate, like its service to the soul. Yet although low, it is perfect in its kind, and is the only use of nature which all men apprehend. The misery of man appears like childish petulance, when we explore the steady and prodigal provision that has been made for his support and delight on this green ball which floats him through the heavens. What angels invented these splendid ornaments, these rich conveniences, this ocean of air above, this ocean of water beneath, this firmament of earth between? this zodiac of lights, this tent of dropping clouds, this striped coat of climates, this fourfold year? Beasts, fire, water, stones, and corn serve him. The field is at once his floor, his work-yard, his play-ground, his garden, and his bed.

> *"More servants wait on man*
> *Than he'll take notice of."*

Nature, in its ministry to man, is not only the material, but is also the process and the result. All the parts incessantly work into each other's hands for the profit of man. The wind sows the seed; the sun evaporates the sea; the wind blows the vapor to the field; the ice, on the other side of the planet, condenses rain on this; the rain feeds the plant; the plant feeds the animal; and thus the endless circulations of the divine charity nourish man.

The useful arts are reproductions or new combinations by the wit of man, of the same natural benefactors. He no longer waits for favoring gales, but by means of steam, he realizes the fable of Æolus's bag, and carries the two and thirty winds in the boiler of his boat. To diminish friction, he paves the road with iron bars, and, mounting a coach with a ship-load of men, animals, and merchandise behind him, he darts through the country, from town to town, like an eagle or a swallow through the air. By the aggregate of these aids, how is the face of the world changed, from the era of Noah to that of Napoleon! The private poor man hath cities, ships, canals, bridges, built for him. He goes to the post-office, and the human race run on his errands; to the book-shop, and the human race read and write of all that happens, for him; to the court-house, and nations repair his wrongs. He sets his house upon the road, and the human race go forth every morning, and shovel out the snow, and cut a path for him.

But there is no need of specifying particulars in this class of uses. The catalogue is endless, and the examples so obvious, that I shall leave them to the reader's reflection, with the general remark, that this mercenary benefit is one which has respect to a farther good. A man is fed, not that he may be fed, but that he may work.

# III

## Beauty

A nobler want of man is served by nature, namely, the love of Beauty.

The ancient Greeks called the world κόσμο, beauty. Such is the constitution of all things, or such the plastic power of the human eye, that the primary forms, as the sky, the mountain, the tree, the animal, give us a delight *in and for themselves*; a pleasure arising from outline, color, motion, and grouping. This seems partly owing to the eye itself. The eye is the best of artists. By the mutual action of its structure and of the laws of light, perspective is produced, which integrates every mass of objects, of what character soever, into a well colored and shaded globe, so that where the particular objects are mean and unaffecting, the landscape which they compose is round and symmetrical. And as the eye is the best composer, so light is the first of painters. There is no object so foul that intense light will not make beautiful. And the stimulus it affords to the sense, and a sort of infinitude which it hath, like space and time, make all matter gay. Even the corpse has its own beauty. But besides this general grace diffused over nature, almost all the individual forms are agreeable to the eye, as is proved by our endless imitations of some of them, as the acorn, the grape, the pine-cone, the wheat-ear, the egg, the wings and forms of most birds, the lion's claw, the serpent, the butterfly, sea-shells, flames, clouds, buds, leaves, and the forms of many trees, as the palm.

For better consideration, we may distribute the aspects of Beauty in a threefold manner.

1. First, the simple perception of natural forms is a delight. The influence of the forms and actions in nature is so needful to man, that, in its lowest functions, it seems to lie on the confines of commodity and beauty. To the body and mind which have been cramped by noxious work or company, nature is medicinal and restores their tone. The tradesman, the attorney comes out of the din and craft of the street and sees the sky and the woods, and is a man again. In their eternal calm, he finds himself. The health of the eye seems to demand a horizon. We are never tired, so long as we can see far enough.

But in other hours, Nature satisfies by its loveliness, and without any mixture of corporeal benefit. I see the spectacle of morning from the hill-top over against my house, from daybreak to sunrise, with emotions which an angel might share. The long slender bars of cloud float like fishes in the sea of crimson light. From the earth, as a shore, I look out into that silent sea. I seem to partake its rapid transformations; the active enchantment reaches my dust, and I dilate and conspire with the morning wind. How does Nature deify us with a few and cheap elements! Give me health and a day, and I will make the pomp of emperors ridiculous. The dawn is my Assyria; the sunset and moonrise my Paphos, and unimaginable realms of faerie; broad noon shall be my England of the senses and the understanding; the night shall be my Germany of mystic philosophy and dreams.

Not less excellent, except for our less susceptibility in the afternoon, was the charm, last evening, of a January sunset. The western clouds divided and subdivided themselves into pink flakes modulated with tints of unspeakable softness, and the air had so much life and sweetness that it was a pain to come within doors. What was it that nature would say? Was there no meaning in the live repose of the valley behind the mill, and which Homer or Shakspeare could not re-form for me in words? The leafless trees become spires of flame in the sunset, with the blue east for their background, and the stars of the dead calices of flowers, and every withered stem and stubble rimed with frost, contribute something to the mute music.

The inhabitants of cities suppose that the country landscape is pleasant only half the year. I please myself with the graces of the winter scenery, and believe that we are as much touched by it as by the genial influences of summer. To the attentive eye, each moment of the year has its own beauty, and in the same field, it beholds, every hour, a picture which was never seen before, and which shall never be seen again. The heavens change every moment, and reflect their glory or gloom on the plains beneath. The state of the crop in the surrounding farms alters the expression of the earth from week to week. The succession of native plants in the pastures and roadsides, which makes the silent clock by which time tells the summer hours, will make even the divisions of the day sensible to a keen observer. The tribes of birds and insects, like the plants punctual to their time, follow each other, and the year has room for all. By watercourses, the variety is greater. In July, the blue pontederia or pickerel-weed blooms in large beds in the shallow parts of our pleasant river, and swarms with yellow butterflies in continual motion. Art cannot rival this pomp of purple and gold. Indeed the river is a perpetual gala, and boasts each month a new ornament.

But this beauty of Nature which is seen and felt as beauty, is the least part. The shows of day, the dewy morning, the rainbow, mountains, orchards in blossom, stars, moonlight, shadows in still water, and the like, if too eagerly hunted, become shows merely, and mock us with their unreality. Go out of the house to see the moon, and 't is mere tinsel; it will not please as when its light shines upon your necessary journey. The beauty that shimmers in the yellow afternoons of October, who ever could clutch it? Go forth to find it, and it is gone; 't is only a mirage as you look from the windows of diligence.

2. The presence of a higher, namely, of the spiritual element is essential to its perfection. The high and divine beauty which can be loved without effeminacy, is that which is found in combination with the human will. Beauty is the mark God sets upon virtue. Every natural action is graceful. Every heroic act is also decent, and causes the place and the bystanders to shine. We are taught by great actions that the universe is the property of every individual in it. Every rational creature has all nature for his

dowry and estate. It is his, if he will. He may divest himself of it; he may creep into a corner, and abdicate his kingdom, as most men do, but he is entitled to the world by his constitution. In proportion to the energy of his thought and will, he takes up the world into himself. "All those things for which men plough, build, or sail, obey virtue;" said Sallust. "The winds and waves," said Gibbon, "are always on the side of the ablest navigators." So are the sun and moon and all the stars of heaven. When a noble act is done,— perchance in a scene of great natural beauty; when Leonidas and his three hundred martyrs consume one day in dying, and the sun and moon come each and look at them once in the steep defile of Thermopylæ; when Arnold Winkelried, in the high Alps, under the shadow of the avalanche, gathers in his side a sheaf of Austrian spears to break the line for his comrades; are not these heroes entitled to add the beauty of the scene to the beauty of the deed? When the bark of Columbus nears the shore of America;—before it the beach lined with savages, fleeing out of all their huts of cane; the sea behind; and the purple mountains of the Indian Archipelago around, can we separate the man from the living picture? Does not the New World clothe his form with her palm-groves and savannahs as fit drapery? Ever does natural beauty steal in like air, and envelope great actions. When Sir Harry Vane was dragged up the Tower-hill, sitting on a sled, to suffer death as the champion of the English laws, one of the multitude cried out to him, "You never sate on so glorious a seat!" Charles II, to intimidate the citizens of London, caused the patriot Lord Russell to be drawn in an open coach through the principal streets of the city on his way to the scaffold. "But," his biographer says, "the multitude imagined they saw liberty and virtue sitting by his side." In private places, among sordid objects, an act of truth or heroism seems at once to draw to itself the sky as its temple, the sun as its candle. Nature stretches out her arms to embrace man, only let his thoughts be of equal greatness. Willingly does she follow his steps with the rose and the violet, and bend her lines of grandeur and grace to the decoration of her darling child. Only let his thoughts be of equal scope, and the frame will suit the picture. A virtuous man is in unison with her works, and makes the central figure of the visible sphere. Homer, Pindar, Socrates, Phocion, associate themselves fitly in our memory with the geography and climate of Greece. The visible heavens and earth sympathize with Jesus. And in common life whosoever has seen a person of powerful character and happy genius, will have remarked how easily he took all things along with him,—the persons, the opinions, and the day, and nature became ancillary to a man.

3. There is still another aspect under which the beauty of the world may be viewed, namely, as it becomes an object of the intellect. Beside the relation of things to virtue, they have a relation to thought. The intellect searches out the absolute order of things as they stand in the mind of God, and without the colors of affection. The intellectual and the active powers seem to succeed each other, and the exclusive activity of the one generates the exclusive activity of the other. There is something unfriendly in each to the other, but they are like the alternate periods of feeding and working in animals; each prepares and will be followed by the other. Therefore does beauty, which, in relation to actions, as we have seen, comes unsought, and comes because it is unsought, remain for the apprehension and pursuit of the intellect; and then again, in its turn, of the active power. Nothing divine dies. All good is eternally reproductive. The beauty of nature re-forms itself in the mind, and not for barren contemplation, but for new creation.

All men are in some degree impressed by the face of the world; some men even to delight. This love of beauty is Taste. Others have the same love in such excess, that, not content with admiring, they seek to embody it in new forms. The creation of beauty is Art.

The production of a work of art throws a light upon the mystery of humanity. A work of art is an abstract or epitome of the world. It is the result or expression of nature, in miniature. For although the works of nature are innumerable and all different, the result or the expression of them all is similar and single. Nature is a sea of forms radically alike and even unique. A leaf, a sunbeam, a landscape, the ocean, make an analogous impression on the mind. What is common to them all,—that perfectness and harmony, is beauty. The standard of beauty is the entire circuit of natural forms,—the totality of nature; which the Italians expressed by defining beauty "il più nell' uno." Nothing is quite beautiful alone; nothing but is beautiful in the whole. A single object is only so far beautiful as it suggests this universal grace. The poet, the painter, the sculptor, the musician, the architect, seek each to concentrate this radiance of the world on one point, and each in his several work to satisfy the love of beauty which stimulates him to produce. Thus is Art a nature passed through the alembic of man. Thus in art does Nature work through the will of a man filled with the beauty of her first works.

The world thus exists to the soul to satisfy the desire of beauty. This element I call an ultimate end. No reason can be asked or given why the soul seeks beauty. Beauty, in its largest and profoundest sense, is one expression for the universe. God is the all-fair. Truth, and goodness, and beauty, are but different faces of the same All. But beauty in nature is not ultimate. It is the herald of inward and eternal beauty, and is not alone a solid and satisfactory good. It must stand as a part, and not as yet the last or highest expression of the final cause of Nature.

## IV

## Language

Language is a third use which Nature subserves to man. Nature is the vehicle of thought, and in a simple, double, and threefold degree.

1. Words are signs of natural facts.

2. Particular natural facts are symbols of particular spiritual facts.

3. Nature is the symbol of spirit.

1. Words are signs of natural facts. The use of natural history is to give us aid in supernatural history; the use of the outer creation, to give us language for the beings and changes of the inward creation. Every word which is used to express a moral or intellectual fact, if traced to its root, is found to be borrowed from some material appearance. *Right* means *straight; wrong* means *twisted. Spirit* primarily means *wind; transgression*, the crossing of a *line; supercilious*, the *raising of the eyebrow*. We say the *heart* to express emotion, the *head* to denote thought; and *thought* and *emotion* are words borrowed from sensible things, and now appropriated to spiritual nature. Most of the process by which this transformation is made, is hidden from us in the remote time when language was framed; but the same tendency may be daily observed in children. Children and savages use only nouns or names of things, which they convert into verbs, and apply to analogous mental acts.

2. But this origin of all words that convey a spiritual import,—so conspicuous a fact in the history of language,—is our least debt to nature. It is not words only that are emblematic; it is things which are emblematic. Every natural fact is a symbol of some spiritual fact. Every appearance in nature corresponds to some state of the mind, and that state of the mind can only be described by presenting that natural appearance as its picture. An enraged man is a lion, a cunning man is a fox, a firm man is a rock, a learned man is a torch. A lamb is innocence; a snake is subtle spite;

flowers express to us the delicate affections. Light and darkness are our familiar expression for knowledge and ignorance; and heat for love. Visible distance behind and before us, is respectively our image of memory and hope.

Who looks upon a river in a meditative hour and is not reminded of the flux of all things? Throw a stone into the stream, and the circles that propagate themselves are the beautiful type of all influence. Man is conscious of a universal soul within or behind his individual life, wherein, as in a firmament, the natures of Justice, Truth, Love, Freedom, arise and shine. This universal soul he calls Reason: it is not mine, or thine, or his, but we are its; we are its property and men. And the blue sky in which the private earth is buried, the sky with its eternal calm, and full of everlasting orbs, is the type of Reason. That which intellectually considered we call Reason, considered in relation to nature, we call Spirit. Spirit is the Creator. Spirit hath life in itself. And man in all ages and countries embodies it in his language as the FATHER.

It is easily seen that there is nothing lucky or capricious in these analogies, but that they are constant, and pervade nature. These are not the dreams of a few poets, here and there, but man is an analogist, and studies relations in all objects. He is placed in the centre of beings, and a ray of relation passes from every other being to him. And neither can man be understood without these objects, nor these objects without man. All the facts in natural history taken by themselves, have no value, but are barren, like a single sex. But marry it to human history, and it is full of life. Whole floras, all Linnæus' and Buffon's volumes, are dry catalogues of facts; but the most trivial of these facts, the habit of a plant, the organs, or work, or noise of an insect, applied to the illustration of a fact in intellectual philosophy, or in any way associated to human nature, affects us in the most lively and agreeable manner. The seed of a plant,—to what affecting analogies in the nature of man is that little fruit made use of, in all discourse, up to the voice of Paul, who calls the human corpse a seed,—"It is sown a natural body; it is raised a spiritual body." The motion of the earth round its axis and round the sun, makes the day and the year. These are certain amounts of brute light and heat. But is there no intent of an analogy between man's life and the seasons? And do the seasons gain no grandeur or pathos from that analogy? The instincts of the ant are very unimportant considered as the ant's; but the moment a ray of relation is seen to extend from it to man, and the little drudge is seen to be a monitor, a little body with a mighty heart, then all its habits, even that said to be recently observed, that it never sleeps, become sublime.

Because of this radical correspondence between visible things and human thoughts, savages, who have only what is necessary, converse in figures. As we go back in history, language becomes more picturesque, until its infancy, when it is all poetry; or all spiritual facts are represented by natural symbols. The same symbols are found to make the original elements of all languages. It has moreover been observed, that the idioms of all languages approach each other in passages of the greatest eloquence and power. And as this is the first language, so is it the last. This immediate dependence of language upon nature, this conversion of an outward phenomenon into a type of somewhat in human life, never loses its power to affect us. It is this which gives that piquancy to the conversation of a strong-natured farmer or backwoodsman, which all men relish.

A man's power to connect his thought with its proper symbol, and so to utter it, depends on the simplicity of his character, that is, upon his love of truth and his desire to communicate it without loss. The corruption of man is followed by the corruption of language. When simplicity of character and the sovereignty of ideas is broken up by the prevalence of secondary desires,—the desire of riches, of pleasure, of power, and of praise,—and duplicity and falsehood take place of simplicity and truth, the power over nature as an interpreter of the will is in a degree lost; new imagery ceases to be created, and old words are perverted to stand for things which are not; a paper currency is employed, when there is no bullion in the vaults. In due time the fraud is manifest, and words lose all power to stimulate the understanding or the affections. Hundreds of writers may be found in every long-civilized nation who for a short time believe and make others believe that they see and utter truths, who do not of themselves clothe one thought in its natural garment, but who feed unconsciously on the language created by the primary writers of the country, those, namely, who hold primarily on nature.

But wise men pierce this rotten diction and fasten words again to visible things; so that picturesque language is at once a commanding certificate that he who employs it is a man in alliance with truth and God. The moment our discourse rises above the ground line of familiar facts and is inflamed with passion or exalted by thought, it clothes itself in images. A man conversing in earnest, if he watch his intellectual processes, will find that a material image more or less luminous arises in his mind, contemporaneous with every thought, which furnishes the vestment of the thought. Hence, good writing and brilliant discourse are perpetual allegories. This imagery is spontaneous. It is the blending of experience with the present action of the mind. It is proper creation. It is the working of the Original Cause through the instruments he has already made.

These facts may suggest the advantage which the country-life possesses, for a powerful mind, over the artificial and curtailed life of cities. We know more from nature than we can at will communicate. Its light flows into the mind evermore, and we forget its presence. The poet, the orator, bred in the woods, whose senses have been nourished by their fair and appeasing changes, year after year, without design and without heed,— shall not lose their lesson altogether, in the roar of cities or the broil of politics. Long hereafter, amidst agitation and terror in national councils,—in the hour of revolution,—these solemn images shall reappear in their morning lustre, as fit symbols and words of the thoughts which the passing events shall awaken. At the call of a noble sentiment, again the woods wave, the pines murmur, the river rolls and shines, and the cattle low upon the mountains, as he saw and heard them in his infancy. And with these forms, the spells of persuasion, the keys of power are put into his hands.

3. We are thus assisted by natural objects in the expression of particular meanings. But how great a language to convey such pepper-corn informations! Did it need such noble races of creatures, this profusion of forms, this host of orbs in heaven, to furnish man with the dictionary and grammar of his municipal speech? Whilst we use this grand cipher to expedite the affairs of our pot and kettle, we feel that we have not yet put it to its use, neither are able. We are like travellers using the cinders of a volcano to roast their eggs. Whilst we see that it always stands ready to clothe what we would say, we cannot avoid the question whether the characters are not significant of themselves. Have mountains, and waves, and skies, no significance but what we consciously give them when we employ them as emblems of our thoughts? The world is emblematic. Parts of speech are metaphors, because the whole of nature is a metaphor of the human mind. The laws of moral nature answer to those of matter as face to face in a glass. "The visible world and the relation of its parts, is the dial plate of the invisible." The axioms of physics translate the laws of ethics. Thus, "the whole is greater than its part;" "reaction is equal to action;" "the smallest weight may be made to lift the greatest, the difference of weight being compensated by time;" and many the like pro-

positions, which have an ethical as well as physical sense. These propositions have a much more extensive and universal sense when applied to human life, than when confined to technical use.

In like manner, the memorable words of history and the proverbs of nations consist usually of a natural fact, selected as a picture or parable of a moral truth. Thus; A rolling stone gathers no moss; A bird in the hand is worth two in the bush; A cripple in the right way will beat a racer in the wrong; Make hay while the sun shines; 'T is hard to carry a full cup even; Vinegar is the son of wine; The last ounce broke the camel's back; Long-lived trees make roots first;—and the like. In their primary sense these are trivial facts, but we repeat them for the value of their analogical import. What is true of proverbs, is true of all fables, parables, and allegories.

This relation between the mind and matter is not fancied by some poet, but stands in the will of God, and so is free to be known by all men. It appears to men, or it does not appear. When in fortunate hours we ponder this miracle, the wise man doubts if at all other times he is not blind and deaf;

> "Can such things be,
> And overcome us like a summer's cloud,
> Without our special wonder?"

for the universe becomes transparent, and the light of higher laws than its own shines through it. It is the standing problem which has exercised the wonder and the study of every fine genius since the world began; from the era of the Egyptians and the Brahmins to that of Pythagoras, of Plato, of Bacon, of Leibnitz, of Swedenborg. There sits the Sphinx at the road-side, and from age to age, as each prophet comes by, he tries his fortune at reading her riddle. There seems to be a necessity in spirit to manifest itself in material forms; and day and night, river and storm, beast and bird, acid and alkali, preexist in necessary Ideas in the mind of God, and are what they are by virtue of preceding affections in the world of spirit. A Fact is the end or last issue of spirit. The visible creation is the terminus or the circumference of the invisible world. "Material objects," said a French philosopher, "are necessarily kinds of *scoriæ* of the substantial thoughts of the Creator, which must always preserve an exact relation to their first origin; in other words, visible nature must have a spiritual and moral side."

This doctrine is abstruse, and though the images of "garment," "scoriæ," "mirror," etc., may stimulate the fancy, we must summon the aid of subtler and more vital expositors to make it plain. "Every scripture is to be interpreted by the same spirit which gave it forth,"—is the fundamental law of criticism. A life in harmony with Nature, the love of truth and of virtue, will purge the eyes to understand her text. By degrees we may come to know the primitive sense of the permanent objects of nature, so that the world shall be to us an open book, and every form significant of its hidden life and final cause.

A new interest surprises us, whilst, under the view now suggested, we contemplate the fearful extent and multitude of objects; since "every object rightly seen, unlocks a new faculty of the soul." That which was unconscious truth, becomes, when interpreted and defined in an object, a part of the domain of knowledge,—a new weapon in the magazine of power.

# V

## Discipline

In view of the significance of nature, we arrive at once at a new fact, that nature is a discipline. This use of the world includes the preceding uses, as parts of itself.

Space, time, society, labor, climate, food, locomotion, the animals, the mechanical forces, give us sincerest lessons, day by day, whose meaning is unlimited. They educate both the Understanding and the Reason. Every property of matter is a school for the understanding,—its solidity or resistance, its inertia, its extension, its figure, its divisibility. The understanding adds, divides, combines, measures, and finds nutriment and room for its activity in this worthy scene. Meantime, Reason transfers all these lessons into its own world of thought, by perceiving the analogy that marries Matter and Mind.

1. Nature is discipline of the understanding in intellectual truths. Our dealing with sensible objects is a constant exercise in the necessary lessons of difference, of likeness, of order, of being and seeming, of progressive arrangement; of ascent from particular to general; of combination to one end of manifold forces. Proportioned to the importance of the organ to be formed, is the extreme care with which its tuition is provided,—a care pretermitted in no single case. What tedious training, day

after day, year after year, never ending, to form the common sense; what continual reproduction of annoyances, inconveniences, dilemmas; what disputing of prices, what reckonings of interest,—and all to form the Hand of the mind;—to instruct us that "good thoughts are no better than good dreams, unless they be executed!"

The same good office is performed by Property and its filial systems of debt and credit. Debt, grinding debt, whose iron face the widow, the orphan, and the sons of genius fear and hate;—debt, which consumes so much time, which so cripples and disheartens a great spirit with cares that seem so base, is a preceptor whose lessons cannot be foregone, and is needed most by those who suffer from it most. Moreover, property, which has been well compared to snow,—"if it fall level to-day, it will be blown into drifts to-morrow,"—is the surface action of internal machinery, like the index on the face of a clock. Whilst now it is the gymnastics of the understanding, it is hiving, in the foresight of the spirit, experience in profounder laws.

The whole character and fortune of the individual are affected by the least inequalities in the culture of the understanding; for example, in the perception of differences. Therefore is Space, and therefore Time, that man may know that things are not huddled and lumped, but sundered and individual. A bell and a plough have each their use, and neither can do the office of the other. Water is good to drink, coal to burn, wool to wear; but wool cannot be drunk, nor water spun, nor coal eaten. The wise man shows his wisdom in separation, in gradation, and his scale of creatures and of merits is as wide as nature. The foolish have no range in their scale, but suppose every man is as every other man. What is not good they call the worst, and what is not hateful, they call the best.

In like manner, what good heed Nature forms in us! She pardons no mistakes. Her yea is yea, and her nay, nay.

The first steps in Agriculture, Astronomy, Zoology (those first steps which the farmer, the hunter, and the sailor take), teach that Nature's dice are always loaded; that in her heaps and rubbish are concealed sure and useful results.

How calmly and genially the mind apprehends one after another the laws of physics! What noble emotions dilate the mortal as he enters into the councils of the creation, and feels by knowledge the privilege to BE! His insight refines him. The beauty of nature shines in his own breast.

Man is greater that he can see this, and the universe less, because Time and Space relations vanish as laws are known.

Here again we are impressed and even daunted by the immense Universe to be explored. "What we know is a point to what we do not know." Open any recent journal of science, and weigh the problems suggested concerning Light, Heat, Electricity, Magnetism, Physiology, Geology, and judge whether the interest of natural science is likely to be soon exhausted.

Passing by many particulars of the discipline of nature, we must not omit to specify two.

The exercise of the Will, or the lesson of power, is taught in every event. From the child's successive possession of his several senses up to the hour when he saith, "Thy will be done!" he is learning the secret that he can reduce under his will not only particular events, and so conform all facts to his character. Nature is thoroughly mediate. It is made to serve. It receives the dominion of man as meekly as the ass on which the Savior rode. It offers all its kingdoms to man as the raw material which he may mould into what is useful. Man is never weary of working it up. He forges the subtile and delicate air into wise and melodious words, and gives them wing as angels of persuasion and command. One after another his victorious thought comes up with and reduces all things, until the world becomes at last only a realized will,—the double of the man.

2. Sensible objects conform to the premonitions of Reason and reflect the conscience. All things are moral; and in their boundless changes have an unceasing reference to spiritual nature. Therefore is nature glorious with form, color, and motion; that every globe in the remotest heaven, every chemical change from the rudest crystal up to the laws of life, every change of vegetation from the first principle of growth in the eye of a leaf, to the tropical forest and antediluvian coal-mine, every animal function from the sponge up to Hercules, shall hint or thunder to man the laws of right and wrong, and echo the Ten Commandments. Therefore is Nature ever the ally of Religion: lends all her pomp and riches to the religious sentiment. Prophet and priest, David, Isaiah, Jesus, have drawn deeply from this source. This ethical character so penetrates the bone and marrow of nature, as to seem the end for which it is made. What ever private purpose is answered by any member or part, this is its public and universal function, and is never omitted. Nothing in nature is exhausted in

its first use. When a thing has served an end to the uttermost, it is wholly new for an ulterior service. In God, every end is converted into a new means. Thus the use commodity, regarded by itself, is mean and squalid. But it is to the mind an education in the doctrine of Use, namely, that a thing is good only so far as it serves; that a conspiring of parts and efforts to the production of an end is essential to any being. The first and gross manifestation of this truth is our inevitable and hated training in values and wants, in corn and meat.

It has already been illustrated, that every natural process is a version of a moral sentence. The moral law lies at the centre of nature and radiates to the circumference. It is the pith and marrow of every substance, every relation, and every process. All things with which we deal, preach to us. What is a farm but a mute gospel? The chaff and the wheat, weeds and plants, blight, rain, insects, sun,—it is a sacred emblem from the first furrow of spring to the last stack which the snow of winter overtakes in the fields. But the sailor, the shepherd, the miner, the merchant, in their several resorts, have each an experience precisely parallel, and leading to the same conclusion; because all organizations are radically alike. Nor can it be doubted that this moral sentiment which thus scents the air, grows in the grain, and impregnates the waters of the world, is caught by man and sinks into his soul. The moral influence of nature upon every individual is that amount of truth which it illustrates to him. Who can estimate this? Who can guess how much firmness the sea-beaten rock has taught the fisherman? how much tranquillity has been reflected to man from the azure sky, over whose unspotted deeps the winds forevermore drive flocks of stormy clouds, and leave no wrinkle or stain? how much industry and providence and affection we have caught from the pantomime of brutes? What a searching preacher of self-command is the varying phenomenon of Health!

Herein is especially apprehended the unity of Nature,—the unity in variety,—which meets us everywhere. All the endless variety of things make an identical impression. Xenophanes complained in his old age, that, look where he would, all the things hastened back to Unity. He was weary of seeing the same entity in the tedious variety of forms. The fable of Proteus has a cordial truth. A leaf, a drop, a crystal, a moment of time, is related to the whole, and partakes of the perfection of the whole. Each particle is a microcosm, and faithfully renders the likeness of the world.

Not only resemblances exist in things whose analogy is obvious, as when we detect the type of the human hand in the flipper of the fossil saurus, but also in objects wherein there is great superficial unlikeness. Thus architecture is called "frozen music," by De Staël and Goethe. Vitruvius thought an architect should be a musician. "A Gothic church," said Coleridge, "is a petrified religion." Michael Angelo maintained, that, to an architect, a knowledge of anatomy is essential. In Haydn's oratorios, the notes present to the imagination not only motions, as of the snake, the stag, and the elephant, but colors also; as the green grass. The law of harmonic sounds reappears in the harmonic colors. The granite is differenced in its laws only by the more less of heat from the river that wears it away. The river, as it flows, resembles the air that flows over it; the air resembles the light which traverses it with more subtile currents; the light resembles the heat which rides with it through Space. Each creature is only a modification of the other; the likeness in them is more than the difference, and their radical law is one and the same. A rule of one art, or a law of one organization, holds true throughout nature. So intimate is this Unity, that, it is easily seen, it lies under the undermost garment of Nature, and betrays its source in Universal Spirit. For it pervades Thought also. Every universal truth which we express in words, implies or supposes every other truth. *Omne verum vero consonat*. It is like a great circle on a sphere, comprising all possible circles; which, however, may be drawn and comprise it in like manner. Every such truth is the absolute Ens seen from one side. But it has innumerable sides.

The central Unity is still more conspicuous in actions. Words are finite organs of the infinite mind. They cannot cover the dimensions of what is in truth. They break, chop, and impoverish it. An action is the perfection and publication of thought. A right action seems to fill the eye, and to be related to all nature. "The wise man, in doing one thing, does all; or, in the one thing he does rightly, he sees the likeness of all which is done rightly."

Words and actions are not the attributes of brute nature. They introduce us to the human form, of which all other organizations appear to be degradations. When this appears among so many that surround it, the spirit prefers it to all others. It says, "From such as this have I drawn joy and knowledge; in such as this have I found and beheld myself; I will speak to it; it can speak again; it can yield me thought already formed and alive." In fact, the eye,—the mind,—is always accompanied by these forms, male and female; and these are incomparably the richest informations of the power and order that lie at the heart of things. Unfortunately every one of them bears the marks as of some injury; is marred and superficially defective. Nevertheless, far different from the deaf and dumb nature around them, these all rest like fountain-pipes on the unfathomed sea of thought and virtue whereto they alone, of all organizations, are the entrances.

It were a pleasant inquiry to follow into detail their ministry to our education, but where would it stop? We are associated in adolescent and adult life with some friends, who, like skies and waters, are coextensive with our idea; who, answering each to a certain affection of the soul, satisfy our desire on that side; whom we lack power to put at such focal distance from us, that we can mend or even analyze them. We cannot choose but love them. When much intercourse with a friend has supplied us with a standard of excellence, and has increased our respect for the resources of God who thus sends a real person to outgo our ideal; when he has, moreover, become an object of thought, and, whilst his character retains all its unconscious effect, is converted in the mind into solid and sweet wisdom,—it is a sign to us that his office is closing, and he is commonly withdrawn from our sight in a short time.

# VI

## Idealism

Thus is the unspeakable but intelligible and practicable meaning of the world conveyed to man, the immortal pupil, in every object of sense. To this one end of Discipline, all parts of nature conspire.

A noble doubt perpetually suggests itself,—whether this end be not the Final Cause of the Universe; and whether nature outwardly exists. It is a sufficient account of that Appearance we call the World, that God will teach a human mind, and so makes it the receiver of a certain number of congruent sensations, which we call sun and moon, man and woman, house and trade. In my utter impotence to test the authenticity of the report of my senses, to know whether the impressions they make on me correspond with outlying objects, what a difference does it make, whether Orion is up there in heaven, or some god paints the image in the firmament of the soul? The relations of parts and the end of the whole remaining the same, what is the difference, whether land and sea interact, and worlds revolve and intermingle without number or end,—deep yawning under deep, and galaxy balancing galaxy, throughout absolute space,—or whether, without relations of time and space, the same appearances are inscribed in the constant faith of man? Whether nature enjoy a substantial existence without, or is only in the apocalypse of the mind, it is alike useful and alike venerable to me. Be it what it may, it is ideal to me so long as I cannot try the accuracy of my senses.

The frivolous make themselves merry with the Ideal theory, as if its consequences were burlesque; as if it affected the stability of nature. It surely does not. God never jests with us, and will not compromise the end of nature by permitting any inconsequence in its procession. Any distrust of the permanence of laws would paralyze the faculties of man. Their permanence is sacredly respected, and his faith therein is perfect. The wheels and springs of man are all set to the hypothesis of the permanence of nature. We are not built like a ship to be tossed, but like a house to stand. It is a natural consequence of this structure, that so long as the active powers predominate over the reflective, we resist with indignation any hint that nature is more short-lived or mutable than spirit. The broker, the wheelwright, the carpenter, the tollman, are much displeased at the intimation.

But whilst we acquiesce entirely in the permanence of natural laws, the question of the absolute existence of nature still remains open. It is the uniform effect of culture on the human mind, not to shake our faith in the stability of particular phenomena, as of heat, water, azote; but to lead us to regard nature as phenomenon, not a substance; to attribute necessary existence to spirit; to esteem nature as an accident and an effect.

To the senses and the unrenewed understanding, belongs a sort of instinctive belief in the absolute existence of nature. In their view man and nature are indissolubly joined. Things are ultimates, and they never look beyond their sphere. The presence of Reason mars this faith. The first effort of thought tends to relax this despotism of the senses which binds us to nature as if we were a part of it, and shows us nature aloof, and, as it were, afloat. Until this higher agency intervened, the animal eye sees, with wonderful accuracy, sharp outlines and colored surfaces. When the eye of Reason opens, to outline and surface are at once added grace and expression. These proceed from imagination and affection, and abate somewhat of the angular distinctness of objects. If the Reason be stimulated to more earnest vision, outlines and surfaces become transparent, and are no longer seen; causes and spirits are seen through them.

The best moments of life are these delicious awakenings of the higher powers, and the reverential withdrawing of nature before its God.

Let us proceed to indicate the effects of culture.

1. Our first institution in the Ideal philosophy is a hint from Nature herself.

Nature is made to conspire with spirit to emancipate us. Certain mechanical changes, a small alteration in our local position, apprizes us of a dualism. We are strangely affected by seeing the shore from a moving ship, from a balloon, or through the tints of an unusual sky. The least change in our point of view gives the whole world a pictorial air. A man who seldom rides, needs only to get into a coach and traverse his own town, to turn the street into a puppet show. The men, the women,—talking, running, bartering, fighting,—the earnest mechanic, the lounger, the beggar, the boys, the dogs, are unrealized at once, or, at least, wholly detached from all relation to the observer, and seen as apparent, not substantial beings. What new thoughts are suggested by seeing a face of country quite familiar, in the rapid movement of the railroad car! Nay, the most wanted objects, (make a very slight change in the point of vision,) please us most. In a camera obscura, the butcher's cart, and the figure of one of our own family amuse us. So a portrait of a well-known face gratifies us. Turn the eyes upside down, by looking at the landscape through your legs, and how agreeable is the picture, though you have seen it any time these twenty years!

In these cases, by mechanical means, is suggested the difference between the observer and the spectacle—between man and nature. Hence arises a pleasure mixed with awe; I may say, a low degree of the sublime is felt, from the fact, probably, that man is hereby apprized that whilst the world is a spectacle, something in himself is stable.

# *from* Walden

*Henry David Thoreau*

## Economy

Let us consider for a moment what most of the trouble and anxiety which I have referred to is about and how much it is necessary that we be troubled, or at least careful. It would be some advantage to live a primitive and frontier life, though in the midst of an outward civilization, if only to learn what are the gross necessaries of life and what methods have been taken to obtain them; or even to look over the old day-books of the merchants, to see what it was that men most commonly bought at the stores, what they stored, that is, what are the grossest groceries. For the improvements of ages have had but little influence on the essential laws of man's existence: as our skeletons, probably, are not to be distinguished from those of our ancestors.

By the words, *necessary of life*, I mean whatever, of all that man obtains by his own exertions, has been from the first, or from long use has become, so important to human life that few, if any, whether from savageness, or poverty, or philosophy, ever attempt to do without it. To many creatures there is in this sense but one necessary of life, Food. To the bison of the prairie it is a few inches of palatable grass, with water to drink; unless he seeks the Shelter of the forest or the mountain's shadow. None of the brute creation requires more than Food and Shelter. The necessaries of life for man in this climate may, accurately enough, be distributed under the several heads of Food, Shelter, Clothing, and Fuel; for not till we have secured these are we prepared to entertain the true problems of life with freedom and a prospect of success. Man has invented, not only houses, but clothes and cooked food; and possibly from the accidental discovery of the warmth of fire, and the consequent use of it, at first a luxury, arose the present necessity to sit by it. We observe cats and dogs acquiring the same second nature. By proper Shelter and Clothing we legitimately retain our own internal heat; but with an excess of these, or of Fuel, that is, with an external heat greater than our own internal, may not cookery properly be said to begin? Darwin, the naturalist, says of the inhabitants of Tierra del Fuego, that while his own party, who were well clothed and

566

sitting close to a fire, were far from too warm, these naked savages, who were farther off, were observed, to his great surprise, "to be streaming with perspiration at undergoing such a roasting." So, we are told, the New Hollander goes naked with impunity, while the European shivers in his clothes. Is it impossible to combine the hardiness of these savages with the intellectualness of the civilized man? According to Liebig, man's body is a stove, and food the fuel which keeps up the internal combustion in the lungs. In cold weather we eat more, in warm less. The animal heat is the result of a slow combustion, and disease and death take place when this is too rapid: or for want of fuel. or from some defect in the draught, the fire goes out. Of course the vital heat is not to be confounded with fire; but so much for analogy. It appears, therefore, from the above list, that the expression, *animal life*, is nearly synonymous with the expression, *animal heat*; for while Food may be regarded as the Fuel which keeps up the fire within us,—and Fuel serves only to prepare that Food or to increase the warmth of our bodies by addition from without,—Shelter and Clothing also serve only to retain the *heat* thus generated and absorbed.

The grand necessity, then, for our bodies, is to keep warm, to keep the vital heat in us. What pains we accordingly take, not only with our Food, and Clothing, and Shelter, but with our beds, which are our nightclothes, robbing the nests and breasts of birds to prepare this shelter within a shelter, as the mole has its bed of grass and leaves at the end of its burrow! The poor man is wont to complain that this is a cold world; and to cold, no less physical than social, we refer directly a great part of our ails. The summer, in some climates, makes possible to man a sort of Elysian life. Fuel, except to cook his Food, is then unnecessary; the sun is his fire, and many of the fruits are sufficiently cooked by its rays; while Food generally is more various, and more easily obtained, and Clothing and Shelter are wholly or half unnecessary. At the present day, and in this country, as I find by my own experience, a few implements, a knife, an axe, a spade, a wheelbarrow, etc., and for the studious, lamplight, stationery, and access to a few books, rank next to necessaries, and can all be obtained at a trifling cost. Yet some, not wise, go to the other side of the globe, to barbarous and unhealthy regions, and devote themselves to trade for ten or twenty years, in order that they may live,—that is, keep comfortably warm,—and die in New England at last. The luxuriously rich are not simply kept comfortably warm, but unnaturally hot: as I implied before, they are cooked, of course *à la mode*.

Most of the luxuries, and many of the so-called comforts of life, are not only not indispensable, but positive hindrances to the elevation of mankind. With respect to luxuries and comforts, the wisest have ever lived a more simple and meagre life than the poor. The ancient philosophers, Chinese, Hindoo, Persian, and Greek, were a class than which none has been poorer in outward riches, none so rich in inward. We know not much about them. It is remarkable that we know so much of them as we do. The same is true of the more modern reformers and benefactors of their race. None can be an impartial or wise observer of human life but from the vantage ground of what we should call voluntary poverty. Of a life of luxury the fruit is luxury, whether in agriculture, or commerce, or literature, or art. There are nowadays professors of philosophy, but not philosophers. Yet it is admirable to profess because it was once admirable to live. To be a philosopher is not merely to have subtle thoughts, nor even to found a school, but so to love wisdom as to live according to its dictates, a life of simplicity, independence, magnanimity, and trust. It is to solve some of the problems of life, not only theoretically, but practically. The success of great scholars and thinkers is commonly a courtier-like success, not kingly, not manly. They make shift to live merely by conformity, practically as their fathers did, and are in no sense the progenitors of a nobler race of men. But why do men degenerate ever? What makes families run out? What is the nature of the luxury which enervates and destroys nations? Are we sure that there is none of it in our own lives? The philosopher is in advance of his age even in the outward form of his life. He is not fed, sheltered, clothed, warmed, like his contemporaries. How can a man be a philosopher and not maintain his vital heat by better methods than other men?

When a man is warmed by the several modes which I have described, what does he want next? Surely not more warmth of the same kind, as more and richer food, larger and more splendid houses, finer and more abundant clothing, more numerous, incessant, and hotter fires, and the like. When he has obtained those things which are necessary to life, there is another alternative than to obtain the superfluities; and that is, to adventure on life now, his vacation from humbler toil having commenced. The soil, it appears, is suited to the seed, for it has sent its radicle downward, and it may now send its shoot upward also with confidence. Why has man rooted himself thus firmly in the earth, but that he may rise in the same proportion into the heavens above?—for the nobler plants are valued for the fruit they bear at last in the air and light, far from the ground, and are not treated like the humbler esculents, which, though they may be biennials, are cultivated only till they have perfected their root, and often cut down at top for this purpose, so that most would not know them in their flowering season.

I do not mean to prescribe rules to strong and valiant natures, who will mind their own affairs whether in heaven or hell, and perchance build more magnificently and spend more lavishly than the richest, without ever impoverishing themselves, not knowing how they live,—if, indeed, there are any such, as has been dreamed nor to those who find their encouragement and inspiration in precisely the present condition of things, and cherish it with the fondness and enthusiasm of lovers,—and, to some extent, I reckon myself in this number; I do not speak to those who are well employed, in whatever circumstances, and they know whether they are well employed or not;—but mainly to the mass of men who are discontented, and idly complaining of the hardness of their lot or of the times, when they might improve them. There are some who complain most energetically and inconsolably of any, because they are, as they say, doing their duty. I also have in my mind that seemingly wealthy, but most terribly impoverished class of all, who have accumulated dross, but know not how to use it, or get rid of it, and thus have forged their own golden or silver fetters.

• • •

However, if one designs to construct a dwelling-house, it behooves him to exercise a little Yankee shrewdness, lest after all he find himself in a workhouse, a labyrinth without a clue, a museum, an almshouse, a prison, or a splendid mausoleum instead. Consider first how slight a shelter is absolutely necessary. I have seen Penobscot Indians, in this town, living in tents of thin cotton cloth, while the snow was nearly a foot deep around them, and I thought that they would be glad to have it deeper to keep out the wind. Formerly, when how to get my living honestly, with freedom left for my proper pursuits, was a question which vexed me even more than it does now, for unfortunately I am become somewhat callous, I used to see a large box by the railroad, six feet long by three wide, in which the laborers locked up their tools at night; and it suggested to me that every man who was hard pushed might get such a one for a dollar, and, having bored a few auger holes in it, to admit the air at least, get into it when it rained and at night, and hook down the lid, and so have freedom in his love, and in his soul be free. This did not appear the worst, nor by any means a despicable alternative. You could sit up as late as you pleased, and, whenever you got up, go abroad without any landlord or house-lord dogging you for rent. Many a man is harassed to death to pay the rent of a larger and more luxurious box who would not have frozen to death in such a box as this. I am far from jesting. Economy is a subject which admits of being treated with levity, but it cannot so be disposed of. A comfortable house for a rude and hardy race, that lived mostly out of doors, was once made here almost entirely of such materials as Nature furnished ready to their hands. Gookin, who was superintendent of the Indians subject to the Massachusetts Colony, writing in 1674, says, "The best of their houses are covered very neatly, tight and warm, with barks of trees, slipped from their bodies at those seasons when the sap is up, and made into great flakes, with pressure of weighty timber, when they are green. . . . The meaner sort are covered with mats which they make of a kind of bulrush, and are also indifferently tight and warm, but not so good as the former. . . . Some I have seen, sixty or a hundred feet long and thirty feet broad. . . . I have often lodged in their wigwams, and found them as warm as the best English houses." He adds that they were commonly carpeted and lined within with well-wrought embroidered mats, and were furnished with various utensils. The Indians had advanced so far as to regulate the effect of the wind by a mat suspended over the hole in the roof and moved by a string. Such a lodge was in the first instance constructed in a day or two at most, and taken down and put up in a few hours; and every family owned one, or its apartment in one.

In the savage state every family owns a shelter as good as the best, and sufficient for its coarser and simpler wants; but I think that I speak within bounds when I say that, though the birds of the air have their nests, and the foxes their holes, and the savages their wigwams, in modern civilized society not more than one half the families own a shelter. In the large towns and cities, where civilization especially prevails, the number of those who own a shelter is a very small fraction of the whole. The rest pay an annual tax for this outside garment of all, become indispensable summer and winter, which would buy a village of Indian wigwams, but now helps to keep them poor as long as they live. I do not mean to insist here on the disadvantage of hiring compared with owning, but it is evident that the savage owns his shelter because it costs so little, while the civilized man hires his commonly because he cannot afford to own it; nor can he, in the long run, any better afford to hire. But, answers one, by merely paying this tax the poor civilized man secures an abode which is a palace compared with the savage's. An annual rent of from twenty-five to a hundred dollars (these are the country rates) entitles him to the benefit of the improvements of centuries, spacious apartments, clean paint and paper, Rumford fireplace, back plastering, Venetian blinds, copper pump, spring lock, a commodious cellar, and many other things. But how happens it that he who is said to enjoy these things is so commonly a poor civilized man, while the savage, who has them not, is rich as a savage? If it is asserted that civilization is a real advance in the condition of man,—and I think that it is, though only the wise improve their advantages,—it must be shown that it has produced better dwellings without making them more costly; and the cost of a thing is the amount of what I will call life which is required to be exchanged for it, immediately or in the long run. An average house in this neighborhood costs perhaps eight hundred dollars, and to lay up this sum will take from ten to fifteen years of the laborer's life, even if he is not encumbered with a family,—estimating the pecuniary value of every man's labor at one dollar a day, for if some receive more, others receive less;—so that he must have spent more than half his life commonly before his wigwam will he earned. If we suppose him to pay a rent instead, this is but a doubtful choice of evils. Would the savage have been wise to exchange his wigwam for a palace on these terms?

• • •

## Higher Laws

Such is oftenest the young man's introduction to the forest, and the most original part of himself. He goes thither at first as a hunter and fisher, until at last, if he has the seeds of a better life in him, he distinguishes his proper objects, as a poet or naturalist it may be, and leaves the gun and fish-pole behind. The mass of men are still and always young in this respect. In some countries a hunting parson is no uncommon sight. Such a one might make a good shepherd's dog, but is far from being the Good Shepherd. I have been surprised to consider that the only obvious employment, except wood-chopping, ice-cutting, or the like business, which ever to my knowledge detained at Walden Pond for a whole half-day any of my fellow-citizens, whether fathers or children of the town, with just one exception, was fishing. Commonly they did not think that they were lucky, or well paid for their time, unless they got a long string of fish, though they had the opportunity of seeing the pond all the while. They might go there a thousand times before the sediment of fishing would sink to the bottom and leave their purpose pure; but no doubt such a clarifying process would be going on all the while. The Governor and his Council faintly remember the pond, for they went a-fishing there when they were boys; but now they are too old and dignified to go a-fishing, and so they know it no more forever. Yet even they expect to go to heaven at last. If the legislature regards it, it is chiefly to regulate the number of hooks to be used there; but they know nothing about the hook of hooks with which to angle for the pond itself, impaling the legislature for a bait. Thus, even in civilized communities, the embryo man passes through the hunter stage of development.

I have found repeatedly, of late years, that I cannot fish without falling a little in self-respect. I have tried it again and again. I have skill at it, and, like many of my fellows, a certain instinct for it, which revives from time to time, but always when I have done I feel that it would have been better if I had not fished. I think that I do not mistake. It is a faint intimation, yet so are the first streaks of morning. There is unquestionably this instinct in me which belongs to the lower orders of creation; yet with every year I am less a fisherman, though without more humanity or even wisdom; at present I am no fisherman at all. But I see that if I were to live in a wilderness I should again he tempted to become a fisher and hunter in earnest. Beside, there is something essentially unclean about this diet and all flesh, and I began to see where housework commences, and whence the endeavor, which costs so much, to wear a tidy and respectable appearance each day, to keep the house sweet and free from all ill odors and sights. Having been my own butcher and scullion and cook, as well as the gentleman for whom the dishes were served up, I can speak from an unusually complete experience. The practical objection to animal food in my case was its uncleanness; and besides. when I had caught and cleaned and cooked and eaten my fish, they seemed not to have fed me essentially. It was insignificant and unnecessary, and cost more than it came to. A little bread or a few potatoes would have done as well, with less trouble and filth. Like many of my contemporaries, I had rarely for many years used animal food, or tea, or coffee, etc.; not so much because of any ill effects which I had traced to them, as because they were not agreeable to my imagination. The repugnance to animal food is not the effect of experience, but is an instinct. It appeared more beautiful to live low and fare hard in many respects; and though I never did so, I went far enough to please my imagination. I believe that every man who has ever been earnest to preserve his higher or poetic faculties in the best condition has been particularly inclined to abstain from animal food, and from much food of any kind. It is a significant fact, stated by entomologists,—I find it in Kirby and Spence,—that "some insects in their perfect state, though furnished with organs of feeding, make no use of them;" and they lay it down as "a general rule, that almost all insects in this state eat much less than in that of larvae. The voracious caterpillar when transformed into a butterfly . . . and the gluttonous maggot when become a fly" content themselves with a drop or two of honey or some other sweet liquid. The abdomen under the wings of the butterfly still represents the larva. This is the tidbit which tempts his insectivorous fate. The gross feeder is a man in the larva state; and there are whole nations in that condition, nations without fancy or imagination, whose vast abdomens betray them.

It is hard to provide and cook so simple and clean a diet as will not offend the imagination; but this, I think, is to be fed when we feed the body; they should both sit down at the same table. Yet perhaps this may be done. The fruits eaten temperately need not make us ashamed of our appetites, nor interrupt the worthiest pursuits. But put an extra condiment into your dish, and it will poison you. It is not worth the while to live by rich cookery. Most men would feel shame if caught preparing with their own hands precisely such a dinner, whether of animal or vegetable food, as is every day prepared for them by others. Yet till this is otherwise we are not civilized, and, if gentlemen and ladies, are not true men and women. This certainly suggests what change is to be made. It may be vain to ask why the imagination will not be reconciled to flesh and fat. I am satisfied that it is not. Is it not a reproach that man is a carnivorous animal? True, he can and does live, in a great measure, by preying on other animals; but this is a miserable way,—as any one who will go to snaring rabbits. or slaughtering lambs, may learn,—and he will be regarded as a benefactor of his race who shall teach man to confine himself to a more innocent and wholesome diet. Whatever my own practice may be, I have no doubt that it is a part of the destiny of the human race, in its gradual improvement, to leave off eating animals, as surely as the savage tribes have left off eating each other when they came in contact with the more civilized.

If one listens to the faintest but constant suggestions of his genius, which are certainly true, he sees not to what extremes, or even insanity, it may lead him; and yet that way, as he grows more resolute and faithful, his road lies. The faintest assured objection which one healthy man feels will at length prevail over the arguments and customs of mankind. No man ever followed. his genius till it misled him. Though the result were bodily weakness, yet perhaps no one can say that the consequences were to be regretted, for these were a life in conformity to higher principles. If the day and the night are such that you greet them with joy, and life emits a fragrance like flowers and sweet-scented herbs, is more elastic, more starry, more immortal,—that is your success. All nature is your congratulation, and you have cause momentarily to bless yourself. The greatest gains and values are farthest from being appreciated. We easily come to doubt if they exist. We soon forget them. They are the highest reality. Perhaps the facts most astounding and most real are never communicated by man to man. The true harvest of my daily life is somewhat as intangible and indescribable as the tints of morning or evening. It is a little star-dust caught, a segment of the rainbow which I have clutched.

Yet, for my part, I was never unusually squeamish; I could sometimes eat a fried rat with a good relish, if it were necessary. I am glad to have drunk water so long, for the same reason that I prefer the natural sky to an opium-eater's heaven. I would fain keep sober always; and there are infinite degrees of drunkenness. I believe that water is the only drink for a wise man: wine is not so noble a liquor; and think of dashing the hopes of a morning with a cup of warm coffee, or of an evening with a dish of tea! Ah, how low I fall when I am tempted by them! Even music may be intoxicating. Such apparently slight causes destroyed Greece and Rome, and will destroy England and America. Of all ebriosity, who does not prefer to be intoxicated by the air he breathes? I have found it to be the most serious objection to coarse labors long continued, that they compelled me to eat and drink coarsely also. But to tell the truth, I find myself at present somewhat less particular in these respects. I carry less religion to the table, ask no blessing; not because I am wiser than I was, but, I am obliged to confess, because, however much it is to be regretted, with years I have grown more coarse and indifferent. Perhaps these questions are entertained only in youth, as most believe of poetry. My practice is "nowhere," my opinion is here. Nevertheless I am far from regarding myself as one of those privileged ones to whom the Ved refers to when it says that "he who has true faith in the Omnipresent Supreme Being may eat all that exists," that is, is not bound to inquire what is his food, or who prepares it; and even in their case it is to be observed, as a Hindoo commentator has remarked, that the Vedant limits this privilege to "the time of distress."

Who has not sometimes derived an inexpressible satisfaction from his food in which appetite had no share? I have been thrilled to think that I owed a mental perception to the commonly gross sense of taste, that I have been inspired through the palate, that some berries which I had eaten on a hillside had fed my genius. "The soul not being mistress of herself," says Thseng-tseu, "one looks, and one does not see; one listens, and one does not hear; one eats, and one does not know the savor of food." He who distinguishes the true savor of his food can never be a glutton; he who does not cannot be otherwise. A puritan may go to his brown-bread crust with as gross an appetite as ever an alderman to his turtle. Not that food which entereth into the mouth defileth a man, but the appetite with which it is eaten. It is neither the quality nor the quantity, but the devotion to sensual savors; when that which is eaten is not a viand to sustain our animal, or inspire our spiritual life, but food for the worms that possess us. If the hunter has a taste for mud-turtles, muskrats, and other such savage tidbits, the fine lady indulges a taste for jelly made of a calf's foot, or for sardines from over the sea, and they are even. He goes to the mill-pond, she to her preserve-pot. The wonder is how they, how you and I, can live this slimy, beastly life, eating and drinking.

Our whole life is startlingly moral. There is never an instant's truce between virtue and vice. Goodness is the only investment that never fails. In the music of the harp which trembles round the world it is the insisting on this which thrills us. The harp is the travelling patterer for the Universe's Insurance Company, recommending its laws, and our little goodness is all the assessment that we pay. Though the youth at last grows indifferent, the laws of the universe are not indifferent, but are forever on the side of the most sensitive. Listen to every zephyr for some reproof, for it is surely there, and he is unfortunate who does not hear it. We cannot touch a string or move a stop but the charming moral transfixes us. Many an irksome noise, go a long way off, is heard as music, a proud, sweet satire on the meanness of our lives.

We are conscious of an animal in us, which awakens in proportion as our higher nature slumbers. It is reptile and sensual, and perhaps cannot be wholly expelled: like the worms which, even in life and health, occupy our bodies. Possibly we may withdraw from it, but never change its nature. I fear that it may enjoy a certain health of its own; that we may be well, yet not pure. The other day I picked up the lower jaw of a hog, with white and sound teeth and tusks, which suggested that there was an animal health and vigor distinct from the spiritual. This creature succeeded by other means than temperance and purity. "That in which men differ from brute beasts," says Mencius, "is a thing very inconsiderable; the common herd lose it very soon; superior men preserve it carefully." Who knows what sort of life would result if we had attained to purity? If I knew so wise a man as could teach me purity I would go to seek him forthwith. "A command over our passions, and over the external senses of the body, and good acts, are declared by the Ved to be indispensable in the mind's approximation to God." Yet the spirit can for the time pervade and control every member and function of the body, and transmute what in form is the grossest sensuality into purity and devotion. The generative energy, which, when we are loose, dissipates and makes us unclean, when we are continent invigorates and inspires us. Chastity is the flowering of man; and what are called Genius, Heroism, Holiness, and the like, are but various fruits which succeed it. Man flows at once to God when the channel of purity is open. By turns our purity inspires and our impurity casts us down. He is blessed who is assured that the animal is dying out in him day by day, and the divine being established. Perhaps there is none but has cause for shame on account of the inferior and brutish nature to which he is allied. I fear that we are such gods or demigods only as fauns and satyrs, the divine allied to beasts, the creatures of appetite, and that, to some extent, our very life is our disgrace.—

"How happy's he who hath due place assigned
To his beasts and disafforested his mind!

Can use his horse, goat, wolf, and ev'ry beast,
And is not ass himself to all the rest!
Else man not only is the herd of swine,
But he's those devils too which did incline
Them to a headlong rage, and made them worse."

All sensuality is one, though it takes many forms; all purity is one. It is the same whether a man eat, or drink, or cohabit, or sleep sensually. They are but one appetite, and we only need to see a person do any one of these things to know how great a sensualist he is. The impure can neither stand nor sit with purity. When the reptile is attacked at one mouth of his burrow, he shows himself at another. If you would be chaste, you must be temperate. What is chastity? How shall a man know if he is chaste? He shall not know it. We have heard of this virtue, but we know not what it is. We speak conformably to the rumor which we have heard. From exertion come wisdom and purity; from sloth ignorance and sensuality. In the student sensuality is a sluggish habit of mind. An unclean person is universally a slothful one, one who sits by a stove, whom the sun shines on prostrate, who reposes without being fatigued. If you would avoid uncleanness, and all the sins, work earnestly, though it be at cleaning a stable. Nature is hard to be overcome, but she must be overcome. What avails it that you are Christian, if you are not purer than the heathen, if you deny yourself no more, if you are not more religious? I know of many systems of religion esteemed heathenish whose precepts fill the reader with shame, and provoke him to new endeavors, though it be to the performance of rites merely.

I hesitate to say these things, but it is not because of the subject,—I care not how obscene my words are,—but because I cannot speak of them without betraying my impurity. We discourse freely without shame of one form of sensuality, and are silent about another. We are so degraded that we cannot speak simply of the necessary functions of human nature. In earlier ages, in some countries, every function was reverently spoken of and regulated by law. Nothing was too trivial for the Hindoo lawgiver, however offensive it may be to modern taste. He teaches how to eat, drink, cohabit, void excrement and urine, and the like, elevating what is mean, and does not falsely excuse himself by calling these things trifles.

Every man is the builder of a temple, called his body, to the god he worships, after a style purely his own, nor can he get off by hammering marble instead. We are all sculptors and painters, and our material is our own flesh and blood and bones. Any nobleness begins at once to refine a man's features, any meanness or sensuality to imbrute them.

John Farmer sat at his door one September evening, after a hard day's work, his mind still running on his labor more or less. Having bathed, he sat down to re-create his intellectual man. It was a rather cool evening, and some of his neighbors were apprehending a frost. He had not attended to the train of his thoughts long when he heard some one playing on a flute, and that sound harmonized with his mood. Still he thought of his work; but the burden of his thought was, that though this kept running in his head, and he found himself planning and contriving it against his will, yet it concerned him very little. It was no more than the scurf of his skin, which was constantly shuffled off. But the notes of the flute came home to his ears out of a different sphere from that he worked in, and suggested work for certain faculties which slumbered in him. They gently did away with the street, and the village, and the state in which he lived. A voice said to him,—Why do you stay here and live this mean moiling life, when a glorious existence is possible for you? Those same stars twinkle over other fields than these.—But how to come out of this condition and actually migrate thither? All that he could think of was to practice some new austerity, to let his mind descend into his body andredeem it, and treat himself with ever increasing respect.

# *from* Song of the Open Road

## *Walt Whitman*

### 1

Afoot and light-hearted, I take to the open road,
Healthy, free, the world before me,
The long brown path before me, leading wherever I choose.

Henceforth I ask not good-fortune—I myself am good fortune;
Henceforth I whimper no more, postpone no more, need nothing,
Strong and content, I travel the open road.

The earth—that is sufficient;
I do not want the constellations any nearer;
I know they are very well where they are;
I know they suffice for those who belong to them.

(Still here I carry my old delicious burdens;
I carry them, men and women—I carry them with me wherever I go;
I swear it is impossible for me to get rid of them;
I am filled with them, and I will fill them in return.)

### 2

You road I enter upon and look around! I believe you are not all that is
        here;
I believe that much unseen is also here.

Here the profound lesson of reception, neither preference or denial;
The black with his woolly head, the felon, the diseased, the illiterate
        person, are not denied;
The birth, the hasting after the physician, the beggar's tramp, the
        drunkard's stagger, the laughing party of mechanics,
The escaped youth, the rich person's carriage, the fop, the eloping couple,
The early market man, the hearse, the moving of furniture into the
        town, the return back from the town,
They pass—I also pass—anything passes—none can be interdicted;
None but are accepted—none but are dear to me.

### 3

You air that serves me with breath to speak!
You objects that call from diffusion my meanings, and give them shape!
You light that wraps me and all things in delicate equable showers!
You paths worn in the irregular hollows by the roadsides!
I think you are latent with unseen existences—you are so dear to me.
You flagg'd walks of the cities! you strong curbs at the edges!
You ferries! you planks and posts of wharves! you timber-lined sides!
      you distant ships!
You rows of houses! you window-pierc'd façades! you roofs!
You porches and entrances! you copings and iron guards!
You windows whose transparent shells might expose so much!
You doors and ascending steps! you arches!
You gray stones of interminable pavements! you trodden crossings!
From all that has been near you, I believe you have imparted to your
      selves, and now would impart the same secretly to me;
From the living and the dead I think you have peopled your impassive
      surfaces, and the spirits thereof would be evident and amicable
      with me

### 4

The earth expanding right hand and left hand,
The picture alive, every part in its best light,
The music falling in where it is wanted, and stopping where it is not
      wanted,
The cheerful voice of the public road—the gay fresh sentiment of the road.

O highway I travel! O public road! do you say to me, *Do not leave me?*
Do you say, *Venture not? If you leave me, you are lost?*
Do you say, *I am already prepared—I am well-beaten and undenied—adhere
      to me?*

O public road! I say back, I am not afraid to leave you—yet I love you;
You express me better than I can express myself;
You shall be more to me than my poem.

I think heroic deeds were all conceiv'd in the open air, and all great
      poems also;
I think I could stop here myself, and do miracles;
(My judgments, thoughts, I henceforth try by the open air, the road;)

I think whatever I shall meet on the road I shall like, and whoever
     beholds me shall like me;
I think whoever I see must be happy.

## 5

From this hour, freedom!
From this hour I ordain myself loos'd of limits and imaginary lines,
Going where I list, my own master, total and absolute,
Listening to others, and considering well what they say,
Pausing, searching, receiving, contemplating,
Gently, but with undeniable will, divesting myself of the holds that
     would hold me.

I inhale great draughts of space;
The east and the west are mine, and the north and the south are mine.

I am larger, better than I thought;
I did not know I held so much goodness.
All seems beautiful to me;
I can repeat over to men and women, You have done such good to me, I
     would do the same to you.

I will recruit for myself and you as I go;
I will scatter myself among men and women as I go;
I will toss the new gladness and roughness among them;
Whoever denies me, it shall not trouble me;
Whoever accepts me, he or she shall be blessed, and shall bless me.

## 6

Now if a thousand perfect men were to appear, it would not amaze me;
Now if a thousand beautiful forms of women appear'd, it would not
     astonish me.

Now I see the secret of the making of the best persons,
It is to grow in the open air, and to eat and sleep with the earth.

Here a great personal deed has room;
A great deed seizes upon the hearts of the whole race of men,
Its effusion of strength and will overwhelms law, and mocks all authority
     and all argument against it.

Here is the test of wisdom;
Wisdom is not finally tested in schools;
Wisdom cannot be pass'd from one having it, to another not having it;
Wisdom is of the Soul, is not susceptible of proof, is its own proof,
Applies to all stages and objects and qualities, and is content,
Is the certainty of the reality and immortality of things, and the excellence
        of things;
Something there is in the float of the sight of things that provokes it out
        of the Soul.

Now I reexamine philosophies and religions,
They may prove well in lecture-rooms, yet not prove at all under the
        spacious clouds, and along the landscape and flowing currents.
Here is realization;
Here is a man tallied—he realizes here what he has in him;
The past, the future, majesty, love—if they are vacant of you, you are
        vacant of them.

Only the kernel of every object nourishes;
Where is he who tears off the husks for you and me?
Where is he that undoes stratagems and envelopes for you and me?

Here is adhesiveness—it is not previously fashion'd—it is apropos;
Do you know what it is, as you pass, to be loved by strangers?
Do you know the talk of those turning eye-balls?

7

Here is the efflux of the Soul;
The efflux of the Soul comes from within, through embower'd gates,
        ever provoking questions:
These yearnings, why are they? These thoughts in the darkness, why
        are they?
Why are there men and women that while they are nigh me, the
        sun-light expands my blood?
Why, when they leave me, do my pennants of joy sink flat and lank?
Why are there trees I never walk under, but large and melodious
        thoughts descend upon me?
(I think they hang there winter and summer on those trees, and always
        drop fruit as I pass;)
What is it I interchange so suddenly with strangers?

What with some driver, as I ride on the seat by his side?
What with some fisherman, drawing his seine by the shore, as I walk
      by, and pause?
What gives me to be free to a woman's or man's good-will?
      What gives them to be free to mine?

### 8

The efflux of the Soul is happiness—here is happiness;
I think it pervades the open air, waiting at all times;
Now it flows unto us—we are rightly charged.
Here rises the fluid and attaching character;
The fluid and attaching character is the freshness and sweetness of man
      and woman;
(The herbs of the morning sprout no fresher and sweeter every day out
      of the roots of themselves, than it sprouts fresh and sweet con-
      tinually out of itself. )

Toward the fluid and attaching character exudes the sweat of the love of
      young and old;
From it falls distill'd the charm that mocks beauty and attainments;
Toward it heaves the shuddering longing ache of contact.

### 9

Allons! whoever you are, come travel with me!
Traveling with me, you find what never tires.

The earth never tires;
The earth is rude, silent, incomprehensible at first—Nature is rude and
      incomprehensible at first;
Be not discouraged—keep on—there are divine things, well envelop'd;
I swear to you there are divine things more beautiful than words can tell.

Allons! we must not stop here!
However sweet these laid-up stores—however convenient this
      dwelling, we cannot remain here;
However shelter'd this port, and however calm these waters, we must
      not anchor here;
However welcome the hospitality that surrounds us, we are permitted
      to receive it but a little while.

## 10

Allons! the inducements shall be greater;
We will sail pathless and wild seas;
We will go where winds blow, waves dash, and the Yankee clipper
      speeds by under full sail.

Allons! with power, liberty, the earth, the elements!
Health, defiance, gayety, self-esteem, curiosity;
Allons! from all formules!
From your formules, O bat-eyed and materialistic priests!
The stale cadaver blocks up the passage—the burial waits no longer.

Allons! yet take warning!
He traveling with me needs the best blood, thews, endurance;
None may come to the trial, till he or she bring courage and health.

Come not here if you have already spent the best of yourself;
Only those may come, who come in sweet and determin'd bodies;
No diseas'd person—no rum-drinker or venereal taint is permitted here.


I and mine do not convince by arguments, similes, rhymes;
We convince by our presence.

## 11

Listen! I will be honest with you;
I do not offer the old smooth prizes, but offer rough new prizes;
These are the days that must happen to you:

You shall not heap up what is called riches,
You shall scatter with lavish hand all that you earn or achieve,
You but arrive at the city to which you were destin'd—you hardly settle
      yourself to satisfaction, before you are call'd by an irresistible
      call to depart,
You shall be treated to the ironical smiles and mocking of those who
      remain behind you;
What beckonings of love you receive, you shall only answer with pas-
      sionate kisses of parting,
You shall not allow the hold of those who spread their reach'd hands
      toward you.

## 12

Allons! after the GREAT COMPANIONS! and to belong to them!
They too are on the road! they are the swift and majestic men; they are
the greatest women.
Over that which hinder'd them—over that which retarded—passing
impediments large or small,
Committers of crimes, committers of many beautiful virtues,
Enjoyers of calms of seas, and storms of seas,
Sailors of many a ship, walkers of many a mile of land,
Habitués of many distant countries, habitués of far-distant dwellings,
Trusters of men and women, observers of cities, solitary toilers,
Pausers and contemplators of tufts, blossoms, shells of the shore,
Dancers at wedding dances, kissers of brides, tender helpers of chil
dren, bearers of children,
Soldiers of revolts, standers by gaping graves, lowerers down of coffins,
Journeyers over consecutive seasons, over the years—the curious years,
each emerging from that which preceded it,
Journeyers as with companions, namely, their own diverse phases,
Forth-steppers from the latent unrealized baby-days,
Journeyers gayly with their own youth—Journeyers with their bearded
and well-grain'd manhood,
Journeyers with their womanhood, ample, unsurpass'd, content,
Journeyers with their own sublime old age of manhood or womanhood,
Old age, calm, expanded, broad with the haughty breadth of the universe,
Old age, flowing free with the delicious near-by freedom of death.

## 13

Allons! to that which is endless, as it was beginningless,
To undergo much, tramps of days, rests of nights,
To merge all in the travel they tend to, and the days and nights they
tend to,
Again to merge them in the start of superior journeys;
To see nothing anywhere but what you may reach it and pass it,
To conceive no time, however distant, but what you may reach it and
pass it,
To look up or down no road but it stretches and waits for you—however
long, but it stretches and waits for you;
To see no being, not God's or any, but you also go thither,
To see no possession but you may possess it—enjoying all without labor

or purchase—abstracting the feast, yet not abstracting one
    particle of it;
To take the best of the farmer's farm and the rich man's elegant villa,
    and the chaste blessings of the well-married couple, and fruits
    of orchards and flowers of gardens,
To take to your use out of the compact cities as you pass through,
To carrying buildings and streets with you afterward wherever you go,
To gather the minds of men out of their brains as you encounter them—
    to gather the love out of their hearts,
To take your lovers on the road with you, for all that you leave them
    behind you,
To know the universe itself as a road—as many roads—as roads for
    traveling souls.


## 14

The Soul travels;
The body does not travel as much as the soul;
The body has just as great a work as the soul, and parts away at  last for
    journeys of the soul.

All parts away for the progress of souls;
All religion, all solid things, arts, government,—all that was or is
    apparent upon this globe or any globe, falls into niches and
    corners  before the procession of Souls along the grand roads of
    the universe.

Of the progress of the souls of men and women along the grand roads
    of the universe, all other progress is the needed emblem and
    sustenance.

Forever alive, forever forward,
Stately, solemn, sad, withdrawn, baffled, mad, turbulent, feeble,
    dissatisfied,
Desperate, proud, fond, sick, accepted by men, rejected by men,
They go! they go! I know that they go, but I know not where they go;
But I know that they go toward the best—toward something great.

## 15

Allons! whoever your are! come forth!
You must not stay sleeping and dallying there in the house, though you
          built it, or though it has been built for you.
Allons! out of the dark confinement!
It is useless to protest—I know all, and expose it.

Behold, through you as bad as the rest,
Through the laughter, dancing, dining, supping, of people,
Inside of dresses and ornaments, inside of those wash'd and trimm'd
          faces,
Behold a secret silent loathing and despair.

No husband, no wife, no friend, trusted to hear the confession; Another
self, a duplicate of every one, skulking and hiding it goes,
Formless and wordless through the streets of the cities, polite and bland
          in the parlors,
In the cars of rail-roads, in steamboats, in the public assembly, Home to
the houses of men and women, at the table, in the bed-room, everwhere,
Smartly attired, countenance smiling, form upright, death under the
          breast-bones, hell under the skull-bones,
Under the broadcloth and gloves, under the ribbons and artificial flowers,
Keeping fair with the customs, speaking not a syllable of itself,
Speaking of anything else, but never of itself.

## 16

Allons! through struggles and wars!
The goal that was named cannot be countermanded.

Have the past struggles succeeded?
What has succeeded? yourself? your nation? nature?
Now understand me well—It is provided in the essence of things, that
          from any fruition of success, no matter what, shall come forth
          something to make a greater struggle necessary.

My call is the call of battle—I nourish active rebellion;
He going with me must go well arm'd;
He going with me goes often with spare diet, poverty, angry enemies,
          desertions.

## 17

Allons! the road is before us!
It is safe—I have tried it—my own feet have tried it well.

Allons! be not detain'd!
Let paper remain on the desk unwritten, and the book on the shelf
       unopen'd!
Let the tools remain in the workshop! let the money remain unearn'd!
Let the school stand! mind not the cry of the teacher!
Let the preacher preach in his pulpit! let the lawyer plead in the court,
       and the judge expound the law.

Mon enfant! I give you my hand!
I give you my love, more precious than money,
I give you myself, before preaching or law;
Will you give me yourself? will you come travel with me?
Shall we stick by each other as long as we live?

# Selected Writings

*John Muir*

## "God's First Temples."

### How Shall We Preserve Our Forests?

The Question Considered by John Muir, the California Geologist—The Views of a Practical man and a Scientific Observer—A Profoundly Interesting Article.

(Communicated to the *Record-Union*)

**Eds. Record-Union:** The forests of coniferous trees growing on our mountain ranges are by far the most destructible of the natural resources of California. Our gold, and silver, and cinnabar are stored in the rocks, locked up in the safest of all banks, so that notwithstanding the world has been making a run upon them for the last twenty-five years, they still pay out steadily, and will probably continue to do so centuries hence, like rivers pouring from perennial mountain fountains. The riches of our magnificent soil beds are also comparatively safe, because even the most barbarous methods of wildcat farming cannot effect complete destruction, and however great the impoverishment produced, full restoration of fertility is always possible to the enlightened farmer. But our forest belts are being burned and cut down and wasted like a field of unprotected grain, and once destroyed can never be wholly restored even by centuries of persistent and painstaking cultivation.

**The practical importance** of the preservation of our forests is augmented by their relations to climate, soil and streams. Strip off the woods with their underbrush from the mountain flanks, and the whole state, the lowlands as well as the highlands, would gradually change into a desert. During rainfalls, and when the winter snow was melting, every stream would become a destructive torrent oveflowing its banks, stripping off and carrying away the fertile soils, filling up the lower river channels, and overspreading the lowland fields with detritus to a vastly more destructive degree than all the washings from hydraulic mines concerning which we now hear so much. Dripping forests give rise to moist sheets and currents of air, and the sod of grasses and underbrush thus fostered, together with the roots of trees themselves, absorb and hold back rains and melting snow, yet allowing them to doze and percolate and flow gently in useful fertilizing streams. Indeed every pine needle and rootlet, as well as fallen trunks and large clasping roots, may by regarded as dams, hoarding the bounty of storm clouds, and dispensing it as blessings all through the summer, instead of allowing it to gather and rush headlong in short-lived devastating floods. Streams taking their rise in deep woods flow unfailingly as those derived from the eternal ice and snow of the Alps. So constant indeed and apparent is the relationship between forests and never-failing springs, that effect is frequently mistaken for cause, it being often asserted that fine forests will grow only along stream sides were their roots are well watered, when in fact the forests themselves produce many of the streams flowing through them.

**The main forest belt** of the Sierra is restricted to the western flank, and extends unbrokenly from one end of the range to the other at an elevation of from three to eight thousand feet above sea level. The great master existence of these noble woods is *Sequoia gigantea*, or Big Tree. Only two species of sequoia are known to exist in the world. Both belong to California, one being found only in the Sierra, the other a (*Sequoia sempervirens*) in the Coast Ranges, although no less than five distinct fossil species have been discovered in the tertiary and cretaceous rocks of Greenland. I would like to call attention to this noble tree, with special references to its preservation. The species extends from the well-known Calaveras groves on the north, to the head of Deer Creek on the south, near the big bend of the Kern River, a distance of about two hundred miles, at an elevation above sea level of from about five to eight thousand feet. From the Calaveras to the South Fork of Kings River it occurs only in small isolated groves, and so sparsely and irregularly distributed that two gaps occur nearly forty miles in width, the one between the Calaveras and Tuolumne groves, the other between those of the Fresno and Kings rivers. From Kings River the belt extends across the broad, rugged basins of the Kaweah and Tule rivers to its southern boundary on Deer Creek, interrupted only by deep, rocky canyons, the width of this portion of the belt being from three to ten miles.

**In the northern groves** few young trees or saplings are found ready to take the places of the failing old ones, and because these ancient, childless sequoias are the only ones known to botanists, the species has been generally regarded as doomed to speedy extinction, as being nothing more than expiring remnant of an ancient flora, and that therefore there is no use trying to save it or to prolong its few dying days. This, however, is in the main a mistaken notion, for the Sierra as it now exists never had an ancient flora. All the species now growing on the range have been planted since the close of the glacial period, and the Big Tree has never formed a greater part of these post-glacial forests than it does today, however widely it may have been distributed throughout pre-glacial forests.

**In tracing the belt** southward, all the phenomena bearing upon its history goes to show that the dominion of *Sequoia gigantea*, as king of California trees, is not yet passing away. No tree in the woods seems more firmly established, or more safely settled in accordance with climate and soil. They fill the woods and form the principal tree, growing heartily on solid ledges, along water courses, in the deep, moist soil of meadows, and on avalanche and glacial debris, with a multitude of thrifty seedlings and saplings crowding around the aged, ready to take their places and rule the woods.

Nevertheless nature in her grandly deliberate way keeps up a rotation of forest crops. Species develop and die like individuals, animal as well as plant. Man himself will as surely become extinct as sequoia or mastodon, and be at length known only as a fossil. Changes of this kind are, however, exceedingly slow in their movements, and, as far as the lives of individuals are concerned, such changes have no appreciable effect. Sequoia seems scarcely further past prime as a species than its companion firs (*Picea amabilis* and *P. grandis*), and judging from its present condition and its ancient history, as far as I have been able to decipher it, our sequoia will live and flourish gloriously until A.D. 15,000 at least—probably for longer—that is, if it be allowed to remain in the hands of nature.

**Waste and Destruction.** But waste and pure destruction are already taking place at a terrible rate, and unless protective measures be speedily invented and enforced, in a few years this noblest tree species in the world will present only a few hacked and scarred remnants. The great enemies of forests are fire and the ax. The destructive effects of these, as compared with those caused by the operations of nature, are instantaneous. Floods undermine and kill many a tree, storm winds bend and break, landslips and avalanches overwhelm whole groves, lightning shatters and burns, but the combined effects of all these amount only to a wholesome beauty-producing culture. Last summer I found some five sawmills located in or near the lower edge of the sequoia belt, all of which saw more or less of the Big Tree into lumber. One of these (Hyde's), situated on the North Fork of the Kaweah, cut no less than 2,000,000 feet of sequoia lumber last season. Most of the Fresno Big Trees are doomed to feed the mills recently erected near them, and a company has been formed by Chas. Converse to cut the noble forest on the South Fork of Kings River. In these milling operations waste far exceeds use. After the choice young manageable trees have been felled, the woods are cleared of limbs and refuse by burning, and in these clearing fires, made with reference to further operations, all the young seedlings and saplings are destroyed, together with many valuable fallen trees and old trees, too large to cut, thus effectually cutting off all hopes of a renewal of the forest.

**These ravages**, however, of mill fires and mill axes are small as compared with those of the "sheepmen's" fires. Incredible numbers of sheep are driven to the mountain pastures every summer, and in order to make easy paths and to improve the pastures, running fires are set everywhere to burn off the old logs and underbrush. These fires are far more universal and destructive than would be guessed. They sweep through nearly the entire forest belt of the range from one extremity to the other, and in the dry weather, before the coming on of winter storms, are very destructive to all kinds of young trees, and especially to sequoia, whose loose, fibrous bark catches and burns at once. Excepting the Calaveras, I, last summer, examined every sequoia grove in the range, together with the main belt extending across the basins of Kaweah and Tule, and found everywhere the most deplorable waste from this cause. Indians burn off underbrush to facilitate deer-hunting. Campers of all kinds often permit fire to run, so also do millmen, but the fires of "sheepmen" probably form more than ninety per cent of all destructive fires that sweep the woods.

**Fire, then, is the arch destroyer** of our forests, and sequoia forests suffer most of all. The young trees are most easily fire-killed; the old are most easily burned, and the prostrate trunks, which *never rot* and would remain valuable until our tenth centennial, are reduced to ashes.

In European countries, especially in France, Germany, Italy, and Austria, the economics of forestry have been carefully studied under the auspices of Government, with the most beneficial results. Whether our loose-jointed Government is really able or willing to do anything in the matter remains to be seen. If our law makers were to discover and enforce any method tending to lessen even in a small degree the destruction going on, they would thus cover a multitude of legislative sins in the eyes of every tree lover. I am satisfied, however, that the question can be intelligently discussed only after a careful survey of our forests has been made, together with studies of the forces now acting upon them.

A law was constructed some years ago making the cutting down of sequoias over sixteen feet in diameter illegal. A more absurd and short-sighted piece of legislation could not be conceived. All the young trees might be cut and burned, and all the old ones might be burned but not cut.

John Muir
Sacramento *Record-Union*, February 5, 1876

## Need of a Park

I fancy the time is not distant when this wonderful region will be opened to the world—when a road will be built up the South Fork of Kings River through the sequoia groves, into the great canyon, and thence across the divide and down the Middle Fork Canyon to Tehipite; thence through the valley and down the canyon to the confluence of the Middle and South forks, and up to the sequoia groves to the point of beginning. Some of the sequoia groves were last year included in the national reservations of Sequoia and General Grant parks. But all of this wonderful Kings river region, together with the Kaweah and Tule sequoias, should be compre-hended in one grand national park. This region contains no mines of con-sequence, it is too high and too rocky for agriculture, and even the lumber industry need suffer no unreasonable restriction. Let our law-givers then make haste before it is too late to set apart this surpassingly glorious region for the recreation and well-being of humanity, and all the world will rise up and call them blessed.

"A Rival of the Yosemite," *Century Magazine*,
November 1891

## The Sierra Reserve

The wildest health and pleasure grounds accessible and available to tourists seeking escape from care and dust and early death are the parks and reservations of the West. There are four national parks—the Yellowstone, Yosemite, General Grant, and Sequoia—all within easy reach, and thirty forest reservations, a magnificent realm of woods, most of which, by railroads and trails and open ridges, is also fairly accessible, not only to the determined traveler rejoicing in difficulties, but to those (may their tribe increase) who, not tired, not sick, just naturally take wing every summer in search of wildness. The forty million acres of these reserves are in the main unspoiled as yet, though sadly wasted and threatened on their more open margins by the ax and fire of the lumberman and prospector, and by hoofed locust, which, like the winged ones, devour every leaf within reach, while the shepherds and owners set fires with the intention of making a blade of grass grow in the place of every tree, but with the result of killing both the grass and the trees.

The Sierra of California is the most openly beautiful and useful of all the forest reserves, and the largest, excepting the Cascade Reserve of Oregon and the Bitter Root of Montana and Idaho. It embraces over four million acres of the grandest scenery and grandest trees on the continent, and its forests are planted just where they do the most good, not only for beauty, but for farming in the great San Joaquin Valley beneath them. It extends southward from the Yosemite National Park to the end of the range, a distance of nearly two hundred miles. No other coniferous forest in the world contains so many species or so many large and beautiful trees— *Sequoia gigantea*, king of conifers, "the noblest of a noble race," as Sir Joseph Hooker well says; the sugar pine, king of all the world's pines, living or extinct; the yellow pine, next rank, which here reaches most perfect development, forming noble towers of verdure two hundred feet high; the mountain pine, which braves the coldest blasts far up the mountains on grim, rocky slopes; and five others, flourishing each in its place, making eight species of pine in one forest, which is still further enriched by the great Douglas spruce, libocedrus, two species of silver fir, large trees and exquisitely beautiful, the Paton hemlock, the most graceful of evergreens, the curious tumion, oaks of many species, maples, alders, poplars, and flowering dogwood, all fringed with flowery underbrush, manzanita, ceanothus, wild rose, cherry, chestnut, and rhododendron. Wandering at random through these friendly, approachable woods, one comes here and there to the loveliest lily gardens, some of the lilies ten feet high, and the smoothest gentian meadows, and yosemite valleys known only to mountaineers. Once I spent a night by a campfire on Mount Shasta with Asa Gray and Sir Joseph Hooker, and, knowing that they were acquainted with all the great forests of the world, I asked whether they knew any coniferous forest that rivaled that of the Sierra. They unhesitatingly said: "No. In the beauty and grandeur of individual trees, and in number and variety of species, the Sierra forests surpass all others."

This Sierra Reserve, proclaimed by the President of the United States in September, 1893, is worth the most thoughtful care of the government for its own sake, without considering its value as the fountain of the rivers on which the fertility of the great San Joaquin Valley depends. Yet it gets no care at all. In the fog of tariff, silver, and annexation politics it is left wholly unguarded, though the management of the adjacent national parks by a few soldiers shows how well and how easily it can be preserved. In the meantime, lumbermen are allowed to spoil it at their will, and sheep in uncountable ravenous hordes to trample it and devour every green leaf within reach; while the shepherds, like destroying angels, set innumerable fires, which burn not only the undergrowth of seedlings on which the permanence of the forest depends, but countless thousands of the venerable giants. If every citizen could take one walk through this reserve, there would be no more trouble about its care; for only in darkness does vandalism flourish.

"The Wild Parks and Forest Reservations of the West,"
*Atlantic Monthly*, January 1898

• • •

## THE WORK OF PRESERVATION

Martinez, January 10, 1899

[To Theodore P. Lukens]

. . . The sheep owners in particular are already giving trouble & promise more next season. I have just learned from Mr. Bartlett, Forest Supervisor of Sierra Reservation, that 200,000 sheep invaded & desolated the reservation last summer under a tempory concession made by the Secretary Bliss & now thus encouraged certain land & timber speculators combined with the sheep owners have sent on agents to Washington to obtain leases of the entire Reservation for sheep grazing during the coming season. We must at once get to work in quick hearty opposition to this, or soon there will be complete surrender at Washington & destruction of the forest & other interests depending on them . . .

Martinez, January 15, 1907

[To William Colby]

I herewith return the draft of a club report on Kings River region with my hearty approval excepting the first 2 pages of the MS in which the Yosemite & Kings River regions are compared. Every possible aid & encouragement should be given by the club for the preservation, road & trail building, etc. for the development of the magnificent Kings River region. But unjust one-sided comparisons seeking to build up & glorify one region at the expense of lowering the other is useless work & should be left to real estate agents, promoters, rival hotel & stage owners, etc. Certainly the Club has nothing to do with such stuff, "tremendous advantages" "wealth & variety of mountain sculpture" depending on greater "depths & heights" etc. suggest boys with eyes to depth & height of butter & honey seeing tremendous advantages in one slice of bread over another cut from the same loaf . . .

Los Angeles, January 16, 1911<br>325 West Adams Street

[To William Colby]

. . . I am now at work on the Kings River yosemites, and I would like to have the part of the Kings River region which ought to be added to the General Grant and Sequoia National Parks definitely described, because I wish to recommend the preservation of the region in the Yosemite Guidebook.

And please tell me how much of the new road to the Kings River canyon has been actually built, and describe its course, where it starts from, where it runs, and where it strikes the river below the mouth of the canyon.

Please tell me also what sort of a trail is the one which runs up Copper Creek and over the divide to Simpson Meadows and down to Tehipite, and also the trails out of the lower end of Tehipite on both sides.

I am afraid I am putting you to lots of trouble, but you are much more familiar with these roads and trails than I am, and I want to get them right. I find in this Yosemite book that it is taking in so much it is going to be difficult to keep it within bounds, and I want to make the description of roads and trails as short as possible . . .

## Natural Boundaries

So far as I am able to see at present only fire and the ax threaten the existence of these noblest of God's trees. In nature's keeping they are safe, but through the agency of man destruction is making rapid progress, while in the work of protection only a good beginning has been made. The Fresno Grove, the Tuolumne, Merced and Mariposa groves are under the protection of the Federal Government in the Yosemite National Park. So are the General Grant and Sequoia national parks; the latter, established twenty-one years ago, has an area of 240 square miles and is efficiently guarded by a troop of cavalry under the direction of the Secretary of the Interior; so also are the small General Grant National Park, established at the same time with an area of four square miles, and the Mariposa Grove, about the same size and the small Merced and Tuolumne group. Perhaps more than half of all the Big Trees have been thoughtlessly sold and are now in the hands of speculators and millmen. It appears, therefore, that far the largest and important section of protected Big Trees is in the great Sequoia National Park, now easily accessible by rail to Lemon Cove and thence by trail to other parts of the park; but large as it is it should be made much larger. Its natural eastern boundary is the high Sierra and northern and southern boundaries are the Kings and Kern rivers. Thus could be included the sublime scenery on the headwaters of these rivers and perhaps nine-tenths of all the Big Trees in existence. All private claims within these bounds should be gradually extinguished by purchase by the Government. The Big Tree, leaving all its higher uses out of the count, is a tree of life to the dwellers of the plain dependent on irrigation, a never-failing spring, sending living waters to the lowland. For every grove cut down a stream is dried up. Therefore all California is crying, "Save the trees of the fountains." Nor, judging by the signs of the times, is it likely that the cry will cease until the salvation of all that is left of *Sequoia gigantea* is made sure.

*The Yosemite*, 1912

# The Buffalo

*Francis Parkman*

FOUR DAYS on the Platte, and yet no buffalo! Last years' signs of them were provokingly abundant; and wood being extremely scarce, we found an admirable substitute in the *bois de vache*, which burns like peat, producing no unpleasant effects. The wagons one morning had left the camp; Shaw and I were already on horseback, but Henry Chatillon still sat cross-legged by the dead embers of the fire, playing pensively with the lock of his rifle, while his sturdy Wyandot pony stood quietly behind him, looking over his head. At last he got up, patted the neck of the pony (which, from an exaggerated appreciation of his merits, he had christened "Five Hundred Dollar"), and then mounted, with a melancholy air.

"What is it, Henry?"

"Ah, I feel lonesome; I never been here before but I see away yonder over the buttes, and down there on the prairie, black—all black with buffalo."

In the afternoon he and I left the party in search of an antelope, until, at the distance of a mile or two on the right, the tall white wagons and the little black specks of horsemen were just visible, so slowly advancing that they seemed motionless; and far on the left rose the broken line of scorched, desolate sand-hills. The vast plain waved with tall rank grass, that swept our horses' bellies; it swayed to and fro in billows with the light breeze, and far and near antelope and wolves were moving through it, the hairy backs of the latter alternately appearing and disappearing as they bounded awkwardly along; while the antelope, with the simple curiosity peculiar to them, would often approach us closely, their little horns and white throats just visible above the grasstops, as they gazed eagerly at us with their round black eyes.

I dismounted, and amused myself with firing at the wolves. Henry attentively scrutinized the surrounding landscape, at length he gave a shout, and called on me to mount again, pointing in the direction of the sand-hills. A mile and a half from us two black specks slowly traversed the bare glaring face of one of them, and disappeared behind the summit. "Let us go!" cried Henry, belaboring the sides of "Five Hundred Dollar;"

598

and I following in his wake, we galloped rapidly through the rank grass toward the base of the hills.

From one of their openings descended a deep ravine, widening as it issued on the prairie. We entered it, and galloping up, in a moment were surrounded by the bleak sand-hills. Half of their steep sides were bare; the rest were scantily clothed with clumps of grass, and various uncouth plants, conspicuous among which appeared the reptile-like prickly-pear. They were gashed with numberless ravines, and as the sky had suddenly darkened, and a cold gusty wind arisen, the strange shrubs and the dreary hills looked doubly wild and desolate. But Henry's face was all eagerness. He tore off a little hair from the piece of buffalo-robe under his saddle, and threw it up, to show the course of the wind. It blew directly before us. The game were therefore to leeward, and it was necessary to make our best speed to get round them.

We scrambled from this ravine, and, galloping away through the hollows, soon found another, winding like a snake among the hills, and so deep that it completely concealed us. We rode up the bottom of it, glancing through the bushes at its edge, till Henry abruptly jerked his rein, and slid out of his saddle. Full a quarter of a mile distant, on the outside of the farthest hill, a long procession of buffalo were walking, in Indian file, with the utmost gravity and deliberation; then more appeared, clambering from a hollow not far off, and ascending, one behind the other, the grassy slope of another hill; then a shaggy head and a pair of short broken horns issued out of a ravine close at hand, and with a slow, stately step, one by one, the enormous brutes came into view, taking their way across the valley, wholly unconscious of an enemy. In a moment Henry was worming his way, lying flat on the ground, through grass and prickly-pears, towards his unsuspecting victims. He had with him both my rifle and his own. He was soon out of sight, and still the buffalo kept issuing into the valley. For a long time all was silent, I sat holding his horse, and wondering what he was about, when suddenly, in rapid succession, came the sharp reports of the two rifles, and the whole line of buffalo, quickening their pace into a clumsy trot, gradually disappeared over the ridge of the hill. Henry rose to his feet, and stood looking after them.

"You have missed them," said I.

"Yes," said Henry; "let us go." He descended into the ravine, loaded the rifles, and mounted his horse.

We rode up the hill after the buffalo. The herd was out of sight when we reached the top, but lying on the grass, not far off, was one quite lifeless, and another violently struggling in the death-agony.

"You see I miss him!" remarked Henry. He had fired from a distance of more than a hundred and fifty yards, and both balls had passed through the lungs, the true mark in shooting buffalo.

The darkness increased, and a driving storm came on. Tying our horses to the horns of the victims, Henry began the bloody work of dissection, slashing away with the science of a connoisseur, while I vainly tried to imitate him. Old Hendrick recoiled with horror and indignation when I endeavored to tie the meat to the strings of raw hide, always carried for this purpose, dangling at the back of the saddle. After some difficulty we overcame his scruples; and, heavily burdened with the more eligible portions of the buffalo, we set out on our return. Scarcely had we emerged from the labyrinth of gorges and ravines, and issued upon the open prairie, when the prickling sleet came driving, gust upon gust, directly in our faces. It was strangely dark, though wanting still an hour of sunset. The freezing storm soon penetrated to the skin, but the uneasy trot of our heavy-gaited horses kept us warm enough, as we forced them unwillingly in the teeth of the sleet and rain, by the powerful suasion of our Indian whips. The prairie in this place was hard and level. A flourishing colony of prairie-dogs had burrowed into it in every direction and the little mounds of fresh earth around their holes were about as numerous as the hills in a cornfield; but not a yelp was to be heard; not the nose of a single citizen was visible; all had retired to the depths of their burrows, and we envied them their dry and comfortable habitations. An hour's hard riding showed us our tent dimly looming through the storm, one side puffed out by the force of the wind, and the other collapsed in proportion, while the disconsolate horses stood shivering close around, and the wind kept up a dismal whistling in the boughs of three old half-dead trees above. Shaw, like a patriarch, sat on his saddle in the entrance, with a pipe in his mouth and his arms folded, contemplating, with cool satisfaction, the piles of meat that we flung on the ground before him. A dark and dreary night succeeded; but the sun rose with a heat so sultry and languid that the captain excused himself on that account from waylaying an old buffalo bull, who with stupid gravity was walking over the prairie to drink at the river. So much for the climate of the Platte.

But it was not the weather alone that had produced this sudden abatement of the sportsman-like zeal which the captain had always professed. He had been out on the afternoon before, together with several members of his party; but their hunting was attended with no other result than the loss of one of their best horses, severely injured by Sorel, in vainly chasing a wounded bull. The captain, whose ideas of hard riding were all derived from transatlantic sources, expressed the utmost amazement at the feats of Sorel, who went leaping ravines, and dashing at full speed up and down the sides of precipitous hills, lashing his horse with the recklessness of a Rocky Mountain rider. Unfortunately for the poor animal, he was the property of R——, against whom Sorel entertained an unbounded aversion. The Captain himself, it seemed, had also attempted to "run" a buffalo, but though a good and practiced horseman, he had soon given over the attempt, being astonished and utterly disgusted at the nature of the ground he was required to ride over.

"Here's old Papin and Frederic, down from Fort Laramie," shouted Henry, as we returned from a reconnoitring tour on the next morning. We had for some days expected this encounter. Papin was the *bourgeois*, or "boss," of Fort Laramie. He had come down the river with the buffalo-robes and the beaver, the produce of the last winter's trading. I had among our baggage a letter which I wished to commit to their hands; so requesting Henry to detain the boats if he could until my return, I set out after the wagons. They were about four miles in advance. In half an hour I overtook them, got the letter, trotted back upon the trail, and looking carefully, as I rode, saw a patch of broken storm-blasted trees, and, moving near them, some little black specks like men and horses. Arriving at the place, I found a strange assembly. The boats, eleven in number, deep-laden with the skins, hugged close to the shore, to escape being borne down by the swift current. The rowers, swarthy ignoble Mexicans, turned their brutish faces upward to look, as I reached the bank. Papin sat in the middle of one of the boats, upon the canvas covering that protected the cargo. He was a stout, robust fellow, with a little gray eye, that had a peculiarly sly twinkle. "Frederic," also, stretched his tall raw-boned proportions close by the *bourgeois*, and "mountain men" completed the group: some lounging in the boats, some strolling on shore, some attired in gayly-painted buffalo robes, like Indian dandies; some with hair saturated with red paint, and plastered with glue to their temples; and one bedaubed with vermilion upon the forehead and each cheek. They were a mongrel race; yet the French blood seemed to predominate: in a few, indeed, might be seen the black snaky eye of the Indian half-breed, and, one and all, they seemed to aim at assimilating themselves to their red associates.

I shook hands with the *bourgeois*, and delivered the letter; then the boats swung round into the stream and floated away. They had reason for haste, for already the voyage from Fort Laramie had occupied a full month, and the river was growing daily more shallow. Fifty times a day the boats had been aground; indeed, those who navigate the Platte invariably spend half their time upon sandbars. Two of these boats, the property of private traders, afterwards separating from the rest, got hopelessly involved in the shallows, not very far from the Pawnee villages, and were soon surrounded by a swarm of the inhabitants. They carried off everything that they thought valuable, including most of the robes; and amused themselves by tying up the men left on guard, and soundly whipping them with sticks.

We encamped that night upon the bank of the river. Among the emigrants was an overgrown boy, some eighteen years old, with a head as round and about as large as a pumpkin, and fever-and-ague fits had dyed his face of a corresponding color. He wore an old white hat, tied under his chin with a handkerchief; his body was short and stout, but his legs were of disproportioned and appalling length. I observed him at sunset, breasting the hill with gigantic strides, and standing against the sky on the summit, like a colossal pair of tongs. In a moment after we heard him screaming frantically behind the ridge, and nothing doubting that he was in the clutches of Indians or grizzly bears, some of the party caught up their rifles and ran to the rescue. His outcries, however, were but an ebullition of joyous excitement, he had chased two wolf pups to their burrow, and was on his knees, grubbing away like a dog at the mouth of the hole, to get at them.

Before morning he caused more serious disquiet in the camp. It was his turn to hold the middle-guard; but no sooner was he called up than he coolly arranged a pair of saddle-bags under a wagon, laid his head upon them, closed his eyes, opened his mouth, and fell asleep. The guard on our side of the camp, thinking it no part of his duty to look after the cattle of the emigrants, contented himself with watching our own horses and mules; the wolves, he said, were unusually noisy; but still no mischief was anticipated until the sun rose, when not a hoof or horn was in sight. The cattle were gone. While Tom was quietly slumbering, the wolves had driven them away.

Then we reaped the fruits of R——'s precious plan of travelling in company with emigrants. To leave them in their distress was not to be thought of, and we felt bound to wait until the cattle could be searched for, and, if possible, recovered. But the reader may be curious to know what punishment awaited the faithless Tom. By the wholesome law of the prairie, he who falls asleep on guard is condemned to walk all day, leading his horse by the bridle; and we found much fault with our companions for not enforcing such a sentence on the offender. Nevertheless, had he been one of our own party, I have no doubt that he would in like manner have escaped scot-free. But the emigrants went farther than mere forbearance: they decreed that since Tom couldn't stand guard without falling asleep, he shouldn't stand guard at all, and henceforward his slumbers were unbroken. Establishing such a premium on drowsiness could have no very beneficial effect upon the vigilance of our sentinels; for it is far from agreeable, after riding from sunrise to sunset to feel your slumbers interrupted by the butt of a rifle nudging your side, and a sleepy voice growling in your ear that you must get up, to shiver and freeze for three weary hours at midnight.

"Buffalo! buffalo!" It was but a grim old bull, roaming the prairie by himself in misanthropic seclusion, but there might be more behind the hills. Dreading the monotony and languor of the camp, Shaw and I saddled our horses, buckled our holsters in their places, and set out with Henry Chatillon in search of the game. Henry, not intending to take part in the chase, but merely conducting us, carried his rifle with him, while we left ours behind as encumbrances. We rode for some five or six miles, and saw no living thing but wolves, snakes, and prairie-dogs.

"This won't do at all," said Shaw.

"What won't do?"

"There's no wood about here to make a litter for the wounded man: I have an idea that one of us will need something of the sort before the day is over."

There was some foundation for such an idea for the ground was none of the best for a race, and grew worse continually as we proceeded; indeed, it soon became desperately bad, consisting of abrupt hills and deep hollows, cut by frequent ravines not easy to pass. At length, a mile in advance, we saw a band of bulls. Some were scattered grazing over a green declivity, while the rest were crowded together in the wide hollow below. Making a circuit, to keep out of sight, we rode towards them, until we ascended a hill, within a furlong of them, beyond which nothing intervened that could possibly screen us from their view. We dismounted behind the ridge, just out of sight, drew our saddle-girths, examined our pistols, and mounting again, rode over the hill, and descended at a canter towards them, bending close to our horses' necks. Instantly they took the alarm: those on the hill descended, those below gathered into a mass, and the whole got into motion, shouldering each other along at a clumsy gallop. We followed, spurring our horses to full speed; and as the herd rushed, crowding and trampling in terror through an opening in the hills, we were close at their heels, half suffocated by the clouds of dust. But as we drew near, their alarm and speed increased; our horses, being new to the work, showed signs of the utmost fear, bounding violently aside as we approached, and refusing to enter among the herd. The buffalo now broke into several small bodies, scampering over the hills in different directions, and I lost sight of Shaw; neither of us knew where the other had gone. Old Pontiac ran like a frantic elephant up hill and down hill, his ponderous hoofs striking the prairie like sledge-hammers. He showed a curious mixture of eagerness and terror, straining to overtake the panic-stricken herd, but constantly recoiling in dismay as we drew near. The fugitives, indeed, offered no very attractive spectacle, with their shaggy manes and the tattered remnants of their last winter's hair covering their backs in irregular shreds and patches, and flying off in the wind as they ran. At length I urged my horse close behind a bull, and after trying in vain, by blows and spurring, to bring him alongside, I fire from this disadvantageous position. At the report Pontiac swerved so much that I was again thrown a little behind the game. The bullet, entering too much in the rear, failed to disable the bull; for a buffalo requires to be shot at particular points, or he will certainly escape. The herd ran up a hill, and I followed in pursuit. As Pontiac rushed headlong down on the other side, I saw Shaw and Henry descending the hollow on the right, at a leisurely gallop; and in front, the buffalo were just disappearing behind the crest of the next hill, their short tails erect, and their hoofs twinkling through a cloud of dust.

At that moment I heard Shaw and Henry shouting to me; but the muscles of a stronger arm than mine could not have checked at once the furious course of Pontiac, whose mouth was as insensible as leather. Added to this, I rode him that morning with a snaffle, having the day before, for the benefit of my other horse, unbuckled from my bridle the curb which I commonly used. A stronger and hardier brute never trod the prairie; but the novel sight of the buffalo filled him with terror, and when at full speed he was almost incontrollable. Gaining the top of the ridge, I saw nothing of the buffalo; they had all vanished amid the intricacies of the hills and hollows. Reloading my pistols, in the best way I could, I galloped on until I saw them again scuttling along the base of the hill, their panic somewhat abated. Down went Pontiac among them, scattering them to the right and left; and then we had another long chase. About a dozen bulls were before us, scouring over the hills, rushing down the declivities with tremendous weight and impetuosity and then laboring with a weary gallop upward. Still Pontiac, in spite of spurring and beating, would not close with them. One bull at length fell a little behind the rest, and by dint of much effort, I urged my horse within six or eight yards of his side. His back was darkened with sweat: he was panting heavily while his tongue lolled out a foot from his jaws. Gradually I came up abreast of him, urging Pontiac with leg and rein nearer to his side, when suddenly he did what buffalo in such circumstances will always do: he slackened his gallop, and turning towards us, with an aspect of mingled rage and distress, lowered his huge, shaggy head for a charge. Pontiac, with a snort, leaped aside in terror, nearly throwing me to the ground, as I was wholly unprepared for such an evolution. I raised my pistol in a passion to strike him on the head, but thinking better of it, fired the bullet after the bull, who had resumed his flight; then drew rein, and determined to rejoin my companions. It was high time. The breath blew hard from Pontiac's nostrils, and the sweat rolled in big drops down his sides: I myself felt as if drenched in warm water. Pledging myself to take my revenge at a future opportunity, I looked about for some indications to show me where I was, and what course I ought to pursue; I might as well have looked for landmarks in the midst of the ocean. How many miles I had run, or in what direction, I had no idea; and around me the prairie was rolling in steep swells and pitches, without a single distinctive feature to guide me. I had a little compass hung at my neck; and ignorant that the Platte at this point diverged considerably from its easterly course, I thought that by keeping to the northward I should certainly reach it. So I turned and rode about two hours in that direction. The prairie changed as I advanced, softening away into easier undulations, but nothing like the Platte appeared, nor any sign of a human being: the same wild endless expanse lay around me still; and to all appearance I was as far from my object as ever. I began now to think myself in danger of being lost, and, reining in my horse, summoned the scanty share of woodcraft that I possessed (if that term is applicable upon the prairie) to extricate me. It occurred to me that the buffalo might prove my best guides. I soon found one of the paths made by them in their passage to the river: it ran nearly at right angles to my course; but turning my horse's head in the direction it indicated, his freer gait and erected ears assured me that I was right.

But in the meantime my ride had been by no means a solitary one. The face of the country was dotted far and wide with countless hundreds of buffalo. They trooped along in files and columns, bulls, cows, and calves, on the green faces of the declivities in front. They scrambled away over the hills to the right and left; and far off, the pale blue swells in the extreme distance were dotted with innumerable specks. Sometimes I surprised shaggy old bulls grazing alone, or sleeping behind the ridges I ascended. They would leap up at my approach, stare stupidly at me through their tangled manes, and then gallop heavily away. The antelope were very numerous; and as they are always bold when in the neighborhood of buffalo, they would approach to look at me, gaze intently with their great round eyes, then suddenly leap aside, and stretch lightly away over the prairie, as swiftly as a racehorse. Squalid, ruthan-like wolves sneaked through the hollows and sandy ravines. Several times I passed through villages of prairie-dogs, who sat, each at the mouth of his burrow, holding his paws before him in a supplicating attitude, and yelping away most vehemently, whisking his little tail with every squeaking cry he uttered. Prairie-dogs are not fastidious in their choice of companions; various long checkered snakes were sunning themselves in the midst of the village, and demure little gray owls, with large white ring around each eye, were perched side by side with the rightful inhabitants. The prairie teemed with life. Again and again I looked toward the crowded hillsides, and was sure I saw horsemen; and riding near, with a mixture of hope and dread, for Indians were abroad, I found them transformed into a group of buffalo. There was nothing in human shape amid all this vast congregation of brute forms.

When I turned down the buffalo path, the prairie seemed changed; only a wolf or two glided by at intervals, like conscious felons never looking to the right or left. Being now free from anxiety, I was at leisure to observe minutely the objects around me; and here, for the first time, I noticed insects wholly different from any of the varieties found farther to the eastward. Gaudy butterflies fluttered about my horse's head; strangely formed beetles, glittering with metallic lustre, were crawling upon plants that I had never seen before; multitudes of lizards, too, were darting like lightning over the sand.

I had run to a great distance from the river. It cost me a long ride on the buffalo path, before I saw, from the ridge of a sand-hill, the pale surface of the Platte glistening in the midst of its desert valley, and the faint outline of the hills beyond waving along the sky. From where I stood, not a tree nor a bush nor a living thing was visible throughout the whole extent of the sun-scorched landscape. In half an hour I came upon the trail, not far from the river; and seeing that the party had not yet passed, I turned eastward to meet them, old Pontiac's long swinging trot again assuring me that I was right in doing so. Having been slightly ill on leaving camp in the morning, six or seven hours of rough riding had fatigued me extremely. I soon stopped, therefore, flung my saddle on the ground, and with my head resting on it and my horse's trail-rope tied loosely to my arm, lay waiting the arrival of the party, speculating meanwhile on the extent of the injuries Pontiac had received. At length the white wagon coverings rose from the verge of the plain. By a singular coincidence, almost at the same moment two horsemen appeared coming down from the hills. They were Shaw and Henry, who had searched for me a while in the morning, but well knowing the futility of the attempt in such a broken country, had placed themselves on the top of the highest hill they could find, and picketing their horses near them, as a signal to me, had lain down and fallen asleep. The stray cattle had been recovered, as the emigrants told us, about noon. Before sunset, we pushed forward eight miles farther.

> "June 7, 1846.—Four men are missing: R——, Sorel, and two emigrants. They set out this morning after buffalo, and have not yet made their appearance; whether killed or lost, we cannot tell."

I find the above in my note-book, and well remember the council held on the occasion. Our fire was the scene of it; for the superiority of Henry Chatillon's experience and skill made him the resort of the whole camp upon every question of difficulty. He was moulding bullets at the fire, when the captain drew near, with a perturbed and careworn expression of countenance, faithfully reflected on the heavy features of Jack, who followed close behind. Then the emigrants came straggling from their wagons towards the common centre. Various suggestions were made, to account for the absence of the four men, and one or two of the emigrants declared that, when out after the cattle, they had seen Indians dogging them, and crawling like wolves along the ridges of the hills. At this the captain slowly shook his head with double gravity, and solemnly remarked,—

"It's a serious thing to be travelling through this cursed wilderness;" an opinion in which Jack immediately expressed thorough coincidence. Henry would not commit himself by declaring any positive opinion.

"Maybe he only followed the buffalo too far; maybe Indian kill him; maybe he got lost; I cannot tell."

With this the auditors were obliged to rest content; the emigrants, not in the least alarmed, though curious to know what had become of their comrades, walked back to their wagons, and the captain betook himself pensively to his tent. Shaw and I followed his example.

# *from* The American Mind

## *Henry Steele Commager*

Yet these three scholars had intellectually much in common. All came from that same Middle Border which nourished Ward and Veblen and Commons and Patten and Pound and so many other seminal thinkers of the new century. All were caught up, in youth, in the swift currents of liberalism and reform, though where the views of Turner and Parrington were colored by the agrarian radicalism of the nineties, those of Beard were illuminated by English and European radicalism and, eventually, by German historical philosophy. All three accepted the doctrine of evolution but as continuity rather than progress; all agreed in awarding environment a more influential role than heredity and in assigning to economy the dominant role in environment.

Of the three, Turner was first on the scene, and he remains in many respects the most influential. Himself relatively unproductive, he inspired a larger volume of historical writing than any other scholar of his generation. The most modest of men, he was most ambitious in his claims and the most successful in establishing them. The least chauvinistic of scholars, he was the most aggressively American, the most insistent upon the unique value of the American historical experience. Alert to the dangers inherent in unregulated individualism and with a tender social conscience, through his celebration of the pioneer virtues he gave aid and comfort to the champions of rugged individualism in the post-frontier era. Not primarily a philosophical historian, his influence was philosophical, for he was concerned with a point of view rather than with the view itself.

That point of view was the frontier, moving inexorably across the continent. Yet Turner was not the historian of the frontier—that he left to others—but the historian of America, who took his vantage point along the frontier. To this vantage point he had made his way, originally, not so much with the aid of the historians' surveying instruments as by instinct. The frontier, indeed, was in his blood. He had grown up in a Wisconsin not far removed from the wilderness stage. As a boy he had watched in fascination while the city fathers of Portage uncovered the graves of early French pioneers; from the old settlers he had heard stories of frontier days, and he was on the first train that puffed its way into the northern woods. His brief experience at the Johns Hopkins did not abate his zeal for the study of the West, and when he returned to Wisconsin, it was to the university that housed the great Draper collection of western history, that encouraged the pioneer work of Reuben Gold Thwaites, and that boasted such scholars as Ely, Commons, and Ross. Here he saw a pioneer democracy adjust itself to the realities of modern industrial capitalism; here he watched Robert LaFollette battle against corporate greed and exploitation; here he formulated his ideas about the significance of the frontier and of sectionalism. He was never really happy outside his Middle West, and for all his broad Americanism, for all his later years in Cambridge and in California, he was almost parochial in his conviction that the Mississippi Valley had somehow taken out a patent on democracy and on Americanism.

Turner's epoch-making paper on the "Significance of the Frontier in American History" appeared the year of Parkman's death. Turner was, in a sense, Parkman's successor, and there could be no better illustration of the difference between the old history and the new than that afforded by the work of these two historians of the West. Parkman's narrative was spacious, poetic, varicolored, and bold, its pages vibrant with life and with heroic deeds, tense with conspiracy and politics and war. Turner was incapable of narrative, eschewed color, ignored individuals except where they served as types, shunned heroism and drama except the heroism of unnamed pioneers and the drama of social evolution, and contented himself with analysis. The stately forests and glistening lakes and rushing waters, the frowning mountains and sweeping plains, which had served as a magnificent backdrop to Parkman's history, with Turner moved into the foreground and became the very stuff of history; but the romantic characters—the black-robed priests and plumed warriors and *couriers-de-boils* and painted savages—vanished from the scene, their place usurped by impersonal institutions. Of all the fifty-some essays which Turner wrote, not one was biographical, and it is not a little curious that a historian so zealous to celebrate individualism should so consistently have ignored the individual.

Yet in this Turner was consistent enough. It was the frontier, after all, that was the hero of his story, the frontier that had molded the great individuals, the frontier that had distinguished American from Old World history and thus given meaning to its story:

The wilderness masters the colonist. It finds him a European in dress, industries, tools, modes of travel, and thought. It takes him from the railroad car and puts him in the birch canoe. It strips off the garments of civilization and arrays him in the hunting shirt and the moccasin. It puts him in the log cabin of the Cherokee and the Iroquois and runs an Indian palisade around him. Before long he has gone to planting Indian corn and plowing with a sharp stick; he shouts the war cry and takes the scalp in orthodox Indian fashion. In short, at the frontier the environment is at first too strong for the man. . . . Little by little he transforms the wilderness, but the outcome is not the old Europe, not simply the development of Germanic germs, any more than the first phenomenon was a case of reversion to the Germanic mark. The fact is, that here is a new product that is American. . . . The advance of the frontier has meant a steady movement away from the influence of Europe, a steady growth of independence on American lines. And to study this advance, the men who grew up under these conditions, and the political, economic, and social results of it, is to study the really American part of our history. (*Significance of the Frontier in American History*)

All this was clearly in the evolutionary stream—an effort to explain the development of institutions from the simple to the complex—but it was just as clearly not the kind of evolution that John Fiske was teaching. For where Fiske emphasized inheritance, Turner emphasized environment; where Fiske liked to find the genesis of the New England town in the folkgemot of primitive Germany, or of liberty in Magna Carta, or of federalism in the leagues of the Greek city-states, Turner insisted that the American environment accounted sufficiently for these and for most other American institutions:

American democracy is fundamentally the outcome of the experiences of the American people in dealing with the West. Western democracy through the whole of its earlier period tended to the production of a society of which the most distinctive fact was the freedom of the individual to rise under conditions of social mobility, and whose ambition was the freedom and well-being of the masses. . . . American democracy was born of no theorist's dream; it was not carried in the *Susan Constant* to Virginia, nor in the *Mayflower* to Plymouth. It came out of the American forest, and it gained new strength each time it touched a new frontier. Not the constitution, but free land, and an abundance of natural resources open to a fit people, made the democratic type of society in America for three centuries. (*Frontier in American History*, pp. 266, 293)

It was inevitable that such a formula should appeal to a people who felt instinctively that they had created more than they had inherited and that they owed little to the Old World. It was a nationalistic formula, for it suggested that democracy and freedom and the institutions that gave them meaning were largely American inventions; insofar as it did not inquire into the experience of other peoples with their frontiers, it was almost parochial. It was a democratic formula, for it presented American history as a creative act and one in which all had participated, the humble and obscure as well as the famous. It gave to each new generation an equal chance, made every American a contributor, and made the contribution a continuous one. It fitted the individualistic temper of the time, revealing what had been achieved in the past by individual enterprise and fortitude, yet it gave some support to the forces of progressivism for it made clear that the individualism of the pioneer had necessarily been accommodated to the security and prosperity of the community. It fitted the pragmatic mood, for it submitted American institutions and ideals to the test of experience and accepted as American what had come out of the crucible of experience. It appeared to be a scientific formula, for it rejected all a priori notions and discovered the nature of the American character and of American institutions by laboratory tests, and for all its celebration of individualism it made clear that the processes of history were controlled by grand, impersonal forces. It justified optimism, for if out of such rude and awkward beginnings Nature and man had fashioned a great civilization, what might not be achieved in the future? Nor did the emphasis on the role of environment detract in any way from the satisfaction felt for the American achievement; it was, after all, as gratifying to discover that America had molded Washington as that Washington had fathered America, that America had created Lincoln as that Lincoln had preserved America.

It was ominous, to be sure, to be reminded that the frontier had gone, for with it much of the old America seemed to have vanished, the America of freedom and individualism, the America of the second chance. Sectionalism rather than the frontier held the key to the future, and if American sections were comparable to European nations, as Turner insisted, could America hope to avoid the rivalries and wars that had for so long plagued the Old World? Turner assessed soberly enough the problems that confronted twentieth-century America—urbanization, industrialism, class conflicts, the rise of the giant corporation—but his deep-rooted optimism did not permit discouragement, and his study of "Sections and the Nation" ended on a lyrical note which revealed how transcendental the new scientific history could be:

There are American ideals. . . . It is inconceivable that we should follow the evil path of Europe, and place our reliance upon triumphant force. We shall not become cynical, and convinced that sections, like European nations, must dominate their neighbors and strike first and hardest. However profound the economic changes, we shall not give up our American ideals and our hopes for man, which had their origin in our own pioneering experience, in favor of any mechanical solution offered by doctrinaires educated in Old World grievances. Rather, we shall find strength to build from our past a nobler structure, in which each section will find its place as a fit room in a worthy house. We shall courageously maintain the American system expressed by nation-wide parties, acting under sectional and class compromises. We shall continue to present to our sister continent of Europe the underlying ideas of America as a better way of solving difficulties. We shall point to the *Pax Americana* and seek the path of peace on earth to men of good will. (*Sections in American History*, p. 339, Holt)

# *from* Brave New World

*Aldous Huxley*

A squat grey building of only thirty-four stories. Over the main entrance the words, CENTRAL LONDON HATCHERY AND CONDITIONING CENTRE, and, in a shield, the World State's motto, COMMUNITY, IDENTITY, STABILITY.

The enormous room on the ground floor faced towards the north. Cold for all the summer beyond the panes, for all the tropical heat of the room itself, a harsh thin light glared through the windows, hungrily seeking some draped lay figure, some pallid shape of academic goose-flesh, but finding only the glass and nickel and bleakly shining porcelain of a laboratory. Wintriness responded to wintriness. The overalls of the workers were white, their hands gloved with a pale corpse-coloured rubber. The light was frozen, dead, a ghost. Only from the yellow barrels of the microscopes did it borrow a certain rich and living substance, lying along the polished tubes like butter, streak after luscious streak in long recession down the work tables.

"And this," said the Director opening the door, "is the Fertilizing Room."

Bent over their instruments, three hundred Fertilizers were plunged, as the Director of Hatcheries and Conditioning entered the room, in the scarcely breathing silence, the absent-minded, soliloquizing hum or whistle, of absorbed concentration. A troop of newly arrived students, very young, pink and callow, followed nervously, rather abjectly, at the Director's heels. Each of them carried a notebook, in which, whenever the great man spoke, he desperately scribbled. Straight from the horse's mouth. It was a rare privilege. The D. H. C. for Central London always made a point of personally conducting his new students round the various departments.

"Just to give you a general idea," he would explain to them. For of course some sort of general idea they must have, if they were to do their work intelligently—though as little of one, if they were to be good and happy members of society, as possible. For particulars, as every one knows, make for virtue and happiness; generalities are intellectually necessary evils. Not philosophers but fretsawyers and stamp collectors compose the backbone of society.

"To-morrow," he would add, smiling at them with a slightly menacing geniality, "you'll be settling down to serious work. You won't have time for generalities. Meanwhile. . ."

Meanwhile, it was a privilege. Straight from the horse's mouth into the notebook. The boys scribbled like mad.

Tall and rather thin but upright, the Director advanced into the room. He had a long chin and big rather prominent teeth, just covered, when he was not talking, by his full, floridly curved lips. Old, young? Thirty? Fifty? Fifty-five? It was hard to say. And anyhow the question didn't arise; in this year of stability, a.f. 632, it didn't occur to you to ask it.

"I shall begin at the beginning," said the D.H.C. and the more zealous students recorded his intention in their notebooks: *Begin at the beginning.* "These," he waved his hand, "are the incubators." And opening an insulated door he showed them racks upon racks of numbered test-tubes. "The week's supply of ova. Kept," he explained, "at blood heat; whereas the male gametes," and here he opened another door, "they have to be kept at thirty-five instead of thirty-seven. Full blood heat sterilizes." Rams wrapped in theremogene beget no lambs.

Still leaning against the incubators he gave them, while the pencils scurried illegibly across the pages, a brief description of the modern fertilizing process; spoke first, of course, of its surgical introduction—"the operation undergone voluntarily for the good of Society, not to mention the fact that it carries a bonus amounting to six months' salary"; continued with some account of the technique for preserving the excised ovary alive and actively developing; passed on to a consideration of optimum temperature, salinity, viscosity; referred to the liquor in which the detached and ripened eggs were kept; and, leading his charges to the work tables, actually showed them how this liquor was drawn off from the test-tubes; how it was let out drop by drop onto the specially warmed slides of the microscopes; how the eggs which it contained were inspected for abnormalities, counted and transferred to a porous receptacle; how (and he now took them to watch the operation) this receptacle was immersed in a warm bouillon containing free-swimming spermatozoa—at a minimum concentration of one hundred thousand per cubic centimetre, he insisted; and how, after ten minutes, the container was lifted out of the liquor and its contents re-examined; how, if any of the eggs remained unfertilized, it was again immersed, and, if necessary, yet again; how the fertilized ova went back to the incubators; where the Alphas and Betas remained until definitely bottled; while the Gammas, Deltas and Epsilons were brought out again, after only thirty-six hours, to undergo Bokanovsky's Process.

"Bokanovsky's Process," repeated the Director, and the students underlined the words in their little notebooks.

One egg, one embryo, one adult—normality. But a bokanovskified egg will bud, will proliferate, will divide. From eight to ninety-six buds, and every bud will grow into a perfectly formed embryo, and every embryo into a full-sized adult. Making ninety-six human beings grow where only one grew before. Progress.

"Essentially," the D.H.C. concluded, "bokanovskification consists of a series of arrests of development. We check the normal growth and, paradoxically enough, the egg responds by budding."

*Responds by budding.* The pencils were busy.

He pointed. On a very slowly moving band a rack-full of test-tubes was entering a large metal box, another, rack-full was emerging. Machinery faintly purred. It took eight minutes for the tubes to go through, he told them. Eight minutes of hard X-rays being about as much as an egg can stand. A few died; of the rest, the least susceptible divided into two; most put out four buds; some eight; all were returned to the incubators, where the buds began to develop; then, after two days, were suddenly chilled, chilled and checked. Two, four, eight, the buds in their turn budded; and having budded were dosed almost to death with alcohol; consequently burgeoned again and having budded—bud out of bud out of bud—were thereafter—further arrest being generally fatal—left to develop in peace. By which time the original egg was in a fair way to becoming anything from eight to ninety-six embryos—a prodigious improvement, you will agree, on nature. Identical twins—but not in piddling twos and threes as in the old viviparous days, when an egg would sometimes accidentally divide; actually by dozens, by scores at a time.

"Scores," the Director repeated and flung out his arms, as though he were distributing largesse. "Scores."

But one of the students was fool enough to ask where the advantage lay.

"My good boy!" The Director wheeled sharply round on him. "Can't you see? Can't you see?" He raised a hand; his expression was solemn. "Bokanovsky's Process is one of the major instruments of social stability!"

*Major instruments of social stability.*

Standard men and women; in uniform batches. The whole of a small factory staffed with the products of a single bokanovskified egg.

"Ninety-six identical twins working ninety-six identical machines!" The voice was almost tremulous with enthusiasm. "You really know where you are. For the first time in history." He quoted the planetary motto. "Community, Identity, Stability." Grand words. "If we could bokanovskify indefinitely the whole problem would be solved."

Solved by standard Gammas, unvarying Deltas, uniform Epsilons. Millions of identical twins. The principle of mass production at last applied to biology.

"But, alas," the Director shook his head, "we can't bokanovskify indefinitely."

Ninety-six seemed to be the limit; seventy-two a good average. From the same ovary and with gametes of the same male to manufacture as many batches of identical twins as possible—that was the best (sadly a second best) that they could do. And even that was difficult.

"For in nature it takes thirty years for two hundred eggs to reach maturity. But our business is to stabilize the population at this moment, here and now. Dribbling out twins over a quarter of a century—what would be the use of that?"

Obviously, no use at all. But Podsnap's Technique had immensely accelerated the process of ripening. They could make sure of at least a hundred and fifty mature eggs within two years. Fertilize and bokanovskify—in other words, multiply by seventy-two—and you get an average of nearly eleven thousand brothers and sisters in a hundred and fifty batches of identical twins, all within two years of the same age.

"And in exceptional cases we can make one ovary yield us over fifteen thousand adult individuals."

Beckoning to a fair-haired, ruddy young man who happened to be passing at the moment. "Mr. Foster," he called. The ruddy young man approached. "Can you tell us the record for a single ovary, Mr. Foster?"

"Sixteen thousand and twelve in this Centre," Mr. Foster replied without hesitation. He spoke very quickly, had a vivacious blue eye, and took an evident pleasure in quoting figures. "Sixteen thousand and twelve; in one hundred and eighty-nine batches of identicals. But of course they've done much better," he rattled on, "in some of the tropical Centres. Singapore has often produced over sixteen thousand five hundred; and Mombasa has actually touched the seventeen thousand mark. But then they have unfair advantages. You should see the way a negro ovary responds to pituitary! It's quite astonishing, when you're used to working with European material. Still," he added, with a laugh (but the light of combat was in his eyes and the lift of his chin was challenging), "still, we mean to beat them if we can. I'm working on a wonderful Delta-Minus ovary at this moment. Only just eighteen months old. Over twelve thousand seven hundred children already, either decanted or in embryo. And still going strong. We'll beat them yet."

"That's the spirit I like!" cried the Director, and clapped Mr. Foster on the shoulder. "Come along with us, and give these boys the benefit of your expert knowledge."

Mr. Foster smiled modestly. "With pleasure." They went.

In the Bottling Room all was harmonious bustle and ordered activity. Flaps of fresh sow's peritoneum ready cut to the proper size came shooting up in little lifts from the Organ Store in the sub-basement. Whizz and then, click! the lift-hatches flew open; the bottle-liner had only to reach out a hand, take the flap, insert, smooth-down, and before the lined bottle had had time to travel out of reach along the endless band, whizz, click! another flap of peritoneum had shot up from the depths, ready to be slipped into yet another bottle, the next of that slow interminable procession on the band.

Next to the Liners stood the Matriculators. The procession advanced; one by one the eggs were transferred from their test-tubes to the larger containers; deftly the peritoneal lining was slit, the morula dropped into place, the saline solution poured in . . . and already the bottle had passed, and it was the turn of the labellers. Heredity, date of fertilization, membership of Bokanovsky Group—details were transferred from test-tube to bottle. No longer anonymous, but named, identified, the procession marched slowly on; on through an opening in the wall, slowly on into the Social Predestination Room.

"Eighty-eight cubic metres of card-index," said Mr. Foster with relish, as they entered.

"Containing *all* the relevant information," added the Director.

"Brought up to date every morning."

"And co-ordinated every afternoon."

"On the basis of which they make their calculations."

"So many individuals, of such and such quality," said Mr. Foster.

"Distributed in such and such quantities."

"The optimum Decanting Rate at any given moment."

"Unforeseen wastages promptly made good."

"Promptly," repeated Mr. Foster. "If you knew the amount of overtime I had to put in after the last Japanese earthquake!" He laughed goodhumouredly and shook his head.

"The Predestinators send in their figures to the Fertilizers."

"Who give them the embryos they ask for."

"And the bottles come in here to be predestined in detail."

"After which they are sent down to the Embryo Store."

"Where we now proceed ourselves."

And opening a door Mr. Foster led the way down a staircase into the basement.

The temperature was still tropical. They descended into a thickening twilight. Two doors and a passage with a double turn insured the cellar against any possible infiltration of the day.

"Embryos are like photograph film," said Mr. Foster waggishly, as he pushed open the second door. "They can only stand red light."

And in effect the sultry darkness into which the students now followed him was visible and crimson, like the darkness of closed eyes on a summer's afternoon. The bulging flanks of row on receding row and tier above tier of bottles glinted with innumerable rubies, and among the rubies moved the dim red spectres of men and women with purple eyes and all the symptoms of lupus. The hum and rattle of machinery faintly stirred the air.

"Give them a few figures, Mr. Foster," said the Director, who was tired of talking.

Mr. Foster was only too happy to give them a few figures.

Two hundred and twenty metres long, two hundred wide, ten high. He pointed upwards. Like chickens drinking, the students lifted their eyes towards the distant ceiling.

Three tiers of racks: ground floor level, first gallery, second gallery.

The spidery steel-work of gallery above gallery faded away in all directions into the dark. Near them three red ghosts were busily unloading demijohns from a moving staircase.

The escalator from the Social Predestination Room.

Each bottle could be placed on one of fifteen racks, each rack, though you couldn't see it, was a conveyor traveling at the rate of thirty-three and a third centimetres an hour. Two hundred and sixty-seven days at eight metres a day. Two thousand one hundred and thirty-six metres in all. One circuit of the cellar at ground level, one on the first gallery, half on the second, and on the two hundred and sixty-seventh morning, daylight in the Decanting Room. Independent existence—so called.

"But in the interval," Mr. Foster concluded, "we've managed to do a lot to them. Oh, a very great deal." His laugh was knowing and triumphant.

"That's the spirit I like," said the Director once more. "Let's walk around. You tell them everything, Mr. Foster."

Mr. Foster duly told them.

Told them of the growing embryo on its bed of peritoneum. Made them taste the rich blood surrogate on which it fed. Explained why it had to be stimulated with placentin and thyroxin. Told them of the corpus luteum extract. Showed them the jets through which at every twelfth metre from zero to 2040 it was automatically injected. Spoke of those gradually increasing doses of pituitary administered during the final ninety-six metres of their course. Described the artificial maternal circulation installed in every bottle at Metre 112; showed them the reservoir of blood-surrogate, the centrifugal pump that kept the liquid moving over the placenta and drove it through the synthetic lung and waste product filter. Referred to the embryo's troublesome tendency to anæmia, to the massive doses of hog's stomach extract and foetal foal's liver with which, in consequence, it had to be supplied.

Showed them the simple mechanism by means of which, during the last two metres out of every eight, all the embryos were simultaneously shaken into familiarity with movement. Hinted at the gravity of the so-called "trauma of decanting," and enumerated the precautions taken to minimize, by a suitable training of the bottled embryo, that dangerous shock. Told them of the test for sex carried out in the neighborhood of Metre 200. Explained the system of labelling—a T for the males, a circle for the females and for those who were destined to become freemartins a question mark, black on a white ground.

"For of course," said Mr. Foster, "in the vast majority of cases, fertility is merely a nuisance. One fertile ovary in twelve hundred—that would really be quite sufficient for our purposes. But we want to have a good choice. And of course one must always have an enormous margin of safety. So we allow as many as thirty per cent of the female embryos to develop normally. The others get a dose of male sex-hormone every twenty-four metres for the rest of the course. Result: they're decanted as freemartins—structurally quite normal (except," he had to admit, "that they *do* have the slightest tendency to grow beards), but sterile. Guaranteed sterile. Which brings us at last," continued Mr. Foster, "out of the realm of mere slavish imitation of nature into the much more interesting world of human invention."

He rubbed his hands. For of course, they didn't content themselves with merely hatching out embryos: any cow could do that.

"We also predestine and condition. We decant our babies as socialized human beings, as Alphas or Epsilons, as future sewage workers or future. . ." He was going to say "future World controllers," but correcting himself, said "future Directors of Hatcheries," instead.

The D.H.C. acknowledged the compliment with a smile.

They were passing Metre 320 on Rack 11. A young Beta-Minus mechanic was busy with screwdriver and spanner on the blood-surrogate pump of a passing bottle. The hum of the electric motor deepened by fractions of a tone as he turned the nuts. Down, down. . . A final twist, a glance at the revolution counter, and he was done. He moved two paces down the line and began the same process on the next pump.

"Reducing the number of revolutions per minute," Mr. Foster explained. "The surrogate goes round slower; therefore passes through the lung at longer intervals; therefore gives the embryo less oxygen. Nothing like oxygen-shortage for keeping an embryo below par." Again he rubbed his hands.

"But why do you want to keep the embryo below par?" asked an ingenuous student.

"Ass!" said the Director, breaking a long silence. "Hasn't it occurred to you that an Epsilon embryo must have an Epsilon environment as well as an Epsilon heredity?"

It evidently hadn't occurred to him. He was covered with confusion.

"The lower the caste," said Mr. Foster, "the shorter the oxygen." The first organ affected was the brain. After that the skeleton. At seventy per cent of normal oxygen you got dwarfs. At less than seventy eyeless monsters.

"Who are no use at all," concluded Mr. Foster.

Whereas (his voice became confidential and eager), if they could discover a technique for shortening the period of maturation what a triumph, what a benefaction to Society!

"Consider the horse."

They considered it.

Mature at six; the elephant at ten. While at thirteen a man is not yet sexually mature; and is only full-grown at twenty. Hence, of course, that fruit of delayed development, the human intelligence.

"But in Epsilons," said Mr. Foster very justly, "we don't need human intelligence."

Didn't need and didn't get it. But though the Epsilon mind was mature at ten, the Epsilon body was not fit to work till eighteen. Long years of superfluous and wasted immaturity. If the physical development could be speeded up till it was as quick, say, as a cow's, what an enormous saving to the Community!

"Enormous!" murmured the students. Mr. Foster's enthusiasm was infectious.

He became rather technical; spoke of the abnormal endocrine co-ordination which made men grow so slowly; postulated a germinal mutation to account for it. Could the effects of this germinal mutation be undone? Could the individual Epsilon embryo be made a revert, by a suitable technique, to the normality of dogs and cows? That was the problem. And it was all but solved.

Pilkington, at Mombasa, had produced individuals who were sexually mature at four and full-grown at six and a half. A scientific triumph. But socially useless. Six-year-old men and women were too stupid to do even Epsilon work. And the process was an all-or-nothing one; either you failed to modify at all, or else you modified the whole way. They were still trying to find the ideal compromise between adults of twenty and adults of six. So far without success. Mr. Foster sighed and shook his head.

Their wanderings through the crimson twilight had brought them to the neighborhood of Metre 170 on Rack 9. From this point onwards Rack 9 was enclosed and the bottles performed the remainder of their journey in a kind of tunnel, interrupted here and there by openings two or three metres wide.

"Heat conditioning," said Mr. Foster.

Hot tunnels alternated with cool tunnels. Coolness was wedded to discomfort in the form of hard X-rays. By the time they were decanted the embryos had a horror of cold. They were predestined to emigrate to the tropics, to be miners and acetate silk spinners and steel workers. Later on their minds would be made to endorse the judgment of their bodies. "We condition them to thrive on heat," concluded Mr. Foster. "Our colleagues upstairs will teach them to love it."

"And that," put in the Director sententiously, "that is the secret of happiness and virtue—liking what you've *got* to do. All conditioning aims at that: making people like their unescapable social destiny."

In a gap between two tunnels, a nurse was delicately probing with a long fine syringe into the gelatinous contents of a passing bottle. The students and their guides stood watching her for a few moments in silence.

"Well, Lenina," said Mr. Foster, when at last she withdrew the syringe and straightened herself up.

The girl turned with a start. One could see that, for all the lupus and the purple eyes, she was uncommonly pretty.

"Henry!" Her smile flashed redly at him—a row of coral teeth.

"Charming, charming," murmured the Director and, giving her two or three little pats, received in exchange a rather deferential smile for himself.

"What are you giving them?" asked Mr. Foster, making his tone very professional.

"Oh, the usual typhoid and sleeping sickness."

"Tropical workers start being inoculated at Metre 150," Mr. Foster explained to the students. "The embryos still have gills. We immunize the fish against the future man's diseases." Then, turning back to Lenina, "Ten to five on the roof this afternoon," he said, "as usual."

"Charming," said the Director once more, and, with a final pat, moved away after the others.

On Rack 10 rows of next generation's chemical workers were being trained in the toleration of lead, caustic soda, tar, chlorine. The first of a batch of two hundred and fifty embryonic rocketplane engineers was just passing the eleven hundred metre mark on Rack 3. A special mechanism kept their containers in constant rotation. "To improve their sense of balance," Mr. Foster explained. "Doing repairs on the outside of a rocket in mid-air is a ticklish job. We slacken off the circulation when they're right way up, so that they're half starved, and double the flow of surrogate when they're upside down. They learn to associate topsy-turvydom with well-being; in fact, they're only truly happy when they're standing on their heads.

"And now," Mr. Foster went on, "I'd like to show you some very interesting conditioning for Alpha Plus Intellectuals. We have a big batch of them on Rack 5. First Gallery level," he called to two boys who had started to go down to the ground floor.

"They're round about Metre 900," he explained. "You can't really do any useful intellectual conditioning till the foetuses have lost their tails. Follow me."

But the Director had looked at his watch. "Ten to three," he said. "No time for the intellectual embryos, I'm afraid. We must go up to the Nurseries before the children have finished their afternoon sleep."

Mr. Foster was disappointed. "At least one glance at the Decanting Room," he pleaded.

"Very well then." The Director smiled indulgently. "Just one glance."

•  •  •

The journey was quite uneventful. The Blue Pacific Rocket was two and a half minutes early at New Orleans, lost four minutes in a tornado over Texas, but flew into a favourable air current at Longitude 95 West, and was able to land at Santa Fe less than forty seconds behind schedule time.

"Forty seconds on a six and a half hour flight. Not so bad," Lenina conceded.

They slept that night at Santa Fe. The hotel was excellent—incomparably better, for example, than that horrible Aurora Bora Palace in which Lenina had suffered so much the previous summer. Liquid air, television, vibro-vacuum massage, radio, boiling caffeine solution, hot contraceptives, and eight different kinds of scent were laid on in every bedroom. The synthetic music plant was working as they entered the hall and left nothing to be desired. A notice in the lift announced that there were sixty Escalator-Squash-Racquet Courts in the hotel, and that Obstacle and Electro-magnetic Golf could both be played in the park.

"But it sounds simply too lovely," cried Lenina. "I almost wish we could stay here. Sixty Escalator-Squash Courts . . ."

"There won't be any in the Reservation," Bernard warned her. "And no scent, no television, no hot water even. If you feel you can't stand it, stay here till I come back."

Lenina was quite offended. "Of course I can stand it. I only said it was lovely here because . . . well, because progress *is* lovely, isn't it?"

"Five hundred repetitions once a week from thirteen to seventeen," said Bernard wearily, as though to himself.

"What did you say?"

"I said that progress was lovely. That's why you mustn't come to the Reservation unless you really want to."

"But I do want to."

"Very well, then," said Bernard; and it was almost a threat.

Their permit required the signature of the Warden of the Reservation, at whose office next morning they duly presented themselves. An Epsilon-Plus negro porter took in Bernard's card, and they were admitted almost immediately.

The Warden was a blond and brachycephalic Alpha-Minus, short, red, moon-faced, and broad-shouldered, with a loud booming voice, very well adapted to the utterance of hypnopædic wisdom. He was a mine of irrelevant information and unasked-for good advice. Once started, He went on and on—boomingly.

". . . five hundred and sixty thousand square kilometres, divided into four distinct Sub-Reservations, each surrounded by a high-tension wire fence."

At this moment, and for no apparent reason, Bernard suddenly remembered that he had left the Eau de Cologne tap in his bathroom wide open and running.

". . . supplied with current from the Grand Canyon hydro-electric station."

"Cost me a fortune by the time I get back." With his mind's eye, Bernard saw the needle on the scent meter creeping round and round, antlike, indefatigably. "Quickly telephone to Helmholtz Watson."

". . . upwards of five thousand kilometres of fencing at sixty thousand volts."

"You don't say so," said Lenina politely, not knowing in the least what the Warden had said, but taking her cue from his dramatic pause. When the Warden started booming, she had inconspicuously swallowed half a gramme of *soma*, with the result that she could now sit, serenely not listening, thinking of nothing at all, but with her large blue eyes fixed on the Walden's face in an expression of rapt attention.

"To touch the fence is instant death," pronounced the Warden solemnly. "There is no escape from a Savage Reservation."

The word "escape" was suggestive. "Perhaps," said Bernard, half rising, "we ought to think of going." The little black needle was scurrying, an insect, nibbling through time, eating into his money.

"No escape," repeated the Warden, waving him back into his chair; and as the permit was not yet countersigned, Bernard had no choice but to obey. "Those who are born in the Reservation—and remember, my dear young lady," he added, leering obscenely at Lenina, and speaking in an improper whisper, "remember that, in the Reservation, children still are born, yes, actually born, revolting as that may seem . . ." (He hoped that this reference to a shameful subject would make Lenina blush; but she only smiled with simulated intelligence and said, "You don't say so!" Disappointed the Warden began again.) "Those, I repeat, who are born in the Reservation are destined to die there."

Destined to die . . . A decilitre of Eau de Cologne every minute. Six litres an hour. Perhaps," Bernard tried again, "we ought . . "

Leaning forward, the Director tapped the table with his forefinger. "You ask me how many people live in the Reservation. And I reply"—triumphantly —"I reply that we do not know. We can only guess."

"You don't say so."

"My dear young lady, I do say so."

Six times twenty-four—no, it would be nearer six times thirty-six. Bernard was pale and trembling with impatience. But inexorably the booming continued.

". . . about sixty thousand Indians and half-breeds . . . absolute savages . . . our inspectors occasionally visit . . . otherwise, no communication whatever with the civilized world . . . still preserve their repulsive habits and customs . . . marriage, if you know what that is, my dear young lady; families . . . no conditioning . . . monstrous superstitions . . . Christianity and totemism and ancestor worship . . . extinct languages, such as Zuñi and Spanish and Athapascan . . . pumas, porcupines and other ferocious animals . . . infectious diseases . . . priests . . . lizards . . . "

"You don't say so?"

They got away at last. Bernard dashed to the telephone. Quick, quick; but it took him nearly three minutes to get on to Helmholtz Watson. "We might be among the savages already," he complained, "Damned incompetence!"

"Have a gramme," suggested Lenina.

He refused, preferring his anger. And at last, thank Ford, he was through and, yes, it was Heimholtz; Heimholtz, to whom he explained what had happened, and who promised to go round at once, at once, and turn off the tap, yes, at once, but took this opportunity to tell him what the D.H.C. had said, in public, yesterday evening. . .

"What? He's looking out for some one to take my place?" Bernard's voice was agonized. "So it's actually decided? Did he mention Iceland? You say he did? Ford! Iceland . . ." He hung up the receiver and turned back to Lenina. His face was pale, his expression utterly dejected.

"What's the matter?" she asked.

"The matter?" He dropped heavily into a chair. "I'm going to be sent to Iceland."

Often in the past he had wondered what it would be like to be subjected (*soma*-less and with nothing but his own inward resources to rely on) to some great trial, some pain, some persecution; he had even longed for affliction. As recently as a week ago, in the Director's office, he had imagined himself courageously resisting, stoically accepting suffering without a word. The Director's threats had actually elated him, made him feel larger than life. But that, as he now realized, was because he had not taken the threats quite seriously; he had not believed that, when it came to the point, the D.H.C. would ever do anything. Now that it looked as though the threats were really to be fulfilled, Bernard was appalled. Of that imagined stoicism, that theoretical courage, not a trace was left.

He raged against himself—what a fool!—against the Director—how unfair not to give him that other chance, that other chance which, he now had no doubt at all, he had always intended to take. And Iceland, Iceland. . .

Lenina shook her head. "Was and will make me ill," she quoted, "I take a gramme and only am."

In the end she persuaded him to swallow four tablets of *soma*. Five minutes later roots and fruits were abolished; the flower of the present rosily blossomed. A message from the porter announced that, at the Warden's orders, a Reservation Guard had come round with a plane and was waiting on the roof of the hotel. They went up at once. An octoroon in Gamma-green uniform saluted and proceeded to recite the morning's programme.

A bird's-eye view of ten or a dozen of the principal pueblos, then a landing for lunch in the valley of Malpais. The rest-house was comfortable there, and up at the pueblo the savages would probably be celebrating their summer festival. It would be the best place to spend the night.

They took their seats in the plane and set off. Ten minutes later they were crossing the frontier that separated the civilization from savagery. Uphill and down, across the deserts of salt and sand, through forests, into the violet depth of the canyons, over crag and peak and table-topped mesa, the fence marched on and on, irresistibly the straight line, the geometrical symbol of triumphant human purpose. And at its foot, here and there, a mosaic of white bones, a still unrotted carcase dark on the tawny ground marked the place where deer or steer, puma or porcupine or coyote, or the greedy turkey buzzards drawn down by the whiff of carrion and fulminated as though by a poetic justice, had come too close to the destroying wires.

"They never learn," said the green-uniformed pilot, pointing down at the skeletons on the ground below them. "And they never will learn," he added and laughed, as though he had somehow scored a personal triumph over the electrocuted animals.

Bernard also laughed; after two grammes of *soma* the joke seemed, for some reason, good. Laughed and then, almost immediately, dropped off to sleep, and sleeping was carried over Taos and Tesuque; over Nambe and Picuris and Pojoaque, over Sia and Cochiti, over Laguna and Acoma and the Enchanted Mesa, over Zuñi and Cibola and Ojo Caliente, and woke at last to find the machine standing on the ground, Lenina carrying the suit-cases into a small square house, and the Gamma-green octoroon talking incomprehensibly with a young Indian.

"Malpais," explained the pilot, as Bernard stepped out. "This is the rest-house. And there's a dance this afternoon at the pueblo. He'll take you there." He pointed to the sullen young savage. "Funny, I expect." He grinned. "Everything they do is funny." And with that he climbed into the plane and started up the engines. "Back to-morrow. And remember," he added reassuringly to Lenina, "they're perfectly tame; savages won't do you any harm. They've got enough experience of gas bombs to know that they mustn't play any tricks." Still laughing, he threw the helicopter screws into gear, accelerated, and was gone.

The mesa was like a ship becalmed in a strait of lion-coloured dust. The channel wound between precipitous banks, and slanting from one wall to the other across the valley ran a streak of green—the river and its field. On the plow of that stone ship in the centre of the strait, and seemingly a part of it, a shaped and geometrical outcrop of the naked rock, stood the pueblo of Malpais. Block above block, each story smaller than the one below, the tall houses rose like stepped and amputated pyramids into the blue sky. At their feet lay a straggle of low buildings, a criss-cross of walls; and on three sides the precipices fell sheer into the plain. A few columns of smoke mounted perpendicularly into the windless air and were lost.

"Queer," said Lenina. "Very queer." It was her ordinary word of condemnation. "I don't like it. And I don't like that man." She pointed to the Indian guide who had been appointed to take them up to the pueblo. Her feeling was evidently reciprocated; the very back of the man, as he walked along before them, was hostile, sullenly contemptuous.

"Besides," she lowered her voice, "he smells."

Bernard did not attempt to deny it. They walked on.

Suddenly it was as though the whole air had come alive and were pulsing, pulsing with the indefatigable movement of blood. Up there, in Malpais, the drums were being beaten. Their feet fell in with the rhythm of that mysterious heart; they quickened their pace. Their path led them to the foot of the precipice. The sides of the great mesa ship towered over them, three hundred feet to the gunwale.

"I wish we could have brought the plane," said Lenina, looking up resentfully at the blank impending rock-face. "I hate walking. And you feel so small when you're on the ground at the bottom of a hill."

They walked along for some way in the shadow of the mesa, rounded a projection, and there, in a water-worn ravine, was the way up the companion ladder. They climbed. It was a very steep path that zigzagged from side to side of the gully. Sometimes the pulsing of the drums was all but inaudible, at others they seemed to be beating only just round the corner.

When they were half-way up, an eagle flew past so close to them that the wind of his wings blew chill on their faces. In a crevice of the rock lay a pile of bones. It was all oppressively queer, and the Indian smelt stronger and stronger. They emerged at last from the ravine into the full sunlight. The top of the mesa was a flat deck of stone.

"Like the Charing-T Tower," was Lenina's comment. But she was not allowed to enjoy her discovery of this reassuring resemblance for long. A padding of soft feet made them turn round. Naked from throat to navel, their dark brown bodies painted with white lines ("like asphalt tennis courts," Lenina was later to explain), their faces inhuman with daubings of scarlet, black and ochre, two Indians came running along the path. Their black hair was braided with fox fur and red flannel. Cloaks of turkey feathers fluttered from their shoulders; huge feather diadems exploded gaudily round their heads. With every step they took came the clink and rattle of their silver bracelets, their heavy necklaces of bone and turquoise beads. They came on without a word, running quietly in their deerskin moccasins. One of them was holding a feather brush; the other carried, in either hand, what looked at a distance like three or four pieces of thick rope. One of the ropes writhed uneasily, and suddenly Lenina saw that they were snakes.

The men came nearer and nearer; their dark eyes looked at her, but without giving any sign of recognition, any smallest sign that they had seen her or were aware of her existence. The writhing snake hung limp again with the rest. The men passed.

"I don't like it," said Lenina. "I don't like it."

She liked even less what awaited her at the entrance to the pueblo, where their guide had left them while he went inside for instructions. The dirt, to start with, the piles of rubbish, the dust, the dogs, the flies. Her face wrinkled up into a grimace of disgust. She held her handkerchief to her nose.

"But how can they live like this?" she broke out in a voice of indignant incredulity. (It wasn't possible.)

Bernard shrugged his shoulders philosophically. "Anyhow," he said, "they've been doing it for the last five or six thousand years. So I suppose they must be used to it by now."

"But cleanliness is next to fordliness," she insisted.

"Yes, and civilization is sterilization," Bernard went on, concluding on a tone of irony the second hypnopædic lesson in elementary hygiene. "But

these people have never heard of Our Ford, and they aren't civilized. So
there's no point in . . ."

"Oh!" She gripped his arm. "Look."

An almost naked Indian was very slowly climbing down the ladder from
the first-floor terrace of a neighbouring house—rung after rung, with the
tremulous caution of extreme old age. His face was profoundly wrinkled
and black, like a mask of obsidian. The toothless mouth had fallen in. At
the corners of the lips, and on each side of the chin, a few long bristles
gleamed almost white against the dark skin. The long unbraided hair
hung down in grey wisps round his face. His body was bent and emaciated to the bone, almost fleshless. Very slowly he came down, pausing at
each rung before he ventured another step.

"What's the matter with him?" whispered Lenina.

Her eyes were wide with horror and amazement.

"He's old, that's all," Bernard answered as carelessly as he could. He too
was startled; but he made an effort to seem unmoved.

"Old?" she repeated. "But the Director's old; lots of people are old;
they're not like that."

"That's because we don't allow them to be like that. We preserve them
from diseases. We keep their internal secretions artificially balanced at a
youthful equilibrium. We don't permit their magnesium-calcium ratio to
fall below what it was at thirty. We give them transfusion of young blood.
We keep their metabolism permanently stimulated. So, of course, they
don't look like that. Partly," he added, "because most of them die long
before they reach this old creature's age. Youth almost unimpaired till
sixty, and then, crack! the end."

But Lenina was not listening. She was watching the old man. Slowly,
slowly he came down. His feet touched the ground. He turned. In their
deep sunken orbits his eyes were still extraordinarily bright. They looked
at her for a long moment expressionlessly, without surprise, as though
she had not been there at all. Then slowly, with bent back, the old man
hobbled past them and was gone.

"But it's terrible," Lenina whispered. "It's awful. We ought not to have
come here." She felt in her pocket for her *soma*—only to discover that, by

some unprecedented oversight, she had left the bottle down at the rest-house. Bernard's pockets were also empty.

Lenina was left to face the horrors of Malpais unaided. They came crowding in on her thick and fast. The spectacle of two young women giving the breast to their babies made her blush and turn away her face. She had never seen anything so indecent in her life. And what made it worse was that, instead of tactfully ignoring it, Bernard proceeded to make open comments on this revoltingly viviparous scene. Ashamed, now that the effects of the *soma* had worn off, of the weakness he had displayed that morning in the hotel, he went out of his way to show himself strong and unorthodox.

"What a wonderfully intimate relationship," he said, deliberately outrageous. "And what an intensity of feeling it must generate! I often think one may have missed something in not having had a mother. And perhaps you've missed something in not being a mother, Lenina. Imagine yourself sitting there with a little baby of your own. . . ."

"Bernard! How can you?" The passage of an old woman with ophthalmia and a disease of the skin distracted her from her indignation.

"Let's go away," she begged. "I don't like it."

But at this moment their guide came back and, beckoning to them to follow, led the way down the narrow street between the houses. They rounded a corner. A dead dog was lying on a rubbish heap; a woman with a goitre was looking for lice in the hair of a small girl. Their guide halted at the foot of a ladder, raised his hand perpendicularly, then darted it horizontally forward. They did what he mutely commanded—climbed the ladder and walked through the doorway, to which it gave access, into a long narrow room, rather dark and smelling of smoke and cooked grease and long-worn, long-unwashed clothes. At the further end of the room was another doorway, through which came a shaft of sunlight and the noise, very loud and close, of the drums.

They stopped across the threshold and found themselves on a wide terrace. Below them, shut in by the tall houses, was the village square, crowded with Indians. Bright blankets, and feathers in black hair, and the glint of turquoise, and dark skins shining with heat. Lenina put her handkerchief to her nose again. In the open space at the centre of the square were two circular platforms of masonry and trampled clay—the roofs, it was evident, of underground chambers; for in the centre of each platform was an open hatchway, with a ladder emerging from the lower darkness. A sound of subterranean flute playing came up and was almost lost in the steady remorseless persistence of the drums.

Lenina liked the drums. Shutting her eyes she abandoned herself to their soft repeated thunder, allowed it to invade her consciousness more and more completely, till at last there was nothing left in the world but that one deep pulse of sound. It reminded her reassuringly of the synthetic noises made at Solidarity Services and Ford's Day celebrations. "Orgy-porgy," she whispered to herself. These drums beat out just the same rhythms.

There was a sudden startling burst of singing— hundreds of male voices crying out fiercely in harsh metallic unison. A few long notes and silence, the thunderous silence of the drums; then shrill, in a neighing treble, the woman's answer. Then again the drums; and once more the men's deep savage affirmation of their manhood.

Queer—yes. The place was queer, so was the music, so were the clothes and the goitres and the skin diseases and the old people. But the performance itself—there seemed to be nothing specially queer about that.

"It reminds me of a lower-caste Community Sing," she told Bernard.

But a little later it was reminding her a good clear less of that innocuous function. For suddenly there had swarmed up from those round chambers underground a ghastly troop of monsters. Hideously masked or painted out of all semblance of humanity, they had tramped out a strange limping dance round the square; round and again round, singing as they went, round and round—each time a little faster; and the drums had changed and quickened their rhythm, so that it became like the pulsing of fever in the ears; and the crowd had begun to sing with the dancers, louder and louder; and first one woman had shrieked, and then another and another, as though they were being killed; and then suddenly the leader of the dancers broke out of the line, ran to a big wooden chest which was standing at one end of the square, raised the lid and pulled out a pair of black snakes. A great yell went up from the crowd, and all the other dancers ran towards him with outstretched hands. He tossed the snakes to the first-comers, then clipped back into the chest for more. More and more, black snakes and brown and mottled—he flung them out. And then the dance began again on a different rhythm. Round and round they went with their snakes, snakily, with a soft undulating movement at the knees and hips. Round and round. Then the leader gave a signal, and one after another, all the snakes were flung down in the middle of the square; an old man came up from underground and sprinkled them with corn meal, and from the other hatchway came a woman and sprinkled them with water from a black jar. Then the old man lifted his hand and, startlingly, terrifyingly, there was absolute silence. The drums stopped beating, life seemed to have come to an end. The old man pointed towards the two hatchways that gave entrance to the lower world. And slowly, raised by invisible hands from below, there emerged from the one a painted image of an eagle, from the other that of a man, naked, and nailed to a cross. They hung there, seemingly self-sustained, as though watching. The old man clapped his hands. Naked but for a white cotton breech-cloth, a boy of about eighteen stepped out of the crowd and stood before him, his hands crossed over his chest, his head bowed. The old man made the sign of the cross over him and turned away. Slowly, the boy began to walk round the writhing heap of snakes. He had completed the first circuit and was half-way through the second when, from among the dancers, a tall man wearing the mask of a coyote and holding in his hand a whip of plaited leather, advanced towards him. The boy moved on as though unaware of the other's existence. The coyote-man raised his whip; there was a long moment of expectancy, then a swift movement, the whistle of the lash and its loud flat-sounding impact on the flesh. The boy's body quivered; but he made no sound, he walked on at the same slow, steady pace. The coyote struck again, again; and at every blow at first a gasp, and then a deep groan went up from the crowd. The boy walked on. Twice, thrice, four times round he went. The blood was streaming. Five times round, six times round. Suddenly Lenina covered her face with her hands and began to sob. "Oh, stop them, stop them!" she implored. But the whip fell and fell inexorably. Seven times round. Then all at once the boy staggered and, still without a sound, pitched forward on to his face. Bending over him, the old man touched his back with a long white feather, held it up for it moment, crimson, for the people to see, then shook it thrice over the snakes. A few drops fell, and suddenly the drums broke out again into a panic of hurrying notes; there was a great shout. The dancers rushed forward, picked up the snakes and ran out of the square. Men, women, children, all the crowd ran after them. A minute later the square was empty, only the boy remained, prone where he had fallen, quite still. Three old women came out of one of the houses, and with some difficulty lifted him and carried him in. The eagle and the man on the cross kept guard for a little while over the empty pueblo; then, as though they had seen enough, sank slowly down through their hatchways, out of sight, into the nether world.

Lenina was still sobbing. "Too awful," she kept repeating, and all Bernard's consolations were in vain. "Too awful! That blood!" She shuddered. "Oh, I wish I had my *soma*."

# Elixirs of Death

*Rachel Carson*

For the first time in the history of the world, every human being is now subjected to contact with dangerous chemicals, from the moment of conception until death. In the less than two decades of their use, the synthetic pesticides have been so thoroughly distributed throughout the animate and inanimate world that they occur virtually everywhere. They have been recovered from most of the major river systems and even from streams of groundwater flowing unseen through the earth. Residues of these chemicals linger in soil to which they may have been applied a dozen years before. They have entered and lodged in the bodies of fish, birds, reptiles, and domestic and wild animals so universally that scientists carrying on animal experiments find it almost impossible to locate subjects free from such contamination. They have been found in fish in remote mountain lakes, in earthworms burrowing in soil, in the eggs of birds—and in man himself. For these chemicals are now stored in the bodies of the vast majority of human beings, regardless of age. They occur in the mother's milk, and probably in the tissues of the unborn child.

All this has come about because of the sudden rise and prodigious growth of an industry for the production of man-made or synthetic chemicals with insecticidal properties. This industry is a child of the Second World War. In the course of developing agents of chemical warfare, some of the chemicals created in the laboratory were found to be lethal to insects. The discovery did not come by chance: insects were widely used to test chemicals as agents of death for man.

The result has been a seemingly endless stream of synthetic insecticides. In being man-made—by ingenious laboratory manipulation of the molecules, substituting atoms, altering their arrangement—they differ sharply from the simpler insecticides of prewar days. These were derived from naturally occurring minerals and plant products—compounds of arsenic, copper, lead, manganese, zinc, and other minerals, pyrethrum from the dried flowers of chrysanthemums, nicotine sulphate from some of the relatives of tobacco, and rotenone from leguminous plants of the East Indies.

637

What sets the new synthetic insecticides apart is their enormous biological potency. They have immense power not merely to poison but to enter into the most vital processes of the body and change them in sinister and often deadly ways. Thus, as we shall see, they destroy the very enzymes whose function is to protect the body from harm, they block the oxidation processes from which the body receives its energy, they prevent the normal functioning of various organs, and they may initiate in certain cells the slow and irreversible change that leads to malignancy.

Yet new and more deadly chemicals are added to the list each year and new uses are devised so that contact with these materials has become practically worldwide. The production of synthetic pesticides in the United States soared from 124,259,000 pounds in 1947 to 637,666,000 pounds in 1960—more than a fivefold increase. The wholesale value of these products was well over a quarter of a billion dollars. But in the plans and hopes of the industry this enormous production is only a beginning.

A Who's Who of pesticides is therefore of concern to us all. If we are going to live so intimately with these chemicals—eating and drinking them, taking them into the very marrow of our bones—we had better know something about their nature and their power.

Although the Second World War marked a turning away from inorganic chemicals as pesticides into the wonder world of the carbon molecule, a few of the old materials persist. Chief among these is arsenic, which is still the basic ingredient in a variety of weed and insect killers. Arsenic is a highly toxic mineral occurring widely in association with the ores of various metals, and in very small amounts in volcanoes, in the sea, and in spring water. Its relations to man are varied and historic. Since many of its compounds are tasteless, it has been a favorite agent of homicide from long before the time of the Borgias to the present. Arsenic is present in English chimney soot and along with certain aromatic hydrocarbons is considered responsible for the carcinogenic (or cancer-causing) action of the soot, which was recognized nearly two centuries ago by an English physician. Epidemics of chronic arsenical poisoning involving whole populations over long periods are on record. Arsenic-contaminated environments have also caused sickness and death among horses, cows, goats, pigs, deer, fishes, and bees; despite this record arsenical sprays and dusts are widely used. In the arsenic-sprayed cotton country of southern United States beekeeping as an industry has nearly died out. Farmers using arsenic dusts over long periods have been afflicted with chronic arsenic poisoning; livestock have been poisoned by crop sprays or weed killers containing arsenic. Drifting arsenic dusts from blueberry lands have spread over neighboring farms, contaminating streams, fatally poisoning bees and cows, and causing human illness. "It is scarcely possible . . . to handle arsenicals with more utter disregard of the general health than that which has been practiced in our country in recent years," said Dr. W. C. Hueper, of the National Cancer Institute, an authority on environmental cancer. "Anyone who has watched the dusters and sprayers of arsenical insecticides at work must have been impressed by the almost supreme carelessness with which the poisonous substances are dispensed."

Modern insecticides are still more deadly. The vast majority fall into one of two large groups of chemicals. One, represented by DDT, is known as the "chlorinated hydrocarbons." The other group consists of the organic phosphorus insecticides, and is represented by the reasonably familiar malathion and parathion. All have one thing in common. As mentioned above, they are built on a basis of carbon atoms, which are also the indispensable building blocks of the living world, and thus classed as "organic." To understand them, we must see of what they are made, and how, although linked with the basic chemistry of all life, they lend themselves to the modifications which make them agents of death.

The basic element, carbon, is one whose atoms have an almost infinite capacity for uniting with each other in chains and rings and various other configurations, and for becoming linked with atoms of other substances. Indeed, the incredible diversity of living creatures from bacteria to the great blue whale is largely due to this capacity of carbon. The complex protein molecule has the carbon atom as its basis, as have molecules of fat, carbohydrates, enzymes, and vitamins. So, too, have enormous numbers of nonliving things, for carbon is not necessarily a symbol of life.

Some organic compounds are simply combinations of carbon and hydrogen. The simplest of these is methane, or marsh gas, formed in nature by the bacterial decomposition of organic matter under water. Mixed with air in proper proportions, methane becomes the dreaded "fire damp" of coal mines. Its structure is beautifully simple, consisting of one carbon atom to which four hydrogen atoms have become attached:

```
H               H
 \             /
  \    C      /
  /    ‖      \
 /             \
H               H
```

Chemists have discovered that it is possible to detach one or all of the hydrogen atoms and substitute other elements. For example, by substituting one atom of chlorine for one of hydrogen we produce methyl chloride:

```
H               Cl
 \             /
  \    C      /
  /           \
 /             \
H               H
```

Take away three hydrogen atoms and substitute chlorine and we have the anesthetic chloroform:

```
H               Cl
 \             /
  \    C      /
  /           \
 /             \
Cl              Cl
```

Substitute chlorine atoms for all of the hydrogen atoms and the result is carbon tetrachloride, the familiar cleaning fluid:

```
Cl              Cl
 \             /
  \    C      /
  /           \
 /             \
Cl              Cl
```

In the simplest possible terms, these changes rung upon the basic molecule of methane illustrate what a chlorinated hydrocarbon is. But this illustration gives little hint of the true complexity of the chemical world of the hydrocarbons, or of the manipulations by which the organic chemist creates his infinitely varied materials. For instead of the simple methane molecule with its single carbon atom, he may work with hydrocarbon molecules consisting of many carbon atoms, arranged in rings or chains, with side chains or branches, holding to themselves with chemical bonds not merely simple atoms of hydrogen or chlorine but also a wide variety of chemical groups. By seemingly slight changes the whole character of the substance is changed; for example, not only what is attached but the place of attachment to the carbon atom is highly important. Such ingenious manipulations have produced a battery of poisons of truly extraordinary power.

DDT (short for dichloro-diphenyl-trichloro-ethane) was first synthesized by a German chemist in 1874, but its properties as an insecticide were not discovered until 1939. Almost immediately DDT was hailed as a means of stamping out insect-borne disease and winning the farmers' war against crop destroyers overnight. The discoverer, Paul Müller of Switzerland, won the Nobel Prize.

DDT is now so universally used that in most minds the product takes on the harmless aspect of the familiar. Perhaps the myth of the harmlessness of DDT rests on the fact that one of its first uses was the wartime dusting of many thousands of soldiers, refugees, and prisoners, to combat lice. It is widely believed that since so many people came into extremely intimate contact with DDT and suffered no immediate ill effects the chemical must certainly be innocent of harm. This understandable misconception arises from the fact that—unlike other chlorinated hydrocarbons—DDT *in powder form* is not readily absorbed through the skin. Dissolved in oil, as it usually is, DDT is definitely toxic. If swallowed, it is absorbed slowly through the digestive tract; it may also be absorbed through the lungs. Once it has entered the body it is stored largely in organs rich in fatty substances (because DDT itself is fat-soluble) such as the adrenals, testes, or thyroid. Relatively large amounts are deposited in the liver, kidneys, and the fat of the large, protective mesenteries that enfold the intestines.

This storage of DDT begins with the smallest conceivable intake of the chemical (which is present as residues on most foodstuffs) and continues until quite high levels are reached. The fatty storage depots act as biological magnifiers, so that an intake of as little as $\frac{1}{10}$ of 1 part per million in the diet results in storage of about 10 to 15 parts per million, an increase of one hundredfold or more. These terms of reference, so commonplace to the chemist or the pharmacologist, are unfamiliar to most of us. One part in a million sounds like a very small amount—and so it is. But such substances are so potent that a minute quantity can bring about vast changes in the body. In animal experiments, 3 parts per million has been found to inhibit an essential enzyme in heart muscle; only 5 parts per million has brought about necrosis or disintegration of liver cells; only 2.5 parts per million of the closely related chemicals dieldrin and chlordane did the same.

This is really not surprising. In the normal chemistry of the human body there is just such a disparity between cause and effect. For example, a quantity of iodine as small as two ten-thousandths of a gram spells the difference between health and disease. Because these small amounts of pesticides are cumulatively stored and only slowly excreted, the threat of chronic poisoning and degenerative changes of the liver and other organs is very real.

Scientists do not agree upon how much DDT can be stored in the human body. Dr. Arnold Lehman, who is the chief pharmacologist of the Food and Drug Administration, says there is neither a floor below which DDT is not absorbed nor a ceiling beyond which absorption and storage ceases. On the other hand, Dr. Wayland Hayes of the United States Public Health Service contends that in every individual a point of equilibrium is reached, and that DDT in excess of this amount is excreted. For practical purposes it is not particularly important which of these men is right. Storage in human beings has been well investigated, and we know that the average person is storing potentially harmful amounts. According to various studies, individuals with no known exposure (except the inevitable dietary one) store an average of 5.3 parts per million to 7.4 parts per million; agricultural workers 17.1 parts per million, and workers in insecticide plants as high as 648 parts per million! So the range of proven storage is quite wide and, what is even more to the point, the minimum figures are above the level at which damage to the liver and other organs or tissues may begin.

One of the most sinister features of DDT and related chemicals is the way they are passed on from one organism to another through all the links of the food chains. For example, fields of alfalfa are dusted with DDT; meal is later prepared from the alfalfa and fed to hens; the hens lay eggs which contain DDT. Or the hay, containing residues of 7 to 8 parts per million, may be fed to cows. The DDT will turn up in the milk in the amount of about 3 parts per million, but in butter made from this milk the concentration may run to 65 parts per million. Through such a process of transfer, what started out as a very small amount of DDT may end as a heavy concentration. Farmers nowadays find it difficult to obtain uncontaminated fodder for their milk cows, though the Food and Drug Administration forbids the presence of insecticide residues in milk shipped in interstate commerce.

The poison may also be passed on from mother to offspring. Insecticide residues have been recovered from human milk in samples tested by Food and Drug Administration scientists. This means that the breast-fed human infant is receiving small but regular additions to the load of toxic chemicals building up in his body. It is by no means his first exposure, however: there is good reason to believe this begins while he is still in the womb. In experimental animals the chlorinated hydrocarbon insecticides freely cross the barrier of the placenta, the traditional protective shield between the embryo and harmful substances in the mother's body. While the quantities so received by human infants would normally be small, they are not unimportant because children are more susceptible to poisoning than adults. This situation also means that today the average individual almost certainly starts life with the first deposit of the growing load of chemicals his body will be required to carry thenceforth.

All these facts—storage at even low levels, subsequent accumulation, and occurrence of liver damage at levels that may easily occur in normal diets, caused Food and Drug Administration scientists to declare as early as 1950 that it is "extremely likely the potential hazard of DDT has been underestimated." There has been no such parallel situation in medical history. No one yet knows what the ultimate consequences may be.

Chlordane, another chlorinated hydrocarbon, has all these unpleasant attributes of DDT plus a few that are peculiarly its own. Its residues are long persistent in soil, on foodstuffs, or on surfaces to which it may be applied. Chlordane makes use of all available portals to enter the body. It may be absorbed through the skin, may be breathed in as a spray or dust, and of course is absorbed from the digestive tract if residues are swallowed. Like all other chlorinated hydrocarbons, its deposits build up in the body in cumulative fashion. A diet containing such a small amount of chlordane as 2.5 parts per million may eventually lead to storage of 75 parts per million in the fat of experimental animals.

So experienced a pharmacologist as Dr. Lehman has described chlordane in 1950 as "one of the most toxic of insecticides—anyone handling it could be poisoned." Judging by the carefree liberality with which dusts for lawn treatments by suburbanites are laced with chlordane, this warning has not been taken to heart. The fact that the suburbanite is not instantly stricken has little meaning, for the toxins may sleep long in his body, to become manifest months or years later in an obscure disorder almost impossible to trace to its origins. On the other hand, death may strike quickly. One victim who accidentally spilled a 25 per cent industrial solution on the skin developed symptoms of poisoning within 40 minutes and died before medical help could be obtained. No reliance can be placed on receiving advance warning which might allow treatment to be had in time.

Heptachlor, one of the constituents of chlordane, is marketed as a separate formulation. It has a particularly high capacity for storage in fat. If the diet contains as little as $1/10$ of 1 part per million there will be measurable amounts of heptachlor in the body. It also has the curious ability to undergo change into a chemically distinct substance known as heptachlor epoxide. It does this in soil and in the tissues of both plants and animals. Tests on birds indicate that the epoxide that results from this change is more toxic than the original chemical, which in turn is four times as toxic as chlordane.

As long ago as the mid-1930s a special group of hydrocarbons, the chlorinated naphthalenes, was found to cause hepatitis, and also a rare and almost invariably fatal liver disease in persons subjected to occupational exposure. They have led to illness and death of workers in electrical industries; and more recently, in agriculture, they have been considered a cause of a mysterious and usually fatal disease of cattle. In view of these antecedents, it is not surprising that three of the insecticides that are related to this group are among the most violently poisonous of all the hydrocarbons. These are dieldrin, aldrin, and endrin.

Dieldrin, named for a German chemist, Diels, is about 5 times as toxic as DDT when swallowed but 40 times as toxic when absorbed through the skin in solution. It is notorious for striking quickly and with terrible effect at the nervous system, sending the victims into convulsions. Persons thus poisoned recover so slowly as to indicate chronic effects. As with other chlorinated hydrocarbons, these long-term effects include severe damage to the liver. The long duration of its residues and the effective insecticidal action make dieldrin one of the most used insecticides today, despite the appalling destruction of wildlife that has followed its use. As tested on quail and pheasants, it has proved to be about 40 to 50 times as toxic as DDT.

There are vast gaps in our knowledge of how dieldrin is stored or distributed in the body, or excreted, for the chemists' ingenuity in devising insecticides has long ago outrun biological knowledge of the way these poisons affect the living organism. However, there is every indication of long storage in the human body, where deposits may lie dormant like a slumbering volcano, only to flare up in periods of physiological stress when the body draws upon its fat reserves. Much of what we do know has been learned through hard experience in the antimalarial campaigns carried out by the World Health Organization. As soon as dieldrin was substituted for DDT in malaria-control work (because the malaria mosquitoes had become resistant to DDT), cases of poisoning among the spraymen began to occur. The seizures were severe—from half to all (varying in the different programs) of the men affected went into convulsions and several died. Some had convulsions as long as four months after the last exposure.

Aldrin is a somewhat mysterious substance, for although it exists as a separate entity it bears the relation of alter ego to dieldrin. When carrots are taken from a bed treated with aldrin they are found to contain residues of dieldrin. This change occurs in living tissues and also in soil. Such alchemistic transformations have led to many erroneous reports, for if a chemist, knowing aldrin has been applied, tests for it he will be deceived into thinking all residues have been dissipated. The residues are there, but they are dieldrin and this requires a different test.

Like dieldrin, aldrin is extremely toxic. It produces degenerative changes in the liver and kidneys. A quantity the size of an aspirin tablet is enough to kill more than 400 quail. Many cases of human poisonings are on record, most of them in connection with industrial handling.

Aldrin, like most of this group of insecticides, projects a menacing shadow into the future, the shadow of sterility. Pheasants fed quantities too small to kill them nevertheless laid few eggs, and the chicks that hatched soon died. The effect is not confined to birds. Rats exposed to aldrin had fewer pregnancies and their young were sickly and short-lived. Puppies born of treated mothers died within three days. By one means or another, the new generations suffer for the poisoning of their parents. No one knows whether the same effect will be seen in human beings, yet this chemical has been sprayed from airplanes over suburban areas and farmlands.

Endrin is the most toxic of all the chlorinated hydrocarbons. Although chemically rather closely related to dieldrin, a little twist in its molecular structure makes it 5 times as poisonous. It makes the progenitor of all this group of insecticides, DDT, seem by comparison almost harmless. It is 15 times as poisonous as DDT to mammals, 30 times as poisonous to fish, and about 300 times as poisonous to some birds.

In the decade of its use, endrin has killed enormous numbers of fish, has fatally poisoned cattle that have wandered into sprayed orchards, has poisoned wells, and has drawn a sharp warning from at least one state health department that its careless use is endangering human lives.

In one of the most tragic cases of endrin poisoning there was no apparent carelessness; efforts had been made to take precautions apparently considered adequate. A year-old child had been taken by his American parents to live in Venezuela. There were cockroaches in the house to which they moved, and after a few days a spray containing endrin was used. The baby and the small family dog were taken out of the house before the spraying was done about nine o'clock one morning. After the spraying the floors were washed. The baby and dog were returned to the house in midafternoon. An hour or so later the dog vomited, went into convulsions, and died. At 10 p.m. on the evening of the same day the baby also vomited, went into convulsions, and lost consciousness. After that fateful contact with endrin, this normal, healthy child became little more than a vegetable—unable to see or hear, subject to frequent muscular spasms, apparently completely cut off from contact with his surroundings. Several months of treatment in a New York hospital failed to change his condition or bring hope of change. "It is extremely doubtful," reported the attending physicians, "that any useful degree of recovery will occur."

The second major group of insecticides, the alkyl or organic phosphates, are among the most poisonous chemicals in the world. The chief and most obvious hazard attending their use is that of acute poisoning of people applying the sprays or accidentally coming in contact with drifting spray, with vegetation coated by it, or with a discarded container. In Florida, two children found an empty bag and used it to repair a swing. Shortly thereafter both of them died and three of their playmates became ill. The bag had once contained an insecticide called parathion, one of the organic phosphates; tests established death by parathion poisoning. On another occasion two small boys in Wisconsin, cousins, died on the same night. One had been playing in his yard when spray drifted in from an adjoining field where his father was spraying potatoes with parathion; the other had run playfully into the barn after his father and had put his hand on the nozzle of the spray equipment.

The origin of these insecticides has a certain ironic significance. Although some of the chemicals themselves—organic esters of phosphoric acid—had been known for many years, their insecticidal properties remained to be discovered by a German chemist, Gerhard Schrader, in the late 1930's. Almost immediately the German government recognized the value of these same chemicals as new and devastating weapons in man's war against his own kind, and the work on them was declared secret. Some became the deadly nerve gases. Others, of closely allied structure, became insecticides.

The organic phosphorus insecticides act on the living organism in a peculiar way. They have the ability to destroy enzymes—enzymes that perform necessary functions in the body. Their target is the nervous system, whether the victim is an insect or a warm-blooded animal. Under normal conditions, an impulse passes from nerve to nerve with the aid of a "chemical transmitter" called acetylcholine, a substance that performs an essential function and then disappears. Indeed, its existence is so ephemeral that medical researchers are unable, without special procedures, to sample it before the body has destroyed it. This transient nature of the transmitting chemical is necessary to the normal functioning of the body. If the acetylcholine is not destroyed as soon as a nerve impulse has passed, impulses continue to flash across the bridge from nerve to nerve, as the chemical exerts its effects in an ever more intensified manner. The movements of the whole body become uncoordinated: tremors, muscular spasms, convulsions, and death quickly result.

This contingency has been provided for by the body. A protective enzyme called cholinesterase is at hand to destroy the transmitting chemical once it is no longer needed. By this means a precise balance is struck and the body never builds up a dangerous amount of acetylcholine. But on contact with the organic phosphorus insecticides, the protective enzyme is destroyed, and as the quantity of the enzyme is reduced that of the transmitting chemical builds up. In this effect, the organic phosphorus compounds resemble the alkaloid poison muscarine, found in a poisonous mushroom, the fly amanita.

Repeated exposures may lower the cholinesterase level until an individual reaches the brink of acute poisoning, a brink over which he may be pushed by a very small additional exposure. For this reason it is considered important to make periodic examinations of the blood of spray operators and others regularly exposed.

Parathion is one of the most widely used of the organic phosphates. It is also one of the most powerful and dangerous. Honeybees become "wildly agitated and bellicose" on contact with it, perform frantic cleaning movements, and are near death within half an hour: A chemist, thinking to learn by the most direct possible means the dose acutely toxic to human beings, swallowed a minute amount, equivalent to about .00424 ounce. Paralysis followed so instantaneously that he could not reach the antidotes he had prepared at hand, and so he died. Parathion is now said to be a favorite instrument of suicide in Finland. In recent years the State of California has reported an average of more than 200 cases of accidental parathion poisoning annually. In many parts of the world the fatality rate from parathion is startling: 100 fatal cases in India and 67 in Syria in 1958, and an average of 336 deaths per year in Japan.

Yet some 7,000,000 pounds of parathion are now applied to fields and orchards of the United States—by hand sprayers, motorized blowers and dusters, and by airplane. The amount used on California farms alone could, according to one medical authority, "provide a lethal dose for 5 to 10 times the whole world's population."

One of the few circumstances that save us from extinction by this means is the fact that parathion and other chemicals of this group are decomposed rather rapidly. Their residues on the crops to which they are applied are therefore relatively short-lived compared with the chlorinated hydrocarbons. However, they last long enough to create hazards and produce consequences that range from the merely serious to the fatal. In Riverside, California, eleven out of thirty men picking oranges became violently ill and all but one had to be hospitalized. Their symptoms were typical of parathion poisoning. The grove had been sprayed with parathion some two and a half weeks earlier; the residues that reduced them to retching, half-blind, semiconscious misery were sixteen to nineteen days old. And this is not by any means a record for persistence. Similar mishaps have occurred in groves sprayed a month earlier, and residues have been found in the peel of oranges six months after treatment with standard dosages.

The danger to all workers applying the organic phosphorus insecticides in fields, orchards, and vineyards, is so extreme that some states using these chemicals have established laboratories where physicians may obtain aid in diagnosis and treatment. Even the physicians themselves may be in some danger, unless they wear rubber gloves in handling the victims of poisoning. So may a laundress washing the clothing of such victims, which may have absorbed enough parathion to affect her.

Malathion, another of the organic phosphates, is almost as familiar to the public as DDT, being widely used by gardeners, in household insecticides, in mosquito spraying, and in such blanket attacks on insects as the spraying of nearly a million acres of Florida communities for the Mediterranean fruit fly. It is considered the least toxic of this group of chemicals and many people assume they may use it freely and without fear of harm. Commercial advertising encourages this comfortable attitude.

The alleged "safety" of malathion rests on rather precarious ground, although—as often happens—this was not discovered until the chemical had been in use for several years. Malathion is "safe" only because the mammalian liver, an organ with extraordinary protective powers, renders it relatively harmless. The detoxification is accomplished by one of the enzymes of the liver. If, however, something destroys this enzyme or interferes with its action, the person exposed to malathion receives the full force of the poison.

Unfortunately for all of us, opportunities for this sort of thing to happen are legion. A few years ago a team of Food and Drug Administration scientists discovered that when malathion and certain other organic phosphates are administered simultaneously a massive poisoning results—up to 50 times as severe as would be predicted on the basis of adding together the toxicities of the two. In other words, $1/100$ of the lethal dose of each compound may be fatal when the two are combined.

This discovery led to the testing of other combinations. It is now known that many pairs of organic phosphate insecticides are highly dangerous, the toxicity being stepped up or "potentiated" through the combined action. Potentiation seems to take place when one compound destroys the liver enzyme responsible for detoxifying the other. The two need not be given simultaneously. The hazard exists not only for the man who may spray this week with one insecticide and next week with another; it exists also for the consumer of sprayed products. The common salad bowl may easily present a combination of organic phosphate insecticides. Residues well within the legally permissible limits may interact.

The full scope of the dangerous interaction of chemicals is as yet little known, but disturbing findings now come regularly from scientific laboratories. Among these is the discovery that the toxicity of an organic phosphate can be increased by a second agent that is not necessarily an insecticide. For example, one of the plasticizing agents may act even more strongly than another insecticide to make malathion more dangerous. Again, this is because it inhibits the liver enzyme that normally would "draw the teeth" of the poisonous insecticide.

What of other chemicals in the normal human environment? What, in particular, of drugs? A bare beginning has been made on this subject, but already it is known that some organic phosphates (parathion and malathion) increase the toxicity of some drugs used as muscle relaxants, and that several others (again including malathion) markedly increase the sleeping time of barbiturates.

In Greek mythology the sorceress Medea, enraged at being supplanted by a rival for the affections of her husband Jason, presented the new bride with a robe possessing magic properties. The wearer of the robe immediately suffered a violent death. This death-by-indirection now finds its counterpart in what are known as "systemic insecticides." These are chemicals with extraordinary properties which are used to convert plants or animals into a sort of Medea's robe by making them actually poisonous. This is done with the purpose of killing insects that may come in contact with them, especially by sucking their juices or blood.

The world of systemic insecticides is a weird world, surpassing the imaginings of the brothers Grimm—perhaps most closely akin to the cartoon world of Charles Addams. It is a world where the enchanted forest of the fairy tales has become the poisonous forest in which an insect that chews a leaf or sucks the sap of a plant is doomed. It is a world where a flea bites a dog, and dies because the dog's blood has been made poisonous, where an insect may die from vapors emanating from a plant it has never touched, where a bee may carry poisonous nectar back to its hive and presently produce poisonous honey.

The entomologists' dream of the built-in insecticide was born when workers in the field of applied entomology realized they could take a hint from nature: they found that wheat growing in soil containing sodium selenate was immune to attack by aphids or spider mites. Selenium, a naturally occurring element found sparingly in rocks and soils of many parts of the world, thus became the first systemic insecticide.

What makes an insecticide a systemic is the ability to permeate all the tissues of a plant or animal and make them toxic. This quality is possessed by some chemicals of the chlorinated hydrocarbon group and by others of the organophosphorus group, all synthetically produced, as well as by certain naturally occurring substances. In practice, however, most systemics are drawn from the organophosphorus group because the problem of residues is somewhat less acute.

Systemics act in other devious ways. Applied to seeds, either by soaking or in a coating combined with carbon, they extend their effects into the following plant generation and produce seedlings poisonous to aphids and other sucking insects. Vegetables such as peas, beans, and sugar beets are sometimes thus protected. Cotton seeds coated with a systemic insecticide have been in use for some time in California, where 25 farm laborers planting cotton in the San Joaquin Valley in 1959 were seized with sudden illness, caused by handling the bags of treated seeds.

In England someone wondered what happened when bees made use of nectar from plants treated with systemics. This was investigated in areas treated with a chemical called schradan. Although the plants had been sprayed before the flowers were formed, the nectar later produced contained the poison. The result, as might have been predicted, was that the honey made by the bees also was contaminated with schradan.

Use of animal systemics has concentrated chiefly on control of the cattle grub, a damaging parasite of livestock. Extreme care must be used in order to create an insecticidal effect in the blood and tissues of the host without setting up a fatal poisoning. The balance is delicate and government veterinarians have found that repeated small doses can gradually deplete an animal's supply of the protective enzyme cholinesterase, so that without warning a minute additional dose will cause poisoning.

There are strong indications that fields closer to our daily lives are being opened up. You may now give your dog a pill which, it is claimed, will rid him of fleas by making his blood poisonous to them. The hazards discovered in treating cattle would presumably apply to the dog. As yet no one seems to have proposed a human systemic that would make us lethal to a mosquito. Perhaps this is the next step.

So far in this chapter we have been discussing the deadly chemicals that are being used in our war against the insects. What of our simultaneous war against the weeds?

The desire for a quick and easy method of killing unwanted plants has given rise to a large and growing array of chemicals that are known as herbicides, or, less formally, as weed killers. The story of how these chemicals are used and misused will be told in Chapter 6; the question that here concerns us is whether the weed killers are poisons and whether their use is contributing to the poisoning of the environment.

The legend that the herbicides are toxic only to plants and so pose no threat to animal life has been widely disseminated, but unfortunately it is not true. The plant killers include a large variety of chemicals that act on animal tissue as well as on vegetation. They vary greatly in their action on the organism. Some are general poisons, some are powerful stimulants of metabolism, causing a fatal rise in body temperature, some induce malignant tumors either alone or in partnership with other chemicals, some strike at the genetic material of the race by causing gene mutations. The herbicides, then, like the insecticides, include some very dangerous chemicals, and their careless use in the belief that they are "safe" can have disastrous results.

Despite the competition of a constant stream of new chemicals issuing from the laboratories, arsenic compounds are still liberally used, both as insecticides (as mentioned above) and as weed killers, where they usually take the chemical form of sodium arsenite. The history of their use is not reassuring. As roadside sprays, they have cost many a farmer his cow and killed uncounted numbers of wild creatures. As aquatic weed killers in lakes and reservoirs they have made public waters unsuitable for drinking or even for swimming. As a spray applied to potato fields to destroy the vines they have taken a toll of human and nonhuman life.

In England this latter practice developed about 1951 as a result of a shortage of sulfuric acid, formerly used to burn off the potato vines. The Ministry of Agriculture considered it necessary to give warning of the hazard of going into the arsenic-sprayed fields, but the warning was not understood by the cattle (nor, we must assume, by the wild animals and birds) and reports of cattle poisoned by the arsenic sprays came with monotonous regularity. When death came also to a farmer's wife through arsenic-contaminated water, one of the major English chemical companies (in 1959) stopped production of arsenical sprays and called in supplies already in the hands of dealers, and shortly thereafter the Ministry of Agriculture announced that because of high risks to people and cattle restrictions on the use of arsenites would be imposed. In 1961, the Australian government announced a similar ban. No such restrictions impede the use of these poisons in the United States, however.

Some of the "dinitro" compounds are also used as herbicides. They are rated as among the most dangerous materials of this type in use in the United States. Dinitrophenol is a strong metabolic stimulant. For this reason it was at one time used as a reducing drug, but the margin between the slimming dose and that required to poison or kill was slight—so slight that several patients died and many suffered permanent injury before use of the drug was finally halted.

A related chemical, pentachlorophenol, sometimes known as "penta," is used as a weed killer as well as an insecticide, often being sprayed along railroad tracks and in waste areas. Penta is extremely toxic to a wide variety of organisms from bacteria to man. Like the dinitros, it interferes, often fatally, with the body's source of energy, so that the affected organism almost literally burns itself up. Its fearful power is illustrated in a fatal accident recently reported by the California Department of Health. A tank truck driver was preparing a cotton defoliant by mixing diesel oil with pentachlorophenol. As he was drawing the concentrated chemical out of a drum, the spigot accidentally toppled back. He reached in with his bare hand to regain the spigot. Although he washed immediately, he became acutely ill and died the next day.

While the results of weed killers such as sodium arsenite or the phenols are grossly obvious, some other herbicides are more insidious in their effects. For example, the now famous cranberry-weed-killer aminotriazole, or amitrol, is rated as having relatively low toxicity. But in the long run its tendency to cause malignant tumors of the thyroid may be far more significant for wildlife and perhaps also for man.

Among the herbicides are some that are classified as "mutagens," or agents capable of modifying the genes, the materials of heredity. We are rightly appalled by the genetic effects of radiation; how then, can we be indifferent to the same effect in chemicals that we disseminate widely in our environment?

# *from* Societies: Evolutionary and Comparative Perspectives

## Talcott Parsons

Consideration of the social system's relation to its organic base and, through that, to the physical world must begin with the physical requirements of organic life. Here the primordial problems concern the provision of food and shelter, but many other factors are also problematic in all known societies. Ramifying from the relatively simple tools and skills of primitive peoples to the very complex systems of modernity, technology is the socially organized capacity for actively controlling and altering objects of the physical environment in the interest of some human want or need. In limiting cases, the social organization may involve simply teaching skills to individual craftsmen who produce by themselves. But even in such cases, if the technology is important, the craftsman is unlikely to remain totally insulated from practitioners of his craft other than the master who taught him. Furthermore, if his work is specialized, he *must* have some organized relations with consumers of his product and, very likely, with sources of his materials and equipment. Truly, there can be no craft wholly divorced from social organization.

Technological processes obviously serve to meet human needs and wants. They depend on the cultural system for their *techniques*[1]—one person's addition to the total technical lore of his society is always an increment rather than an entirely "new system." Furthermore, technological tasks in this sense are always performed in a socially defined *role*. Products are very generally, though by no means always, the outcome of *collectively* organized processes, not the work of one individual. Thus some executive or coordinating functions must be performed in a broad variety of social-relations with consumers, suppliers, workers, researchers, and the like.

Technology, then, is the primarily physical reference of the complex which includes the *economy* as its primary social system reference. The economy is the aspect of the societal system which functions not just to order technological procedures socially, but more importantly to fit them into the social system and control them in the interests of social units, whether individual or collective.[2] The institutional complexes of property, contract, and the regulation of terms of employment are important integrating elements here. The more strictly economic aspects of the complex are, in primitive and archaic societies, embedded in diffuse structures where kinship, religion, or political interests are paramount. Under certain circumstances, however, markets develop, along with money as a medium of exchange.

Technological organization, then, should be regarded as a boundary-structure between the society as a system and the organic-physical environment. On the societal side of the boundary, the economy is the focal structure, providing linkage with the societal community. Here, as the traditions of economic theory strongly emphasize, the function of *allocation* is central. Resources must be allocated toward the satisfaction of the vast variety of wants present in any society, and opportunities for satisfying wants must be allocated among different categories of the population. As socially organized, technological considerations also apply to the utilization of services. As the services of individuals become a truly mobile and *allocable* resource, they comprise an economic category, as their bracketing with physical goods in the economists' formula "goods and services" makes clear. Once involved (through employment) in an operating organization, however, they become engaged in what is in analytical terms political functioning—organizational processes oriented toward attaining the specific goals of the society or a relevant sub-collectivity.

These considerations imply that technology involves a complex of territorial references parallel to residence. In fact, it differentiates from the residence complex only late in social evolution. Its major concern is the location of "industry." Insofar as personnel perform differentiated occupational or service roles, they must work *where* their services are needed, though this location must be coordinated with residential factors. However, location must also depend on access to materials and equipment and on distribution of output. Industry in the strict sense represents the case in which such economic considerations take primacy. But the location problems of governmental administration or of specialized religious personnel can be analyzed in somewhat similar terms.

## Notes

1    *Skill* is essentially the internalization of certain elements of culture in the *organism*.

2    Talcott Parsons and Neil J. Smelser. *Economy and Society* (Glencoe, Ill: The Free Press, 1956).

# *from* Religion in Social Context

## N. J. Demerath III and Phillip E. Hammond

## Animism and Naturism: The Mystique of Mistakes

One of the early theoretical insights has come to be known as animism, the point of view that sees religion as an explanation for "spirits." Each of us dreams, sees his reflection in quiet water, and has periodic déjà vu experiences. In primitive societies, so the animists argued, these kinds of events generated beliefs in the existence of other realms with other beings. Accepting this premise, primitive man could then conclude that a spirit being lived in him, was released during sleep (and thus appeared in dreams), and permanently escaped from its host's body at time of death. These escaped spirits were especially important because they not only were freer to move about but also "represented" their dead hosts. The spirits of departed chiefs, fathers, mothers-in-law, and so forth thus had to be placated. Rituals for the dead, beliefs about afterlife, and pantheons became natural extensions of the premise regarding spirit beings. Religion, thus, was seen as an irrational response to a rational quest for explanation.

Animism is no longer considered a true explanation of religion. Tylor, with whom the animism theory is chiefly associated, presented the details of this theory in 1871,[1] and the prevailing question in his work was that of the *origin* of religion. Questions incorrectly asked seldom yield answers correctly understood, and Tylor's was no exception; for, as we shall argue toward the end of this chapter, though his answer has great relevance for the sociology of religion, it has little to do with the question of origins. Neanderthal and Cro-Magnon men apparently had religion. At least, archaeological evidence suggests that they took special pains with burial, had "sacred" places, and called upon special powers to help in hunts. But the *beginnings* of beliefs and practices taking place as recently as 50,000 or 100,000 years ago, even when they exist in modified form today, are unlikely ever to be known. As William J. Goode has stated, conjectures about "how, under what conditions, man began to believe in divine beings nearly a million years ago must remain sheer speculation."[2] The fault with animism lay not in its answer but in its question. The ultra-rationalism of Tylor's day was too much reflected in his approach to religion.

• • •

## Society as Source and Consequence of Religious Sentiment

Durkheim's intellectual life was devoted to the issues of morality and social cohesion. His first monograph, *The Division of Labor in Society*, had identified the shifting basis of social cohesion as related to the extent of occupational specialization and mutual interdependency in society.[3] Later, however, Durkheim sought to supplement such structural explanations of solidarity by putting more explicit emphasis on moral factors such as religion itself. In keeping with the evolutionism of his day, he too went to primitive peoples in order to understand religion's "elementary" forms. However, unlike his predecessors, Durkheim sought to "find a means of discerning the ever-present causes upon which the most essential forms of religious thought and practice depend."[4] He was seeking, in other words, not the "very first beginning" but the forces that *maintain* religious sentiment. The other issue, he said, "has nothing scientific about it, and should be resolutely discarded."[5]

The major distinguishing characteristic of religion, Durkheim noted, is that it deals with *sacred*, not *profane*, things. Sacred things are "set apart and forbidden," whereas profane objects are ordinary. Moreover, sacredness may be imputed to almost anything; sacred character, that is, resides not in the object but in the mind of the beholder. Such being the case, the reason why any particular object is made sacred may be quite different from the reason why persons are led to impute sacredness to objects. The separation of the two questions is thus complete, and the Durkheimian theory, as a consequence, takes a radically different direction.

In the case of the central Australian tribe, the sacred sphere is intimately joined with the totem. Specifically, at least four elements of totemism are classed apart: (1) the totemic emblem; (2) the thing (usually an animal or plant) that the emblem symbolizes; (3) the members of the clan possessing the totem; and (4) the ideas or beliefs that, via the totem, explain the cosmos. Animism and naturism accounted for the collective totem by saying it was an extension of individual totems. They theorized that ancestor worship, fear of spirits, or cataclysmic natural events generated in individuals a religious (totemic) response that then spread to the collectivity. Durkheim, however, rejected these explanations[6] and reasoned instead that religious sentiments are generated by social organization, by collective life itself. The totem, that is to say, represents a force found in each individual but not coequal with any one individual, a force that is real (it is universally felt), physical, and morally binding. This force is the force of the clan, and Durkheim's statement led to its now-famous restatement that religion is the worship of society.

## Notes

1    E. B. Tylor, *Primitive Culture*, 2 vols. (New York: Harper & Row, 1958). Volume II contains the discussion of animism.

2    William J. Goode, *Religion Among the Primitives* (New York: Free Press, 1951), p. 22.

3    For this Durkheimian question asked in a contemporary setting, see Phillip E. Hammond, "Secularization, Incorporation, and Social Relations," *American Journal of Sociology*, 72 (September 1966), 188–194.

4    Durkheim, op. cit., p. 20.

5    Ibid.

6    See ibid., pp. 194–215.

# *from* Magic, Science and Religion

## Bronislaw Malinowski

In dealing with the first question, we shall have to examine the "pro-fane" side of life, the arts, crafts and economic pursuits, and we shall attempt to disentangle in it a type of behavior, clearly marked off from magic and religion, based on empirical knowledge and on the confidence in logic. We shall try to find whether the lines of such behavior are defined by traditional rules, known, perhaps even discussed sometimes, and tested. We shall have to inquire whether the sociological setting of the rational and empirical behavior differs from that of ritual and cult. Above all we shall ask, do the natives distinguish the two domains and keep them apart, or is the field of knowledge constantly swamped by superstition, ritualism, magic or religion?

Since in the matter under discussion there is an appalling lack of relevant and reliable observations, I shall have largely to draw upon my own material, mostly unpublished, collected during a few years' field work among the Melanesian and Papuo-Melanesian tribes of Eastern New Guinea and the surrounding archipelagoes. As the Melanesians are reputed, however, to be specially magic-ridden, they will furnish an acid test of the existence of empirical and rational knowledge among savages living in the age of polished stone.

These natives, and I am speaking mainly of the Melanesians who inhabit the coral atolls to the N.E. of the main island, the Trobriand Archipelago and the adjoining groups, are expert fishermen, industrious manufacturers and traders, but they rely mainly on gardening for their subsistence. With the most rudimentary implements, a pointed digging-stick and a small axe, they are able to raise crops sufficient to maintain a dense population and even yielding a surplus, which in olden days was allowed to rot unconsumed, and which at present is exported to feed plantation hands. The success in their agriculture depends—besides the excellent natural conditions with which they are favored—upon their extensive knowledge of the classes of the soil, of the various cultivated plants, of the mutual adaptation of these two factors, and, last not least, upon their knowledge of the importance of accurate and hard work. They have to select the soil and the seedlings, they have appropriately to fix the times for clearing and burning the scrub, for planting and weeding, for training the vines of the yam plants. In all this they are guided by a clear knowledge of weather and seasons, plants and pests, soil and tubers, and by a conviction that this knowledge is true and reliable, that it can be counted upon and must be scrupulously obeyed.

Yet mixed with all their activities there is to be found magic, a series of rites performed every year over the gardens in rigorous sequence and order. Since the leadership in garden work is in the hands of the magician, and since ritual and practical work are intimately associated, a superficial observer might be led to assume that the mystic and the rational behavior are mixed up, that their effects are not distinguished by the natives and not distinguishable in scientific analysis. Is this so really?

Magic is undoubtedly regarded by the natives as absolutely indispensable to the welfare of the gardens. What would happen without it no one can exactly tell, for no native garden has ever been made without its ritual, in spite of some thirty years of European rule and missionary influence and well over a century's contact with white traders. But certainly various kinds of disaster, blight, unseasonable droughts, rains, bush-pigs and locusts, would destroy the unhallowed garden made without magic.

Does this mean, however, that the natives attribute all the good results to magic? Certainly not. If you were to suggest to a native that he should make his garden mainly by magic and scamp his work, he would simply smile on your simplicity. He knows as well as you do that there are natural conditions and causes, and by his observations he knows also that he is able to control these natural forces by mental and physical effort. His knowledge is limited, no doubt, but as far as it goes it is sound and proof against mysticism. If the fences are broken down, if the seed is destroyed or has been dried or washed away, he will have recourse not to magic, but to work, guided by knowledge and reason. His experience has taught him also, on the other hand, that in spite of all his forethought and beyond all his efforts there are agencies and forces which one year bestow unwonted and unearned benefits of fertility, making everything run smooth and well, rain and sun appear at the right moment, noxious insects remain in abeyance, the harvest yields a superabundant crop; and another year again the same agencies bring ill luck and bad chance, pursue him from beginning till end and thwart all his most strenuous efforts and his best-founded knowledge. To control these influences and these only he employs magic.

Thus there is a clear-cut division: there is first the well-known set of conditions, the natural course of growth, as well as the ordinary pests and dangers to be warded off by fencing and weeding. On the other hand there is the domain of the unaccountable and adverse influences, as well as the great unearned increment of fortunate coincidence. The first conditions are coped with by knowledge and work, the second by magic.

This line of division can also be traced in the social setting of work and ritual respectively. Though the garden magician is, as a rule, also the leader in practical activities, these two functions are kept strictly apart. Every magical ceremony has its distinctive name, its appropriate time and its place in the scheme of work, and it stands out of the ordinary course of activities completely. Some of them are ceremonial and have to be attended by the whole community, all are public in that it is known when they are going to happen and anyone can attend them. They are performed on selected plots within the gardens and on a special corner of this plot. Work is always tabooed on such occasions, sometimes only while the ceremony lasts, sometimes for a day or two. In his lay character the leader and magician directs the work, fixes the dates for starting, harangues and exhorts slack or careless gardeners. But the two roles never overlap or interfere: they are always clear, and any native will inform you without hesitation whether the man acts as magician or as leader in garden work.

What has been said about gardens can be paralleled from any one of the many other activities in which work and magic run side by side without ever mixing. Thus in canoe building empirical knowledge of material, of technology, and of certain principles of stability and hydrodynamics, function in company and close association with magic, each yet uncontaminated by the other.

• • •

But besides these natural causes there is the enormous domain of sorcery and by far the most cases of illness and death are ascribed to this. The line of distinction between sorcery and the other causes is clear in theory and in most cases of practice, but it must be realized that it is subject to what could be called the personal perspective. That is, the more closely a case has to do with the person who considers it, the less will it be "natural," the more "magical." Thus a very old man, whose pending death will be considered natural by the other members of the community, will be afraid only of sorcery and never think of his natural fate. A fairly sick person will diagnose sorcery in his own case, while all the others might speak of too much betel nut or overeating or some other indulgence.

• • •

Thus in his relation to nature and destiny, whether he tries to exploit the first or to dodge the second, primitive man recognizes both the natural and the supernatural forces and agencies, and he tries to use them both for his benefit. Whenever he has been taught by experience that effort guided by knowledge is of some avail, he never spares the one or ignores the other. He knows that a plant cannot grow by magic alone, or a canoe sail or float without being properly constructed and managed, or a fight be won without skill and daring. He never relies on magic alone, while, on the contrary, he sometimes dispenses with it completely, as in fire-making and in a number of crafts and pursuits. But he clings to it, whenever he has to recognize the impotence of his knowledge and of his rational technique.

I have given my reasons why in this argument I had to rely principally on the material collected in the classical land of magic, Melanesia. But the facts discussed are so fundamental, the conclusions drawn of such a general nature, that it will be easy to check them on any modern detailed ethnographic record. Comparing agricultural work and magic, the building of canoes, the art of healing by magic and by natural remedies, the ideas about the causes of death in other regions, the universal validity of what has been established here could easily be proved. Only, since no observations have methodically been made with reference to the problem of primitive knowledge, the data from other writers could be gleaned only piecemeal and their testimony though clear would be indirect.

I have chosen to face the question of primitive man's rational knowledge directly: watching him at his principal occupations, seeing him pass from work to magic and back again, entering into his mind, listening to his opinions. The whole problem might have been approached through the avenue of language, but this would have led us too far into questions of logic, semasiology, and theory of primitive languages. Words which serve to express general ideas such as *existence, substance*, and *attribute, cause* and *effect*, the *fundamental* and the *secondary*; words and expressions used in complicated pursuits like sailing, construction, measuring and checking; numerals and quantitative descriptions, correct and detailed classifications of natural phenomena, plants and animals—all this would lead us exactly to the same conclusion: that primitive man can observe and think, and that he possesses, embodied in his language, systems of methodical though rudimentary knowledge.

Similar conclusions could be drawn from an examination of those mental schemes and physical contrivances which could be described as diagrams or formulas. Methods of indicating the main points of the compass, arrangements of stars into constellations, co-ordination of these with the seasons, naming of moons in the year, of quarters in the moon— all these accomplishments are known to the simplest savages. Also they are all able to draw diagrammatic maps in the sand or dust, indicate arrangements by placing small stones, shells, or sticks on the ground, plan expeditions or raids on such rudimentary charts. By co-ordinating space and time they are able to arrange big tribal gatherings and to combine vast tribal movements over extensive areas.[1] The use of leaves, notched sticks, and similar aids to memory is well known and seems to be almost universal. All such "diagrams" are means of reducing a complex and unwieldy bit of reality to a simple and handy form. They give man a relatively easy mental control over it. As such are they not—in a very rudimentary form no doubt—fundamentally akin to developed scientific formulas and "models," which are also simple and handy paraphrases of a complex or abstract reality, giving the civilized physicist mental control over it?

This brings us to the second question: Can we regard primitive knowledge, which, as we found, is both empirical and rational, as a rudimentary stage of science, or is it not at all related to it? If by science be understood a body of rules and conceptions, based on experience and derived from it by logical inference, embodied in material achievements and in a fixed form of tradition and carried on by some sort of social organization—then there is no doubt that even the lowest savage communities have the beginnings of science, however rudimentary.

Most epistemologists would not, however, be satisfied with such a "minimum definition" of science, for it might apply to the rules of an art or craft as well. They would maintain that the rules of science must be laid down explicitly, open to control by experiment and critique by reason. They must not only be rules of practical behavior, but theoretical laws of knowledge. Even accepting this stricture, however, there is hardly any doubt that many of the principles of savage knowledge are scientific in this sense. The native shipwright knows not only practically of buoyancy, leverage, equilibrium, he has to obey these laws not only on water, but while making the canoe he must have the principles in his mind. He instructs his helpers in them. He gives them the traditional rules, and in a crude and simple manner, using his hands, pieces of wood, and a limited technical vocabulary, he explains some general laws of hydrodynamics and equilibrium. Science is not detached from the craft, that is certainly true, it is only a means to an end, it is crude, rudimentary, and inchoate, but with all that it is the matrix from which the higher developments must have sprung.

If we applied another criterion yet, that of the really scientific attitude, the disinterested search for knowledge and for the understanding of causes and reasons, the answer would certainly not be in a direct negative. There is, of course, no widespread thirst for knowledge in a savage community, new things such as European topics bore them frankly and their whole interest is largely encompassed by the traditional world of their culture. But within this there is both the antiquarian mind passionately interested in myths, stories, details of customs, pedigrees, and ancient happenings, and there is also to be found the naturalist, patient and painstaking in his observations, capable of generalization and of connecting long chains of events in the life of animals, and in the marine world or in the jungle. It is enough to realize how much European naturalists have often learned from their savage colleagues to appreciate this interest found in the native for nature. There is finally among the primitives, as every fieldworker well knows, the sociologist, the ideal informant, capable with marvelous accuracy and insight to give the *raison d'être*, the function, and the organization of many a simpler institution in his tribe.

Science, of course, does not exist in any uncivilized community as a driving power, criticizing, renewing, constructing. Science is never consciously made. But on this criterion, neither is there law, nor religion, nor government among savages.

• • •

We may, therefore, lay down the main function of initiation ceremonies: they are a ritual and dramatic expression of the supreme power and value of tradition in primitive societies; they also serve to impress this power and value upon the minds of each generation, and they are at the same time an extremely efficient means of transmitting tribal lore, of insuring continuity in tradition and of maintaining tribal cohesion.

We still have to ask: What is the relation between the purely physiological fact of bodily maturity which these ceremonies mark, and their social and religious aspect? We see at once that religion does something more, infinitely more, than the mere "sacralizing of a crisis of life." From a natural event it makes a social transition, to the fact of bodily maturity it adds the vast conception of entry into manhood with its duties, privileges, responsibilities, above all with its knowledge of tradition and the communion with sacred things and beings. There is thus a creative element in the rites of religious nature. The act establishes not only a social event in the life of the individual but also a spiritual metamorphosis, both associated with the biological event but transcending it in importance and significance.

Initiation is a typically religious act, and we can see clearly here how the ceremony and its purpose are one, how the end is realized in the very consummation of the act. At the same time we can see the function of such acts in society in that they create mental habits and social usages of inestimable value to the group and its civilization.

Another type of religious ceremony, the rite of marriage, is also an end in itself that it creates a supernaturally sanctioned bond, superadded to the primarily biological fact: the union of man and woman for lifelong partnership in affection, economic community, the procreation and rearing of children. This union, monogamous marriage, has always existed in human societies—so modern anthropology teaches in the face of the older fantastic hypotheses of "promiscuity" and "group marriage." By giving monogamous marriage an imprint of value and sanctity, religion offers another gift to human culture. And that brings us to the consideration of the two great human needs of propagation and nutrition.

## 2. Providence in Primitive Life

Propagation and nutrition stand first and foremost among the vital concerns of man. Their relation to religious belief and practice has been often recognized and even overemphasized. Especially sex has been, from some older writers up to the psychoanalytic school, frequently regarded as the main source of religion. In fact, however, it plays an astonishingly insignificant part in religion, considering its force and insidiousness in human life in general. Besides love magic and the use of sex in certain magical performances—phenomena not belonging to the domain of religion—there remain to be mentioned here only acts of licence at harvest festivities or other public gatherings, the facts of temple prostitution and, at the level of barbarism and lower civilization, the worship of phallic divinities. Contrary to what one would expect, in savagery sexual cults play an insignificant role. It must also be remembered that acts of ceremonial licence are not mere indulgence, but that they express a reverent attitude towards the forces of generation and fertility in man and nature, forces on which the very existence of society and culture depends. Religion, the permanent source of moral control, which changes its incidence but remains eternally vigilant, has to turn its attention to these forces, at first drawing them merely into its sphere, later on submitting them to repression, finally establishing the ideal of chastity and the sanctification of askesis.

When we pass to nutrition, the first thing to be noted is that eating is for primitive man an act surrounded by etiquette, special prescriptions and prohibitions, and a general emotional tension to a degree unknown to us. Besides the magic of food, designed to make it go a long way, or to prevent its scarcity in general—and we do not speak here at all of the innumerable forms of magic associated with the procuring of food—food has also a conspicuous role in ceremonies of a distinctly religious character. First-fruit offerings of a ritual nature, harvest ceremonies, big seasonal feasts in which crops are accumulated, displayed, and, in one way or another, sacralized, play an important part among agricultural people. Hunters, again, or fishers celebrate a big catch or the opening of the season of their pursuit by feasts and ceremonies at which food is ritually handled, the animals propitiated or worshipped. All such acts express the joy of the community, their sense of the great value of food, and religion through them consecrates the reverent attitude of man towards his daily bread.

To primitive man, never, even under the best conditions, quite free from the threat of starvation, abundance of food is a primary condition of normal life. It means the possibility of looking beyond the daily worries, of paying more attention to the remoter, spiritual aspects of civilization. If we thus consider that food is the main link between man and his surroundings, that by receiving it he feels the forces of destiny and providence, we can see the cultural, nay, biological importance of primitive religion in the sacralization of food. We can see in it the germs of what in higher types of religion will develop into the feeling of dependence upon Providence, of gratitude, and of confidence in it.

Sacrifice and communion, the two main forms in which food is ritually ministered, can now be held in a new light against the background of man's early attitude of religious reverence towards the providential abundance of food. That the idea of giving, the importance of the exchange of gifts in all phases of social contact, plays a great role in sacrifice seems— in spite of the unpopularity of this theory nowadays—unquestionable in view of the new knowledge of primitive economic psychology.[2] Since the giving of gifts is the normal accompaniment of all social intercourse among primitives, the spirits who visit the village or the demons who haunt some hallowed spot, or divinities when approached are given their due, their share sacrificed from the general plenty, as any other visitors or persons visited would be. But underlying this custom there is a still deeper religious element. Since food is to the savage the token of the beneficence of the world, since plenty gives him the first, the most elementary, inkling of Providence, by sharing in food sacrificially with his spirits or divinities the savage shares with them in the beneficial powers of his Providence already felt by him but not yet comprehended. Thus in primitive societies the roots of sacrificial offerings are to be found in the psychology of gift, which is to the communion in beneficent abundance.

The sacramental meal is only another expression of the same mental attitude, carried out in the most appropriate manner by the act by which life is retained and renewed—the act of eating. But this ritual seems to be extremely rare among lower savages, and the sacrament of communion, prevalent at a level of culture when the primitive psychology of eating is no more, has by then acquired a different symbolic and mystical meaning. Perhaps the only case of sacramental eating, well attested and known with some detail, is the so-called "totemic sacrament" of Central Australian tribes, and this seems to require a somewhat more special interpretation.

## 3. Man's Selective Interest in Nature

This brings us to the subject of totemism, briefly defined in the first section. As may have been seen, the following questions have to be asked about totemism. First, why does a primitive tribe select for its totems a limited number of species, primarily animals and plants; and on what principles is this selection made? Secondly, why is this selective attitude expressed in beliefs of affinity, in cults of multiplication, above all in the negative injunctions of totemic taboos, and again in injunctions of ritual eating, as in the Australian "totemic sacrament"? Thirdly and finally, why with the subdivision of nature into a limited number of selected species does there run parallel a subdivision of the tribe into clans correlated with the species?

The above outlined psychology of the primitive attitude towards food and its abundance and our principle of man's practical and pragmatic outlook lead us directly to an answer. We have seen that food is the primary link between the primitive and providence. And the need of it and the desire for its abundance have led man to economic pursuits, collecting, hunting, fishing, and they endow these pursuits with varied and tense emotions. A number of animal and vegetable species, those which form the staple food of the tribe, dominate the interests of the tribesmen. To primitive man nature is his living larder, to which—especially at the lowest stages of culture—he has to repair directly in order to gather, cook, and eat when hungry. The road from the wilderness to the savage's belly and consequently to his mind is very short, and for him the world is an indiscriminate background against which there stand out the useful, primarily the edible, species of animals or plants. Those who have lived in the jungle with savages, taking part in collecting or hunting expeditions, or who have sailed with them over the lagoons, or spent moonlit nights on sand-banks waiting for the shoals of fish or for the appearance of turtle, know how keen and selective is the savage's interest, how it clings to the indications, trails, and to the habits and peculiarities of his quarry, while it yet remains quite indifferent to any other stimuli. Every such species which is habitually pursued forms a nucleus round which all the interests, the impulses, the emotions of a tribe tend to crystallize. A sentiment of social nature is built round each species, a sentiment which naturally finds its expression in folklore, belief, and ritual.

It must also be remembered that the same type of impulse which makes small children delight in birds, take a keen interest in animals, and shrink from reptiles, places animals in the front rank of nature for primitive man. By their general affinity with man—they move, utter sounds, manifest emotions, have bodies and faces like him—and by their superior powers—the birds fly in the open, the fishes swim under water, reptiles renew their skins and their life and can disappear in the earth—by all this the animal, the intermediate link between men and nature, often his superior in strength, agility, and cunning, usually his indispensable quarry, assumes an exceptional place in the savage's view of the world.

The primitive is deeply interested in the appearance and properties of beasts; he desires to have them and, therefore, to control them as useful and edible things; sometimes he admires and fears them. All these interests meet and, strengthening each other, produce the same effect: the selection, in man's principal preoccupations, of a limited number of species, animal first, vegetable in the second place, while inanimate or man-made things are unquestionably but a secondary formation, an introduction by analogy, of objects which have nothing to do with the substance of totemism.

## Notes

1    Cf. the writer's *Argonauts of the Western Pacific*, chap. xvi.

2    Cf. the writer's *Argonauts of the Western Pacific*, 1923, and the article on "Primitive Economics" in the *Economic Journal*, 1921; as well as Professor Rich. Thurnwald's memoir on "Die Gestaltung der Wirtschftsentwicklung aus ihren Anfangen heraus" in *Erinnerungsgabe fur Max Weber*, 1923.

# *from* My Petition for More Space

## John Hersey

### Chapter 1

As usual at this hour, downtown streets are glutted with busses and cargo conveyors and people shuffling on foot to their jobs. Every square inch of concrete and asphalt is taken up. Wheeled traffic worms along at the stipulated pace. On this sidewalk, at the outer edge of our waitline to the right, one infinity of pedestrians, facing us, inches toward Elm, and another, beyond, toward Chapel. It takes a walker fifteen or twenty minutes to move a single block. This is the familiar suffocating physical crush of the morning hours: breast touches shoulder blade, hip rubs hip, one's shoes are scuffed by others' shoes.

In the street, the busses and cargo vans creep along so close together they almost touch each other. The vans, uniform in design, squarish and chunky, white and immaculate, with no writing on them save for tiny numbers on the operators' doors, look like huge mobile ovens. Across the street, over the tops of these vehicles, I can see the upper part of the wall enclosing the Green. It is a long time since I have stood at the windows in that wall, looking in: at the empty grass, crosscut and gleaming; the score of majestic maples, standing apart, whose leaves turn to each other on stirring air, I think, and whisper, 'Forest! Forest! Forest, brother leaf!'; the vaulting wire cages with great murmurations of sparrows in them; the three nineteenth-century churches, two built of red brick and white wood, one of brownish stone, their spires pointing the way to uninhabited regions above. The public is not admitted inside the wall. The Green—green space, a museum of openness. The lines of citizens waiting on pavements to get to the windows in that wall, just to gaze at the emptiness within, are the longest in the whole city. One can only hope to look through the windows into the Green on a rest day. I have not attempted it for nearly a year.

• • •

The reason I refer to the retired circuitry printer on my left as a grandmother is that she has told me about Robert, her grandson, who is fourteen, who has had a vasectomy and so can be considered a man, and who is one of four hundred pupils in New Haven who have been chosen this year to learn to read. She is proud of him!—even though she regards the skill he has been chosen for as low-grade. She is gray under the eyes, her white hair is unruly, but there is strength in her face, which has in it a trace—dragged long ago through some southeastern European way station—of Mongol or Tartar; a wideness, almond eyes, high cheeks, irrepressible vigor. She could in another century have been a horsewoman, but she has worked at a stamping machine. I like her.

• • •

So I suppose he is. Nowadays it takes great vanity, great force of character, a gift for climbing on others' backs, tirelessness, and doubtless a pinch of talent for a man to become famous. To stay famous is almost impossible: there are too many with that climbing gift, as there are too many of every sort. But who wants any more to be famous? I would like to change places with the Mayor of New Haven, who is not particularly famous, whose name I can hardly think of—it is an Italian name again. I want to be he, for he has the priceless right to enter the Green, to mow its grass, to stand alone on the vast lawn.

The girl turns her head and asks, 'Where do you live?'

'In the Marinson building. You know, out Whitney.'

'Luck.'

'I don't know. It's modern. But'—I put my mouth almost to her ear and whisper; she can surely feel my breath on her neck—'we're on edge. My petition is for more space.'

'*What*? You're going to harm yourself.'

I am foolish. I know. But I have to try. There is a rumor that they are going to cut down everyone's space. Maximum dimensions now for a single person are eight feet by twelve. What you actually get depends on the building; space is allotted in inverse ratio to the quality of the premises. I myself have seven by eleven—it is said to be fairly desirable housing, the Marinson. A person's space is defined by lines painted on the sleeping-hall floor. One must keep all his belongings within his space; trespassing, except during communal hours, even 'trespassing' by accidental knocking over of possessions, is severely punished. We had a violent fight the other night because a sleeping man, stirring in a dream,

stretched his foot across the line into a couple's space while they were—
at least they *said* they were—having sexual union. We are told over and
over: Survival Is Acceptance. With my petition I may, as the girl says, do
myself harm.

*If* I succeed in reaching the petition windows.

The man behind me barks, 'Move it!'

The bureau building, now tantalizingly close, is a relic kept standing by
the Historical Site Preservation Society. A nineteenth-century romanti-
cization of a twelfth-century concept of power, it is stone-built and
sparsely adorned, with squinting arches and Romanesque striations,
dark-brown and light-brown in color, its walls spalled and pocked and
grimed—a fort for men whose trade it is to say: No.

Someone behind us has eaten garlic. Other scents on the morning air: the
delicious perfume of fresh-clipped grass from over the wall across the
street, and acrid whiffs of synthetic resins from the factories down
beyond Wooster Square.

●    ●    ●

He is responsive, his face haggard but mobile. Perhaps he understands
pleasure better than I had thought. . . . *It is strictly forbidden* . . . Their
exchanges go on longer than necessary. They are having quite a conversation.

Indifferent to the outcome of this chat, I turn to the janitor and say in a
loud, unpleasant voice, 'Line's slow this morning.'

Every once in a while, perhaps once a minute, it is possible to shuffle
one's foot two or three inches forward. Sometimes, in this shuffling, one
winds up a bit off balance, but it does not matter: the crowd-pressure
holds you firmly upright. There are sixteen petition windows on the
ground floor of the bureau building. You have to realize that each person
feels keenly the justice of his request, and when the bureau person behind
the bars of the window denies the petition, it is understandable that the
petitioner would wish to argue awhile, first in anger or outrage and later
perhaps in a whining tone—and all this takes time. Each person wants a
fair turn at a window. It takes a few minutes, when you have been waiting in line, let's say, nearly five hours, to absorb a no. This time-taking
backs up the whole column, which is, I would estimate, by now, a quarter of a mile long.

At my remark about the slowness of the line, the janitor is suddenly over-come by self-pity. 'I'm not getting enough to eat,' he says. 'Look. My wife's sick. She's not right. After work, she'd come back to the sleep-ing-hall and Christ, here she'd start yelling at me, throwing junk. All this stuff would land in other people's space. I had to take her up to Con-necticut Valley. The admissions office, they said, "Sign here, lady." She says, "What's this?" They tell her, "This here is a voluntary self-commit-ment form." She says, "Up yours, Jack." They say, "You have to sign it, lady." She jerks her head at me and says, "Get Mr. Big-ass here to sign it." They say, "Come on, lady, regulations." She says, "Voluntary my hine end." I damn near passed out. I mean I really almost fainted. I'm hungry *all the time.'*

•    •    •

Now it is the janitor who is whispering. He inclines his head close to mine, aims his cleaver of a nose at my cheek. 'I heard you, before.'

Is he some kind of operative? Informer? I do not want to exchange whis-pers with this creep in a green coverall with an eagle on his shoulder, and I say out loud, 'Yes, I saw you were eavesdropping.'

But he insists on whispering. 'I mean way before. About your petition. Look, if you louse me up, I'll get you, sure as hell.'

Aloud: 'Have you fallen out of your nest?'

Whisper: 'Suppose we get to the windows exactly the same time, I'm at the window right next to you. The minute you start in, I'm done for.' He suddenly says out loud, 'We're *all* finished.'

His shoulder trembles against my shoulder. He is pale. I do not feel threatened. It is he who feels threatened. I feel depressed.

The space I occupy is near the center of the Marinson sleeping-hall. It is defined by white lines, about an inch wide, painted on the varnished pine boards of the floor. What I think of as the head of my space, because I sleep with my head in that direction, is toward the north; I sleep, in other words, parallel to Whitney Avenue. On my right, lengthwise in the hall, is the passageway, eight inches wide, to the various spaces in our row and the next one. Each person tries to give his space a private style. I have adopted a quite common practice of bunking like a seaman on top of a long chest of drawers. The distinction of my space is that, apart from this chest-bed, it is bare. It is empty. Nothing but uncovered pine boards. No desk, no chair, no rug, no lamps, no TV, no books. Nothing. I have achieved a highly personal style by reducing my property—and my needs—to an absolute minimum. People think I am either pathetically poor or barren in imagination, but I have noticed that whenever I have guests, they get very high in my space, just from being in it. That is because so much of it *is* space. In a sense I have the largest home in New Haven.

But it is not large enough.

The grandmother is nudging me, and I turn toward her.

'You haven't told me what your petition is.'

The janitor's fear and anger at my petition are on my mind; I haven't dealt with him, and I don't relish at this moment the idea of setting the circuitry printer's active tongue in motion. Shall I make something up?

'I think I'd rather not discuss it.'

'You're just like my son—big Robert. He keeps things from me. Deliberately. He does it to hurt me. When little Robert was born, do you know how I found out he had come into this world? Marcia had gone to the hospital—she was having some trouble with the veins in her legs—so I called the hospital, I got the nurses' station on the floor where she was, and they said, "We aren't allowed to give out information. . . . Hold on a minute. We can put you through to your daughter-in-law when she finishes nursing." That's how I found out—they let it slip out that she had little Robert at her breast. He was already a day old. See what I mean?'

I must turn this old talkpot back on herself. 'You're so interested in everyone's petition—what's yours?'

'I'll trade. You first.' She is grinning.

I say, 'I'll bet yours is about this little Robert of yours. Right?'

'It is. Yes, it is. It's about Robert.' She pauses, then, unable to help herself, goes on. 'I don't want him to learn to read. I want him to have a useful skill.'

'I thought you were so proud he'd been chosen.'

'Of course I'm proud. But I'm also interested in his future.'

'Don't his parents have something to say?'

'They want him to read.'

'Do you always go over their heads this way?'

'I have to stay active.'

The girl has turned her head to the left and is listening. I am distracted. A deep part of my attention is drawn to the front of my body. The part of my mind that carries on with the grandmother is the stilted part devoted to manners, courtesy. I answer her only because I feel it would be rude not to. Another part, concerned with survival and courage and hope and aggression, reminds me that the janitor is not at all satisfied with what I have said to him. At the edge of each layer of attention is a clamor of impressions: traffic hum, brick turrets, blue pompon, siren, sparrows, snarls from behind, resins, the nibbling of fear.

The girl says to the grandmother, 'You mean to say you're interfering this way just to keep your mind occupied?'

The glasses, like headlights, swerve and throw their baleful beams at the girl. 'What's the difference? They'll turn me down.'

The girl snorts. 'Then why stand in line this way?'

'I like it. I enter a petition lots of days. I stand on line four, five times a week. You meet people. I'm talking to you right now.'

I say, 'That's a stupid thing to do. Look at the people behind you. You may be keeping somebody away from the windows who really has a hardship case.'

She bathes me with a pitying look. 'You born yesterday? There's lots of us come all the time.'

'Can't you see that hurts everybody?'

'How hurts? Do you think you'd get a yes if I weren't here?'

This waitline, which is agony for most of us, is the grandmother's social life. She makes me feel that my pessimism, like my attention to her words, is shallow.

I laugh and say to her, 'You're a case!'

'Listen,' she says, 'if you'd been through what I've been through . . .'

The girl is laughing, too, now.

The front I put up is earnest and hopeful, but truly I am pessimistic. Bureaucracy attracts such mediocre people; we are in the hands of imbeciles. It would make more sense to put this grandmother in charge of the petition windows than whoever is there now.

•   •   •

I write reports. The job to which I must make my way is in the state building out on Bassett Street, and I write reports for my department. My desklet is in a six-by-six cubicle with walls which do not go to the ceiling—plaster divider three feet high, crinkled acrylic panels above, to a height of five feet six. The four desklets are each two feet square; one tucks one's knees under. From overhead come showers of fluorescent light and of confused sounds from all the other cubicles—a song of typewriters, calculators, duplicators, teletype machines, creaking chairs, shifting feet, clearing throats; murmurs of Acceptance with overtones of Wanting the Day to Be Done.

My reports invariably put a good face on things—their tenor goes against the grain of my pessimistic bias; perhaps that is why I occasionally have an angry stomach.

I doubt if anyone reads my reports. But if one is late I get a warning printout from the computer.

'I wouldn't mind changing jobs myself,' I whisper to the girl—to the right side of her face.

'I suppose everyone wants to,' she whispers. 'I suppose that's why they'll turn me down.'

'But your petition isn't a selfish one.' There is a slight note, I hope a playful one, of mockery in this echoing line.

'It *is* selfish, really,' she whispers, turning my ribbing into an accusation, 'because I don't enjoy what I'm doing now.'

She has told me that she works in a bakery. She squeezes frosting decorations onto cakes—edging, star-shaped kisses, furbelows, bunting swoops; birthday greetings, business messages, consolations. Cakes in the shapes of towers, books, sports cars, beds with covers turned down. Discussing her cakes back when we were getting acquainted, before dawn, she whispered to me, 'A lot of people have the illusion that they can make things happen by eating shapes they connect with those happenings.'

'Why would you like to change jobs?' she now asks me.

'So few higher-ups in my department can read. Who reads my reports? A good writer like me should have more readers!'

• • •

## Chapter 2

'Isn't it hard,' she whispers, veering, 'being separated from your daughter?'

'I see her on rest days'—knowing it is not enough. It took so long—so many waitlines, less crowded ones than this, to be sure, in those days, but slow ones all the same—to get permission to have a child at all. Jill is twelve. I see her in my memory as being three, or perhaps four; her mouth is pursed as she works at weaving colored strips of paper together. She is in the bedlam of a day-care center, sitting cross-legged on the floor with a storm of hundreds of children whirling around her, she is one flake in a blizzard of innocence; yet at her weaving she is poised, serene, concentrated. Her generation does not seem to feel crowded. She floats in her natural medium. Her eyes, her ears work differently from mine. She has perceptions I cannot begin to share: Once, when she was six, she said, 'When Jeremy claps his hands, one hand makes more noise than the other.' In that her mind has been shaped by a more dense and shifting time even than mine, she and I will never understand each other. I adore her, but I cannot alert her. And if she tries to teach me something new, I either refuse to learn or mis-hear her; she strikes chords in an entirely new mode, to which I am deaf.

'What is she like?'

'She looks like me.' My small claim to immortality.

'But that doesn't tell me anything. I can't see your face.'

Of course that is true. Since well before dawn we have been so close-packed that the girl has not been able to turn her head far enough around to get a good look at me. I find this disturbing. The pressure of my body against hers does not tell her what sort of person I am; her sense of me comes only from what she hears in my voice. It is true that I don't know how wide her face is, but at least I can *see*: the wisps of fine hair at her neck, the sky on her skin, the bump that I presume to be related to humor on the left side of her face. The three-quarters rear view shows her to be an easy person—no tense muscles, no started veins. The sight of her flesh so close to my own—her cheek, the side of her neck—makes her real and helps me define her.

She has seemed responsive. I remember how, a while ago, she leaned her head back toward me, when I put out a few sympathetic syllables at her sudden puzzling grief. But how can she come to have any feelings about me—negotiable feelings, I mean—without seeing me and perhaps being encouraged by what she sees?

•   •   •

No one needs to be told that waitlines are slow. We are allowed fifteen minutes at table for breakfast at the Marinson; it takes twenty-five minutes in the cafeteria line to get to the first food racks. We are allowed six minutes on the john; there is a twenty-minute wait in the shitline. There should be more petition windows, no doubt of that. There should be more of everything. But there is not more of everything. That is the first fact of existence.

'My wife,' I whisper, 'was too damned judicious.'

I remember, once, on a rest day, a sunny morning in May, when the dogwood was at its height—we sat over breakfast and discussed a choice: Should we take Jill to Judges' Cave State Park, or should we stay in town and take a chance on a waitline at the public library? Doris considered. She didn't *list* all the pros and cons out loud. It was more a case of 'Let's see . . . . Let me think about it a sec . . ., Mmmm . . .' An atmosphere of good sense, not rushing blindly into things. Many long silences.

•   •   •

The janitor sprays me with spit as he tries to keep his next whisper even more hushed. 'You *can't* ask for more space. You'll have us all in trouble. They'll shut the petition windows. Or something much worse. I'm telling you, you better get out of this line before I get you out.'

I try to be cool. 'Anyone has a right to be in the line.'

'Not to ask *that*. You have no right to spoil everyone else's chances.'

'How would I be spoiling your chances? You're asking for food.'

A torrent is loosed. He forgets to whisper. 'You damn fool, *you know why*. Who cares about food? What kind of space do you think *I* have? When I had to put my wife away, the very day, I mean, Christ, two hours after I got back from Connecticut Valley, they cut me down to a single person's space. I tell you I wasn't home two hours—I was *famished*, just lying down trying to get my strength back—and here comes this twerp in a gray uniform from Allocations. He had two porters with him, and they carted my wife's stuff and my stuff away right then—I had no comeback, he had a warrant all made out—to this single space that they'd just moved some other guy out of, three houses down Willow Street. Look, in the married-couple space we'd had, we were so tight you had to climb over things—you had to move the TV and the vacuum cleaner onto the bed if you wanted to use the table, and the other way around, you know, back and forth. God, we worked hard for things, a lot of years, it's not so easy to give things up when they've come hard. So we had all our stuff piled up as it was. Well, when they put all our junk in a *single* space, it had to be really stacked. I can't get *at* anything now. It isn't any more, you know, moving things back and forth—it's stacking and unstacking. The rocking chair has to be on top of the pile, it isn't steady enough to pile anything on—it *rocks*. You know? I can't get rid of anything. I hope she'll get better. I miss her. I want her back. Let her throw stuff at me. If she comes back we'll get space for two again—but not in any two hours, I'll tell you *that*. I've seen people get married and have to make do with single space for *six months* waiting for what's their everyday right.'

• • •

## Chapter 3

'This the first time you've asked?'

'Yeah.'

'I've been through that meat grinder. I have a child. It's rough. When my wife and I were asking for permission it was done in a different way—they had a special bureau. It was all paperwork then. Fill out a form. Rejected—answers incomplete. Try again. Rejected—insufficient tax stamps. Try again. Rejected—one signature illegible. They never said we couldn't have a baby, just kept finding technicalities.'

'I know,' the young man says. 'Everyone tells me it won't happen the first time. May never. It must be a lot tighter now than when you tried.'

He sees me as an aging man. My pessimism asserts itself. 'It took us three years,' I say, 'even back then.'

'We don't care. We want to try.'

'What makes you want to bring a baby into . . . ?' My chin points in three wide swoops at the stream of people waiting.

# The Case for Human Beings

*Thomas Palmer*

An argument, a human argument, maintains that we ought to be concerned about the disappearance of individual animal species. If it could be directed at the objects of its solicitude, it would go approximately as follows: "You lesser beasts had better watch your step—we'll decide when you can leave." It recognizes that once chromosome patterns combine at the species level, they become unique and irreplaceable—one cannot make a rattlesnake, for instance, out of anything but more rattlesnakes. It looks at the speed at which such patterns are disappearing and shudders to think how empty our grandchildren's world might become, patternwise.

In the past twenty years this argument has conquered much of the world: it may soon become part of the thinking of nearly every school child.

Perhaps because we ourselves are a species, we regard the species level as that at which deaths become truly irreversible. Populations, for instance, can and do fade in and out: when a species dies, however, we call it extinct and retire its name forever, being reasonably certain that it will not reappear in its old form.

Students of evolution have shown that species death, or extinction, is going on all the time, and that it is an essential feature of life history. Species are adapted to their environments: as environments change, some species find themselves in the position of islanders whose islands are washing away, and they go under. Similarly, new islands (or environments) are appearing all the time. and they almost invariably produce new species.

What alarms so many life historians is not that extinctions are occurring but that they appear to be occurring at a greater rate than they have at all but a few times in the past, raising the specter of the sort of wholesale die-offs that ended the reign of the dinosaurs. Do we want, they ask, to exile most of our neighbors to posterity? Exactly how much of our planet's resources do we mean to funnel into people-making? Such questions are serious; they involve choosing among futures, and some of these futures are already with us, in the form of collapsing international fish-

eries, rich grasslands gnawed and trampled into deserts, forests skele-
tonized by windborne acids, and so forth. Thus high rates of extinction
are seen as a symptom of major problems in the way our species operates—problems that may, if we're not careful, be solved for us. A new
word has been coined to define the value most threatened by these over-
heated rates: "biodiversity." As species disappear, biodiversity declines,
and our planet's not-quite-limitless fund of native complexities—so some
argue—declines with it.

The process described above is indeed occurring. Human beings tend to
change environments; when they do, species vanish. The Puritans, for
example, though famous for their efforts to discipline sexuality, imposed
upon Massachusetts an orgy of ecological licentiousness: they introduced
dozens of microbes, weeds, and pests foreign to the region, some of
which played havoc with the natives. Human beings tend to travel everywhere, and to bring their cats, rats, and fleas with them, so that hardly
any environment is truly isolated today, and creatures that evolved in isolated environments have paid a high price. Of the 171 species and sub-
species of birds that have become extinct in the past 300 years, for
example, 155 were island forms.

Since extinction is a particularly final and comprehensive form of death,
species preservation and its corollary, habitat protection, are now seen as
the most important means available to stem the erosion of biodiversity.
So far, so good—but I wonder if these ideas, which emphasize diversity
at the species level, fail to give an adequate picture of recent biological
history. If, for instance, biodiversity is regarded as the chief measure of a
landscape's richness, then the American continents reached their peak of
splendor on the day after the first Siberian spearmen arrived, and have
been deteriorating ever since. More recent developments—such as the
domestication of maize, the rise of civilizations in Mexico and Peru, and
the passage of the U.S. Bill of Rights—are neutral at best, and are essentially invisible since they are the work of a single species, a species no
more or less weighty than any other, and already present at the start of
the interval. But what kind of yardstick measures a handful of skin-clad
hunters against Chicago, Los Angeles, and Caracas, and finds one group
no more "diverse" than the other.

A considerable amount of pessimism is built into this species-based
notion of diversity. Nearly all change on such a scale is change for the
worse—especially human-mediated change. Change involves stress, and

stress causes extinctions; each extinction is another pock in the skin of an Edenic original. This original is frozen in time: more often than not, it is defined as the blissful instant just prior to the arrival of the first human being. In fact, the only way to re-create this instant, and restore biodiversity to its greatest possible richness, would be to arrange for every human being on earth to drop dead tomorrow.

This is not to say that cities are better than coral reefs, or that binary codes are an improvement on genetic ones, but only that "biodiversity" cannot adequately account for the phenomenon of *Homo sapiens*.

Maybe it's time to give up the notion of human beings as intruders, tramplers, and destroyers. We are all of these, there's no doubt about it, but they are not all we are. And yet the same mind-set that interprets human history as little more than a string of increasingly lurid ecological crimes also insists that our species represents the last, best hope of "saving" the planet. Is it any wonder that the future looks bleak?

Here we have the essential Puritan outlook disguised as science—human beings, the sinners, occupy center stage, and cannot move a muscle without risking the direst consequences in a cosmic drama. At stake is the fate of the world; thousands of innocents (other species) rely on the shaky powers of human foresight. One false step—and our ancestors, as we know, have taken almost nothing but false steps—and our dwelling place may be mutilated beyond redemption.

This outlook is realistic in its recognition that our species is different in kind from all others, as any visitor from outer space would admit: it is obnoxious in the limits it places on the organic experiment. Human consciousness—whether in the form of Bach chorales, three-masted schooners, or microwave communications—cannot, in this view, contribute to biodiversity, except by staying as far out of the picture as possible, so as to avoid tainting still-intact landscapes with unnatural influences. The possibility that chorales and schooners might represent positive contributions to biotic richness—that they might, just as much as any rain-forest orchid, embody the special genius of this planet—is never admitted. Somehow an agreement has been reached to exclude whatever is human from the sum of biodiversity—as if the Apollo landings, for example, do not represent an astonishing breakthrough *in strictly biological terms*.

This view has a certain legitimacy as long as its definition of diversity is narrowly chromosomal, or species-based. Those environments richest in species—the tropical forests and the warmwater seas—are, from its perspective, the most diverse and complex, but I would argue that this definition, though accurate enough for most of the history of life, became obsolete about a half million years ago when *Homo sapiens* came on the scene. This creature released organic change from its age-old dependence on genetic recombination and harnessed it to new energies—culture, symbolic language, and imagination. This is becoming more and more evident, nothing has been the same since.

Being reluctant to acknowledge this fact, ecologists, biologists, and environmentalists have had fits trying to introduce our species into their models of the natural world. These models are based on the idea of balance, or equilibrium, wherein each variety of plant or animal plays a limited, genetically prescribed role in the cycling of materials and energy. The roles are not absolutely fixed—natural selection, by sorting and resorting chromosomes, can adapt lines of descent to new ones—but change, by and large, is assumed to be gradual, and millions of years can pass without any notable restructuring of communities.

Human beings cannot be worked into such models. One cannot look at human beings and predict what they will eat, or where they will live, or how many of their children a given landscape will support. If they inhabit a forest, they may burn it down and raise vegetables, or flood it and plant rice, or sell it to a pulp-and-paper manufacturer. They may think of anything; the life their parents led is not a reliable blueprint, but merely a box with a thousand exits. Moralists in search of instructive contrasts will sometimes idealize primitive societies, claiming that they deliberately live "in balance" with their environments, but these examples don't stand up to scrutiny. The Massachuset Indians, for instance, though sometimes presented as sterling conservationists, were the descendants of aboriginal American hunters who appear to have pursued a whole constellation of Ice Age mammals to extinction (including several species of horses). When, in historical times, they were offered metal fishhooks, knives, and firearms, they didn't say, "Thanks, but we prefer rock-chipping."

The revelation that we are not like other creatures in certain crucial respects is an ancient one, and may be nearly as old as humanity; it probably contributed to the idea central to several major religions, that we inhabit a sort of permanent exile. Until recently, however, we could still imagine ourselves encompassed by, if not entirely contained in, landscapes dominated by nonhuman forces—weather, infectious illness, growing seasons, light and darkness, and so forth. This is no longer so: today most human beings lie in artificial wildernesses called cities, and don't raise the food they eat, or know where the water they drink fell as rain. A sort of vertigo has set in—a feeling that a rhythm has been upset, and that soon nothing will be left of the worlds that made us. This feeling is substantiated by population curves, ocean pollution, chemical changes in the earth's atmosphere, vanishing wildlife, mountains of garbage, and numerous other signs that anyone can read. The nineteenth-century conservation movement, which sought to preserve landscapes for largely aesthetic reasons, has become absorbed in the twentieth-century environmental movement, which insists that more is at stake than postcard views. We are, it argues, near to exceeding the carrying capacity of our planet's natural systems, systems whose importance to us will become very obvious when they begin to wobble and fail.

These are not empty warnings. Human communities can and occasionally do self-destruct by overstraining their resource bases. Historical examples include the Easter Islanders, the lowland Maya, and some of the classical-era city-dwellers of the Middle East and North Africa. But if we set aside the equilibrium-based models of the ecologists, and do not limit ourselves to species-bound notions of diversity—in other words, if we seek to include human beings in the landscape of nature, rather than make them outcasts—what sort of picture do we get of the phenomenon of life?

The difference between life and nonlife, according to the biologists, is a matter of degree. A glass of seawater, for instance, contains many of the same materials as a condor (or a green turtle). What makes one alive and the other not are the varying chemical pathways those materials follow. The glass of water contains few internal boundaries, and gases diffuse freely across its surface. In the condor, in contrast, a much more complex array of reactions is in progress, reactions that maintain certain molecular-energy potentials in an oddly elevated state, even though the bird as a whole shows a net energy loss. In other words, both the condor and the glass of water cycle energy, but in the condor the energy goes to support a level of complexity not present in the water.

Perhaps the condor is more like a candle flame—both burn energy, and that burning keeps certain patterns intact. The condor, like the candle, can burn out. But although one can relight the candle, one cannot relight the condor—it is too delicately tuned, too dependent on various internal continuities.

As useful as these distinctions are, they tend to blur under increased magnification. A virus, for instance, is more condorlike than flamelike, because the energy and materials it draws from its surroundings reappear not primarily as heat, light, and simple oxides but as viral protein and nucleic acids—complex substances that the flame cannot construct but only disassemble. And yet most students agree that viruses are not alive, because they cannot build these substances without the aid of the machineries inside a living cell. A certain level of independence is necessary—living things, according to this definition, not only must transform simple compounds into more varied and characteristic ones but also must be able to do so in an atmosphere of nonlife.

Life, for the biologists is uphill or retrograde process—it adds order and complexity to environments whose overall tendency is toward diffusion and disorder. It captures energies released by decay and exploits them for growth and rebirth. It is startlingly anomalous in this respect: so far as we know, it occurs nowhere but on the surface of this planet, and even here its appearance seems to have been a one-time-only event; though many lifelike substances have been produced inside sterile glassware, none has ever quickened into veritable beasthood.

The evidence suggests that life continued to fructify and elaborate itself for several billion years after its appearance. The milestones along the way—the nucleated cell, photosynthesis, sexual reproduction, multicellularity, the internal skeleton, the invasion of the land and sky, and so forth—are usually interpreted as advances, because they added additional layers of complexity, interconnection, and ordered interaction to existing systems. This drama did not proceed without crises—photosynthesis, for instance, probably wiped out entire ecosystems by loading the atmosphere with a deadly poison, free oxygen—but life as a whole laughed at such insults, and continued on its protean way.

If we believe that all life—in contrast to rocks and gases—shares a certain quality of sensitivity, or self-awareness, then *Homo sapiens* was an astonishing and wholly unpredictable leap forward in this respect, because human beings manifested an idea of personhood never before achieved. The exact moment of this discovery is of course problematic, as are most events in evolution, but I would date it from early summer about 60,000 years ago, when a group of Neanderthals living in present-day Iraq lost one of their members, dug a grave for him in the Shanidar Cave of the Zagros Mountain highlands, placed his body inside, and covered it with yarrow blossoms, cornflowers, hyacinths, and mallows. Here, in a gesture of remarkable grace, a group of living creatures betrayed an awareness that creatureliness is a pose, a pose that can't be held forever.

The poignancy of this moment is profound. Though the idea is startling to consider, all the evidence suggests that most of life's history has unfolded unobserved, so to speak. I would bet that the dinosaurs, for instance, did not know that they were reptiles, or that they had faces like their neighbors, or that they once hatched from eggs like their offspring.

Consciousness. Mind. Insight. Here are qualities that, if not exclusively human, seem appallingly rudimentary elsewhere. Primitive peoples distributed them throughout their worlds: we moderns hold to stricter standards of evidence. Does a cloud learn, for instance, to drop rain? Is a seed eager to sprout?

The irruption of thoughtfulness that our species represents is not inexplicable in Darwinian terms. Once our apelike and erect ancestors began using weapons, hunting large animals, and sharing the spoils, the ability to develop plans and communicate them acquired considerable survival value, and was genetically enhanced. This ability, and the tripling in brain weight that accompanied it, turned out to be one of the most revolutionary experiments in the history of gene-sorting. It was as if Nature, after wearing out several billion years tossing off new creatures like nutshells, looked up to see that one had come back, and was eyeing her strangely.

The distance between that moment and today is barely a hiccup, geologically speaking. We are genetically almost indistinguishable from those bear-roasters and mammoth-stickers. But the world is a different place now. Grad students in ecology, for instance, are expected to do a certain amount of "fieldwork," and many of them have to travel hundreds and even thousands of miles before they consider themselves far enough from classrooms to be in the field.

Plainly, our planet contained vast opportunities for creatures willing to shape it consciously toward their ends. The way was clear; we know of no other species that has divined what we've been up to, or has a mind to object. What seems simple to us is far beyond them; it's almost as if we move so fast that we are invisible, and they are still trying to pretend—without much success—that the world is the same as it was before we arrived.

This speed on the uptake appears to be the chief advantage that cultural adaptation has over genetic. When human beings encounter new circumstances, adaptation rarely depends on which individuals are genetically best suited to adjust, passing on their abilities more successfully than others and producing subsequent generations better adapted to the new order. No, human beings tend to cut the loop short by noticing the new, puzzling over it, telling their friends, and attempting to find out immediately whether it is edible, combustible, domesticable, or whatever. In this way we develop traditions that are immaterial, so to speak, in that they evolve on a track largely disengaged from the double helix.

This talent for endless jabber and experiment, and the pooling of useful knowledge it makes possible, means that human beings, unlike orangutans or condors, operate not primarily as individuals scattered over a landscape but as shareholders in a common fund of acquired skills, many of them the work of previous generations. This fund is extraordinarily deep and sophisticated, even among the most isolated bands of hunter-gatherers; when, as in recent times, it has included experience accumulated by thousands or even millions of forebears, it has enabled our species to become the quickest-acting agent of change in life's history. In fact, we might sensibly think of the human species not as five billion distinct selves but as five billion nodes in a single matrix, just as the human body is more commonly considered a unit than an accumulation of cells.

If life, as before noted, is a paradoxical chemical process by which order arises from disorder, and a movement toward uniformity produces more complex local conditions, then human enterprise, though full of disasters for other species, is clearly not outside the main line of development. Equatorial rain forests, for instance, are probably the most diverse and multifaceted communities of species on earth. But are they more densely stuffed with highly refined codes and labels than, say, the Library of Congress? Long ago certain moths learned to communicate over as much as two miles of thick woods by releasing subtle chemicals that prospective mates could detect at levels measured in parts per million; today a currency broker in Tokyo can pick up a phone and hear accurate copies of sounds vocalized a split second earlier by a counterpart on the other side of the world. Which system of signals is more sensitive and flexible?

I am concerned, as is obvious, with an image—the image of our species as a vast, featureless mob of yahoos mindlessly trampling this planet's most ancient and delicate harmonies. This image, which is on its way to becoming an article of faith, is not a completely inaccurate description of present conditions in some parts of the world, but it portrays the human presence as a sort of monolithic disaster, when in fact *Homo sapiens* is the crown of creation, if by creation we mean the explosion of earthly vitality and particularity long ago ignited by a weak solution of amino acids mixing in sunlit waters. Change—dramatic, wholesale change—is one of the most reliable constants of this story. To say that the changes we have brought, and will continue to bring, are somehow alien to the world, and are within a half inch of making its "natural" continuance impossible, displays some contempt, I think, for the forces at work, along with a large dose of inverted pride. Who are we, for instance, to say what's possible and what isn't? Have we already glimpsed the end? Where exactly did things go awry? It's useful to remember that just yesterday our main concern was finding something to eat.

I prefer to suppose that we will be here awhile, and that such abilities as we have, though unprecedented in certain respects, are not regrettable. The human mind, for instance, could never have set itself the task of preserving rare species if earlier minds had not learned how to distinguish light from darkness, or coordinate limbs, or identify mates. Now that we think we know something about our immediate neighborhood, we are beginning to realize what a rare quality life is, and if we think of its multi-billion-year history on earth as a sort of gradual awakening of matter, we must conclude that the dawning of human consciousness represents one of the most extraordinary sunrises on record. Is it any wonder, then that the world is changing?

Perhaps because we have become so expert at interrogating our surroundings, we tremble a little at our own shadows. God, for instance, has become almost a fugitive. We have disassembled the atom; we have paced off the galaxies; He doesn't figure in our equations.

Maybe it would be useful at this point to compare our common birthplace to a fertile hen's egg. Nearly everyone has seen the delicate tracery of blood vessels that begins to spread across the yolk of such an egg within a few hours of laying. Before long a tiny pump starts to twitch rhythmically, and it drives a bright scarlet fluid through these vessels. The egg doesn't know that it is on its way to becoming a chicken. Chickens, for the egg, lie somewhere on the far side of the beginning of time. And yet the egg couldn't be better equipped to make a chicken out of itself.

I would argue that our planet, like the egg, is on a mission of sorts. We don't know what that mission is any more than the nascent nerve cells in the egg know why they are forming a network. All we know is that things are changing rapidly and dramatically.

Today many believe that these changes are often for the worse, and represent a fever or virus from which the body of life will emerge crippled and scarred. We look back with longing on a time, only a moment ago, when the human presence barely dimpled the landscape—when the yolk, so to speak, was at its creamiest, and no angry little eye-spots signaled an intent to devour everything.

I'm not persuaded by this picture—I think it arises from a mistaken belief that the outlines of earthly perfection are already evident. It has inspired a small army of doomsayers—if we burn the forests of the Amazon, we are told, our planet's lungs will give out, and we will slowly asphyxiate. Surely we have better, more practical reasons for not burning them than to stave off universal catastrophe. I can easily imagine similar arguments that would have required the interior of North America to remain empty of cities—and yet I don't think this continent is a poorer place now than it was 20,000 years ago. The more convinced we are that our species is a plague, the more we are obliged to yearn for disasters.

Students of historical psychology have noticed that the end of the world is always at hand. For the Puritan preachers it was to take the form of divine wrath, and they warned that the Wampanoag war was only a foretaste. The Yankees saw it coming in the flood of nineteenth-century immigrants, who meant to drown true Americanism. Today we are more likely to glimpse it in canned aerosols, poisoned winds, and melting ice caps.

Curiously enough, the end of the world always is at hand—the world dies and is reborn on a daily basis. A fertile hen's egg is never today what it was yesterday, or will be tomorrow. Few would deny that the effort to preserve and protect as many as possible of the millions of species now existing represents a fresh and heartening expansion of human ambitions. But to suppose that earthly diversity is past its prime, and that a strenuous program of self-effacement is the best contribution our species has left to offer, is neither good biology nor good history.

# The Lunar Eclipse

*The moon, according to the Hupa, was also a living being, specifically a man: not an abstract, ethereal, symbolic man—not a male principle—but a real, flesh-and-blood, awesomely powerful man. This man had wives and pets, and like men everywhere he hunted deer. The moon's rising and setting, waxing and waning, and especially its eclipses were dramatic, often bloody events in the man's life.*

The one who always travels at night has ten wives in the west and ten wives also where he rises. In the distant west he always comes out to the ocean and hunts the deer which live on the water. He calls them by saying, "wu, wu, wu, wu." He always kills ten and then ten more. Taking ten on his back he carries them to the place where he goes up into the sky. It is there his house is. Then his pets crowd around him, his mountain-lions and his rattlesnakes. He divides the deer among the animals but they are not satisfied with one apiece. They jump on him and eat him besides. They leave only his blood. Then Frog, who stands in the body of her husband, clubs them off and they desist. He goes down in the west, nothing but blood. There his wives brush together the blood and he recovers. He always goes back to the place of rising and there they make him well again.

His pets do not do that way with him every time. Sometimes they get enough and then they quit. When they are not satisfied with the food given them, then they eat him.

HUPA

*Section Five*

# The Nature of Time

# *from* The City of God

## St. Augustine

*St. Augustine of Hippo was born in North Africa in 354. Though born a Christian, he spent much of his youth following the Manichaen philosophy. Later, he converted back to Christianity, becoming one of its foremost interpreters. He died in 430.*

## How These Persons Are to Be Answered, Who Find Fault With the Creation of Man on the Score of Its Recent Date

As to those who are always asking why man was not created during these countless ages of the infinitely extended past, and came into being so lately that, according to Scripture, less than 6000 years have elapsed since he began to be, I would reply to them regarding the creation of man, just as I replied regarding the origin of the world to those who will not believe that it is not eternal, but had a beginning, which even Plato himself most plainly declares, though some think his statement was not consistent with his real opinion. If it offends them that the time that has elapsed since the creation of man is so short, and his years so few according to our authorities, let them take this into consideration, that nothing that has a limit is long, and that all the ages of time being finite, are very little, or indeed nothing at all, when compared to the interminable eternity. Consequently, if there had elapsed since the creation of man, I do not say five or six, but even sixty or six hundred thousand years, or sixty times as many, or six hundred or six hundred thousand times as many, or this sum multiplied until it could no longer be expressed in numbers, the same question could still be put, Why was he not made before? For the past and boundless eternity during which God abstained from creating man is so great, that, compare it with what vast and untold number of ages you please, so long as there is a definite conclusion of this term of time, it is not even as if you compared the minutest drop of water with the ocean that everywhere flows around the globe. For of these two, one indeed is very small, the other incomparably vast, yet both are finite; but that space of time which starts from some beginning, and is limited by some termination, be it of what extent it may, if

694

you compare it with that which has no beginning, I know not whether to say we should count it the very minutest thing, or nothing at all. For, take this limited time, and deduct from the end of it, one by one, the briefest moments (as you might take day by day from a man's life, beginning at the day in which he now lives, back to that of his birth), and though the number of moments you must subtract in this backward movement be so great that no word can express it, yet this subtraction will sometime carry you to the beginning. But if you take away from a time which has no beginning, I do not say brief moments one by one, nor yet hours, or days, or months, or years even in quantities, but terms of years so vast that they cannot be named by the most skillful arithmeticians—take away terms of years as vast as that which we have supposed to be gradually consumed by the deduction of moments—and take them away not once and again repeatedly, but always, and what do you effect, what do you make by your deduction, since you never reach the beginning which has no existence? Wherefore, that which we now demand after five thousand odd years, our descendants might with like curiosity demand after six hundred thousand years, supposing these dying generations of men continue so long to decay and be renewed, and supposing posterity continues as weak and ignorant as ourselves. The same question might have been asked by those who have lived before us and while man was even newer upon earth. The first man himself, in short, might, the day after or the very day of his creation have asked why he was created no sooner. And no matter at what earlier or later period he had been created, this controversy about the commencement of this world's history would have had precisely the same difficulties as it has now.

## Of the Revolution of the Ages, Which Some Philosophers Believe Will Bring All Things Round Again, After a Certain Fixed Cycle, to the Same Order and Form as at First

This controversy some philosophers have seen no other approved means of solving than by introducing cycles of time, in which there should be a constant renewal and repetition of the order of nature; and they have therefore asserted that these cycles will ceaselessly recur, one passing away and another coming, though they are not agreed as to whether one permanent world shall pass through all these cycles, or whether the world shall at fixed intervals die out, and be renewed so as to exhibit a recurrence of the same phenomena—the things which have been, and those which are to be, coinciding. And from this fantastic vicissitude they exempt not even the immortal soul that has attained wisdom, consigning it to a ceaseless transmigration between delusive blessedness and real misery. For how can that be truly called blessed which has no assurance of being so eternally, and is either in ignorance of the truth, and blind to the misery that is approaching, or, knowing it, is in misery and fear? Or if it passes to bliss, and leaves miseries forever, then there happens in time a new thing which time shall not end. Why not, then, the world also? Why may not man, too, be a similar thing? So that, by following the straight path of sound doctrine, we escape, I know not what circuitous paths, discovered by deceiving and deceived sages.

Some, too, in advocating these recurring cycles that restore all things to their original, cite in favor of their supposition what Solomon says in the book of Ecclesiastes: "What is that which hath been? It is that which shall be. And what is that which is done? It is that which shall be done: and there is no new thing under the sun. Who can speak and say, See, this is new? It hath been already of old time, which was before us." This he said either of those things of which he had just been speaking—the succession of generations, the orbit of the sun, the course of rivers—or else of all kinds of creatures. that are born and die. For men were before us, are with us, and shall be after us; and so all living things and all plants. Even monstrous and irregular productions, though differing from one another, and though some are reported as solitary instances, yet resemble one another generally, in so far as they are miraculous and monstrous, and, in this sense, have been, and shall be, and are no new and recent things under the sun. However, some would understand these words as meaning that in the predestination of God all things have already existed, and that thus there is no new thing under the sun. At all events, far be it from any true believer to suppose that by these words of Solomon those cycles are meant, in which, according to those philosophers, the same periods and events of time are repeated; as if, for example, the philosopher Plato, having taught in the school at Athens which is called the Academy, so, numberless ages before, at long but certain intervals, this same Plato and the same school, and the same disciples existed, and so also are to be repeated during the countless cycles that are yet to be—far be it, I say, from us to believe this. For once Christ died for our sins; and, rising from the dead, He dieth no more. "Death hath no more dominion over Him; and we ourselves after the resurrection shall be "ever with the Lord," to whom we now say, as the sacred Psalmist dictates, "Thou shall keep us, O Lord, Thou shall preserve us from this generation." And that too which follows, is, I think, appropriate enough: "The wicked walk *in a circle;*" not because their life is to recur by means of these circles, which these philosophers imagine, but because the path in which their false doctrine now runs is circuitous.

## Of the Creation of the Human Race in Time, and How This Was Effected Without Any New Design or Change of Purpose on God's Part

What wonder is it if, entangled in these circles, they find neither entrance nor egress? For they know not how the human race, and this mortal condition of ours, took its origin, nor how it will be brought to an end, since they cannot penetrate the inscrutable wisdom of God. For, though Himself eternal, and without beginning, yet He caused time to have a beginning; and man, whom He had not previously made He made in time, not from a new and sudden resolution, but by His unchangeable and eternal design. Who can search out the unsearchable depth of this purpose, who can scrutinize the inscrutable wisdom, wherewith God, without change of will, created man, who had never before been, and gave him an existence in time, and increased the human race from one individual? For the Psalmist himself, when he had first said, "Thou shalt keep us, O Lord, Thou shall preserve us from this generation for ever," and had then rebuked those whose foolish and impious doctrine preserves for the soul no eternal deliverance and blessedness adds immediately, "The wicked walk in a circle." Then, as if it were said to him, "What then do you believe, feel, know? Are we to believe that it suddenly occurred to God to create man, whom He had never before made in a past eternity—God, to whom nothing new can occur, and in whom is no changeableness?" the Psalmist goes on to reply, as if addressing God Himself, "According to the depth of Thy wisdom Thou hast multiplied the children of men." Let men, he seems to say, fancy what they please, let them conjecture and dispute as seems good to them, but Thou hast multiplied the children of men according to the depth of thy wisdom, which no man can comprehend. For this is a depth indeed, that God always has been, and that man, whom He had never made before, He willed to make in time, and this without changing His design and will.

## Whether We Are to Believe That God, As He Has Always Been Soverign Lord, Has Always Had Creatures Over Whom He Exercised His Sovereignty; and In What Sense We Can Say That the Creature Has Always Been, and Yet Cannot Say It Is Co-eternal

For my own part, indeed, as I dare not say that there ever was a time when the Lord God was not Lord, so I ought not to doubt that man had no existence before time, and was first created in time. But when I consider what God could be the Lord of, if there was not always some creature, I shrink from making any assertion, remembering my own insignificance, and that it is written, "What man is he that can know the counsel of God? or who can think what the will of the Lord is? For the thoughts of mortal men are timid, and our devices are but uncertain. For the corruptible body presseth down the soul, and the earthly tabernacle weigheth down the mind that museth upon many things."' Many things certainly do I muse upon in this earthly tabernacle, because the one thing which is true among the many, or beyond the many, I cannot find. If, then, among these many thoughts, I say that there have always been creatures for Him to be Lord of, who is always and ever has been Lord, but that these creatures have not always been the same, but succeeded one another (for we would not seem to say that any is co-eternal with the Creator, an assertion condemned equally by faith and sound reason), I must take care lest I fall into the absurd and ignorant error of maintaining that by these successions and changes mortal creatures have always existed, whereas the immortal creatures had not begun to exist until the date of our own world, when the angels were created; if at least the angels are intended by that light which was first made, or, rather, by that heaven of which it is said, "In the beginning God created the heavens and the earth." The angels, at least did not exist before they were created; for if we say that they have always existed, we shall seem to make them co-eternal with the Creator. Again, if I say that the angels were not created in time, but existed before all times, as those over whom God, who has ever been Sovereign, exercised His sovereignty, then I shall be asked whether, if they were created before all time, they, being creatures, could possibly always exist. It may perhaps be replied, Why not always, since that which is in all time may very properly be said to be "always?" Now so true is it that these angels have existed in all time that even before time was they were created; if at least time began with the heavens, and the angels existed before the heavens. And if time was even before the heavenly bodies, not indeed marked by hours, days, months, and years—for these measures of time's periods which are commonly and properly called times, did manifestly begin with the motion of the heavenly bodies, and so God said, when He appointed them, "Let them be for signs, and for seasons, and for days, and for years," if, I say, time was before these heavenly bodies by some changing movement, whose parts succeeded one another and could not exist simultaneously, and if there was some such movement among the angels which necessitated the existence of time, and that they from their very creation should be subject to these temporal changes, then they have existed in all time, for time came into being along with them. And who will say that what was in all time, was not always?

But if I make such a reply, it will be said to me, How, then, are they not co-eternal with the Creator, if He and they always have been? How even can they be said to have been created, if we are to understand that they have always existed? What shall we reply to this? Shall we say that both statements are true? that they always have been, since they have been in all time, they being created along with time, or time along with them, and yet that also they were created? For, similarly, we will not deny that time itself was created, though no one doubts that time has been in all time; for if it has not been in all time, then there was a time when there was no time. But the most foolish person could not make such an assertion. For we can reasonably say there was a time when Rome was not; there was a time when Jerusalem was not; there was a time when Abraham was not; there was a time when man was not, and so on: in fine, if the world was not made at the commencement of time, but after some time had elapsed, we can say there was a time when the world was not. But to say there was a time when time was not, is as absurd as to say there was a man when there was no man; or, this world was when this world was not. For if we are not referring to the same object, the form of expression may be used, as, there was another man when this man was not. Thus we can reasonably say there was another time when this time was not; but not the merest simpleton could say there was a time when there was no time. As, then, we say that time was created, though we also say that it always has been, since in all time time has been, so it does not follow that if the angels have always been, they were therefore not created. For we say that they have always been, because they have been in all time; and we say they have been in all time, because time itself could no wise be without them. For where there is no creature whose changing movements admit of succession, there cannot be time at all. And consequently, even if they have always existed, they were created; neither, if they have always existed, are they therefore co-eternal with the Creator. For He has always existed in unchangeable eternity; while they were created, and are said to have been always, because they have been in all time, time being impossible without the creature. But time passing away by its changefulness, cannot be co-eternal with changeless eternity. And consequently, though the immortality of the angels does not pass in time, does not become past as if now it were not, nor has a future as if it were not yet, still their movements, which are the basis of time, do pass from future to past; and therefore they cannot be co-eternal with the Creator, in whose movement we cannot say that there has been that which now is not, or shall be that which is not yet. Wherefore, if God always has been Lord, He has always had creatures under His dominion—creatures, however, not begotten of Him, but created by Him out of nothing; nor co-eternal with Him, for He was before them though at no time without them, because He preceded them, not by the lapse of time, but by His abiding eternity. But if I make this reply to those who demand how He was always Creator, always Lord, if there were not always a subject creation; or how this was created, and not rather co-eternal with its Creator, if it always was, I fear I may be accused of recklessly affirming what I know not, instead of teaching what I know. I return, therefore, to that which our Creator has seen fit that we should know; and those things which He has allowed the abler men to know in this life, or has reserved to be known in the next by the perfected saints, I acknowledge to be beyond my capacity. But I have thought it right to discuss these matters without making positive assertions, that they who read may be warned to abstain from hazardous questions, and may not deem themselves fit for everything. Let them rather endeavor to obey the wholesome injunction of the apostle, when he says, "For I say, through the grace given unto me, to every man that is among you, not to think of himself more highly than he ought to think; but to think soberly, according as God hath dealt to every man the measure of faith." For if an infant receive nourishment suited to its strength, it becomes capable, as it grows, of taking more; but if its strength and capacity be overtaxed, it dwines away in place of growing.

## How We Are to Understand God's Promise of Life Eternal, Which Was Uttered Before the "Eternal Times."

I own that I do not know what ages passed before the human race was created, yet I have no doubt that no created thing is co-eternal with the Creator. But even the apostle speaks of time as eternal, and this with reference, not to the future, but, which is more surprising, to the past. For he says, "In hope of eternal life, which God that cannot lie promised before the eternal times, but hath in due times manifested His word." You see he says that in the past there have been eternal times, which, however, were not co-eternal with God. And since God before these eternal times not only existed, but also, "promised" life eternal, which He manifested in its own times (that is to say, in due times), what else is this than His word? For this is life eternal. But then, how did He promise; for the promise was made to men, and yet they had no existence before eternal times? Does this not mean that, in His own eternity, and in His co-eternal word, that which was to be in its own time was already predestined and fixed?

## What Defense Is Made By Sound Faith Regarding God's Unchangeable Counsel and Will, Against the Reasonings of Those Who Hold That the Works of God Are Eternally Repeated in Revolving Cycles That Restore All Things As They Were

Of this, too, I have no doubt, that before the first man was created, there never had been a man at all, neither this same man himself recurring by I know not what cycles, and having made I know not how many revolutions, nor any other of similar nature. From this belief I am not frightened by philosophical arguments, among which that is reckoned the most acute which is founded on the assertion that the infinite cannot be comprehended by any mode of knowledge. Consequently, they argue, God has in his own mind finite conceptions of all finite things which He makes. Now it cannot be supposed that His goodness was ever idle; for if it were, there should be ascribed to Him an awakening to activity in time, from a past eternity of inactivity, as if He repented of an idleness that had no beginning, and proceeded, therefore, to make a beginning of work. This being the case, they say it must be that the same things are always repeated, and that as they pass, so they are destined always to return, whether amidst all these changes the world remains the same—the world which has always been, and yet was created—or that the world in these revolutions is perpetually dying out and being renewed; otherwise, if we point to a time when the works of God were begun, it would be believed that He considered His past eternal leisure to be inert and indolent, and therefore condemned and altered it as displeasing to Himself. Now if God is supposed to have been indeed always making temporal things, but different from one another, and one after the other, so, that He thus came at last to make man, whom He had never made before, then it may seem that He made man not with knowledge (for they suppose no knowledge can comprehend the infinite succession of creatures), but at the dictate of the hour, as it struck him at the moment, with a sudden and accidental change of mind. On the other hand, say they, if those cycles be admitted, and if we suppose that the same temporal things are repeated, while the world either remains identical through all these rotations, or else dies away and is renewed, then there is ascribed to God neither the slothful ease of a past eternity, nor a rash and unforeseen creation. And if the same things be not thus repeated in cycles, then they cannot by any science or prescience be comprehended in their endless diversity. Even though reason could not refute, faith would smile at these argumentations, with which the godless endeavor to turn our simple piety from the right way, that we may walk with them "in a circle." But by the help of the Lord our God, even reason, and that readily enough, shatters these revolving circles which conjecture frames. For that which specially leads these men astray to refer their own circles to the straight path of truth, is, that they measure by their own human, changeable, and narrow intellect the divine mind, which is absolutely unchangeable, infinitely capacious, and without succession of thought, counting all things without number. So that saying of the apostle comes true of them, for, "comparing themselves with themselves, they do not understand." For because they do, in virtue of a new purpose, whatever new thing has occurred to them to be done (their minds being changeable), they conclude it is so with God; and thus compare, not God—for they cannot conceive God, but think of one like themselves when they think of Him—not God, but themselves, and not with Him, but with themselves. For our part, we dare not believe that God is affected in one way when He works, in another when He rests. Indeed, to say that He is affected at all, is an abuse of language, since it implies that there comes to be something in His nature which was not there before. For he who is affected is acted upon, and whatever is acted upon is changeable. His leisure, therefore, is no laziness, indolence, inactivity; as in His work is no labor, effort, industry. He can act while He reposes, and repose while He acts. He can begin a new work with (not a new, but) an eternal design; and what He has not made before, He does not now begin to make because He repents of His former repose. But when one speaks of His former repose and subsequent operation (and I know not how men can understand these things), this "former" and "subsequent" are applied only to the things created, which formerly did not exist, and subsequently came into existence. But in God the former purpose is not altered and obliterated by the subsequent and different purpose, but by one and the same eternal and unchangeable will He effected regarding the things He created, both that formerly, so long as they were not, they should not be, and that subsequently, when they began to be, they should come into existence. And thus, perhaps, He would show, in a very striking way, to those who have eyes for such things, how independent He is of what He makes, and how it is of His own gratuitous goodness He creates, since from eternity He dwelt without creatures in no less perfect a blessedness.

## Against Those Who Assert That Things That Are Infinite Cannot Be Comprehended By the Knowledge of God

As for their other assertion, that God's knowledge cannot comprehend things infinite, it only remains for them to affirm, in order that they may sound the depths of their impiety, that God does not know all numbers. For it is very certain that they are infinite; since, no matter of what number you suppose an end to be made, this number can be, I will not say, increased by the addition of one more, but however great it be, and however vast be the multitude of which it is the rational and scientific expression, it can still be not only doubled, but even multiplied. Moreover, each number is so defined by its own properties, that no two numbers are equal. They are therefore both unequal and different from one another; and while they are simply finite, collectively they are infinite. Does God, therefore, not know numbers on account of this infinity; and does His knowledge extend only to a certain height in numbers, while of the rest He is ignorant? Who is so left to himself as to say so? Yet they can hardly pretend to put numbers out of the question, or maintain that they have nothing to do with the knowledge of God; for Plato, their great authority, represents God as framing the world on numerical principles: and in our books also it is said to God, "Thou hast ordered all things in number, and measure, and weight." The prophet also says, "Who bringeth out their host by number." And the Saviour says in the Gospel, "The very hairs of your head are all numbered." Far be it, then, from us to doubt that all number is known to Him "whose understanding," according to the Psalmist, "is infinite." The infinity of number, though there be no numbering of infinite numbers, is yet not incomprehensible by Him whose understanding is infinite. And thus, if everything which is comprehended is defined or made finite by the comprehension of him who knows it, then all infinity is in some ineffable way made finite to God, for it is comprehensible by His knowledge. Wherefore, if the infinity of numbers cannot be infinite to the knowledge of God, by which it is comprehended, what are we poor creatures that we should presume to fix limits to His knowledge, and say that unless the same temporal thing be repeated by the same periodic revolutions, God cannot either foreknow His creatures that He may make them, or know them when He has made them? God, whose knowledge is simply manifold, and uniform in its variety, comprehends all incomprehensibles with so incomprehensible a comprehension, that though He willed always to make His later works novel and unlike what went before them, He could not produce them without order and foresight, nor conceive them suddenly, but by His eternal foreknowledge.

## Of Worlds Without End, or Ages of Ages

I do not presume to determine whether God does so, and whether these times which are called "ages of ages" are joined together in a continuous series, and succeed one another with a regulated diversity, and leave exempt from their vicissitudes only those who are freed from their misery, and abide without end in a blessed immortality; or whether these are called "ages of ages," that we may understand that the ages remain unchangeable in God's unwavering wisdom, and are the efficient causes, as it were, of those ages which are being spent in time. Possibly "ages" is used for "age," so that nothing else is meant by "ages of ages" than by "age of age," as nothing else is meant by "heavens of heavens" than by "heaven of heaven." For God called the firmament, above which are the waters, "Heaven," and yet the psalm says, "Let the waters that are above the *heavens* praise the name of the Lord." Which of these two meanings we are to attach to "ages of ages," or whether there is not some other and better meaning still, is a very profound question; and the subject we are at present handling presents no obstacle to our meanwhile deferring the discussion of it, whether we may be able to determine anything about it, or may only be made more cautious by its further treatment, so as to be deterred from making any rash affirmations in a matter of such obscurity.

For at present we are disputing the opinion that affirms the existence of those periodic revolutions by which the same things are always recurring at intervals of time. Now whichever of these suppositions regarding the "ages of ages" be the true one, it avails nothing for the substantiating of those cycles; for whether the ages of ages be not a repetition of the same world, but different worlds succeeding one another in a regulated connection, the ransomed souls abiding in well-assured bliss without any recurrence of misery, or whether the ages of ages be the eternal causes which rule what shall be and is in time, it equally follows, that those cycles which bring round the same things have no existence; and nothing more thoroughly explodes them than the fact of the eternal life of the saints.

## Of the Impiety of Those Who Assert That the Souls Which Enjoy True and Perfect Blessedness, Must Yet Again and Again in These Periodic Revolutions Return to Labor and Misery

What pious ears could bear to hear that after a life spent in so many and severe distresses (if, indeed, that should be called a life at all which is rather a death, so utter that the love of this present death makes us fear that death which delivers us from it,) that after evils so disastrous, and miseries of all kinds have at length been expiated and finished by the help of true religion and wisdom, and when we have thus attained to the vision of God, and have entered into bliss by the contemplation of spiritual light and participation in His unchangeable immortality, which we burn to attain—that we must at some time lose all this, and that they who do lose it are cast down from that eternity, truth, and felicity to infernal mortality and shameful foolishness, and are involved in accursed woes, in which God is lost, truth held in detestation, and happiness sought in iniquitous impurities? and that this will happen endlessly again and again, recurring at fixed intervals, and in regularly returning periods? and that this everlasting and ceaseless revolution of definite cycles, which remove and restore true misery and deceitful bliss in turn, is contrived in order that God may be able to know His own works, since on the one hand He cannot rest from creating and on the other, cannot know the infinite number of His creatures, if He always makes creatures? Who, I say, can listen to such things? Who can accept or suffer them to be spoken? Were they true, it were not only more prudent to keep silence regarding them, but even (to express myself as best I can) it were the part of wisdom not to know them. For if in the future world we shall not remember these things, and by this oblivion be blessed, why should we now increase our misery, already burdensome enough, by the knowledge of them? If, on the other hand, the knowledge of them will be forced upon us hereafter, now at least let us remain in ignorance, that in the present expectation we may enjoy a blessedness which the future reality is not to bestow; since in this life we are expecting to obtain life everlasting, but in the world to come are to discover it to be blessed, but not everlasting.

And if they maintain that no one can attain to the blessedness of the world to come, unless in this life he has been indoctrinated in those cycles in which bliss and misery relieve one another, how do they avow that the more a man loves God, the more readily he attains to blessedness—they who teach what paralyzes love itself? For who would not be more remiss and lukewarm in his love for a person whom he thinks he shall be forced to abandon, and whose truth and wisdom he shall come to hate; and this, too, after he has quite attained to the utmost and most blissful knowledge of Him that he is capable of? Can any one be faithful in his love, even to a human friend, if he knows that he is destined to become his enemy? God forbid that there be any truth in an opinion which threatens us with a real misery that is never to end, but is often and endlessly to be interrupted by intervals of fallacious happiness. For what happiness can be more fallacious and false than that in whose blaze of truth we yet remain ignorant that we shall be miserable, or in whose most secure citadel we yet fear that we shall be so? For if, on the one hand, we are to be ignorant of coming calamity, then our present misery is not so short-sighted for it is assured of coming bliss. If, on the other hand, the disaster that threatens is not concealed from us in the world to come, then the time of misery which is to be at last exchanged for a state of blessedness, is spent by the soul more happily than its time of happiness, which is to end in a return to misery. And thus our expectation of unhappiness is happy, but of happiness unhappy. And therefore, as we here suffer present ills, and hereafter fear ills that are imminent, it were truer to say that we shall always be miserable than that we can some time be happy.

But these things are declared to be false by the loud testimony of religion and truth; for religion truthfully promises a true blessedness, of which we shall be eternally assured, and which cannot be interrupted by any disaster. Let us therefore keep to the straight path, which is Christ, and, with Him as our Guide and Saviour, let us turn away in heart and mind from the unreal and futile cycles of the godless. Porphyry, Platonist though he was, abjured the opinion of his school, that in these cycles souls are ceaselessly passing away and returning, either being struck with the extravagance of the idea, or sobered by his knowledge of Christianity. As I mentioned in the tenth book, he preferred saying that the soul, as it had been sent into the world that it might know evil, and be purged and delivered from it, was never again exposed to such an experience after it had once returned to the Father. And if he abjured the tenets of his school, how much more ought we Christians to abominate and avoid an opinion so unfounded and hostile to our faith? But having disposed of these cycles and escaped out of them, no necessity compels us to suppose that the human race had no beginning in time, on the ground that there is nothing new in nature which, by I know not what cycles, has not at some previous period existed, and is not hereafter to exist again. For if the soul, once delivered, as it never was before, is never to return to misery, then there happens in its experience something which never happened before; and this, indeed, something of the greatest consequence, to wit, the secure entrance into eternal felicity. And if in an immortal nature there can occur a novelty, which never has been, nor ever shall be, reproduced by any cycle, why is it disputed that the same may occur in mortal natures? If they maintain that blessedness is no new experience to the soul, but only a return to that state in which it has been eternally, then at least its deliverance from misery is something new, since, by their own showing, the misery from which it is delivered is itself, too, a new experience. And if this new experience fell out by accident, and was not embraced in the order of things appointed by Divine Providence, then where are those determinate and measured cycles in which no new thing happens, but all things are reproduced as they were before? If, however, this new experience was embraced in that providential order of nature (whether the soul was exposed to the evil of this world for the sake of discipline, or fell into it by sin), then it is possible for new things to happen which never happened before, and which yet are not extraneous to the order of nature. And if the soul is able by its own imprudence to create for itself a new misery, which was not unforeseen by the Divine Providence, but was provided for in the order of nature along with the deliverance from it, how can we, even with all the rashness of human vanity, presume to deny that God can create new things—new to the world, but not to Him—which He never before created, but yet foresaw from all eternity? If they say that it is indeed true that ransomed souls return no more to misery, but that even so no new thing happens, since there always have been, now are, and ever shall be a succession of ransomed souls, they must at least grant that in this case there are new souls to whom the misery and the deliverance from it are new. For if they maintain that those souls out of which new men are daily being made (from whose bodies, if they have lived wisely, they are so delivered that they never return to misery) are not new, but have existed from eternity, they must logically admit that they are infinite. For however great a finite number of souls there were, that would not have sufficed to make perpetually new men from eternity—men whose souls were to be eternally freed from this mortal state, and never afterwards to return to it. And our philosophers will find it hard to explain how there is an infinite number of souls in an order of nature which they require shall be finite, that it may be known by God.

And now that we have exploded these cycles which were supposed to bring back the soul at fixed periods to the same miseries, what can seem more in accordance with godly reason than to believe that it is possible for God both to create new things never before created, and in doing so, to preserve His will unaltered? But whether the number of eternally redeemed souls can be continually increased or not, let the philosophers themselves decide, who are so subtle in determining where infinity cannot be admitted. For our own part, our reasoning holds in either case. For if the number of souls can be indefinitely increased, what reason is there to deny that what had never before been created, could be created? since the number of ransomed souls never existed before, and has yet not only been once made, but will never cease to be anew coming into being. If, on the other hand, it be more suitable that the number of eternally ransomed souls be definite, and that this number will never be increased, yet this number, whatever it be, did assuredly never exist before, and it cannot increase, and reach the amount it signifies, without having some beginning; and this beginning never before existed. That this beginning, therefore, might be, the first man was created.

# The Cyclical Night

## Jorge Luis Borges

*Jorge Luis Borges was the premiere 20th century Argentine storyteller, essayist and poet. He also served for a time as the national librarian. In his later years, he lost his vision but still continued to write. His themes include time, memory, and human identity. He lived from 1899 until 1986.*

*To Sylvina Bullrich*

They knew it, the fervent pupils of Pythagoras:
that stars and men revolve in a cycle;
the fateful atoms will bring back the vital
gold Aphrodite, Thebans and agoras.

In future epochs, the centaur will oppress
with solid, uncleft hoof the breast of the Lapith;
when Rome is dust, the Minotaur will groan
once more in the endless dark of its stinking palace.

Every sleepless night will come back in minute detail.
This writing hand will be born from the same womb;
and bitter armies will contrive their doom.
(The philologist Nietzsche made this very point.)

I do not know if we will recur in a second
cycle, like numbers in a repeating fraction;
but I know that a vague Pythagorean rotation
night after night leaves me on some ground

in the suburbs of the world. A remote spot
which might be either north or east or south,
but always with these things—a crumbled path,
a miraculous wall, a fig tree giving shade.

This, here, is Buenos Aires. Time which brings
to men either love or money, now leaves to me
no more than this withered rose, this empty tracery
of streets with names from the past recurring

out of my blood: Laprida, Cabrera, Soler, Suárez . . .
names in which secret bugle calls are sounding,
the republics, the horses and the mornings,
glorious victories and dead soldiers.

Ruined squares at night with no one there
are the vast patios of a crumbled palace,
and the single-minded streets implying Space.
They are corridors out of dreams and nameless fear.

It returns, the concave dark of Anaxagoras;
in my human flesh, eternity keeps recurring,
and an endless poem, remembered or still in the writing . . .
"They knew it, the fervent pupils of Pythagoras . . ."

—*Translated by* ALASTAIR REID

# Progress: Its Law and Cause

## Herbert Spencer

*Herbert Spencer was an English philosopher and sociologist. Influenced by the evolutionary ideas of Darwin, he wrote considerably on many scientific and social topics. He lived from 1820 until 1903.*

The current conception of Progress is somewhat shifting and indefinite. Sometimes it comprehends that more than simple growth—as of a nation in the number of its members and the extent of territory over which it has spread. Sometimes it has reference to quantity of material products—as when the advance of agriculture and manufactures is the topic. Sometimes the superior quality of these products is contemplated: and sometimes the new or improved appliances by which they are produced. When, again, we speak of moral or intellectual progress, we refer to the state of the individual or people exhibiting it; while, when the progress of Knowledge, of Science, of Art, is commented upon, we have in view certain abstract results of human thought and action. Not only, however, is the current conception of Progress more or less vague, but it is in great measure erroneous. It takes in not so much the reality of Progress as its accompaniments—not so much the substance as the shadow. That progress in intelligence seen during the growth of the child into the man, or the savage into the philosopher, is commonly regarded as consisting in the greater number of facts known and laws understood: whereas the actual progress consists in those internal modifications of which this increased knowledge is the expression. Social progress is supposed to consist in the produce of a greater quantity and variety of the articles required for satisfying man's wants; in the increasing security of person and property; in widening freedom of action: whereas, rightly understood, social progress consists in those changes of structure in the social organism which have entailed these consequences. The current conception is a teleological one. The phenomena are contemplated solely as bearing on human happiness. Only those changes are held to constitute progress which directly or indirectly tend to heighten human happiness. And they are thought to constitute progress simply *because* they tend to heighten human happiness. But rightly to understand progress, we must inquire what is the nature of these changes, considered apart from our interests. Ceasing, for example, to regard the successive geological modifications that have taken place in the Earth, as modifications that have gradually fitted it for the habitation of Man, and as *therefore* a geological progress, we must seek to determine the character common to these modifications—the law to which they all conform. And similarly in every other case. Leaving out of sight concomitants and beneficial consequences, let us ask what Progress is in itself.

In respect to that progress which individual organisms display in the course of their evolution, this question has been answered by the Germans. The investigations of Wolff, Goethe, and Von Baer, have established the truth that the series of changes gone through during the development of a seed into a tree, or an ovum into an animal, constitute an advance from homogeneity of structure to heterogeneity of structure. In its primary stage, every germ consists of a substance that is uniform throughout, both in texture and chemical composition. The first step is the appearance of a difference between two parts of this substance; or, as the phenomenon is called in physiological language, a differentiation. Each of these differentiated divisions presently begins itself to exhibit some contrast of parts; and by and by these secondary differentiations become as definite as the original one. This process is continuously repeated—is simultaneously going on in all parts of the growing embryo; and by endless such differentiations there is finally produced that complex combination of tissues and organs constituting the adult animal or plant. This is the history of all organisms whatever. It is settled beyond dispute that organic progress consists in a change from the homogeneous to the heterogeneous.

Now, we propose in the first place to show, that this law of organic progress is the law of all progress. Whether it be in the development of the Earth, in the development of Life upon its surface, in the development of Society, of Government, of Manufactures, of Commerce, of Language, Literature, Science, Art, this same evolution of the simple into the complex, through successive differentiations, holds throughout. From the earliest traceable cosmical changes down to the latest results of civilization, we shall find that the transformation of the homogeneous into the heterogeneous, is that in which Progress essentially consists. . . .

Whether an advance from the homogeneous to the heterogeneous is or is not displayed in the biological history of the globe, it is clearly enough displayed in the progress of the latest and most heterogeneous creature—Man. It is alike true that, during the period in which the Earth has been peopled, the human organism has grown more heterogeneous among the civilized divisions of the species; and that the species, as a whole, has been growing more heterogeneous in virtue of the multiplication of races and the differentiation of these races from each other.

In proof of the first of these positions, we may cite the fact that, in the relative development of the limbs, the civilized man departs more widely from the general type of the placental mammalia than do the lower human races. While often possessing well-developed body and arms, the Papuan has extremely small legs: thus reminding us of the quadrumana, in which there is no great contrast in size between the hind and fore limbs. But in the European, the greater length and massiveness of the legs has become very marked—the fore and hind limbs are relatively more heterogeneous. Again, the greater ratio which the cranial bones bear to the facial bones illustrates the same truth. Among the vertebrata in general, progress is marked by an increasing heterogeneity in the vertebral column, and more especially in the vertebrae constituting the skull: the higher forms being distinguished by the relatively larger size of the bones which cover the brain, and the relatively smaller size of those which form the jaw, &c. Now, this characteristic, which is stronger in Man than in any other creature, is stronger in the European than in the savage. Moreover, judging from the greater extent and variety of faculty he exhibits, we may infer that the civilized man has also a more complex or heterogeneous nervous system than the uncivilized man: and indeed the fact is in part visible in the increased ratio which his cerebrum bears to the subjacent ganglia.

If further elucidation be needed, we may find it in every nursery. The infant European has sundry marked points of resemblance to the lower human races; as in the flatness of the alæ of the nose, the depression of its bridge, the divergence and forward opening of the nostrils, the form of the lips, the absence of a frontal sinus, the width between the eyes, the smallness of the legs. Now, as the developmental process by which these traits are turned into those of the adult European, is a continuation of that change from the homogeneous to the heterogeneous displayed during the previous evolution of the embryo, which every physiologist will admit; it follows that the parallel development process by which the like traits of the barbarous races have been turned into those of the civilized races, has also been a continuation of the change from the homogeneous to the heterogeneous. The truth of the second position—that Mankind, as a whole, have become more heterogeneous—is so obvious as scarcely to need illustration. Every work on Ethnology, by its divisions and subdivisions of races, bears testimony to it. Even were we to admit the hypothesis that Mankind originated from several separate stocks, it would still remain true, that as, from each of these stocks, there have sprung many now widely different tribes, which are proved by philological evidence to have had a common origin, the race as a whole is far less homogeneous than it once was. Add to which, that we have, in the Anglo-Americans, an example of a new variety arising within these few generations; and that, if we may trust to the description of observers, we are likely soon to have another such example in Australia.

On passing from Humanity under its individual form, to Humanity as socially embodied, we find the general law still more variously exemplified. The change from the homogeneous to the heterogeneous is displayed equally in the progress of civilization as a whole, and in the progress of every tribe or nation; and is still going on with increasing rapidity. As we see in existing barbarous tribes, society in its first and lowest form is a homogeneous aggregation of individuals having like powers and like functions: the only marked difference of function being that which accompanies difference of sex. Every man is warrior, hunter, fisherman, tool-maker, builder; every woman performs the same drudgeries; every family is self-sufficing. and save for purposes of aggression and defence, might as well live apart from the rest. Very early, however, in the process of social evolution, we find an incipient differentiation between the governing and the governed. Some kind of chieftainship seems coeval with tile first advance from the state of separate wandering families to that of a nomadic tribe. The authority of the strongest makes itself felt among a body of savages as in a herd of animals, or a posse of schoolboys. At first however, it is indefinite, uncertain; is shared by others of scarcely inferior power; and is unaccompanied by any difference in occupation or style of living: the first ruler kills his own game, makes his own weapons, builds his own hut, and economically considered, does not differ from others of his tribe. Gradually, as the tribe progresses, the contrast between the governing and the governed grows more decided. Supreme power becomes hereditary in one family; the head of that family, ceasing to provide for his own wants, is served by others; and he begins to assume the sole office of ruling.

At the same time there has been arising a co-ordinate species of government—that of Religion. As all ancient records and traditions prove, the earliest rulers are regarded as divine personages. The maxims and commands they uttered during their lives are held sacred after their deaths, and are enforced by their divinely-descended successors; who in their turns are promoted to the pantheon of the race, there to be worshipped and propitiated along with their predecessors: the most ancient of whom is the supreme god, and the rest subordinate gods. For a long time these connate form of government—civil and religious—continue closely associated. For many generations the king continues to be the chief priest, and the priesthood to be members of the royal race. For many ages religious law continues to contain more or less of civil regulations, and civil law to possess more or less of religious sanction; and even among the most advanced nations these two controlling agencies are by no means completely differentiated from each other.

Having a common root with these, and gradually diverging from them, we find yet another controlling agency—that of Manners or ceremonial usages. All titles of honour are originally the names of the god-king; afterwards of God and the king; still later of persons of high rank; and finally come, some of them, to be used between man and man. All forms of complimentary address were at first the expressions of submission from prisoners to their conqueror or from subjects to their ruler, either human or divine—expressions that were afterwards used to propitiate subordinate authorities, and slowly descended into ordinary intercourse. All models of salutation were once obeisances made before the monarch and used in worship of him after his death. Presently others of the god-descended race were similarly saluted; and by degrees some of the salutations have become the due of all. Thus, no sooner does the originally homogeneous social mass differentiate into the governed and the governing parts, than this last exhibits an incipient differentiation into religious and secular— Church and State; while at the same time there begins to be differentiated from both, that less definite species of government which rules our daily intercourse—a species of government which, as we may see in heralds' colleges, in books of the peerage, in masters of ceremonies, is not without a certain embodiment of its own. Each of these is itself subject to successive differentiations. In the course of ages, there arises, as among ourselves, a highly complex political organization of monarch, ministers, lords and commons, with their subordinate administrative departments, courts of justice, revenue offices, &c., supplemented in the provinces by municipal governments, county governments, parish or union governments—all of them more or less elaborated. By its side there grows up a highly complex religious organization, with its various grades of officials, from archbishops down to sextons, its colleges, convocations, ecclesiastical courts, &c.; to all which must be added the ever multiplying independent sects, each with its general and local authorities. And at the same time there is developed a highly complex aggregation of customs, manners, and temporary fashions, enforced by society at large, and serving to control those minor transactions between man and man which are not regulated by civil and religious law. Moreover it is to be observed that this ever increasing heterogeneity in the government appliances of each nation, has been accompanied by an increasing heterogeneity in the governmental appliances of different nations; all of which are more or less unlike in their political systems and legislation, in their creeds and religious institutions, in their customs and ceremonial usages.

Simultaneously there has been going on a second differentiation of a more familiar kind; that, namely, by which the mass of the community has been segregated into distinct classes and orders of workers. While the governing part has undergone the complex development above detailed, the governed part has undergone an equally complex development, which has resulted in that minute division of labour characterizing advanced nations. It is needless to trace out this progress from its first stages, up through the caste divisions of the East and the incorporated guilds of Europe, to the elaborate producing and distributing organization existing among ourselves. Political economist have long since described the evolution which, beginning with a tribe whose members severally perform the same actions each for himself, ends with a civilized community whose members severally perform different actions for each other; and they have further pointed out the changes through which the solitary producer of any one commodity is transformed into a combination of producers who, united under a master, take separate parts to the manufacture of such commodity. But there are yet other and higher phases of this advance from the homogeneous to the heterogeneous in the industrial organization of society.

Long after considerable progress has been made in the division of labour among different classes of workers, there is still little or no division of labour among the widely separated parts of the community; the nation continues comparatively homogeneous in the respect that in each district the same occupations are pursued. But when roads and other means of transit become numerous and good, the different districts begin to assume different functions, and to become mutually dependent. The calico manufacture locates itself in this county, the woollen-cloth manufacture in that; silks are produced here, lace there; stockings in one place, shoes in another; pottery, hardware, cutlery, come to have their special towns; and ultimately every locality becomes more or less distinguished from the rest by the leading occupation carried on in it. Nay, more, this subdivision of functions shows itself not only among the different parts of the same nation, but among different nations. That exchange of commodities which free-trade promises so greatly to increase, will ultimately have the effect of specializing, in a greater or less degree, the industry of each people. So that beginning with a barbarous tribe, almost if not quite homogeneous in the functions of its members, the progress has been, and still is, towards an economic aggregation of the whole human race; growing ever more heterogeneous in respect of the separate functions assumed by separate nations, the separate functions assumed by the local sections of each nation, the separate functions assumed by the many kinds of makers and traders in each town, and the separate functions assumed by the workers united in producing each commodity.

Not only is the law thus clearly exemplified in the evolution of the social organism, but it is exemplified with equal clearness in the evolution of all products of human thought and action, whether concrete or abstract, real or ideal. Let us take Language as our first illustration. . . . [Spencer considers the evolution of language, painting, sculpture, poetry, music and musical instruments from their origin in religion.]

But doubtless the reader is already weary of illustrations; and our promise has been amply fulfilled. We believe we have shown beyond question, that that which the German physiologists have found to be the law of organic development, is the law of all development. The advance from the simple to the complex, through a process of successive differentiations, is seen alike in the earliest changes of the Universe to which we can reason our way back; and in the earliest changes which we can inductively establish; it is seen in the geologic and climatic evolution of the Earth, and of every single organism on its surface; it is seen in the evolution of humanity, whether contemplated in the civilized individual, or in the aggregation of races; it is seen in the evolution of Society in respect alike of its political, its religious, and its economical organization; and it is seen in the evolution of all those endless concrete and abstract products of human activity which constitute the environment of our daily life.

From the remotest past which Science can fathom, up to the novelties of yesterday, that in which Progress essentially consists, is the transformation of the homogeneous into the heterogeneous.

And now, from this uniformity of procedure, may we not infer some fundamental necessity whence it results? May we not rationally seek for some all-pervading principle which determines this all-pervading process of things? Does not the universality of the *law* imply a universal *cause*?

That we can fathom such cause, noumenally considered, is not to be supposed. To do this would be to solve that ultimate mystery which must ever transcend human intelligence. But it still may be possible for us to reduce the law of all Progress, above established, from the condition of an empirical generalization, to the condition of a rational generalization. Just as it was possible to interpret Kepler's laws as necessary consequences of the law of gravitation; so it may be possible to interpret this law of Progress, in its multiform manifestations, as the necessary consequence of some similarly universal principle. As gravitation was assignable as the cause of each of the groups of phenomena which Kepler formulated; so may some equally simple attribute of things be assignable as the cause of each of the groups of phenomena formulated in the foregoing pages. We may be able to affiliate all these varied and complex evolutions of the homogeneous into the heterogeneous, upon certain simple facts of immediate experience, which, in virtue of endless repetition, we regard as necessary.

The probability of a common cause, and the possibility of formulating it, being granted, it will be well, before going further, to consider what must be the general characteristics of such cause, and in what direction we ought to look for it. We can with certainty predict that it has a high degree of generality; seeing that it is common to such infinitely varied phenomena: just in proportion to the universality of its application must be the abstractness of its character. We need not expect to see in it an obvious solution of this or that form of Progress; because it equally refers to forms of Progress bearing little apparent resemblance to them: its association with multi-form orders of facts, involves its dissociation from any particular order of facts. Being that which determines Progress of every kind— astronomic, geologic, organic, ethnologic, social, economic, artistic, &c.—it must be concerned with some fundamental attribute possessed in common by these; and must be expressible in terms of this fundamental attribute. The only obvious respect in which all kinds of Progress are alike, is, that they are modes of *change*; and hence, in some characteristic of changes in general, the desired solution will probably be found. We may suspect *a priori* that in some law of change lies the explanation of this universal transformation of the homogeneous into the heterogeneous.

Thus much premised, we pass at once to the statement of the law, which is this:—*Every active force produces more than one change—every cause produces more than one effect.*

Before this law can be duly comprehended, a few examples must be looked at. . . . [Some examples from Chemistry follow.]

. . . This multiplication of results, which is displayed in every event of to-day, has been going on from the beginning; and is true of the grandest phenomena of the universe as of the most insignificant. From the law that every active force produces more than one change, it is an inevitable corollary that through all time there has been an ever-growing complication of things. Starting with the ultimate fact that every cause produces more than one effect, we may readily see that throughout creation there must have gone on, and must still go on, a never-ceasing transformation of the homogeneous into the heterogeneous. But let us trace out this truth in detail. . . . [Spencer applies it to cosmology and biology with tendencies to an increasing variety of species and to the internal differentiation of each one.]

Observe, now, however, a further consequence. There must arise not simply a tendency towards the differentiation of each race of organisms into several races; but also a tendency to the occasional production of a somewhat higher organism. Taken in the mass these divergent varieties which have been caused by fresh physical conditions and habits of life, will exhibit changes quite indefinite in kind and degree; and changes that do not necessarily constitute an advance. Probably in most cases the modified type will be neither more nor less heterogeneous than the original one. In some cases the habits of life adopted being simpler than before, a less heterogeneous structure will result: there will be a retrogradation. But it *must* now and then occur, that some division of a species, falling into circumstances which give it rather more complex experiences, and demand actions somewhat more involved, will have certain of its organs further differentiated in proportionately small degrees,—will become slightly more heterogeneous.

Thus, in the natural course of things, there will from time to time arise an increased heterogeneity both of the Earth's flora and fauna, and of individual races included in them. Omitting detailed explanations, and allowing for the qualifications which cannot here he specified, we think it is clear that geological mutations have all along tended to complicate the forms of life, whether regarded separately or collectively. The same causes which have led to the evolution of the Earth's crust from the simple into the complex, have simultaneously led to a parallel evolution of the Life upon its surface. In this case, as in previous ones, we see that the transformation of the homogeneous into the heterogeneous is consequent upon the universal principle, that every active force produces more than one change. . . .

If the advance of Man towards greater heterogeneity is traceable to the production of many effects by one cause, still more clearly may the advance of Society towards greater heterogeneity be so explained. Consider the growth of an industrial organization. When, as must occasionally happen, some individual of a tribe displays unusual aptitude for making an article of general use—a weapon, for instance—which was before made by each man for himself, there arises a tendency towards the differentiation of that individual into a maker of such weapons. His companions—warriors and hunters all of them,—severally feel the importance of having the best weapons that can be made; and are therefore certain to offer strong inducements to this skilled individual to make weapons for them. He, on the other hand, having not only an unusual faculty, but an unusual liking, for making such weapons (the talent and the desire for any occupation being commonly associated), is predisposed to fulfill these commissions on the offer of an adequate reward: especially as his love of distinction is also gratified. This first specialization of function, once commenced, tends ever to become more decided. On the side of the weapon-maker continued practice gives increased skill—increased superiority to his products: on the side of his clients, cessation of practice entails decreased skill. Thus the influences that determine this division of labour grow stronger in both ways; and the incipient heterogeneity is, on the average of cases, likely to become permanent for that generation, if no longer.

Observe now, however, that this process not only differentiates the social mass into two parts, the one monopolizing, or almost monopolizing, the performance of a certain function, and the other having lost the habit, and in some measure the power, of performing that function; but it tends to imitate other differentiations. The advance we have described implies the introduction of barter,—the maker of weapons has, on each occasion, to be paid in such other articles as he agrees to take in exchange. But he will not habitually take in exchange one kind of article, but many kinds. He does not want mats only, or skins, or fishing gear, but he wants all these; and on each occasion will bargain for the particular things he most needs. What follows? If among the members of the tribe there exist any slight differences of skill in the manufacture of these various things, as there are almost sure to do, the weapon-maker will take from each one the thing which that one excels in making: he will exchange for mats with him whose mats are superior, and will bargain for the fishing gear of whoever has the best. But he who has bartered away his mats or his fishing gear, must make other mats or fishing gear for himself; and in so doing must, in some degree, further develop his aptitude. Thus it results that the small specialties of faculty possessed by various members of the tribe, will tend to grow more decided. If such transactions are from time repeated, these specializations may become appreciable. And whether or not there ensue distinct differentiations of other individuals into makers of particular articles, it is clear that incipient differentiations take place throughout the tribe: the one original cause produces not only the first dual effect, but a number of secondary dual effects, like in kind, but minor in degree. This process, of which traces may be seen among groups of schoolboys, cannot well produce any lasting effects in an unsettled tribe; but where there grows up a fixed and multiplying community, these differentiations become permanent, and increase with each generation. A larger population, involving a greater demand for every commodity, intensifies the functional activity of each specialized person or class; and this renders the specialization more definite where it already exists, and establishes it where it is nascent. By increasing the pressure on the means of subsistence, a larger population again augments these results; seeing that each person is forced more and more to confine himself to that which he can do best, and by which he can gain most. This industrial progress, by aiding future production, opens the way for a further growth of population, which reacts as before: in all which the multiplication of effects is manifest. . . .

Our limits will not allow us to follow out this process in its higher complications: else might we show how the localization of special industries in special parts of a kingdom, as well as the minute subdivision of labour in the making of each commodity, are similarly determined. Or, turning to a somewhat different order of illustrations, we might dwell on the multitudinous changes—material, intellectual, moral,—caused by printing; or the further extensive series of changes wrought by gunpowder. But leaving the intermediate phases of social development, let us take a few illustrations from its most recent and its passing phases. To trace the effects of steam-power, in its manifold applications to mining, navigation, and manufactures of all kinds, would carry us into unmanageable detail. Let us confine ourselves to the latest embodiment of steam-power—the locomotive engine.

This, as the proximate cause of our railway system, has changed the face of the country, the course of trade, and the habits of the people. Consider, first, the complicated sets of changes that precede the making of every railway—the provisional arrangements, the meetings, the registration, the trial section, the parliamentary survey, the lithographed plans, the books of reference, the local deposits and notices, the application to Parliament, the passing Standing-Orders Committee, the first, second, and third readings: each of which brief heads indicates a multiplicity of transactions, and the development of sundry occupations—as those of engineers, surveyors, lithographers, parliamentary agents, sharebrokers; and the creation of sundry others—as those of traffic-takers, reference-takers. Consider, next, the yet more marked changes implied in railway construction—the cutting, embankings, tunnellings, diversions of roads; the building of bridges and stations; the laying down of ballast, sleepers, and rails; the making of engines, tenders, carriages and waggons which processes, acting upon numerous trades, increase the importation of timber, the quarrying of stone, the manufacture of iron, the mining of coal, the burning of bricks: institute a variety of special manufactures weekly advertised in the *Railway Times*; and, finally, open the way to sundry new occupations, as those of drivers, stokers, cleaners, plate-layers, &c., &c. And then consider the changes, more numerous and involved still, which railways in action produce on the community at large. The organization of every business is more or less modified: ease of communication makes it better to do directly what was before done by proxy; agencies are established where previously they would not have paid; goods are obtained from remote wholesale houses instead of near retail ones; and commodities are used which distance once rendered inaccessible. Again, the rapidity and small cost of carriage tend to specialize more than ever the industries of different districts—to confine each manufacture to the parts in which, from local advantages, it can be best carried on. Further, the diminished cost of carriage, facilitating distribution, equalizes prices, and also, on the average, lowers prices: thus bringing divers articles within the means of those before unable to buy them, and so increasing their comforts and improving their habits. At the same time the practice of travelling is immensely extended. Classes who never before thought of it, take annual trips to the sea; visit their distant relations; make tours; and so we are benefited in body, feelings, and intellect. Moreover, the more prompt transmission of letters and of news produces further changes—makes the pulse of the nation faster. Yet more, there arises a wide dissemination of cheap literature through railway book-stalls, and of advertisements in railway carriages: both of them aiding ulterior progress.

And all the innumerable changes here briefly indicated are consequent on the invention of the locomotive engine. The social organism has been rendered more heterogeneous in virtue of the many new occupations introduced, and the many old ones further specialized; prices in every place have been altered; each trader has, more or less, modified his way of doing business; and almost every person has been affected in his actions, thoughts, emotions. . . .

. . . It will be seen that as in each event of to-day, so from the beginning, the decomposition of every expended force into several forces has been perpetually producing a higher complication; that the increase of hetero-geneity so brought about is still going on, and must continue to go on; and that thus Progress is not an accident, not a thing within human con-trol, but a beneficent necessity.

# The New Accelerator

## H. G. Wells

*Best known for "The Time Machine," "The Invisible Man," and "War of the Worlds," the English author Herbert George Wells wrote hundreds of essays and stories. A lifelong socialist, he was interested in ideas for reforming society and establishing equality. He lived from 1866 until 1946.*

Certainly, if ever a man found a guinea when he was looking for a pin it is my good friend Professor Gibberne. I have heard before of investigators overshooting the mark, but never quite to the extent that he has done. He has really, this time at any rate, without any touch of exaggeration in the phrase, found something to revolutionise human life. And that when he was simply seeking an all-round nervous stimulant to bring languid people up to the stresses of these pushful days. I have tasted the stuff now several times, and I cannot do better than describe the effect the thing had on me. That there are astonishing experiences in store for all in search of new sensations will become apparent enough.

Professor Gibberne, as many people know, is my neighbour in Folkestone. Unless my memory plays me a trick, his portrait at various ages has already appeared in *The Strand Magazine*—I think late in 1899; but I am unable to look it up because I have lent that volume to someone who has never sent it back. The reader may, perhaps, recall the high forehead and the singularly long black eyebrows that give such a Mephistophelian touch to his face. He occupies one of those pleasant detached houses in the mixed style that make the western end of the Upper Sandgate Road so interesting. His is the one with the Flemish gables and the Moorish portico, and it is in the room with the mullioned bay window that he works when he is down here, and in which of an evening we have so often smoked and talked together. He is a mighty jester, but, besides, he likes to talk to me about his work; he is one of those men who find a help and stimulus in talking, and so I have been able to follow the conception of the New Accelerator right up from a very early stage. Of course, the greater portion of his experimental work is not done in Folkestone, but in

724

Gower Street, in the fine new laboratory next to the hospital that he has been the first to use.

As everyone knows, or at least as all intelligent people know, the special department in which Gibberne has gained so great and deserved a reputation among physiologists is the action of drugs upon the nervous system. Upon soporifics, sedatives, and anaesthetics he is, I am told, unequalled. He is also a chemist of considerable eminence, and I suppose in the subtle and complex jungle of riddles that centres about the ganglion cell and the axis fibre there are little cleared places of his making, glades of illumination, that, until he sees fit to publish his results, are inaccessible to every other living man. And in the last few years he has been particularly assiduous upon this question of nervous stimulants, and already, before the discovery of the New Accelerator, very successful with them. Medical science has to thank him for at least three distinct and absolutely safe invigorators of unrivalled value to practising men. In cases of exhaustion the preparation known as Gibberne's B Syrup has, I suppose, saved more lives already than any lifeboat round the coast.

"But none of these things begin to satisfy me yet," he told me nearly a year ago. "Either they increase the central energy without affecting the nerves or they simply increase the available energy by lowering the nervous conductivity; and all of them are unequal and local in their operation. One wakes up the heart and viscera and leaves the brain stupefied, one gets at the brain champagne fashion and does nothing good for the solar plexus, and what I want—and what, if it's an earthly possibility, I mean to have—is a stimulant that stimulates all round, that wakes you up for a time from the crown of your head to the tip of your great toe, and makes you go two—or even three to everybody else's one. Eh? That's the thing I'm after."

"It would tire a man," I said.

"Not a doubt of it. And you'd eat double or treble—and all that. But just think what the thing would mean. Imagine yourself with a little phial like this"—he held up a bottle of green glass and marked his points with it—"and in this precious phial is the power to think twice as fast, move twice as quickly, do twice as much work in a given time as you could otherwise do."

"But is such a thing possible?"

"I believe so. If it isn't, I've wasted my time for a year. These various preparations of the hypophosphites, for example, seem to show that something of the sort. . . . Even if it was only one and a half times as fast it would do."

"It *would* do," I said.

"If you were a statesman in a corner, for example, time rushing up against you, something urgent to be done, eh?"

"He could dose his private secretary," I said.

"And gain—double time. And think if *you*, for example, wanted to finish a book."

"Usually," I said, "I wish I'd never begun 'em."

"Or a doctor, driven to death, wants to sit down and think out a case. Or a barrister—or a man cramming for an examination."

"Worth a guinea a drop," said I, "and more—to men like that."

"And in a duel again," said Gibberne, "where it all depends on your quickness in pulling the trigger."

"Or in fencing," I echoed.

"You see," said Gibberne, "if I get it as an all-round thing it will really do you no harm at all—except perhaps to an infinitesimal degree it brings you nearer old age. You will just have lived twice to other people's once——"

"I suppose," I meditated, "in a duel—it would be fair?"

"That's a question for the seconds," said Gibberne.

I harked back further. "And you really think such a thing is possible?" I said.

"As possible," said Gibberne, and glanced at something that went throbbing by the window, "as a motorbus. As a matter of fact——"

He paused and smiled at me deeply, and tapped slowly on the edge of his desk with the green phial. "I think I know the stuff. . . . Already I've got something coming." The nervous smile upon his face betrayed the gravity of his revelation. He rarely talked of his actual experimental work unless things were very near the end. "And it may be, it may be—I shouldn't be surprised—it may even do the thing at a greater rate than twice."

"It will be rather a big thing," I hazarded.

"It will be, I think, rather a big thing."

But I don't think he quite knew what a big thing it was to be, for all that.

I remember we had several subsequent talks about the stuff. "The New Accelerator" he called it, and his tone about it grew more confident on each occasion. Sometimes he talked nervously of unexpected physiological results its use might have, and then he would get a bit unhappy; at others he was frankly mercenary, and we debated long and anxiously how the preparation might be turned to commercial account. " It's a good thing," said Gibberne, "a tremendous thing. I know I'm giving the world something, and I think it only reasonable we should expect the world to pay. The dignity of science is all very well, but I think somehow I must have the monopoly of the stuff for, say, ten years. I don't see why *all* the fun in life should go to the dealers in ham."

My own interest in the coming drug certainly did not wane in the time. I have always had a queer twist towards metaphysics in my mind. I have always been given to paradoxes about space and time, and it seemed to me that Gibberne was really preparing no less than the absolute acceler- ation of life. Suppose a man repeatedly dosed with such a preparation: he would live an active and record life indeed, but he would be an adult at eleven, middle-aged at twenty-five, and by thirty well on the road to senile decay. It seemed to me that so far Gibberne was only going to do for anyone who took his drug exactly what Nature has done for the Jews and Orientals, who are men in their teens and aged by fifty, and quicker in thought and act than we are all the time. The marvel of drugs has always been great to my mind; you can madden a man, calm a man, make him incredibly strong and alert or a helpless log, quicken this passion and allay that, all by means of drugs, and here was a new miracle to be added to this strange armoury of phials the doctors use! But Gibberne was far too eager upon his technical points to enter very keenly into my aspect of the question.

It was the 7th or 8th of August, when he told me the distillation that would decide his failure or success for a time was going forward as we talked, and it was on the 10th that he told me the thing was done and the New Accelerator a tangible reality in the world. I met him as I was going up the Sandgate Hill towards Folkestone—I think I was going to get my hair cut; and he came hurrying down to meet me—I suppose he was coming to my house to tell me at once of his success. I remember that his eyes were unusually bright and his face flushed, and I noted even then the swift alacrity of his step.

"It's done," he cried, and gripped my hand, speaking very fast; "it's more than done. Come up to my house and see."

"Really?"

"Really!" he shouted. "Incredibly! Come up and see."

"And it does—twice!"

"It does more, much more. It scares me. Come up and see the stuff. Taste it! Try it! It's the most amazing stuff on earth." He gripped my arm and, walking at such a pace that he forced me into a trot, went shouting with me up the hill. A whole charabancful of people turned and stared at us in unison after the manner of people in charabancs. It was one of those hot, clear days that Folkestone sees so much of, every colour incredibly bright and every outline hard. There was a breeze, of course, but not so much breeze as sufficed under these conditions to keep me cool and dry. I panted for mercy.

"I'm not walking fast, am I?" cried Gibberne, and slackened his pace to a quick march.

"You've been taking some of this stuff," I puffed.

"No," he said. "At the utmost a drop of water that stood in a beaker from which I had washed out the last traces of the stuff. I took some last night, you know. But that is ancient history, now."

"And it goes twice?" I said, nearing his doorway in a grateful perspiration.

"It goes a thousand times, many thousand times!" cried Gibberne, with a dramatic gesture, flinging open his Early English carved oak gate.

"Phew!" said I, and followed him to the door.

"I don't know how many times it goes," he said, with his latch-key in his hand.

"And you——"

"It throws all sorts of light on nervous physiology, it kicks the theory of vision into a perfectly new shape! . . . Heaven knows how many thousand times. We'll try all that after—The thing is to try the stuff now."

"Try the stuff?" I said, as we went along the passage.

"Rather," said Gibberne, turning on me in his study. "There it is in that little green phial there! Unless you happen to be afraid?"

I am a careful man by nature, and only theoretically adventurous. I *was* afraid. But on the other hand there is pride.

"Well," I haggled. "You say you've tried it?"

"I've tried it," he said, "and I don't look hurt by it, do I? I don't even look livery and I *feel*——"

I sat down. "Give me the potion," I said. "If the worst comes to the worst it will save having my hair cut, and that I think is one of the most hateful duties of a civilised man. How do you take the mixture?"

"With water," said Gibberne, whacking down a carafe.

He stood up in front of his desk and regarded me in his easy chair; his manner was suddenly affected by a touch of the Harley Street specialist. "It's rum stuff, you know," he said.

I made a gesture with my hand.

"I must warn you in the first place as soon as you've got it down to shut your eyes, and open them very cautiously in a minute or so's time. One still sees. The sense of vision is a question of length of vibration, and not of multitude of impacts; but there's a kind of shock to the retina, a nasty giddy confusion just at the time if the eyes are open. Keep 'em shut."

"Shut," I said. "Good!"

"And the next thing is, keep still. Don't begin to whack about. You may fetch something a nasty rap if you do. Remember you will be going several thousand times faster than you ever did before, heart, lungs, muscles, brain—everything—and you will hit hard without knowing it. You won't know it, you know. You'll feel just as you do now. Only everything in the world will seem to be going ever so many thousand times slower than it ever went before. That's what makes it so deuced queer."

"Lor'," I said. "And you mean——"

"You'll see," said he, and took up a measure. He glanced at the material on his desk. "Glasses," he said, "water. All here. Mustn't take too much for the first attempt."

The little phial glucked out its precious contents. "Don't forget what I told you," he said, turning the contents of the measure into a glass in the manner of an Italian waiter measuring whisky. "Sit with the eyes tightly shut and in absolute stillness for two minutes," he said. "Then you will hear me speak."

He added an inch or so of water to the dose in each glass.

"By the bye," he said, "don't put your glass down. Keep it in your hand and rest your hand on your knee. Yes—so. And now——"

He raised his glass.

"The New Accelerator," I said.

"The New Accelerator," he answered, and we touched glasses and drank, and instantly I closed my eyes.

You know that blank non-existence into which one drops when one has taken "gas." For an indefinite interval it was like that. Then I heard Gibberne telling me to wake up, and I stirred and opened my eyes. There he stood as he had been standing, glass still in hand. It was empty, that was all the difference.

"Well?" said I.

"Nothing out of the way?"

"Nothing. A slight feeling of exhilaration, perhaps. Nothing more."

"Sounds?"

"Things are still," I said. "By Jove! yes! They *are* still. Except the sort of faint pat, patter, like rain falling on different things. What is it?"

"Analysed sounds," I think he said, but I am not sure. He glanced at the window. "Have you ever seen a curtain before a window fixed in that way before?"

I followed his eyes, and there was the end of the curtain, frozen, as it were, corner high, in the act of flapping briskly in the breeze.

"No," said I; "that's odd."

"And here," he said, and opened the hand that held the glass. Naturally I winced, expecting the glass to smash. But so far from smashing it did not even seem to stir; it hung in mid-air—motionless. "Roughly speaking," said Gibberne, "an object in these latitudes falls 16 feet in the first second. This glass is falling 16 feet in a second now. Only, you see, it hasn't been falling yet for the hundredth part of a second. That gives you some idea of the pace of my Accelerator." And he waved his hand round and round, over and under the slowly sinking glass. Finally he took it by the bottom, pulled it down and placed it very carefully on the table. "Eh?" he said to me, and laughed.

"That seems all right," I said, and began very gingerly to raise myself from my chair. I felt perfectly well, very light and comfortable, and quite confident in my mind. I was going fast all over. My heart, for example, was beating a thousand times a second, but that caused me no discomfort at all. I looked out of the window. An immovable cyclist, head down and with a frozen puff of dust behind his driving-wheel, scorched to overtake a galloping charabanc that did not stir. I gaped in amazement at this incredible spectacle. "Gibberne," I cried, "how long will this confounded stuff last?"

"Heaven knows!" he answered. "Last time I took it, I went to bed and slept it off. I tell you, I was frightened. It must have lasted some minutes, I think—it seemed like hours. But after a bit it slows down rather suddenly, I believe."

I was proud to observe that I did not feel frightened—I suppose because there were two of us. "Why shouldn't we go out?" I asked.

"Why not?"

"They'll see us."

"Not they. Goodness, no! Why, we shall be going a thousand times faster than the quickest conjuring trick that was ever done. Come along! Which way shall we go? Window, or door?"

And out by the window we went.

Assuredly of all the strange experiences that I have ever had, or imagined, or read of other people having or imagining, that little raid I made with Gibberne on the Folkestone Leas, under the influence of the New Accelerator, was the strangest and maddest of all. We went out by his gate into the road, and there we made a minute examination of the statuesque passing traffic. The tops of the wheels and some of the legs of the horses of this charabanc, the end of the whiplash and the lower jaw of the conductor—who was just beginning to yawn—were perceptibly in motion, but all the rest of the lumbering conveyance seemed still. And quite noiseless except for a faint rattling that came from one man's throat! And as parts of this frozen edifice there were a driver, you know, and a conductor, and eleven people! The effect as we walked about the thing began by being madly queer and ended by being—disagreeable. There they were, people like ourselves and yet not like ourselves, frozen in care- less attitudes, caught in mid-gesture. A girl and a man smiled at one another, a leering smile that threatened to last for evermore; a woman in a floppy capelline rested her arm on the rail and stared at Gibberne's house with the unwinking stare of eternity; a man stroked his moustache like a figure of wax, and another stretched a tiresome stiff hand with extended fingers towards his loosened hat. We stared at them, we laughed at them, we made faces at them, and then a sort of disgust of them came upon us, and we turned away and walked round in front of the cyclist towards the Leas.

"Goodness!" cried Gibberne, suddenly; "look there!"

He pointed, and there at the tip of his finger and sliding down the air with wings flapping slowly and at the speed of an exceptionally languid snail—was a bee.

And so we came out upon the Leas. There the thing seemed madder than ever. The band was playing in the upper stand, though all the sound it made for us was a low-pitched, wheezy rattle, a sort of prolonged last sigh that passed at times into a sound like the slow, muffled ticking of some monstrous clock. Frozen people stood erect; strange, silent, self- conscious-looking dummies hung unstably in mid-stride, promenading upon the grass. I passed close to a poodle dog suspended in the act of leaping, and watched the slow movement of his legs as he sank to earth. "Lord, look here!" cried Gibberne, and we halted for a moment before a magnificent person in white faint-striped flannels, white shoes, and a Panama hat, who turned back to wink at two gaily-dressed ladies he had passed. A wink, studied with such leisurely deliberation as we could afford, is an unattractive thing. It loses any quality of alert gaiety, and one remarks that the winking eye does not completely close, that under its drooping lid appears the lower edge of an eyeball and a line of white. "Heaven give me memory," said I, "and I will never wink again."

"Or smile," said Gibberne, with his eye on the lady's answering teeth.

"It's infernally hot, somehow," said I. "Let's go slower."

"Oh, come along!" said Gibberne.

We picked our way among the Bath chairs in the path. Many of the people sitting in the chairs seemed almost natural in their passive poses, but the contorted scarlet of the bandsmen was not a restful thing to see. A purple-faced gentleman was frozen in the midst of a violent struggle to refold his newspaper against the wind; there were many evidences that all these people in their sluggish way were exposed to a considerable breeze, a breeze that had no existence so far as our sensations went. We came out and walked a little way from the crowd, and turned and regarded it. To see all that multitude changed to a picture, smitten rigid, as it were, into the semblance of realistic wax, was impossibly wonderful. It was absurd, of course; but it filled me with an irrational, an exultant sense of superior advantage. Consider the wonder of it! All that I had said and thought and done since the stuff had begun to work in my veins had happened, so far as those people, so far as the world in general went, in the twinkling of an eye. "The New Accelerator——" I began, but Gibberne interrupted me.

"There's that infernal old woman!" he said.

"What old woman?"

"Lives next door to me," said Gibberne. "Has a lapdog that yaps. Gods! The temptation is strong!"

There is something very boyish and impulsive about Gibberne at times. Before I could expostulate with him he had dashed forward, snatched the unfortunate animal out of visible existence, and was running violently with it towards the cliff of the Leas. It was most extraordinary. The little brute, you know, didn't bark or wriggle or make the slightest sign of vitality. It kept quite stiffly in an attitude of somnolent repose, and Gibberne held it by the neck. It was like running about with a dog of wood. "Gibberne," I cried, "put it down!" Then I said something else. "If you run like that, Gibberne," I cried, "you'll set your clothes on fire. Your linen trousers are going brown as it is!"

He clapped his hand on his thigh and stood hesitating on the verge. "Gibberne," I cried, coming up, "put it down. This heat is too much! It's our running so! Two or three miles a second! Friction of the air!"

"What?" he said, glancing at the dog.

"Friction of the air," I shouted. "Friction of the air. Going too fast. Like meteorites and things. Too hot. And Gibberne! Gibberne! I'm all over pricking and a sort of perspiration. You can see people stirring slightly. I believe the stuff's working off! Put that dog down."

"Eh?" he said.

"It's working off," I repeated. "We're too hot and the stuff's working off! I'm wet through."

He stared at me. Then at the band, the wheezy rattle of whose performance was certainly going faster. Then with a tremendous sweep of the arm he hurled the dog away from him and it went spinning upward, still inanimate, and hung at last over the grouped parasols of a knot of chattering people. Gibberne was gripping my elbow. "By Jove!" he cried. "I believe it is! A sort of hot pricking and—yes. That man's moving his pocket-handkerchief! Perceptibly. We must get out of this sharp."

But we could not get out of it sharply enough. Luckily, perhaps! For we might have run, and if we had run we should, I believe, have burst into flames. Almost certainly we should have burst into flames! You know we had neither of us thought of that. . . . But before we could even begin to run the action of the drug had ceased. It was the business of a minute fraction of a second. The effect of the New Accelerator passed like the drawing of a curtain, vanished in the movement of a hand. I heard Gibberne's voice in infinite alarm. "Sit down," he said, and flop, down upon the turf at the edge of the Leas I sat—scorching as I sat. There is a patch of burnt grass there still where I sat down. The whole stagnation seemed to wake up as I did so, the disarticulated vibration of the band rushed together into a blast of music, the promenaders put their feet down and walked their ways, the papers and flags began flapping, smiles passed into words, the winker finished his wink and went on his way complacently, and all the seated people moved and spoke.

The whole world had come alive again, was going as fast as we were, or rather we were going no faster than the rest of the world. It was like slowing down as one comes into a railway station. Everything seemed to spin round for a second or two, I had the most transient feeling of nausea, and that was all. And the little dog which had seemed to hang for a moment when the force of Gibberne's arm was expended fell with a swift acceleration clean through a lady's parasol!

That was the saving of us. Unless it was for one corpulent old gentleman in a Bath chair, who certainly did start at the sight of us and afterwards regarded us at intervals with a darkly suspicious eye, and finally, I believe, said something to his nurse about us, I doubt if a solitary person remarked our sudden appearance among them. Plop! We must have appeared abruptly. We ceased to smoulder almost at once, though the turf beneath me was uncomfortably hot. The attention of everyone—including even the Amusements' Association band, which on this occasion, for the only time in its history, got out of tune—was arrested by the amazing fact, and the still more amazing yapping and uproar caused by the fact, that a respectable, over-fed lapdog sleeping quietly to the east of the bandstand should suddenly fall through the parasol of a lady on the west—in a slightly singed condition due to the extreme velocity of its movements through the air. In these absurd days, too, when we are all trying to be as psychic and silly and superstitious as possible! People got up and trod on other people, chairs were overturned, the Leas policeman ran. How the matter settled itself, I do not know—we were much too anxious to disentangle ourselves from the affair and get out of range of the eye of the old gentleman in the Bath chair to make minute inquiries. As soon as we were sufficiently cool and sufficiently recovered from our giddiness and nausea and confusion of mind to do so we stood up and, skirting the crowd, directed our steps back along the road below the Metropole towards Gibberne's house. But amidst the din I heard very distinctly the gentleman who had been sitting beside the lady of the ruptured sunshade using quite unjustifiable threats and language to one of those chair-attendants who have "Inspector" written on their caps. "If you didn't throw the dog," he said, "who *did*?"

The sudden return of movement and familiar noises, and our natural anxiety about ourselves (our clothes were still dreadfully hot, and the fronts of the thighs of Gibberne's white trousers were scorched a drabbish brown), prevented the minute observations I should have liked to make on all these things. Indeed, I really made no observations of any scientific value on that return. The bee, of course, had gone. I looked for that cyclist, but he was already out of sight as we came into the Upper Sandgate Road or hidden from us by traffic; the charabanc, however, with its people now all alive and stirring, was clattering along at a spanking pace almost abreast of the nearer church.

We noted, however, that the window-sill on which we had stepped in getting out of the house was slightly singed and that the impressions of our feet on the gravel of the path were unusually deep.

So it was I had my first experience of the New Accelerator. Practically we had been running about and saying and doing all sorts of things in the space of a second or so of time. We had lived half an hour while the band had played, perhaps, two bars. But the effect it had upon us was that the whole world had stopped for our convenient inspection. Considering all things, and particularly considering our rashness in venturing out of the house, the experience might certainly have been much more disagreeable than it was. It showed, no doubt, that Gibberne has still much to learn before his preparation is a manageable convenience, but its practicability it certainly demonstrated beyond all cavil.

Since that adventure he has been steadily bringing its use under control, and I have several times, and without the slightest bad result, taken measured doses under his direction; though I must confess I have not yet ventured abroad again while under its influence. I may mention, for example, that this story has been written at one sitting and without interruption, except for the nibbling of some chocolate, by its means. I began at 6:25, and my watch is now very nearly at the minute past the half-hour. The convenience of securing a long, uninterrupted spell of work in the midst of a day full of engagements cannot be exaggerated. Gibberne is now working at the quantitative handling of his preparation, with especial reference to its distinctive effects upon different types of constitution. He then hopes to find a Retarder with which to dilute its present rather excessive potency. The Retarder will, of course, have the reverse effect to the Accelerator; used alone it should enable the patient to spread a few seconds over many hours of ordinary time, and so to maintain an apathetic inaction, a glacierlike absence of alacrity, amidst the most animated or irritating surroundings. The two things together must necessarily work an entire revolution in civilised existence. It is the beginning of our escape from that Time Garment of which Carlyle speaks. While this Accelerator will enable us to concentrate ourselves with tremendous impact upon any moment or occasion that demands our utmost sense and vigour, the Retarder will enable us to pass in passive tranquillity through infinite hardship and tedium. Perhaps I am a little optimistic about the Retarder, which has indeed still to be discovered, but about the Accelerator there is no possible sort of doubt whatever. Its appearance upon the market in a convenient, controllable, and assimilable form is a matter of the next few months. It will be obtainable of all chemists and druggists, in small green bottles, at a high but, considering its extraordinary qualities, by no means excessive price. Gibberne's Nervous Accelerator it will be called, and he hopes to be able to supply it in three strengths: one in 200, one in 900, and one in 2000, distinguished by yellow, pink, and white labels respectively.

No doubt its use renders a great number of very extraordinary things possible; for, of course, the most remarkable and, possibly, even criminal proceedings may be effected with impunity by thus dodging, as it were, into the interstices of time. Like all potent preparations it will be liable to abuse. We have, however, discussed this aspect of the question very thoroughly, and we have decided that this is purely a matter of medical jurisprudence and altogether outside our province. We shall manufacture and sell the Accelerator, and, as for the consequences—we shall see.

# The Secret Miracle

*Jorge Luis Borges*

> And God made him die during the
> course of a hundred years and then
> He revived him and said:
> "How long have you been here?"
> "A day, or part of a day," he replied.
> —*The Koran*, II 261

On the night of March 14, 1939, in an apartment on the Zelternergasse in Prague, Jaromir Hladík, author of the unfinished tragedy *The Enemies*, of a *Vindication of Eternity*, and of an inquiry into the indirect Jewish sources of Jakob Boehme, dreamt a long-drawn-out chess game. The antagonists were not two individuals, but two illustrious families. The contest had begun many centuries before. No one could any longer describe the forgotten prize, but it was rumored that it was enormous and perhaps infinite. The pieces and the chessboard were set up in a secret tower. Jaromir (in his dream) was the first-born of one of the contending families. The hour for the next move, which could not be postponed, struck on all the clocks. The dreamer ran across the sands of a rainy desert and he could not remember the chessmen or the rules of chess. At this point he awoke. The din of the rain and the clangor of the terrible clocks ceased. A measured unison, sundered by voices of command, arose from the Zelternergasse. Day had dawned, and the armored vanguards of the Third Reich were entering Prague.

On the nineteenth, the authorities received an accusation against Jaromir Hladík; on the same day, at dusk, he was arrested. He was taken to a barracks, aseptic and white, on the opposite bank of the Moldau. He was unable to refute a single one of the charges made by the Gestapo: his maternal surname was Jaroslavski, his blood was Jewish, his study of Boehme was Judaizing, his signature had helped to swell the final census of those protesting the *Anschluss*. In 1928, he had translated the *Sepher Yezirah* for the publishing house of Hermann Barsdorf; the effusive catalogue issued by this firm had exaggerated, for commercial reasons, the translator's renown; this catalogue was leafed through by Julius Rothe, one of the officials in whose hands lay Hladík's fate. The man does not exist who, outside his own specialty, is not credulous: two or three adjectives in Gothic script sufficed to convince Julius Rothe of Hladík's preeminence, and of the need for the death penalty, *pour encourager les autres*. The execution was set for the twenty-ninth of March, at nine in the morning. This delay (whose importance the reader will appreciate later) was due to a desire on the part of the authorities to act slowly and impersonally, in the manner of planets or vegetables.

Hladík's first reaction was simply one of horror. He was sure he would not have been terrified by the gallows, the block, or the knife; but to die before a firing squad was unbearable. In vain he repeated to himself that the pure and general act of dying, not the concrete circumstances, was the dreadful fact. He did not grow weary of imagining these circumstances: he absurdly tried to exhaust all the variations. He infinitely anticipated the process, from the sleepless dawn to the mysterious discharge of the rifles. Before the day set by Julius Rothe, he died hundreds of deaths, in courtyards whose shapes and angles defied geometry, shot down by changeable soldiers whose number varied and who sometimes put an end to him from close up and sometimes from far away. He faced these imaginary executions with true terror (perhaps with true courage). Each simulacrum lasted a few seconds. Once the circle was closed, Jaromir returned interminably to the tremulous eve of his death. Then he would reflect that reality does not tend to coincide with forecasts about it. With perverse logic he inferred that to foresee a circumstantial detail is to prevent its happening. Faithful to this feeble magic, he would invent, *so that they might not happen*, the most atrocious particulars. Naturally, he finished by fearing that these particulars were prophetic. During his wretched nights he strove to hold fast somehow to the fugitive substance of time. He knew that time was precipitating itself toward the dawn of the twenty-ninth. He reasoned aloud: *I am now in the night of the twenty-second. While this night lasts (and for six more nights to come) I am invulnerable, immortal.* His nights of sleep seemed to him deep, dark pools into which he might submerge. Sometimes he yearned impatiently for the firing squad's definitive volley, which would redeem him, for better or for worse, from the vain compulsion of his imagination. On the twenty-eighth, as the final sunset reverberated across the high barred windows, he was distracted from all these abject considerations by thought of his drama, *The Enemies*.

Hladík was past forty. Apart from a few friendships and many habits, the problematic practice of literature constituted his life. Like every writer, he measured the virtues of other writers by their performance, and asked that they measure him by what he conjectured or planned. All of the books he had published merely moved him to a complex repentance. His investigation of the work of Boehme, of Ibn Ezra, and of Fludd was essentially a product of mere application; his translation of the *Sepher Yezirah* was characterized by negligence, fatigue, and conjecture. He judged his *Vindication of Eternity* to be perhaps less deficient: the first volume is a history of the diverse eternities devised by man, from the immutable Being of Parmenides to the alterable past of Hinton; the second volume denies (with Francis Bradley) that all the events in the universe make up a temporal series. He argues that the number of experiences possible to man is not infinite, and that a single "repetition" suffices to demonstrate that time is a fallacy. . . . Unfortunately, the arguments that demonstrate this fallacy are not any less fallacious. Hladík was in the habit of running through these arguments with a certain disdainful perplexity. He had also written a series of expressionist poems; these, to the discomfiture of the author, were included in an anthology in 1924, and there was no anthology of later date which did not inherit them. Hladík was anxious to redeem himself from his equivocal and languid past with his verse drama, *The Enemies*. (He favored the verse form in the theater because it prevents the spectators from forgetting unreality, which is the necessary condition of art.)

This opus preserved the dramatic unities (time, place, and action). It transpires in Hradcany, in the library of the Baron Roemerstadt, on one of the last evenings of the nineteenth century. In the first scene of the first act, a stranger pays a visit to Roemerstadt. (A clock strikes seven, the vehemence of a setting sun glorifies the window panes, the air transmits familiar and impassioned Hungarian music.) This visit is followed by others; Roemerstadt does not know the people who come to importune him, but he has the uncomfortable impression that he has seen them before: perhaps in a dream. All the visitors fawn upon him, but it is obvious—first to the spectators of the drama, and then to the Baron himself—that they are secret enemies, sworn to ruin him. Roemerstadt manages to outwit, or evade, their complex intrigues. In the course of the dialogue, mention is made of his betrothed, Julia de Weidenau, and of a certain Jaroslav Kubin, who at one time had been her suitor. Kubin has now lost his mind and thinks he is Roemerstadt. . . . The dangers multiply. Roemerstadt, at the end of the second act, is forced to kill one of the conspirators. The third and final act begins. The incongruities gradually mount up: actors who seemed to have been discarded from the play reappear; the man who had been killed by Roemerstadt returns, for an instant. Someone notes that the time of day has not advanced: the clock strikes seven, the western sun reverberates in the high windowpanes, impassioned Hungarian music is carried on the air. The first speaker in the play reappears and repeats the words he had spoken in the first scene of the first act. Roemerstadt addresses him without the least surprise. The spectator understands that Roemerstadt is the wretched Jaroslav Kubin. The drama has never taken place: it is the circular delirium which Kubin unendingly lives and relives.

Hladík had never asked himself whether this tragicomedy of errors was preposterous or admirable, deliberate or casual. Such a plot, he intuited, was the most appropriate invention to conceal his defects and to manifest his strong points, and it embodied the possibility of redeeming (symbolically) the fundamental meaning of his life. He had already completed the first act and a scene or two of the third. The metrical nature of the work allowed him to go over it continually, rectifying the hexameters, without recourse to the manuscript. He thought of the two acts still to do, and of his coming death. In the darkness, he addressed himself to God. *If I exist at all, if I am not one of Your repetitions and errata, I exist as the author of* The Enemies. *In order to bring this drama, which may serve to justify me, to justify You, I need one more year. Grant me that year, You to whom belong the centuries and all time.* It was the last, the most atrocious night, but ten minutes later sleep swept over him like a dark ocean and drowned him.

Toward dawn, he dreamt he had hidden himself in one of the naves of the Clementine Library. A librarian wearing dark glasses asked him: *What are you looking for?* Hladík answered: *God.* The Librarian told him: *God is in one of the letters on one of the pages of one of the 400,000 volumes of the Clementine. My fathers and the fathers of my fathers have sought after that letter. I've gone blind looking for it.* He removed his glasses, and Hladík saw that his eyes were dead. A reader came in to return an atlas. *This atlas is useless,* he said, and handed it to Hladík, who opened it at random. As if through a haze, he saw a map of India. With a sudden rush of assurance, he touched one of the tiniest letters. An ubiquitous voice said: *The time for your work has been granted.* Hladík awoke.

He remembered that the dreams of men belong to God, and that Maimonides wrote that the words of a dream are divine, when they are all separate and clear and are spoken by someone invisible. He dressed. Two soldiers entered his cell and ordered him to follow them.

From behind the door, Hladík had visualized a labyrinth of passageways, stairs, and connecting blocks. Reality was less rewarding: the party descended to an inner courtyard by a single iron stairway. Some soldiers—uniforms unbuttoned—were testing a motorcycle and disputing their conclusions. The sergeant looked at his watch: it was 8:44. They must wait until nine. Hladík, more insignificant than pitiful, sat down on a pile of firewood. He noticed that the soldiers' eyes avoided his. To make his wait easier, the sergeant offered him a cigarette. Hladík did not smoke. He accepted the cigarette out of politeness or humility. As he lit it, he saw that his hands shook. The day was clouding over. The soldiers spoke in low tones, as though he were already dead. Vainly, he strove to recall the woman of whom Julia de Weidenau was the symbol. . . .

The firing squad fell in and was brought to attention. Hladík, standing against the barracks wall, waited for the volley. Someone expressed fear the wall would be splashed with blood. The condemned man was ordered to step forward a few paces. Hladík recalled, absurdly, the preliminary maneuvers of a photographer. A heavy drop of rain grazed one of Hladík's temples and slowly rolled down his cheek. The sergeant barked the final command.

The physical universe stood still.

The rifles converged upon Hladík, but the men assigned to pull the triggers were immobile. The sergeant's arm eternalized an inconclusive gesture. Upon a courtyard flagstone a bee cast a stationary shadow. The wind had halted, as in a painted picture. Hladík began a shriek, a syllable, a twist of the hand. He realized he was paralyzed. Not a sound reached him from the stricken world.

He thought: *I'm in hell, I'm dead.*

He thought: *I've gone mad.*

He thought: *Time has come to a halt.*

Then he reflected that in that case, his thought, too, would have come to a halt. He was anxious to test this possibility: he repeated (without moving his lips) the mysterious Fourth Eclogue of Virgil. He imagined that the already remote soldiers shared his anxiety; he longed to communicate with them. He was astonished that he felt no fatigue, no vertigo from his protracted immobility. After an indeterminate length of time he fell asleep. On awakening he found the world still motionless and numb. The drop of water still clung to his cheek; the shadow of the bee still did not shift in the courtyard; the smoke from the cigarette he had thrown down did not blow away. Another "day" passed before Hladík understood.

He had asked God for an entire year in which to finish his work: His omnipotence had granted him the time. For his sake, God projected a secret miracle: German lead would kill him, at the determined hour, but in his mind a year would elapse between the command to fire and its execution. From perplexity he passed to stupor, from stupor to resignation, from resignation to sudden gratitude.

He disposed of no document but his own memory; the mastering of each hexameter as he added it, had imposed upon him a kind of fortunate discipline not imagined by those amateurs who forget their vague, ephemeral, paragraphs. He did not work for posterity, nor even for God, of whose literary preferences he possessed scant knowledge. Meticulous, unmoving, secretive, he wove his lofty invisible labyrinth in time. He worked the third act over twice. He eliminated some rather too-obvious symbols: the repeated striking of the hour, the music. There were no circumstances to constrain him. He omitted, condensed, amplified; occasionally, he chose the primitive version. He grew to love the courtyard, the barracks; one of the faces endlessly confronting him made him modify his conception of Roemerstadt's character. He discovered that the hard cacophonies which so distressed Flaubert are mere visual superstitions: debilities and annoyances of the written word, not of the sonorous, the sounding one. . . . He brought his drama to a conclusion: he lacked only a single epithet. He found it: the drop of water slid down his cheek. He began a wild cry, moved his face aside. A quadruple blast brought him down.

Jaromir Hladík died on March 29, at 9:02 in the morning.

# Rose R.

*Oliver Sacks*

*Oliver Sacks is a British-born neurologist who currently lives in New York. He has written a number of books chronicling the neurological, psychological and ethical dilemmas faced by his patients. The film* Awakenings *was loosely based on his work. He was born in London in 1933.*

Miss R. was born in New York City in 1905, the youngest child of a large, wealthy and talented family. Her childhood and school-days were free of serious illness, and were marked, from their earliest days, by a love of merriment, games and jokes. High-spirited, talented, full of interests and hobbies, sustained by deep family affection and love, and a sure sense of who and what and why she was, Miss R. steered clear of significant neurotic problems or "identity-crises" in her growing-up period.

On leaving school, Miss R. threw herself ardently into a social and peripatetic life. Airplanes, above all, appealed to her eager, volant and irrepressible spirit; she flew to Pittsburgh and Denver, New Orleans and Chicago, and twice to the California of Hearst and Hollywood (no mean feat in the planes of those days). She went to innumerable parties and shows, was toasted and fêted, and rolled home drunk at night. And between parties and flights she dashed off sketches of the bridges and waterfronts with which New York abounded. Between 1922 and 1926, Miss R. lived in the blaze of her own vitality, and lived more than most other people in the whole of their lives. And this was as well, for at the age of twenty-one she was suddenly struck down by a virulent form of *encephalitis lethargica*—one of its last victims before the epidemic vanished. 1926, then, was the last year in which Miss R. really *lived*.

The night of the sleeping-sickness, and the days which followed it, can be reconstructed in great detail from Miss R.'s relatives, and Miss R. herself. The acute phase announced itself (as sometimes happened: compare Maria G.) by nightmares of a grotesque and terrifying and premonitory nature. Miss R. had a series of dreams about one central theme: she dreamed she was imprisoned in an inaccessible castle, but the castle had the form and shape of herself; she dreamed of enchantments, bewitchments, entrancements; she dreamed that she had become a living, sentient statue of stone; she dreamed that the world had come to a stop; she dreamed that she had fallen into a sleep so deep that nothing could wake her; she dreamed of a death which was different from death. Her family had difficulty waking her the next morning, and when she awoke there was intense consternation: "Rose," they cried, "Wake up! What's the matter? Your expression, your position . . . You're so still and so strange." Miss R. could not answer, but turned her eyes to the wardrobe-mirror, and there she saw that her dreams had come true. The local doctor was brisk and unhelpful: "Catatonia," he said; "*Flexibilitas cerea.* What can you expect with the life she's been leading? She's broken her heart over one of these bums. Keep her quiet and feed her—she'll be fine in a week."

But Miss R. was not to recover for a week, or a year, or forty-three years. She recovered the ability to speak in short sentences, or to make sudden movements before she froze up again. She showed, increasingly, a forced retraction of her neck; and her eyes—a state of almost-continuous oculogyric crisis, broken only by sleep, meals and occasional "releases." She was alert, and seemed to notice what went on around her; she lost none of her affection for her numerous family—and they lost none of their affection for her; but she seemed absorbed and pre-occupied in some unimaginable state. For the most part, she showed no sign of distress, and no sign of anything save intense *concentration:* "She looked," said one of her sisters, "as if she were trying her hardest to remember something—or, maybe, doing her damndest to forget something. Whatever it was, it took all her attention." In her years at home, and subsequently in hospital, her family did their utmost to penetrate this absorption, to learn what was going on with their beloved "kid" sister. With them—and, much later, with me—Miss R. was exceedingly candid, but whatever she said seemed cryptic and gnomic, and yet at the same time disquietingly clear.[1]

When there was only this state, and no other problems, Miss R.'s family could keep her at home: she was no trouble, they loved her, she was simply—elsewhere (or nowhere). But three or four years after her trance-state had started, she started to become rigid on the left side of her body, to lose her balance when walking, and to develop other signs of Parkinsonism. Gradually these symptoms grew worse and worse, until full-time nursing became a necessity. Her siblings left home, and her parents were aging, and it was increasingly difficult to keep her at home. Finally, in 1935, she was admitted to Mount Carmel.

Her state changed little after the age of thirty, and when I first saw her in 1966, my findings coincided with the original notes from her admission. Indeed, the old staff-nurse on her ward, who had known her throughout, said: "It's uncanny, that woman hasn't aged a day in the thirty years I've known her. The rest of us get older—but Rosie's the same." It was true: Miss R. at sixty-one looked thirty years younger; she had raven-black hair, and her face was unlined, as if she had been magically preserved by her trance or her stupor.

She sat upright and motionless in her wheelchair, with little or no spontaneous movement for hours on end. There was no spontaneous blinking, and her eyes stared straight ahead, seemingly indifferent to her environment but completely absorbed. Her gaze, when requested to look in different directions, was full, save for complete inability to converge the eyes. Fixation of gaze lacked smooth and subtle modulation, and was accomplished by sudden, gross movements which seemed to cost her considerable effort. Her face was completely masked and expressionless. The tongue could not be protruded beyond the lip-margins, and its movements, on request, were exceedingly slow and small. Her voice was virtually inaudible, though Miss R. could whisper quite well with considerable effort. Drooling was profuse, saturating a cloth bib within an hour, and the entire skin was oily, sebarrhoeic, and sweating intensely. Akinesia was global, although rigidity and dystonia were strikingly unilateral in distribution. There was intense axial rigidity, no movement of the neck or trunk muscles being possible. There was equally intense rigidity in the left arm, and a very severe dystonic contracture of the left hand. No voluntary movement of this limb was possible. The right arm was much less rigid, but showed great akinesia, all movements being minimal, and decaying to zero after two or three repetitions. Both legs were hypertonic, the left much more so. The left foot was bent inwards in dystonic inversion. Miss R. could not rise to her feet unaided, but when assisted to do so could maintain her balance and take a few small, shuffling, precarious steps, although the tendency to backward-falling and pulsion was very great.

She was in a state of near-continuous oculogyric crisis, although this varied a good deal in severity. When it became more severe, her Parkinsonian "background" was increased in intensity, and an intermittent coarse tremor appeared in her right arm. Prominent tremor of the head, lips and tongue also became evident at these times, and rhythmic movement of buccinators and corrugators. Her breathing would become somewhat stertorous at such times, and would be accompanied by a guttural phonation reminiscent of a pig grunting. Severe crises would always be accompanied by tachycardia and hypertension. Her neck would be thrown back in an intense and sometimes agonising opisthotonic posture. Her eyes would generally stare directly ahead, and could not be moved by voluntary effort: in the severest crises they were forced upwards and fixed on the ceiling.

Miss R.'s capacity to speak or move, minimal at the best of times, would disappear almost entirely during her severer crises, although in her greatest extremity she would sometimes call out, in a strange high-pitched voice, perseverative and palilalic, utterly unlike her husky "normal" whisper: "Doctor, doctor, doctor, doctor . . . help me, help, help, h'lp, h'lp . . . I am in terrible pain, I'm so frightened, so frightened, so frightened . . . I'm going to die, I know it, I know it. I know it, I know it . . ." And at other times, if nobody was near, she would whimper softly to herself, like some small animal caught in a trap. The nature of Miss R.'s pain during her crises was only elucidated later, when speech had become easy: some of it was a local pain associated with extreme opisthotonos, but a large component seemed to be central—diffuse, unlocalizable, of sudden onset and offset, and inseparably coalesced with feelings of dread and threat, in the severest crises a true *angor animi*. During exceptionally severe attacks, Miss R.'s face would become flushed, and her eyes reddened and protruding, and she would repeat "It'll kill me, it'll kill me, it'll kill me . . ." hundreds of times in succession.[2]

Miss R.'s state scarcely changed between 1966 and 1969, and when L-DOPA became available I was in two minds about using it. She was, it was true, intensely disabled, and had been virtually helpless for over forty years. It was her strangeness above all which made me hesitate and wonder—fearing what might happen if I gave her L-DOPA. I had never seen a patient whose regard was so turned away from the world, and so immured in a private, inaccessible world of her own.

I kept thinking of something Joyce wrote about his mad daughter: ". . . fervently as I desire her cure, I ask myself what then will happen when and if she finally withdraws her regard from the lightning-lit revery of her clairvoyance and turns it upon that battered cabman's face, the world . . ."

*Course on L-DOPA*

But I started her on L-DOPA, despite my misgivings, on 18 June 1969. The following is an extract from my diary.

*25 June.* The first therapeutic responses have already occurred, even though the dosage has only been raised to 1.5 Gm. a day. Miss R. has experienced two entire days unprecedently free of oculogyric crises, and her eyes, so still and pre-occupied before, are brighter and more mobile and attentive to her surroundings.

*1 July.* Very real improvements are evident by this date: Miss R. is able to walk unaided down the passage, shows a distinct reduction of rigidity in the left arm and elsewhere, and has become able to speak at a normal conversational volume. Her mood is cheerful, and she has had no oculogyric crises for three days. In view of this propitious response, and the absence of any adverse effects, I am increasing the dosage of L-DOPA to 4 Gm. daily.

*6 July.* Now receiving 4 Gm. L-DOPA. Miss R. has continued to improve in almost every way. When I saw her at lunchtime, she was delighted with everything: "Dr. Sacks!" she called out, "I walked to and from the New Building today" (this is a distance of about six hundred yards). "It's fabulous, it's gorgeous!" Miss R. has now been free from oculogyric crises for eight days, and has shown no akathisia or undue excitement. I too feel delighted at her progress, but for some reason am conscious of obscure forebodings.

*7 July.* Today Miss R. has shown her first signs of unstable and abrupt responses to L-DOPA. Seeing her 3-1/2 hours after her early-morning dose, I was shocked to find her very "down"—hypophonic, somewhat depressed, rigid and akinetic, with extremely small pupils and profuse salivation. Fifteen minutes after receiving her medication she was "up" again—her voice and walking fully restored, cheerful, smiling, talkative, her eyes alert and shining, and her pupils somewhat dilated. I was further disquieted by observing an occasional impulsion to run, although this was easily checked by her.

*8 July.* Following an insomniac night ("I didn't feel in the least sleepy: thoughts just kept rushing through my head"), Miss R. is extremely active, cheerful and affectionate. She seems to be very busy, constantly flying from one place to another, and all her thoughts too are concerned with movement; "Dr. Sacks," she exclaimed breathlessly, "I feel great today. I feel I want to fly. I love you, Dr. Sacks, I love you, I love you. You know, you're the kindest doctor in the world . . . You know I always liked to travel around: I used to fly to Pittsburgh, Chicago, Miami, California . . ." etc. Her skin is warm and flushed, her pupils are again very widely dilated, and her eyes constantly glancing to and fro. Her energy seems limitless and untiring, although I get the impression of exhaustion somewhere beneath the pressured surface. An entirely new symptom has also appeared today, a sudden quick movement of the right hand to the chin, which is repeated two or three times an hour. When I questioned Miss R. about this she said: "It's new, it's odd, it's strange, I never did it before. God knows why I do it. I just suddenly get an urge, like you suddenly got to sneeze or scratch yourself." Fearing the onset of akathisia or excessive emotional excitement, I have reduced the dosage of L-DOPA to 3 Gm. daily.

*9 July.* Today Miss R.'s energy and excitement are unabated, but her mood has veered from elation to anxiety. She is impatient, touchy and extremely demanding. She became much agitated in the middle of the day, asserting that seven dresses had been stolen from her closet, and that her purse had been stolen. She entertained dark suspicions of various fellow-patients: no doubt they had been plotting this for weeks before. Later in the day, she discovered that her dresses were in fact in her closet in their usual position. Her paranoid recriminations instantly vanished: "Wow!" she said, "I must have imagined it all. I guess I better take myself in hand."

*14 July.* Following the excitements and changing moods of 9 July, Miss R.'s state has become less pressured and hyperactive. She has been able to sleep, and has lost the tic-like "wiping" movements of her right hand. Unfortunately, after a two-week remission, her old enemy has re-emerged, and she has experienced two severe oculogyric crises. I observed in these not only the usual staring, but a more bizarre symptom—captivation or enthralment of gaze: in one of these crises she had been forced to stare at one of her fellow-patients, and had felt her eyes "drawn" this way and that, following the movements of this patient around the Ward. "It was uncanny," Miss R. said later. "My eyes were spell-bound. I felt like I was bewitched or something, like a rabbit with a snake." During the periods of "bewitchment" or fascination, Miss R. had the feeling that her "thoughts had stopped," and that she could only

think of one thing, the object of her gaze. If, on the other hand, her attention was distracted, the quality of thinking would suddenly change, the
motionless fascination would be broken up, and she would experience
instead "an absolute torrent of thoughts," rushing through her mind:
these thoughts did not seem to be "her" thoughts, they were not what she
wanted to think, they were "peculiar thoughts" which appeared "by
themselves." Miss R. could not or would not specify the nature of these
intrusive thoughts, but she was greatly frightened by the whole business:
"These crises are different to the ones I used to get," she said. "They are
worse. They are completely *mad!*"[3]

*25 July.* Miss R. has had an astonishing ten days, and has shown phenomena I never thought possible. Her mood has been joyous and elated,
and very salacious. Her social behaviour has remained impeccable, but
she has developed an insatiable urge to sing songs and tell jokes, and has
made very full use of our portable tape-recorder. In the past few days, she
has recorded innumerable songs of an astonishing lewdness, and reams
of "light" verse all dating from the twenties. She is also full of anecdotes
and allusions to "current" figures—to figures who were current in the
mid-1920s. We have been forced to do some archival research, looking at
old newspaper-files in the New York Library. We have found that almost
all of Miss R.'s allusions date to 1926, her last year of real life before her
illness closed round her. Her memory is uncanny, considering she is
speaking of so long ago. Miss R. wants the tape-recorder, and nobody
around; she stays in her room, alone with the tape-recorder; she is looking at everyone as if they didn't exist. She is completely engrossed in her
memories of the twenties, and is doing her best to not-notice anything
later. I suppose one calls this "forced reminiscence," or uncontrollable
nostalgia. *But I also have the feeling, that she feels her "past" as present, and
that, perhaps, it has never felt "past" for her. Is it possible that Miss R. has never,
in fact, moved on from the "past?" Could she still be "in" 1926 forty-three years
later?*[4]

*28 July.* Miss R. sought me out this morning—the first time she has done
so in almost two weeks. Her face has lost its jubilant look; and she looks
anxious and shadowed and slightly bewildered: "Things can't last," she
said. "Something awful is coming. God knows what it is, but it's as bad
as they come." I tried to find out more, but Miss R. shook her head: "It's
just a feeling, I can't tell you more . . ."

*1 August.* A few hours after stating her prediction, Miss R. ran straight into a barrage of difficulties. Suddenly she was ticcing, jammed and blocked; the beautiful smooth flow which had borne her along seemed to break up, and dam, and crash back on itself. Her walking and talking are gravely affected. She is impelled to rush forward for five or six steps, and then suddenly freezes or jams without warning; she continually gets more excited and frustrated, and with increasing excitement the jamming grows worse. If she can moderate her excitement or her impulsion to run, she can still walk the corridor without freezing or jamming. Analogous problems are affecting her speech: she can only speak softly, if she is to speak at all, for with increased vocal impetus she stutters and stops. I have the feeling that Miss R.'s "motor space" is becoming confined, so that she rebounds internally if she moves with too much speed or force. Reducing her L-DOPA to 3 Gm. a day reduced the dangerous hurry-and-block, but led to an intensely severe oculogyric crisis—the worst Miss R. has had since starting L-DOPA. Moreover, her "wiping" tic—which re-appeared on 28th—has grown more severe and more *complex* with each passing hour. From a harmless feather-light brush of the chin, the movement has become a deep circular gouging, her right index-finger scratching incessantly in tight little circles, abrading the skin and making it bleed. Miss R. has been quite unable to stop this compulsion directly, but she can over-ride it by thrusting her tic-hand deep in her pocket and clutching its lining with all of her force. The moment she forgets to do this, the hand flies up and scratches her face.

*August 1969*[5]

During the first week of August, Miss R. continued to have oculogyric crises every day of extreme severity, during which she would be intensely rigid and opisthotonic, anguished, whimpering and bathed in sweat. Her tics of the right hand became almost too fast for the eye to follow, their rate having increased to almost 300 per minute (an estimate confirmed by a slow-motion film). On 6 August, Miss R. showed very obvious palilalia, repeating entire sentences and strings of words again and again: "I'm going round like a record," she said, "which gets stuck in the groove . . ." During the second week of August, her tics became more complex, and were conflated with defensive maneuvers' counter-tics and elaborate rituals. Thus Miss R. would clutch someone's hand, release her grip, touch something nearby, put her hand in her pocket, withdraw it, slap the pocket *three* times, put it back in the pocket, wipe her chin *five* times, clutch someone's hand . . . and move again and again through this stereo-typed sequence.

The evening of 15 August provided the only pleasant interlude in a month otherwise full of disability and suffering. On this evening, quite unexpectedly, Miss R. emerged from her crises and blocking and ticcing, and had a brief return of joyous salacity, accompanied with free-flowing singing and movement. For an hour this evening, she improvised a variety of coprolalic limericks to the tune of "The Sheikh of Araby," accompanying herself on the piano with her uncontractured right hand.

Later this week, her motor and vocal block became absolute. She would suddenly call out to Miss Kohl: "Margie, I . . . Margie, I want . . . Margie! . . . ," completely unable to proceed beyond the first word or two of what she so desperately wanted to say. When she tried to write, similarly, her hand (and thoughts) suddenly stopped after a couple of words. If one asked her to try and say what she wanted, softly and slowly, her face would go blank, and her eyes would shift in a tantalized manner, indicating, perhaps, her frantic inner search for the dislimning thought. Walking became impossible at this time, for Miss R. would find her feet completely stuck to the ground, but the impulse to move would throw her flat on her face. During the last ten days of August, Miss R. seemed to be totally blocked in all spheres of activity; everything about her showed an extremity of tension, which was entirely prevented from finding any outlet. Her face at this time was continually clenched in a horrified, tortured and anguished expression. Her prediction of a month earlier was completely fulfilled: something awful *had* come, and it was as bad as they came.

*1969-1972*

Miss R.'s reactions to L-DOPA since the summer of 1969 have been almost non-existent compared with her dramatic initial reaction. She has been placed on L-DOPA five further times, each with an increase of dose by degrees to about 3.0 Gm. per day. Each time the L-DOPA has procured *some* reduction in her rigidity, oculogyria and general entrancement, but less and less on each succeeding occasion. It has *never* called forth anything resembling the amazing mobility and mood change of July 1969, and in particular has never re-called the extraordinary sense of 1926-ness which she had at that time. When Miss R. has been on L-DOPA for several weeks its advantages invariably become over-weighted by its disadvantages, and she returns to a state of intense "block," crises, and tic-like impulsions. The form of her tics has varied a good deal on different occasions: on one of her periods on L-DOPA her crises were always accompanied by a palilalic verbigeration of the word "Honeybunch!" which she would repeat twenty or thirty times a minute for the entire day.

However deep and strange her pathological state, Miss R. can invariably be "awakened" for a few seconds or minutes by external stimuli, although she is obviously quite unable to generate any such stimuli or calls-to-action for herself. If Miss A.—a fellow-patient with dipsomania—drinks more than twenty times an hour at the water fountain, Miss R. cries "Get away from that fountain, Margaret, or I'll clobber you!" or "Stop sucking that spout, Margaret, we all know what you really want to suck!" Whenever she hears my name being paged she yells out "Dr. Sacks! Dr. Sacks!! They're after you again!," and continues to yell this until I have answered the page.

Miss R. is at her best when she is visited—as she frequently is—by any of her devoted family who fly in from all over the country to see her. At such times she is all agog with excitement, her blank masked face cracks into a smile, and she shows a great hunger for family gossip, though no interest at all in political events or other current "news"; at such times she is able to say a certain amount quite intelligibly, and in particular shows her fondness for jokes and mildly-salacious indiscretions. Seeing Miss R. at this time one realises what a "normal" and charming and alive personality is imprisoned or suspended by her ridiculous illness.

On a number of occasions I have asked Miss R. about the strange "nostalgia" which she showed in July 1969, and how she experiences the world generally. She usually becomes distressed and "blocked" when I ask such questions, but on a few occasions she has given me enough information for me to perceive the almost incredible truth about her. She indicates that in her "nostalgic" state she knew perfectly well that it was 1969 and that she was sixty-four years old, but that she *felt* that it was 1926 and she was twenty-one; she adds that she can't really imagine what it's like being older than twenty-one, because she has never really experienced it. For most of the time, however, there is "nothing, absolutely nothing, no thoughts at all" in her head, as if she is forced to block off an intolerable and insoluble anachronism—the almost half-century gap between her age as felt and experienced (her *ontological* age) and her actual or official age. It seems, in retrospect, as if the L-DOPA must have "de-blocked" her for a few days, and revealed to her a time-gap beyond comprehension or bearing, and that she has subsequently been forced to "re-block" herself and the possibility of any similar reaction to L-DOPA ever happening again. She continues to look much younger than her years; indeed, in a fundamental sense, she *is* much younger than her age. But she is a Sleeping Beauty whose "awakening" was unbearable to her, and who will never be awoken again.

## Notes

1    The following are typical of some of the "dialogues" I had with Miss R.
"What are you thinking about, Rosie?"
"Nothing, just nothing."
"But how can you possibly be thinking of nothing." "It's dead easy, once you know how."
"*How* exactly do you think about nothing."
"One way is to think about the same thing again and again. Like 2=2=2=2; or, I am what I am what I am what I am . . . It's the same thing with my posture. My posture continually leads to itself. Whatever I do or whatever I think leads deeper and deeper into itself . . . And then there are maps."
"Maps? What do you mean?"
"Everything I do is a map of itself, everything I do is a part of itself. Every part leads into itself . . . I've got a thought in my mind, and then I see something in it, like a dot on the skyline. It comes nearer and nearer, and then I see what it is—it's just the same thought as I was thinking before. And then I see another dot, and another, and so on . . . Or I think of a map, then a map of that map then a map of that map of that map, and each map perfect, though smaller and smaller . . . Worlds within worlds within worlds within worlds . . . Once I get going, I can't possibly stop. It's like being caught between mirrors, or echoes or something. Or being caught on a merry-go-round which won't come to a stop."
"And do you have any other ways of thinking about nothing?"
"Oh yes! The dots and maps are positive nothings, but I also think of negative nothings."
"And what are those like, Rosie?"
"That's impossible to say, because they're takings-away. I think of a thought, and it's suddenly gone—like having a picture whipped out of its frame. Or I try to picture something in my mind, but the picture dissolves as fast as I make it. I have a particular idea, but can't keep it in mind; and then I lose the general idea; and then the general idea of a general idea; and

in two or three jumps my mind is a blank—all my thoughts gone, blanked-out or erased."

2    Compare cases cited by Jelliffe (1932): the patient who would cry out in "anguish" during her attacks, but could give no reason for her fear (p. 36), or the patient who would feel every attack to be "a calamity" (p.42).

3    Jelliffe (1932) cites many cases of oculogyric crises with fixation of gaze and attention, and also of crises with reiterative "autochthonous" thinking. Miss R. never vouchsafed the nature of the "mad" thoughts which came to her during her crises at this time, and one would suspect from this reticence that these thoughts were of an inadmissible nature, either sexual or hostile. Jelliffe refers to several patients who were compelled to think of "dirty things" during their crises (pp. 37-8), and to another patient (p. 39) who experienced during his crises "ideas of reference to which he pays no attention."

4    Our earth in 1969
Is not the planet I call mine,
The world. I mean, that gives me strength
To hold off chaos at arm's length.

My Eden landscapes and their climes
Are constructs from Edwardian times . . .

Me alienated? Bosh! It's just
. . . that I feel
Most at home with what is Real.
                    W. H. AUDEN

5    The following is based on notes provided by our speech-pathologist, Miss Marjorie Kohl. I myself was away during August.

# The Lost Mariner

*Oliver Sacks*

*You have to begin to lose your memory, if only in bits and pieces, to realise that memory is what makes our lives. Life without memory is no life at all. . . . Our memory is our coherence, our reason, our feeling, even our action. Without it, we are nothing . . . (I can only wait for the final amnesia, the one that can erase an entire life, as it did my mother's . . .)*

*Luis Buñuel*

This moving and frightening segment in Buñuel's recently translated memoirs raises fundamental questions—clinical, practical, existential, philosophical: what sort of a life (if any), what sort of a world, what sort of a self, can be preserved in a man who has lost the greater part of his memory and, with this, his past, and his moorings in time?

It immediately made me think of a patient of mine in whom these questions are precisely exemplified: charming, intelligent, memoryless Jimmie G., who was admitted to our Home for the Aged near New York City early in 1975, with a cryptic transfer note saying, 'Helpless, demented, confused and disoriented.'[1]

Jimmie was a fine-looking man, with a curly bush of grey hair, a healthy and handsome forty-nine-year-old. He was cheerful, friendly, and warm.

'Hiya, Doc!' he said. 'Nice morning! Do I take this chair here?' He was a genial soul, very ready to talk and to answer any questions I asked him. He told me his name and birth date, and the name of the little town in Connecticut where he was born. He described it in affectionate detail, even drew me a map. He spoke of the houses where his family had lived—he remembered their phone numbers still. He spoke of school and school days, the friends he'd had, and his special fondness for mathematics and science. He talked with enthusiasm of his days in the navy— he was seventeen, had just graduated from high school when he was drafted in 1943. With his good engineering mind he was a 'natural' for radio and electronics, and after a crash course in Texas found himself assistant radio operator on a submarine. He remembered the names of various submarines on which he had served, their missions, where they were stationed, the names of his shipmates. He remembered Morse code, and was still fluent in Morse tapping and touch-typing.

A full and interesting early life, remembered vividly, in detail, with affection. But there, for some reason, his reminiscences stopped. He recalled, and almost relived, his war days and service, the end of the war, and his thoughts for the future. He had come to love the navy, thought he might stay in it. But with the GI Bill, and support, he felt he might do best to go to college. His older brother was in accountancy school and engaged to a girl, a 'real beauty,' from Oregon.

With recalling, reliving, Jimmie was full of animation; he did not seem to be speaking of the past but of the present, and I was very struck by the change of tense in his recollections as he passed from his school days to his days in the navy. He had been using the past tense, but now used the present—and (it seemed to me) not just the formal or fictitious present tense of recall, but the actual present tense of immediate experience.

A sudden, improbable suspicion seized me.

'What year is this, Mr G.?' I asked, concealing my perplexity under a casual manner.

'Forty-five, man. What do you mean?' He went on, 'We've won the war, FDR's dead, Truman's at the helm. There are great times ahead.'

'And you, Jimmie, how old would you be?'

Oddly, uncertainly, he hesitated a moment, as if engaged in calculation.

'Why, I guess I'm nineteen, Doc. I'll be twenty next birthday.'

Looking at the gray-haired man before me, I had an impulse for which I have never forgiven myself—it was, or would have been, the height of cruelty had there been any possibility of Jimmie's remembering it.

'Here,' I said, and thrust a mirror toward him. 'Look in the mirror and tell me what you see. Is that a nineteen-year-old looking out from the mirror?'

He suddenly turned ashen and gripped the sides of the chair. 'Jesus Christ,' he whispered. 'Christ, what's going on? What's happened to me? Is this a nightmare? Am I crazy? Is this a joke?'—and he became frantic, panicked.

'It's okay, Jimmie,' I said soothingly. 'It's just a mistake. Nothing to worry about. Hey!' I took him to the window. 'Isn't this a lovely spring day. See the kids there playing baseball?' He regained his colour and started to smile, and I stole away, taking the hateful mirror with me.

Two minutes later I re-entered the room. Jimmie was still standing by the window, gazing with pleasure at the kids playing baseball below. He wheeled around as I opened the door, and his face assumed a cheery expression.

'Hiya, Doc!' he said. 'Nice morning! You want to talk to me—do I take this chair here?' There was no sign of recognition on his frank, open face.

'Haven't we met before, Mr G.?' I asked casually.

'No, I can't say we have. Quite a beard you got there. I wouldn't forget *you*, Doc!'

'Why do you call me "Doc"?'

'Well, you are a doc, ain't you?'

'Yes, but if you haven't met me, how do you know what I am?'

'You *talk* like a doc. I can *see* you're a doc.'

'Well, you're right, I am. I'm the neurologist here.'

'Neurologist? Hey, there's something wrong with my nerves? And "here"—where's "here"? What is this place anyhow?'

'I was just going to ask you—where do you think you are?'

'I see these beds, and these patients everywhere. Looks like a sort of hospital to me. But hell, what would I be doing in a hospital—and with all these old people, years older than me. I feel good, I'm strong as a bull. Maybe I *work* here . . . Do I work? What's my job? . . . No, you're shaking your head, I see in your eyes I don't work here. If I don't work here, I've been *put* here. Am I a patient, am I sick and don't know it, Doc? It's crazy, it's scary . . . Is it some sort of joke?'

'You don't know what the matter is? You really don't know? You remember telling me about your childhood, growing up in Connecticut, working as a radio operator on submarines? And how your brother is engaged to a girl from Oregon?'

'Hey, you're right. But I didn't tell you that, I never met you before in my life. You must have read all about me in my chart.'

'Okay,' I said. 'I'll tell you a story. A man went to his doctor complaining of memory lapses. The doctor asked him some routine questions, and then said, "These lapses. What about them?" "What lapses?" the patient replied.'

'So that's my problem,' Jimmie laughed. 'I kinda thought it was. I do find myself forgetting things, once in a while—things that have just happened. The past is clear, though.'

'Will you allow me to examine you, to run over some tests?'

'Sure,' he said genially. 'Whatever you want.'

On intelligence testing he showed excellent ability. He was quick-witted, observant, and logical, and had no difficulty solving complex problems and puzzles—no difficulty, that is, if they could be done quickly. If much time was required, he forgot what he was doing. He was quick and good at tic-tac-toe and checkers, and cunning and aggressive—he easily beat me. But he got lost at chess—the moves were too slow.

Homing in on his memory, I found an extreme and extraordinary loss of recent memory—so that whatever was said or shown to him was apt to be forgotten in a few seconds' time. Thus I laid out my watch, my tie, and my glasses on the desk, covered them, and asked him to remember these. Then, after a minute's chat, I asked him what I had put under the cover. He remembered none of them—or indeed that I had even asked him to remember. I repeated the test, this time getting him to write down the names of the three objects; again he forgot, and when I showed him the paper with his writing on it he was astounded, and said he had no recollection of writing anything down, though he acknowledged that it was his own writing, and then got a faint 'echo' of the fact that he had written them down.

He sometimes retained faint memories, some dim echo or sense of familiarity. Thus five minutes after I had played tic-tac-toe with him, he recollected that 'some doctor' had played this with him 'a while back'—whether the 'while back' was minutes or months ago he had no idea. He then paused and said, 'It could have been you!' When I said it *was* me, he seemed amused. This faint amusement and indifference were very characteristic, as were the involved cogitations to which he was driven by being so disoriented and lost in time. When I asked Jimmie the time of the year, he would immediately look around for some clue—I was careful to remove the calendar from my desk—and would work out the time of year, roughly, by looking through the window.

It was not, apparently, that he failed to register in memory, but that the memory traces were fugitive in the extreme, and were apt to be effaced within a minute, often less, especially if there were distracting or competing stimuli, while his intellectual and perceptual powers were preserved, and highly superior.

Jimmie's scientific knowledge was that of a bright high school graduate with a penchant for mathematics and science. He was superb at arithmetical (and also algebraic) calculations, but only if they could be done with lightning speed. If there were many steps, too much time, involved, he would forget where he was, and even the question. He knew the elements, compared them, and drew the periodic table—but omitted the transuranic elements.

'Is that complete?' I asked when he'd finished.

'It's complete and up-to-date, sir, as far as I know.'

'You wouldn't know any elements beyond uranium?'

'You kidding? There's ninety-two elements, and uranium's the last.'

I paused and flipped through a *National Geographic* on the table. 'Tell me the planets,' I said, 'and something about them.' Unhesitatingly, confidently, he gave me the planets—their names, their discovery, their distance from the sun, their estimated mass, character, and gravity.

'What is this?' I asked, showing him a photo in the magazine I was holding.

'It's the moon,' he replied.

'No, it's not,' I answered. 'It's a picture of the earth taken from the moon.'

'Doc, you're kidding! Someone would've had to get a camera up there!'

'Naturally.'

'Hell! You're joking—how the hell would you do that?'

Unless he were a consummate actor, a fraud simulating an astonishment he did not feel, this was an utterly convincing demonstration that he was still in the past. His words, his feelings, his innocent wonder, his struggle to make sense of what he saw, were precisely those of an intelligent young man in the forties faced with the future, with what had not yet happened, and what was scarcely imaginable. 'This more than anything else,' I wrote in my notes, 'persuades me that his cut-off around 1945 is genuine . . . What I showed him, and told him, produced the authentic amazement which it would have done in an intelligent young man of the pre-Sputnik era.'

I found another photo in the magazine and pushed it over to him.

'That's an aircraft carrier,' he said. 'Real ultramodern design. I never saw one quite like that.'

'What's it called?' I asked.

He glanced down, looked baffled, and said, 'The *Nimitz!*'

'Something the matter?'

'The hell there is!' he replied hotly. 'I know 'em all by name, and *I don't know a Nimitz*. . . . Of course there's an Admiral Nimitz, but I never heard they named a carrier after him.'

Angrily he threw the magazine down.

He was becoming fatigued, and somewhat irritable and anxious, under the continuing pressure of anomaly and contradiction, and their fearful implications, to which he could not be entirely oblivious. I had already, unthinkingly, pushed him into panic, and felt it was time to end our session. We wandered over to the window again, and looked down at the sunlit baseball diamond; as he looked his face relaxed, he forgot the *Nimitz*, the satellite photo, the other horrors and hints, and became absorbed in the game below. Then, as a savoury smell drifted up from the dining room, he smacked his lips, said 'Lunch!,' smiled, and took his leave.

And I myself was wrung with emotion—it was heartbreaking, it was absurd, it was deeply perplexing, to think of his life lost in limbo, dissolving.

'He is, as it were,' I wrote in my notes, 'isolated in a single moment of being, with a moat or lacuna of forgetting all round him . . . He is man without a past (or future), stuck in a constantly changing, meaningless moment.' And then, more prosaically, 'The remainder of the neurological examination is entirely normal. Impression: probably Korsakov's syndrome, due to alcoholic degeneration of the mammillary bodies.' My note was a strange mixture of facts and observations, carefully noted and itemised, with irrepressible meditations on what such problems might 'mean,' in regard to who and what and where this poor man was—whether, indeed, one could speak of an 'existence,' given so absolute a privation of memory or continuity.

I kept wondering, in this and later notes—unscientifically—about 'a lost soul,' and how one might establish some continuity, some roots, for he was a man without roots, or rooted only in the remote past.

'Only connect'—but how could he connect, and how could we help him to connect? What was life without connection? 'I may venture to affirm,' Hume wrote, 'that we are nothing but a bundle or collection of different sensations, which succeed each other with an inconceivable rapidity, and are in a perpetual flux and movement.' In some sense, he had been reduced to a 'Humean' being—I could not help thinking how fascinated Hume would have been at seeing in Jimmie his own philosophical 'chimaera' incarnate, a gruesome reduction of a man to mere disconnected, incoherent flux and change.

Perhaps I could find advice or help in the medical literature—a literature which, for some reason, was largely Russian, from Korsakov's original thesis (Moscow, 1887) about such cases of memory loss, which are still called 'Korsakov's syndrome,' to Luria's *Neuropsychology of Memory* (which appeared in translation only a year after I first saw Jimmie). Korsakov wrote in 1887:

> Memory of recent events is disturbed almost exclusively; recent impressions apparently disappear soonest, whereas impressions of long ago are recalled properly, so that the patient's ingenuity, his sharpness of wit, and his resourcefulness remain largely unaffected.

To Korsakov's brilliant but spare observations, almost a century of further research has been added—the richest and deepest, by far, being Luria's. And in Luria's account science became poetry, and the pathos of radical lostness was evoked. 'Gross disturbances of the organization of impressions of events and their sequence in time can always be observed in such patients,' he wrote. 'In consequence, they lose their integral experience of time and begin to live in a world of isolated impressions.' Further, as Luria noted, the eradication of impressions (and their disorder) might spread backward in time—in the most serious cases—even to relatively distant events.

Most of Luria's patients, as described in this book, had massive and serious cerebral tumours, which had the same effects as Korsakov's syndrome, but later spread and were often fatal. Luria included no cases of 'simple' Korsakov's syndrome, based on the self-limiting destruction that Korsakov described—neuron destruction, produced by alcohol, in the tiny but crucial mammillary bodies, the rest of the brain being perfectly preserved. And so there was no long-term follow-up of Luria's cases.

I had at first been deeply puzzled, and dubious, even suspicious, about the apparently sharp cut-off in 1945, a point, a date, which was also symbolically so sharp. I wrote in a subsequent note:

> There is a great blank. We do not know what happened then—or subsequently . . . We must fill in these 'missing' years—from his brother, or the navy, or hospitals he has been to . . . Could it be that he sustained some massive trauma at this time, some massive cerebral or emotional trauma in combat, in the war, and that *this* may have affected him ever since? . . . was the war his 'high point,' the last time he was really alive, and existence since one long anti-climax?[2]

We did various tests on him (EEG, brain scans), and found no evidence of massive brain damage, although atrophy of the tiny mammillary bodies would not show up on such tests. We received reports from the navy indicating that he had remained in the navy until 1965, and that he was perfectly competent at that time.

Then we turned up a short nasty report from Bellevue Hospital, dated 1971, saying that he was 'totally disoriented . . . with an advanced organic brain-syndrome, due to alcohol' (cirrhosis had also developed by this time). From Bellevue he was sent to a wretched dump in the Village, a so-called 'nursing home' whence he was rescued—lousy, starving—by our Home in 1975.

We located his brother, whom Jimmie always spoke of as being in accountancy school and engaged to a girl from Oregon. In fact he had married the girl from Oregon, had become a father and grandfather, and been a practicing accountant for thirty years.

Where we had hoped for an abundance of information and feeling from his brother, we received a courteous but somewhat meagre letter. It was obvious from reading this—especially reading between the lines—that the brothers had scarcely seen each other since 1943, and gone separate ways, partly through the vicissitudes of location and profession, and partly through deep (though not estranging) differences of temperament. Jimmie, it seemed, had never 'settled down,' was 'happy-go-lucky,' and 'always a drinker.' The navy, his brother felt, provided a structure, a life, and the real problems started when he left it, in 1965. Without his habitual structure and anchor Jimmie had ceased to work, 'gone to pieces,' and started to drink heavily. There had been some memory impairment, of the Korsakov type, in the middle and especially the late Sixties, but not so severe that Jimmie couldn't 'cope' in his nonchalant fashion. But his drinking grew heavier in 1970.

Around Christmas of that year, his brother understood, he had suddenly 'blown his top' and become deliriously excited and confused, and it was at this point that he had been taken into Bellevue. During the next month, the excitement and delirium died down, but he was left with deep and bizarre memory lapses, or 'deficits,' to use the medical jargon. His brother had visited him at this time—they had not met for twenty years—and, to his horror, Jimmie not only failed to recognise him, but said, 'Stop joking! You're old enough to be my father. My brother's a young man, just going through accountancy school.'

When I received this information, I was more perplexed still: why did Jimmie not remember his later years in the navy, why did he not recall and organise his memories until 1970? I had not heard then that such patients might have a retrograde amnesia (see Postscript). 'I wonder, increasingly,' I wrote at this time, 'whether there is not an element of hysterical or fugal amnesia—whether he is not in flight from something too awful to recall,' and I suggested he be seen by our psychiatrist. Her report was searching and detailed—the examination had included a sodium amytal test, calculated to 'release' any memories which might be repressed. She also attempted to hypnotize Jimmie, in the hope of eliciting memories repressed by hysteria—this tends to work well in cases of hysterical amnesia. But it failed because Jimmie could not be hypnotized, not because of any 'resistance,' but because of his extreme amnesia, which caused him to lose track of what the hypnotist was saying. (Dr. M. Homonoff, who worked on the amnesia ward at the Boston Veterans Administration hospital, tells me of similar experiences—and of his feeling that this is absolutely characteristic of patients with Korsakov's, as opposed to patients with hysterical amnesia.)

'I have no feeling or evidence,' the psychiatrist wrote, 'of any hysterical or "put-on" deficit. He lacks both the means and the motive to make a façade. His memory deficits are organic and permanent and incorrigible, though it is puzzling they should go back so long.' Since, she felt, he was 'unconcerned . . . manifested no special anxiety . . . constituted no management problem,' there was nothing she could offer, or any therapeutic 'entrance' or 'lever' she could see.

At this point, persuaded that this was, indeed, 'pure' Korsakov's, uncomplicated by other factors, emotional or organic, I wrote to Luria and asked his opinion. He spoke in his reply of his patient Bel[3] whose amnesia had retroactively eradicated ten years. He said he saw no reason why such a retrograde amnesia should not thrust backward decades, or almost a whole lifetime. 'I can only wait for the final amnesia,' Buñuel writes, 'the one that can erase an entire life.' But Jimmie's amnesia, for whatever reason, had erased memory and time back to 1945—roughly—and then stopped. Occasionally, he would recall something much later, but the recall was fragmentary and dislocated in time. Once, seeing the word 'satellite' in a newspaper headline, he said offhandedly that he'd been involved in a project of satellite tracking while on the ship *Chesapeake Bay*, a memory fragment coming from the early or mid-Sixties. But, for all practical purposes, his cut-off point was during the mid- (or late) Forties, and anything subsequently retrieved was fragmentary, unconnected. This was the case in 1975, and it is still the case now nine years later.

What could we do? What should we do? 'There are no prescriptions,' Luria wrote, 'in a case like this. Do whatever your ingenuity and your heart suggest. There is little or no hope of any recovery in his memory. But a man does not consist of memory alone. He has feeling, will, sensibilities, moral being—matters of which neuropsychology cannot speak. And it is here, beyond the realm of an impersonal psychology, that you may find ways to touch him, and change him. And the circumstances of your work especially allow this, for you work in a Home, which is like a little world, quite different from the clinics and institutions where I work. Neuropsychologically, there is little or nothing you can do; but in the realm of the Individual, there may be much you can do.'

Luria mentioned his patient Kur as manifesting a rare self-awareness, in which hopelessness was mixed with an odd equanimity. 'I have no memory of the present,' Kur would say. 'I do not know what I have just done or from where I have just come . . . I can recall my past very well, but I have no memory of my present.' When asked whether he had ever seen the person testing him, he said, 'I cannot say yes or no, I can neither affirm nor deny that I have seen you.' This was sometimes the case with Jimmie; and, like Kur, who stayed many months in the same hospital, Jimmie began to form 'a sense of familiarity'; he slowly learned his way around the home—the whereabouts of the dining room, his own room, the elevators, the stairs, and in some sense recognised some of the staff, although he confused them, and perhaps had to do so, with people from the past. He soon became fond of the nursing sister in the Home; he recognised her voice, her footfalls, immediately, but would always say that she had been a fellow pupil at his high school, and was greatly surprised when I addressed her as 'Sister.'

'Gee!' he exclaimed, 'the damnedest things happen. I'd never have guessed you'd become a religious, Sister!'

Since he's been at our Home—that is, since early 1975—Jimmie has never been able to identify anyone in it consistently. The only person he truly recognises is his brother, whenever he visits from Oregon. These meetings are deeply emotional and moving to observe—the only truly emotional meetings Jimmie has. He loves his brother, he recognises him, but he cannot understand why he looks so old: 'Guess some people age fast,' he says. Actually his brother looks much younger than his age, and has the sort of face and build that change little with the years. These are true meetings, Jimmie's only connection of past and present, yet they do nothing to provide any sense of history or continuity. If anything they emphasise—at least to his brother, and to others who see them together—that Jimmie still lives, is fossilised, in the past.

All of us, at first, had high hopes of helping Jimmie—he was so personable, so likable, so quick and intelligent, it was difficult to believe that he might be beyond help. But none of us had ever encountered, even imagined, such a power of amnesia, the possibility of a pit into which everything, every experience, every event, would fathomlessly drop, a bottomless memory-hole that would engulf the whole world.

I suggested, when I first saw him, that he should keep a diary, and be encouraged to keep notes every day of his experiences, his feelings, thoughts, memories, reflections. These attempts were foiled, at first, by his continually losing the diary: it had to be attached to him—somehow. But this too failed to work: he dutifully kept a brief daily notebook but could not recognise his earlier entries in it. He does recognise his own writing, and style, and is always astounded to find that he wrote something the day before.

Astounded—and indifferent—for he was a man who, in effect, had no 'day before.' His entries remained unconnected and unconnecting and had no power to provide any sense of time or continuity. Moreover, they were trivial—'Eggs for breakfast,' 'Watched ballgame on TV'—and never touched the depths. But were there depths in this unmemoried man, depths of an abiding feeling and thinking, or had he been reduced to a sort of Humean drivel, a mere succession of unrelated impressions and events?

Jimmie both was and wasn't aware of this deep, tragic loss in himself, loss *of* himself. (If a man has lost a leg or an eye, he knows he has lost a leg or an eye; but if he has lost a self—himself—he cannot know it, because he is no longer there to know it.) Therefore I could not question him intellectually about such matters.

He had originally professed bewilderment at finding himself amid patients, when, as he said, he himself didn't feel ill. But what, we wondered, did he feel? He was strongly built and fit, he had a sort of animal strength and energy, but also a strange inertia, passivity, and (as everyone remarked) 'unconcern'; he gave all of us an overwhelming sense of 'something missing,' although this, if he realised it, was itself accepted with an odd 'unconcern.' One day I asked him not about his memory, or past, but about the simplest and most elemental feelings of all:

'How do you feel?'

'How do I feel,' he repeated, and scratched his head. 'I cannot say I feel ill. But I cannot say I feel well. I cannot say I feel anything at all.'

'Are you miserable?' I continued.

'Can't say I am.'

'Do you enjoy life?'

'I can't say I do . . . '

I hesitated, fearing that I was going too far, that I might be stripping a man down to some hidden, unacknowledgeable, unbearable despair.

'You don't enjoy life,' I repeated, hesitating somewhat. 'How then *do* you feel about life?'

'I can't say that I feel anything at all.'

'You feel alive though?'

'Feel alive? Not really. I haven't felt alive for a very long time.'

His face wore a look of infinite sadness and resignation.

Later, having noted his aptitude for, and pleasure in, quick games and puzzles, and their power to 'hold' him, at least while they lasted, and to allow, for a while, a sense of companionship and competition—he had not complained of loneliness, but he looked so alone; he never expressed sadness, but he looked so sad—I suggested he be brought into our recreation programs at the Home. This worked better—better than the diary. He would become keenly and briefly involved in games, but soon they ceased to offer any challenge: he solved all the puzzles, and could solve them easily; and he was far better and sharper than anyone else at games. And as he found this out, he grew fretful and restless again, and wandered the corridors, uneasy and bored and with a sense of indignity—games and puzzles were for children, a diversion. Clearly, passionately, he wanted something to do: he wanted to do, to be, to feel—and could not; he wanted sense, he wanted purpose—in Freud's words, 'Work and Love.'

Could he do 'ordinary' work? He had 'gone to pieces,' his brother said, when he ceased to work in 1965. He had two striking skills—Morse code and touch-typing. We could not use Morse, unless we invented a use; but good typing we could use, if he could recover his old skills—and this would be real work, not just a game. Jimmie soon did recover his old skill and came to type very quickly—he could not do it slowly—and found in this some of the challenge and satisfaction of a job. But still this was superficial tapping and typing; it was trivial, it did not reach to the depths. And what he typed, he typed mechanically—he could not hold the thought—the short sentences following one another in a meaningless order.

One tended to speak of him, instinctively, as a spiritual casualty—a 'lost soul': was it possible that he had really been 'de-souled' by a disease? 'Do you think he *has* a soul?' I once asked the Sisters. They were outraged by my question, but could see why I asked it. 'Watch Jimmie in chapel,' they said, 'and judge for yourself.'

I did, and I was moved, profoundly moved and impressed, because I saw here an intensity and steadiness of attention and concentration that I had never seen before in him or conceived him capable of. I watched him kneel and take the Sacrament on his tongue, and could not doubt the fullness and totality of Communion, the perfect alignment of his spirit with the spirit of the Mass. Fully, intensely, quietly, in the quietude of absolute concentration and attention, he entered and partook of the Holy Communion. He was wholly held, absorbed, by a feeling. There was no forgetting, no Korsakov's then, nor did it seem possible or imaginable that there should be; for he was no longer at the mercy of a faulty and fallible mechanism—that of meaningless sequences and memory traces—but was absorbed in an act, an act of his whole being, which carried feeling and meaning in an organic continuity and unity, a continuity and unity so seamless it could not permit any break.

Clearly Jimmie found himself, found continuity and reality, in the absoluteness of spiritual attention and act. The sisters were right—he did find his soul here. And so was Luria, whose words now came back to me: 'A man does not consist of memory alone. He has feeling, will, sensibility, moral being . . . It is here . . . you may touch him, and see a profound change.' Memory, mental activity, mind alone, could not hold him; but moral attention and action could hold him completely.

But perhaps 'moral' was too narrow a word—for the aesthetic and dramatic were equally involved. Seeing Jim in the chapel opened my eyes to other realms where the soul is called on, and held, and stilled, in attention and communion. The same depth of absorption and attention was to be seen in relation to music and art: he had no difficulty, I noticed, 'following' music or simple dramas, for every moment in music and art refers to, contains, other moments. He liked gardening, and had taken over some of the work in our garden. At first he greeted the garden each day as new, but for some reason this had become more familiar to him than the inside of the Home. He almost never got lost or disoriented in the garden now; he patterned it, I think, on loved and remembered gardens from his youth in Connecticut.

Jimmie, who was so lost in extensional 'spatial' time, was perfectly organised in Bergsonian 'intentional' time; what was fugitive, unsustainable, as formal structure, was perfectly stable, perfectly held, as art or will. Moreover, there was something that endured and survived. If Jimmie was briefly 'held' by a task or puzzle or game or calculation, held in the purely mental challenge of these, he would fall apart as soon as they were done, into the abyss of his nothingness, his amnesia. But if he were held in emotional and spiritual attention—in the contemplation of nature or art, in listening to music, in taking part in the Mass in chapel—the attention, its 'mood,' its quietude, would persist for a while, and there would be in him a pensiveness and peace we rarely, if ever, saw during the rest of his life at the Home.

I have known Jimmie now for nine years—and neuropsychologically, he has not changed in the least. He still has the severest, most devastating Korsakov's, cannot remember isolated items for more than a few seconds, and has a dense amnesia going back to 1945. But humanly, spiritually, he is at times a different man altogether—no longer fluttering, restless, bored, and lost, but deeply attentive to the beauty and soul of the world, rich in all the Kierkegaardian categories—the aesthetic, the moral, the religious, the dramatic. I had wondered, when I first met him, if he were not condemned to a sort of 'Humean' froth, a meaningless fluttering on the surface of life, and whether there was any way of transcending the incoherence of his Humean disease. Empirical science told me there was not—but empirical science, empiricism, takes no account of the soul, no account of what constitutes and determines personal being. Perhaps there is a philosophical as well as a clinical lesson here: that in Korsakov's, or dementia, or other such catastrophes, however great the organic damage and Humean dissolution, there remains the undiminished possibility of reintegration by art, by communion, by touching the human spirit: and this can be preserved in what seems at first a hopeless state of neurological devastation.

*Postscript*

I know now that retrograde amnesia, to some degree, is very common, if not universal, in cases of Korsakov's. The classical Korsakov's syndrome—a profound and permanent, but 'pure,' devastation of memory caused by alcoholic destruction of the mammillary bodies—is rare, even among very heavy drinkers. One may, of course, see Korsakov's syndrome with other pathologies, as in Luria's patients with tumours. A particularly fascinating case of an acute (and mercifully transient) Korsakov's syndrome has been well described only very recently in the so-called Transient Global Amnesia (TGA) which may occur with migraines, head injuries or impaired blood supply to the brain. Here, for a few minutes or hours, a severe and singular amnesia may occur, even though the patient may continue to drive a car, or, perhaps, to carry on medical or editorial duties, in a mechanical way. But under this fluency lies a profound amnesia—every sentence uttered being forgotten as soon as it is said, everything forgotten within a few minutes of being seen, though long-established memories and routines may be perfectly preserved.

Further, there may be a profound retrograde amnesia in such cases. My colleague Dr. Leon Protass tells me of such a case seen by him recently, in which the patient, a highly intelligent man, was unable for some hours to remember his wife or children, to remember that he had a wife or children. In effect, he lost thirty years of his life—though, fortunately, for only a few hours. Recovery from such attacks is prompt and complete— yet they are, in a sense, the most horrifying of 'little strokes' in their power absolutely to annul or obliterate decades of richly lived, richly achieving, richly memoried life. The horror, typically, is only felt by others—the patient, unaware, amnesiac for his amnesia, may continue what he is doing, quite unconcerned, and only discover later that he lost not only a day (as is common with ordinary alcoholic 'blackouts'), but half a lifetime, and never knew it. The fact that one can lose the greater part of a lifetime has peculiar, uncanny horror.

In adulthood, life, higher life, may be brought to a premature end by strokes, senility, brain injuries, etc., but there usually remains the consciousness of life lived, of one's past. This is usually felt as a sort of compensation: 'At least I lived fully, tasting life to the full, before I was brain-injured, stricken, etc.' This sense of the life lived before, which may be either a consolation or a torment, is precisely what is taken away in retrograde amnesia. The 'final amnesia, the one that can erase a whole life' that Buñuel speaks of may occur, perhaps, in a terminal dementia, but not, in my experience, suddenly, in consequence of a stroke. But there is a different, yet comparable, sort of amnesia, which can occur suddenly— different in that it is not 'global' but 'modality-specific.'

Thus, in one patient under my care, a sudden thrombosis in the posterior circulation of the brain caused the immediate death of the visual parts of the brain. Forthwith this patient became completely blind—but did not know it. He looked blind—but he made no complaints. Questioning and testing showed, beyond doubt, that not only was he centrally or 'cortically' blind, but he had lost all visual images and memories, lost them totally—yet had no sense of any loss. Indeed, he had lost the very idea of seeing—and was not only unable to describe anything visually, but bewildered when I used words such as 'seeing' and 'light.' He had become, in essence, a non-visual being. His entire lifetime of seeing, of visuality, had, in effect, been stolen. His whole visual life had, indeed, been erased—and erased permanently in the instant of his stroke. Such a visual amnesia, and (so to speak) blindness to the blindness, amnesia for the amnesia, is in effect a 'total' Korsakov's, confined to visuality.

A still more limited, but none the less total, amnesia may be displayed with regard to particular forms of perception, as in the last chapter, 'The Man who Mistook his Wife for a Hat.' There there was an absolute 'prosopagnosia,' or agnosia for faces. This patient was not only unable to recognise faces, but unable to imagine or remember any faces—he had indeed lost the very idea of a 'face,' as my more afflicted patient had lost the very idea of 'seeing' or 'light.' Such syndromes were described by Anton in the 1890s. But the implication of these syndromes—Korsakov's and Anton's—what they entail and must entail for the world, the lives, the identities of affected patients, has been scarcely touched on even to this day.

In Jimmie's case, we had sometimes wondered how he might respond if taken back to his home town—in effect, to his pre-amnesia days—but the little town in Connecticut had become a booming city with the years. Later I did have occasion to find out what might happen in such circumstances, though this was with another patient with Korsakov's, Stephen R., who had become acutely ill in 1980 and whose retrograde amnesia went back only two years or so. With this patient, who also had severe seizures, spasticity and other problems necessitating in-patient care, rare weekend visits to his home revealed a poignant situation. In hospital he could recognise nobody and nothing, and was in an almost ceaseless frenzy of disorientation. But when his wife took him home, to his house which was in effect a 'time-capsule' of his pre-amnesia days, he felt instantly at home. He recognised everything, tapped the barometer, checked the thermostat, took his favourite armchair, as he used to do. He spoke of neighbours, shops, the local pub, a nearby cinema, as they had been in the mid-Seventies. He was distressed and puzzled if the smallest changes were made in the house. ('You changed the curtains today!' he once expostulated to his wife. 'How come? So suddenly? They were green this morning.' But they had not been green since 1978.) He recognised most of the neighbouring houses and shops—they had changed little between 1978 and 1983—but was bewildered by the 'replacement' of the cinema ('How could they tear it down and put up a supermarket *overnight?*'). He recognised friends and neighbours—but found them oddly older than he expected ('Old so-and-so! He's really showing his age. Never noticed it before. How come everyone's showing their age today?'). But the real poignancy, the horror, would occur when his wife brought him back—brought him, in a fantastic and unaccountable manner (so he felt), to a strange home he had never seen, full of strangers, and then left him. 'What are you doing?' he would scream, terrified and confused. 'What in the hell is this place? What the hell's going on?' These scenes were almost unbearable to watch, and must have seemed like madness, or nightmare, to the patient. Mercifully perhaps he would forget them within a couple of minutes.

Such patients, fossilised in the past, can only be at home, oriented, in the past. Time, for them, has come to a stop. I hear Stephen R. screaming with terror and confusion when he returns—screaming for a past which no longer exists. But what can we do? Can we create a time-capsule, a fiction? Never have I known a patient so confronted, so tormented, by anachronism, unless it was the 'Rose R.' of *Awakenings* (see 'Incontinent Nostalgia,' Chapter Fifteen).

Jimmie has reached a sort of calm; William (Chapter Twelve) continually confabulates; but Stephen has a gaping time-wound, an agony that will never heal.

## Notes

1    After writing and publishing this history I embarked with Dr. Elkhonon Goldberg—a pupil of Luria and editor of the original (Russian) edition of *The Neuropsychology of Memory*—on a close and systematic neuropsychological study of this patient. Dr. Goldberg has presented some of the preliminary findings at conferences, and we hope in due course to publish a full account.

2    In his fascinating oral history *The Good War* (1985) Studs Terkel transcribes countless stories of men and women, especially fighting men, who felt World War II as intensely real—by far the most real and significant time of their lives—and everything since as pallid in comparison. Such men tend to dwell on the war and to relive its battles, comradeship, moral certainties and intensity. But this dwelling on the past and relative hebetude towards the present—this emotional dulling of current feeling and memory—is nothing like Jimmie's organic amnesia. I recently had occasion to discuss the question

with Terkel: 'I've met thousands of men,' he told me, 'who feel they've just been "marking time" since '45—but I never met anyone for whom time terminated, like your amnesiac Jimmie.'

3  See A.R. Luria, *The Neuropsychology of Memory* (1976), pp. 250–2.

# A Matter of Identity

*Oliver Sacks*

'What'll it be today?' he says, rubbing his hands. 'Half a pound of Virginia, a nice piece of Nova?'

(Evidently he saw me as a customer—he would often pick up the phone on the ward, and say 'Thompson's Delicatessen.')

'Oh Mr. Thompson!' I exclaim, 'and who do you think I am?'

'Good heavens, the light's bad—I took you for a customer. As if it isn't my old friend Tom Pitkins . . . Me and Tom' (he whispers in an aside to the nurse) 'was always going to the races together.'

'Mr. Thompson, you are mistaken again.'

'So I am,' he rejoins, not put out for a moment. 'Why would you be wearing a white coat if you were Tom? You're Hymie, the kosher butcher next door. No bloodstains on your coat though. Business bad today? You'll look like a slaughterhouse by the end of the week!'

Feeling a bit swept away myself in this whirlpool of identities, I finger the stethoscope dangling from my neck.

'A stethoscope!' he exploded. 'And you pretending to be Hymie! You mechanics are all starting to fancy yourselves as doctors, what with your white coats and stethoscopes—as if you need a stethoscope to listen to a car! So, you're my old friend Manners from the Mobil station up the block, come in to get your boloney-and-rye . . .'

William Thompson rubbed his hands again, in his salesman-grocer's gesture, and looked for the counter. Not finding it, he looked at me strangely again.

'Where am I?' he said, with a sudden scared look. 'I thought I was in my shop, doctor. My mind must have wandered . . . You'll be wanting my shirt off, to sound me as usual?'

'No, not the usual. I'm *not* your usual doctor.'

'Indeed you're not. I could see that straightaway! You're not my usual chest-thumping doctor. And, by God, you've a beard! You look like Sigmund Freud—have I gone bonkers, round the bend?'

'No, Mr. Thompson. Not round the bend. Just a little trouble with your memory—difficulties remembering and recognising people.'

'My memory has been playing me some tricks,' he admitted. 'Sometimes I make mistakes—I take somebody for somebody else . . . What'll it be now—Nova or Virginia?'

So it would happen, with variations, every time—with improvisations, always prompt, often funny, sometimes brilliant, and ultimately tragic. Mr. Thompson would identify me—misidentify, pseudo-identify me—as a dozen different people in the course of five minutes. He would whirl, fluently, from one guess, one hypothesis, one belief, to the next, without any appearance of uncertainty at any point—he never knew who I was, or what and where *he* was, an ex-grocer, with severe Korsakov's, in a neurological institution.

He remembered nothing for more than a few seconds. He was continually disoriented. Abysses of amnesia continually opened beneath him, but he would bridge them, nimbly, by fluent confabulations and fictions of all kinds. For him they were not fictions, but how he suddenly saw, or interpreted, the world. Its radical flux and incoherence could not be tolerated, acknowledged, for an instant—there was, instead, this strange, delirious, quasi-coherence, as Mr. Thompson, with his ceaseless, unconscious, quick-fire inventions continually improvised a world around him—an Arabian Nights world, a phantasmagoria, a dream, of ever-changing people, figures, situations—continual, kaleidoscopic mutations and transformations. For Mr. Thompson, however, it was not an issue of ever-changing, evanescent fancies and illusion, but a wholly normal, stable and factual world. So far as *he* was concerned, there was nothing the matter.

On one occasion, Mr. Thompson went for a trip, identifying himself at the front desk as 'the Revd. William Thompson,' ordering a taxi, and taking off for the day. The taxi-driver, whom we later spoke to, said he had never had so fascinating a passenger, for Mr. Thompson told him one story after another, amazing personal stories full of fantastic adventures. 'He seemed to have been everywhere, done everything, met everyone. I could hardly believe so much was possible in a single life,' he said. 'It is not exactly a single life,' we answered. 'It is all very curious—a matter of identity.'[1]

Jimmie G., another Korsakov's patient, had long since *cooled down* from his acute Korsakov's syndrome, and seemed to have settled into a state of permanent lostness (or, perhaps, a permanent now-seeming dream or reminiscence of the past). But Mr. Thompson, only just out of hospital—his Korsakov's had exploded just three weeks before, when he developed a high fever, raved, and ceased to recognise all his family—was still on the boil, was still in an almost frenzied confabulatory delirium (of the sort sometimes called 'Korsakov's psychosis,' though it is not really a psychosis at all), continually creating a world and self, to replace what was continually being forgotten and lost. Such a frenzy may call forth quite brilliant powers of invention and fancy—a veritable confabulatory genius—*for such a patient must literally make himself (and his world) up every moment*. We have, each of us, a life-story, an inner narrative—whose continuity, whose sense, is our lives. It might be said that each of us constructs and lives, a 'narrative', and that this narrative *is* us, our identities.

If we wish to know about a man, we ask 'what is his story—his real, inmost story?'—for each of us is a biography, a story. Each of us *is* a singular narrative, which is constructed, continually, unconsciously, by, through, and in us—through our perceptions, our feelings, our thoughts, our actions; and, not least, our discourse, our spoken narrations. Biologically, physiologically, we are not so different from each other; historically, as narratives—we are each of us unique.

To be ourselves we must *have* ourselves—possess, if need be re-possess, our life-stories. We must 'recollect' ourselves, recollect the inner drama, the narrative, of ourselves. A man *needs* such a narrative, a continuous inner narrative, to maintain his identity, his self.

This narrative need, perhaps, is the clue to Mr. Thompson's desperate tale-telling, his verbosity. Deprived of continuity, of a quiet, continuous, inner narrative, he is driven to a sort of narrational frenzy—hence his ceaseless tales, his confabulations, his mythomania. Unable to maintain a genuine narrative or continuity, unable to maintain a genuine inner world, he is driven to the proliferation of pseudo-narratives, in a pseudo-continuity, pseudo-worlds peopled by pseudo-people, phantoms.

What is it *like* for Mr. Thompson? Superficially, he comes over as an ebullient comic. People say 'He's a riot'. And there *is* much that is farcical in such a situation, which might form the basis of a comic novel.[2] It *is* comic, but not just comic—it is terrible as well. For here is a man who, in some sense, is desperate, in a frenzy. The world keeps disappearing, losing meaning, vanishing—and he must seek meaning, *make* meaning, in a desperate way, continually inventing, throwing bridges of meaning over abysses of meaninglessness, the chaos that yawns continually beneath him.

But does Mr. Thompson himself know this, feel this? After finding him 'a riot,' 'a laugh,' 'loads of fun,' people are disquieted, even terrified, by something in him. 'He never stops,' they say. 'He's like a man in a race, a man trying to catch something which always eludes him.' And, indeed, he can never stop running, for the breach in memory, in existence, in meaning, is never healed, but has to be bridged, to be 'patched,' every second. And the bridges, the patches, for all their brilliance, fail to work—because they *are* confabulations, fictions, which cannot do service for reality, while also failing to correspond with reality. Does Mr. Thompson feel *this*? Or, again, what *is* his 'feeling of reality'? Is he in a torment all the while—the torment of a man lost in unreality, struggling to rescue himself, but sinking himself, by ceaseless inventions, illusions, themselves quite unreal? It is certain that he is not at ease—there is a tense, taut look on his face all the while, as of a man under ceaseless inner pressure; and occasionally, not too often, or masked if present, a look of open, naked, pathetic bewilderment. What saves Mr. Thompson in a sense, and in another sense damns him, *is* the forced or defensive superficiality of his life: the way in which it is, in effect, reduced to a surface, brilliant, shimmering, iridescent, ever-changing, but for all that a surface, a mass of illusions, a delirium, without depth.

And with this, no feeling *that* he has lost feeling (for the feeling he has lost), no feeling *that* he has lost the depths, that unfathomable, mysterious, myriad-levelled depth which somehow defines identity or reality. This strikes everyone who has been in contact with him for any time—that under his fluency, even his frenzy, is a strange loss of feeling—that feeling, or judgment, which distinguishes between 'real' and 'unreal,' 'true' and 'untrue' (one cannot speak of 'lies' here, only of 'non-truth'), important and trivial, relevant or irrelevant. What comes out, torrentially, in his ceaseless confabulation, has, finally, a peculiar quality of indifference . . .

as if it didn't really matter what he said, or what anyone else did or said; as if nothing really mattered any more.

A striking example of this was presented one afternoon, when William Thompson, jabbering away, of all sorts of people who were improvised on the spot, said: 'And there goes my younger brother, Bob, past the window', in the same, excited, but even and indifferent tone, as the rest of his monologue. I was dumbfounded when, a minute later, a man peeked round the door, and said: 'I'm Bob, I'm his younger brother—I think he saw me passing by the window.' Nothing in William's tone or manner— nothing in his exuberant, but unvarying and indifferent, style of monologue—had prepared me for the possibility of . . . reality. William spoke of his brother, who *was* real, in precisely the same tone, or lack of tone, in which he spoke of the unreal—and now, suddenly, out of the phantoms, a real figure appeared! Further, he did not treat his younger brother as 'real'—did not display any real emotion, was not in the least oriented or delivered from his delirium—but, on the contrary, instantly treated his brother *as* unreal, effacing him, losing him, in a further whirl of delirium—utterly different from the rare but profoundly moving times when Jimmie G. met *his* brother, and while with him was unlost. This was intensely disconcerting to poor Bob—who said 'I'm Bob, not Rob, not Dob,' to no avail whatever. In the midst of confabulations—perhaps some strand of memory, of remembered kinship, or identity, was still holding, (or came back for an instant)—William spoke of his *elder* brother, George, using his invariable present indicative tense.

'But George died nineteen years ago!' said Bob, aghast.

'Aye, George is always the joker!' William quipped, apparently ignoring, or indifferent to, Bob's comment and went on blathering of George in his excited, dead way, insensitive to truth, to reality, to propriety, to everything—insensitive too to the manifest distress of the living brother before him.

It was this which convinced me, above everything, that there was some ultimate and total loss of inner reality, of feeling and meaning, of soul, in William—and led me to ask the Sisters, as I had asked them of Jimmie G. 'Do you think William *has* a soul? Or has he been pithed, scooped-out, de-souled, by disease?'

This time, however, they looked worried by my question, as if something of the sort were already in their minds: they could not say 'Judge for yourself. See Willie in Chapel,' because his wise-cracking, his confabulations continued even there. There is an utter pathos, a sad *sense* of lostness, with Jimmie G. which one does not feel, or feel directly, with the effervescent Mr. Thompson. Jimmie has *moods*, and a sort of brooding (or, at least, yearning) sadness, a depth, a soul, which does not seem to be present in Mr. Thompson. Doubtless, as the Sisters said, he had a soul, an immortal soul, in the theological sense; could be seen, and loved, as an individual by the Almighty; but, they agreed, something very disquieting had happened to him, to his spirit, his character, in the ordinary, human sense.

It is *because* Jimmie is 'lost' that he *can* be redeemed or found, at least for a while, in the mode of a genuine emotional relation. Jimmie is in despair, a quiet despair (to use or adapt Kierkegaard's term), and therefore he has the possibility of salvation, of touching base, the ground of reality, the feeling and meaning he has lost, but still recognises, still yearns for . . .

But for William—with his brilliant, brassy surface, the unending joke which he substitutes for the world (which if it covers over a desperation, is a desperation he does not feel); for William with his manifest indifference to relation and reality caught in an unending verbosity, there may be nothing 'redeeming' at all—his confabulations, his apparitions, his frantic search for meanings, being the ultimate barrier *to* any meaning.

Paradoxically, then, William's great gift—for confabulation—which has been called out to leap continually over the ever-opening abyss of amnesia—William's great gift is also his damnation. If only he could be *quiet*, one feels, for an instant; if only he could stop the ceaseless chatter and jabber; if only he could relinquish the deceiving surface of illusions—then (ah then!) reality might seep in; something genuine, something deep, something true, something felt, could enter his soul.

For it is not memory which is the final, 'existential' casualty here (although his memory is wholly devastated); it is not memory only which has been so altered in him, but some ultimate capacity for feeling which is gone; and this is the sense in which he is 'de-souled.'

Luria speaks of such indifference as 'equalisation'—and sometimes seems to see it as the ultimate pathology, the final destroyer of any world, any self. It exerted, I think, a horrified fascination on him, as well as constituting an ultimate therapeutic challenge. He was drawn back to this theme again and again—sometimes in relation to Korsakov's and memory, as in *The Neuropsychology of Memory*, more often in relation to frontal-lobe syndromes, especially in *Human Brain and Psychological Processes*, which contains several full-length case-histories of such patients, fully comparable in their terrible coherence and impact to 'the man with a shattered world,—comparable, and, in a way, more terrible still, because they depict patients who do not realise that anything has befallen them, patients who have lost their own reality, without knowing it, patients who may not suffer, but be the most God-forsaken of all. Zazetsky (in *The Man with a Shattered World*) is constantly described as a *fighter*, always (even passionately) conscious of his state, and always fighting 'with the tenacity of the damned' to recover the use of his damaged brain. But William (like Luria's frontal-lobe patients) is so damned he does not know he is damned, for it is not just a faculty, or some faculties, which are damaged, but the very citadel, the self, the soul itself. William is 'lost,' in this sense, far more than Jimmie—for all his brio; one never feels, or rarely feels, that there is a *person* remaining, whereas in Jimmie there is plainly a real, moral being, even if disconnected most of the time. In Jimmie, at least, re-connection is *possible*—the therapeutic challenge can be summed up as 'Only connect.'

Our efforts to 're-connect' William all fail—even increase his confabulatory pressure. But when we abdicate our efforts, and let him be, he sometimes wanders out into the quiet and undemanding garden which surrounds the Home, and there, in his quietness, he recovers his own quiet. The presence of others, other people, excite and rattle him, force him into an endless, frenzied, social chatter, a veritable delirium of identity-making and -seeking; the presence of plants, a quiet garden, the non-human order, making no social or human demands upon him, allow this identity-delirium to relax, to subside; and by their quiet, non-human self-sufficiency and completeness allow him a rare quietness and self-sufficiency of his own, by offering (beneath, or beyond, all merely human identities and relations) a deep wordless communion with Nature itself, and with this the restored sense of being in the world, being real.

## Notes

1     A very similar story is related by Luria in *The Neurospychology of Memory* (1976), in which the spell-bound cabdriver only realised that his exotic passenger was ill when he gave him, for a fare, a temperature chart he was holding. Only then did he realise that this Scheherazade, this spinner of 1001 tales, was one of those strange patients' at the Neurological Institute.

2    Indeed such a novel has been written. Shortly after 'The Lost Mariner' (Chapter Two) was published, a young writer named David Gilman sent me the manuscript of his book *Croppy Boy*, the story of an amnesiac like Mr. Thompson, who enjoys the wild and unbridled license of creating identities, new selves, as he whims, and as he must—an astonishing imagination of an amnesiac genius, told with positively Joycean richness and gusto. I do not know whether it has been published; I am very sure it should be. I could not help wondering whether Mr. Gilman had actually met (and studied) a 'Thompson'—as I have often wondered whether Borges' 'Funes,' so uncannily similar to Luria's Mnemonist, may have been based on a personal encounter with such a mnemonist.

# *from* Time Travel

## Martin Gardner

*Martin Gardner is an American science writer. Born in 1914, he is well known for his science columns, philosophical essays and math puzzles. He currently lives in North Carolina.*

*"It's against reason," said Filby.*
*"What reason?" said the Time Traveller.*

—*H.G. Wells*, The Time Machine

H. G. Wells's short novel *The Time Machine*, an undisputed master-piece of science fiction, was not the first story about a time machine. That distinction belongs to "The Clock That Went Backward," a pioneering but mediocre yarn by Edward Page Mitchell, an editor of the New York *Sun*. It was published anonymously in the *Sun* on September 18, 1881, seven years before young Wells (he was only 22) wrote the first version of his famous story.

Mitchell's tale was so quickly forgotten that science-fiction buffs did not even know of its existence until Sam Moskowitz reprinted it in his anthology of Mitchell's stories, *The Crystal Man* (1973). Nor did anyone pay much attention to Wells's fantasy when it was serialized in 1888 in *The Science Schools Journal* under the horrendous title "The Chronic Argonauts." Wells himself was so ashamed of this clumsily written tale that he broke it off after three installments and later destroyed all the copies he could find. A completely rewritten version, "The Time Traveller's Story," was serialized in *The New Review* beginning in 1894. When it came out as a book in 1895, it brought Wells instant recognition.

One of the many remarkable aspects of Wells's novella is the introduction in which the Time Traveller (his name is not revealed, but in Wells's first version he is called Dr. Nebo-gipfel) explains the theory behind his invention. Time is a fourth dimension. An instantaneous cube cannot exist. The cube we see is at each instant a cross section of a "fixed and unalterable" four-dimensional cube having length, breadth, thickness, and duration. "There is no difference between Time and any of the three dimensions of

Space," says the Time Traveller, "except that our consciousness moves along it." If we could view a person from outside our space-time (the way human history is viewed by the Eternals in Isaac Asimov's *The End of Eternity* or by the Tralfamadorians in Kurt Vonnegut's *Slaughterhouse-Five*), we would see that person's past, present, and future all at once, just as in 3-space we see all parts of a wavy line that traces on a time chart the one-dimensional spatial movements of mercury in a barometer.

Reading these remarks today, one might suppose that Wells had been familiar with Hermann Minkowski's great work of tidying up Einstein's special theory of relativity. The line along which our consciousness crawls is, of course, our "world line": the line that traces our movements in 3-space on a four-dimensional Minkowski space-time graph. (*My World Line* is the title of George Gamow's autobiography.) But Wells's story appeared in its final form ten years before Einstein published his first paper on relativity!

When Wells wrote his story, he regarded the Time Traveller's theories as little more than metaphysical hanky-panky designed to make his fantasy more plausible. A few decades later physicists were taking such hanky-panky with the utmost seriousness. The notion of an absolute cosmic time, with absolute simultaneity between distant events, was swept out of physics by Einstein's equations. Virtually all physicists now agree that if an astronaut were to travel to a distant star and back, moving at a velocity close to that of light, he could in theory travel thousands of years into the earth's future. Kurt Gödel constructed a rotating cosmological model in which one can, in principle, travel to any point in the world's past as well as future, although travel to the past is ruled out as physically impossible. In 1965 Richard P. Feynman received a Nobel prize for his space-time approach to quantum mechanics in which antiparticles are viewed as particles momentarily moving into the past.

Hundreds of science-fiction stories have been written about time travel, many of them raising questions about time and causality that are as profound as they are sometimes funny. To give the most hackneyed example, suppose you traveled back to last month and shot yourself through the head. Not only do you know before making the trip that nothing like this happened but, assuming that somehow you could murder your earlier self, how could you exist next month to make the trip? Fredric Brown's "First Time Machine" opens with Dr. Grainger exhibiting his machine to three friends. One of them uses the device to go back sixty years and kill his hated grandfather when the man was a youth. The story ends sixty years later with Dr. Grainger showing his time machine to two friends.

It must not be thought that logical contradictions arise only when people travel in time. The transportation of anything can lead to paradox. There is a hint of this in Wells's story. When the Time Traveller sends a small model of his machine into the past or the future (he does not know which), his guests raise two objections. If the time machine went into the future, why do they not see it now, moving along its world line? If it went into the past, why did they not see it there before the Time Traveller brought it into the room?

One of the guests suggests that perhaps the model moves so fast in time it becomes invisible, like the spokes of a rotating wheel. But what if a time-traveling object stops moving? If you have no memory of a cube on the table Monday, how could you send it back to Monday's table on Tuesday? And if on Tuesday you go into the future, put the cube on the table Wednesday, then return to Tuesday, what happens on Wednesday if on Tuesday you destroy the cube?

Objects carried back and forth in time are sources of endless confusion in certain science-fiction tales. Sam Mines once summarized the plot of his own story, "Find the Sculptor," as follows: "A scientist builds a time machine, goes 500 years into the future. He finds a statue of himself commemorating the first time traveler. He brings it back to his own time and it is subsequently set up in his honor. You see the catch here? It had to be set up in his own time so that it would be there waiting for him when he went into the future to find it. He had to go into the future to bring it back so it could be set up in his own time. Somewhere a piece of the cycle is missing. When was the statue made?"

A splendid example of how paradox arises, even when nothing more than messages go back in time, is provided by the conjecture that tachyons, particles moving faster than light, might actually exist. Relativity theory leaves no escape from the fact that anything moving faster than light would move backward in time. This is what inspired A. H. Reginald Buller, a Canadian botanist, to write his often quoted limerick:

> *There was a young lady named Bright*
> *Who traveled much faster than light.*
> *She started one day*

> *In the relative way,*
> *And returned on the previous night.*

Tachyons, if they exist, clearly cannot be used for communication. G. A. Benford, D. L. Book, and W. A. Newcomb (of "Newcomb's paradox," the topic of two chapters in my *Knotted Doughnuts and Other Mathematical Entertainments*, W. H. Freeman and Company, 1986), have chided physicists who are searching for tachyons for overlooking this. In "The Tachyonic Antitelephone," they point out that certain methods of looking for tachyons are based on interactions that make possible, in theory, communication by tachyons. Suppose physicist Jones on the earth is in communication by tachyonic antitelephones with physicist Alpha in another galaxy. They make the following agreement. When Alpha receives a message from Jones, he will reply immediately. Jones promises to send a message to Alpha at three o'clock earth time, if and only if he has not received a message from Alpha by one o'clock. Do you see the difficulty? Both messages go back in time. If Jones sends his message at three, Alpha's reply could reach him before one. "Then," as the authors put it, "the exchange of messages will take place if and only if it does not take place . . . a genuine . . . causal contradiction." Large sums of money have already gone down the drain, the authors believe, in efforts to detect tachyons by methods that imply tachyonic communication and are therefore doomed to failure.

Time dilation in relativity theory, time travel in Gödel's cosmos, and reversed time in Feynman's way of viewing antiparticles are so carefully hedged by other laws that contradictions cannot arise. In most time-travel stories the paradoxes are skirted by leaving out any incident that would generate a paradox. In some stories, however, logical contradictions explicitly arise. When they do, the author may leave them paradoxical to bend the reader's mind or may try to escape from paradox by making clever assumptions.

Before discussing ways of avoiding the paradoxes, brief mention should be made of what might be called pseudo-time-travel stories in which there is no possibility of contradiction. There can be no paradox, for example, if one simply observes the past but does not interact with it. The electronic machine in Eric Temple Bell's "Before the Dawn," which extracts motion pictures of the past from imprints left by light on ancient rocks, is as free of possible paradox as watching a video tape of an old television show. And paradox cannot arise if a person travels into the future by going into suspended animation, like Rip van Winkle, or Woody Allen in his motion picture *Sleeper*, or the sleepers in such novels as Edward Bellamy's *Looking Backward* or Wells's *When the Sleeper Wakes*. No paradox can arise if one dreams of the past (as in Mark Twain's *A Connecticut Yankee at King Arthur's Court*, or in the 1986 motion picture *Peggy Sue Got Married*), or goes forward in a reincarnation, or lives for a while in a galaxy where change is so slow in relation to earth time that when he returns, centuries on the earth have gone by. But when someone actually travels to the past or the future, interacts with it and returns, enormous difficulties arise.

In certain restricted situations paradox can be avoided by invoking Minkowski's "block universe," in which all history is frozen, as it were, by one monstrous space-time graph on which all world lines are eternal and unalterable. From this deterministic point of view one can allow certain kinds of time travel in either direction, although one must pay a heavy price for it. Hans Reichenbach, in a muddled discussion in *The Philosophy of Space and Time* (Dover, 1957, pp. 140–142), puts it this way: Is it possible for a person's world line to "loop" in the sense that it returns him to a spot in space-time, a spot very close to where he once had been and where some kind of interaction, such as speech, occurs between the two meeting selves? Reichenbach argues that this cannot be ruled out on logical grounds; it can only be ruled out on the ground that we would have to give up two axioms that are strongly confirmed by experience: (1) A person is a unique individual who maintains his identity as he ages, and (2) a person's world line is linearly ordered so that what he considers "now" is always a unique spot along the line. (Reichenbach does not mention it, but we would also have to abandon any notion of free will.) If we are willing to give up these things, says Reichenbach, we can imagine without paradox certain kinds of loops in a person's world line.

Reichenbach's example of a consistent loop is as follows. One day you meet a man who looks exactly like you but who is older. He tells you he is your older self who has traveled back in time. You think him insane and walk on. Years later you discover how to go back in time. You visit your younger self. You are compelled to tell him exactly what your older duplicate had told you when you were younger. Of course, he thinks that you are insane. You separate. Each of you leads a normal life until the day comes when your younger self makes the trip back in time.

Hilary Putnam, in "It Ain't Necessarily So," argues in similar fashion that such world-line loops need not be contradictory. He draws a Feynman graph (See Figure 1) on which particle pair-production and pair-annihilation are replaced by person pair-production and pair-annihilation. The zigzag line is the world line of time traveler Smith. At time $t_2$ he goes back to $t_1$, converses with his younger self, then continues to lead a normal life. How would this be observed by someone whose world line is normal? Simply put a ruler at the bottom of the chart, its edge parallel to the space axis, and move it slowly upward. At $t_0$ you see young Smith. At $t_1$ an older Smith suddenly materializes out of thin air in the same room along with an anti-Smith, who is seated in his time machine and living backward. (If he is smoking, you see his cigarette butt lengthen into a whole cigarette, and so on.) Perhaps the two forward Smiths converse. Finally, at $t_2$, young Smith, backward Smith, and the backward-moving time machine vanish. The older Smith and his older time machine continue on their way. The fact that we can draw a space-time diagram of these events, Putnam insists, is proof that they are logically consistent.

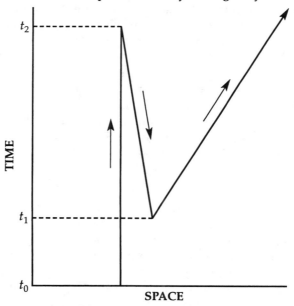

FIGURE 1 Feynman graph for a time traveler to the past.

It is true that they are consistent, but note that Putnam's scenario, like Reichenbach's, involves such weak interaction between the Smiths that it evades the deeper contradictions that arise in time-travel fiction. What happens if the older Smith kills the younger Smith? Will Putnam kindly supply a Feynman graph?

There is only one good way out, and science-fiction scribblers have been using it for more than half a century. According to Sam Moskowitz, the device was first explicitly employed to resolve time-travel paradoxes by David R. Daniels in "Branches of Time," a tale that appeared in *Wonder Stories* in 1934. The basic idea is as simple as it is fantastic. Persons can travel to any point in the future of their universe, with no complications, but the moment they enter the past, the universe splits into two parallel worlds, each with its own time track. Along one track rolls the world as if no looping had occurred. Along the other track spins the newly created universe, its history permanently altered. When I say "newly created," I speak, of course, from the standpoint of the time traveler's consciousness. For an observer in, say, a fifth dimension the traveler's world line simply switches from one space-time continuum to another on a graph that depicts all the universes branching like a tree in a metauniverse.

Forking time paths appear in many plays, novels, and short stories by non-science-fiction writers. J. B. Priestley uses it in his popular play *Dangerous Corner*, as Lord Dunsany had done earlier in his play If: Mark Twain discusses it in *The Mysterious Stranger*. Jorge Luis Borges plays with it in his "Garden of Forking Paths." But it was the science-fiction writers who sharpened and elaborated the concept.

Let us see how it works. Suppose you go back to the time of Napoleon in Universe 1 and assassinate him. The world forks. You are now in Universe 2. If you like, you can return to the present of Universe 2, a universe in which Napoleon had been mysteriously murdered. How much would this world differ from the old one? Would you find a duplicate of yourself there? Maybe.

Maybe not. Some stories assume that the slightest alteration of the past would introduce new causal chains that would have a multiplying effect and produce vast historical changes. Other tales assume that history is dominated by such powerful overall forces that even major alterations of the past would damp out and the future would soon be very much the same.

In Ray Bradbury's "A Sound of Thunder," Eckels travels back to an ancient geological epoch under elaborate precautions to prevent any serious alteration of the past. For example, he wears an oxygen mask to prevent his microbes from contaminating animal life. But Eckels violates a prohibition and accidentally steps on a living butterfly. When he returns to the present, he notices subtle changes in the office of the firm that arranged his trip. He is killed for having illegally altered the future.

Hundreds of other stories by fantasy and science-fiction writers have played variations on this theme. One of the saddest is Lord Dunsany's "Lost" (in *The Fourth Book of Jorkens*, 1948). A man travels to his past, by way of an Oriental charm, to right some old mistakes. Of course, this alters history. When he gets back to the present, he is missing his wife and home. "Lost! Lost!" he cries. "Don't go back down the years trying to alter anything. Don't even wish to. . . . And, mind you, the whole length of the Milky Way is more easily traveled than time, amongst whose terrible ages I am lost."

It is easy to see that in such a metacosmos of branching time paths, it is not possible to generate paradox. The future is no problem. If you travel to next week, you merely vanish for a week and reappear in the future a week younger than you would have been. But if you go back and murder yourself in your crib, the universe obligingly splits. Universe 1 goes on as before, with you vanishing from it when you grow up and make the trip back. Perhaps this happens repeatedly, each cycle creating two new worlds. Perhaps it happens only once. Who knows? In any case, Universe 2 with you and the dead baby in it rolls on. You are not annihilated by your deed, because now you are an alien from Universe 1 living in Universe 2.

In such a metacosmos it is easy (as many science-fiction writers have done) to fabricate duplicates of yourself. You can go back a year in Universe 1, live for a year with yourself in Universe 2, then again go back a year to visit two replicas of yourself in Universe 3. Clearly, by repeating such loops you can create as many replicas of yourself as you please. They are genuine replicas, not pseudo-replicas as in the scenarios by Reichenbach and Putnam. Each has his independent world line. History might become extremely chaotic, but there is one type of event that can never occur: a logically contradictory one.

This vision of a metacosmos containing branching worlds may seem crazy, but respectable physicists have taken it quite seriously. In Hugh

Everett III's Ph.D. thesis "'Relative State' Formulation of Quantum Mechanics" (*Reviews of Modern Physics* 29, July 1957, pp. 454–462) he outlines a metatheory in which the universe at every micromicroinstant branches into countless parallel worlds, each a possible combination of microevents that could occur as a result of microlevel uncertainty. The paper is followed by John A. Wheeler's favorable assessment in which he points out that classical physicists were almost as uncomfortable at first with the radical notions of general relativity.

"If there are infinite universes," wrote Fredric Brown in *What Mad Universe*, "then all possible combinations must exist. Then, somewhere, *everything must be true*. . . . There is a universe in which Huckleberry Finn is a real person, doing the exact things Mark Twain described him as doing. There are, in fact, an infinite number of universes in which a Huckleberry Finn is doing every possible variation of what Mark Twain might have described him as doing. . . . And infinite universes in which the states of existence are such that we would have no words or thoughts to describe them or to imagine them."

What if the universe never forks? Suppose there is only one world, this one, in which all world lines are linearly ordered and objects preserve their identity, come what may. Brown considers this possibility in his story "Experiment." Professor Johnson holds a brass cube in his hand. It is six minutes to three o'clock. At exactly three, he tells his colleagues, he will place the cube on his time machine's platform and send it five minutes into the past.

"Therefore," he remarks, "the cube should, at five minutes before three, vanish from my hand and appear on the platform, five minutes before I place it there."

"How can you place it there, then?" asked one of his colleagues.

"It will, as my hand approaches, vanish from the platform and appear in my hand to be placed there."

At five minutes to three the cube vanishes from Professor Johnson's hand and appears on the platform, having been sent back five minutes in time by his future action of placing the cube on the platform at three.

"See? Five minutes before I shall place it there, it is there!"

"But," says a frowning colleague, "what if, now that it has already appeared five minutes before you place it there, you should change your mind about doing so and not place it there at three o'clock? Wouldn't there be a paradox of some sort involved?"

Professor Johnson thinks this is an interesting idea. To see what happens, he does not put the cube on the platform at three.

There is no paradox. The cube remains. But the entire universe, including Professor Johnson, his colleagues, and the time machine, disappears.

## Addendum

J. A. Lindon, a British writer of comic verse, sent me his sequel to the limerick about Miss Bright:

> When they questioned her, answered Miss Bright,
> "I was there when I got home that night;
>      So I slept with myself,
>      Like two shoes on a shelf,
> Put-up relatives shouldn't be tight!"

Ned Block wrote to say he had heard the following blue version from a student at M.I.T.:

> There was a young couple named Bright
> Who could make love much faster than light.
>      They started one day
>      In the relative way,
> And came on the previous night.

Many readers called attention to two difficulties that could arise from time travel in either direction. If travelers stay at the same spot in space-time, relative to the universe, the earth would no longer be where it was. They might find themselves in empty space, or inside something solid. In the latter case, would the solid body prevent them from arriving? Would one or the other be shoved aside? Would there be an explosion?

The second difficulty is thermodynamic. After the time traveler departs, the universe will have lost a bit of mass-energy. When he arrives, the universe gains back the same amount. During the interval between leaving and arriving, the universe would seem to be violating the law of mass-energy conservation.

I mentioned briefly what is now called the "many-worlds interpretation" of QM (quantum mechanics). The best reference is a 1973 collection of papers on the topic, edited by Bryce DeWitt and Neill Graham. Assuming that the universe constantly splits into billions of parallel worlds, the interpretation provides an escape from the indeterminism of the Copenhagen interpretation of QM, as well as from the many paradoxes that plague it.

Some physicists who favor the many-worlds interpretation have argued that the countless duplicate selves and parallel worlds produced by the forking paths are not "real," but only artifacts of the theory. In this interpretation of the many-worlds interpretation, the theory collapses into no more than a bizarre way of saying the same things that are said in the Copenhagen interpretation. Everett himself, in his original 1957 thesis, added in proof this famous footnote:

> In reply to a preprint of this article some correspondents have raised the question of the "transition from possible to actual," arguing that in "reality," there is—as our experience testifies—no such splitting of observer states, so that only one branch can ever actually exist. Since this point may occur to other readers the following is offered in explanation.

> The whole issue of the transition from "possible" to "actual" is taken care of in the theory in a very simple way—there is no such transition, nor is such a transition necessary for the theory to be in accord with our experience. From the viewpoint of the theory all elements of a superposition (all "branches") are "actual," none any more "real" than the rest. It is unnecessary to suppose that all but one are somehow destroyed, since all the separate elements of a superposition individually obey the wave equation with complete indifference to the presence or absence ("actuality" or not) of any other elements. This total lack of effect of one branch on another also implies that no observer will ever be aware of any "splitting" process.

> Arguments that the world picture presented by this theory is contradicted by experience, because we are unaware of any branching process, are like the criticism of the Copernican theory that the mobility of the earth as a real physical fact is incompatible with the common sense interpretation of nature because we feel no such motion. In both cases the argument fails when it is shown that the theory itself predicts that our experience will be what it in fact is. (In the Copernican case the addition of Newtonian physics was required to be able to show that the earth's inhabitants would be unaware of any motion of the earth.)

The many-worlds interpretation has been called a beautiful theory nobody can believe. Nevertheless, a number of top physicists have indeed accepted—some still do—its outrageous multiplicity of logically possible worlds. Here is DeWitt defending it in "Quantum Mechanics and Reality," a 1970 article reprinted in the collection he edited with Graham:

> The obstacle to taking such a lofty view of things, of course, is that it forces us to believe in the reality of all the simultaneous worlds . . . in each of which the measurement has yielded a different outcome. Nevertheless, this is precisely what [the inventors of the theory] would have us believe. . . . This universe is constantly splitting into a stupendous number of branches, all resulting from the measurementlike interactions between its myriads of components. Moreover, every quantum transition taking place on every star, in every galaxy, in every remote corner of the universe is splitting our local world on earth into myriads of copies of itself.

> I still recall vividly the shock I experienced on first encountering this multi-world concept. The idea of $10^{100+}$ slightly imperfect copies of oneself all constantly splitting into further copies, which ultimately become unrecognizable, is not easy to reconcile with commonsense.

Although John Wheeler originally supported the many-worlds interpretation, he has since abandoned it. I quote from the first chapter of his *Frontiers of Time* (Center for Theoretical Physics, 1978):

> Imaginative Everett's thesis is, and instructive, we agree. We once subscribed to it. In retrospect, however, it looks like the wrong track. First, this formulation of quantum mechanics denigrates the quantum. It denies from the start that the quantum character of nature is any clue to the plan of physics. Take this Hamiltonian for the world, that Hamiltonian, or any other Hamiltonian, this formulation says. I am a principle too lordly to care which, or why there should be any Hamiltonian at all. You give me whatever world you please, and in return I give you back many worlds. Don't look to me for help in understanding this universe.

> Second, its infinitely many unobservable worlds make a heavy load of metaphysical baggage. They would seem to defy Mendeleev's demand of any proper scientific theory, that it should "expose itself to destruction."

> Wigner, Weizsacker, and Wheeler have made objections in more detail, but also in quite contrasting terms, to the relative-state or many-worlds interpretation of quantum mechanics. It is hard to name anyone who conceives of it as a way to uphold determinism.

In the paper titled "Rotating Cylinders and the Possibility of Global Causality Violation," physicist Frank Tipler raised the theoretical possibility of constructing a machine that would enable one to go forward or backward in time. (Tipler is one of the few remaining enthusiasts for the many-worlds interpretation, and the coauthor of a controversial book, *The Anthropic Cosmological Principle*, Oxford University Press, 1986). Taking off from Gödel's rotating cosmos and from recent work on the space-time pathologies surrounding black holes, Tipler imagines a massive cylinder, infinitely long, and rotating so rapidly that its surface moves faster than half the speed of light. Space-time near the cylinder would be so distorted that, according to Tipler's calculations, astronauts could orbit the cylinder, going with or against its spin, and travel into their past or future.

Tipler speculated on the possibility that such a machine could be built with a cylinder of finite length and mass, but later concluded that such a device was impossible to construct with any known forms of matter and force. Such doubts did not inhibit Poul Anderson from using Tipler's cylinder for time travel in his novel *The Avatar*, nor did it stop Robert Forward from writing "How to Build a Time Machine" (*Omni*, May 1980). "We already know the theory," *Omni* editors commented above Forward's backward article, "All that's needed is some advanced engineering."

I close with two pearls of wisdom from the stand-up comic "Professor" Irwin Corey: "The past is behind us, and the future lies ahead."

# A Sound of Thunder

### Ray Bradbury

*Ray Bradbury, an American science fiction writer, was born in 1920. The author of numerous novels, plays, and short stories, he is best known for* Fahrenheit 451 *and the* Martian Chronicles. *His themes include small town life and the perils of conformity.*

The sign on the wall seemed to quaver under a film of sliding warm water. Eckels felt his eyelids blink over his stare, and the sign burned in this momentary darkness:

> TIME SAFARI, INC.
> SAFARIS TO ANY YEAR IN THE PAST.
> YOU NAME THE ANIMAL.
> WE TAKE YOU THERE.
> YOU SHOOT IT.

A warm phlegm gathered in Eckels' throat; he swallowed and pushed it down. The muscles around his mouth formed a smile as he put his hand slowly out upon the air, and in that hand waved a check for ten thousand dollars to the man behind the desk.

"Does this safari guarantee I come back alive?"

"We guarantee nothing," said the official, "except the dinosaurs." He turned. "This is Mr. Travis, your Safari Guide in the Past. He'll tell you what and where to shoot. If he says no shooting, no shooting. If you disobey instructions, there's a stiff penalty of another ten thousand dollars, plus possible government action, on your return."

Eckels glanced across the vast office at a mass and tangle, a snaking and humming of wires and steel boxes, at an aurora that flickered now orange, now silver, now blue. There was a sound like a gigantic bonfire burning all of Time, all the years and all the parchment calendars, all the hours piled high and set aflame.

A touch of the hand and this burning would, on the instant, beautifully reverse itself. Eckels remembered the wording in the advertisements to

796

the letter. Out of chars and ashes, out of dust and coals, like golden sala-manders, the old years, the green years, might leap; roses sweeten the air, white hair turn Irish-black, wrinkles vanish; all, everything fly back to seed, flee death, rush down to their beginnings, suns rise in western skies and set in glorious casts, moons eat themselves opposite to the custom, all and everything cupping one in another like Chinese boxes, rabbits into hats, all and everything returning to the fresh death, the seed death, the green death, to the time before the beginning. A touch of-a hand might do it, the merest touch of a hand.

"Unbelievable." Eckels breathed, the light of the Machine on his thin face. "A real Time Machine." He shook his head. "Makes you think. If the election had gone badly yesterday, I might be here now running away from the results. Thank God Keith won. He'll make a fine President of the United States."

"Yes," said the man behind the desk. "We're lucky. If Deutscher had gotten in, we'd have the worst kind of dictatorship. There's an anti-everything man for you, a militarist, anti-Christ, anti-human, anti-intellectual. People called us up, you know, joking but not joking. Said if Deutscher became President they wanted to go live in 1492. Of course it's not our business to conduct Escapes, but to form Safaris. Anyway, Keith's President now. All you got to worry about is—"

"Shooting my dinosaur," Eckels finished it for him.

"A *Tyrannosaurus rex*. The Tyrant Lizard, the most incredible monster in history. Sign this release. Anything happens to you, we're not responsible. Those dinosaurs are hungry."

Eckels flushed angrily. "Trying to scare me!"

"Frankly, yes. We don't want anyone going who'll panic at the first shot. Six Safari leaders were killed last year, and a dozen hunters. We're here to give you the severest thrill a *real* hunter ever asked for. Traveling you back sixty million years to bag the biggest game in all of Time. Your personal check's still there. Tear it up."

Mr. Eckels looked at the check. His fingers twitched.

"Good luck," said the man behind the desk. "Mr. Travis, he's all yours."

They moved silently across the room, taking their guns with them, toward the Machine, toward the silver metal and the roaring light.

First a day and then a night and then a day and then a night, then it was day-night-day-night-day. A week, a month, a year, a decade! A.D. 2055. A.D. 2019. 1999! 1957! Gone!

The Machine roared.

They put on their oxygen helmets and tested the intercoms.

Eckels swayed on the padded seat, his face pale, his jaw stiff. He felt the trembling in his arms and he looked down and found his hands tight on the new rifle. There were four other men in the Machine. Travis, the Safari Leader, his assistant, Lesperance, and two other hunters, Billings and Kramer. They sat looking at each other, and the years blazed around them.

"Can these guns get a dinosaur cold?" Eckels felt his mouth saying.

"If you hit them right," said Travis on the helmet radio. "Some dinosaurs have two brains, one in the head, another far down the spinal column. We stay away from those. That's stretching luck. Put your first two shots into the eyes, if you can, blind them, and go back into the brain."

The Machine howled. Time was a film run backward. Suns fled and ten million moons fled after them. "Think," said Eckels. "Every hunter that ever lived would envy us today. This makes Africa seem like Illinois."

The Machine slowed; its scream fell to a murmur. The Machine stopped.

The sun stopped in the sky.

The fog that had enveloped the Machine blew away and they were in an old time, a very old time indeed, three hunters and two Safari Heads with their blue metal guns across their knees.

"Christ isn't born yet," said Travis. "Moses has not gone to the mountain to talk with God. The Pyramids are still in the earth, waiting to be cut out and put up. *Remember* that. Alexander, Caesar, Napoleon, Hitler—none of them exists."

The man nodded.

"That"—Mr. Travis pointed—"is the jungle of sixty million two thousand and fifty-five years before President Keith."

He indicated a metal path that struck off into green wilderness, over streaming swamp, among giant ferns and palms.

"And that," he said, "is the Path, laid by Time Safari for your use. It floats six inches above the earth. Doesn't touch so much as one grass blade, flower, or tree. It's an antigravity metal. Its purpose is to keep you from touching this world of the past in any way. Stay on the Path. Don't go off it. I repeat. *Don't go off.* For *any* reason! If you fall off, there's a penalty. And don't shoot any animal we don't okay."

"Why?" asked Eckels.

They sat in the ancient wilderness. Far birds' cries blew on a wind, and the smell of tar and an old salt sea, moist grasses, and flowers the color of blood.

"We don't want to change the Future. We don't belong here in the Past. The government doesn't *like* us here. We have to pay big graft to keep our franchise. A Time Machine is finicky business. Not knowing it, we might kill an important animal, a small bird, a roach, a flower even, thus destroying an important link in a growing species."

"That's not clear," said Eckels.

"All right," Travis continued, "say we accidentally kill one mouse here. That means all the future families of this one particular mouse are destroyed, right?"

"Right."

"And all the families of the families of the families of that one mouse! With a stamp of your foot, you annihilate first one, then a dozen, then a thousand, a million, a *billion* possible mice!"

"So they're dead," said Eckels. "So what?"

"So what?" Travis snorted quietly. "Well, what about the foxes that'll need those mice to survive? For want of ten mice, a fox dies. For want of ten foxes, a lion starves. For want of a lion, all manner of insects, vultures, infinite billions of life forms are thrown into chaos and destruction. Eventually it all boils down to this: fifty-nine million years later, a caveman, one of a dozen on the *entire world*, goes hunting wild boar or saber-toothed tiger for food. But you, friend, have *stepped* on all the tigers in that region. By stepping on *one* single mouse. So the caveman starves. And the caveman, please note, is not just *any* expendable man, no! He is an *entire future nation*. From his loins would have sprung ten sons. From *their* loins one hundred sons, and thus onward to a civilization. Destroy this one man, and you destroy a race, a people, an entire history of life. It is comparable to slaying some of Adam's grandchildren. The stomp of your foot, on one mouse, could start an earthquake, the effects of which could shake our earth and destinies down through Time, to their very foundations. With the death of that one caveman, a billion others yet unborn are throttled in the womb. Perhaps Rome never rises on its seven hills. Perhaps Europe is forever a dark forest, and only Asia waxes healthy and teeming. Step on a mouse and you crush the Pyramids. Step on a mouse and you leave your print, like a Grand Canyon, across Eternity. Queen Elizabeth might never be born, Washington might not cross the Delaware, there might never be a United States at all. So be careful. Stay on the Path. *Never* step off!"

"I see," said Eckels. "Then it wouldn't pay for us even to touch the *grass*?"

"Correct. Crushing certain plants could add up infinitesimally. A little error here would multiply in sixty million years, all out of proportion. Of course maybe our theory is wrong. Maybe Time can't be changed by us. Or maybe it can be changed only in little subtle ways. A dead mouse here makes an insect imbalance there, a population disproportion later, a bad harvest further on, a depression, mass starvation, and, finally, a change in social temperament in farflung countries. Something much more subtle, like that. Perhaps only a soft breath, a whisper, a hair, pollen on the air, such a slight, slight change that unless you looked close you wouldn't see it. Who knows? Who really can say he knows? We don't know. We're guessing. But until we do know for certain whether our messing around in Time *can* make a big roar or a little rustle in history, we're being careful. This Machine, this Path, your clothing and bodies, were sterilized, as you know, before the journey. We wear these oxygen helmets so we can't introduce our bacteria into an ancient atmosphere."

"How do we know which animals to shoot?"

"They're marked with red paint," said Travis. "Today, before our journey, we sent Lesperance here back with the Machine. He came to this particular era and followed certain animals."

"Studying them?"

"Right," said Lesperance. "I track them through their entire existence, noting which of them lives longest. Very few. How many times they mate. Not often. Life's short. When I find one that's going to die when a tree falls on him, or one that drowns in a tar pit, I note the exact hour, minute, and second. I shoot a paint bomb. It leaves a red patch on his side. We can't miss it. Then I correlate our arrival in the Past so that we meet the Monster not more than two minutes before he would have died anyway. This way, we kill only animals with no future, that are never going to mate again. You see how *careful* we are?"

"But if you came back this morning in Time," said Eckels eagerly, "you must've bumped into us, our Safari! How did it turn out? Was it successful? Did all of us get through—alive?"

Travis and Lesperance gave each other a look.

"That'd be a paradox," said the latter. "Time doesn't permit that sort of mess—a man meeting himself. When such occasions threaten, Time steps aside. Like an airplane hitting an air pocket. You felt the Machine jump just before we stopped? That was us passing ourselves on the way back to the Future. We saw nothing. There's no way of telling *if* this expedition was a success, *if we* got our monster, or whether all of us—meaning *you,* Mr. Eckels—got out alive."

Eckels smiled palely.

"Cut that," said Travis sharply. "Everyone on his feet!"

They were ready to leave the Machine.

The jungle was high and the jungle was broad and the jungle was the entire world forever and forever. Sounds like music and sounds like flying tents filled the sky, and those were pterodactyls soaring with cavernous gray wings, gigantic bats of delirium and night fever. Eckels, balanced on the narrow Path, aimed his rifle playfully.

"Stop that!" said Travis. "Don't even aim for fun, blast you! If your guns should go off—"

Eckels flushed. "Where's our *Tyrannosaurus*?"

Lesperance checked his wristwatch. "Up ahead. We'll bisect his trail in sixty seconds. Look for the red paint! Don't shoot till we give the word. Stay on the path. *Stay on the Path!*"

They moved forward in the wind of morning.

"Strange," murmured Eckels. "Up ahead, sixty million years, Election Day over. Keith made President. Everyone celebrating. And here we are, a million years lost, and they don't exist. The things we worried about for months, a lifetime, not even born or thought of yet."

"Safety catches off, everyone!" ordered Travis. "You, first shot, Eckels. Second, Billings. Third, Kramer."

"I've hunted tiger, wild boar, buffalo, elephant, but now, this is *it*," said Eckels. "I'm shaking like a kid."

"Ah," said Travis.

Everyone stopped.

Travis raised his hand. "Ahead," he whispered. "In the mist. There he is. There's His Royal Majesty now."

The jungle was wide and full of twitterings, rustlings, murmurs, and sighs.

Suddenly it all ceased, as if someone had shut a door.

Silence.

A sound of thunder.

Out of the mist, one hundred yards away, came *Tyrannosaurus rex*.

"It," whispered Eckels. "It . . ."

"Sh!"

It came on great oiled, resilient, striding legs. It towered thirty feet above half of the trees, a great evil god, folding its delicate watchmaker's claws close to its oily reptilian chest. Each lower leg was a piston, a thousand pounds of white bone, sunk in thick ropes of muscle, sheathed over in a gleam of pebbled skin like the mail of a terrible warrior. Each thigh was a ton of meat, ivory, and steel mesh. And from the great breathing cage of the upper body those two delicate arms dangled out front, arms with hands which might pick up and examine men like toys, while the snake neck coiled. And the head itself, a ton of sculptured stone, lifted easily upon the sky. Its mouth gaped, exposing a fence of teeth like daggers. Its eyes rolled, ostrich eggs, empty of all expression save hunger. It closed its mouth in a death grin. It ran, its pelvic bones crushing aside trees and bushes, its taloned feet clawing damp earth, leaving prints six inches deep wherever it settled its weight. It ran with a gliding ballet step, far too poised and balanced for its ten tons. It moved into a sunlit arena warily, its beautifully reptilian hands feeling the air.

"Why, why," Eckels twitched his mouth. "It could reach up and grab the moon."

"Sh!" Travis jerked angrily. "He hasn't seen us yet."

"It can't be killed." Eckels pronounced this verdict quietly, as if there could be no argument. He had weighed the evidence and this was his considered opinion. The rifle in his hands seemed a cap gun. "We were fools to come. This is impossible."

"Shut up!" hissed Travis.

"Nightmare."

"Turn around," commanded Travis. "Walk quietly to the Machine. We'll remit one half your fee."

"I didn't realize it would be this *big*," said Eckels. "I miscalculated, that's all. And now I want out."

"It *sees* us!"

'There's the red paint on its chest!"

The Tyrant Lizard raised itself. Its armored flesh glittered like a thousand green coins. The coins, crusted with slime, steamed. In the slime, tiny insects wriggled, so that the entire body seemed to twitch and undulate, even while the monster itself did not move. It exhaled. The stink of raw flesh blew down the wilderness.

"Get me out of here," said Eckels. "It was never like this before. I was always sure I'd come through alive. I had good guides, good safaris, and safety. This time, I figured wrong. I've met my match and admit it. This is too much for me to get hold of."

"Don't run," said Lesperance. "Turn around. Hide in the Machine."

"Yes." Eckels seemed to be numb. He looked at his feet as if trying to make them move. He gave a grunt of helplessness.

"Eckels!"

He took a few steps, blinking, shuffling.

"Not *that* way!"

The Monster, at the first motion, lunged forward with a terrible scream. It covered one hundred yards in six seconds. The rifles jerked up and blazed fire. A windstorm from the beast's mouth engulfed them in the stench of slime and old blood. The Monster roared, teeth glittering with sun.

Eckels, not looking back, walked blindly to the edge of the Path, his gun limp in his arms, stepped off the Path, and walked, not knowing it, in the jungle. His feet sank into green moss. His legs moved him, and he felt alone and remote from the events behind.

The rifles cracked again. Their sound was lost in shriek and lizard thunder. The great level of the reptile's tail swung up, lashed sideways. Trees exploded in clouds of leaf and branch. The Monster twitched its jeweler's hands down to fondle at the men, to twist them in half, to crush them like berries, to cram them into its teeth and its screaming throat. Its boulder-stone eyes leveled with the men. They saw themselves mirrored. They fired at the metallic eyelids and the blazing black iris.

Like a stone idol, like a mountain avalanche, *Tyrannosaurus* fell. Thundering, it clutched trees, pulled them with it. It wrenched and tore the metal Path. The men flung themselves back and away. The body hit, ten tons of cold flesh and stone. The guns fired. The Monster lashed its armored tail, twitched its snake jaws, and lay still. A fount of blood spurted from its throat. Somewhere inside, a sac of fluids burst. Sickening gushes drenched the hunters. They stood, red and glistening.

The thunder faded.

The jungle was silent. After the avalanche, a green peace. After the nightmare, morning.

Billings and Kramer sat on the pathway and threw up. Travis and Lesperance stood with smoking rifles, cursing steadily.

In the Time Machine, on his face, Eckels lay shivering. He had found his way back to the Path, climbed into the Machine.

Travis came walking, glanced at Eckels, took cotton gauze from a metal box, and returned to the others, who were sitting on the Path.

"Clean up."

They wiped the blood from their helmets. They began to curse too. The Monster lay, a hill of solid flesh. Within, you could hear the sighs and murmurs as the furthest chambers of it died, the organs malfunctioning, liquids running a final instant from pocket to sac to spleen, everything shutting off, closing up forever. It was like standing by a wrecked locomotive or a steam shovel at quitting time, all valves being released or levered tight. Bones cracked; the tonnage of its own flesh, off balance, dead weight, snapped the delicate forearms, caught underneath. The meat settled, quivering.

Another cracking sound. Overhead, a gigantic tree branch broke from its heavy mooring, fell. It crashed upon the dead beast with finality.

"There." Lesperance checked his watch. "Right on time. That's the giant tree that was scheduled to fall and kill this animal originally." He glanced at the two hunters. "You want the trophy picture?"

"What?"

"We can't take a trophy back to the Future. The body has to stay right here where it would have died originally, so the insects, birds, and bacteria can get at it, as they were intended to. Everything in balance. The body stays. But we can take a picture of you standing near it."

The two men tried to think, but gave up, shaking their heads.

They let themselves be led along the metal Path. They sank wearily into the Machine cushions. They gazed back at the ruined Monster, the stagnating mound, where already strange reptilian birds and golden insects were busy at the steaming armor.

A sound on the floor of the Time Machine stiffened them. Eckels sat there, shivering.

"I'm sorry," he said at last.

"Get up!" cried Travis.

Eckels got up.

"Go out on that Path alone," said Travis. He had his rifle pointed. "You're not coming back in the Machine. We're leaving you here!"

Lesperance seized Travis's arm. "Wait—"

"Stay out of this!" Travis shook his hand away. "This fool nearly killed us. But it isn't *that* so much, no. It's his *shoes*! Look at them! He ran off the Path. That *ruins* us! We'll forfeit! Thousands of dollars of insurance! We guarantee no one leaves the Path. He left it. Oh, the fool! I'll have to report to the government. They might revoke our licence to travel. Who knows *what* he's done to Time, to History!"

"Take it easy, all he did was kick up some dirt."

"How do we *know*?" cried Travis. "We don't know anything! It's all a mystery! Get out here, Eckels!"

Eckels fumbled his shirt. "I'll pay anything. A hundred thousand dollars!"

Travis glared at Eckels' checkbook and spat. "Go out there. The Monster's next to the Path. Stick your arms up to your elbows in his mouth. Then you can come back with us."

"That's unreasonable!"

"The Monster's dead, you idiot. The bullets. The bullets can't be left behind. They don't belong in the Past; they might change anything. Here's my knife. Dig them out!"

The jungle was alive again, full of the old tremorings and bird cries. Eckels turned slowly to regard the primeval garbage dump, that hill of nightmares and terror. After a long time, like a sleepwalker he shuffled out along the Path.

He returned, shuddering, five minutes later, his arms soaked and red to the elbows. He held out his hands. Each held a number of steel bullets. Then he fell. He lay where he fell, not moving.

"You didn't have to make him do that," said Lesperance.

"Didn't I? It's too early to tell." Travis nudged the still body. "He'll live. Next time he won't go hunting game like this. Okay." He jerked his thumb wearily at Lesperance. "Switch on. Let's go home."

1492. 1776. 1812.

They cleaned their hands and faces. They changed their caking shirts and pants. Eckels was up and around again, not speaking. Travis glared at him for a full ten minutes.

"Don't look at me," cried Eckels. "I haven't done anything."

"Who can tell?"

"Just ran off the Path, that's all, a little mud on my shoes—what do you want me to do—get down and pray?"

"We might need it. I'm warning you, Eckels, I might kill you yet. I've got my gun ready."

"I'm innocent. I've done nothing!"

1999. 2000. 2055.

The Machine stopped.

"Get out," said Travis.

The room was there as they had left it. But not the same as they had left it. The same man sat behind the same desk. But the same man did not quite sit behind the same desk.

Travis looked around swiftly. "Everything okay here?" he snapped.

"Fine. Welcome home!"

Travis did not relax. He seemed to be looking at the very atoms of the air itself, at the way the sun poured through the one high window.

"Okay, Eckels, get out. Don't ever come back."

Eckels could not move.

"You heard me," said Travis. "What are you *staring* at?"

Eckels stood smelling of the air, and there was a thing to the air, a chemical taint so subtle, so slight, that only a faint cry of his subliminal senses warned him it was there. The colors, white, gray, blue, orange, in the wall, in the furniture, in the sky beyond the window, were . . . were . . . And there was a *feel*. His flesh twitched. His hands twitched. He stood drinking the oddness with the pores of his body. Somewhere, someone must have been screaming one of those whistles that only a dog can hear. His body screamed silence in return. Beyond this room, beyond this wall, beyond this man who was not quite the same man seated at this desk that was not quite the same desk . . . lay an entire world of streets and people. What sort of world it was now, there was no telling. He could feel them moving there, beyond the walls, almost, like so many chess pieces blown in a dry wind. . . .

But the immediate thing was the sign painted on the office wall, the same sign he had read earlier today on first entering.

Somehow, the sign had changed:

TYME SEFARI INC.
SEFARIS TU ANY YEER EN THE PAST.
YU NAIM THE ANIMALL.
WEE TAEKYUTHAIR.
YU SHOOT ITT.

Eckels felt himself fall into a chair. He fumbled crazily at the thick slime on his boots. He held up a clod of dirt, trembling, "No, it *can't* be. Not a *little* thing like that. No!"

Embedded in the mud, glistening green and gold and black, was a butterfly, very beautiful and very dead.

"Not a little thing like *that*! Not a butterfly!" cried Eckels.

It fell to the floor, an exquisite thing, a small thing that could upset balances and knock down a line of small dominoes and then big dominoes and then gigantic dominoes, all down the years across Time. Eckels' mind whirled. It *couldn't* change things. Killing one butterfly couldn't be *that* important! Could it?

His face was cold. His mouth trembled, asking: "Who—Who won the presidential election yesterday?"

The man behind the desk laughed. "You joking? You know very well. Deutscher, of course. Who else? Not that fool weakling Keith. We got an iron man now, a man with guts!" The official stopped. "What's wrong?"

Eckels moaned. He dropped to his knees. He scrabbled at the golden butterfly with shaking fingers. "Can't we," he pleaded to the world, to himself, to the officials, to the Machine, "can't we take it *back*, can't we *make* it alive again? Can't we start over? Can't we—"

He did not move. Eyes shut, he waited, shivering. He heard Travis breathe loud in the room; he heard Travis shift his rifle, click the safety catch, and raise the weapon.

There was a sound of thunder.

# The Garden of Forking Paths

*Jorge Luis Borges*

To Victoria Ocampo

*In his* A History of the World War *(page 212), Captain Liddell Hart reports that a planned offensive by thirteen British divisions, supported by fourteen hundred artillery pieces, against the German line at Serre-Montauban, scheduled for July 24, 1916, had to be postponed until the morning of the 29th. He comments that torrential rain caused this delay—which lacked any special significance. The following deposition, dictated by, read over, and then signed by Dr. Yu Tsun, former teacher of English at the Tsingtao Hochschule, casts unsuspected light upon this event. The first two pages are missing.*

. . . and I hung up the phone. Immediately I recollected the voice that had spoken in German. It was that of Captain Richard Madden. Madden, in Viktor Runeberg's office, meant the end of all our work and—though this seemed a secondary matter, *or should have seemed so to me*—of our lives also. His being there meant that Runeberg had been arrested or murdered.[1] Before the sun set on this same day, I ran the same risk. Madden was implacable. Rather, to be more accurate, he was obliged to be implacable. An Irishman in the service of England, a man suspected of equivocal feelings if not of actual treachery, how could he fail to welcome and seize upon this extraordinary piece of luck—the discovery, capture and perhaps the deaths of two agents of Imperial Germany?

I went up to my bedroom. Absurd though the gesture was I closed and locked the door. I threw myself down on my narrow iron bed, and waited on my back. The never changing rooftops filled the window, and the hazy six o'clock sun hung in the sky. It seemed incredible that this day, a day without warnings or omens, might be that of my implacable death. In despite of my dead father, in despite of having been a child in one of the symmetrical gardens of Hai Feng, was I to die now?

Then I reflected that all things happen, happen to one, precisely *now*. Century follows century, and things happen only in the present. There are countless men in the air, on land and at sea, and all that really happens happens to me. . . . The almost unbearable memory of Madden's long horseface put an end to these wandering thoughts.

In the midst of my hatred and terror (now that it no longer matters to me to speak of terror, now that I have outwitted Richard Madden, now that my neck hankers for the hangman's noose), I knew that the fast-moving and doubtless happy soldier did not suspect that I possessed the Secret—the name of the exact site of the new British artillery park on the Ancre. A bird streaked across the misty sky and, absently, I turned it into an airplane and then that airplane into many in the skies of France, shattering the artillery park under a rain of bombs. If only my mouth, before it should be silenced by a bullet, could shout this name in such a way that it could be heard in Germany. . . . My voice, my human voice, was weak. How could it reach the ear of the Chief? The ear of that sick and hateful man who knew nothing of Runeberg or of me except that we were in Staffordshire. A man who, sitting in his arid Berlin office, leafed infinitely through newspapers, looking in vain for news from us. I said aloud, "I must flee."

I sat up on the bed, in senseless and perfect silence, as if Madden was already peering at me. Something—perhaps merely a desire to prove my total penury to myself—made me empty out my pockets. I found just what I knew I was going to find. The American watch, the nickel-plated chain and the square coin, the key ring with the useless but compromising keys to Runeberg's office, the notebook, a letter which I decided to destroy at once (and which I did not destroy), a five shilling piece, two single shillings and some pennies, a red and blue pencil, a handkerchief—and a revolver with a single bullet. Absurdly I held it and weighed it in my hand, to give myself courage. Vaguely I thought that a pistol shot can be heard for a great distance.

In ten minutes I had developed my plan. The telephone directory gave me the name of the one person capable of passing on the information. He lived in a suburb of Fenton, less than half an hour away by train.

I am a timorous man. I can say it now, now that I have brought my incredibly risky plan to an end. It was not easy to bring about, and I know that its execution was terrible. I did not do it for Germany—no! Such a barbarous country is of no importance to me, particularly since it had degraded me by making me become a spy. Furthermore, I knew an Englishman—a modest man—who, for me, is as great as Goethe. I did not speak with him for more than an hour, but during that time, he *was* Goethe.

I carried out my plan because I felt the Chief had some fear of those of my race, of those uncountable forebears whose culmination lies in me. I wished to prove to him that a yellow man could save his armies. Besides, I had to escape the Captain. His hands and voice could, at any moment, knock and beckon at my door.

Silently, I dressed, took leave of myself in the mirror, went down the stairs, sneaked a look at the quiet street, and went out. The station was not far from my house, but I thought it more prudent to take a cab. I told myself that I thus ran less chance of being recognized. The truth is that, in the deserted street, I felt infinitely visible and vulnerable. I recall that I told the driver to stop short of the main entrance. I got out with a painful and deliberate slowness.

I was going to the village of Ashgrove, but took a ticket for a station further on. The train would leave in a few minutes, at eight-fifty. I hurried, for the next would not go until half past nine. There was almost no one on the platform. I walked through the carriages. I remember some farmers, a woman dressed in mourning, a youth deep in Tacitus' *Annals* and a wounded, happy soldier.

At last the train pulled out. A man I recognized ran furiously, but vainly, the length of the platform. It was Captain Richard Madden. Shattered, trembling, I huddled in the distant corner of the seat, as far as possible from the fearful window.

From utter terror I passed into a state of almost abject happiness. I told myself that the duel had already started and that I had won the first encounter by besting my adversary in his first attack—even if it was only for forty minutes—by an accident of fate. I argued that so small a victory prefigured a total victory. I argued that it was not so trivial, that were it not for the precious accident of the train schedule, I would be in prison or dead. I argued, with no less sophism, that my timorous happiness was proof that I was man enough to bring this adventure to a successful conclusion. From my weakness I drew strength that never left me.

I foresee that man will resign himself each day to new abominations, that soon only soldiers and bandits will be left. To them I offer this advice: *Whosoever would undertake some atrocious enterprise should act as if it were already accomplished, should impose upon himself a future as irrevocable as the past.*

Thus I proceeded, while with the eyes of a man already dead, I contemplated the fluctuations of the day which would probably be my last, and watched the diffuse coming of night.

The train crept along gently, amid ash trees. It slowed down and stopped, almost in the middle of a field. No one called the name of a station. "Ashgrove?" I asked some children on the platform. "Ashgrove," they replied. I got out.

A lamp lit the platform, but the children's faces remained in a shadow. One of them asked me: "Are you going to Dr. Stephen Albert's house?" Without waiting for my answer, another said: "The house is a good distance away but you won't get lost if you take the road to the left and bear to the left at every crossroad." I threw them a coin (my last), went down some stone steps and started along a deserted road. At a slight incline, the road ran downhill. It was a plain dirt way, and overhead the branches of trees intermingled, while a round moon hung low in the sky as if to keep me company.

For a moment I thought that Richard Madden might in some way have divined my desperate intent. At once I realized that this would be impossible. The advice about turning always to the left reminded me that such was the common formula for finding the central courtyard of certain labyrinths. I know something about labyrinths. Not for nothing am I the great-grandson of Ts'ui Pên. He was Governor of Yunnan and gave up temporal power to write a novel with more characters than there are in the *Hung Lou Mêng,* and to create a maze in which all men would lose themselves. He spent thirteen years on these oddly assorted tasks before he was assassinated by a stranger. His novel had no sense to it and nobody ever found his labyrinth.

Under the trees of England I meditated on this lost and perhaps mythical labyrinth. I imagined it untouched and perfect on the secret summit of some mountain; I imagined it drowned under rice paddies or beneath the sea; I imagined it infinite, made not only of eight-sided pavilions and of twisting paths but also of rivers, provinces and kingdoms. . . . I thought of a maze of mazes, of a sinuous, ever growing maze which would take in both past and future and would somehow involve the stars.

Lost in these imaginary illusions I forgot my destiny—that of the hunted. For an undetermined period of time I felt myself cut off from the world, an abstract spectator. The hazy and murmuring countryside, the moon, the decline of the evening, stirred within me. Going down the gently sloping road I could not feel fatigue. The evening was at once intimate and infinite.

The road kept descending and branching off, through meadows misty in the twilight. A high-pitched and almost syllabic music kept coming and going, moving with the breeze, blurred by the leaves and by distance.

I thought that a man might be an enemy of other men, of the differing moments of other men, but never an enemy of a country: not of fireflies, words, gardens, streams, or the West wind.

Meditating thus I arrived at a high, rusty iron gate. Through the railings I could see an avenue bordered with poplar trees and also a kind of summer house or pavilion. Two things dawned on me at once, the first trivial and the second almost incredible: the music came from the pavilion and that music was Chinese. That was why I had accepted it fully, without paying it any attention. I do not remember whether there was a bell, a push-button, or whether I attracted attention by clapping my hands. The stuttering sparks of the music kept on.

But from the end of the avenue, from the main house, a lantern approached; a lantern which alternately, from moment to moment, was crisscrossed or put out by the trunks of the trees; a paper lantern shaped like a drum and colored like the moon. A tall man carried it. I could not see his face for the light blinded me.

He opened the gate and spoke slowly in my language.

"I see that the worthy Hsi P'eng has troubled himself to see to relieving my solitude. No doubt you want to see the garden?"

Recognizing the name of one of our consuls, I replied, somewhat taken aback.

"The garden?"

"The garden of forking paths."

Something stirred in my memory and I said, with incomprehensible assurance:

"The garden of my ancestor, Ts'ui Pên."

"Your ancestor? Your illustrious ancestor? Come in."

The damp path zigzagged like those of my childhood. When we reached the house, we went into a library filled with books from both East and West. I recognized some large volumes bound in yellow silk—manuscripts of the Lost Encyclopedia which was edited by the Third Emperor of the Luminous Dynasty. They had never been printed. A phonograph record was spinning near a bronze phoenix. I remember also a rose-glazed jar and yet another, older by many centuries, of that blue color which our potters copied from the Persians. . . .

Stephen Albert was watching me with a smile on his face. He was, as I have said, remarkably tall. His face was deeply lined and he had gray eyes and a gray beard. There was about him something of the priest, and something of the sailor. Later, he told me he had been a missionary in Tientsin before he "had aspired to become a Sinologist."

We sat down, I upon a large, low divan, he with his back to the window and to a large circular clock. I calculated that my pursuer, Richard Madden, could not arrive in less than an hour. My irrevocable decision could wait.

"A strange destiny," said Stephen Albert, "that of Ts'ui Pên—Governor of his native province, learned in astronomy, in astrology and tireless in the interpretation of the canonical books, a chess player, a famous poet and a calligrapher. Yet he abandoned all to make a book and a labyrinth. He gave up all the pleasures of oppression, justice, of a well-stocked bed, of banquets, and even of erudition, and shut himself up in the Pavilion of the Limpid Sun for thirteen years. At his death, his heirs found only a mess of manuscripts. The family, as you doubtless know, wished to consign them to the fire, but the executor of the estate—a Taoist or a Buddhist monk—insisted on their publication."

"Those of the blood of Ts'ui Pên," I replied, "still curse the memory of that monk. Such a publication was madness. The book is a shapeless mass of contradictory rough drafts. I examined it once upon a time: the hero dies in the third chapter, while in the fourth he is alive. As for that other enterprise of Ts'ui Pên . . . his Labyrinth. . . ."

"Here is the Labyrinth," Albert said, pointing to a tall, lacquered writing cabinet.

"An ivory labyrinth?" I exclaimed. "A tiny labyrinth indeed . . . ! "

"A symbolic labyrinth," he corrected me. "An invisible labyrinth of time. I, a barbarous Englishman, have been given the key to this transparent mystery. After more than a hundred years most of the details are irrecoverable, lost beyond all recall, but it isn't hard to image what must have happened. At one time, Ts'ui Pên must have said; 'I am going into seclusion to write a book,' and at another, 'I am retiring to construct a maze.' Everyone assumed these were separate activities. No one realized that the book and the labyrinth were one and the same. The Pavilion of the Limpid Sun was set in the middle of an intricate garden. This may have suggested the idea of a physical maze.

"Ts'ui Pên died. In all the vast lands which once belonged to your family, no one could find the labyrinth. The novel's confusion suggested that *it* was the labyrinth. Two circumstances showed me the direct solution to the problem. First, the curious legend that Ts'ui Pên had proposed to create an infinite maze, second, a fragment of a letter which I discovered."

Albert rose. For a few moments he turned his back to me. He opened the top drawer in the high black and gilded writing cabinet. He returned holding in his hand a piece of paper which had once been crimson but which had faded with the passage of time: it was rose colored, tenuous, quadrangular. Ts'ui Pên's calligraphy was justly famous. Eagerly, but without understanding, I read the words which a man of my own blood had written with a small brush: "I leave to various future times, but not to all, my garden of forking paths."

I handed back the sheet of paper in silence. Albert went on:

"Before I discovered this letter, I kept asking myself how a book could be infinite. I could not imagine any other than a cyclic volume, circular. A volume whose last page would be the same as the first and so have the possibility of continuing indefinitely. I recalled, too, the night in the middle of *The Thousand and One Nights* when Queen Scheherezade, through a magical mistake on the part of her copyist, started to tell the story of *The Thousand and One Nights*, with the risk of again arriving at the night upon which she will relate it, and thus on to infinity. I also imagined a Platonic hereditary work, passed on from father to son, to which each individual would add a new chapter or correct, with pious care, the work of his elders.

"These conjectures gave me amusement, but none seemed to have the remotest application to the contradictory chapters of Ts'ui Pên. At this point, I was sent from Oxford the manuscript you have just seen.

"Naturally, my attention was caught by the sentence, 'I leave to various future times, but not to all, my garden of forking paths.' I had no sooner read this, than I understood. *The Garden of Forking Paths* was the chaotic novel itself. The phrase 'to various future times, but not to all' suggested the image of bifurcating in time, not in space. Rereading the whole work confirmed this theory. In all fiction, when a man is faced with alternatives he chooses one at the expense of the others. In the almost unfathomable Ts'ui Pên, he chooses—simultaneously—all of them. He thus *creates* various futures, various times which start others that will in their turn branch out and bifurcate in other times. This is the cause of the contradictions in the novel.

"Fang, let us say, has a secret. A stranger knocks at his door. Fang makes up his mind to kill him. Naturally there are various possible outcomes. Fang can kill the intruder, the intruder can kill Fang, both can be saved, both can die and so on and so on. In Ts'ui Pên's work, all the possible solutions occur, each one being the point of departure for other bifurcations. Sometimes the pathways of this labyrinth converge. For example, you come to this house; but in other possible pasts you are my enemy; in others my friend.

"If you will put up with my atrocious pronunciation, I would like to read you a few pages of your ancestor's work."

His countenance, in the bright circle of lamplight, was certainly that of an ancient, but it shone with something unyielding, even immortal.

With slow precision, he read two versions of the same epic chapter. In the first, an army marches into battle over a desolate mountain pass. The bleak and somber aspect of the rocky landscape made the soldiers feel that life itself was of little value, and so they won the battle easily. In the second, the same army passes through a palace where a banquet is in progress. The splendor of the feast remained a memory throughout the glorious battle, and so victory followed.

With proper veneration I listened to these old tales, although perhaps with less admiration for them in themselves than for the fact that they had been thought out by one of my own blood, and that a man of a distant empire had given them back to me, in the last stage of a desperate adventure, on a Western island. I remember the final words, repeated at the end of each version like a secret command: "Thus the heroes fought, with tranquil heart and bloody sword. They were resigned to killing and to dying."

At that moment I felt within me and around me something invisible and intangible pullulating. It was not the pullulation of two divergent, parallel, and finally converging armies, but an agitation more inaccessible, more intimate, prefigured by them in some way. Stephen Albert continued:

"I do not think that your illustrious ancestor toyed idly with variations. I do not find it believable that he would waste thirteen years laboring over a never ending experiment in rhetoric. In your country the novel is an inferior genre; in Ts'ui Pên's period, it was a despised one. Ts'ui Pên was a fine novelist but he was also a man of letters who, doubtless, considered himself more than a mere novelist. The testimony of his contemporaries attests to this, and certainly the known facts of his life confirm his leanings toward the metaphysical and the mystical. Philosophical conjectures take up the greater part of his novel. I know that of all problems, none disquieted him more, and none concerned him more than the profound one of time. Now then, this is the *only* problem that does not figure in the pages of *The Garden*. He does not even use the word which means *time*. How can these voluntary omissions be explained?"

I proposed various solutions, all of them inadequate. We discussed them. Finally Stephen Albert said: "In a guessing game to which the answer is chess, which word is the only one prohibited?" I thought for a moment and then replied:

"The word is *chess*."

"Precisely," said Albert. "*The Garden of Forking Paths* is an enormous guessing game, or parable, in which the subject is time. The rules of the game forbid the use of the word itself. To eliminate a word completely, to refer to it by means of inept phrases and obvious paraphrases, is perhaps the best way of drawing attention to it. This, then, is the tortuous method of approach preferred by the oblique Ts'ui Pên in every meandering of his interminable novel. I have gone over hundreds of manuscripts, I have corrected error introduced by careless copyists, I have worked out the plan from this chaos, I have restored, or believe I have restored, the original. I have translated the whole work. I can state categorically that not once has the word *time* been used in the whole book.

"The explanation is obvious. *The Garden of Forking Paths* is a picture, incomplete yet not false, of the universe such as Ts'ui Pên conceived it to be. Differing from Newton and Schopenhauer, your ancestor did not think of time as absolute and uniform. He believed in an infinite series of times, in a dizzily growing, ever spreading network of diverging, converging and parallel times. This web of time—the strands of which approach one another, bifurcate, intersect or ignore each other through the centuries embraces *every* possibility. We do not exist in most of them. In some you exist and not I, while in others I do, and you do not, and in yet others both of us exist. In this one, in which chance has favored me, you have come to my gate. In another, you, crossing the garden, have found me dead. In yet another, I say these very same words, but am an error, a phantom."

"In all of them," I enunciated, with a tremor in my voice. "I deeply appreciate and am grateful to you for the restoration of Ts'ui Pên's garden."

"Not in *all*," he murmured with a smile. "Time is forever dividing itself toward innumerable futures and in one of them I am your enemy."

Once again I sensed the pullulation of which I have already spoken. It seemed to me that the dew-damp garden surrounding the house was infinitely saturated with invisible people. All were Albert and myself, secretive, busy and multiform in other dimensions of time. I lifted my eyes and the short nightmare disappeared. In the black and yellow garden there was only a single man, but this man was as strong as a statue and this man was walking up the path and he was Captain Richard Madden.

"The future exists now," I replied. "But I am your friend. Can I take another look at the letter?"

Albert rose from his seat. He stood up tall as he opened the top drawer of the high writing cabinet. For a moment his back was again turned to me. I had the revolver ready. I fired with the utmost care: Albert fell without a murmur, at once. I swear that his death was instantaneous, as if he had been struck by lightning.

What remains is unreal and unimportant. Madden broke in and arrested me. I have been condemned to hang. Abominably, I have yet triumphed! The secret name of the city to be attacked got through to Berlin. Yesterday it was bombed. I read the news in the same English newspapers which were trying to solve the riddle of the murder of the learned Sinologist Stephen Albert by the unknown Yu Tsun. The Chief, however, had already solved this mystery. He knew that my problem was to shout, with my feeble voice, above the tumult of war, the name of the city called Albert, and that I had no other course open to me than to kill someone of that name. He does not know, for no one can, of my infinite penitence and sickness of the heart.

—*Translated by* Helen Temple *and* Ruthven Todd

# Note

1   A malicious and outlandish statement. In point of fact, Captain Richard Madden had been attacked by the Prussian spy Hans Rabener, alias Viktor Runeberg, who drew an automatic pistol when Madden appeared with orders for the spy's arrest. Madden, in self defense, had inflicted wounds of which the spy later died.—*Note by the manuscript editor.*

# All You Zombies—

*Robert A. Heinlein*

*Robert Heinlein was one of the best known science fiction writers of the 20th century. His most famous work,* Stranger in a Strange Land, *served as an anthem of the changing sexual mores of the 1960s. Born in the United States, he lived from 1907 until 1988.*

2217 Time Zone V (EST) 7 Nov 1970 NYC—"Pop's Place": I was polishing a brandy snifter when the Unmarried Mother came in. I noted the time—10:17 P.M. zone five or eastern time November 7th, 1970. Temporal agents always notice time & date; we must.

The Unmarried Mother was a man twenty-five years old, no taller than I am, immature features and a touchy temper. I didn't like his looks—I never had—but he was a lad I was here to recruit, he was my body. I gave him my best barkeep's smile.

Maybe I'm too critical. He wasn't swish; his nickname came from what he always said when some nosy type asked him his line: "I'm an unmarried mother." If he felt less than murderous he would add: "—at four cents a word. I write confession stories."

If he felt nasty, he would wait for somebody to make something of it. He had a lethal style of in-fighting, like a female cop—one reason I wanted him. Not the only one.

He had a load on and his face showed that he despised people more than usual. Silently I poured him a double shot of Old Underwear and left the bottle. He drank, poured another.

I wiped the bar top. "How's the 'Unmarried Mother' racket?"

His fingers tightened on the glass and he seemed about to throw it at me; I felt for the sap under the bar. In temporal manipulation you try to figure everything, but there are so many factors that you never take needless risks.

I saw him relax that tiny amount they teach you to watch for in the Bureau's training school. "Sorry," I said. "Just asking. 'How's business?' Make it 'How's the weather?'"

He looked sour. "Business is okay. I write 'em, they print 'em, I eat."

I poured myself one, leaned toward him, "Matter of fact," I said, "you write a nice stick—I've sampled a few. You have an amazingly sure touch with the woman's angle."

It was a slip I had to risk; he never admitted what pennames he used. But he boiled enough to pick up only the last. "'Woman's angle!'" he repeated with a snort. "Yeah, I know the woman's angle. I should."

"So?" I said doubtfully. "Sisters?"

"No. You wouldn't believe me if I told you."

"Now, now," I answered mildly, "bartenders and psychiatrists learn that nothing is stranger than the truth. Why, son, if you heard the stories I do—well, you'd make yourself rich. Incredible."

"You don't know what 'incredible' means!"

"So? Nothing astonishes me. I've always heard worse."

He snorted again. "Want to bet the rest of the bottle?"

"I'll bet a full bottle." I placed one on the bar.

"Well—" I signaled my other bartender to handle the trade. We were at the far end, a single-stool space that I kept private by loading the bar top by it with jars of pickled eggs and other clutter. A few were at the other end watching the fights and somebody was playing the juke box—private as a bed where we were. "Okay," he began, "to start with, I'm a bastard."

"No distinction around here," I said.

"I mean it," he snapped. "My parents weren't married."

"Still no distinction," I insisted. "Neither were mine."

"When—" He stopped, gave me the first warm look I ever saw on him. "You mean that?"

"I do. A one-hundred-percent bastard. In fact," I added, "No one in my family ever marries. All bastards."

"Don't try to top me—*you're* married." He pointed at my ring.

"Oh, that." I showed it to him. "It just looks like a wedding ring; I wear it to keep women off." That ring is an antique I bought in 1985 from a fellow operative—he had fetched it from pre-Christian Crete. "The Worm Ouroboros . . . the World Snake that eats its own tail forever without end. A symbol of the Great Paradox."

He barely glanced at it. "If you're really a bastard, you know how it feels. When I was a little girl—"

"Wups!" I said. "Did I hear you correctly?"

"Who's telling this story? When I was a little girl—Look, ever hear of Christine Jorgenson? Or Roberta Cowell?"

"Uh, sex change cases. You're trying to tell me—"

"Don't interrupt or swelp me, I won't talk. I was a foundling, left at an orphanage in Cleveland in 1945 when I was a month old. When I was a little girl, I envied kids with parents. Then, when I learned about sex— and, believe me, Pop, you learn fast in an orphanage—"

"I know."

"—I made a solemn vow that any kid of mine would have both a pop and a mom. It kept me 'pure,' quite a feat in that vicinity—I had to learn to fight to manage it. Then I got older and realized I stood darned little chance of getting married—for the same reason I hadn't been adopted." He scowled. "I was horse-faced and buck-toothed, flat-chested and straight-haired."

"You don't look any worse than I do."

"Who cares how a barkeep looks? Or a writer? But people wanting to adopt pick little blue-eyed golden-haired morons. Later on, the boys want bulging breasts, a cute face, and an Oh-you-wonderful-male manner." He shrugged. "I couldn't compete. So I decided to join the W.E.N.C.H.E.S."

"Eh?"

"Women's Emergency National Corps, Hospitality & Entertainment Section, what they now call 'Space Angels'—Auxiliary Nursing Group, Extraterrestrial Legions."

I knew both terms, once I had them chronized. Although we now use still a third name; it's that elite military service corps: Women's Hospitality Order Refortifying & Encouraging Spacemen. Vocabulary shift is the worst hurdle in timejumps—did you know that "service station" once meant a dispensary for petroleum fractions? Once on an assignment in the Churchill Era a woman said to me, "Meet me at the service station next door"—which is *not* what it sounds; a "service station" (then) wouldn't have a bed in it.

He went on: "It was when they first admitted you can't send men into space for months and years and not relieve the tension. You remember how the wowsers screamed?—that improved my chances, volunteers were scarce. A gal had to be respectable, preferably virgin (they liked to train them from scratch), above average mentally, and stable emotionally. But most volunteers were old hookers, or neurotics who would crack up ten days off Earth. So I didn't need looks; if they accepted me, they would fix my buck teeth, put a wave in my hair, teach me to walk and dance and how to listen to a man pleasingly, and everything else—plus training for the prime duties. They would even use plastic surgery if it would help—nothing too good for Our Boys.

"Best yet, they made sure you didn't get pregnant during your enlistment—and you were almost certain to marry at the end of your hitch. Same way today, A.N.G.E.L.S. marry spacers—they talk the language.

"When I was eighteen I was placed as a 'mother's helper.' This family simply wanted a cheap servant but I didn't mind as I couldn't enlist till I was twenty-one. I did housework and went to night school—pretending to continue my high school typing and shorthand but going to a charm class instead, to better my chances for enlistment.

"Then I met this city slicker with his hundred dollar bills." He scowled. "The no-good actually did have a wad of hundred dollar bills. He showed me one night, told me to help myself.

"But I didn't. I liked him. He was the first man I ever met who was nice to me without trying to take my pants off. I quit night school to see him oftener. It was the happiest time of my life.

"Then one night in the park my pants did come off."

He stopped. I said, "And then?"

"And then *nothing*! I never saw him again. He walked me home and told me he loved me—and kissed me good-night and never came back." He looked grim. "If I could find him, I'd kill him!"

"Well," I sympathized, "I know how you feel. But killing him—just for doing what comes naturally—hmm . . . Did you struggle?"

"Huh? What's that got to do with it?"

"Quite a bit. Maybe he deserves a couple of broken arms for running out on you, but—"

"He deserves worse than that! Wait till you hear. Somehow I kept anyone from suspecting and decided it was all for the best. I hadn't really loved him and probably would never love anybody—and I was more eager to join the W.E.N.C.H.E.S. than ever. I wasn't disqualified, they didn't insist on virgins. I cheered up.

"It wasn't until my skirts got tight that I realized."

"Pregnant?"

"The bastard had me higher 'n a kite! Those skinflints I lived with ignored it as long as I could work—then kicked me out and the orphanage wouldn't take me back. I landed in a charity ward surrounded by other big bellies and trotted bedpans until my time came.

"One night I found myself on an operating table, with a nurse saying, 'Relax. Now breathe deeply.'

"I woke up in bed, numb from the chest down. My surgeon came in. 'How do you feel?' he says cheerfully.

"'Like a mummy.'

"'Naturally. You're wrapped like one and full of dope to keep you numb. You'll get well—but a Caesarian isn't a hangnail.'

"'Caesarian?' I said. 'Doc—*did I lose the baby?*'

"'Oh, no. Your baby's fine.'

"'Oh. Boy or girl?'

"'A healthy little girl. Five pounds, three ounces.'

"I relaxed. It's something, to have made a baby. I told myself I would go somewhere and tack 'Mrs.' on my name and let the kid think her papa was dead—no orphanage for *my* kid!

"But the surgeon was talking. 'Tell me, uh—' He avoided my name '—did you ever think your glandular setup was odd?'

"I said, 'Huh? Of course not. What are you driving at?'

"He hesitated. 'I'll give you this in one dose, then a hypo to let you sleep off your jitters. You'll have 'em.'

"'Why?' I demanded.

"'Ever hear of that Scottish physician who was female until she was thirty-five?—then had surgery and became legally and medically a man? Got married. All okay.'

"'What's that got to do with me?'

"'That's what I'm saying. You're a man.'

"I tried to sit up. '*What?*'

"'Take it easy. When I opened you, I found a mess. I sent for the Chief of Surgery while I got the baby out, then we held a consultation with you on the table—and worked for hours to salvage what we could. You had two full sets of organs, both immature, but with the female set well enough developed that you had a baby. They could never be any use to you again, so we took them out and rearranged things so that you can develop properly as a man.' He put a hand on me. 'Don't worry. You're young, your bones will readjust, we'll watch your glandular balance— and make a fine young man out of you.'

"I started to cry. 'What about my *baby*?'

"'Well, you can't nurse her, you haven't milk enough for a kitten. If I were you, I wouldn't see her—put her up for adoption.'

"'*No!*'

"He shrugged. 'The choice is yours; you're her mother—well, her parent. But don't worry now; we'll get you well first.'

"Next day they let me see the kid and I saw her daily—trying to get used to her. I had never seen a brand-new baby and had no idea how awful they look—my daughter looked like an orange monkey. My feeling changed to cold determination to do right by her. But four weeks later that didn't mean anything."

"Eh?"

"She was snatched."

"'Snatched?' "

The Unmarried Mother almost knocked over the bottle we had bet. "Kidnapped—stolen from the hospital nursery!" He breathed hard. "How's that for taking the last thing a man's got to live for?"

"A bad deal," I agreed. "Let's pour you another. No clues?"

"Nothing the police could trace. Somebody came to see her, claimed to be her uncle. While the nurse had her back turned, he walked out with her."

"Description?"

"Just a man, with a face-shaped face, like yours or mine." He frowned. "I think it was the baby's father. The nurse swore it was an older man but he probably used makeup. Who else would swipe my baby? Childless women pull such stunts—but whoever heard of a man doing it?"

"What happened to you then?"

"Eleven more months of that grim place and three operations. In four months I started to grow a beard; before I was out I was shaving regularly . . . and no longer doubted that I was male." He grinned wryly. "I was staring down nurses' necklines."

"Well," I said, "seems to me you came through okay. Here you are, a normal man, making good money, no real troubles. And the life of a female is not an easy one."

He glared at me. "A lot you know about it!"

"So?"

"Ever hear the expression 'a ruined woman'?"

"Mmm, years ago. Doesn't mean much today."

"I was as ruined as a woman can be; that bastard *really* ruined me—I was no longer a woman . . . and I didn't know *how* to be a man."

"Takes getting used to, I suppose."

"You have no idea. I don't mean learning how to dress, or not walking into the wrong rest room, I learned those in the hospital. But how could I *live*? What job could I get? Hell, I couldn't even drive a car. I didn't know a trade; I couldn't do manual labor—too much scar tissue, too tender.

"I hated him for having ruined me for the W.E.N.C.H.E.S., too, but I didn't know how much until I tried to join the Space Corps instead. One look at my belly and I was marked unfit for military service. The medical officer spent time on me just from curiosity; he had read about my case.

"So I changed my name and came to New York. I got by as a fry cook, then rented a typewriter and set myself up as a public stenographer—what a laugh! In four months I typed four letters and one manuscript. The manuscript was for *Real Life Tales* and a waste of paper, but the goof who wrote it, sold it. Which gave me an idea; I bought a stack of confession magazines and studied them." He looked cynical. "Now you know how I get the authentic woman's angle on an unmarried-mother story . . . through the only version I haven't sold—the true one. Do I win the bottle?"

I pushed it toward him. I was upset myself, but there was work to do. I said, "Son, you still want to lay hands on that so-and-so?"

His eyes lighted up—a feral gleam.

"Hold it!" I said. "You wouldn't kill him?"

He chuckled nastily. "Try me."

"Take it easy. I know more about it than you think I do. I can help you. I know where he is."

He reached across the bar. "*Where is he?*"

I said softly, "Let go my shirt, sonny—or you'll land in the alley and we'll tell the cops you fainted." I showed him the sap.

He let go. "Sorry, but where is he?" He looked at me. "And how do you know so much?"

"All in good time. There are records—hospital records, orphanage records, medical records. The matron of your orphanage was Mrs. Fetherage—right? She was followed by Mrs. Gruenstein—right? Your name, as a girl, was 'Jane'—right? And you didn't tell me any of this—right?"

I had him baffled and a bit scared. "What's this? You trying to make trouble for me?"

"No indeed. I've your welfare at heart. I can put this character in your lap. You do to him as you see fit—and I guarantee that you'll get away with it. But I don't think you'll kill him. You'd be nuts—and you aren't nuts. Not quite."

He brushed it aside. "Cut the noise. *Where is he?*"

I poured him a short one; he was drunk but anger was offsetting it. "Not so fast. I do something for you—you do something for me."

"Uh . . . what?"

"You don't like your work. What would you say to high pay, steady work, unlimited expense account, your own boss on the job, and lots of variety and adventure?"

He stared. "I'd say, 'Get those goddam reindeer off my roof! Shove it, Pop—there's no such job.' "

"Okay, put it this way: I hand him to you, you settle with him, then try my job. If it's not all I claim—well, I can't hold you."

He was wavering; the last drink did it. "When d'yuh d'liver 'im?" he said thickly.

"If it's a deal—*right now!*"

He shoved out his hand. "It's a deal!"

I nodded to my assistant to watch both ends, noted the time—2300—started to duck through the gate under the bar—when the juke box blared out: "*I'm My Own Granpaw!*" The service man had orders to load it with old Americana and classics because I couldn't stomach the "music" of 1970, but I hadn't known that tape was in it. I called out, "Shut that off! Give the customer his money back." I added, "Storeroom, back in a moment," and headed there with my Unmarried Mother following.

It was down the passage across from the johns, a steel door to which no one but my day manager and myself had a key; inside was a door to an inner room to which only I had a key. We went there.

He looked blearily around at windowless walls. "Where is 'e?"

"Right away." I opened a case, the only thing in the room; it was a U.S.F.F. Co-ordinates Transformer Field Kit, series 1992, Mod. II—a beauty, no moving parts, weight twenty-three kilos fully charged, and shaped to pass as a suitcase. I had adjusted it precisely earlier that day; all I had to do was to shake out the metal net which limits the transformation field.

Which I did. "Wha's that?" he demanded.

"Time machine," I said and tossed the net over us.

"Hey!" he yelled and stepped back. There is a technique to this; the net has to be thrown so that the subject will instinctively step back *onto* the metal mesh, then you close the net with both of you inside completely— else you might leave shoe soles behind or a piece of foot, or scoop up a slice of floor. But that's all the skill it takes. Some agents con a subject into the net; I tell the truth and use that instant of utter astonishment to flip the switch. Which I did.

*1030-V-3 April 1963—Cleveland, Ohio—Apex Bldg.:* "Hey!" he repeated "Take this damn thing off!"

"Sorry," I apologized and did so, stuffed the net into the case, closed it. "You said you wanted to find him."

"But—You said that was a time machine!"

I pointed out a window. "Does that look like November? Or New York?" While he was gawking at new buds and spring weather, I re-opened the case, took out a packet of hundred dollar bills, checked that the numbers and signatures were compatible with 1963. The Temporal Bureau doesn't care how much you spend (it costs nothing) but they don't like unneces- sary anachronisms. Too many mistakes and a general court martial will exile you for a year in a nasty period, say 1974 with its strict rationing and forced labor. I never make such mistakes, the money was okay. He turned around and said, "What happened?"

"He's here. Go outside and take him. Here's expense money." I shoved it at him and added, "Settle him, then I'll pick you up."

Hundred dollar bills have a hypnotic effect on a person not used to them. He was thumbing them unbelievingly as I eased him into the hall, locked him out. The next jump was easy, a small shift in era.

*1700-V-10 March 1964—Cleveland—Apex Bldg.:* There was a notice under the door saying that my lease expired next week; otherwise the room looked as it had a moment before. Outside, trees were bare and snow threatened; I hurried, stopping only for contemporary money and a coat, hat and topcoat I had left there when I leased the room. I hired a car, went to the hospital. It took twenty minutes to bore the nursery attendant to the point where I could swipe the baby without being noticed; we went to the Apex Building. This dial setting was more involved as the building did not yet exist in 1945. But I had precalculated it.

*0100-V-20 Sept 1945—Cleveland—Skyview Motel*: Field kit, baby, and I arrived in a motel outside town. Earlier I had registered as "Gregory Johnson, Warren, Ohio," so we arrived in a room with curtains closed, windows locked, and doors bolted, and the floor cleared to allow for waver as the machine hunts. You can get a nasty bruise from a chair where it shouldn't be—not the chair of course, but backlash from the field.

No trouble. Jane was sleeping soundly; I carried her out, put her in a grocery box on the seat of a car I had provided earlier, drove to the orphanage, put her on the steps, drove two blocks to a "service station" (the petroleum products sort) and phoned the orphanage, drove back in time to see them taking the box inside, kept going and abandoned the car near the motel—walked to it and jumped forward to the Apex Building in 1963.

*2200-V24 April 1963—Cleveland—Apex Bldg.*: I had cut the time rather fine—temporal accuracy depends on span, except on return to zero. If I had it right, Jane was discovering, out in the park this balmy spring night, that she wasn't quite as "nice" a girl as she had thought. I grabbed a taxi to the home of those skinflints, had the hackie wait around a corner while I lurked in shadows.

Presently I spotted them down the street, arms around each other. He took her up on the porch and made a long job of kissing her goodnight—longer than I had thought. Then she went in and he came down the walk, turned away. I slid into step and hooked an arm in his. "That's all, son," I announced quietly. "I'm back to pick you up."

"*You!*" He gasped and caught his breath.

"Me. Now you know who *he* is—and after you think it over you'll know who *you* are . . . and if you think hard enough, you'll figure out who the baby is . . . and who *I* am."

He didn't answer, he was badly shaken. It's a shock to have it proved to you that you can't resist seducing yourself. I took him to the Apex Building and we jumped again.

*2300-VII-12 Aug 1985—Sub Rockies Base*: I woke the duty sergeant, showed my I.D., told the sergeant to bed him down with a happy pill and recruit him in the morning. The sergeant looked sour but rank is rank, regardless of era; he did what I said—thinking, no doubt, that the next time we met he might be the colonel and I the sergeant. Which can happen in our corps. "What name?" he asked.

I wrote it out. He raised his eyebrows. "Like so, eh? *Hmm*—"

"You just do your job, Sergeant." I turned to my companion. "Son, your troubles are over. You're about to start the best job a man ever held—and you'll do well. I *know*."

"But—"

"'But' nothing. Get a night's sleep, then look over the proposition. You'll like it."

"That you will!" agreed the sergeant. "Look at me—born in 1917—still around, still young, still enjoying life." I went back to the jump room, set everything on preselected zero.

*2301-V-7 Nov 1970—NYC—"Pop's Place"*: I came out of the storeroom carrying a fifth of Drambuie to account for the minute I had been gone. My assistant was arguing with the customer who had been playing *"I'm My Own Granpaw!"* I said, "Oh, let him play it, then unplug it." I was very tired.

It's rough, but somebody must do it and it's very hard to recruit anyone in the later years, since the Mistake of 1972. Can you think of a better source than to pick people all fouled up where they are and give them well-paid, interesting (even though dangerous) work in a necessary cause? Everybody knows now why the Fizzle War of 1963 fizzled. The bomb with New York's number on it didn't go off, a hundred other things didn't go as planned—all arranged by the likes of me.

But not the Mistake of '72; that one is not our fault—and can't be undone; there's no paradox to resolve. A thing either is, or it isn't, now and forever amen. But there won't be another like it; an order dated "1992" takes precedence any year.

I closed five minutes early, leaving a letter in the cash register telling my day manager that I was accepting his offer, so see my lawyer as I was leaving on a long vacation. The Bureau might or might not pick up his payments, but they want things left tidy. I went to the room back of the storeroom and forward to 1993.

*2200-VII-12 Jan 1993—Sub Rockies Annex—HQ Temporal DOL*: I checked in with the duty officer and went to my quarters, intending to sleep for a week. I had fetched the bottle we bet (after all, I won it) and took a drink before I wrote my report. It tasted foul and I wondered why I had ever liked Old Underwear. But it was better than nothing; I don't like to be cold sober, I think too much. But I don't really hit the bottle either; other people have snakes—I have people.

I dictated my report: forty recruitments all okayed by the Psych Bureau—counting my own, which I knew would be okayed. I was here, wasn't I? Then I taped a request for assignment to operations; I was sick of recruiting. I dropped both in the slot and headed for bed.

My eye fell on "The By-Laws of Time," over my bed:

*Never Do Yesterday What Should Be Done Tomorrow.*
*If At Last you Do Succeed, Never Try Again.*
*A Stitch in Time Saves Nine Billion.*
*A Paradox May be Paradoctored.*
*It is Earlier When You Think.*
*Ancestors Are Just People.*
*Even Jove Nods.*

They didn't inspire me the way they had when I was a recruit; thirty subjective-years of time-jumping wears you down. I undressed and when I got down to the hide I looked at my belly. A Caesarian leaves a big scar but I'm so hairy now that I don't notice it unless I look for it.

Then I glanced at the ring on my finger.

The Snake That Eats Its Own Tail, Forever and Ever . . . I *know* where *I* came from—but *where did all you zombies come from?*

I felt a headache coming on, but a headache powder is one thing I do not take. I did once—and you all went away.

So I crawled into bed and whistled out the light.

*You* aren't really there at all. There isn't anybody but me—Jane—here alone in the dark.

I miss you dreadfully!

# All the Myriad Ways

*Larry Niven*

*Larry Niven is an American science fiction writer. Born in 1938, he has written numerous stories, including the well-known "Ringworld Series." He currently lives in California.*

There were timelines branching and branching, a mega-universe of universes, millions more every minute. Billions? Trillions? Trimble didn't understand the theory, though God knows he'd tried. The universe split every time someone made a decision. Split, so that every decision ever made could go both ways. Every choice made by every man, woman and child on Earth was reversed in the universe next door. It was enough to confuse any citizen, let alone Detective-Lieutenant Gene Trimble, who had other problems to worry about.

Senseless suicide, senseless crime. A city-wide epidemic. It had hit other cities too. Trimble suspected that it was world wide, that other nations were simply keeping it quiet.

Trimble's sad eyes focused on the clock. Quitting time. He stood up to go home and slowly sat down again. For he had his teeth in the problem, and he couldn't let go.

Not that he was really accomplishing anything.

But if he left now, he'd only have to take it up again tomorrow.

Go, or stay?

And the branchings began again. Gene Trimble thought of other universes parallel to this one, and a parallel Gene Trimble in each one. Some had left early. Many had left on time, and were now halfway home to dinner, out to a movie, watching a strip show, racing to the scene of another death. Streaming out of police headquarters in all their multitudes, leaving a multitude of Trimbles behind them. Each of these trying to deal, alone, with the city's endless, inexplicable parade of suicides.

Gene Trimble spread the morning paper on his desk. From the bottom drawer he took his gun-cleaning equipment, then his .45. He began to take the gun apart.

The gun was old but serviceable. He'd never fired it except on the target range and never expected to. To Trimble, cleaning his gun was like knitting, a way to keep his hands busy while his mind wandered off. Turn the screws, don't lose them. Lay the parts out in order.

Through the closed door to his office came the sounds of men hurrying. Another emergency? The department couldn't handle it all. Too many suicides, too many casual murders, not enough men.

Gun oil. Oiled rag. Wipe each part. Put it back in place.

Why would a man like Ambrose Harmon go off a building?

In the early morning light he lay, more a stain than man, thirty-six stories below the edge of his own penthouse roof. The pavement was splattered red for yards around him. The stains were still wet. Harmon had landed on his face. He wore a bright silk dressing gown and a sleeping jacket with a sash.

Others would take samples of his blood, to learn if he had acted under the influence of alcohol or drugs. There was little to be learned from seeing him in his present condition.

"But why was he up so early?" Trimble wondered. For the call had come in at 8:03, just as Trimble arrived at headquarters.

"So late, you mean." Bentley had beaten him to the scene by twenty minutes. "We called some of his friends. He was at an all-night poker game. Broke up around six o'clock."

"Did Harmon lose?"

"Nope. He won almost five hundred bucks."

"That fits," Trimble said in disgust. "No suicide note?"

"Maybe they've found one. Shall we go up and see?"

"We won't find a note," Trimble predicted.

Even three months earlier Trimble would have thought, *How incredible!* or *Who could have pushed him?* Now, riding up in the elevator, he thought only, *Reporters.* For Ambrose Harmon was news. Even among this past year's epidemic of suicides, Ambrose Harmon's death would stand out like Lyndon Johnson in a lineup.

He was a prominent member of the community, a man of dead and wealthy grandparents. Perhaps the huge inheritance, four years ago, had gone to his head. He had invested tremendous sums to back harebrained quixotic causes.

Now, because one of the harebrained causes had paid off, he was richer than ever. The Crosstime Corporation already held a score of patents on inventions imported from alternate time tracks. Already those inventions had started more than one industrial revolution. And Harmon was the money behind Crosstime. He would have been the world's next billionaire—had he not walked off the balcony.

They found a roomy, luxuriously furnished apartment in good order, and a bed turned down for the night. The only sign of disorder was Harmon's clothing—slacks, sweater, a silk turtleneck shirt, knee-length shoesocks, no underwear—piled on a chair in the bedroom. The toothbrush had been used.

He got ready for bed, Trimble thought. He brushed his teeth, and then he went out to look at the sunrise. A man who kept late hours like that, he wouldn't see the sunrise very often. He watched the sunrise, and when it was over, he jumped.

"Why?"

They were all like that. Easy, spontaneous decisions. The victim-killers walked off bridges or stepped from their balconies or suddenly flung themselves in front of subway trains. They strolled halfway across a freeway, or swallowed a full bottle of laudanum. None of the methods showed previous planning. Whatever was used, the victim had had it all along; he never actually went out and bought a suicide weapon. The victim rarely dressed for the occasion, or used makeup, as an ordinary suicide would. Usually there was no note.

Harmon fit the pattern perfectly.

"Like Richard Corey," said Bentley.

"Who?"

"Richard Corey, the man who had everything. 'And Richard Corey, one calm summer night, Went home and put a bullet through his head.' You know what I think?"

"If you've got an idea, let's have it."

"The suicides all started about a month after Crosstime got started. I think one of the Crosstime ships brought back a new bug from some alternate timeline."

"A suicide bug?"

Bentley nodded.

"You're out of your mind."

"I don't think so. Gene, do you know how many Crosstime pilots have killed themselves in the last year? More than twenty percent!"

"Oh?"

"Look at the records. Crosstime has about twenty vehicles in action now, but in the past year they've employed sixty-two pilots. Three disappeared. Fifteen are dead, and all but two died by suicide."

"I didn't know that." Trimble was shaken.

"It was bound to happen sometime. Look at the alternate worlds they've found so far. The Nazi world. The Red Chinese world, half bombed to death. The ones that are totally bombed, and Crosstime can't even find out who did it. The one with the Black Plague mutation, and no penicillin until Crosstime came along. Sooner or later—"

"Maybe, maybe. I don't buy your bug, though. If the suicides are a new kind of plague, what about the other crimes?"

"Same bug."

"Uh, uh. But I think we'll check up on Crosstime."


Trimble's hands finished with the gun and laid it on the desk. He was hardly aware of it. Somewhere in the back of his mind was a prodding sensation: the *handle*, the piece he needed to solve the puzzle.

He spent most of the day studying Crosstime, Inc. News stories, official handouts, personal interviews. The incredible suicide rate among Crosstime pilots could not be coincidence. He wondered why nobody had noticed it before.

It was slow going. With Crosstime travel, as with relativity, you had to throw away reason and use only logic. Trimble had sweated it out. Even the day's murders had not distracted him.

They were typical, of a piece with the preceding eight months' crime wave. A man had shot his foreman with a gun bought an hour earlier, then strolled off toward police headquarters. A woman had moved through the back row of a dark theater, using an ice pick to stab members of the audience through the backs of their seats. She had chosen only young men. They had killed without heat, without concealment; they had surrendered without fear or bravado. Perhaps it was another kind of suicide.

Time for coffee, Trimble thought, responding unconsciously to a dry throat plus a fuzziness of the mouth plus slight fatigue. He set his hands to stand up, and—

The image came to him in an endless row of Trimbles, lined up like the repeated images in facing mirrors. But each image was slightly different. He would go get the coffee *and* he wouldn't *and* he would send somebody for it, and someone was about to bring it without being asked. Some of the images were drinking coffee, a few had tea or milk, some were smoking, some were leaning too far back with their feet on the desks (and a handful of these were toppling helplessly backward), some were, like this present Trimble, introspecting with their elbows on the desk. Damn Crosstime anyway.

He'd have had to check Harmon's business affairs, even without the Crosstime link. There might have been a motive there, for suicide or murder, though it had never been likely.

In the first place, Harmon had cared nothing for money. The Crosstime group had been one of many. At the time that project had looked as hairbrained as the rest: a handful of engineers and physicists and philosophers determined to prove that the theory of alternate time tracks was reality.

In the second place, Harmon had no business worries.

Quite the contrary.

Eleven months ago an experimental vehicle had touched one of the worlds of the Confederate States of America and returned. The universes of alternate choice were within reach. And the pilot had brought back an artifact.

From that point on, Crosstime travel had more than financed itself. The Confederate world's "stapler," granted an immediate patent, had bought two more ships. A dozen miracles had originated in a single, technologically advanced timeline, one in which the catastrophic Cuban War had been no more than a wet firecracker. Lasers, oxygen-hydrogen rocket motors, computers, strange plastics—the list was still growing. And Crosstime held all the patents.

In those first months the vehicles had gone off practically at random. Now the pinpointing was better. Vehicles could select any branch they preferred. Imperial Russia, Amerindian America, the Catholic Empire, the dead worlds. Some of the dead worlds were hells of radioactive dust and intact but deadly artifacts. From these worlds Crosstime pilots brought strange and beautiful works of art which had to be stored behind leaded glass.

The latest vehicles could reach worlds so like this one that it took a week of research to find the difference. In theory they could get even closer. There was a phenomenon called 'the broadening of the bands' . . .

And that had given Trimble the shivers.

When a vehicle left its own present, a signal went on in the hangar, a signal unique to that ship. When the pilot wanted to return, he simply cruised across the appropriate band of probabilities until he found the signal. The signal marked his own unique present.

Only it didn't. The pilot always returned to find a clump of signals, a broadened band. The longer he stayed away, the broader was the signal band. His own world had continued to divide after his departure, in a constant stream of decisions being made both ways.

Usually it didn't matter. Any signal the pilot chose represented the world he had left. And since the pilot himself had a choice, he naturally returned to them all. But—

There was a pilot by the name of Gary Wilcox. He had been using his vehicle for experiments, to see how close he could get to his own timeline and still leave it. Once, last month, he had returned twice.

Two Gary Wilcoxes, two vehicles. The vehicles had been wrecked— their hulls intersected. For the Wilcoxes it could have been sticky, for Wilcox had a wife and family. But one of the duplicates had chosen to die almost immediately.

Trimble had tried to call the other Gary Wilcox. He was too late. Wilcox had gone skydiving a week ago. He'd neglected to open his parachute.

Small wonder, thought Trimble. At least Wilcox had had motive. It was bad enough, knowing about the other Trimbles, the ones who had gone home, the ones drinking coffee, et cetera. But—suppose someone walked into the office right now, and it was Gene Trimble?

It could happen.

Convinced as he was that Crosstime was involved in the suicides, Trimble—some other Trimble—might easily have decided to take a trip in a Crosstime vehicle. A short trip. He could land *here*.

Trimble closed his eyes and rubbed at the corners with his fingertips. In some timeline, very close, someone had thought to bring him coffee. Too bad this wasn't it.

It didn't do to think too much about these alternate timelines. There were too many of them. The close one could drive you buggy, but the ones farther off were just as bad.

Take the Cuba War. Atomics had been used, *here*, and now Cuba was uninhabited, and some American cities were gone, and some Russian. It could have been worse.

Why wasn't it? How could we luck out? Intelligent statesmen? Faulty bombs? A humane reluctance to kill indiscriminately?

No. There was no luck anywhere. Every decision was made both ways. For every wise choice you bled your heart out over, you had made all the other choices too. And so it went, all through history.

Civil wars unfought on some worlds were won by either side on others. Elsewhere, another animal had first done murder with an antelope femur. Some worlds were still all nomad; civilization had lost out. If every choice was cancelled elsewhere, why make a decision at all?

Trimble opened his eyes and saw the gun.

That gun, too, was endlessly repeated on endless desks. Some of the images were dirty with years of neglect. Some smelled of gunpowder, fired recently, a few at living targets. Some were loaded. All were as real as this one.

A number of these were about to go off by accident.

A proportion of these were pointed, in deadly coincidence at Gene Trimble.

See the endless rows of Gene Trimble, each at his desk. Some were bleeding and cursing as men run into the room following the sound of the gunshot. Many are already dead.

Was there a bullet in there? Nonsense.

He looked away. The gun was empty.

Trimble loaded it. At the base of his mind he felt the touch of the *handle*. He would find what he was seeking.

He put the gun back on his desk, pointing away from him, and he thought of Ambrose Harmon, coming home from a late night. Ambrose Harmon. who had won five hundred dollars at poker. Ambrose Harmon, exhausted, seeing the lightening sky as he prepared for bed. Going out to watch the dawn.

Ambrose Harmon, watching the slow dawn, remembering a two thousand dollar pot. He'd bluffed. In some other branching of time, he had lost.

Thinking that in some other branching of time, that two thousand dollars included his last dime. It was certainly possible. If Crosstime hadn't paid off, he might have gone through the remains of his fortune in the past four years. He liked to gamble.

Watching the dawn, thinking of all the Ambrose Harmons on that roof. Some were penniless this night, and they had not come out to watch the dawn.

Well, why not? If he stepped over the edge, here and now, another Ambrose Harmon would only laugh and go inside.

If he laughed and went inside, other Ambrose Harmons would fall to their deaths. Some were already on their way down. One changed his mind too late, another laughed as he fell. . . .

Well, why not? . . .

Trimble thought of another man, a nonentity, passing a firearms store. Branching of timelines, he thinks, looking in; and he thinks of the man who took his foreman's job. Well, why not? . . .

Trimble thought of a lonely woman making herself a drink at three in the afternoon. She thinks of myriads of alter egos, with husbands, lovers, children, friends. Unbearable, to think that all the might-have-beens were as real as herself. As real as this ice pick in her hand. Well, why not? . . .

And she goes out to a movie, but she takes the ice pick.

And the honest citizen with a carefully submerged urge to commit rape, just once. Reading his newspaper at breakfast, and there's another story from Crosstime: they've found a world line in which Kennedy the First was assassinated. Strolling down a street, he thinks of world lines and infinite branchings, of alter egos already dead, or jailed, or President. A girl in a mini-skirt passes, and she has nice legs. Well, why not? . . .

Casual murder, casual suicide, casual crime. Why not? If alternate universes are a reality, then cause and effect are an illusion. The law of averages is a fraud. You can do anything, and one of you will, or did.

Gene Trimble looked at the clean and loaded gun on his desk. Well, why not? . . .

And he ran out of the office shouting, "Bentley, listen. I've got the answer. . . ."

And he stood up slowly and left the office shaking his head. This was the answer, and it wasn't any good. The suicides, murders, casual crimes would continue. . . .

And he suddenly laughed and stood up. Ridiculous! Nobody dies for a philosophical point! . . .

And he reached for the intercom and told the man who answered to bring him a sandwich and some coffee. . . .

And picked the gun off the newspapers, looked at it for a long moment, then dropped it in the drawer. His hands began to shake. On a world line very close to this one. . . .

And he picked the gun off the newspapers, put it to his head and

fired. The hammer fell on an empty chamber.
fired. The gun jerked and blasted a hole in the ceiling.
fired. The bullet tore a furrow in his scalp.
fired. The bullet took off the top of his head.

*Section Six*

# The Modern Self

# *from* Song of Myself

*Walt Whitman*

## 1

I celebrate myself, and I sing myself,
And what I assume you shall assume,
For every atom belonging to me as good belongs to you.

I loafe and invite my soul,
I lean and loafe at my ease observing a spear of summer grass.

My tongue, every atom of my blood, form'd from this soil, this air,
Born here of parents born here from parents the same, and their parents
    the same,
I, now thirty-seven years old in perfect health begin,
Hoping to cease not till death.

Creeds and schools in abeyance,
Retiring back a while sufficed at what they are, but never forgotten,
I harbor for good or bad, I permit to speak at every hazard,
Nature without check with original energy.

## 2

Houses and rooms are full of perfumes, the shelves are crowded with
    perfumes,
I breathe the fragrance myself and know it and like it,
The distillation would intoxicate me also, but I shall not let it.

The atmosphere is not a perfume, it has no taste of the distillation, it is
    odorless,
It is for my mouth forever, I am in love with it,
I will go to the bank by the wood and become undisguised and naked,
I am mad for it to be in contact with me.

844

The smoke of my own breath
Echoes, ripples, buzz'd whispers, love-root, silk-thread, crotch and vine,
My respiration and inspiration, the beating of my heart, the passing of
    blood and air through my lungs,
The sniff of green leaves and dry leaves, and of the shore and dark-col-
    or'd sea-rocks, and of hay in the barn,
The sound of the belch'd words of my voice loos'd to the eddies of the
    wind,
A few light kisses, a few embraces, a reaching around of arms,
The play of shine and shade on the trees as the supple boughs wag,
The delight alone or in the rush of the streets, or along the fields and
    hill-sides,
The feeling of health, the full-moon trill, the song of me rising from bed
    and meeting the sun.

Have you reckon'd a thousand acres much? have you reckon'd the earth
    much?
Have you practis'd so long to learn to read?
Have you felt so proud to get at the meaning of poems?

Stop this day and night with me and you shall possess the origin of all
    poems,
You shall possess the good of the earth and sun, (there are millions of
    suns left,)
You shall no longer take things at second or third hand, nor look through
    the eyes of the dead, nor feed on the spectres in books
You shall not look through my eyes either, nor take things from me,
You shall listen to all sides and filter them from your self.


3

I have heard what the talkers were talking, the talk of the beginning and
    the end,
But I do not talk of the beginning or the end.

There was never any more inception than there is now,
Nor any more youth or age than there is now,
And will never be any more perfection than there is now,
Nor any more heaven or hell than there is now.

Urge and urge and urge,
Always the procreant urge of the world.
Out of the dimness opposite equals advance, always substance and
     increase, always sex,
Always a knit of identity, always distinction, always a breed of life.

To elaborate is no avail, learn'd and unlearn'd feel that it is so.

Sure as the most certain sure, plumb in the uprights, well entretied,
     braced in the beams,
Stout as a horse, affectionate, haughty, electrical,
I and this mystery here we stand.

Clear and sweet is my soul, and clear and sweet is all that is not my soul.

Lack one lacks both, and the unseen is proved by the seen,
Till that becomes unseen and receives proof in its turn.
Showing the best and dividing it from the worst age vexes age,
Knowing the perfect fitness and equanimity of things, while they discuss
I am silent, and go bathe and admire myself.

Welcome is every organ and attribute of me, and of any man hearty and
     clean,
Not an inch nor a particle of an inch is vile, and none shall be less famil-
     iar than the rest.

I am satisfied—I see, dance, laugh, sing;

As the hugging and loving bed-fellow sleeps at my side through the
     night, and withdraws at the peep of the day with stealthy tread,

Leaving me baskets cover'd with white towels swelling the house with
     their plenty,

Shall I postpone my acceptation and realization and scream at my eyes,
That they turn from gazing after and down the road,
And forthwith cipher and show me to a cent,
Exactly the value of one and exactly the value of two, and which is ahead?

## 4

Trippers and askers surround me,
People I meet, the effect upon me of my early life or the ward and city I
   live in, or the nation,
The latest dates, discoveries, inventions, societies, authors old and new,
My dinner, dress, associates, looks, compliments, dues,
The real or fancied indifference of some man or woman I love,
The sickness of one of my folks or of myself, or ill-doing or loss or lack of
   money, or depressions or exaltations
Battles, the horrors of fratricidal war, the fever of doubtful news, the fit-
   ful events;
These come to me days and nights and go from me again.
But they are not the Me myself.

Apart from the pulling and hauling stands what I am,
Stands amused, complacent, compassionating, idle, unitary,
Looks down, is erect, or bends an arm on an impalpable certain rest,
Looking with side-curved head curious what will come next,
Both in and out of the game and watching and wondering at it.

Backward I see in my own days where I sweated through fog with lin-
   guists and contenders,
I have no mockings or arguments, I witness and wait.

## 5

I believe in you my soul, the other I am must not abase itself to you,
And you must not be abased to the other.

Loafe with me on the grass, loose the stop from your throat,
Not words, not music or rhyme I want, not custom or lecture, not even
   the best,
Only the lull I like, the hum of your valvèd voice.
I mind how once we lay such a transparent summer morning,
How you settled your head athwart my hips and gently turn'd over upon me,
And parted the shirt from my bosom-bone, and plunged your tongue to
   my bare-stript heart,
And reach'd till you felt my beard, and reach'd till you held my feet.

Swiftly arose and spread around me the peace and knowledge that pass
    all the argument of the earth,
And I know that the hand of God is the promise of my own,
And I know that the spirit of God is the brother of my own,
And that all the men ever born are also my brothers, and the women my
    sisters and lovers,
And that a kelson of the creation is love,
And limitless are leaves stiff or drooping in the fields,
And brown ants in the little wells beneath them,
And mossy scabs of the worm fence, heap'd stones, elder, mullein and
    poke-weed.

## 6

A child said What is the grass? fetching it to me with full hands,
How could I answer the child? I do not know what it is any more than he.

I guess it must be the flag of my disposition, out of hopeful green stuff
    woven.

Or I guess it is the handkerchief of the Lord,
A scented gift and remembrancer designedly drops,
Bearing the owner's name some way in the corners, that we may see and
    remark, and say *Whose?*

Or I guess the grass is itself a child, the produced babe of the vegetation.

Or I guess it is a uniform hieroglyphic,
And it means, Sprouting alike in broad zones and narrow zones,
Growing among black folks as among white,
Kanuck, Tuckahoe, Congressman, Cuff, I give them the same, I receive
    them the same.

And now it seems to me the beautiful uncut hair of graves.

Tenderly will I use you curling grass,
It may be you transpire from the breasts of young men,
It may be if I had known them I would have loved them,

It may be you are from old people, or from offspring taken soon out of
   their mothers' laps,
And here you are the mothers' laps.

This grass is very dark to be from the white heads of old mothers,
Darker than the colorless beards of old men,
Dark to come from under the faint red roofs of mouths.
O I perceive after all so many uttering tongues,
And I perceive they do not come from the roofs of mouths for nothing.

I wish I could translate the hints about the dead young men and women,
And the hints about old men and mothers, and the offspring taken soon
   out of their laps.

What do you think has become of the young and old men?
And what do you think has become of the women and children ?

They are alive and well somewhere,
The smallest sprout shows there is really no death,
And if ever there was it led forward life, and does not wait at the end to
   arrest it,
And ceas'd the moment life appear'd.

All goes onward and outward, nothing collapses,
And to die is different from what any one supposed, and luckier.

# Dover Beach

*Matthew Arnold*

The sea is calm tonight.
The tide is full, the moon lies fair
Upon the straits—on the French coast the light
Gleams and is gone; the cliffs of England stand,
Glimmering and vast, out in the tranquil bay.
Come to the window, sweet is the night air!
Only, from the long line of spray
Where the sea meets the moon-blanched land,
Listen! you hear the grating roar
Of pebbles which the waves draw back, and fling,
At their return, up the high strand,
Begin, and cease, and then again begin,
With tremulous cadence slow, and bring
The eternal note of sadness in.

Sophocles long ago
Heard it on the Aegean, and it brought
Into his mind the turbid ebb and flow
Of human misery; we
Find also in the sound a thought,
Hearing it by this distant northern sea.

The Sea of Faith
Was once, too, at the full, and round earth's shore
Lay like the folds of a bright girdle furled.
But now I only hear
Its melancholy, long, withdrawing roar,
Retreating, to the breath
Of the night wind, down the vast edges drear
And naked shingles of the world.

Ah, love, let us be true
To one another! for the world, which seems
To lie before us like a land of dreams,

So various, so beautiful, so new,
Hath really neither joy, nor love, nor light,
Nor certitude, nor peace, nor help for pain;
And we are here as on a darkling plain
Swept with confused alarms of struggle and flight,
Where ignorant armies clash by night.

# The Tables Turned

*William Wordsworth*

## An Evening Scene on the Same Subject

Up! up! my Friend, and quit your books;
Or surely you'll grow double:
Up! up! my Friend, and clear your looks;
Why all this toil and trouble?

The sun, above the mountain's head,
A freshening lustre mellow
Through all the long green fields has spread,
His first sweet evening yellow.

Books! 'tis a dull and endless strife:
Come, hear the woodland linnet,
How sweet his music! on my life,
There's more of wisdom in it.

And hark! how blithe the throstle sings!
He, too, is no mean preacher:
Come forth into the light of things,
Let Nature be your Teacher.

She has a world of ready wealth,
Our minds and hearts to bless—
Spontaneous wisdom breathed by health,
Truth breathed by cheerfulness.

One impulse from a vernal wood
May teach you more of man,
Of moral evil and of good,
Than all the sages can.

Sweet is the lore which Nature brings;
Our meddling intellect
Mis-shapes the beauteous forms of things:—
We murder to dissect.                    MAKE IT
                                         MORE COMPLICATED

Enough of Science and of Art;
Close up those barren leaves;
Come forth, and bring with you a heart
That watches and receives.        CURIOSITY


SIMPLICITY   IS   HAPPINESS

# Expostulation and Reply

*William Wordsworth*

"Why, William, on that old grey stone,
Thus for the length of half a day,
Why, William, sit you thus alone,
And dream your time away?

"Where are your books?—that light bequeathed
To Beings else forlorn and blind!
Up! up! and drink the spirit breathed
From dead men to their kind.

"You look round on your Mother Earth,
As if she for no purpose bore you;
As if you were her first-born birth,
And none had lived before you!"

One morning thus, by Esthwaite lake,
When life was sweet, I knew not why,
To me my good friend Matthew spake,
And thus I made reply.

"The eye—it cannot choose but see;
We cannot bid the ear be still;
Our bodies feel, where'er they be,
Against or with our will.

"Nor less I deem that there are Powers
Which of themselves our minds impress;
That we can feed this mind of ours
In a wise passiveness.

"Think you, 'mid all this mighty sum
Of things for ever speaking,
That nothing of itself will come,
But we must still be seeking?

"—Then ask not wherefore, here, alone,
Conversing as I may,
I sit upon this old grey stone,
And dream my time away."

Spring 1798

# The Soldier

*Rupert Brooke*

If I should die, think only this of me:
    That there's some corner of a foreign field
That is for ever England. There shall be
    In that rich earth a richer dust concealed;
A dust whom England bore, shaped, made aware,
    Gave, once, her flowers to love, her ways to roam,
A body of England's, breathing English air,
    Washed by the rivers, blest by suns of home.

And think, this heart, all evil shed away,
    A pulse in the eternal mind, no less
        Gives somewhere back the thoughts by England given;
Her sights and sounds; dreams happy as her day;
    And laughter, learnt of friends; and gentleness,
        In hearts at peace, under an English heaven.

# Anthem for Doomed Youth

*Wilfred Owen*

What passing-bells for these who die as cattle?
  —Only the monstrous anger of the guns.
  Only the stuttering rifles' rapid rattle
Can patter out their hasty orisons.
No mockeries now for them; no prayers nor bells;
  Nor any voice of mourning save the choirs,—
The shrill, demented choirs of wailing shells;
  And bugles calling for them from sad shires.

What candles may be held to speed them all?
  Not in the hands of boys, but in their eyes
Shall shine the holy glimmers of good-byes.
  The pallor of girls' brows shall be their pall;
Their flowers the tenderness of patient minds,
And each slow dusk a drawing-down of blinds.

# Disabled

*Wilfred Owen*

He sat in a wheeled chair, waiting for dark,
And shivered in his ghastly suit of grey,
Legless, sewn short at elbow. Through the park
Voices of boys rang saddening like a hymn,
Voices of play and pleasure after day,
Till gathering sleep had mothered them from him.
                        • • •
About this time Town used to swing so gay
When glow-lamps budded in the light blue trees,
And girls glanced lovelier as the air grew dim,—
In the old times, before he threw away his knees,
Now he will never feel again how slim
Girls' waists are, or how warm their subtle hands;
All of them touch him like some queer disease.
                        • • •
There was an artist silly for his face,
For it was younger than his youth, last year.
Now, he is old; his back will never brace;
He's lost his colour very far from here,
Poured it down shell-holes till the veins ran dry,
And half his lifetime lapsed in the hot race
And leap of purple spurted from his thigh.

One time he liked a blood-smear down his leg,
After the matches, carried shoulder-high.
It was after football, when he'd drunk a peg,
He thought he'd better join. —He wonders why.
Someone had said he'd look a god in kilts,
That's why; and may be, too, to please his Meg;
Aye, that was it, to please the giddy jilts
He asked to join. He didn't have to beg;
Smiling they wrote his lie; aged nineteen years.
Germans he scarcely thought of; all their guilt,
And Austria's, did not move him. And no fears

Of Fear came yet. He thought of jewelled hilts
For daggers in plaid socks; of smart salutes;
And care of arms; and leave; and pay arrears;
Esprit de corps; and hints for young recruits.
And soon, he was drafted out with drums and cheers.

• • •

Some cheered him home, but not as crowds cheer Goal.
Only a solemn man who brought him fruits
*Thanked* him; and then inquired about his soul.

• • •

Now, he will spend a few sick years in institutes,
And do what things the rules consider wise,
And take whatever pity they may dole.
To-night he noticed how the women's eyes
Passed from him to the strong men that were whole.
How cold and late it is! Why don't they come
And put him into bed? Why don't they come?

# The Last Laugh

*Wilfred Owen*

'O Jesus Christ! I'm hit,' he said; and died.
Whether he vainly cursed, or prayed indeed,
The Bullets chirped—In vain! vain! vain!
Machine-guns chuckled, —Tut-tut! Tut-tut!
And the Big Gun guffawed.

Another sighed, —'O Mother, mother! Dad!
Then smiled, at nothing, childlike, being dead.
    And the lofty Shrapnel-cloud
    Leisurely gestures,—Fool!
    And the falling splinters tittered.

'My Love!' one moaned. Love-languid seemed his mood,
Till, slowly lowered, his whole face kissed the mud.
    And the Bayonets' long teeth grinned;
    Rabbles of Shells hooted and groaned;
    And the Gas hissed.

# Base Details

*Siegfried Sassoon*

If I were fierce, and bald, and short of breath,
   I'd live with scarlet Majors at the Base,
And speed glum heroes up the line to death.
   You'd see me with my puffy petulant face,
Guzzling and gulping in the best hotel,
   Reading the Roll of Honour. 'Poor young chap,'
I'd say —'I used to know his father well;
   Yes, we've lost heavily in this last scrap.'
And when the war is done and youth stone dead,
I'd toddle safely home and die — in bed.

# The General

*Siegfried Sassoon*

'Good-morning; good-morning!' the General said
When we met him last week on our way to the line.
Now the soldiers he smiled at are most of 'em dead,
And we're cursing his staff for incompetent swine.
'He's a cheery old card,' grunted Harry to Jack
As they slogged up to Arras with rifle and pack.
• • •
But he did for them both by his plan of attack.

# Everyone Sang

*Siegfried Sassoon*

Everyone suddenly burst out singing;
And I was filled with such delight
As prisoned birds must find in freedom,
Winging wildly across the white
Orchards and dark-green fields; on—on—and out of sight.
Everyone's voice was suddenly lifted;
And beauty came like the setting sun:
My heart was shaken with tears; and horror
Drifted away . . . O, but Everyone
Was a bird; and the song was wordless; the singing will
    never be done.

# The Love Song of J. Alfred Prufrock

*T. S. Eliot*

Let us go then, you and I,
When the evening is spread out against the sky
Like a patient etherized upon a table;
Let us go, through certain half-deserted streets.
The muttering retreats
Of restless nights in one-night cheap hotels
And sawdust restaurants with oyster-shells:
Streets that follow like a tedious argument
Of insidious intent
To lead you to an overwhelming question . . .
Oh, do not ask, "What is it?"
Let us go and make our visit.

In the room the women come and go
Talking of Michelangelo.

The yellow fog that rubs its back upon the window-panes,
The yellow smoke that rubs its muzzle on the window-panes
Licked its tongue into the corners of the evening,
Lingered upon the pools that stand in drains,
Let fall upon its back the soot that falls from chimneys,
Slipped by the terrace, made a sudden leap,
And seeing that it was a soft October night,
Curled once about the house, and fell asleep.

And indeed there will be time
For the yellow smoke that slides along the street,
Rubbing its back upon the window-panes;
There will be time, there will be time
To prepare a face to meet the faces that you meet;
There will be time to murder and create,
And time for all the works and days of hands
That lift and drop a question on your plate;
Time for you and time for me,

And time yet for a hundred indecisions,
And for a hundred visions and revisions,
Before the taking of a toast and tea.

In the room the women come and go
Talking of Michelangelo.

And indeed there will be time
To wonder, "Do I dare?" and, "Do I dare?"
Time to turn back and descend the stair,
With a bald spot in the middle of my hair—
(They will say: "How his hair is growing thin!")
My morning coat, my collar mounting firmly to the chin,
My necktie rich and modest, but asserted by a simple pin—
(They will say: "But how his arms and legs are thin!")
Do I dare
Disturb the universe?
In a minute there is time
For decisions and revisions which a minute will reverse.

For I have known them all already, known them all—
Have known the evenings, mornings, afternoons,
I have measured out my life with coffee spoons,
I know the voices dying with a dying fall
Beneath the music from a farther room.
        So how should I presume?

And I have known the eyes already, known them all—
The eyes that fix you in a formulated phrase.
And when I am formulated, sprawling on a pin,
When I am pinned and wriggling on the wall,
Then how should I begin
To spit out all the butt-ends of my days and ways?
        And how should I presume?

And I have known the arms already, known them all—
Arms that are braceleted and white and bare
(But in the lamplight, downed with light brown hair!)
Is it perfume from a dress
That makes me so digress?

Arms that lie along a table, or wrap about a shawl.
          And should I then presume?
          And how should I begin?


Shall I say, I have gone at dusk through narrow streets
And watched the smoke that rises from the pipes
Of lonely men in shirt-sleeves, leaning out of windows? . . .

I should have been a pair of ragged claws
Scuttling across the floors of silent seas.


And the afternoon, the evening, sleeps so peacefully!
Smoothed by long fingers,
Asleep . . . tired . . . or it malingers,
Stretched on the floor, here beside you and me.
Should I, after tea and cakes and ices,
Have the strength to force the moment to its crisis?
But though I have wept and fasted, wept and prayed,
Though I have seen my head (grown slightly bald) brought in upon a
          platter,
I am no prophet—and here's no great matter;
I have seen the moment of my greatness flicker,
And I have seen the eternal Footman hold my coat, and snicker,
And in short, I was afraid.

And would it have been worth it, after all,
After the cups, the marmalade, the tea,
Among the porcelain, among some talk of you and me,
Would it have been worth while,
To have bitten off the matter with a smile,
To have squeezed the universe into a ball
To roll it towards some overwhelming question,
To say: "I am Lazarus, come from the dead,
Come back to tell you all, I shall tell you all"—
If one, settling a pillow by her head,
          Should say: "That is not what I meant at all.
          That is not it, at all."

And would it have been worth it, after all,
Would it have been worth while,
After the sunsets and the dooryards and the sprinkled streets,
After the novels, after the teacups, after the skirts that trail along the floor—
And this, and so much more?—
It is impossible to say just what I mean!
But as if a magic lantern threw the nerves in patterns on a screen:
Would it have been worth while
If one, settling a pillow or throwing off a shawl,
And turning toward the window, should say:
      "That is not it at all,
      That is not what I meant, at all."


No! I am not Prince Hamlet, nor was meant to be;
Am an attendant lord, one that will do
To swell a progress, start a scene or two,
Advise the prince; no doubt, an easy tool,
Deferential, glad to be of use,
Politic, cautious, and meticulous;
Full of high sentence, but a bit obtuse;
At times, indeed, almost ridiculous—
Almost, at times, the Fool.

I grow old . . . I grow old . . .
I shall wear the bottoms of my trousers rolled.

Shall I part my hair behind? Do I dare to eat a peach?
I shall wear white flannel trousers, and walk upon the beach.
I have heard the mermaids singing, each to each.

I do not think that they will sing to me.

I have seen them riding seaward on the waves
Combing the white hair of the waves blown back
When the wind blows the water white and black.

We have lingered in the chambers of the sea
By sea-girls wreathed with seaweed red and brown
Till human voices wake us, and we drown.

# Apostrophe to Man

## (on reflecting that the world is ready to go to war again)

*Edna St. Vincent Millay*

Detestable race, continue to expunge yourself, die out.
Breed faster, crowd, encroach, sing hymns, build bombing planes;
Make speeches, unveil statues, issue bonds, parade;
Convert again into explosives the bewildered ammonia and distracted
       cellulose;
Convert again into putrescent matter drawing flies
The hopeful bodies of the young, exhort,
Pray, pull long faces, be earnest, be all but overcome, be photographed;
Confer, perfect your formulae, commercialize
Bacteria harmful to human tissue,
Put death on the market;
Breed, crowd, encroach, expand, expunge yourself, die out,
*Homo* called *sapiens*.

# *from* Civilization and Its Discontents

## *Sigmund Freud*

The element of truth behind all this, which people are so ready to disavow, is that men are not gentle creatures who want to be loved, and who at the most can defend themselves if they are attacked: they are, on the contrary, creatures among whose instinctual endowments is to be reckoned a powerful share of aggressiveness. As a result, their neighbour is for them not only a potential helper or sexual object, but also someone who tempts them to satisfy their aggressiveness on him, to exploit his capacity for work without compensation, to use him sexually without his consent, to seize his possessions, to humiliate him, to cause him pain, to torture and to kill him. Homo homini lupus. Who, in the face of all his experience of life and of history, will have the courage to dispute this assertion? As a rule this cruel aggressiveness waits for some provocation or puts itself at the service of some other purpose, whose goal might also have been reached by milder measures. In circumstances that are favourable to it, when the mental counter-forces which ordinarily inhibit it are out of action, it also manifests itself spontaneously and reveals man as a savage beast to whom consideration towards his own kind is something alien. Anyone who calls to mind the atrocities committed during racial migrations or the invasions of the Huns, or by the people known as Mongols under Jenghiz Khan and Tamerlane, or at the capture of Jerusalem by the pious Crusaders, or even, indeed, the horrors of the recent World War—anyone who calls these things to mind will have to bow humbly before the truth of this view.

The existence of this inclination to aggression, which we can detect in ourselves and justly assume to be present in others, is the factor which disturbs our relations with our neighbour and which forces civilization into such a high expenditure [of energy]. In consequence of this primary mutual hostility of human beings, civilized society is perpetually threatened with disintegration. The interest of work in common would not hold it together: instinctual passions are stronger than reasonable interests. Civilization has to use its utmost efforts in order to set limits to man's aggressive instincts and to hold the manifestations of them in check by psychical reaction-formations.

Hence, therefore, the use of methods intended to incite people into iden-
tifications and aim-inhibited relationships of love, hence the restriction
upon sexual life, and hence too the ideal's commandment  to love one's
neighbour as oneself—a commandment which is really justified by the
fact that nothing else runs so strongly counter to the original nature of
man. In spite of every effort, these endeavours of civilization have not so
far achieved very much. It hopes to prevent the crudest excesses of brutal violence by itself assuming the right to use violence against criminals,
but the law is not able to lay hold of the more cautious and refined manifestations of human aggressiveness.

•   •   •

The fateful question for the human species  seems to me to be whether
and to what extent their cultural development will succeed in mastering
the disturbance of their communal life by the human instinct of aggression and self destruction. It may be that in this respect precisely the present time deserves a special interest. Men have gained control over the
forces of nature to such an extent that with their help they would have no
difficulty in exterminating one another to the last man. They know this,
and hence comes a large part of their current unrest, their unhappiness
and their mood of anxiety. And now it is to be expected that the other of
the two 'Heavenly Powers,' eternal Eros, will make an effort to assert
himself in the struggle with his equally immortal adversary. But who can
foresee with what success and with what result?

# *from* The Myth of Sisyphus

## *Albert Camus*

The gods had condemned Sisyphus to ceaselessly rolling a rock to the top of a mountain, whence the stone would fall back of its own weight. They had thought with some reason that there is no more dreadful punishment than futile and hopeless labor.

If one believes Homer, Sisyphus was the wisest and most prudent of mortals. According to another tradition, however, he was disposed to practice the profession of highwayman. I see no contradiction in this. Opinions differ as to the reasons why he became the futile laborer of the underworld. To begin with, he is accused of a certain levity in regard to the gods. He stole their secrets. Ægina, the daughter of Æsopus, was carried off by Jupiter. The father was shocked by that disappearance and complained to Sisyphus. He, who knew of the abduction, offered to tell about it on condition that Æsopus would give water to the citadel of Corinth. To the celestial thunderbolts he preferred the benediction of water. He was punished for this in the underworld. Homer tells us also that Sisyphus had put Death in chains. Pluto could not endure the sight of his deserted, silent empire. He dispatched the god of war, who liberated Death from the hands of her conqueror.

It is said also that Sisyphus, being near to death, rashly wanted to test his wife's love. He ordered her to cast his unburied body into the middle of the public square. Sisyphus woke up in the underworld. And there, annoyed by an obedience so contrary to human love, he obtained from Pluto permission to return to earth in order to chastise his wife. But when he had seen again the face of this world, enjoyed water and sun, warm stones and the sea, he no longer wanted to go back to the infernal darkness. Recalls, signs of anger, warnings were of no avail. Many years more he lived facing the curve of the gulf, the sparkling sea, and the smiles of earth. A decree of the gods was necessary. Mercury came and seized the impudent man by the collar and, snatching him from his joys, led him forcibly back to the underworld, where his rock was ready for him.

You have already grasped that Sisyphus is the absurd hero. He *is*, as much through his passions as through his torture. His scorn of the gods, his hatred of death, and his passion for life won him that unspeakable penalty in which the whole being is exerted toward accomplishing nothing. This is the price that must be paid for the passions of this earth. Nothing is told us about Sisyphus in the underworld. Myths are made for the imagination to breathe life into them. As for this myth, one sees merely the whole effort of a body straining to raise the huge stone, to roll it and push it up a slope a hundred times over; one sees the face screwed up, the cheek tight against the stone, the shoulder bracing the clay-covered mass, the foot wedging it, the fresh start with arms outstretched, the wholly human security of two earth-clotted hands. At the very end of his long effort measured by skyless space and time without depth, the purpose is achieved. Then Sisyphus watches the stone rush down in a few moments toward that lower world whence he will have to push it up again toward the summit. He goes back down to the plain.

It is during that return, that pause, that Sisyphus interests me. A face that toils so close to stones is already stone itself! I see that man going back down with a heavy yet measured step toward the torment of which he will never know the end. That hour like a breathing-space which returns as surely as his suffering, that is the hour of consciousness. At each of those moments when he leaves the heights and gradually sinks toward the lairs of the gods, he is superior to his fate. He is stronger than his rock.

If this myth is tragic, that is because its hero is conscious. Where would his torture be indeed if at every step the hope of succeeding upheld him? The workman of today works every day in his life at the same tasks, and this fate is no less absurd. But it is tragic only at the rare moments when it becomes conscious. Sisyphus, proletarian of the gods, powerless and rebellious, knows the whole extent of his wretched condition: it is what he thinks of during his descent. The lucidity that was to constitute his torture at the same time crowns his victory. There is no fate that cannot be surmounted by scorn.

If the descent is thus sometimes performed in sorrow, it can also take place in joy. This word is not too much. Again I fancy Sisyphus returning toward his rock, and the sorrow was in the beginning. When the images of earth cling too tightly to memory, when the call of happiness becomes too insistent, it happens that melancholy rises in man's heart: this is the rock's victory, this is the rock itself. The boundless grief is too heavy to bear. These are our nights of Gethsemane. But crushing truths perish from being acknowledged. Thus, Œdipus at the outset obeys fate without knowing it. But from the moment he knows, his tragedy begins. Yet at the same moment, blind and desperate, he realizes that the only bond linking him to the world is the cool hand of a girl. Then a tremendous remark rings out: "Despite so many ordeals, my advanced age and the nobility of my soul make me conclude that all is well." Sophocles' Œdipus, like Dostoevsky's Kirilov, thus gives the recipe for the absurd victory. Ancient wisdom confirms modern heroism.

One does not discover the absurd without being tempted to write a manual of happiness. "What! by such narrow ways—?" There is but one world, however. Happiness and the absurd are two sons of the same earth. They are inseparable. It would be a mistake to say that happiness necessarily springs from the absurd discovery. It happens as well that the feeling of the absurd springs from happiness. "I conclude that all is well," says Œdipus, and that remark is sacred. It echoes in the wild and limited universe of man. It teaches that all is not, has not been, exhausted. It drives out of this world a god who had come into it with dissatisfaction and a preference for futile sufferings. It makes of fate a human matter, which must be settled among men.

All Sisyphus' silent joy is contained therein. His fate belongs to him. His rock is his thing. Likewise, the absurd man, when he contemplates his torment, silences all the idols. In the universe suddenly restored to its silence, the myriad wondering little voices of the earth rise up. Unconscious, secret calls, invitations from all the faces, they are the necessary reverse and price of victory. There is no sun without shadow, and it is essential to know the night. The absurd man says yes and his effort will henceforth be unceasing. If there is a personal fate, there is no higher destiny, or at least there is but one which he concludes is inevitable and despicable. For the rest, he knows himself to be the master of his days. At that subtle moment when man glances backward over his life, Sisyphus returning toward his rock, in that slight pivoting he contemplates that series of unrelated actions which becomes his fate, created by him, combined under his memory's eye and soon sealed by his death. Thus, convinced of the wholly human origin of all that is human, a blind man eager to see who knows that the night has no end, he is still on the go. The rock is still rolling.

I leave Sisyphus at the foot of the mountain! One always finds one's burden again. But Sisyphus teaches the higher fidelity that negates the gods and raises rocks. He too concludes that all is well. This universe henceforth without a master seems to him neither sterile nor futile. Each atom of that stone, each mineral flake of that night-filled mountain, in itself forms a world. The struggle itself toward the heights is enough to fill a man's heart. One must imagine Sisyphus happy.

# *from* Existentialism Is a Humanism

## *Jean-Paul Sartre*

For in truth this is of all teachings the least scandalous and the most austere: it is intended strictly for technicians and philosophers. All the same, it can easily be defined.

The question is only complicated because there are two kinds of existentialists. There are, on the one hand, the Christians, amongst whom I shall name Jaspers and Gabriel Marcel, both professed Catholics; and on the other the existential atheists, amongst whom we must place Heidegger as well as the French existentialists and myself. What they have in common is simply the fact that they believe that *existence* comes before *essence*—or, if you will, that we must begin from the subjective. What exactly do we mean by that?

If one considers an article of manufacture as, for example, a book or a paper-knife—one sees that it has been made by an artisan who had a conception of it; and he has paid attention, equally, to the conception of a paper-knife and to the pre-existent technique of production which is a part of that conception and is, at bottom, a formula. Thus the paper-knife is at the same time an article producible in a certain manner and one which, on the other hand, serves a definite purpose, for one cannot suppose that a man would produce a paper-knife without knowing what it was for. Let us say, then, of the paper-knife that its essence—that is to say the sum of the formulae and the qualities which made its production and its definition possible—precedes its existence. The presence of such-and-such a paper-knife or book is thus determined before my eyes. Here, then, we are viewing the world from a technical standpoint, and we can say that production precedes existence.

When we think of God as the creator, we are thinking of him, most of the time, as a supernal artisan. Whatever doctrine we may be considering, whether it be a doctrine like that of Descartes, or of Leibnitz himself, we always imply that the will follows, more or less, from the understanding or at least accompanies it, so that when God creates he knows precisely what he is creating. Thus, the conception of man in the mind of God is comparable to that of the paper-knife in the mind of the artisan: God makes man according to a procedure and a conception, exactly as the artisan manufactures a paper-knife, following a definition and a formula. Thus each individual man is the realisation of a certain conception which dwells in the divine understanding. In the philosophic atheism of the eighteenth century, the notion of God is suppressed, but not, for all that, the idea that essence is prior to existence; something of that idea we still find everywhere, in Diderot, in Voltaire and even in Kant. Man possesses a human nature; that "human nature," which is the conception of human being, is found in every man; which means that each man is a particular example of an universal conception, the conception of Man. In Kant, this universality goes so far that the wild man of the woods, man in the state of nature and the bourgeois are all contained in the same definition and have the same fundamental qualities. Here again, the essence of man precedes that historic existence which we confront in experience.

Atheistic existentialism, of which I am a representative, declares with greater consistency that if God does not exist there is at least one being whose existence comes before its essence, a being which exists before it can be defined by any conception of it. That being is man or, as Heidegger has it, the human reality. What do we mean by saying that existence precedes essence? We mean that man first of all exists, encounters himself, surges up in the world—and defines himself afterwards. If man as the existentialist sees him is not definable, it is because to begin with he is nothing. He will not be anything until later, and then he will be what he makes of himself. Thus, there is no human nature, because there is no God to have a conception of it. Man simply is. Not that he is simply what he conceives himself to be, but he is what he wills, and as he conceives himself after already existing—as he wills to be after that leap towards existence. Man is nothing else but that which he makes of himself. That is the first principle of existentialism. And this is what people call its "subjectivity," using the word as a reproach against us. But what do we mean to say by this, but that man is of a greater dignity than a stone or a table? For we mean to say that man primarily exists—that man is, before all else, something which propels itself towards a future and is aware that it is doing so. Man is, indeed, a project which possesses a subjective life, instead of being a kind of moss, or a fungus or a cauliflower. Before that projection of the self nothing exists; not even in the heaven of intelligence: man will only attain existence when he is what he purposes to be. Not, however, what he may wish to be. For what we usually understand by wishing or willing is a conscious decision taken—much more often than not—after we have made ourselves what we are. I may wish to join a party, to write a book or to marry—but in such a case what is usually called my will is probably a manifestation of a prior and more spontaneous decision. If, however, it is true that existence is prior to essence, man is responsible for what he is. Thus, the first effect of existentialism is that it puts every man in possession of himself as he is, and places the entire responsibility for his existence squarely upon his own shoulders. And, when we say that man is responsible for himself, we do not mean that he is responsible only for his own individuality, but that he is responsible for all men. The word "subjectivism" is to be understood in two senses, and our adversaries play upon only one of them. Subjectivism means, on the one hand, the freedom of the individual subject and, on the other, that man cannot pass beyond human subjectivity. It is the latter which is the deeper meaning of existentialism. When we say that man chooses himself, we do mean that every one of us must choose himself; but by that we also mean that in choosing for himself he chooses for all men. For in effect, of all the actions a man may take in order to create himself as he wills to be, there is not one which is not creative, at the same time, of an image of man such as he believes he ought to be. To choose between this or that is at the same time to affirm the value of that which is chosen; for we are unable ever to choose the worse. What we choose is always the better; and nothing can he better for us unless it is better for all. If, moreover, existence precedes essence and we will to exist at the same time as we fashion our image, that image is valid for all and for the entire epoch in which we find ourselves. Our responsibility is thus much greater than we had supposed, for it concerns mankind as a whole. If I am a worker, for instance, I may choose to join a Christian rather than a Communist trade union. And if, by that membership, I choose to signify that resignation is, after all, the attitude that best becomes a man, that man's kingdom is not upon this earth, I do not commit myself alone to that view. Resignation is my will for everyone, and my action is, in consequence, a commitment on behalf of all mankind. Or if, to take a more personal case, I decide to marry and to have children, even though this decision proceeds simply from my situation, from my passion or my desire, I am thereby committing not only myself, but humanity as a whole, to the practice of monogamy. I am thus responsible for myself and for all men, and I am creating a certain image of man as I would have him to be. In fashioning myself I fashion man.

This may enable us to understand what is meant by such terms—perhaps a little grandiloquent—as anguish, abandonment and despair. As you will soon see, it is very simple. First, what do we mean by anguish? The existentialist frankly states that man is in anguish. His meaning is as follows—When a man commits himself to anything, fully realising that he is not only choosing what he will be, but is thereby at the same time a legislator deciding for the whole of mankind—in such a moment a man cannot escape from the sense of complete and profound responsibility. There are many, indeed, who show no such anxiety. But we affirm that they are merely disguising their anguish or are in flight from it. Certainly, many people think that in what they are doing they commit no one but themselves to anything: and if you ask them, "What would happen if everyone did so?" they shrug their shoulders and reply, "Everyone does not do so." But in truth, one ought always to ask oneself what would happen if everyone did as one is doing; nor can one escape from that disturbing thought except by a kind of self-deception. The man who lies in self-excuse by saying "Everyone will not do it," must be ill at ease in his conscience, for the act of lying implies the universal value which it denies. By its very disguise his anguish reveals itself. This is the anguish that Kierkegaard called "the anguish of Abraham." You know the story: An angel commanded Abraham to sacrifice his son: and obedience was obligatory if it really was an angel who had appeared and said "Thou Abraham shalt sacrifice thy son." But anyone in such a case would wonder first whether it was indeed an angel and secondly whether I am really Abraham. Where are the proofs? A certain mad woman who suffered from hallucinations said that people were telephoning to her and giving her orders. The doctor asked "But who is it that speaks to you?" She replied: "He says it is God." And what indeed could prove to her that it was God? If an angel appears to me what is the proof that it is an angel; or if I hear voices who can prove that they proceed from heaven and not from hell or from my own subconsciousness or some pathological condition? Who can prove that they are really addressed to me?

Who, then, can prove that I am the proper person to impose by my own choice, my conception of man upon mankind? I shall never find any proof whatever; there will be no sign to convince me of it. If a voice speaks to me, it is still I myself who must decide whether the voice is or is not that of an angel. If I regard a certain course of action as good, it is only I who choose to say that it is good and not bad. There is nothing to show that I am Abraham: nevertheless I also am obliged at every instant to perform actions which are examples. Everything happens to every man as though the whole human race had its eyes fixed upon what he is doing and regulated its conduct accordingly. So every man ought to say "Am I really a man who has the right to act in such a manner that humanity regulates itself by what I do?" If a man does not say that, he is dissembling his anguish. Clearly, the anguish with which we are concerned here is one that could lead to quietism or inaction. It is anguish pure and simple of the kind well known to all those who have borne responsibilities. When, for instance, a military leader takes upon himself the responsibility for an attack and sends a number of men to their death, he chooses to do it and at bottom he alone chooses. No doubt he acts under a higher command, but its orders, which are more general, require interpretation by him and upon that interpretation depends the life of ten, fourteen or twenty men. In making the decision, he cannot but feel a certain anguish. All leaders know that anguish. It does not prevent their acting, on the contrary it is the very condition of their action, for the action presupposes that there is a plurality of possibilities, and in choosing one of these, they realise that it has value only because it is chosen. Now it is anguish of that kind which existentialism describes, and moreover, as we shall see, makes explicit through direct responsibility towards other men who are concerned. Far from being a screen which could separate us from action, it is a condition of action itself.

And when we speak of "abandonment"—a favourite word of Heidegger—we only mean to say that God does not exist and that it is necessary to draw the consequences of his absence right to the end. The existentialist is strongly opposed to a certain type of secular moralism which seeks to suppress God at the least possible expense. Towards 1880, when the French professors endeavoured to formulate a secular morality, they said something like this:—God is a useless and costly hypothesis, so we will do without it. However, if we are to have morality, a society and a law-abiding world, it is essential that certain values should be taken seriously; they must have an *a priori* existence ascribed to them. It must be considered obligatory *a priori* to be honest, not to lie, not to beat one's wife, to bring up children and so forth; so we are going to do a little work on this subject, which will enable us to show that these values exist all the same, inscribed in an intelligible heaven although, of course, there is no God. In other words—and this is, I believe, the purport of all that we in France call radicalism—nothing will be changed if God does not exist; we shall re-discover the same norms of honesty, progress and humanity, and we shall have disposed of God as an out-of-date hypothesis which will die away quietly of itself. The existentialist, on the contrary, finds it extremely embarrassing that God does not exist, for there disappears with Him all possibility of finding values in an intelligible heaven. There can no longer be any good *a priori*, since there is no infinite and perfect consciousness to think it. It is nowhere written that "the good" exists, that one must be honest or must not lie, since we are now upon the plane where there are only men. Dostoievsky once wrote "If God did not exist, everything would be permitted"; and that, for existentialism, is the starting point. Everything is indeed permitted if God does not exist, and man is in consequence forlorn, for he cannot find anything to depend upon either within or outside himself. He discovers forthwith, that he is without excuse. For if indeed existence precedes essence, one will never be able to explain one's action by reference to a given and specific human nature; in other words, there is no determinism— man is free, man *is* freedom. Nor, on the other hand, if God does not exist, are we provided with any values or commands that could legitimise our behaviour. Thus we have neither behind us, nor before us in a luminous realm of values, any means of justification or excuse. We are left alone, without excuse. That is what I mean when I say that man is condemned to be free. Condemned, because he did not create himself, yet is nevertheless at liberty, and from the moment that he is thrown into this world he is responsible for everything he does. The existentialist does not believe in the power of passion. He will never regard a grand passion as a destructive torrent upon which a man is swept into certain actions as by fate, and which, therefore, is an excuse for them. He thinks that man is responsible for his passion. Neither will an existentialist think that a man can find help through some sign being vouchsafed upon earth for his orientation: for he thinks that the man himself interprets the sign as he chooses. He thinks that every man, without any support or help whatever, is condemned at every instant to invent man. As Ponge has written in a very fine article "Man is the future of man." That is exactly true. Only, if one took this to mean that the future is laid up in Heaven, that God knows what it is, it would be false, for then it would no longer even be a future. If, however, it means that whatever man may now appear to be there is a future to be fashioned, a virgin future that awaits him—then it is a true saying. But in the present one is forsaken.

As an example by which you may the better understand this state of abandonment, I will refer to the case of a pupil of mine who sought me out in the following circumstances. His father was quarrelling with his mother and was also inclined to be a "collaborator"; his elder brother had been killed in the German offensive of 1940 and this young man, with a sentiment somewhat primitive but generous, burned to avenge him. His mother was living alone with him, deeply afflicted by the semi-treason of his father and by the death of her eldest son, and her one consolation was in this young man. But he, at this moment, had the choice between going to England to join the Free French Forces or of staying near his mother and helping her to live. He fully realised that this woman lived only for him and that his disappearance—or perhaps his death—would plunge her into despair. He also realised that, concretely and in fact, every action he performed on his mother's behalf would be sure of effect in the sense of aiding her to live, whereas anything he did in order to go and fight would be an ambiguous action which might vanish like water into sand and serve no purpose. For instance, to set out for England he would have to wait indefinitely in a Spanish camp on the way through Spain; or, on arriving in England or in Algiers he might be put into an office to fill up forms. Consequently, he found himself confronted by two very different modes of action: the one concrete, immediate but directed towards only one individual; and the other an action addressed to an end infinitely greater, a national collectivity, but for that very reason ambiguous—and it might be frustrated on the way. At the same time, he was hesitating between two kinds of morality; on the one side the morality of sympathy, of personal devotion and, on the other side, a morality of wider scope but of more debatable validity. He had to choose between those two. What could help him to choose? Could the Christian doctrine? No. Christian doctrine says: Act with charity, love your neighbour, deny yourself for others, choose the way which is hardest, and so forth. But which is the harder road? To whom does one owe the more brotherly love, the patriot or the mother? Which is the more useful aim, the general one of fighting in and for the whole community, or the precise aim of helping one particular person to live? Who can give an answer to that *a priori*? No one. Nor is it given in any ethical scripture. The Kantian ethic says, Never regard another as a means but always as an end. Very well; if I remain with my mother, I shall he regarding her as the end and not as a means: but by the same token I am in danger of treating as means those who are fighting on my behalf; and the converse is also true, that if I go to the aid of the combatants I shall be treating them as the end at the risk of treating my mother as a means.

If values are uncertain, if they are still too abstract to determine the particular, concrete case under consideration, nothing remains but to trust in our instincts. That is what this young man tried to do; and when I saw him he said, "In the end, it is feeling that counts; the direction in which it is really pushing me is the one I ought to choose. If I feel that I love my mother enough to sacrifice everything else for her—my will to be avenged, all my longings for action and adventure—then I stay with her. If, on the contrary, I feel that my love for her is not enough, I go." But how does one estimate the strength of a feeling? The value of his feeling for his mother was determined precisely by the fact that he was standing by her. I may say that I love a certain friend enough to sacrifice such or such a sum of money for him, but I cannot prove that unless I have done it. I may say, "I love my mother enough to remain with her," if actually I have remained with her. I can only estimate the strength of this affection if I have performed an action by which it is defined and ratified. But if I then appeal to this affection to justify my action, I find myself drawn into a vicious circle.

What is at the very heart and centre of existentialism is the absolute character of the free commitment, by which every man realises himself in realising a type of humanity—a commitment always understandable, to no matter whom in no matter what epoch—and its bearing upon the relativity of the cultural pattern which may result from such absolute commitment. One must observe equally the relativity of Cartesians and the absolute character of the Cartesian commitment. In this sense you may say, if you like, that every one of us makes the absolute by breathing, by eating, by sleeping or by behaving in any fashion whatsoever. There is no difference between free being—being as self-committal, as existence choosing its essence—and absolute being. And there is no difference whatever between being as an absolute, temporarily localised—that is, localised in history—and universally intelligible being.

. . . Existentialism is nothing else but an attempt to draw the full conclusions from a consistently atheistic position. . . . Not that we believe God does exist, but we think that the real problem is not that of His existence; what man needs is to find himself again and to understand that nothing can save him from himself, not even a valid proof of the existence of God. In this sense existentialism is optimistic, it is a doctrine of action, and it is only by self-deception, by confusing their own despair with ours that Christians can describe us as without hope.